Products Liability Law

Products Liability Law

Cases, Commentary, and Conundra

Tim Kaye

PROFESSOR,
STETSON UNIVERSITY COLLEGE OF LAW

CAROLINA ACADEMIC PRESS
Durham, North Carolina

ISBN: 978-1-59460-842-1
LCCN: 2012940585

Carolina Academic Press
700 Kent Street
Durham, North Carolina 27701
Telephone (919) 489-7486
Fax (919) 493-5668
www.cap-press.com

Cover photo credits: bakery display © Missing35mm/iStockphoto; prescription bottle
© DNY59/iStockphoto; wood chipper © kryczka/iStockphoto

Printed in the United States of America
2021 Printing

Summary of Contents

Contents

Part II: Product Defects

Chapter 6 · Manufacturing Defects

List of Figures

Table of Cases

Table of Statutes and Other Authorities

Preface

In a dissenting opinion in *New State Ice Co. v. Liebmann*, 285 U.S. 262, 311; 52 S.Ct. 371, 386–87 (1932), Justice Louis D. Brandeis famously observed that: "It is one of the happy incidents of the federal system that a single courageous state may, if its citizens choose, serve as a laboratory; and try novel social and economic experiments without risk to the rest of the country." In no area of the law is this more true than in products liability.

Indeed, the very notion of a new, discrete body of products liability law essentially came about from an "experiment" in California. But "experimentation" in cases of defective products has not ended there. Some states have tried strict liability as the yardstick for all products liability claims, albeit with different explanations as to what that notion entails. Other states have asserted (or re-asserted) various different notions of fault as essential to (some types of) products liability claims; and they have then differed as to whether this should be measured by a "consumer expectations" or "risk-utility" standard, or whether both these tests should be available as alternatives within the same jurisdiction. One state requires that both tests be satisfied, treating the latter as a question of law for the court, and the former as a question of fact for the jury.

Similarly, different states have tried different approaches regarding the circumstances in which substantial remedial measures to a product may be produced as evidence to sustain the claim of a product defect. Even the admissibility or otherwise of expert evidence is judged against different criteria in different states. And scientific uncertainty as to whether, and how, allegedly toxic agents can cause harm has led to a whole series of different approaches to proof of causation of harm, including tests applicable solely to asbestos cases that are not applied elsewhere.

Overlaid on this patchwork of judicial experimentation among the states is a federal blanket of rulings on multi-district litigation, pre-emption, bankruptcy, punitive damages, and the rules of evidence. This blanket shows the extent to which the Supreme Court has been prepared to adopt the rest of Brandeis's view, which has often been overlooked. For he was not, in fact, waxing eloquent in support of unconfined experiments with the law by the judiciary of the various states. On the contrary, the sentences that immediately follow the above quotation from Brandeis's judgment read as follows:

> This Court has the power to prevent an experiment. We may strike down the statute which embodies it on the ground that, in our opinion, the measure is arbitrary, capricious, or unreasonable. We have power to do this, because the due process clause has been held by the Court applicable to matters of substantive law as well as to matters of procedure. But, in the exercise of this high power, we must be ever on our guard, lest we erect our prejudices into legal principles. If we would guide by the light of reason, we must let our minds be bold. (285 U.S. at 311, 52 S.Ct. at 387.)

Above everything else, then, products liability law is really about a struggle for power—and not just about a struggle for power between the parties to specific litigation, but also about struggles for power between one state and another, between the states and the federal government, between judge and jury, and among the judiciary itself. These struggles are often, moreover, less about what kinds of legal submissions may be successful, and more about who gets to decide.

One of the ramifications of this combination of a patchwork of state experimentation, subject to periodic federal intervention, is that the body of law it produces is best conceived not as fixed, black-letter rules that can be learned by rote, but as a body of policy-driven, fact-specific decision-making around a consistent set of themes. Many of these themes are lucidly highlighted by the Restatement (Third) of Torts: Products Liability, to which regular reference is made throughout this book. Yet it frequently remains open to question whether that Restatement's black-letter sections really do represent the law.

Another important consideration to be borne in mind is that, even if the decision-making around these themes varies from one state to another, there are (and have been) discernible trends (often nationwide) as to the direction in which the case law is headed. For this reason, recent cases predominate among those extracted here, while the older cases that are discussed have been chosen to highlight the ways in which the law has changed since they were decided.

One of the consequences of this emphasis on thematic trends is that many of the questions that are posed throughout the book are designed to encourage the reader to identify those trends in the particular area of the law then under discussion. Another is the inclusion of discussions of areas of the law that are not typically covered in books on products liability law, but which have nevertheless become matters of significant importance in products liability litigation. Chapter 16, in particular, is devoted to considering what happens when a manufacturer of defective products enters bankruptcy protection. In these recessionary times, omitting this important topic—and its consequences for the availability of compensation, whether through liability- or self-insurance—would surely amount to a refusal to recognize one of the most important, albeit also most unfortunate, trends of all.

An area of products liability law that could certainly benefit from a new trend and more "experiments" is its rhetoric. Comprehension of the area is currently impeded both by pompous Latinisms that have little connection to the Ancient Romans (though perhaps the worst of all, *syllabi*—which embodies so many linguistic, historical, and etymological errors that it is hard to know where to begin in identifying them all—seems sadly endemic throughout American law) and by wholly misleading terminology expressed in English (such as "implied assumption of risk"). The bizarre tendency to call every legal doctrine a "rule" when it is really no such thing (as in, for example, the "economic loss rule") is another such impediment. Perhaps worst of all is the lazy usage of the phrase "strict liability," which has now become so pervasive that it is impossible to know, without added verbiage, whether the speaker or writer is referring to fault-based or no-fault liability. I would happily laud any bench who resolved to eradicate these linguistic nightmares, especially one who ordered that the terminology of strict liability be once again restricted solely to cases of no-fault liability.

In the continued absence of that particular experiment, products liability lawyers are compelled to work with a lexicon that is neither as sharp nor as granular as it should be. One of the ways in which I have tried to overcome this problem is by supplementing the text with frequent flowcharts and other graphics, which are designed to be particularly useful to "visual" learners. Sometimes I wish that judgments were set out in such a manner. A picture may paint a thousand words, although it is admittedly unlikely that any diagrams will be as eloquent as Justice Brandeis. They do, however, seldom strive to be pompous.

Tim Kaye
Tampa, FL
April 2012

Acknowledgments

The contents of this book have been tried, amended, and thoroughly shaped by discussions in my Products Liability classes at Stetson University College of Law. I should like to thank all the students in those classes for engaging positively with the material, for asking penetrating questions, and for offering different perspectives and important insights. Eric Briley, Chrissy Carpenter, Patrick Causey, Stephen Farkas, Dawn Hunter, Patrick Plamondon, Michael Schuette, Daniel Strader, Elizabeth Stringer, and Douglas Wieland deserve particular mention as first among equals in this regard, while my research assistants, Michelle Mos (née Searce) and Margaret "Peggy" Peters, went well beyond the call of duty in locating materials and providing critical assessments of them.

I have been fortunate indeed to find so supportive an environment as Stetson University College of Law in which to write this book. A scholarship grant facilitated the preparation of the manuscript. Terri Radwan improved my understanding of bankruptcy law. In their very different ways, Marco Jimenez, Candace Zierdt, and Jamie Fox have kept me thinking about, and re-evaluating, contract law. Ann Piccard, Jim and Millie Brown—and, from further afield, Tadas Klimas—have been a constant source of support and encouragement. So too has Bob Bickel, who is a fountain of knowledge and ideas about tort law, and with whom I have had countless enjoyable discussions about Life, the Universe, and Everything. Above all, my wife, Jan, continues to put up with me—albeit often from the safety of a tennis court! I like to think it has something to do with love.

Working with Carolina Academic Press has been as smooth as any author can wish for. I must particularly thank Linda Lacy for her wise counsel and suggestions; Tim Colton for dealing with technical matters so helpfully, and for re-creating the flowcharts in a publishable format; and Karen Clayton (despite the demands of her menagerie of cats, dogs, and fish) for typesetting the manuscript with such efficiency and good humor.

I should also like to thank the following authors and publishers for granting permission to enable me to include excerpts from the following publications:

American Law Institute, Restatement, Second, Torts, § 285(b), § 291, § 310 and Illustration 2, § 311, § 328D, § 388, § 395, § 402A and Caveat and Comments *h* and *i*, § 402B and Caveat, § 526, § 531, § 539, § 540, § 542, § 545A, § 557A and Illustration 1. Copyright © 1965, 1977 by The American Law Institute. Reprinted by permission. All rights reserved.

American Law Institute, Restatement (Third) of Torts: Products Liability, § 1 and Comment *a*, § 2 and Comment *i*, § 3, § 4 and Comment *e*, § 5, § 6 and Comments *b* and *d*, § 7, § 8, § 9, § 16, § 17, § 19, § 20. Copyright © 1998 by The American Law Institute. Reprinted by permission. All rights reserved.

Ausness, Richard C., From Caveat Emptor to Strict Liability: A Review of Products Liability in Florida, 24 U.L. Rev. 410, 410, 411–13. Copyright © 1972 by the Florida Law Review. Reprinted by permission.

Boivin, Denis, Strict Products Liability Revisited, 33 Osgoode Hall L.J. 487, 491–92. Copyright © 1995 by Denis Boivin. Reprinted by permission.

Bonney, Paul R., Manufacturers' Strict Liability for Handgun Injuries: An Economic Analysis, 73 Geo. L.J. 1437, 1456–57 and note 167. Copyright © 1985 by Paul R. Bonney. Reprinted by permission.

Brennan, Troyen A., Causal Chains and Statistical Links: The Role of Scientific Uncertainty in Hazardous-Substance Litigation, 73 Cornell L. Rev. 469, 479–83, 483, 484–85; 486; 489–91; 500–501. Copyright © 1988 by the Cornell Law Review. Reprinted by permission.

Fede, Andrew, Legal Protection for Slave Buyers in the U.S. South: A Caveat Concerning Caveat Emptor, 31 Am. J. Legal Hist. 322, 322–23, 327, 328–29, 331–33, 334–35, 336. Copyright © 1987 by the American Journal of Legal History. Reprinted by permission.

Gardner, Sheldon, & Robert Kuehl, Acquiring an Historical Understanding of Duties to Disclose, Fraud, and Warranties, 104 Com. L.J. 168, 173–76. Copyright © 1999 by the Commercial Law League of America. Reprinted by permission.

Gifford, Donald G., The Challenge to the Individual Causation Requirement in Mass Products Torts, 62 Wash. & Lee L. Rev. 873, 875–81. Copyright © 2005 Donald G. Gifford. Reprinted by permission of Donald G. Gifford and the Washington and Lee Law Review.

Green, Michael D., D. Michal Freedman, & Leon Gordis, Reference Guide on Epidemiology, in Reference Manual on Scientific Evidence, 3d ed., pp. 551–54. Copyright © 2011 by the National Academy of Sciences. Reprinted with permission from the National Academy of Sciences, Courtesy of the National Academies Press, Washington, D.C.

Johnston, Susan Power, & Katherine Porter, Extension of Section 524(g) of the Bankruptcy Code to Nondebtor Parents, Affiliates, and Transaction Parties, 59 Bus. Lawyer 503, 510–11, 511, 512, 513–14, 514–15, 515–16. Copyright © 2004 by Susan Power Johnston & Katherine Porter. Reprinted by permission.

McGarity, Thomas O., Proposal for Linking Culpability and Causation to Ensure Corporate Accountability for Toxic Risks, 26 Wm. & Mary Envtl. L. & Policy Rev. 1, 1–3, 4–6. Copyright © 2001 by Thomas O. McGarity. Reprinted by permission.

Pridgen, Dee, & Ivan L. Preston, Enhancing the Flow of Information in the Marketplace: From Caveat Emptor to Virginia Pharmacy and Beyond at the Federal Trade Commission, 14 Ga. L. Rev. 635, 641, 642–45, 646. Copyright © 1980 by the Georgia Law Review. Reprinted by permission.

Stapleton, Jane, Product Liability, p. 11, London, UK: Butterworths. Copyright © 1994 by Jane Stapleton. Reprinted by permission.

Stapleton, Jane, Two Causal Fictions at the Heart of U.S. Asbestos Doctrine, 122 L.Q. Rev. 189, 189–95. Copyright © 2006 by Jane Stapleton. Reprinted by permission.

Uniform Commercial Code, § 2-103, § 2-104, § 2-105(1), § 2-302, § 2-313, § 2-314, § 2-315, § 2-316, § 2-318, § 2-718, § 2-719, § 2-725. Copyright © 2011 by The American Law Institute and the National Conference of Commissioners on Uniform State Laws. Reproduced by permission of the Permanent Editorial Board for the Uniform Commercial Code. All rights reserved.

Viscusi, W. Kip, Reforming Products Liability, pp. 114–16, Cambridge, Mass.: Harvard University Press. Copyright © 1991 by the President and Fellows of Harvard College. Reprinted by permission.

Walker, Vern R., *Restoring the Individual Plaintiff to Tort Law by Rejecting the Junk Logic about Specific Causation*, 56 Ala. L. Rev. 381, 381–86. Copyright © 2004 by the Alabama Law Review. Reprinted by permission.

In order to make these extracts easier to follow, internal citations have been omitted without indication. I have adopted the same approach to the case extracts.

Part I

The Development of Products Liability Law

Chapter 1

An Introduction to Products Liability Law

Elements and Themes

The law of products liability straddles the boundary between contracts and torts. On the one hand, products liability cases tend to arise out of contractual relationships, even if those contracts are not always between the plaintiff and defendant. Sometimes they arise from a chain of relationships, such as those involving manufacturer, retailer, and consumer, or those involving a pharmaceuticals manufacturer, physician and patient. Unlike the law of contracts, however, and much more like regular torts cases, products liability cases are restricted to instances where the plaintiff claims to have suffered—or to be likely to suffer—personal injury.

This means that, although this book addresses the field of law known as "products liability," this field actually encompasses six different forms of action. These are, in the order in which we shall tackle them in this book:

- Breach of warranty (which may itself be subdivided into breaches of express warranties, and breaches of implied warranties);
- Misrepresentation (which may also be subdivided into fraudulent, negligent, and innocent misrepresentations);
- Negligence (albeit restricted to cases of negligence in the creation or distribution of a product);
- Manufacturing defects;
- Design defects;
- Failures to warn.

The first of these forms of action sounds in contracts, whereas the others are all types of torts (though misrepresentations often induce the representee to enter into a contract). Naturally, each of these forms of action requires proof of a different set of elements, and the disparate nature of the claims involved can sometimes get confusing. Nevertheless, they do share a common core that helps us to define what constitutes the field of products liability law. No matter which of these claims are made, a *prima facie* case of products liability essentially requires proof, on a preponderance of the evidence, of the existence of each of the following five elements:

1. A product;
2. Sold, or otherwise distributed, by someone in the business of selling or distributing that type of product;

3

3.   Which, at the time of sale or distribution, contained some type of defect;

4.   Which defect caused—or is likely to cause—physical injury or damage;

5.   To the consumer or a reasonably foreseeable third party.

The significance of these elements may be easier to grasp by looking at the flowchart in Figure 1.1. It should be noted that, even if there is a *prima facie* case of one form of products liability, this does not preclude a plaintiff's use of others if more than one can be applied to the facts of the case. Indeed, virtually every case of alleged products liability involves consideration of multiple theories.

We shall shortly go on to consider each of these five elements in more detail. As we do so, you will be introduced to a number of themes that are characteristic of products lia-

Figure 1.1 *The Five Elements Required for a Prima Facie Case of Products Liability*

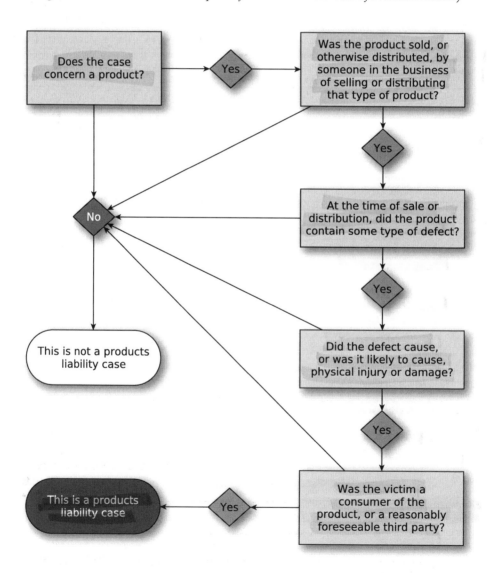

bility law, and which will be developed throughout the rest of the book. These themes include the following:

- The distinction between questions of law and questions of fact;
- The extent to which it is appropriate to allow the substantive law of products liability to be trumped by matters of procedure;
- The question of who should bear the cost of the victim's injuries when neither the victim nor anyone else was at fault;
- The floodgates issue;
- The extent to which products liability law should take account of macro public policy issues such as a need to protect the public, or a need to bolster (or avoid undermining) American business or the American economy.

These themes are important because they tend to dictate how the parties frame a case. For example, plaintiffs' attorneys will tend to emphasize questions of fact, because these will be determined by a jury who, they hope, will be so dismayed by evidence about the victim's injury and/or lack of care by the defendant, that the plaintiff will not just win the case but also be awarded significant compensation and, perhaps, punitive damages. Defendants' attorneys, by contrast, will tend to focus much more heavily on questions of law, since these are matters for the court and so amenable to summary judgment, thus rendering a jury trial unnecessary. Indeed, even where the potentially dispositive issue in a particular case (such as factual causation) would normally be considered as a matter of fact for the jury, defendants' attorneys will typically try to argue that there is so little evidence to support the plaintiff's contentions that, once again, the matter is amenable to summary judgment by the court in the defendant's favor as a matter of law.

It can hardly be emphasized too strongly how much defendants' attorneys focus on winning products liability lawsuits on motions for summary judgment. Another means by which they may be able to achieve the same objective is by having the case dismissed on a matter of procedure. This then renders moot the substantive merits of the case. We will look at an unusual example of such a case later in this Chapter, in *J. McIntyre Machinery, Ltd. v. Nicastro*, 131 S.Ct. 2780 (2011).

Some of these themes raise questions of public policy, but in rather different ways. They have also tended to be addressed differently by the courts according to era and jurisdiction. Thus, as will be seen in Chapters 2, 3, and 5, the courts used to take the view that victims had no right of redress unless they could establish that their injuries were the product of someone else's fault—and, even then, they could do so only in very limited circumstances. Chapter 6 indicates how the tide turned so as to put the burden of the risk of injury more on manufacturers and distributors, while Chapters 7 and 8 show how the courts currently struggle to articulate a consistent approach to this issue.

Underlying this struggle with consistency are the fear of "opening the floodgates" (which will be addressed further in this Chapter) and the larger policy questions of the extent to which the courts should be concerned either to protect the public at large from faulty products, or with the potential impact that their decisions might have on American business or the American economy. In many ways, all these issues are interrelated. Yet, while there is no doubt that the courts must take heed of potential floodgates problems, there is considerable controversy as to when these problems are likely, in practice, to arise. Indeed, many commentators greeted the very creation of a special body of products liability law with the warning that this would open the floodgates to "crushing liability" on American business, and that this would ruin the economy and the competitiveness of American businesses. In fact, however, the rise of products liability law from the 1940s onwards coincided with unprecedented economic growth to the extent that, in the eyes of many historians, the twentieth century may rightly be regarded as the "American century."

Some commentators have argued that the creation of products liability law was, in fact, one of the reasons for this American economic success, because it made it uneconomic for businesses to rely on old, unsafe methods and products, and instead encouraged innovation on a hitherto unseen scale. Perhaps this was so, although the contention needs to be treated with some caution because it rests on an unproven claim of cause-and-effect; ironically, those who had previously forecast the doom of the opening of the floodgates had been equally sure that they understood the cause-and-effect relationship between the law and the economy, and they were quite clearly wrong.

A Product

The first question to be addressed is what constitutes a product. Although technological development may alter our view of specific items over time, the question of what constitutes a product clearly goes to the root of any body of law called Products Liability. Determination of this issue is therefore a systemic issue rather than one of fact and degree, and so is a matter of law for the court to decide rather than a question of fact for a jury. As a systemic matter, consistency is key. The disjuncture in terminology between the Restatement (Third) of Torts: Products Liability (referred to hereinafter as the Products Liability Restatement) on the one hand, and the Uniform Commercial Code (UCC) on the other, is therefore unfortunate to say the least. In fact, the UCC does not talk of "products" at all, but instead follows English common (and statutory) law in talking of "goods." Article 2-105(1) of the UCC defines "goods" as:

> all things (including specially manufactured goods) which are movable at the time of identification to the contract for sale other than the money in which the price is to be paid, investment securities and things in action. "Goods" also includes the unborn young of animals and growing crops and other identified things attached to realty as described in the section on goods to be severed from realty.

Unlike the law of contracts, which was imported from England some time ago, much of the law of products liability law has been home-grown since the Second World War. For that reason, it developed autonomously and with its own terminology. For most practical purposes, the terms "goods" and "products" are effectively synonymous. (Animals may be an exception, as will be discussed below.) However, the Products Liability Restatement provides a definition of "product" that is somewhat more precise.

Restatement (Third) of Torts: Products Liability (1998)

§ 19. Definition of "Product"

For purposes of this Restatement:

(a) A product is tangible personal property distributed commercially for use or consumption. Other items, such as real property and electricity, are products when the context of their distribution and use is sufficiently analogous to the distribution and use of tangible personal property that it is appropriate to apply the rules stated in this Restatement.

(b) Services, even when provided commercially, are not products.

(c) Human blood and human tissue, even when provided commercially, are not subject to the rules of this Restatement.

Notes

1. *Electricity.* As this definition implies, there have been cases where the courts have been prepared to extend the definition of "products" to include electricity. In *Ransome v. Wisconsin Elec. Power Co.,* 87 Wis.2d 605, 275 N.W.2d 641 (1979), the owners of a house which was destroyed by fire as a result of an electricity overload were permitted by the Wisconsin Supreme Court to bring a products liability action against the electric power company on the grounds that, when the electricity passed through the electric meter and into the house, it was in an unreasonably dangerous condition (at 4,800 volts). This view was considered persuasive by the Connecticut Supreme Court in *Carbone v. Connecticut Light & Power Co.,* 482 A.2d 722 (1984). However, it was not followed by the Ohio Supreme Court in *Otte v. Dayton Power & Light Co.,* 37 Ohio St.3d 33, 37–38; 523 N.E.2d 835, 839–40 (1988), where Wright J. declared:

> We must note that there are a scattering of cases that have determined electricity is a product for strict liability purposes. Some have reached the curious conclusion that electricity passing through a consumer's meter becomes a product, but electricity not passing that point is a service. Although this distinction is convenient for Section 402A [of the Second Restatement of Torts] analysis purposes, we find it unsupported by both logic and common sense. The jurisdictions finding electricity to be a product with no meter distinction fail to recognize that electricity is not manufactured and that it undergoes a substantial change in form before entering the home. We decline the invitation to follow such logic.

2. *Real property.* Similarly, although the definition of "products" may extend to real property, whether such an expansive application of the term is appropriate will depend very much on the context. The relevant features include not just the particular factual matrix of the case, but also the precise manner in which the relevant law has been brought into force within a given jurisdiction. In *Association of Unit Owners of Bridgeview Condominiums v. Dunning,* 187 Or.App. 595, 618; 69 P.3d 788, 801 (2003), Landau P.J., giving judgment for the Oregon Court of Appeals, commented:

> In any event, the courts of other jurisdictions have split on the question whether section 402A extends to entire buildings.... Those courts that have expanded the concept of "product" to encompass buildings have done so as a matter of policy. In contrast, as we have explained, we are constrained to determine the issue as a matter of statutory construction, focusing instead on what the legislature most likely intended when it enacted the product liability law.

3. *Human blood and tissue.* The exclusion of human blood and tissue from the definition of products is explained by the Products Liability Restatement's Reporters both in *Comment c* to § 19 and in their notes on *Comment c*:

> Although human blood and human tissue meet the formal requisites of Subsection (a), they are specifically excluded from the coverage of this Restatement. Almost all the litigation regarding such products has dealt with contamination of human blood and blood-related products by the hepatitis virus or the HIV virus. Absent a special rule dealing with human blood and tissue, such contamination presumably would be subject to the rules of §§ 1 and 2(a). Those Sections impose strict liability when a product departs from

its intended design even though all possible care was exercised in the preparation and marketing of the product.... In recent years, however, legislatures and courts alike have concluded that public policy concerns behind the availability of both human blood and tissue outweigh the risks inherent in their supply. Thus, in almost all states, liability of human blood and tissue suppliers is limited through legislation.

4. *Alternatives.* The exclusion of blood and human tissue from products liability law does not necessarily mean that a victim of contaminated blood or tissue will have no right to compensation. Where legislation governs the situation in the relevant jurisdiction, that will dictate what rights or immunities exist; otherwise (such as in cases of cosmetic surgery) the victim will have to fall back on the ordinary common law of contracts or torts.

5. *Intangible property.* There is also the difficult question of whether the tangible medium through which (obviously intangible) ideas and information are conveyed can be the subject of a products liability claim. *Comment d* to § 19 argues that:

> [With] information in media such as books, maps, and navigational charts[, p]laintiffs allege that the information delivered was false and misleading, causing harm when actors relied on it. They seek to recover against publishers in strict liability in tort based on product defect, rather than on negligence or some form of misrepresentation. Although a tangible medium such as a book, itself clearly a product, delivers the information, the plaintiff's grievance in such cases is with the information, not with the tangible medium. Most courts, expressing concern that imposing strict liability for the dissemination of false and defective information would significantly impinge on free speech have, appropriately, refused to impose strict products liability in these cases. One area in which some courts have imposed strict products liability involves false information contained in maps and navigational charts. In that context the falsity of the factual information is unambiguous and more akin to a classic product defect. However, the better view is that false information in such documents constitutes a misrepresentation that the user may properly rely upon.

6. *Maps and charts.* In *Saloomey v. Jeppesen & Co.*, 707 F.2d 671, 676–77 (2nd Cir., C.A.Conn., 1983) Judge Davis, writing for the court, which was unanimous on this point, found that:

> We believe that the trial court did not err in classifying appellant's charts as products. The charts, as produced by Jeppesen and supplied to Wahlund by Braniff, reached Wahlund without any individual tailoring or substantial change in contents—they were simply mass-produced. The comments to § 402A ... envision strict liability against sellers of such items in these circumstances. By publishing and selling the charts, Jeppesen undertook a special responsibility, as seller, to insure that consumers will not be injured by the use of the charts; Jeppesen is entitled—and encouraged—to treat the burden of accidental injury as a cost of production to be covered by liability insurance. This special responsibility lies upon Jeppesen in its role as designer, seller and manufacturer.
>
> Appellant's position that its navigational charts provide no more than a service ignores the mass-production aspect of the charts. Though a "product" may not include mere provision of architectural design plans or any similar form of data supplied under individually-tailored service arrangements, the mass production and marketing of these charts requires Jeppesen to bear the costs of accidents that are proximately caused by defects in the charts.

Saloomey was, however, distinguished by the Court of Appeals of Texas in the following case.

Way v. Boy Scouts of America

856 S.W.2d 230 (1993) (Court of Appeals of Texas)

WHITTINGTON, J. Jan Way, individually and on behalf of the estate of Rocky William Miller, deceased, sued the Boy Scouts of America, National Shooting Sports Foundation, Inc., and Remington Arms Company, Inc. claiming that a supplement on shooting sports published in Boys' Life magazine caused the death of her son. Way's twelve-year-old son, Rocky, read the supplement on shooting sports and was later killed when the rifle he and several friends were playing with accidentally discharged. We must decide whether Texas law, under these circumstances, recognizes a cause of action for publication of an article or advertisement that causes harm to a reader. In the trial court, appellees separately moved for summary judgment. The trial court granted appellees' motions for summary judgment. Appellant contends the trial court erred in granting summary judgment. Because we conclude that Texas law does not recognize a cause of action for publication of an article or advertisement that causes harm under these circumstances, we affirm the trial court's judgment....

In reviewing a summary judgment record, we apply the following standards:

1. The movant for summary judgment has the burden of showing that there is no genuine issue of material fact and that it is entitled to judgment as a matter of law.

2. In deciding whether there is a disputed material fact issue precluding summary judgment, evidence favorable to the non-movant will be taken as true.

3. Every reasonable inference must be indulged in favor of the non-movant and any doubts resolved in its favor.

[The] cases [like *Saloomey*] involved aircraft charts and flight maps that erroneously depicted data necessary for the navigation and operation of an airplane. In those cases, the charts were physically used in the operation of the aircraft at the time of the accident. The inaccurate data directly caused or was alleged to have caused the accidents in question in the same manner in which a broken compass or an inaccurate altimeter would have caused a plane to crash.

Here, Way is not complaining about the physical properties of the supplement. She alleges the ideas and information contained in the magazine encouraged children to engage in activities that were dangerous. These are intangible characteristics, not tangible properties. The Ninth Circuit explained the distinction between tangible and intangible aspects of a publication as follows:

> A book containing Shakespeare's sonnets consists of two parts, the material and the print therein, and the ideas and expression thereof. The first may be a product, but the second is not. The latter, were Shakespeare alive, would be governed by copyright laws; the laws of libel, to the extent consistent with the First Amendment; and the laws of misrepresentation, negligent misrepresentation, negligence, and mistake. These doctrines applicable to the second part are aimed at the delicate issues that arise with respect to intangibles such as ideas and expression. Products liability law is geared to the tangible world. *Winter v. G.P. Putnam's Sons*, 938 F.2d 1033, 1034 (9th Cir.1991).

In *Winter*, the plaintiffs consulted *The Encyclopedia of Mushrooms* in gathering and cooking mushrooms. After eating the mushrooms, they became sick. The plaintiffs analogized their case to the ones involving defective aeronautical charts to support their cause of action for products liability. The *Winter* court rejected this argument. The court found the aeronautical charts to be highly technical tools similar to a compass. In contrast, the court found the *Encyclopedia of Mushrooms* to be like a book on how to use a compass or aeronautical chart. The court further found that although the chart itself is like a physical product, the how-to-use book is pure thought and expression. The court concluded there was no basis for a products liability action....

We conclude that the ideas, thoughts, words, and information conveyed by the magazine and the shooting sports supplement are not products within the meaning of the Restatement (Second) of Torts.

Judgment affirmed.

Notes

1. *Freedom of speech.* Underlying the concern about the implications of allowing the words of a book to be construed as a "product" is the fear that such a decision would have a "chilling" effect on freedom of speech. Thus in *Smith v. Linn*, 563 A.2d 123 (1989), the Superior Court of Pennsylvania held that a diet book which advocated *The Last Chance Diet* of liquid protein was protected by the First Amendment of the Constitution of the United States. The plaintiff had argued that, since his wife had died from cardiac failure (allegedly as a result of following the diet), the book was so false and dangerous as to be tantamount to shouting "Fire" in a crowded theater and was therefore unworthy of First Amendment protection. The Court rejected the analogy as "inapposite." *Linn* was followed in *Gorran v. Atkins Nutritionals, Inc.*, 464 F.Supp.2d 315, 324–25 (2006), where the plaintiff alleged that he had undergone an angioplasty—a surgical procedure to unclog a coronary artery—because of his following the *Atkins Diet*. The court held:

> The intangible qualities of a book, however—the ideas and expressions—are not products for purposes of products liability law. Imposing liability for physical injuries caused by the ideas contained in a book would "inhibit those who wish to share thoughts and theories," for no author would write on a topic that could potentially result in physical injury to the reader.

2. *Computer software.* If maps are products, but the self-help instructions in books are not, where does that leave computer software? There have been no definitive cases so far, although *Winter* suggested in passing (938 F.2d at 1035) that software might constitute a product. The question was left open in the Products Liability Restatement, though *Comment d* noted that software is considered a "good" under the UCC. Whether that advances the argument very far is open to doubt. After all, books are clearly "goods" under the UCC. Treating software like books would mean that a CD, DVD or memory stick containing digital code would be considered a product, but not the code itself.

On the other hand, it could be argued that, unlike ideas, there is simply no meaningful way to separate the digital code from the tangible good that contains it. Thus the CD, DVD or memory stick and the digital code which it contains are best conceived as an integrated whole. See *Retail Systems, Inc. v. CNA Insurance Companies*, 469 N.W.2d 735, 737 (Minn. App., 1991):

> The data on the tape was of permanent value and was integrated completely with the physical property of the tape. Like a motion picture, where the information and the celluloid medium are integrated, so too were the tape and data integrated at the moment the tape was lost.

This argument suggests an analogy with a map. Just as a paper map cannot be separated from the information it conveys, so the electronic media on which data is stored cannot be separated in any tangible sense from the data itself. Indeed, the standard methods for erasing data are either to over-write it with other data—when it may actually remain recoverable and so part of the media on which it is stored—or to de-magnetize the disk, which effectively destroys both data and disk. Moreover, both maps and software are frequently (though not always) mass-produced.

Yet there is a further complication. So far as software downloaded from the internet is concerned, this is delivered by a series of high-speed electronic pulses of electricity. Since electricity which has passed through the consumer's meter is capable of being a product, it could be argued that there is no reason for treating software delivered by this method any differently from that transported on disk or memory stick. Such a view did not, however, find favor in *America Online, Inc. v. St. Paul Mercury Insurance Co.*, 207 F. Supp. 2d 459, 462, 467 (E.D. Va., 2002), where District Judge Lee reasoned:

> First, the Court holds that computer data, software and systems are not "tangible" property in the common sense understanding of the word. The plain and ordinary meaning of the term "tangible" is property that can be touched. Computer data, software and systems are incapable of perception by any of the senses and are therefore intangible. Accordingly, St. Paul has no duty to defend AOL against allegations in the underlying complaint alleging harm to consumers' computer data, software and systems. By the same token, the Court finds that the computer itself is tangible property because it is obviously a tactile, corporeal item. Because the claims in the underlying complaint allege the loss of use of consumers' computers, such claims are potentially covered by the parties' insurance policy....

> [T]he plain and ordinary meaning of the word tangible is something that is capable of being touched or perceptible to the senses. Computer data, software, and systems do not have or possess physical form and are therefore not tangible property as understood by the [insurance] Policy.

> Computer data can be transmitted and stored in a variety of ways, but none of them renders the data capable of being touched. A "bit" on a computer disk or hard drive is not palpable. Electrical impulses that carry computer data may be observable with the aid of a computer, but they are invisible to the human eye. An ordinary person understands the term "tangible" to include something she can touch, such as a chair or a book, not an imperceptible piece of data or software that can only be perceived with the help of a computer.

3. *Components.* It is important to note that a component of a larger product can itself be classed as a product.

Restatement (Third) of Torts: Products Liability (1998)

§ 5. Liability of Commercial Seller or Distributor of Product Components for Harm Caused by Products Into Which Components Are Integrated

One engaged in the business of selling or otherwise distributing product components who sells or distributes a component is subject to liability for harm to persons or property caused by a product into which the component is integrated if:

(a) the component is defective in itself, as defined in this Chapter, and the defect causes the harm; or

(b) (1) the seller or distributor of the component substantially participates in the integration of the component into the design of the product; and

(2) the integration of the component causes the product to be defective, as defined in this Chapter; and

(3) the defect in the product causes the harm.

Jimenez v. Superior Court

58 P.3d 450 (2002) (Supreme Court of California)

KENNARD, J. In 1988, developer McMillin Scripps II completed the Galleria and Renaissance housing developments in the Scripps Ranch area of San Diego. Viking Industries, Inc. (Viking) manufactured the windows in the Galleria development; T.M. Cobb Company (Cobb) manufactured the windows in the Renaissance development.

Plaintiffs Filipina and Nestor Jimenez, owners of one of the Galleria homes, brought this action against window manufacturers Viking and Cobb, and also against two companies (Medallion Industries, Inc., and Minnoch Supply Co.) that had supplied and installed the windows. On behalf of themselves and all homeowners in the Galleria and Renaissance developments, plaintiffs asserted that defendants had "designed, developed, manufactured, produced, supplied and placed into the stream of commerce" defective windows installed in the Galleria and Renaissance homes, and that the defects caused property damage. They alleged strict liability and negligence causes of action.

Window manufacturer Cobb moved for summary adjudication of the strict liability cause of action. Cobb argued that the manufacturer of a product installed in a mass-produced home, unless it has ownership or control over the housing development, cannot be held strictly liable to a homeowner for a defective or dangerous condition in the home. In response, plaintiffs conceded that Cobb did not own or control the Renaissance housing development, but they argued that manufacturers of component parts of mass-produced houses are strictly liable for damages caused by those component parts, including damage to other parts of the houses in which they are installed. Plaintiffs asserted that the allegedly defective windows installed in their home had damaged the "stucco, insulation, framing, drywall, paint, wall coverings, floor coverings, baseboards, and other parts of the home."

The trial court granted window manufacturer Cobb's motion for summary adjudication. The parties later stipulated, and the trial court ordered, that the ruling also applied to window manufacturer Viking. Plaintiffs petitioned the Court of Appeal for a writ of mandate.

The Court of Appeal issued a writ directing the trial court to vacate its order granting the defense motion for summary adjudication. It held that the doctrine of strict products liability applied to manufacturers of defective component parts installed in mass-produced homes, and that this strict liability extended to injuries to other parts of the house in which the defective component was installed. We granted the petitions for review of defendant window manufacturers Cobb and Viking....

In 1969, the Court of Appeal in *Kriegler v. Eichler Homes, Inc.* (1969) 269 Cal.App.2d 224 applied strict products liability to mass-produced homes. There, the plaintiff homeowner successfully sued the developer of mass-produced homes in strict liability for damages caused by the failure of a radiant heating system in the home. The Court of Appeal affirmed the judgment. It pointed out that a developer of defective mass-produced homes, like a manufacturer, retailer, or supplier of another product, is responsible for dangerous conditions in its own products and is in a better economic position to bear the resulting loss than the consumer, who justifiably relied on the developer's expertise in constructing mass-produced homes. The *Kriegler* court explained:

> We think, in terms of today's society, there are no meaningful distinctions between Eichler's mass production and sale of homes and the mass production and sale of automobiles and that the pertinent overriding policy considerations are the same.

Thereafter, the Court of Appeal in *La Jolla Village Homeowners' Assn. v. Superior Court* (1989) 212 Cal.App.3d 1131 (*La Jolla Village*) held that a subcontractor hired by a developer cannot be strictly liable for defects in mass-produced homes, unless it also owns or controls the housing development. Although earlier decisions had concluded that strict products liability did not apply to ordinary subcontractors because they provided services rather than products, the *La Jolla Village* court suggested a broader subcontractor exception, under which strict products liability did not apply to "subcontractors in the typical real estate construction project *regardless of whether they provided 'services' or a 'product.'*" Courts in later cases have disagreed on the soundness of this expansion.

The Court of Appeal in this case was the same Court of Appeal (that is, the same division of the same appellate district) that decided *La Jolla Village*. Interestingly, the Court of Appeal in this case criticized its own earlier statement in *La Jolla Village* that even subcontractors who provide products generally cannot be strictly liable in tort for defects in mass-produced houses. The court characterized its earlier statement as "overstated" and "dictum" and this time concluded that subcontractors providing products may be strictly liable for defects in mass-produced homes. The court retained the limitation, consistent with established law, that persons providing only services are not subject to strict products liability.

Citing *La Jolla Village*, defendant window manufacturers contend that because they merely supplied component parts (the windows) of mass-produced homes, not the completed homes themselves, they should not be subject to strict products liability. They argue that extending strict products liability to component manufacturers would not serve the purposes of strict products liability. We disagree.

Δargument
✱

The policies underlying strict products liability in tort, restated in our decision in *Vandermark*, 61 Cal.2d 256, are equally applicable to component manufacturers and suppliers. Like manufacturers, suppliers, and retailers of complete products, component manufacturers and suppliers are "an integral part of the overall producing and marketing enterprise," may in a particular case "be the only member of that enterprise reasonably available to the injured plaintiff," and may be in the best position to ensure product safety. And component manufacturers and suppliers, like manufacturers, suppliers, and retailers of complete products, can adjust the costs of liability in the course of their continuing business relationship with other participants in the overall manufacture and marketing enterprise. For purposes of strict products liability, there are "no meaningful distinctions" between, on the one hand, component manufacturers and suppliers and, on the other hand, manufacturers and distributors of complete products; for both groups, the "overriding policy considerations are the same."

Defendant window manufacturers here argue that subjecting them to strict liability would be improper because they had no physical control over the windows at the time of the alleged harm. In support, they cite *Preston v. Goldman* (1986) 42 Cal.3d 108. But that case is distinguishable. At issue there was the negligence liability of a former landowner for a dangerous property condition that caused injury after the land was sold. It did *not* involve strict liability for defects in mass-produced homes, which is at issue here. In any event, we have never held or implied that strict products liability applies only to those injuries that defective products cause while still under the manufacturer's ownership or control. Rarely, if ever, are defective products still in the control of a manufacturer, distributor, or retailer at the time of injury to the consumer. What matters is whether the windows were defective when they left the factory, and whether these alleged defects caused the injuries.

Insisting that they should not be held strictly liable, defendant window manufacturers point out that their windows are shipped in parts, assembled by others, and installed by others. They rely on language in subdivision (1)(b) of section 402A of the Restatement Second of Torts. That subdivision says that the seller of a defective product "is subject to liability for physical harm thereby caused to the ultimate user or consumer, or to his property, if ... (b) *it is expected to and does reach the user or consumer without substantial change in the condition in which it is sold.*" (Italics added.) The mere assembly of a product that is sold in parts is not a "substantial change" in the product within the meaning of the Restatement. The issue is not whether the product was sold fully assembled or in parts, but rather whether the defect that resulted in the alleged damage existed when the windows left the manufacturers' control. To the extent defendants argue that any defect in their windows resulted from improper assembly or installation, their argument is not properly before us here. A motion for summary adjudication may be granted only if there is no triable issue of material fact. Defendants' motion for summary adjudication did not rely on a claim of improper assembly or installation....

Finally, defendant window manufacturers contend that applying strict liability to them would "open the litigation floodgates." They predict a massive increase in litigation as manufacturers and distributors of component products used in the mass production of homes bring actions and cross actions against each other for indemnity and other claims. We are not convinced. The same dire predictions were made in response to the original development of strict products liability. As we have explained, the policy reasons favoring strict products liability for component manufacturers are the same as for other participants in the general enterprise of manufacturing and marketing consumer goods, and these interests, including the incentives for improved product safety, outweigh the burden imposed by increased litigation.

Holding

Accordingly, we hold that the manufacturers of component parts, here windows, that are installed in mass-produced homes can be subject to strict products liability in tort when their defective products cause harm.

Notes

1. *Floodgates.* Note the reference by Kennard J to the "litigation floodgates." This is an issue to which we shall regularly return. For the moment, it is important to distinguish two issues here which are often conflated.

2. *Floods of lawsuits.* One issue is the notion that "floods" of lawsuits will be brought because plaintiffs (advised, of course, by their attorneys) find that they have the opportunity to recover compensation when formerly that would not have been possible. This may be called the threat of floods of lawsuits. Naturally, such a threat will arise only if a significant increase occurs in the number of plaintiffs who find that they have a realistic chance of success in seeking compensation for an injury suffered.

3. *Floods of trials.* The second issue is that "floods" of claims will reach the courtroom, rather than being settled through negotiation, thus causing far more work for the courts

(perhaps to the extent that there will be an unmanageable backlog of cases and so the courts will be unable to cope). This may be called the threat of floods of trials. This is by no means the same sort of threat as that of floods of lawsuits. In fact, if the threat of floods of lawsuits is genuine, then defendants will generally settle out of court because they will realize that there is little prospect of a successful defense. The threat of floods of trials, however, will be valid only if there is such confusion or ambiguity in the law that *both* plaintiffs and defendants believe that they have a reasonable chance of success in any litigation. In such circumstances, neither side will have a significant incentive to settle before trial, and so the courts would risk being flooded with more cases.

4. *Lawsuits and trials.* It is particularly important to realize that the threat of floods of trials does not necessarily imply a threat of floods of lawsuits. It can occur just as easily when a change in the law is made which appears perhaps—but not definitively—to give defendants a chance to resist a claim where previously they had none. While it is normally defendants who make a "floodgates" assertion, it must be emphasized that there is actually no reason why it cannot be made by plaintiffs against defendants who seek to resist liability. (Whether such assertions are actually valid will, like every other "floodgates" argument, be a matter of law for the court to judge in the circumstances of the particular case.)

Unfortunately, judges, attorneys, academics and politicians are all guilty of sloppy usage—which probably reflects sloppy thinking—when they talk of the "floodgates" argument. The validity of any such assertion can really be assessed only once it has first been established whether it is a "floods of lawsuits" or a "floods of trials" claim.

5. *Raw materials.* In *Garza v. Asbestos Corp., Ltd.*, 161 Cal. App. 4th 651 (2008), an appellate court in California dismissed an appeal from a supplier of asbestos from a judgment in favor of a worker and his wife for personal injury and loss of consortium. They had alleged that the worker's exposure to asbestos and asbestos-containing products caused him severe and permanent lung damage (asbestosis), as well as increased risk and fear of developing mesothelioma and lung cancer. Among other arguments made on appeal the defendants, ACL, contended that their asbestos was not a "product," but a raw material, and that it was only through the asbestos-buying corporation's production process that the asbestos had become incorporated into a finished (insulation) product. ACL argued that this meant that any products liability claim should therefore have been made only against the insulation manufacturer and any subsequent distributors.

The Superior Court, however, affirmed both the verdict in favor of the plaintiffs and its previous judgment in *Arena v. Owens-Corning Fiberglass Corp.*, 63 Cal.App.4th 1178 (1998). It repeated the reasoning in *Arena* that, because incorporating raw asbestos into an insulation product does not substantially alter ACL's own product (i.e., its asbestos), ACL remained responsible under products liability law for any defects in that product.

6. *Asbestos.* As will be seen regularly through this course, exposure to dangerous asbestos products has been a regular source not only of product liability suits, but also of questions as to how—and to what extent—courts should adapt standard axioms of tort law so as to deal meaningfully with claims arising from this particular hazard.

Board of Education of City of Chicago v. A, C And S, Inc. *Don't have to read*

546 N.E.2d 580 (1989) (Supreme Court of Illinois)

RYAN, J. The issue presented in this case is whether the plaintiffs, 34 school districts, have sufficiently pleaded a cause of action to recover the removal and repair costs of asbestos-containing material (ACM) in their buildings from the various defendants who are or were involved at some level of the manufacturing and distribution chain of ACM. The circuit court of Cook County granted the defendants' motion to dismiss each of the 13 causes of action alleged in the plaintiffs' complaints. The appellate court ... reversed on the strict liability, negligence, intentional and negligent misrepresentation, restitution, consumer fraud and breach of warranty counts. The remaining four counts were not raised on appeal. We agree with the appellate court that these complaints allege sufficient facts to survive a motion to dismiss as to the negligence, strict liability and negligent misrepresentation counts, but affirm the trial court's dismissal of the other counts....

Each of the three complaints essentially allege the same facts; in fact, the Chicago and Evanston complaints are nearly identical. The trial court, therefore, based its rulings using the Chicago complaint as the court's outline. Preliminarily, the facts alleged which are common to each count are that asbestos is a known carcinogen which can lead to lung cancer and other serious diseases; a disturbance or deterioration of ACMs causes the release of asbestos fibers into the air, where they may remain for long periods of time; defendants obscured medical and scientific data as to the link between asbestos and disease; defendants ignored and failed to act upon available medical and scientific data; by failing to warn, the defendants induced plaintiffs to purchase large quantities of asbestos products between 1946 and 1972; and the failure to warn deprived plaintiffs of a knowledgeable choice of alternatives. Plaintiffs admit that it may be impossible to identify a specific defendant with the products in a specific school, but allege that the existence of asbestos products in the schools continues to present a danger to the health and welfare of students, school personnel and others. It is also alleged that undertaking the corrective action required ... will be very costly.

The first two causes of action sound in tort—strict products liability and negligence. The parties and both the appellate and circuit courts dealt with the sufficiency of these counts together. The linchpin for both of these causes is whether the complaints sufficiently allege that asbestos has caused damage to other property or injury to persons so as to fall within a tort claim, as opposed to a contract cause of action. The defendants contend that the plaintiffs have, if anything, only suffered economic loss, which is recoverable in contract and not in tort. They argue that there is only alleged a risk of harm to people and no actual harm is pleaded. Further, they contend that no property damage is alleged in the complaint. The plaintiffs counter that there is alleged property damage to the extent that the buildings are contaminated with a toxic substance which renders them unsafe for their normal use....

Perhaps it is difficult, and may appear somewhat artificial, to fit a claim for asbestos damage within the framework which has been established for more traditional tort or contract actions. Indeed, the nature of the "defect" and the "damage" caused by asbestos is unique from most of the cases we have addressed. Nonetheless, we do believe that this complaint has alleged sufficient facts to establish a tort action ...

It is alleged in these complaints that friable asbestos exists in plaintiffs' buildings and asbestos has been released throughout the schools. We need not, in ruling on this motion to dismiss, determine whether the amounts of friable asbestos which exist in the buildings are harmful. Our focus is to take as true the facts alleged in the complaints and determine whether they sufficiently state a claim.

We conclude that it would be incongruous to argue there is no damage to other property when a harmful element exists throughout a building or an area of a building which by law must be corrected and at trial may be proven to exist at unacceptably dangerous levels. The view that asbestos fibers may contaminate a building sufficiently to allege damage to property has been recently adopted in a number of cases. A claim of property damages to the city hall of Greenville, South Carolina, caused by asbestos contamination was held actionable in tort in *City of Greenville v. W.R. Grace & Co.*, 827 F.2d 975 (4th Cir.1987). In *City of Greenville*, ACM was attached to steel beams in the building. The negligence action survived a motion to dismiss, and at trial, evidence was presented establishing its defective nature and that asbestos fibers had been released into ceiling tiles, ventilation and elevator shafts, carpets and computer equipment. The jury held in favor of the city and awarded damages. On appeal, the court held that the property damage alleged was sufficient for a tort action. In affirming the denial of a judgment notwithstanding the verdict, the court held that from the evidence presented the jury could have reasonably found that the product was unreasonably dangerous and defective and "that the city hall was contaminated by significant amounts of asbestos." ...

The ACMs involved in this case include acoustic plaster, acoustic tile, boiler insulation, pipe insulation and spray-on fireproofing. The fact that these are used in construction and have been installed in a building does not detract from their nature as products separate from the actual structure. We cannot accept the defendant's argument that these ACMs have become permanent fixtures upon real property, indistinguishable from the buildings themselves, and to do so would defeat the underlying policy reasons for imposing tort or recovery.

Our holding is not influenced by the fact that these ACMs performed the insulation or fire-proofing purposes satisfactorily. A product may adequately perform its intended purposes yet still cause personal injury or damage to other property. Therefore, the plaintiffs should be given a chance to prove that friable asbestos exists within the buildings and that the remaining criteria, other than whether physical harm is alleged, for either a strict products liability or a negligence action exists.

Affirmed in part and reversed in part.

Questions

1. Is computer software best considered as a product or not? If not, what is it?

2. Is it best to address these questions (a) by applying tests laid down in other cases, such as *Saloomey*, *Winter*, and *American Online*, or (b) by analogizing between computer software and some other item about which the courts have already made a decision, or (c) by considering the functions that the software performs in each specific context?

3. Is an in-car satellite navigation system that gives the driver audible advice as to where to go a product or a service?

4. How real are the so-called "floodgates" problems?

5. Which sort of floodgates claim was being made in *Jimenez v. Superior Court*?

6. Should raw materials be capable of being classified as products?

7. Many products, such as flat-packed furniture, are sold or distributed together with instructions as to how the items should be assembled. If one or more of these instructions is faulty, so that the assembled product is defective, and that defect subsequently causes injury to someone using it, is any resultant claim properly conceived as relating to a defective product, or would it implicate some other area of law?

Sale or Other Distribution

The Products Liability Restatement explains in two stages what is involved in this element of products liability law.

Restatement (Third) of Torts: Products Liability (1998)

§ 1. Liability of Commercial Seller or Distributor for Harm Caused by Defective Products

One engaged in the business of selling or otherwise distributing products who sells or distributes a defective product is subject to liability for harm to persons or property caused by the defect.

§ 20. Definition of "One Who Sells or Otherwise Distributes"

For purposes of this Restatement:

(a) One sells a product when, in a commercial context, one transfers ownership thereto either for use or consumption or for resale leading to ultimate use or consumption. Commercial product sellers include, but are not limited to, manufacturers, wholesalers, and retailers.

(b) One otherwise distributes a product when, in a commercial transaction other than a sale, one provides the product to another either for use or consumption or as a preliminary step leading to ultimate use or consumption. Commercial nonsale product distributors include, but are not limited to, lessors, bailors, and those who provide products to others as a means of promoting either the use or consumption of such products or some other commercial activity.

(c) One also sells or otherwise distributes a product when, in a commercial transaction, one provides a combination of products and services and either the transaction taken as a whole, or the product component thereof, satisfies the criteria in Subsection (a) or (b).

Notes

1. *Question of fact or law?* The issue of whether there has been a sale or other distribution is normally considered to be one of fact for the jury, subject to the judge's reserve power to rule as a matter of law when there is insufficient evidence to support a contrary verdict. However, in *Agurto v. Guhr*, 887 A.2d 159, 166 (2005) (see below), the Superior Court of New Jersey held that resolving the issue of whether someone is a "product seller" necessarily "requires a determination as to whether defendant has a duty that results in his being subject to principles of strict liability." Since duty is undoubtedly a systemic issue of law and is therefore a matter for the court, it followed that the question of whether someone is a "product seller" is also one for the court rather than for the jury.

2. *Sale and the UCC.* The Restatement clearly goes beyond the definition of a "sale" provided in Article 2-106(1) of the Uniform Commercial Code (UCC), which describes it as "the passing of title from the seller to the buyer for a price." The Restatement is itself defective, however, in failing to take sufficient note of the Reporters' own *Comment c*: "The rule stated in this Section applies only to manufacturers and other commercial sellers and distributors who are *engaged in the business of selling or otherwise distributing the type of product* that harmed the plaintiff" (emphasis added). It is arguable whether employing the more precise terminology of "merchant" used in the Uniform Commercial Code would

be preferable, as well as aiding consistency between commercial law and products liability law.

Uniform Commercial Code — Article 2 — Sales (1952)

§ 2-104(1). Definitions: "Merchant"

"Merchant" means a person that deals in goods of the kind or otherwise by his occupation holds himself out as having knowledge or skill peculiar to the practices or goods involved in the transaction or to which the knowledge or skill may be attributed by the person's employment of an agent or broker or other intermediary that holds itself out by occupation as having the knowledge or skill.

Note

It seems possible that employing the UCC terminology of "merchant" rather than that in § 20 of the *Restatement (Third) of Torts* would make a substantive difference to the law in at least some cases.

Agurto v. Guhr

887 A.2d 159 (2005) (Superior Court of New Jersey)

S.L. REISNER, J.A.D. Plaintiff, an employee of Baker Adhesive Co., was seriously injured when his arm was drawn into a glue mixing machine that Baker had bought from defendant Valer Guhr. Plaintiff sued Guhr under the Product Liability Act, *N.J.S.A.* 2A:58C-1 to -11, contending that Guhr was a product seller who was strictly liable for any defect in the mixing machine. The trial judge granted Guhr's motion for summary judgment, concluding that the evidence was insufficient to establish that he was a product seller as defined in the Act.

We conclude that the trial judge erroneously viewed the evidence in the light most favorable to the defendant, contrary to the well-established summary judgment standard. Giving plaintiff the benefit of all favorable inferences, he was entitled to a trial on the issue of whether defendant was a product seller. Because defendant's alleged status as a seller under the Act is an issue of duty which the court must decide, and since it is a discrete issue readily separable from the underlying personal injury suit, the trial judge should have conducted a bench trial on the issue pursuant to *R.* 4:46-3(b)....

We briefly review the facts and procedural history of this matter. This action arose from an accident that occurred on October 30, 2000, while plaintiff, Jose Agurto, was operating a glue mixer or "disperser" at his place of employment, Baker Adhesive Company. While he was working on the mixer, the machine grabbed his shirt and pulled him in. As a result, his right arm became caught in the vat, was crushed, and had to be amputated. He sued Guhr, the seller of the mixer, and Special Machinery Corp., the manufacturer, on claims of strict liability and negligence.

The facts relating to the strict liability claim are as follows. Guhr obtained the machine in 1992 from a company called Malcom-Nickol in lieu of payment for work he had done for that company. He kept the machine in his warehouse for five years and then sold it to Baker in 1997. The machine was manufactured by Special Machinery Corp., an entity that was defunct by the time of plaintiff's lawsuit. Hence, Guhr was not protected by the exemption in the Product Liability Act for a seller that can identify the manufacturer of the defective product.

At his deposition Guhr testified that he was an electrician who worked as an independent contractor providing installation and maintenance services for Baker and similar companies. He testified that he worked on production and packaging machinery, such as "[r]ibbon blenders, dryers, dispersers [and] pumps." He admitted selling the machine in question to Baker and he admitted having additional machines in his warehouse.

In Guhr's deposition, he also admitted having sold at least three machines to other companies besides Baker since 2000, although he claimed that sales of machinery were a very small part of his business. He claimed he could not recall how many machines he had sold between 1995 and 2000.

Stewart, the president of Baker, testified at one point in his deposition that Guhr "[b]ought equipment for us and maintained it." He testified that "if we needed a machine, we would just go to Valer Guhr and say we needed a machine." But later in his deposition he testified that Baker had bought machines from Guhr. He was asked "Do you know how many other machines, if any, Baker Adhesive has purchased from Mr. Guhr over whatever period of time?" He answered "[p]robably all of them." He was then asked "[a]nd by that you mean to say that Baker Adhesive has probably purchased all of the mixing machines from Mr. Guhr at one point or another?" He responded "I would think so, yes." He also testified that Guhr was called to his company on an average of once a month to perform maintenance and repairs on the machinery.

After the depositions were completed, defendant moved for summary judgment. In a certification that was not provided to plaintiff's counsel until the day of the motion argument, Guhr attested that he had "occasionally put [Baker] in touch with used machine dealers for the purchase of dispersers. I have not profited from any purchase of machinery made by Baker Adhesive." In supplemental answers to interrogatories, also served on plaintiff on the day of the argument, he attested "I have not sold machines to anyone in the past 15 years. At time [sic] I may have placed companies interested in buying machine [sic] with machine dealers, but I have not sold any machines." He also stated that

> [t]o the best of my recollection over the past 15 years [the disperser in question] is the only machine that I sold to Baker. Over the past 20 years or so, I have placed Baker in touch with distributors ... and facilitated Bakers' [sic] purchase of 3–4 machines, but they were not sold by Valer Guhr.

The trial judge granted summary judgment based on his conclusion that although there was some apparent contradiction in Stewart's testimony as to whether Baker purchased additional machinery from Guhr, his use of the word "probably" made his testimony too indefinite to create a material dispute of fact. The lack of any documentation that Guhr made other sales to Baker also led the judge to conclude that the record could not support a finding that Guhr was a product seller under the Act.

In deciding a motion for summary judgment, the trial court must determine whether the evidence, when viewed in a light most favorable to the non-moving party, would permit a rational fact-finder to resolve the dispute in the non-moving party's favor. The trial court cannot decide issues of fact but must decide whether there are any such issues of fact. Our review of a trial court's summary judgment decision is *de novo* ...

The critical issue in this case is whether Guhr was acting as a product seller when he sold the mixing machine to Baker. The Product Liability Act defines the term "product seller" as follows:

Question Presented

> "Product seller" means any person who, *in the course of a business conducted for that purpose: sells;* distributes; leases; *installs;* prepares or assembles a manufacturer's product according to the manufacturer's plan, intention, design, specifications or formulations; blends; packages; labels; markets; *repairs; maintains or otherwise is involved in placing a product in the line of commerce* (emphasis added).

As we recognized in *Becker v. Tessitore,* "[t]his definition encompasses entities within a product's chain of distribution and is consistent with most prior New Jersey case law ... and the common law" and hence we look to pre-Act cases in construing the Act.

Looking to case law that predated the Act, we find that strict liability has been applied to sellers of used equipment.

Strict liability may also apply to a broker who takes possession of goods, or exercises control over them, and then transfers them to a buyer.

There is also a recognized exception for the "casual" or "occasional" seller of goods. This exception is discussed in the *Restatement (Third) of Torts* § 1 (1998). In the comments to this section, it is noted that the seller does not have to exclusively sell or distribute the product as long as the sale is not occasional or casual. *Restatement (Third) of Torts* § 1 comment c (1998). The exception applies to occasional sales outside the regular course of the seller's business. For example, an occasional sale of a business's surplus equipment is not covered under this rule.

In light of the New Jersey cases in which this exception has been applied, we conclude that the term "occasional" does not mean "once in a while." It means that the selling of the goods at issue is not part of the "purpose" of the seller's business under *N.J.S.A.* 2A:58C-8. For example, in *Santiago v. E.W. Bliss Div.,* we declined to apply strict liability to a company that sold one of its punch presses after using the machine in its telephone equipment business for twenty-three years. We recognized that "the rule of strict liability does not apply to an occasional seller who is not engaged in that activity *as a part of its business*" (emphasis added). The defendant in *Santiago* did not manufacture or sell punch presses as part of its business; it only used the punch press to make telephone equipment. Hence, although it happened to sell off one of its used punch presses, it was not a "seller" of punch presses for purposes of strict liability.

Similarly, in *Allen v. Nicole, Inc.,* defendant Jones, an amusement ride operator, purchased an amusement ride from the manufacturer and after two months of use, sold it to defendant Nicole, Inc., an operator of amusement rides. In the regular course of Jones' business, he had occasionally traded equipment with manufacturers and other ride operators. But the court held that this activity did not make him a seller for purposes of strict liability:

> In the case at bar defendant Jones, if he may be viewed as a seller, is even more a consumer of the equipment, for it is not the sale but the use of the equipment which constitutes his business. His disposal of less favored rides does not rise to the level of being a business of selling.

Guhr does not dispute that if he were in the business of selling used machinery, the Act would apply to him. His contention is that he is not, and never has been, in the business of such sales. He contends that his business was not "conducted for the purpose" of selling used equipment. *N.J.S.A.* 2A:58C-8. Rather he seeks to bring his activity within the exceptions for brokers or facilitators of sales, or for occasional sales. While he may ultimately be entitled to the benefit of one or both exceptions, the murky and contradictory state of this record does not entitle him to summary judgment....

Reversed and remanded.

Notes

Auctioneers. In *New Texas Auto Auction Services, L.P. v. Gomez De Hernandez*, 249 S.W.3d 400, 402 (2008), the Supreme Court of Texas held that an auctioneer could not be considered to be a "product seller" since, as Justice Brister put it:

> While they are obviously engaged in sales, the only thing they sell for their own account is their services; the items they auction are generally sold for others. In this case, the court of appeals held an auto auctioneer could be liable in both strict liability and negligence for auctioning a defective car. But product-liability law requires those who *place* products in the stream of commerce to stand behind them; it does not require everyone who *facilitates* the stream to do the same.

In *New Texas* the auctioneer had actually acquired the title of the defective vehicle that it sold, but the Court held that that was irrelevant because (a) it did not normally do so, and did so on this occasion only because of an arbitrator's order; and (b) the occasional sale of its own goods did not amount to its running a *business* selling products.

Questions

1. If the trial judge in *Agurto v. Guhr* had been required to apply the definition of "merchant" in § 2-104(1) of the UCC rather than that of "product seller" under the New Jersey legislation (which apparently bears the same meaning as § 20 of the Products Liability Restatement), what do you think he would have decided?

2. Why does § 20 of the Products Liability Restatement bear a different meaning from that of "merchant" in § 2-104(1) of the UCC?

3. Does the case of *Agurto v. Guhr* suggest that, if the definition of "merchant" in § 2-104(1) of the UCC had been applicable, this might have caused a "flood of claims" but avoided a "flood of trials"?

4. Would it have been preferable to describe the seller or distributor as a "merchant," as defined in § 2-104(1) of the UCC?

J. McIntyre Machinery, Ltd. v. Nicastro
131 S.Ct. 2780 (2011) (SCOTUS)

KENNEDY, J. This case arises from a products-liability suit filed in New Jersey state court. Robert Nicastro seriously injured his hand while using a metal-shearing machine manufactured by J. McIntyre Machinery, Ltd. (J. McIntyre). The accident occurred in New Jersey, but the machine was manufactured in England, where J. McIntyre is incorporated and operates. The question here is whether the New Jersey courts have jurisdiction over J. McIntyre, notwithstanding the fact that the company at no time either marketed goods in the State or shipped them there. Nicastro was a plaintiff in the New Jersey trial court and is the respondent here; J. McIntyre was a defendant and is now the petitioner.

At oral argument in this Court, Nicastro's counsel stressed three primary facts in defense of New Jersey's assertion of jurisdiction over J. McIntyre.

First, an independent company agreed to sell J. McIntyre's machines in the United States. J. McIntyre itself did not sell its machines to buyers in this country beyond the U.S. distributor, and there is no allegation that the distributor was under J. McIntyre's control.

Second, J. McIntyre officials attended annual conventions for the scrap recycling industry to advertise J. McIntyre's machines alongside the distributor. The conventions took place in various States, but never in New Jersey.

Third, no more than four machines (the record suggests only one), including the machine that caused the injuries that are the basis for this suit, ended up in New Jersey.

In addition to these facts emphasized by petitioner, the New Jersey Supreme Court noted that J. McIntyre held both United States and European patents on its recycling technology. It also noted that the U.S. distributor "structured [its] advertising and sales efforts in accordance with" J. McIntyre's "direction and guidance whenever possible," and that "at least some of the machines were sold on consignment to" the distributor.

In light of these facts, the New Jersey Supreme Court concluded that New Jersey courts could exercise jurisdiction over petitioner without contravention of the Due Process Clause. Jurisdiction was proper, in that court's view, because the injury occurred in New Jersey; because petitioner knew or reasonably should have known "that its products are distributed through a nationwide distribution system that might lead to those products being sold in any of the fifty states"; and because petitioner failed to "take some reasonable step to prevent the distribution of its products in this State."

Both the New Jersey Supreme Court's holding and its account of what it called "[t]he stream-of-commerce doctrine of jurisdiction," were incorrect, however....

A court may subject a defendant to judgment only when the defendant has sufficient contacts with the sovereign "such that the maintenance of the suit does not offend 'traditional notions of fair play and substantial justice.'" *International Shoe Co. v. Washington*, 326 U.S. 310, 316, 66 S.Ct. 154, 90 L.Ed. 95 (1945) (quoting *Milliken v. Meyer*, 311 U.S. 457, 463, 61 S.Ct. 339, 85 L.Ed. 278 (1940)).... In products-liability cases like this one, it is the defendant's purposeful availment that makes jurisdiction consistent with "traditional notions of fair play and substantial justice." ...

Two principles are implicit in the foregoing. First, personal jurisdiction requires a forum-by-forum, or sovereign-by-sovereign, analysis. The question is whether a defendant has followed a course of conduct directed at the society or economy existing within the jurisdiction of a given sovereign, so that the sovereign has the power to subject the defendant to judgment concerning that conduct. Personal jurisdiction, of course, restricts "judicial power not as a matter of sovereignty, but as a matter of individual liberty," for due process protects the individual's right to be subject only to lawful power. *Insurance Corp.*, 456 U.S., at 702, 102 S.Ct. 2099. But whether a judicial judgment is lawful depends on whether the sovereign has authority to render it.

The second principle is a corollary of the first. Because the United States is a distinct sovereign, a defendant may in principle be subject to the jurisdiction of the courts of the United States but not of any particular State. This is consistent with the premises and unique genius of our Constitution.... For jurisdiction, a litigant may have the requisite relationship with the United States Government but not with the government of any individual State. That would be an exceptional case, however. If the defendant is a domestic domiciliary, the courts of its home State are available and can exercise general jurisdiction. And if another State were to assert jurisdiction in an inappropriate case, it would upset the federal balance, which posits that each State has a sovereignty that is not subject to unlawful intrusion by other States. Furthermore, foreign corporations will often target or concentrate on particular States, subjecting them to specific jurisdiction in those forums....

In this case, petitioner directed marketing and sales efforts at the United States. It may be that, assuming it were otherwise empowered to legislate on the subject, the Congress could authorize the exercise of jurisdiction in appropriate courts. That circumstance is not presented in this case, however, and it is neither necessary nor appropriate to address here any constitutional concerns that might be attendant to that exercise of power. Nor is it necessary to determine what substantive law might apply were Congress to authorize jurisdiction in a federal court in New Jersey.... Here the question concerns the authority of a New Jersey state court to exercise jurisdiction, so it is petitioner's purposeful contacts with New Jersey, not with the United States, that alone are relevant.

Respondent has not established that J. McIntyre engaged in conduct purposefully directed at New Jersey. Recall that respondent's claim of jurisdiction centers on three facts: The distributor agreed to sell J. McIntyre's machines in the United States; J. McIntyre officials attended trade shows in several States but not in New Jersey; and up to four machines ended up in New Jersey. The British manufacturer had no office in New Jersey; it neither paid taxes nor owned property there; and it neither advertised in, nor sent any employees to, the State. Indeed, after discovery the trial court found that the "defendant does not have a single contact with New Jersey short of the machine in question ending up in this state." App. to Pet. for Cert. 130a. These facts may reveal an intent to serve the U.S. market, but they do not show that J. McIntyre purposefully availed itself of the New Jersey market.

It is notable that the New Jersey Supreme Court appears to agree, for it could "not find that J. McIntyre had a presence or minimum contacts in this State — in any jurisprudential sense — that would justify a New Jersey court to exercise jurisdiction in this case." 201 N.J., at 61, 987 A.2d, at 582.

ROBERTS, CJ, SCALIA and THOMAS, JJ concurred. BREYER and ALITO, JJ concurred in the judgment.

GINSBURG, J, joined by SOTOMAYOR and KAGAN, JJ (dissenting). A foreign industrialist seeks to develop a market in the United States for machines it manufactures. It hopes to derive substantial revenue from sales it makes to United States purchasers. Where in the United States buyers reside does not matter to this manufacturer. Its goal is simply to sell as much as it can, wherever it can. It excludes no region or State from the market it wishes to reach. But, all things considered, it prefers to avoid products liability litigation in the United States. To that end, it engages a U.S. distributor to ship its machines stateside. Has it succeeded in escaping personal jurisdiction in a State where one of its products is sold and causes injury or even death to a local user?

Under this Court's pathmarking precedent in *International Shoe Co. v. Washington*, 326 U.S. 310, 66 S.Ct. 154, 90 L.Ed. 95 (1945), and subsequent decisions, one would expect the answer to be unequivocally, "No." But instead, six Justices of this Court, in divergent opinions, tell us that the manufacturer has avoided the jurisdiction of our state courts, except perhaps in States where its products are sold in sizeable quantities. Inconceivable as it may have seemed yesterday, the splintered majority today "turn[s] the clock back to the days before modern long-arm statutes when a manufacturer, to avoid being haled into court where a user is injured, need only Pilate-like wash its hands of a product by having independent distributors market it." Weintraub, *A Map Out of the Personal Jurisdiction Labyrinth*, 28 U.C. Davis L. Rev. 531, 555 (1995).

On October 11, 2001, a three-ton metal shearing machine severed four fingers on Robert Nicastro's right hand....

[T]he constitutional limits on a state court's adjudicatory authority derive from considerations of due process, not state sovereignty....

[I]n *International Shoe* itself, and decisions thereafter, the Court has made plain that legal fictions, notably "presence" and "implied consent," should be discarded, for they conceal the actual bases on which jurisdiction rests....

The modern approach to jurisdiction over corporations and other legal entities, ushered in by *International Shoe*, gave prime place to reason and fairness. Is it not fair and reasonable, given the mode of trading of which this case is an example, to require the international seller to defend at the place its products cause injury? Do not litigational convenience and choice-of-law considerations point in that direction? On what measure of reason and fairness can it be considered undue to require McIntyre UK to defend in New Jersey as an incident of its efforts to develop a market for its industrial machines anywhere and everywhere in the United States? Is not the burden on McIntyre UK to defend in New Jersey fair, i.e., a reasonable cost of transacting business internationally, in comparison to the burden on Nicastro to go to Nottingham, England to gain recompense for an injury he sustained using McIntyre's product at his workplace in Saddle Brook, New Jersey?

McIntyre UK dealt with the United States as a single market. Like most foreign manufacturers, it was concerned not with the prospect of suit in State X as opposed to State Y, but rather with its subjection to suit anywhere in the United States....

In sum, McIntyre UK, by engaging McIntyre America to promote and sell its machines in the United States, "purposefully availed itself" of the United States market nationwide, not a market in a single State or a discrete collection of States. McIntyre UK thereby availed itself of the market of all States in which its products were sold by its exclusive distributor. "Th[e] 'purposeful availment' requirement," this Court has explained, simply "ensures that a defendant will not be haled into a jurisdiction solely as a result of 'random,' 'fortuitous,' or 'attenuated' contacts." *Burger King*, 471 U.S., at 475, 105 S.Ct. 2174. Adjudicatory authority is appropriately exercised where "actions by the defendant himself" give rise to the affiliation with the forum. *Ibid.* How could McIntyre UK not have intended, by its actions targeting a national market, to sell products in the fourth largest destination for imports among all States of the United States and the largest scrap metal market?

Reversed.

Questions

1. Note the difference in the characterization by the plurality and dissent of the victim's injury. Do both judgments "spin" the facts and, if so, do their respective "spins" make the judgments more or less persuasive?

2. Would it be accurate to characterize the decision in *Nicastro* as finding that McIntyre UK was not a product seller?

3. Do foreign products manufacturers understand the distinction between exporting to the United States (in the hope of selling as many of their products as possible, wherever they are used) and exporting to specific states? If your answer to this question is "No," does the Supreme Court's invocation of a notion of "purposeful availment" make sense?

4. Does *Nicastro* place domestic US manufacturers and distributors at a competitive disadvantage compared to foreign businesses? Does *Nicastro* encourage foreign manu-

facturers to export to the US? In either case, is the potential economic impact of the decision something about which the Supreme Court should be concerned, or is it simply a matter of economic policy, and so solely the province of politicians?

5. Can domestic US businesses organize themselves in a way to take advantage of the decision in *Nicastro*?

6. Does *Nicastro* mean that the residents of less populous states are more likely to find themselves without a remedy when injured by a defective product than residents of more populous states?

7. As § 1 of the Products Liability Restatement suggests, the liability of a distributor in a products liability case is strict, since it may well have no control (or even influence) over the design or manufacturing of the products it sells, yet it can still be held liable for the injuries caused if one of these products proves defective. Is the notion in *Nicastro* of "purposeful availment" compatible with that notion of strict liability?

Types of Defects

A determination that the product in question was defective at the time of the sale or other distribution is a matter of fact for the jury. However, it will frequently have to be guided by expert testimony and, as will be seen in Part V, the issue of whether such testimony should be admitted leaves broad discretion to the judge. In any event, the plaintiff will have to explain which type(s) of defect are being alleged. This is important not simply because the elements required to prove each type of defect are quite different, but also because the nature of the defect dictates whether the defendant is facing a claim involving fault or not. Nicholas J. McBride & Roderick Bagshaw, Tort Law 764–65 (2nd ed., 2005) have suggested a helpful categorization of defective products into six different types:

> First: a manufactured product that does not conform to its intended design and as a result is more dangerous to use than would otherwise be the case. It is customary to say that such a product suffers from a *manufacturing defect*. An example of such a product is a tin of food where the inner lining of the tin is scratched, making the food inside dangerous to eat.
>
> Second: a manufactured product that conforms to its intended design but it could be designed to a higher safety standard. It is customary to say that such a product suffers from a *design defect*. An example of such a product is a car that is not fitted with airbags.
>
> Third: a manufactured product that is dangerous to use but which cannot be made any safer than it is. We can say that such a product is *inherently dangerous*. An example of such a product is a cigarette.
>
> Fourth: a natural product that is contaminated or infected with some dangerous substance, or otherwise diseased in some way. As the product is natural, and therefore not designed or manufactured, it would be inappropriate to say that it suffers from a *manufacturing defect*, though it is analogous to such a product. Instead, we will say that such a product is *dangerously abnormal*. An example of such a product is a cancerous kidney or a dog that is infested with fleas.
>
> Fifth: a product that does not carry a[n appropriate] warning as to how it should be used. We can say that such a product suffers from a *marketing defect*.

An example of such a product is a box of paracetamol that does not warn that the paracetamol should not be taken in conjunction with other medicine or by those who suffer kidney problems.

Sixth: a product that *may* be dangerous to use but it is impossible to tell whether it is or not. We can say that such a product is *potentially harmful.* An example of such a product is a bag of blood that may or may not carry a virus that will trigger Creutzfeld-Jakob Disease (CJD) in a patient who is given the blood. The blood may be perfectly safe or it may be deadly but it is impossible to know which it is.

Notes

1. *US and UK.* Although the extract above was written as a means of explaining the approach of the Consumer Protection Act 1987 in the United Kingdom, this typology may also be useful in explaining current products liability law in the United States. Note, however, that what McBride and Bagshaw term "marketing defects" are called "failures to warn" in US products liability law.

2. *Dangerously abnormal products.* In *Beyer v. Aquarium Supply Co.*, 94 Misc. 2d 336, 337; 404 N.Y.S.2d 778 (1977), the New York Supreme Court held that a diseased hamster was a product for the purposes of products liability law, reasoning that:

> The purpose for imposing this doctrine in the products liability field is to distribute fairly equitably the inevitable consequences of commercial enterprise and to promote the marketing of safe products. Accordingly, there is no reason why a breeder, distributor or vendor who places a diseased animal in the stream of commerce should be less accountable for his actions than one who markets a defective manufactured product.

Similarly, the Supreme Court of Connecticut held in *Worrell v. Sachs*, 41 Conn. Supp. 179; 563 A.2d 1387 (1989) that a parasite-infested puppy (which carried a disease which caused the buyers' child to go blind) qualified as a product.

However, in *Anderson v. Farmers Hybrid Companies, Inc.*, 87 Ill. App. 3d 493, 501; 408 N.E.2d 1194 (1980), while the Appellate Court for the Third District of Illinois accepted that pigs are "goods," it declined to treat them as products. This was because:

> Living creatures, such as the swine in the instant case, are by their nature in a constant process of internal development and growth and they are also participants in a constant interaction with the environment around them as part of their development. Thus, living creatures have no fixed nature in the same sense as ... mushrooms can be said to have a fixed nature at the time they enter the stream of commerce.

The Supreme Court of South Dakota claimed to follow *Anderson* in the dog-bite case of *Blaha v. Stuard*, 2002 SD 19; 640 N.W.2d 85 (2002). It is submitted, however, that *Blaha* can be justified without going this far. An animal can surely be a product while at the same time recognizing that its propensity to behave in a certain manner is not the stuff of products liability law. An animal that is disease-ridden or parasite-infested at the point of sale is clearly defective for a reason that has nothing to do with its "nature" or personality traits. There seems little to gain by insisting on a semantic distinction between "goods" and "products."

3. *Terminology: inherently or abnormally dangerous?* While McBride and Bagshaw talk of "dangerously abnormal" products, that juxtaposition of adverb and adjective is reversed in the US, where the phrase in common usage is "abnormally dangerous." How-

ever, since the issue in both *Beyer* and *Worrell* was the preliminary one of whether an animal could qualify as a product, neither court considered what might be the appropriate
terminology to describe any defect in a natural product. This vacuum has led to a collapsing
of any terminological distinction between inherently dangerous products and abnormally
dangerous products. In *District of Columbia v. Beretta, U.S.A., Corp.*, 847 A.2d 1127
(2004), for example, the court addressed the question of whether certain firearms are
potentially inherently or abnormally dangerous, thus apparently treating those epithets
as interchangeable.

4. *Blood and human tissue.* The McBride-Bagshaw typology suggests a plausible reason explaining why blood and human tissue are not covered by US products liability law
under § 19(c) of the Products Liability Restatement (1998).

5. *Relevant test.* All this means that US products liability law recognizes four types of
defects, namely (i) manufacturing defects, (ii) design defects, (iii) failures to warn and (iv)
inherently dangerous products. As will become clear in Part II, the law takes a different
approach in relation to each type of issue.

Causation of Physical Harm

Determinations concerning both causation and harm are ordinarily matters of fact for
the jury. However, not only will the jury often need to be guided by expert evidence—
on whose admissibility the court will be required to rule—but the court will also need
to be sure that there is sufficient evidence to sustain a finding that the defendant caused
the plaintiff physical harm. It may seem odd to say this, since the sustaining of physical
harm should clearly be provable with appropriate evidence. So far as the law is concerned,
however, not everything that the layperson might consider to be physical harm is properly characterized as such.

The reason for this complication is the courts' view of the respective merits of actions
in the laws of contracts and torts. As will be seen from the rest of Part I, the action for a
breach of contract regarding a defective product was established well before the notion
of products liability in torts. While the latter has consistently been gaining ground since
the Second World War, it remains true that the courts have been reluctant to allow it to
usurp entirely the purpose and role of contract law. Indeed, it has often been asserted
that contract law exists to protect the legitimate expectations of the parties, whereas tort
law—including products liability law—is designed to provide some redress for innocent victims who have sustained injury.

On this basis, although a product supplied under a contract, but which fails to work
properly, is clearly defective, the loss involved is one that should be remedied by means
of contract law rather than tort law. This is because the loss involved is one of expectation, since the product does not do what was legitimately expected of it. Equally, since
no other injury has been sustained, there can be no question of suing for a tort. The position remains the same if the defect in the product damages the product itself, since all
this does is again render the product unable to do what was legitimately expected of it.
But if the product damages something else, then compensation for the latter injury is recoverable in tort.

For example, a new electrical product with defective wiring might simply not work. That
will amount to a simple breach of contract. Moreover, if the wiring causes a short-circuit

that causes an internal circuit board to burn out, that is still properly to be dealt with in the law of contract, since the only loss suffered by the consumer is still one of expectation: the product just fails to work. On the other hand, if the faulty wiring were to cause the product to catch fire and destroy the consumer's kitchen, then the damage to the kitchen would be compensable in tort.

Unfortunately, the clarity of this approach has been blurred by four complicating factors. One of these is a matter of mixed law and fact; the other three are pure issues of law. As to the factual matter, where a defective product is a component part of a larger product, the question arises of whether that larger item should be treated as one, integrated whole. If so, as Comment *e* to § 21 of the Products Liability Restatement points out, any damage that the component does to other components within the whole will be treated by the law as damage to the product itself. This, of course, then raises the question of when the courts will deem that a specific product is indeed part of an integrated whole, and when it is not.

The second complicating factor relates to the manner in which the courts have expressed this distinction between losses that are properly recoverable in contracts and those that are compensable in torts. For, although the courts regularly explain their decisions along the lines already discussed, they also have a regrettable tendency to refer to this issue by the misleading shorthand of the "economic loss rule." This phrase suggests that purely economic losses are recoverable only in contracts and not in torts, while physical harm is compensable in torts but not contracts. As we have seen, this is not entirely true, because a product that was itself damaged (or that damaged part of a larger, integrated whole) clearly involves the sustaining of physical harm, yet is recoverable only in contracts. Thus the terminology of the "economic loss rule" makes sense only once it is understood that "economic loss" in this context really means loss of expectation, where the victim simply did not get what he was expecting to receive from the transaction.

The third complicating factor is that the various jurisdictions have not adopted a unified approach to this issue, so that the very notion of an economic loss "rule" is highly misleading. Some states restrict the applicability of the doctrine to specific types of cases, others have virtually abandoned it altogether, and still others seem determined to cling to it in every conceivable instance.

The fourth, and final, complicating factor is that, despite its name, the so-called "economic loss rule" has never barred a victim from recovering for economic losses which are consequential on the sustaining of physical harm. Thus, to return to the scenario of the burnt-out kitchen, a householder who had to move into a hotel while repairs were carried out would—in every jurisdiction—be able to claim compensation for both the hotel bills and the associated, additional living expenses, because such economic loss would be consequential on physical harm. This is recognized by § 21 of the Products Liability Restatement.

Jimenez v. Superior Court

58 P.3d 450 (2002) (Supreme Court of California)

[For the facts of this case, see above.] KENNARD, J. Two years after our 1963 decision in *Greenman*, ... 59 Cal.2d 57, which held that manufacturers are strictly liable in tort for injuries that their defective products cause to consumers, we decided *Seely v. White Motor Co.* (1965) 63 Cal.2d 9 (*Seely*). In that case, the plaintiff purchased a truck for use in his business, but he discovered that the truck bounced violently, preventing normal use of the truck for his business. Eventually the truck overturned when its brakes failed. The plaintiff then sued the truck manufacturer to recover the cost of repairing the damage to the truck caused by the accident, the amount he had paid on the purchase price, and business profits he lost because of the truck's bouncing problem. The action was tried to the court, which found that the bouncing problem was a defect in the truck for which the manufacturer was responsible under its written warranty, but that this problem had not caused the accident in which the truck overturned. The court awarded the plaintiff damages for breach of warranty, consisting of the amount paid on the purchase price of the truck and lost business profits attributable to the bouncing problem.

The truck manufacturer appealed, and we affirmed the judgment. We rejected a contention that strict products liability had entirely superseded the law governing product warranties. We explained:

> The distinction that the law has drawn between tort recovery for physical injuries and warranty recovery for economic loss is not arbitrary and does not rest on the "luck" of one plaintiff in having an accident causing physical injury. The distinction rests, rather, on an understanding of the nature of the responsibility a manufacturer must undertake in distributing his products.

We concluded that the nature of this responsibility meant that a manufacturer could appropriately be held liable for physical injuries (including both personal injury and damage to property other than the product itself), regardless of the terms of any warranty. But the manufacturer could not be held liable for "the level of performance of his products in the consumer's business unless he agrees that the product was designed to meet the consumer's demands."

This reasoning ultimately outlined the framework of our economic loss rule, which the United States Supreme Court later adopted in large part for purposes of tort liability under admiralty jurisdiction. As we stressed in *Seely,* recovery under the doctrine of strict liability is limited solely to "physical harm to person or property." Damages available under strict products liability do not include economic loss, which includes damages for inadequate value, costs of repair and replacement of the defective product or consequent loss of profits—without any claim of personal injury or damages to other property ... Most recently, in *Aas v. Superior Court* (2000) 24 Cal.4th 627, 632, we applied the economic loss rule in a negligence action by homeowners against the developer, contractor, and subcontractors who built their dwellings. In *Aas,* the plaintiffs alleged that their homes suffered from many construction defects, but they conceded that many of the defects had caused no bodily injury or property damage. The trial court barred them from introducing evidence of the defects that had caused no injury to persons or property. We upheld the trial court's ruling. We explained that under the economic loss rule, "appreciable, nonspeculative, present injury is an essential element of a tort cause of action." "Construction defects that have not ripened into property damage, or at least into involuntary out-of-pocket losses," we held, "do not comfortably fit the definition of 'appreciable harm'—an essential element of a negligence claim."

In summary, the economic loss rule allows a plaintiff to recover in strict products liability in tort when a product defect causes damage to "other property," that is, property *other than the product itself.* The law of contractual warranty governs damage to the product itself.

To apply the economic loss rule, we must first determine what the product at issue is. Only then do we find out whether the injury is to the product itself (for which recovery is barred by the economic loss rule) or to property other than the defective product (for which plaintiffs may recover in tort). Defendant window manufacturers argue that here the "product" is the entire house in which their windows were installed, and that the damage caused to other parts of the house by the allegedly defective windows is damage to the product itself within the economic loss rule, thus precluding application of strict liability. We disagree.

California decisional law has long recognized that the economic loss rule does not necessarily bar recovery in tort for damage that a defective product (e.g., a window) causes to other portions of a larger product (e.g., a house) into which the former has been incorporated. In *Aas v. Superior Court, supra,* 24 Cal.4th at page 641, we observed that "the concept of recoverable physical injury or property damage" had over time "expanded to include damage to one part of a product caused by another, defective part." The list of examples we gave included *Stearman v. Centex Homes* (2000) 78 Cal.App.4th 611, in which the Court of Appeal affirmed a judgment making a builder strictly liable in tort for damages that a defective foundation caused to the interior and exterior of a home. *Aas* also cited with approval the part of *Casey v. Overhead Door Corp.,* 74 Cal.App.4th 112, in which the Court of Appeal affirmed a nonsuit for the defendant on a tort claim for defective windows only because the plaintiffs had failed to prove that the windows damaged other property. The nonsuit would not have been proper, the Court of Appeal explained, had the plaintiffs been able to support their assertion that the windows had "caused damage to the drywall and framing and resulted in insect infestation and damage to personal property." Defendants' argument here that the house is the relevant product for purposes of applying the economic loss rule is inconsistent with these and other decisions recognizing that the duty of a product manufacturer to prevent property damage does not necessarily end when the product is incorporated into a larger product.

Applying this principle to the facts before us here, we conclude that the manufacturer of a defective window installed in a mass-produced home may be held strictly liable in tort for damage that the window's defect causes to other parts of the home in which it is installed. We have no occasion here to consider whether defective raw materials should be treated in the same manner as component parts or whether there may be situations in which the economic loss rule would bar recovery for damages that a defective component part causes to other portions of the finished product of which it is a part. We hold only that, under California decisional law, the economic loss rule does not bar a homeowner's recovery in tort for damage that a defective window causes to other parts of the home in which it has been installed....

Judgment of the Court of Appeals affirmed.

Gunkel v. Renovations, Inc. and J & N Stone, Inc.

822 N.E.2d 150 (2005) (Supreme Court of Indiana)

BOEHM, J. We hold that damages recoverable in tort for a defective product or service are governed by the "economic loss" doctrine whether or not the product or service is supplied in a transaction subject to either the Products Liability Act or the Uniform Commercial Code, or both. Under the doctrine, physical injuries and damages to other property are recoverable in tort, but damages to the defective product itself are not. Whether damaged property is "other property" turns on whether it was acquired by the plaintiff as a component of the defective product or was acquired separately....

The theory underlying the economic loss doctrine is that the failure of a product or service to live up to expectations is best relegated to contract law and to warranty either express or implied. The buyer and seller are able to allocate these risks and price the product or service accordingly....

We think that the theory supporting the economic loss doctrine supplies the answer to whether damage to "other property" is involved. Only the supplier furnishing the defective property or service is in a position to bargain with the purchaser for allocation of the risk that the product or service will not perform as expected. If a component is sold to the first user as a part of the finished product, the consequences of its failure are fully within the rationale of the economic loss doctrine. It therefore is not "other property." But property acquired separately from the defective good or service is "other property," whether or not it is, or is intended to be, incorporated into the same physical object. Although we express our reasoning slightly differently, we align ourselves with the courts that have concluded that the "product" is the product purchased by the plaintiff, not the product furnished by the defendant. The cases that have used this formulation have typically involved claims by a first user of a finished product that includes a component supplied by the defendant where the purchaser had no dealings with the defendant. A frequently cited example is *King v. Hilton-Davis*, 855 F.2d 1047 (3d Cir.1988), where a farmer sued the manufacturer of a chemical used to treat the seed potatoes that the farmer purchased from a supplier. The Third Circuit applied Pennsylvania law but followed the United States Supreme Court's reasoning in *East River Steamship Corp. v. Transamerica Delaval, Inc.*, 476 U.S. 858, 106 S.Ct. 2295, 90 L.Ed.2d 865 (1986), finding that there was no reason to give purchasers a broader tort remedy against the remote supplier than the purchaser could assert against the manufacturer of the assembled defective product. Similarly, a purchaser of a complete aircraft is remitted to warranty remedies and has no tort remedy against a component supplier even if the entire aircraft is damaged by a defective component.

Here we have the obverse situation. The Gunkels did deal directly with J & N. The same formulation of the demarcation between contract and tort remedies is controlling-property acquired by the plaintiff separately from the defective goods or services is "other property" whose damage is recoverable in tort. That formulation excludes from "other property" other parts of a finished product damaged by components supplied to the seller by other manufactures and imported into the seller's product. But it does make property acquired separately "other property" for purposes of the economic loss rule even if the defective product is to be incorporated into a completed product for use or resale.

The Court of Appeals held that here the "product" is the entire house on which the stone façade was installed. Under this view, the damage caused to other parts of the house by the alleged defect in the façade is damage to the product itself and is barred by the economic loss rule. As will be seen from the foregoing, we disagree. The economic loss rule does not bar recovery in tort for damage that a separately acquired defective product or service causes to other portions of a larger product into which the former has been incorporated. See, e.g., *Jimenez v. Superior Court*. The product or service purchased from J & N was the façade added to the exterior of the Gunkels' home by J & N. J & N installed the façade under an arrangement with the Gunkels that was independent of the contract with Renovations to build the home. Therefore, the economic loss rule precludes tort recovery for damage to the façade itself, but tort recovery for damage to the home, and its parts, caused by the allegedly negligent installation of the façade is not limited by the economic loss rule.

Summary judgment as to the negligence claim is reversed. This case is remanded for further proceedings consistent with this opinion.

Questions

1. What is the difference between "pure" and "consequential" economic loss?

2. Why are pure and consequential losses often treated differently in cases of products liability?

3. What is the position if a product defect causes a risk of future physical harm, but no such damage has yet been sustained?

Frank v. DaimlerChrysler Corp.

292 A.D.2d 118 (2002)
(Appellate Division, Supreme Court of New York)

NARDELLI, J.P. In this appeal, we are asked to determine whether the Supreme Court properly dismissed, for failure to state a cause of action, plaintiffs' proposed class action, which is based upon a purported defect in the front seat backrests of certain vehicles.

Plaintiffs commenced this proposed class action in June 1999 on behalf of themselves and all New York residents who own a "Class Vehicle," which includes various specified automobiles manufactured by defendants Ford Motor Company ("Ford"), General Motors Corporation ("General Motors"), and Saturn Corporation ("Saturn"), between 1993 and 1998. The class, as defined by plaintiffs, is estimated at 1,000,000 people and specifically excludes those individuals who allegedly suffered personal injuries as a result of the claimed "defect." The defect is defined by plaintiffs as a design utilizing a "single recliner mechanism" ("SRM"), which is a manually adjustable lever that fixes the angle of the seat backrest, and which is located only on the outboard side of the front seats.

Plaintiffs aver that the backrest, as designed, is unreasonably dangerous because "it is unstable and susceptible to rearward collapse in the event of a rear-end collision," in that if a Class Vehicle is struck from the rear by another vehicle "the force of the occupant's body against the backrest of the seat can result in the rearward collapse of the backrest," which in turn "can result … in neck and back injuries, paraplegia, quadriplegia, and even death." Plaintiffs further maintain that the seat defect was aggravated by certain additional design flaws, and that defendants knew or should have known of the hazardous condition, yet "made a conscious and deliberate decision" against implementing an improved design, which would have included an additional recliner mechanism on the inboard side of the seats.

Plaintiffs continue that defendants "knowingly and intentionally concealed from the public the foreseeable risk of harm from seat collapses" and that as a result, plaintiffs "suffered economic loss" in that the Class Vehicles and seats did not meet reasonable consumer expectations and posed an unreasonable risk of serious injury or death in the event of a rear-end collision. Plaintiffs maintain that class members were therefore compelled to "incur the expense of alternate transportation, or the expense of correcting the Defect."

Plaintiffs sought compensatory damages "measured by the cost of correcting the Defect, not to exceed $5,000 for each Class Vehicle," and interposed seven causes of action sounding in, respectively: (1) negligence; (2) strict liability; (3) breach of the implied warranty of merchantability; (4) negligent concealment and misrepresentation; (5) fraud; (6) unfair or deceptive business practices in violation of General Business Law ("GBL") §§ 349 and 350; and (7) civil conspiracy. Ford, General Motors and Saturn subsequently moved to dismiss the complaint for failure to state a cause of action and failure to state the fraud claims with sufficient particularity. The motion court, in an order entered on or about May 30, 2000, granted the motions and dismissed the complaint in its entirety. Plaintiffs appeal and we now affirm....

Plaintiffs herein, with regard to the issue of damages, have, as previously noted, specifically excluded from the putative class "all persons who have suffered personal injury as a result of the rearward collapse of a seat." Indeed, plaintiffs do not allege that they have been in the type of accident that allegedly triggers the defect; that the seat back in any of the vehicles they own had, in fact, collapsed; or that they have suffered an injury as the result of the anticipated malfunction. In sum, plaintiffs maintain that if their vehicles were to become involved in accidents, and if the accidents were rear-end collisions, and if the accidents were severe enough, their front-end seats might deform or collapse rearward and, consequently, the hypothetical malfunction might cause them to be injured. Thus, while plaintiffs claim that the defect is "presently manifested," they essentially argue that the breach of duty, the purported design defect, is itself the injury, and their damages as well, as they do not allege any actual malfunction.

Plaintiffs' claims, which defendants characterize as "tendency to fail" types of claims, have been addressed, in one form or another, by the United States District Court for the Southern District of New York, as well as a number of other courts in various jurisdictions. In *Feinstein v. Firestone Tire and Rubber Company*, 535 F.Supp. 595, plaintiff interposed causes of action sounding in breach of implied warranty of merchantability, strict liability, negligence, reckless disregard, fraud and deceit, arising out of allegations that defendant's "Firestone 500" steel-belted radial tires "will suffer blowouts, tread separation and chunking, steel belt separation, or shifting, bead distortion, sidewalk blisters and cracks, and out of round conditions." Plaintiffs, as a result of the foregoing, sought "replacement on a fairly adjusted basis of all Radial 500 tires ... with steel-belted radial tires which are safe and free of defects or the equivalent in dollars".

The District Court, in addressing motions for class certification, held that those plaintiffs whose tires had not malfunctioned could not maintain a cause of action for breach of implied warranty of merchantability since "[t]ires which lived full, productive lives were, by demonstration and definition, 'fit for the ordinary purposes' for which they were used; hence they were 'merchantable' under UCC § 2-314". Plaintiffs, in other words, failed to establish the necessary element of damage, and the court rejected plaintiffs' argument "that a 'common' defect which never manifests itself 'ipso facto caused economic loss' and breach of implied warranty," notwithstanding the fact that reports by the National Highway Traffic Safety Administration ("NHTSA"), and the House Committee on Interstate and Foreign Commerce, indicated that some of the tires had failed, or the fact that other complainants had commenced actions for actual injury or death, or that Firestone had entered into a voluntary recall program concerning the tires in question. The court further opined that "[l]iability does not exist in a vacuum; there must be a showing of some damages, which then may lead to further issues of quantum". The court, in conclusion, declined to certify the proposed class with respect to the remaining causes of action for the very same reasons....

Courts, other than New York's Southern District, have reached the same conclusion in cases involving various alleged defects in automobiles. In *American Suzuki Motor Corporation v. Superior Court*, 37 Cal.App.4th 1291, 44 Cal.Rptr.2d 526, the California Court of Appeals had before it a class action wherein plaintiffs alleged that the design of the Samurai, a sport utility vehicle manufactured by Suzuki, "'create[d] an unacceptable risk of a deadly roll-over accident when driven under reasonably anticipated and foreseeable driving conditions ...'". The plaintiffs, like those herein, did not allege that they had suffered any personal injuries or property damage as the result of the purported design defect and the issue, as framed by the court in *American Suzuki*, was whether plaintiffs could state a cause of action for breach of implied warranty where "they have suffered no personal injury or property damage from a vehicle they claim is defectively designed, and it is impliedly conceded that their vehicles have—since the date of purchase—remained fit for their ordinary purpose". In dismissing plaintiffs' breach of implied warranty claims, the court found that:

> [T]he evidence presented demonstrated that only a small percentage of the Samurais sold during the class period have been involved in rollover accidents, and real parties have impliedly conceded that nearly all of them have not. Because the vast majority of the Samurais sold to the putative class "did what they were supposed to do for as long as they were supposed to do it," we conclude that these vehicles remained fit for their ordinary purpose. This being so, their owners are not entitled to assert a breach of implied warranty action against Suzuki ...

Public policy concerns, in our view, also dictate that we reject plaintiffs' claims, for it would be manifestly unfair to require a manufacturer to become, in essence, an indemnifier for a loss that may never occur. Plaintiffs' argument, basically, is that as an accident becomes foreseeably possible, upon the occurrence of certain contingencies, due to a design aspect of a product, the manufacturer must retrofit the product or otherwise make the consumer whole. However, under such a schematic, as soon as it can be demonstrated, or alleged, that a better design exists, a suit can be brought to force the manufacturer to upgrade the product or pay an amount to every purchaser equal to the alteration cost. Such "no injury" or "peace of mind" actions would undoubtedly have a profound effect on the marketplace, as they would increase the cost of manufacturing, and therefore the price of everyday goods to compensate those consumers who claim to have a better design, or a fear certain products might fail.

This is not to say that plaintiffs, to the extent that they may have some legitimate concerns, are not without recourse. The National Traffic and Motor Vehicle Safety Act (49 USC § 30101, *et seq.*) provides, inter alia, that "[a]ny interested person" may petition the NHTSA to conduct an investigation into whether a motor vehicle contains a safety related defect or fails to comply with a safety standard. If the NHTSA determines that such a defect does exist, it will direct the manufacturer to repair, replace or recall the vehicle at no charge to the owner. If the consumer's petition is denied, the NHTSA must publish the reasons for such action, and the party whose petition has been denied may obtain judicial review of the NHTSA's decision. It is our finding herein that the remedy which will not only best promote consumer safety, but will also address the parties' concerns regarding the possible consequences of a rear-end collision if the purported defect is not remedied, is to petition the NHTSA for a defect investigation.

Order affirmed.

Note

Products liability and battery. While claims based on product liability laws will not normally be successful where plaintiffs have yet to sustain physical damage, this does not mean that the only avenue of recourse open to those whose bodily integrity has been violated will be a complaint to an administrative agency or body responsible for criminal law enforcement. In *Mink v. University of Chicago*, 460 F.Supp. 713 (1978), pregnant women had been given the drug diethylstilbestrol (DES) during their prenatal care at the University's Lying-In Hospital in the early 1950s as part of a double blind study to determine the value of DES in preventing miscarriages. The women were not told they were part of an experiment, nor that were being given DES. They claimed that as a result of their taking DES, their daughters had developed abnormal cervical cellular formations and were exposed to an increased risk of vaginal or cervical cancer, while the plaintiffs themselves—and their sons—suffered reproductive tract and other abnormalities and an increased risk of cancer.

The women brought claims, alleging products liability and battery, against both the university and Eli Lilly. The District Court granted the defendants' motions to dismiss the products liability claims on the grounds that the plaintiffs' exposure to a risk of harm did not state a claim for physical injury, while there was no evidence that they had suffered any of the alleged "abnormalities." The claim for battery was allowed to proceed, however, since this did not require proof of harm but, rather, the unjustified touching of a person without her consent.

A Consumer or Reasonably Foreseeable Third Party

The determination of who qualifies as a consumer or other foreseeable third party for the purposes of products liability laws is effectively the products liability version of establishing to whom a duty of care is owed. Since the issue of duty is always a matter of law for the court, so too is this (just like the question of what constitutes a "product").

Stegemoller v. A, C And S, Inc.
767 N.E.2d 974 (2002) (Supreme Court of Indiana)

SHEPARD, CJ. Ramona Stegemoller allegedly contracted a disease as a result of contact with asbestos fibers brought home on the person and clothing of her husband Lee, a union insulator. The trial court dismissed the Stegemollers' suit on the basis that Ramona lacked standing under Indiana's Product Liability Act. The Court of Appeals affirmed.... We granted transfer, ... and now hold that she has standing as a bystander under the Act....

The Act governs actions by users or consumers against manufacturers or sellers for physical harm caused by products. For purposes of the Act, "consumer" includes "any bystander injured by the product who would reasonably be expected to be in the vicinity of the product during its reasonably expected use." § 34-6-2-29. Who qualifies under this statutory definition is a legal question, to be decided by the court.

The manufacturers and other defendants would have us hold that Mrs. Stegemoller lacks standing under the Act and cannot otherwise maintain a negligence claim because the Act "provides the sole and exclusive remedy for personal injuries allegedly caused by a product." They say the claim falls outside the Act because Mrs. Stegemoller was not in the vicinity of the product. They reason that the product at issue is insulation material that contains asbestos, not residue such as fibers from that material, and that Mrs. Stegemoller was not in the vicinity of the industrial jobsite where the insulation material was used.

This is too narrow a view. The normal, expected use of asbestos products entails contact with its migrating and potentially harmful residue. We conclude that divorcing the underlying product from fibers or other residue it may discharge is not consistent with the Act.

The manufacturers further argue that Mrs. Stegemoller was not in the product's vicinity during its "reasonably expected use." Again, their reading is too restrictive. In *Butler v. City of Peru*, 733 N.E.2d 912, 914, 919 (Ind.2000), we held that a maintenance worker who was electrocuted while trying to restore power to an electrical outlet was a user or consumer as defined in the Act. Implicit in that holding was the assumption that maintenance may be part of a product's reasonably expected use.

The same is true of customary clean-up activities. Here, the reasonably expected use of asbestos products encompasses the cleansing of asbestos residue from one's person and clothing at the end of the workday.

We therefore hold, taking into account the nature of asbestos products, that Mrs. Stegemoller has a cognizable claim as a bystander under the Act.

We reverse the dismissal of this action and direct that it be reinstated.

DICKSON, SULLIVAN, BOEHM, and RUCKER, JJ., concur.

Notes

1. *Floodgates revisited.* A similar decision was reached by the Fifth District Appeal Court of Illinois in *Simpkins v. CSX Corp.*, 929 N.E.2d 1257 (2010). The court held that an employer owes a duty to protect the family of its employee from the dangers of "take-home" asbestos exposure. In its defense, CSX raised the floodgates argument, contending that recognizing such a duty would expose employers to limitless liability to the entire world. Citing both *Olivo v. Owens-Illinois, Inc.*, 186 N.J. 394, 895 A.2d 1143 (2006) and *Satterfield v. Breeding Insulation Co.*, 266 S.W.3d 347 (Tenn.2008), however, the court held that such a burden would not arise if a duty were owed only to the immediate families of a company's employees.

2. *Foreseeability.* The court in *Simpkins* (929 N.E.2d 1257, 1265) justified its distinction on the grounds of foreseeability:

> It is certainly foreseeable that the wife of an asbestos-exposed worker would also be exposed to asbestos dust through washing his clothing. It is also foreseeable that other members of the household could be exposed. It is not necessarily foreseeable that any person who shares a cab with the asbestos worker would inhale asbestos dust and develop mesothelioma.

Of course, foreseeability is not a criterion that permits of hard-and-fast rules because it is very fact-specific. Accordingly, the court also noted that: "Should a proper case arise, we can consider whether the duty extends to others who regularly come into contact with employees who are exposed to asbestos-containing products." (929 N.E.2d 1257, 1266).

3. *Is foreseeability the appropriate criterion for duty?* The New York courts have taken a rather different view. In the state where Chief Justice Cardozo's opinion in *Palsgraf* still stands, the Court of Appeals of New York held in *Holdampf v. A.C. & S., Inc. (In re New York City Asbestos Litigation)*, 840 N.E.2d 115; 806 N.Y.S.2d 146 (2005), that foreseeability is *not* the basis for determining *whether* a duty exists, but simply determines the scope of the duty *if* it is held to exist. But a duty can exist only if there is a relationship between the defendant on the one hand and either the plaintiff or a third-party tortfeasor on the other. Since no third-party tortfeasor was involved in *Holdampf*, and the employer had no relationship with its employees' spouses, the employer could not be under a duty to protect a wife from exposure to asbestos.

4. *Interpreting and applying statutes.* It might be thought that the question of whether a duty extends beyond users and consumers of products to third parties would be clearer when a state has a statute that contains an express provision on the matter. Unfortunately, however, that is not necessarily true. Facts similar to those in *Simpkins* presented themselves the same year in *Boley v. Goodyear Tire & Rubber Co.*, 929 N.E.2d 448 (2010). The wife of a Goodyear employee died of mesothelioma, allegedly after breathing in asbestos dust from her husband's work clothes when she shook them out before laundering them. Unlike in *Simpkins*, a majority of the Supreme Court of Ohio held that Goodyear did not owe a duty to prevent asbestos dust being carried home on the clothes of its employees. But this was because of its interpretation of § 2307.94.1(A)(1) of the Ohio Revised Code, which expressly provides that:

> A premises owner is not liable for any injury to any individual resulting from asbestos exposure unless that individual's alleged exposure occurred while the individual was at the premises owner's property.

Justice Pfeifer dissented. He pointed out that the immediately prior provision in the Code, § 2307.94.1(A), said:

> The following apply to all tort actions for asbestos claims brought against a premises owner to recover damages or other relief for exposure to asbestos on the premises owner's property.

This meant, he argued, that the statute was merely imposing a requirement for premises liability claims. Since the claim in *Boley* was obviously not a premises liability claim, the statute was entirely irrelevant.

Questions

1. Is there a need for a discrete body of products liability law, or can the whole field be effectively regulated by standard doctrines of contracts and torts?

2. Do the five factors which dictate whether or not a case falls within the parameters of products liability make sense? Why (not)?

3. If the 2010 *Deepwater Horizon* oil blowout in the Gulf of Mexico, off the coast of Louisiana, turns out to have been at least partly caused by the failure of a blowout prevention device, which victims would count as reasonably foreseeable for the purposes of products liability law, and therefore be owed a duty by the device's manufacturer?

4. What is the preferable interpretation of the pertinent parts of the Ohio Revised Code in *Boley*? Do you arrive at this view because of the plain words of the statute, or because of some policy consideration, or both? If a policy consideration affects your reasoning, what is the policy concerned?

Chapter 2

The Historical Origins of Products Liability Law

Contracts and the Doctrine of Privity

The law of products liability is of comparatively recent vintage. All reasonably orderly societies have some form of criminal law—to set the boundaries of socially acceptable conduct—and real property law, which defines who is entitled to use specific areas of land and the buildings constructed thereon. So property law was traditionally concerned not with ownership, but with possession of land. This is because, under the common law system, which the early settlers brought with them from England, all land was considered to be owned by the Crown.

In his ground-breaking book, The Division of Labor in Society, the French sociologist, Emile Durkheim, argued that a society's laws can be treated as an "index" or indicator of its degree of social development. A society whose legal system is comprised almost entirely of property and criminal law is likely to be very static, since such laws effectively protect the *status quo* without providing the means for significant social change. For industrialization to take hold, some individuals need to be able to accumulate sufficient wealth to buy well-situated land (typically near sources of fresh water) and raw materials, as well as to employ a large workforce. This was made possible by the development in the late eighteenth century of a new body of what we now call contract law, which facilitated the buying and selling of both personal and real property.

The development of the law of contracts thus paved the way for the Industrial Revolution, which in turn ushered in an era of large-scale manufacture of products consumed by persons other than those who produced them. While this new and more dynamic society certainly generated hitherto unknown wealth, the products created also contained new (and often unforeseen) potential to cause serious harm to those who used or consumed them. Yet the law of torts, at least in the form that we recognize today, did not emerge until the 1870s. Until then, anyone who sought compensation for an injury allegedly caused by someone else had to look to the law of contracts for a remedy—although that was seldom forthcoming. One of the major obstacles to recovery was the doctrine of privity.

Winterbottom v. Wright
(1842) 10 M & W 109; 152 E.R. 402 (Court of Exchequer)

The declaration stated, that the defendant was a contractor for the supply of mailcoaches, and had in that character contracted for hire and reward with the Postmaster-General, to provide the mail-coach for the purpose of conveying the mailbags from Hartford, in the county of Chester, to Holyhead: That the defendant, under and by virtue of the said contract, had agreed with the said Postmaster-General that the said mail-coach should, during the said contract, be kept in a fit, proper, safe, and secure state and condition for the said purpose, and took upon himself, to wit, under and by virtue of the said contract, the sole and exclusive duty, charge, care, and burden of the repairs, state, and condition of the said mailcoach; and it had become and was the sole and exclusive duty of the defendant, to wit, under and by virtue of his said contract, to keep and maintain the said mail-coach in a fit, proper, safe, and secure state and condition for the purpose aforesaid: That Nathaniel Atkinson and other persons, having notice of the said contract, were under contract with the Postmaster-General to convey the said mail-coach from Hartford to Holyhead, and to supply horses and coachmen for that purpose, and also, not on any pretence whatever, to use or employ any other coach or carriage whatever than such as should be so provided, directed, and appointed by the Postmaster-General: That the plaintiff, being a mail-coachman, and thereby obtaining his livelihood, and whilst the said several contracts were in force, having notice thereof, and trusting to and confiding in the contract made between the defendant and the Postmaster-General, and believing that the said coach was in a fit, safe, secure, and proper state and condition for the purpose aforesaid, and not knowing and having no means of knowing to the contrary thereof, hired himself to the said Nathaniel Atkinson and his co-contractors as mailcoachman, to drive and take the conduct of the said mail-coach, which but for the said contract of the defendant he would not have done. The declaration then averred, that the defendant so improperly and negligently conducted himself, and so utterly disregarded his aforesaid contract, and so wholly neglected and failed to perform his duty in this behalf, that heretofore, to wit, on the 8th of August, 1840, whilst the plaintiff, as such mail-coachman so hired, was driving the said mail-coach from Hartford to Holyhead, the same coach, being a mail-coach found and provided by the defendant under his said contract, and the defendant then acting under his said contract, and having the means of knowing and then well knowing all the aforesaid premises, the said mail-coach being then in a frail, weak, and infirm, and dangerous state and condition, to wit, by and through certain latent defects in the state and condition thereof, and unsafe and unfit for the use and purpose aforesaid, and from no other cause, circumstance, matter or thing whatsoever, gave way and broke down, whereby the plaintiff was thrown from his seat, and in consequence of injuries then received, had become lamed for life.

To this declaration the defendant pleaded several pleas, to two of which there were demurrers; but as the Court gave no opinion as to their validity, it is not necessary to state them.

LORD ABINGER, C.B. I am clearly of opinion that the defendant is entitled to our judgment. We ought not to permit a doubt to rest upon this subject, for our doing so might be the means of letting in upon us an infinity of actions. This is an action of the first impression, and it has been brought in spite of the precautions which were taken, in the judgment of this Court in the case of *Levy* v. *Langridge*, to obviate any notion that such an action could be maintained. We ought not to attempt to extend the principle of that decision, which, although it has been cited in support of this action, wholly fails as an authority in its favour; for there the gun was bought for the use of the son, the plaintiff in that action, who could not make the bargain himself, but was really and substantially the party contracting. Here the action is brought simply because the defendant was a contractor with a third person; and it is contended that thereupon he became liable to every body who might use the carriage. If there had been any ground for such an action, there certainly would have been some precedent of it; but with the exception of actions against innkeepers, and some few other persons, no case of a similar nature has occurred in practice. That is a strong circumstance, and is of itself a great authority against its maintenance.

It is however contended, that this contract being made on the behalf of the public by the Postmaster-General, no action could be maintained against him, and therefore the plaintiff must have a remedy against the defendant. But that is by no means a necessary consequence—he may be remediless altogether. There is no privity of contract between these parties; and if the plaintiff can sue, every passenger, or even any person passing along the road, who was injured by the upsetting of the coach, might bring a similar action. Unless we confine the operation of such contracts as this to the parties who entered into them, the most absurd and outrageous consequences, to which I can see no limit, would ensue. Where a party becomes responsible to the public, by undertaking a public duty, he is liable, though the injury may have arisen from the negligence of his servant or agent. So, in cases of public nuisances, whether the act was done by the party as a servant, or in any other capacity, you are liable to an action at the suit of any person who suffers. Those, however, are cases where the real ground of the liability is the public duty, or the commission of the public nuisance. There is also a class of cases in which the law permits a contract to be turned into a tort; but unless there has been some public duty undertaken, or public nuisance committed, they are all cases in which an action might have been maintained upon the contract. Thus, a carrier may be sued either in assumpsit or case; but there is no instance in which a party, who was not privy to the contract entered into with him, can maintain any such action. The plaintiff in this case could not have brought an action on the contract; if he could have done so, what would have been his situation, supposing the Postmaster-General had released the defendant? that would, at all events, have defeated his claim altogether. By permitting this action, we should be working this injustice, that after the defendant had done everything to the satisfaction of his employer, and after all matters between them had been adjusted, and all accounts settled on the footing of their contract, we should subject them to be ripped open by this action of tort being brought against him.

ALDERSON, B. I am of the same opinion. The contract in this case was made with the Postmaster-General alone; and the case is just the same as if he had come to the defendant and ordered a carriage, and handed it at once over to Atkinson. If we were to hold that the plaintiff could sue in such a case, there is no point at which such actions would stop. The only safe rule is to confine the right to recover to those who enter into the contract: if we go one step beyond that, there is no reason why we should not go fifty. The only real argument in favour of the action is, that this is a case of hardship; but that might have been obviated, if the plaintiff had made himself a party to the contract. Then it is urged that it falls within the principle of the case of *Levy* v. *Langridge*. But the principle of that case was simply this, that the father having bought the gun for the very purpose of being used by the plaintiff, the defendant made representations by which he was induced to use it. There a distinct fraud was committed on the plaintiff; the falsehood of the representation was also alleged to have been within the knowledge of the defendant who made it, and he was properly held liable for the consequences. How are the facts of that case applicable to those of the present? Where is the allegation of misrepresentation or fraud in this declaration? It shews nothing of the kind. Our judgment must therefore be for the defendant.

GURNEY, B. concurred.

ROLFE, B. The breach of the defendant's duty, stated in this declaration, in his omission to keep the carriage in a safe condition; and when we examine the mode in which that duty is alleged to have arisen, we find a statement that the defendant took upon himself, to wit, under and by virtue of the said contract, the sole and exclusive duty, charge, care, and burden of the repairs, state and condition of the said mail-coach, and, during all the time aforesaid, it had become and was the sole and exclusive duty of the defendant, to wit, under and by virtue of his said contract, to keep and maintain the said mail-coach in a fit, proper, safe, and secure state and condition. The duty, therefore, is shewn to have arisen solely from the contract; and the fallacy consists in the use of that word "duty." If a duty to the Postmaster-General be meant, that is true; but if a duty to the plaintiff be intended (and in that sense the word is evidently used), there was none. This is one of those unfortunate cases in which there certainly has been *damnum*, but it is *damnum absque injuria*; it is, no doubt, a hardship upon the plaintiff to be without a remedy, but by that consideration we ought not to be influenced. Hard cases, it has been frequently observed, are apt to introduce bad law.

Judgment for the defendant.

Notes

1. *Breadth of applicability.* As Professors Gray and Gifford have noted, H. Shulman et al., Law of Torts: Cases and Materials 759–60 (4th ed., 2003):

> This case comes down to us, and has been consistently treated, as the leading case for the proposition that a manufacturer or seller is not liable to a remote purchaser with whom he is not in "privity of contract" for harm caused by the lack of care on his part in putting out the product; because, it is said, the manufacturer or seller is not under a duty to the remote purchaser—not in privity of contract—to exercise care. It is enlightening toward an understanding of the development of law to see how far the case supports this proposition for which alone the case is remembered.... But, of course, the opinions may express a common-sense judgment of much wider applicability.

2. *New and old law.* The law of products liability covers a certain set of unintentional accidents. As *Winterbottom* demonstrates, the common law of England did not typically provide any remedy for the victims of such accidents, unless they could prove that their injuries were caused by a breach of contract to which both they and the defendant were parties. Thus actions for accidental personal injury had little chance of success.

3. *Approach to case of first impression.* It is instructive to note how the judges of the Court of Exchequer approached this case of first impression. Abinger C.B. starts from the proposition that, if the law recognized such a claim, then there would be instances of it already in the law reports. If taken literally, this is a nonsensical remark. In any case of first impression, the law has *by definition* decided neither whether the plaintiff has a valid claim nor whether the defendant has a good defense. What Abinger C.B.'s remark really demonstrates is the common law's use of the device of a rebuttable presumption. When presented with a case of first impression, the common law presumes that the claim is invalid unless that presumption can be effectively rebutted by the plaintiff's presentation of a strong policy reason why this new type of claim should be recognized.

This is a particularly important lesson to learn; students often begin their studies of the law believing that for every wrong there is a remedy. Yet in *Winterbottom*, while both Abinger C.B. and (even more explicitly) Rolfe B. are certainly prepared to accept that the defendant perpetrated an injury, the idea that the plaintiff must therefore have a remedy against the defendant is rejected as "by no means a necessary consequence." Note that Rolfe B. expresses the reason for the lack of a remedy from the perspective of both defendant and plaintiff, so that (a) the defendant owed the plaintiff no duty, and (b) the plaintiff did not suffer a legally-recognized injury.

4. *Potentially unlimited liability.* There were probably many reasons for the historical denial of liability for accidental personal injury. One was certainly that articulated in *Winterbottom* by Abinger C.B.:

> We ought not to permit a doubt to rest upon this subject, for our doing so might be the means of letting in upon us an infinity of actions.... Unless we confine the operation of such contracts as this to the parties who entered into them, the most absurd and outrageous consequences, to which I can see no limit, would ensue.

This may be seen as a precursor to Cardozo C.J.'s famous warning in the New York Court of Appeals in the case of *Ultramares Corporation v. Touche*, 255 N.Y. 170, 179 (1931), that the law should be wary of "expos[ing defendants] to a liability in an indeterminate amount for an indeterminate time to an indeterminate class." The "floodgates" argument, discussed in Chapter 1 in the context of *Jimenez v. Superior Court*, 58 P.3d 450 (2002), may be seen as a modern label applied to the same assertion. But which version of the "floodgates" argument does Abinger C.B. appear to have had in mind in *Winterbottom*?

5. *Context.* Although it has since been has been superseded by more recent case law, *Winterbottom* is a useful case for the historical context that it provides. Without this context, it is tempting to fall into the trap of assuming that the law of products liability (or the wider law of torts more generally) consists of a fixed body of rules, when in fact it is dynamic and so apt to be modified to deal with what are perceived to be new problems that arise as society changes. One of the most important tasks for a student of products liability is to identify current trends in the law, which will then make it easier to predict the outcome of future cases.

6. *California.* California is often said to be the state which takes to the extreme the idea that for every wrong there is a remedy. This may be at least partly because that very principle is actually enshrined in § 3523 of the California Civil Code. Yet, while it has already been observed both that it is important to discern the trends in the law and that *Winterbottom* is no longer followed, it is equally important to realize that, even now, American courts tend to approach cases of first impression with a degree of skepticism similar to that of Abinger C.B. and his brethren. Indeed, the phrase *damnum absque injuria* is itself sometimes still used to justify the rejection of a plaintiff's claim—even in California.

Mega Life and Health Ins. Co. v. Superior Court

92 Cal. Rptr. 3d 399 (2009) (Fourth DCA, California)

RICHLI, ACTING P.J. It is often said—and is codified in California law—that "[f]or every wrong there is a remedy." (Civ.Code, § 3523.) But this statute does not create substantive rights or an unbounded right to damages. Instead, "[this] wholesome maxim of jurisprudence ... can obviously have no application to any but legal wrongs or those wrongs for which the law authorizes or sanctions redress." "A tort ... involves a violation of a *legal duty*, imposed by statute, contract, or otherwise, owed by the defendant to the person injured. Without such a duty, any injury is '*damnum absque injuria*' — injury without wrong." The proposition that courts should strain to provide remedies for every "wrong" in the moral sense flies directly in the face of this longstanding authority that only *legal* wrongs must be redressed.

California courts have explicitly rejected the concept of universal duty. "It must not be forgotten that 'duty' got into our law for the very purpose of combatting what was then feared to be a dangerous delusion ... viz., that the law might countenance legal redress for all foreseeable harm." Instead, whether to recognize a new "legal wrong" or "tort" is often governed by policy factors. In making these determinations, both the courts and the Legislature must weigh concepts of "public policy," as well as problems inherent in measuring loss, and "floodgates" concerns, in addition to the traditional element of foreseeability.

As a result of these weighings, modern law, if not replete with examples of "wrongs" for which there is no remedy, at least offers numerous examples....

Notes

1. *Historical perspective.* Acquiring a historical perspective on the laws of contracts and torts is very important if trends are to be identified. One problem that has to be confronted, however, is that judges (and some academics) are prone to oversimplification and exaggeration. It is just so tempting to use a neat phrase or glib assertion instead of engaging in painstaking analysis and explanation, especially if others are apparently impressed by the recitation of a Latin phrase as if it contained the "Answer to the Ultimate Question of Life, the Universe, and Everything." (That is, of course, 42: see Douglas Adams, The Hitchhiker's Guide to the Galaxy.) In fact, they tend to be half-truths at best, and can sometimes be seriously misleading.

2. *Latinisms.* The truth is that Latin phrases are often either alarmingly mistranslated, or else used to obfuscate a simple idea (in pursuit of a desire to sound more sophisticated). Indeed, most Latinisms expressed by lawyers today were never uttered by the ancient Romans, but were dreamed up during the Renaissance by a fashionable elite who thought that they added a greater touch of eloquence. However, as Sir William Erle noted in *Brand v. H. & C.R. Co.*, L.R. 2 Q.B. 223, 247: "[Such a] maxim ... is no help to decision, as it cannot be applied till the decision is made."

The phrase *damnum absque injuria* is more literally translated as "damage without injustice." The idea that usage of this Latinism is supposed to convey is that while someone may suffer a real loss, it will not be compensable unless it arose through someone else's breach of the law. It is surely better and clearer to express that idea in standard English.

3. *Caveat emptor.* Surely one of the most pernicious Latinisms has been that of *caveat emptor.* Literally translated as "Let the buyer beware," it was adopted to convey the idea that ancient law had long ago determined that it was up to the buyer to work out for him- or herself whether the product in question was free from material defects. The seller was thus under no duty to disclose any flaw in a product unless responding to a buyer's direct question on the matter. Yet, as Kevin M. Teeven, A History of the Anglo-American Common Law of Contract 136 (1990), has pointed out:

> *Caveat emptor* was an indigenous development unique to the common law—there was no such rule in the civil law or law merchant. The term was first used when Fitzherbert wrote about the purchase of a horse in 1534: "if he be tame and have been rydden upon, then *caveat emptor*". *Caveat emptor* may have first appeared in the common law courts in response to the upsurge of itinerant merchants where buyers had to be aware that the seller would not be around to answer complaints. The impersonality of developing market forces was breaking down local customary protection based on status. The forty shilling rule forced more of these cases before less sympathetic common law judges. In the influential *caveat emptor* case of *Chandelor v. Lopus* (1604), a goldsmith "affirmed" it to be a precious bezoar stone, but the court held that, excepting victuals, there was

no liability unless there was an express warranty. As the defendant's attorney argued, "if there is no warranty ... an action on the case does not lie, even though he is deceived: for *caveat emptor*". There was a concern that a distinction be drawn between puffery, "for everyone in selling his wares will affirm that his wares are good," and a binding promise of quality, the difference being a jury question. Popham, C.J. added: "This case is a dangerous case, and may be the cause of a multitude of actions if it be understood that a bare affirmation by the seller causes the action."

4. *Indeterminacy.* Note that claims for breach of contract are not nowadays generally considered to raise problems of indeterminacy, since the parties to the contract are easily identified. Yet Popham C.J.'s upholding in *Chandelor* of the principle of *caveat emptor* was still underlined by his fear that any other conclusion would lead to a "multitude of actions." This was clearly a precursor to the concern about the possibility of an "infinity of actions" which so exercised Abinger C.B. in *Winterbottom*.

5. *Infinity, indeterminacy and public policy.* The law of products liability may be seen as a battleground in which plaintiffs and their legal counsel regularly strive to push back the boundaries which have traditionally denied a victim compensation. While plaintiffs may be able to point to good public policy reasons in favor of recognizing a new form of legal obligation where none had existed before, such reasons will seldom be enough in themselves to convince a court to permit such cases to proceed. In every case in which a hitherto-unrecognized claim is made, judges—especially those sitting in the highest appellate courts—will also need to consider whether allowing such a case to proceed would expose defendants to the risks of indeterminacy of which Abinger C.B. and Cardozo C.J. were so conscious. As we shall see, such indeterminacy can arise both in areas of substantive law (such as deciding on appropriate tests of defect or causation) and in matters of procedure (such as ascertaining the reliability of expert evidence). Plaintiffs who can demonstrate that their claim, though apparently novel, can be sufficiently confined so as to avoid raising the prospect of indeterminate liability or unbounded speculation will undoubtedly be placing themselves in a more advantageous position.

6. *Latinisms (again).* As Teeven points out, *caveat emptor* is not actually a doctrine that originates from ancient Rome at all. As noted above, this is true of almost all legal Latinisms. Since the common law did not derive from the laws of the ancient Romans, most Latinisms were actually invented *in England* during the Renaissance, when usage of Latin was considered the mark of an educated man (since, of the relatively few who could read, even fewer could read Latin). Latinisms were thus nothing more than an indicator of social class. The title of a famous article by Walton Hamilton, *The Ancient Maxim of Caveat Emptor*, 40 Yale L.J. 1133, 1156, 1178 (1931), was therefore intended to be ironic. Hamilton wrote:

> An adage was never fitted more neatly to the part than *caveat emptor*; it is, among many excellent examples, the ideal legal maxim. It is brief, concise, of meaning all compact. Its terms are too broad to be pent up within the narrow confines of rules of law; they are an easy focus for judicial thought, a principle to be invoked when the going is difficult, a guide to be followed amid the battling uncertainties of litigation. The phrase seems to epitomise centuries of experience; it is written in the language of Rome, the great law-giver; it comes with the repute of the classics and with the prestige of authority....

> We must, however, turn from England to America to witness the real triumph of *caveat emptor*. In the new republic the tradition of authority did not linger long

after the war for independence, the intellectual individualism was reinforced by the spirit of the frontier, an emerging industrial system was not to be shackled by formal control, and the courts were quite loath to take up the shock of business friction.

Sheldon Gardner & Robert Kuehl, Acquiring an Historical Understanding of Duties to Disclose, Fraud, and Warranties
104 Com. L.J. 168 (1999)

During the Middle Ages, sellers pledged their faith to buyers, who would consider the pledge valuable only because it was bolstered by the seller's willingness to forsake his honor and even his hope of salvation should he not perform in good faith.... [D]isclosure was crucial, for the failure to disclose created a basis for fraud....

Celebrating the individual and the value of his labor, the Protestant Reformation spawned Calvinism, which brought with it new ways of looking at capitalism. The growing affinity toward the Calvinist view of hard work and capitalist competition loosened the Catholic Church's hold over merchants. The Enlightenment, with its exaltation of reason, further relaxed the Church's control of the marketplace. While not nominally tolerated, fraud became very difficult to prove during this period, given courts' friendly reception to capitalistic activities. Despite this trend, a minority of courts went so far as to *heighten* the duty of disclosure and broaden the scope of common-law fraud.

Adam Smith, a product of the Enlightenment, proclaimed *laissez faire*, advocating market control of the economy and preferring private ordering by contract to public ordering by regulation. For him, much like for the Jews and Romans, a promise to act in good faith was implied in every contract. Moreover, he thought that a man's enlightened self-interest would force that man to honor his promises. The governmental desire to refrain from interfering in the marketplace during this period created a perspective wherein courts defined fraud more narrowly, making it more difficult for buyers to raise claims.

The ubiquitous acceptance of Smith's philosophy enabled the doctrine of *caveat emptor* to thrive. This doctrine was predicated upon the notion that nearly every transaction contains uncertainty. Two other factors underlying the doctrine included (1) the balanced bargaining positions of buyers and their sellers, whose products were usually easily examinable, and (2) the sentiment that sellers were not in the business of furnishing information. Buyers, under *caveat emptor*, were deemed to have been aware of the risks they assumed, and were thought to be able to protect themselves accordingly. Even the most strident supporters of *caveat emptor*, however, never meant for the doctrine to protect fraudulent activities. What the doctrine did do was marginalize fraud, placing a heavier burden on purchasers to inspect goods before buying them.

In this country, in 1817, the case of *Laidlaw v. Organ* 15 U.S. 178 (1817) was one of the first to deal with the issue of nondisclosure. To date, it remains one of the most important and intriguing cases in the area. Interestingly, this case focused on whether a *buyer* had a duty to disclose. That buyer was Hector Organ, who was negotiating to acquire a large quantity of tobacco from Francis Girault, a partner in Peter Laidlaw & Co., a New Orleans tobacco broker. The night before the close of the deal, Organ heard from his brother that American and England had signed the Treaty of Ghent, ending the War of 1812. Prior to the treaty, the British blockade of eastern ports, such as New Orleans, made trade with other countries nearly impossible. This, in turn, depressed the price of exportable commodities such as tobacco. When news of peace reached everyone, the cost of tobacco jumped astronomically, because it could then go to more profitable markets, particularly Europe. Girault, lacking knowledge of the treaty, sold Organ the tobacco at the lower price. Within hours of the sale, Girault learned of the armistice and refused to deliver the tobacco.

The evidence adduced at trial suggested that, during the morning of the sale, Girault asked Organ "if there was any news which was calculated to enhance the price or value of the article about to be purchased." The record did not reflect how Organ responded to this question, if at all. The District Court of Louisiana, finding no evidence that Organ had said or done anything to lull Girault into believing that any such news did not exist, ruled in favor of Organ.

The Supreme Court concluded that Organ was not bound to communicate his knowledge of the treaty. It remanded the case to the district court, which refused to allow the jury to decide whether Girault had asked Organ the question mentioned above, and, if so, how Organ replied. The Court held that a buyer is not required to disclose knowledge of extrinsic conditions (1) "where the means of intelligence are equally accessible to both parties" and (2) where each party to the transaction "take[s] care not to say or do any thing tending to impose upon the other."

So, even with a society around it that was embracing *caveat emptor*, the Court was still concerned about fraud and, presumably, would not have tolerated such activity in the form of silence or prevarication on the part of either the buyer or the seller when a crucial question was asked, the answer to which would have affected either party's consent or consideration. Many view *Laidlaw* as a declaration of *caveat emptor* and the notion that silence is not actionable. However, as noted above, the holding has two important restrictions. Here, it seems, the buyer or seller must not only beware the other person's misconduct, but also his own.

Several decades after *Laidlaw*, the Gilded Age brought about a panoply of abuses, subsidies, and extravagances in support of big business. As Mark Twain depicted in the satirical novel that gave the age its name, this era of shallowness and corruption was marked by an "anything goes" mentality. During Reconstruction, the law protected sellers as the Northern economy exploded, overwhelming the economies of the defeated South and West. This political partiality toward industrial growth dwarfed biases toward buyers. As a result, the seller's duty to disclose was minimized.

Notes

1. *Adam Smith and good faith.* Gardner and Kuehl talk of the "ubiquitous acceptance of Smith's philosophy [that] enabled the doctrine of *caveat emptor* to thrive." Yet, what was— and is still regularly taken to be— "Smith's philosophy" is, at best, only a half-truth. For, as Gardner and Kuehl note, Adam Smith believed that "a promise to act in good faith was implied in every contract." In other words, *laissez faire*— "leave to do," or minimal government intervention— was to be preferred *precisely because* every contract had a moral component: "a promise to act in good faith." However, the bastardization of Smith's views saw— and still sees— him cited regularly in support of the amoral proposition that "anything goes" in business. Although the Uniform Commercial Code has several provisions requiring the parties to a contract to act in "good faith," § 2-103(1)(b) defines this only as "honesty in fact and the observance of reasonable commercial standards of fair dealing in the trade." There is thus no general pre-contractual obligation at common law to

disclose relevant information, unless specifically asked to do so (although certain types of contract, such insurance, may be treated as requiring full disclosure of material facts by the parties).

2. *Good faith and the civil law world.* In civil law systems, however, the parties must *deal* in good faith. In other words, pre-contractual bargaining must also be conducted in good faith. It is this civil law view that has been incorporated into the United Nations Convention on Contracts for the International Sale of Goods (C.I.S.G.) 1980, according to section 13 of which "all parties are admonished ... to promote ... the observance of good faith in international trade." Since the United States has ratified the C.I.S.G., the Supremacy Clause of the Constitution dictates that the C.I.S.G. has the force of federal law and so supersedes U.C.C.-based state law for contracts between a U.S. entity and an entity based in another Contracting State (unless the parties have drafted a term which specifies otherwise).

3. *Indeterminacy (again).* The verdict of the Supreme Court in *Laidlaw* was given by Marshall C.J., who declared (at 15 U.S. 178, 194):

> The question in this case is, whether the intelligence of extrinsic circumstances, which might influence the price of the commodity, and which was exclusively within the knowledge of the vendee, ought to have been communicated by him to the vendor? The court is of opinion that he was not bound to communicate it. It would be difficult to circumscribe the contrary doctrine within proper limits, where the means of intelligence are equally accessible to both parties. But at the same time, each party must take care not to say or do any thing tending to impose upon the other.

The same concern for unlimited or indeterminate liability that underlay *Winterbottom* was thus also at the root of the decision in *Laidlaw*. If a duty to disclose had been imposed, Marshall C.J. doubted that it would have been possible to lay down what precisely should have been disclosed. So instead, he simply required that the parties refrain from actively misleading each other (which would implicate the law of misrepresentation, which is tackled in the next Chapter).

Questions

1. If courts decide against finding liability on the grounds that this might cause a flood of either lawsuits or trials, does this mean that a defendant effectively has immunity to injure many individuals, but may be liable if causing injury to a smaller number of victims? If so, is this just?

2. Should there be (as there is in many civil law jurisdictions) a pre-contractual duty to bargain in good faith?

Overcoming Caveat Emptor

As we have seen, nineteenth-century victims injured by a defective product typically faced a two-pronged obstacle to any compensation. In the absence of fraud, a claim could only be brought against a supplier or manufacturer if the latter were in privity of contract with the victim. Yet, even when there was such privity, victims were then faced with a second difficulty, namely the doctrine of *caveat emptor*.

Unlike the requirement of privity, however, which was seen as a mandatory rule, *caveat emptor* operated more like a rebuttable presumption which could be defeated if the defendant had warranted — or was deemed by the courts to have warranted — the fitness of the defective product. While the courts' views as to what constituted such a warranty fluctuated from one era to another, this state of the law essentially continued until 1913, when Washington became the first state to dispense with the requirement of privity in cases of defective food. It is represented in Figure 2.1.

Figure 2.1 The State of the Law on Products Liability Until 1913

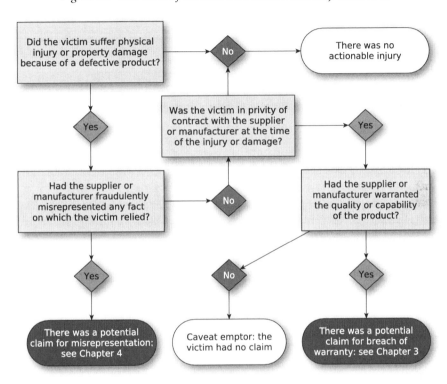

It is common to attribute much of the growth of the doctrine of warranty to the reforming British judge, Lord Mansfield. As long ago as *Stuart v. Wilkins* (1778), for example, Mansfield declared that: "A warranty extends to all faults known and unknown to seller." *Stuart* was a case of express warranty, but Mansfield even went so far as, in Teeven's words, to

> flirt[] with the notion of an implied warranty of quality in holding a brewer to an obligation to sell quality beer in 1781 and in implying a warranty of seaworthiness in a marine insurance contract the next year. There was a widespread recognition of an implied duty of quality in the eighteenth century under statutes, mercantile custom and local court rulings ...
>
> The zenith of caveat emptor would occur, however, in the nineteenth century, and so these early developments in implied warranty would be narrowly applied and not extended until toward the end of that century. (A History of the Anglo-American Common Law of Contract 139, 140 (1990).)

Mansfield is also known for his judgment in *Somersett's Case* (1772) 20 State Tr 1; (1772) Lofft 1, where he held that slavery in England was unlawful. Unhappily, as the next extract from Andrew Fede's article suggests, it seems that the vitality of the doctrine of warranty in the United States stems at least partially from an antebellum desire to preserve the institution of slavery.

Andrew Fede,
Legal Protection for Slave Buyers in the U.S. South:
A Caveat Concerning Caveat Emptor
31 Am. J. Legal Hist. 322 (1987)

The doctrine of *caveat emptor*—let the buyer beware—achieved its "real triumph" in the sales law of the antebellum United States, according to Walton Hamilton's seminal article on the history of that ancient maxim. Hamilton's interpretation is only half correct, however, because *caveat emptor*'s conquest of the law of the antebellum South was not as resounding as in the North. Both statutes and cases of the nineteenth century South protected slave buyers during *caveat emptor*'s antebellum heyday. The reason for this distinction is suggested by Karl Llewellyn, who called antebellum sales law "common law made by the Ellenboroughs—and the horse." Like Hamilton, however, Llewellyn omitted southern sales law from his study, and this is a significant omission. By ignoring southern law, these great scholars failed to see that the law in the common law South differed, and that it was different because it was made by judges, horses, and slaves.

The slaves' influence on sales law, however, was akin to that of horses, rather than to that of other persons. Slave masters legally bought and sold bondsmen in the antebellum South; to the commercial law, slaves were ordinary but valuable articles of commerce. The law in the South was indeed protective of the slave buyer's interest, in contrast to the law that protected the interests of sellers in the North. One issue best illustrates the distinction between *caveat emptor* and *caveat venditor*, and it arose in the sale of slaves, as it does in the sale of both ordinary livestock and inanimate chattels. If an illness or defect exists at the time of a sale of an item, and the flaw is not observable by reasonable and ordinary means, all is well with the transaction until the defect manifests itself after delivery. If neither the buyer nor the seller knew of the deficiency, who should bear the loss? A related issue concerns imperfections known to the seller but not observable to the buyer. Is the seller required to disclose what he knows of the defect before delivery, and if he does not, will he risk liability to the buyer? ...

[Hamilton's] interpretation relegates Southern slave law to, at best, a footnote—an odd exception to the general pattern. Consequently, the picture of nineteenth century "American" law that it presents is distorted; *caveat emptor* did not rule supreme before the Civil War. In fact, the South Carolina courts protected slave buyers to a greater degree than the modern law of sales protects purchasers, and applied this rule to non-slave transactions as well. Additionally, the other southern states, although less consumer oriented than South Carolina, had a law of slave sales that more closely resembles modern sales law ...

In the first half of the nineteenth century, the North and South grew further apart, both legally and in the non-law context. As a part of this development, the nineteenth century Southerners harbored no difficulty in treating slaves like property—not people—and protecting the interests of the buyers of property as valuable as slaves. Consequently, "consumer protection" is not a twentieth century invention; a doctrine analogous to modern consumer protection was adopted by the southern antebellum courts and legislatures as they balanced the social, political and economic interests that were affected by slave sales. Of course modern consumer protection did not grow out of this aspect of the law of slavery; nevertheless, the southern courts and legislatures present an interesting trend contrary to *caveat emptor*....

In this regard, the "most southern" state of all was South Carolina. Since this was the state with the highest percentage of slave population, it was the scene of much slave buying from the colonial days until the Civil War. It follows that South Carolina, with so many slave consumers, would be the most consumer oriented state. In fact, while the doctrine of *caveat emptor* reigned in the North, it was explicitly and repeatedly rejected by the South Carolina courts in favor of the rule that a sound price implies a sound product — an implied warranty of soundness.

The first leading case is *Timrod v. Shoolbred*, decided in 1793. The seller brought an action of assumpsit to recover from the buyer the value of a family of slaves purchased. One of the slaves "broke out with the smallpox, the day after the sale and died; and, consequently, must have taken the infection previous to the day of sale." The report also states that it was "proved that the negroes were taken from a house where the small-pox had been, but it did not appear that the plaintiff knew that either of these negroes had taken the infection."

The defendant offered to pay for the slaves purchased, less the value of Stepney, the slave who died, but the seller refused to accept this offer, and sued for the full price. The jury reached a verdict for the plaintiff, less the value of Stepney, thereby vindicating the buyer's position.

The court also enunciated the theory that would allow cases such as this to go to South Carolina juries throughout the era of *caveat emptor* the warranty of soundness implied from the payment of a sound price:

> In every contract all imaginable fairness ought to be observed, especially in the sale of negroes, which are a valuable species of property in this country. It has been decided, often, in our courts, that selling for a sound price, raises, in law, a warranty of the soundness of the thing sold; and if it turns out otherwise it is a good ground for the action of assumpsit, to recover back the money paid.... This warranty extends to all faults, known and unknown to the seller; and although, in general, it principally relates to title and qualifications, and not to longevity, yet, in some cases, it ought to be construed to extend to the latter. For if the negro sold had about him, at the time of sale, the seeds of a disorder generally difficult of cure, and which occasioned his death, it would be unreasonable to say that the purchaser shall sustain the loss. Though if the disorder had been contracted afterwards, it must be at the risk of the purchaser.

Therefore, even if the seller made no express warranty of soundness, or any statement whatsoever, the buyer could have his case go to the jury if he proved the slave was unsound when sold, and that he did not know of the hidden defect. This rule was not a threat to the bargain struck by the parties to a slave sale because the burden of proof was on the buyer, and mere inadequacy of consideration was not a sufficient ground to void a contract. Moreover, during the antebellum period the courts refined this rule and further defined the rights of buyers and sellers of slaves.

The first limitation was that the defect had to be unknown to the buyer at the time of sale. The purpose of the rule was to protect the buyer from "latent" defects or diseases; therefore, if the buyer was told of or could observe the defect, he could not benefit from the implied warranty of soundness. A second limitation was engrafted on the rule in an 1845 decision. In a ruling out of step with precedent, the court required that the buyer pay a "sound price." Therefore, a buyer who paid less than full value for a slave was unprotected by the implied warranty of soundness. A "discount buyer" had to elicit an express warranty to obtain relief, unless the seller was guilty of deceit or fraudulent concealment of a disease or defect.

Another limitation was established in *Smith v. McCall*. It was there held that the implied warranty did not extend to the "moral qualities" of the slave....

It was held in 1821 in *Wells v. Spears* that if the seller gave the buyer an express written warranty of title, this alone would not, as a matter of law, exclude the implied warranty of soundness. Writing for the court, Judge John S. Richardson noted that "many authorities have been adduced to shew, that where there has been one warranty expressed, other warranties are excluded." Nevertheless, he found that it had been repeatedly held in his state that when a seller gives a bill of sale with such a warranty, this would not exclude the warranty of soundness. The court noted:

> It would be inconvenient, and would probably be a misconstruction of the real intention of the parties to such bills of sale, were we at this day to decide that the express warranty of title excludes the implied warranty of soundness.

Instead, the court left this question of intention for the jury, as a general rule.

This approach comports with the modern interpretation of the parol evidence rule, but it would have been an anathema to the majority of nineteenth century jurists. Judge Evans, in 1843, while reaffirming the *Wells* rule, noted:

> The general rule of evidence is, that where the parties put their contract in writing, that is the only evidence of what they intended, and everything else is excluded.

Yet, the court majority stated it had "no inclination to depart" from the *Wells* doctrine. Although Judges Nott and John B. O'Neall dissented from this rule, they were in the distinct minority.

Similarly modern in approach was the South Carolina courts' position on disclaimer of the implied warranty of soundness. An explicit disclaimer or limitation of this warranty could exclude it, but it was held that what constituted a valid disclaimer was ordinarily a question for the jury. Consequently, in *Rodrigues v. Habersham* the majority, with Judge O'Neall dissenting, upheld a jury verdict for the buyer based upon the implied warranty theory, although there was no allegation that the defendant knew the slave was seriously ill when sold. Judge Evans affirmed the result below although it was proved that:

> The defendant refused to insert a clause of warranty in the deed, but went on to assign as a reason, "that he never required it when he bought, and would not insert it when he sold" — "that the price was a good one, and sufficient evidence that he thought the negro sound."

Therefore, as in modern law, a case would be decided as a matter of law in favor of disclaimer of the implied warranty only if the disclaimer was in writing or was unambiguous and clearly proved by the seller....

Furthermore, South Carolina courts were unique among the common law states because the sound price rule was also applied to sales of non-slave goods and real estate....

Notes

1. *Torts and contracts.* Much of this Chapter has illustrated that litigation over defective products has historically straddled the line between the laws of contracts and torts.

Indeed, the current position in most non-US common law jurisdictions is that they are just as prepared to entertain claims for physical injury within the law of contracts as within the law of torts. For a useful discussion of the approach in the UK and Canada, for example, see Bryan Finlay, Marie-Andrée Vermette & Brydie Bethell, *Convergence of Contract and Tort: Damages in the Age of Concurrent Liability* in Special Lectures 2005: The Modern Law of Damages (2006).

2. *Product liability as a tort.* As the full name of the *Restatement of the Law (Third) Torts: Products Liability* implies, however, products liability law within the United States is considered as falling essentially within the law of torts. Indeed, it may be said that the United States remains almost obsessive among common law jurisdictions in seeking to maintain such a rigid distinction between contracts and torts. The Restatement, for example, does not tackle issues of warranty, since they are part of the law of contracts and thus beyond its domain. As will be seen, this insistence on rigid labeling distinctions is apt, on occasion, to lead to some rather idiosyncratic decisions. Such idiosyncrasies arise because many—perhaps even most—of those who have an arguable claim in tort for physical injury caused by a defective product also have potentially an equally plausible contractual claim for breach of warranty. For this reason, it is important to note that the law of warranty in contracts remains very important in deciding many claims that are concerned with defective products.

3. *Distinguishing product liability claims in tort from those for breach of warranty.* However, the fact that many product liability claims can be framed as claims for breach of warranty does not mean that the two are synonymous. As was explained in Chapter 1, products liability claims are restricted to those for physical injury (and consequential losses). Product liability claims framed in tort are subject to the so-called "economic loss" rule, which disallows claims made for purely economic harm (as well as for damage caused purely to the defective product itself). In contrast, claims framed as breaches of warranty can extend to cover both of these forms of harm because—rather than being concerned with life, limb or property—the law of contract's primary rule is to protect the sanctity of the bargain. It therefore follows that many claims for breach of warranty go beyond the sphere of products liability.

4. *Orthodoxy and myopia?* Teeven presents what might be called the orthodox view of the move from *caveat emptor* to ideas of warranty. But he does point out that "in the US … there [was] also evidence of an earlier eighteenth century judicial interest in intervening to construct fair bargains." In fact, such "judicial interest" in the US continued well into the nineteenth century, at least in the South. Whether this has been overlooked or "forgotten" for reasons of political expediency is a matter for conjecture.

Questions

1. Should a fair price for a product be taken as an implied warranty that the product is free of material defects? If so, what constitutes a "fair price"?

2. As this Chapter has shown, liability of a supplier or manufacturer was strict (i.e. required no fault) if the case could be brought within the law of contract (assumpsit) but, otherwise—and therefore outside contract law—required proof of either the defendant's intention to mislead or knowledge of the product defect. Which is the better approach?

3. Should it be possible to disclaim liability for product defects, even when they are known to the supplier or manufacturer?

Chapter 3

Warranties

Express Contractual Warranties

As we saw in Chapter 2, the giving of a warranty rebutted the presumption of *caveat emptor* that otherwise prevailed, especially in the antebellum North. Moreover, the predisposition towards the notion of *caveat emptor* meant that courts in the North were slow to find that any warranty had been given. Indeed, although Lord Holt C.J. had held in the old English case of *Cross v. Gardner*, (1689) Cart. 90, that "[a]n affirmation at the time of a sale is a warranty, provided it appears on evidence to be so intended," it had become typical for the courts to require explicit use of the actual word "warranty" before the existence of a warranty would be recognized. Judicial views in the North began to change, however, after the Civil War.

Hawkins v. Pemberton

6 Sickels 198 (1872) (Court of Appeals of New York)

EARL, C.J. This action was brought against the defendants as purchasers of an article called, at the time of the sale, blue vitriol, to recover damages for refusing to take and pay for the same, and upon the trial the court refused to submit the evidence to the jury and ordered a verdict for the plaintiff....

It is unquestioned that there was a warranty that the article was sound and in good order, and I am quite clear that there was no breach of this warranty. It was good, sound saltzburger or mixed vitriol. It was just as it was made; not damaged, or in any way out of order. It was in its natural, normal condition, and it could not be said of such an article that it was unsound.

Did the plaintiff warrant the article to be blue vitriol? It is unquestioned that at the time of the sale, through his auctioneer, he represented it to be blue vitriol, and that the defendants bought it as such, relying upon that representation. To constitute a warranty, it is not necessary that the word warranty should be used. It is a general rule that whatever a seller represents, at the time of a sale, is a warranty.

In *Stone v. Denny* it is said that the courts in their later decisions

manifested a strong disposition to construe liberally, in favor of the vendee, the language used by the vendor in making any affirmation as to his goods, and have been disposed to treat such affirmations as warranties whenever the language would reasonably authorize the inference that the vendee so understood it.

In *Oneida Manufacturing Society v. Lawrence* (4 Cowen, 440) Chief Justice Savage says:

There is no particular phraseology necessary to constitute a warranty. The assertion or affirmation of a vendor concerning the article sold must be positive and unequivocal. It must be a representation which the vendee relies on, and which is understood by the parties as an absolute assertion, and not the expression of an opinion.

And generally, where the representation is not in writing, the question of warranty is to be submitted to the jury.

It is not true, as sometimes stated, that the representation, in order to constitute a warranty, must have been intended by the vendor, as well as understood by the vendee, as a warranty. If the contract be in writing and it contains a clear warranty, the vendor will not be permitted to say that he did not intend what his language clearly and explicitly declares; and so if it be by parol, and the representation as to the character or quality of the article sold be positive, not mere matter of opinion or judgment, and the vendee understands it as a warranty, and he relies upon it and is induced by it, the vendor is bound by the warranty, no matter whether he intended it to be a warranty or not. He is responsible for the language he uses, and cannot escape liability by claiming that he did not intend to convey the impression which his language was calculated to produce upon the mind of the vendee.

Here it is not questioned that the language used was sufficient to constitute a warranty that the article sold was sound and in good order; and why should it not as well extend to the character of the article? When a buyer purchases an article whose true character he cannot discover by any examination which it is practicable for him to make at the time, why may he not rely upon the positive representation of the seller as to its character as well as to its quality and condition? I can discover no distinction in principle in the two kinds of representation; and yet it is claimed in behalf of the plaintiff that there is a distinction, and certain cases are cited to uphold it, which I will proceed briefly to consider....

The cases of *Seixas v. Woods* and of *Swett v. Colgate* have been frequently cited in our courts, and have doubtless influenced, and it may be controlled, the decisions in other cases. The propositions of law announced in them are sufficiently correct; but in view of the rules of law, as now settled in this and other States, I am of opinion that the law was not properly applied to the facts appearing in those cases.

Here there was a positive representation that the article sold was blue vitriol; the plaintiff meant the purchasers to understand that it was blue vitriol, and he sold it as such. The defendants relied upon the representation, believing it to be blue vitriol, and bought it as such. If upon these facts the court was not authorized to hold as matter of law that there was a warranty, it was at least bound to submit the question of warranty to the jury....

The only remaining question to be considered is, whether there was a breach of this warranty, and this can need but little discussion. The article sold, if it was known at all in market, was known by another name. It had only from seventeen to twenty-five per cent of blue vitriol in it. It was not an inferior article of blue vitriol, but a different substance with a small admixture of blue vitriol.

The judgment should, therefore, be reversed and a new trial granted, costs to abide event.

All concur. Judgment reversed.

Notes

1. *The objective approach. Hawkins* shows the courts not only moving away from a ready reliance on the notion of *caveat emptor*, but also towards the view that the seller's

position should be judged solely according to his conduct rather than according to his actual intent or knowledge. Thus whether a warranty was given was to be judged according to what the seller did, and not according to what he knew or intended; and (once it was held that such a warranty had been given) whether it was breached was to be judged according to what was supplied, rather than the intentions of the supplier. Adjudicating upon a person's legal position in this way, rather than according to their subjective thoughts, is generally known in the law of contract as taking the objective approach. Whether an offer to contract has been made and accepted is judged in similar fashion.

2. *Strict liability.* Allied with this objective approach is the designation of liability for breach of warranty as strict. Once the existence of a warranty (whether express or implied) has been established, the law is interested only in the objective fact of whether it has been complied with. Since breach of warranty is a matter of strict liability, there is no need to evaluate the apparent reasons for non-compliance, so that the state of mind of the parties is irrelevant.

3. *Quality, or lack of quality?* Perhaps the softening of judicial attitudes regarding the giving of a warranty was influenced by sellers' increasingly sharp practices. The irony is that the giving of a warranty was not always seen as an indication of quality or longevity, a position which itself led to other developments. In fact, as Arvinder P.S. Loomba, *Historical Perspective on Warranty*, in Product Warranty Handbook 42 (Blischke & Prabhakar Murthy eds., 1995) has pointed out, in the nineteenth century:

> [D]eceit associated with the sale of goods, such as misbranding, adulteration, and misrepresentation, became widespread. This, in part, led to a trend of dishonest manufacturers offering warranties on products without any intention of honoring them. Because of this, consumers started perceiving a warranty of any sort on products to be an indication of poor quality.
>
> In the next few decades, independent product testing organizations emerged throughout America partly to curb such deceitful practices. Examples of these organizations include Underwriters Laboratory, an independent testing agency sponsored by various insurance companies and underwriters, which tested electrical appliances; the Good Housekeeping Institute, run by the *Good Housekeeping* magazine, which tested household goods; and Consumers' Research, a consumer-sponsored organization, which led to the formation of Consumers Union, publisher of *Consumer Reports*. Seals of approval from organizations such as these served as a symbol of acceptable quality in terms of product reliability and the credibility of the manufacturer's own warranty.

We shall see in Chapter 4—specifically, in the case of *Hanberry v. Hearst Corporation*, 39 A.L.R.3d 173 (1969)—that these "seals of approval" have themselves been called into question in products liability litigation.

4. *Uniform Sales Act of 1906.* Throughout the twentieth century, there were various attempts to regulate the wording and effect of warranties. The first attempt of significance was the Uniform Sales Act, which was drafted on behalf of the National Conference of Commissioners on Uniform State Laws (NCCUSL) by Samuel Williston. Note how he reflected the approach of *Hawkins*, which abandoned the requirement of special language to create an express warranty, in section 12 of the Act, which stated:

> Any affirmation of fact or any promise by the seller relating to the goods is an express warranty if the natural tendency of such affirmation or promise is to induce the buyer to purchase the goods, and if the buyer purchases the goods relying thereon.

5. *Partial success.* Although Williston was one of the leading contract scholars of his day, by 1947 still only 34 states had adopted the Uniform Sales Act. Those that had not adopted it were primarily in the less-industrialized South. The limited success of the Act created momentum for the drafting of a new legal instrument to replace it, so that the new one would be assimilated by all the states. This is what brought about NCCUSL's promulgation of the Uniform Commercial Code (UCC) in 1952.

6. *Additional requirement.* While section 12 of the Uniform Sales Act made both the existence and breach of an express warranty *necessary* for a successful claim, it considered these elements *insufficient.* The plaintiff also had to show *reliance* on the warranty. This approach was, however, subsequently superseded by § 2-313 of the UCC, which adopts a different formulation where the warranty is "part of the basis of the bargain."

Uniform Commercial Code — Article 2 — Sales (1952)

§ 2-313. Express Warranties by Affirmation, Promise, Description, Sample.

(1) Express warranties by the seller are created as follows:

(a) Any affirmation of fact or promise made by the seller to the buyer which relates to the goods and becomes part of the basis of the bargain creates an express warranty that the goods shall conform to the affirmation or promise.

(b) Any description of the goods which is made part of the basis of the bargain creates an express warranty that the goods shall conform to the description.

(c) Any sample or model which is made part of the basis of the bargain creates an express warranty that the whole of the goods shall conform to the sample or model.

(2) It is not necessary to the creation of an express warranty that the seller use formal words such as "warrant" or "guarantee" or that he have a specific intention to make a warranty, but an affirmation merely of the value of the goods or a statement purporting to be merely the seller's opinion or commendation of the goods does not create a warranty.

Notes

1. *The objective approach revisited.* We saw in *Hawkins v. Pemberton* that an express warranty at common law did not depend on the subjective knowledge or intent of the party providing it, but on that party's conduct. The UCC confirms that position. This means that it is somewhat misleading to say that contract law is always concerned with obligations taken on voluntarily, or by choice, since the party providing an express warranty may have no idea of that fact.

2. *Express warranty as consideration.* Making an express warranty "part of the basis of the bargain" essentially means that it becomes part of the consideration provided by the seller, in return for the payment provided as consideration by the buyer. So the warranty becomes part of what the seller was selling. This analysis of the bargain is depicted in Figure 3.1.

Figure 3.1 Express Contractual Warranties

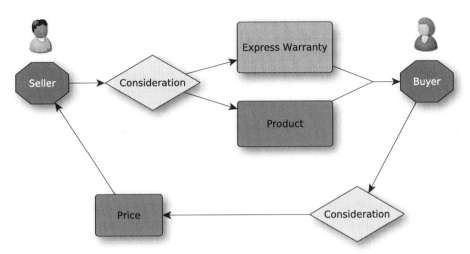

3. **Breach of warranty as breach of contract.** Treating an express warranty in this way essentially means treating a breach of warranty as just as much a breach of contract as any failure to provide the other forms of consideration (i.e. failure either to provide the product, or to pay the purchase price). Of course, in order to become part of the contract, the statement construed as a warranty must be made either before, or at the time that, the contract is formed.

Stang v. Hertz Corp.

490 P.2d 475 (1971) (Court of Appeals of New Mexico)

WOOD, C.J. The automobile accident involved in this case occurred when a tire blew out. The tire, manufactured by Firestone Tire & Rubber Company, was mounted on a car belonging to Hertz Corporation. The car had been rented by a nun, and Catherine Lavan, also a nun, was a passenger in the car when the blowout occurred. Catherine Lavan suffered injuries in the accident resulting in her death. Prior appellate decisions were concerned with damages in wrongful death actions. Subsequent to the appellate decisions, the case was tried and submitted to a jury as against Firestone. The verdict was in favor of Firestone. There is no appeal from this verdict. The trial court directed a verdict in favor of Hertz. The dispositive issues in this appeal concern the liability of Hertz. Plaintiffs contend there were issues for the jury concerning: (1) an express warranty and (2) strict liability in tort.

Express warranty

Plaintiffs assert the rental agreement contains an express warranty. They rely on a statement that the "vehicle" was in good mechanical condition. Defendant contends that "vehicle" does not include tires because twice in the rental agreement "tires" were referred to in a sense separate from "vehicle." Apart from the rental agreement, a Hertz representative, in a conversation with one of the nuns, stated: "you have got good tires." Plaintiffs contend this statement was also an express warranty as to the tires. Defendant asserts this statement was no more than "puffing."

It is not necessary to answer these contentions. Section 50A-2-313(1), N.M.S.A.1953 [replicates UCC § 2-313(1)] ...

We assume there is no distinction between "seller," as used in the statute, and defendant's status as lessor. Under § 50A-2-313(1), above, the affirmation of fact (the rental agreement) creates an express warranty if it "becomes part of the basis of the bargain." Similarly, the description of the goods (the reference to good tires) creates an express warranty if the description "is made part of the basis of the bargain."

There is no evidence that any of the nuns relied on, or in any way considered, the terms of the rental agreement before agreeing to the rental. The comment concerning "good tires" was made after the car had been rented. There is no evidence that either the terms of the rental agreement or the reference to "good tires" were part of the basis of the bargain. There was insufficient evidence for the question of express warranty to be submitted to the jury.

Directed verdict in favor of Hertz affirmed. (Affirmed on the issue of express warranty, but reversed on other grounds by Stang v. Hertz *83 N.M. 730, 497 P.2d 732 (1972).)*

express warranty wasn't basis of the bargain

Questions

1. Was the court in *Stang* right to *assume* that "there is no distinction between "seller," as used in the statute, and defendant's status as lessor"?

2. Would the issue of express warranty in *Stang* have been decided any differently under the Uniform Sales Act?

3. What is the difference between (a) requiring reliance by the buyer, and (b) requiring a statement of the seller to become part of the basis of the bargain, in order for a claim for breach of warranty to be successful?

Torres v. Northwest Engineering Co.

949 P.2d 1004 (1997) (Court of Appeals of Hawai'i)

WATANABE, J. This lawsuit arises from an industrial accident in which a crane manufactured and sold by Defendant-Appellee Northwest Engineering Company (Northwest) tipped over and crushed its operator, Fernando Torres (Torres). Torres subsequently died from injuries he sustained in the accident....

Northwest insists, however, that the existence of an express warranty was not established as a matter of law because (1) Plaintiffs failed to adduce any evidence that Wailuku *relied* on the thirty (30)-inch width of the crane's treads as part of the "basis of its bargain" with Northwest to purchase the Northwest Model 41 crane; and (2) "Plaintiffs presented absolutely no evidence that Wailuku ... even received the Northwest product literature ... upon which their claim for breach of express warranty was based, much less that Wailuku ... specifically considered or relied upon any affirmation of fact or description contained in the documents in deciding to purchase [crane] C204."

The arguments of the parties raise an issue which has divided courts across the country whether, under UCC 2-313, a buyer's *reliance* on a seller's affirmations, promises, descriptions or models (collectively, "seller's statements") is required for an express warranty to arise....

In examining this issue, we note as a historical preface, that under Section 12 of the Uniform Sales Act (USA), the plaintiff in an express warranty case was required to prove that he or she "relied" on a seller's warranty in purchasing the goods. When the UCC was adopted, the language of Section 12 of the USA was substantially retained; however, the

USA's "reliance" test was substituted with a new test that required the plaintiff to prove that the seller's statements became "part of the basis of the bargain" between the buyer and seller (basis of the bargain test) (UCC 2-313).

The UCC does not define "basis of the bargain," and one scholar has expressed that the term "[m]ost probably … is an indefinable concept." (M. Foran, *Williston on Sales* § 17-7, at 12 (5th ed., 1994)). As a result, much litigation has arisen over the years regarding the meaning and proper application of the "basis of the bargain" test….

After examining the history of, and the Official Comments to, UCC 2-313, as well as the case law and legal treatises regarding the basis of the bargain test, we agree with those jurisdictions that have concluded that reliance is not an essential element of a breach of express warranty claim under the UCC. We reach this conclusion for several reasons.

First, according to Comment 4 to UCC 2-313, as set forth in the Comments to the 1962 Official Text of the UCC (Official Comments),

> the whole purpose of the law of warranty is to determine what it is that the seller has in essence agreed to sell, [and therefore,] the policy is adopted of those cases which refuse except in unusual circumstances to recognize a material deletion of the seller's obligation. Thus, a contract is normally a contract for a sale of something describable and described.

If the purpose of the law of warranty is to determine what a seller has agreed to sell, it should not matter that the buyer did not rely on a seller's statements in purchasing particular goods. The seller is bound to deliver, and the buyer to accept, goods that conform to the seller's statements or descriptions of what is being sold. The gist of a breach of express warranty action thus focuses on (1) what the seller agreed to sell; and (2) whether the product delivered by the seller complied with the statements or description of what the seller agreed to sell.

Second, Official Comments 3 and 8 to UCC 2-313 explain that,

> 3. The present section deals with affirmations of fact by the seller, descriptions of the goods or exhibitions of samples, exactly as any other part of a negotiation which ends in a contract is dealt with. No specific intention to make a warranty is necessary if any of these factors is made part of the basis of the bargain. In actual practice *affirmations of fact made by the seller about the goods during a bargain are regarded as part of the description of those goods; hence no particular reliance on such statements need be shown in order to weave them into the fabric of the agreement.* Rather, any fact which is to take such affirmations, once made, out of the agreement requires clear affirmative proof. The issue normally is one of fact….

> 8. Concerning affirmations of value or a seller's opinion or commendation under subsection (2), the basic question remains the same: What statements of the seller have in the circumstances and in objective judgment become part of the basis of the bargain? As indicated above, *all of the statements of the seller do so unless good reason is shown to the contrary….* (emphases added).

The foregoing comments reflect a clear intent on the part of the framers of the UCC that a buyer need not show reliance on a seller's statements in order for such statements to become "part of the basis of the bargain" between the seller and buyer. It is not necessary, therefore, for a buyer to show that he or she would not have entered into the agreement absent the seller's statements or even that the sellers statements were a dominant factor inducing the agreement. Rather, the dispositive issue is whether the seller's statements became "part of the basis of the bargain."

Third, the framers of the UCC purposely abandoned the USA reliance test in favor of the basis of the bargain test. In light of this change, it would be illogical, in our view, to construe the basis of the bargain test as requiring a buyer's reliance on a seller's statements. On the other hand, as Official Comment 3 makes clear, a buyer's *nonreliance* on a seller's statements would be relevant to show that the seller's statements did not become a part of the basis of the bargain between the buyer and seller....

The Official Comments to UCC 2-313 express the general notion that statements about goods made by a seller to a buyer during the bargaining process are *presumed* to be a part of the "basis of the bargain" between a seller and buyer. For example, Official Comment 3 states that

> in actual practice *affirmations of fact made by the seller about the goods during a bargain are regarded as part of the description of those goods;* hence no particular reliance on such statements need be shown in order to weave them into the fabric of the agreement. Rather, *any fact which is to take such affirmations, once made, out of the agreement requires clear affirmative proof* (emphases added).

Also, Official Comment 6 states in relevant part that "in general, the presumption is that any sample or model just as any affirmation of fact is intended to become a basis of the bargain." Finally, Official Comment 8 provides:

> Concerning affirmations of value or a seller's opinion or commendation under subsection (2), the basic question remains the same: What statements of the seller have in the circumstances and in objective judgment become part of the basis of the bargain? *As indicated above, all of the statements of the seller do so unless good reason is shown to the contrary....* (emphasis added).

In light of the foregoing comments, we conclude, as other jurisdictions have, that under the UCC, a seller's statements to a buyer regarding goods sold, made during the bargaining process, are presumptively part of the basis of the bargain between the seller and buyer. Therefore, the burden is on the seller to prove that the resulting bargain did not rest at all on the seller's statements.

Affirmed in part, vacated in part, and remanded.

Notes

1. *Differing presumptions.* With the application of the doctrine of *caveat emptor,* the courts effectively adopted a rebuttable presumption that any risk that the goods might be somehow defective was to be borne by the buyer. According to UCC §2-313, as interpreted in *Torres,* the doctrine of express warranty also makes use of a rebuttable presumption. But in this case, the presumptive risk is shifted from the buyer to the seller.

2. *Not automatic.* There is, however, one way in which the two presumptions are not analogous. *Caveat emptor* applied automatically unless rebutted; an express warranty can only be presumed if the seller has actually said something about the quality of the item involved in the transaction (although such statements can, of course, be in writing instead of—or in addition to—being made orally).

Questions

1. When might the presumption that a seller's statement becomes a part of the basis of the bargain be overcome?

2. Are the circumstances in which such a presumption is overcome determined by the nature of the statement or the circumstances in which the statement is given (or both)? Give examples.

Implied Contractual Warranties

Express warranties are precisely what their name suggests: warranties that have been stated expressly by the seller (even if the party concerned did not realize that the law considered the express statement to be a warranty). Unless they constitute mere "puffery" — the lawful exaggeration of which the court in *Torres* was mindful — or they are in contravention of other law, such as consumer protection legislation, the courts' duty is simply to apply them.

Implied warranties, however, are imposed by the law irrespective of the seller's behavior. Like many express warranties, implied warranties are therefore not the product of a seller's subjective choice or intent. The distinction between them is that, whereas the existence or otherwise of an express warranty is usually a question of fact, implied warranties come into existence as a matter of law. This does not mean that every contract of the same type necessarily contains the same implied warranties. In fact, implied warranties usually operate as "default rules," which specify that a particular warranty exists, *unless* the parties have overridden it by express agreement. By the end of the nineteenth century, English common law had settled upon a number of "default" implied warranties.

Jane Stapleton, Product Liability
(1994)

[British] judges proceeded to construct solutions to the new wave of disputes about goods by the implication of terms in the sale contract, for example by holding that in general a seller of a good must be taken implicitly to warrant his title. The two such implied terms of most importance later in the context of product liability were the implied warranty of merchantability and, where a particular purpose had been made known to the seller, the implied warranty of fitness for that particular purpose. Comparable developments occurred in the U.S. where there is also evidence of an earlier eighteenth century judicial interest in intervening to construct fair bargains.

What were the market phenomena which provoked this interventionist approach? Probably the most important factor was that, as the industrial revolution accelerated, there was an increased incidence of sales of new goods where reasonable opportunities for inspection of the goods by the buyer were not feasible for one of a number of reasons. Sometimes the nature of the new types of good made inspection difficult or impossible at least without expert technical advice, which was often in short supply. Even if the intrinsic nature of the good did not produce this situation, the volume of transactions and the new forms in which products were packaged and delivered often did. But most importantly of all, inspection was often rendered difficult if not impossible — at least for commercial buyers in the chain — by the increasing number of contracts formed between parties acting at a distance, in some cases before the relevant goods had come into existence, and the speed at which goods were passed down the lengthening commercial chain. In such circumstances these traditionally-minded judges seemed impressed by the reality of the buyer's reliance on the superior knowledge and commercial integrity of the seller and perhaps on the apparently increased reliability and safety of goods. They saw it as the common law's duty to construct a fair bargain to protect such reliance of those "necessarily ignorant" of the quality of the goods they bought for a price which had presumably been accepted on the basis of this reliance. To modern minds this seems common sense. As Prosser noted in 1943, "it cannot reasonably be thought that the buyer is willing to pay good money for whatever the seller will give him and remain completely at the seller's mercy". In any case, the implied terms as to quality also seemed to be in line with sellers' increasing appreciation of the value of goodwill and their correspondingly increased acceptance of responsibility for quality—a point supported by the fact that by the 1860s much of the vast trade in Indian cotton was conducted on an express standard term of merchantability.

Although the tussle between the new laissez-faire contract ideas and those of the traditionalists continued for some decades, the latter's view eventually came to predominate so that by 1893 Chambers had no difficulty in formulating the implied warranties of merchantability and fitness for purpose as the accepted common law position.

Notes

1. *Sale of Goods Act.* 1893 is significant because that was the year in which the Sale of Goods Act became law in England. This is important because, rather than the law of warranty in operation in the antebellum American South, it was this English Sale of Goods Act of 1893 upon which Williston subsequently modeled the U.S. Uniform Sales Act of 1906, which itself later formed the basis of the Uniform Commercial Code.

2. *Warranty or condition?* There were, however, two significant differences in the drafting of the Uniform Sales Act as compared to the Sale of Goods Act. The first is that the English Act referred to implied "conditions," whereas the U.S. Act referred to implied "warranties." The latter was simply a stylistic choice by Williston. In English law, a breach of warranty would not permit the injured party to rescind the contract, whereas a breach of condition would provide that remedy (though a person might instead elect to continue with the contract and just claim damages). In section 69 of the Uniform Sales Act, however, Williston set out the remedies available for breach of warranty so as to make them essentially identical to those available for breach of condition in England.

3. *Substantive distinction between American and English law.* The second difference is that Williston omitted a significant phrase in section 15(1) of his Uniform Sales Act. This omission made it possible for a buyer—if he made clear to the seller the purpose to which he intended to put the product in question—to bring a claim against a seller for a breach of an implied warranty that the product was fit for that purpose, even if the seller was not in the business of selling such products. The UCC continues to follow Williston's approach.

Uniform Commercial Code—Article 2—Sales (1952)

§ 2-315. Implied Warranty: Fitness for Particular Purpose.

Where the seller at the time of contracting has reason to know any particular purpose for which the goods are required and that the buyer is relying on the seller's skill or judgment to select or furnish suitable goods, there is unless excluded or modified under the next section an implied warranty that the goods shall be fit for such purpose.

Notes

1. *Implied warranties of merchantability and fitness for a particular purpose.* The notion of a "particular" purpose in §2-315 refers to a specialized, non-standard use of the goods in question. This is why the seller must know of the intention to use the goods in this manner in order for the implied warranty to become applicable. The implied warranty of merchantability in §2-314, discussed further below, is applicable to the ordinary use of the goods concerned, and so does not require that the seller knows of the intended usage.

2. *Contracts versus torts.* It is interesting that, while the requirement that the seller was in the business of selling such products is not applicable when the issue of whether a product is fit for a specific purpose is dealt with in *contracts*, such a requirement has arguably become part of the law of products liability in *torts*. Unfortunately, as pointed out in Chapter 1, there is some confusion within the Products Liability Restatement on this point. While section 1 of the *Restatement* talks of the imposition of liability for a defective product on any person "engaged in the business of selling or otherwise distributing products," *Comment c* purports to confine such activity to "manufacturers and other commercial sellers and distributors *who are engaged in the business of selling or otherwise distributing the type of product that harmed the plaintiff*" (my emphasis). No such limiting language appears in section 1 itself.

3. *Restatement versus UCC.* As suggested in Chapter 1, this confusion could have been avoided if section 1 of the *Restatement* had simply adopted the UCC terminology of "merchant," and then applied the definition of that term to be found in §2-104 of the UCC. See *Smith v. Stewart*, below.

Uniform Commercial Code—Article 2—Sales (1952)

§2-104. Definitions: "Merchant"

(1) "Merchant" means a person that deals in goods of the kind or otherwise holds itself out by occupation as having knowledge or skill peculiar to the practices or goods involved in the transaction or to which the knowledge or skill may be attributed by the person's employment of an agent or broker or other intermediary that holds itself out by occupation as having the knowledge or skill.

§2-103. Definitions and Index of Definitions.

(1) In this Article unless the context otherwise requires

(a) "*Buyer*" means a person who buys or contracts to buy goods.

(b) "*Good faith*" in the case of a merchant means honesty in fact and the observance of reasonable commercial standards of fair dealing in the trade.

(c) "*Receipt*" of goods means taking physical possession of them.

(d) "*Seller*" means a person who sells or contracts to sell goods.

§2-314. Implied Warranty: Merchantability; Usage of Trade.

(1) Unless excluded or modified (Section 2-316), a warranty that the goods shall be merchantable is implied in a contract for their sale if the seller is a merchant with respect to goods of that kind. Under this section the serving for value of food or drink to be consumed either on the premises or elsewhere is a sale.

(2) Goods to be merchantable must be at least such as

(a) pass without objection in the trade under the contract description; and

(b) in the case of fungible goods, are of fair average quality within the description; and

(c) are fit for the ordinary purposes for which such goods are used; and

(d) run, within the variations permitted by the agreement, of even kind, quality and quantity within each unit and among all units involved; and

(e) are adequately contained, packaged, and labeled as the agreement may require; and

(f) conform to the promise or affirmations of fact made on the container or label if any.

(3) Unless excluded or modified (Section 2-316) other implied warranties may arise from course of dealing or usage of trade.

Notes

1. *Tests of merchantability.* Although § 2-314(2) provides a list of six factors to be taken into account in determining whether the goods involved are merchantable. However, many of these factors have little applicability to transactions with consumers, and are more relevant to dealings between businesses.

2. *Merchant and implied warranty.* In *Smith v. Stewart*, 233 Kan. 904, 667 P.2d 358 (1983), a dentist had sold his boat to another pleasure sailor with an express warranty that if it was found within six months to have dry rot, then he would pay for its repair. Three days after taking delivery, the purchaser found that the boat's fuel tank was leaking. He claimed that the seller should recompense him for the repair to the fuel tank under theories of breach of an implied warranty of merchantability and fitness for a particular purpose. The Supreme Court of Kansas disagreed on both counts. On the claim for breach of an implied warranty of merchantability, it noted that:

> Defendant-seller is a dentist practicing in Overland Park, Kansas. There is no allegation defendant was in the boat-selling business at the time of the sale or any other time. The transaction herein involved the casual sale of seller's personal pleasure craft. Clearly the district court did not err in holding "the seller [defendant] does not meet the requirement of being a merchant in respect to boats."

The claim for breach of an implied warranty of fitness for a particular purpose also failed because, as the Court pointed out that:

> Defendant-seller operated the boat as a personal pleasure craft on an inland lake. Plaintiff-buyer purchased the boat for like use. Such usage is well within the ordinary purpose of such goods. There is no allegation that plaintiff's intended usage of the boat was for a particular purpose as opposed to an ordinary purpose. In his motion for relief from the judgment, plaintiff concedes [§ 2-315 of the UCC] "applies only when the buyer indicates to the seller that he intends to use the goods in a manner not *customarily* made for the goods." Taking plaintiff's allegations relative to the dangerous conditions resulting from the leaky fuel tank as true, the defect rendered the boat unfit for ordinary purposes as opposed to unfit for a particular purpose.
>
> Under the uncontroverted facts herein, we conclude plaintiff has failed to state a claim of breach of implied warranty of fitness for a particular purpose ...

3. *Goods or services?* The UCC makes no distinction between goods supplied under a contract for the sale of goods alone, and goods supplied under a hybrid contract for the supply of both goods and services. Nevertheless, parties have sometimes argued that goods

supplied as a "package" with labor or other services should not be considered as warranted where it is the supply of services that forms the predominant purpose of the transaction.

In *Anthony Pools v. Sheehan*, 295 Md. 285, 455 A.2d. 434 (1983), for example, the Court of Appeals of Maryland had to adjudicate upon a claim involving the defendants' installation of a swimming pool and diving board at the plaintiff's home. A couple of months after the completion of the installation, the plaintiff emerged from the pool and walked along the diving board, but slipped and fell, striking the coping of the pool. It turned out that the skid-resistant material built into the surface of the board did not extend right to the edge, and the plaintiff brought a claim for breach of the implied warranty of merchantability. The defendants countered that, while they had designed and manufactured the board, the contract was predominantly for the supply of services, and that a warranty should not therefore be attached to any goods supplied.

The Court disagreed, holding that a mechanical application of a "predominant purpose" test would lead to arbitrary results. It favored instead the application of "a more policy oriented approach" which looks to the substance of mixed or hybrid transactions. In this case, the transaction was really partly for services, and partly for the supply of goods (including the board); there was simply no valid reason for denying the applicability of an implied warranty of merchantability to the latter.

4. *Implied warranties and the bargain.* Express contractual warranties have to become "part of the basis of the bargain" in order to be enforceable. As shown above, this means that an express warranty becomes part of the consideration provided by the seller. The effect of the UCC (as effected through state statutes) is to make an implied warranty just as much a part of the consideration provided by the seller. This position is depicted graphically in Figure 3.2.

Figure 3.2 Implied Contractual Warranties

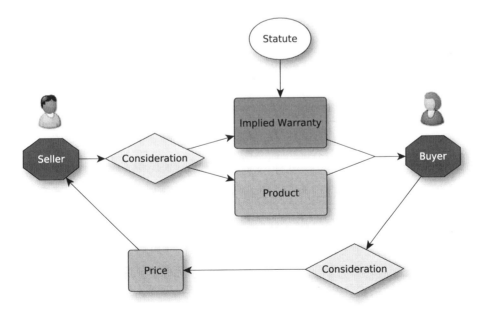

5. *Implied versus express warranties.* Implied warranties can exist without express warranties, or alongside express warranties. As will be seen below, an appropriately-worded express warranty can sometimes have the effect of preventing an implied warranty from being provided.

Question

Does the sale of a known carcinogen, such as cigarettes, automatically involve the breach of an implied warranty of merchantability?

Hypothetical

Those addicted to cigarettes often smoke to help to keep them calm, or to steady their nerves. These are certainly among the reasons that Mitch smokes cigarettes. Last week, Mitch bought a pack of his regular brand, but it turns out that, because of an error in the manufacturing process, a batch of cigarettes (including this pack) were filled only with a harmless vegetable product and flavoring, so that they actually contained no tobacco at all. Unfortunately, having smoked a couple of the cigarettes in the pack, Mitch subsequently injured himself when working with machinery at work because his hands were insufficiently steady. If he is able to establish causation, would he be able, in principle, to bring a claim against the cigarette manufacturer for the breach of an express warranty and/or breach of an implied warranty of either merchantability or fitness for purpose?

Warranties to Third Parties

The original idea of a warranty, as reflected in the Uniform Sales Act of 1906, was clearly that it involved a statement made by one party to a contract to another about the quality of goods that were the subject-matter of that contract. William L. Prosser, *Strict Liability to the Consumer in California*, 18 Hastings L.J. 9, 10–11, 12, 14–15 (1966), traced how this apparently contractual doctrine became transformed so that third parties were also able to claim the benefit of a product warranty:

> The rule of strict liability, without privity and without negligence, began … with cases of defective food and drink. It came as the aftermath of a prolonged and violent national agitation over defective food: and the first decisions followed immediately upon the heels of the political overturn of 1912. There was considerable historical support for the idea that the seller of food incurred a more or less undefined special responsibility to the immediate purchaser, which nineteenth-century cases had called a special implied warranty. In extending this special responsibility to the consumer who was not in privity, the courts initially were a great deal more clear as to the result to be achieved than as to any theory which would support it; and for another fourteen years there was resort to a remarkable variety of highly ingenious, and equally unconvincing, notions of fictitious agencies, third-party beneficiary contract, and the like, plucked out of thin air as devices to get around the fact that there was no contract between the plaintiff and the defendant. Finally, in 1927 the Mississippi court came up with the idea of a "warranty" running with the goods from the manufacturer to the consumer, by analogy to a contract running with the land. For more than thirty years after that date, until Justice Traynor upset the apple cart in 1963, the strict liability continued to be identified with warranty, which was necessarily a warranty without a contract.…

[T]he "warranty" was not the one made on the original sale, and did not run with the goods, but was a new and independent one made directly to the consumer; ... it did not arise out of or depend upon any contract, but was imposed by law, in tort, as a matter of policy; and ... it was subject to rules of its own....

In 1960 there came in New Jersey the landmark decision in *Henningsen v. Bloomfield Motors, Inc.*, which entered into the first full discussion of the rule, and held the manufacturer and the retailer of an automobile to a warranty of safety to the ultimate driver. The citadel of privity fell. What followed was unquestionably the most sudden and spectacular overturn of a well-established rule of law in the entire history of the law of torts.

Henningsen v. Bloomfield Motors, Inc.

161 A.2d 69 (1960) (Supreme Court of New Jersey)

FRANCIS, J. Plaintiff Claus H. Henningsen purchased a Plymouth automobile, manufactured by defendant Chrysler Corporation, from defendant Bloomfield Motors, Inc. His wife, plaintiff Helen Henningsen, was injured while driving it and instituted suit against both defendants to recover damages on account of her injuries. Her husband joined in the action seeking compensation for his consequential losses. The complaint was predicated upon breach of express and implied warranties and upon negligence. At the trial the negligence counts were dismissed by the court and the cause was submitted to the jury for determination solely on the issues of implied warranty of merchantability. Verdicts were returned against both defendants and in favor of the plaintiffs. Defendants appealed and plaintiffs cross-appealed from the dismissal of their negligence claim. The matter was certified by this court prior to consideration in the Appellate Division....

The record indicates that Mr. Henningsen intended the car as a Mother's Day gift to his wife. He said the intention was communicated to the dealer. When the purchase order or contract was prepared and presented, the husband executed it alone. His wife did not join as a party....

The new Plymouth was turned over to the Henningsens on May 9, 1955.... Mr. Henningsen drove it from the dealer's place of business in Bloomfield to their home in Keansburg. On the trip nothing unusual appeared in the way in which it operated. Thereafter, it was used for short trips on paved streets about the town. It had no servicing and no mishaps of any kind before the event of May 19. That day, Mrs. Henningsen drove to Asbury Park. On the way down and in returning the car performed in normal fashion until the accident occurred. She was proceeding north on Route 36 in Highlands, New Jersey, at 20–22 miles per hour. The highway was paved and smooth, and contained two lanes for northbound travel. She was riding in the right-hand lane. Suddenly she heard a loud noise "from the bottom, by the hood." It "felt as if something cracked." The steering wheel spun in her hands; the car veered sharply to the right and crashed into a highway sign and a brick wall. No other vehicle was in any way involved. A bus operator driving in the left-hand lane testified that he observed plaintiffs' car approaching in normal fashion in the opposite direction; "all of a sudden (it) veered at 90 degrees ... and right into this wall." As a result of the impact, the front of the car was so badly damaged that it was impossible to determine if any of the parts of the steering wheel mechanism or workmanship or assembly were defective or improper prior to the accident. The condition was such that the collision insurance carrier, after inspection, declared the vehicle a total loss. It had 468 miles on the speedometer at the time.

The insurance carrier's inspector and appraiser of damaged cars, with 11 years of experience, advanced the opinion, based on the history and his examination, that something definitely went "wrong from the steering wheel down to the front wheels" and that the untoward happening must have been due to mechanical defect or failure; "something down there had to drop off or break loose to cause the car" to act in the manner described.

As has been indicated, the trial court felt that the proof was not sufficient to make out a Prima facie case as to the negligence of either the manufacturer or the dealer. The case was given to the jury, therefore, solely on the warranty theory, with results favorable to the plaintiffs against both defendants....

Of course such sales, whether oral or written, may be accompanied by an express warranty. Under the broad terms of the Uniform Sale of Goods Law any affirmation of fact relating to the goods is an express warranty if the natural tendency of the statement is to induce the buyer to make the purchase. And over the years since the almost universal adoption of the act, a growing awareness of the tremendous development of modern business methods has prompted the courts to administer that provision with a liberal hand. Solicitude toward the buyer plainly harmonizes with the intention of the Legislature. That fact is manifested further by the later section of the act which preserves and continues any permissible implied warranty, despite an express warranty, unless the two are inconsistent.

The uniform act codified, extended and liberalized the common law of sales. The motivation in part was to ameliorate the harsh doctrine of Caveat emptor, and in some measure to impose a reciprocal obligation on the seller to beware. The transcendent value of the legislation, particularly with respect to implied warranties, rests in the fact that obligations on the part of the seller were imposed by operation of law, and did not depend for their existence upon express agreement of the parties. And of tremendous significance in a rapidly expanding commercial society was the recognition of the right to recover damages on account of personal injuries arising from a breach of warranty. The particular importance of this advance resides in the fact that under such circumstances strict liability is imposed upon the maker or seller of the product. Recovery of damages does not depend upon proof of negligence or knowledge of the defect.

As the Sales Act and its liberal interpretation by the courts threw this protective cloak about the buyer, the decisions in various jurisdictions revealed beyond doubt that many manufacturers took steps to avoid these ever increasing warranty obligations. Realizing that the act governed the relationship of buyer and seller, they undertook to withdraw from actual and direct contractual contact with the buyer. They ceased selling products to the consuming public through their own employees and making contracts of sale in their own names. Instead, a system of independent dealers was established; their products were sold to dealers who in turn dealt with the buying public, ostensibly solely in their own personal capacity as sellers. In the past in many instances, manufacturers were able to transfer to the dealers burdens imposed by the act and thus achieved a large measure of immunity for themselves. But, as will be noted in more detail hereafter, such marketing practices, coupled with the advent of large scale advertising by manufacturers to promote the purchase of these goods from dealers by members of the public, provided a basis upon which the existence of express or implied warranties was predicated, even though the manufacturer was not a party to the contract of sale.

The general observations that have been made are important largely for purposes of perspective. They are helpful in achieving a point from which to evaluate the situation now presented for solution. Primarily, they reveal a trend and a design in legislative and judicial thinking toward providing protection for the buyer....

With these considerations in mind, we come to a study of the express warranty on the reverse side of the purchase order signed by Claus Henningsen. At the outset we take notice that it was made only by the manufacturer and that by its terms it runs directly to Claus Henningsen. On the facts detailed above, it was to be extended to him by the dealer as the agent of Chrysler Corporation. The consideration for this warranty is the purchase of the manufacturer's product from the dealer by the ultimate buyer....

Preliminarily, it may be said that the express warranty against defective parts and workmanship is not inconsistent with an implied warranty of merchantability. Such warranty cannot be excluded for that reason.

Chrysler points out that an implied warranty of merchantability is an incident of a contract of sale. It concedes, of course, the making of the original sale to Bloomfield Motors, Inc., but maintains that this transaction marked the terminal point of its contractual connection with the car. Then Chrysler urges that since it was not a party to the sale by the dealer to Henningsen, there is no privity of contract between it and the plaintiffs, and the absence of this privity eliminates any such implied warranty.

There is no doubt that under early common-law concepts of contractual liability only those persons who were parties to the bargain could sue for a breach of it. In more recent times a noticeable disposition has appeared in a number of jurisdictions to break through the narrow barrier of privity when dealing with sales of goods in order to give realistic recognition to a universally accepted fact. The fact is that the dealer and the ordinary buyer do not, and are not expected to, buy goods, whether they be foodstuffs or automobiles, exclusively for their own consumption or use. Makers and manufacturers know this and advertise and market their products on that assumption; witness, the "family" car, the baby foods, etc. The limitations of privity in contracts for the sale of goods developed their place in the law when marketing conditions were simple, when maker and buyer frequently met face to face on an equal bargaining plane and when many of the products were relatively uncomplicated and conducive to inspection by a buyer competent to evaluate their quality. With the advent of mass marketing, the manufacturer became remote from the purchaser, sales were accomplished through intermediaries, and the demand for the product was created by advertising media. In such an economy it became obvious that the consumer was the person being cultivated. Manifestly, the connotation of "consumer" was broader than that of "buyer." He signified such a person who, in the reasonable contemplation of the parties to the sale, might be expected to use the product. Thus, where the commodities sold are such that if defectively manufactured they will be dangerous to life or limb, then society's interests can only be protected by eliminating the requirement of privity between the maker and his dealers and the reasonably expected ultimate consumer. In that way the burden of losses consequent upon use of defective articles is borne by those who are in a position to either control the danger or make an equitable distribution of the losses when they do occur....

Most of the cases where lack of privity has not been permitted to interfere with recovery have involved food and drugs....

In fact, the rule as to such products has been characterized as an exception to the general doctrine. But more recently courts, sensing the inequity of such limitation, have moved into broader fields: home permanent wave set, soap detergent, inflammable cowboy suit (by clear implication), exploding bottle, defective emery wheel, defective wire rope, defective cinder blocks. We see no rational doctrinal basis for differentiating between a fly in a bottle of beverage and a defective automobile. The unwholesome beverage may bring illness to one person, the defective car, with its great potentiality for harm to the driver, occupants, and others, demands even less adherence to the narrow barrier of privity....

Under modern conditions the ordinary layman, on responding to the importuning of colorful advertising, has neither the opportunity nor the capacity to inspect or to determine the fitness of an automobile for use; he must rely on the manufacturer who has control of its construction, and to some degree on the dealer who, to the limited extent called for by the manufacturer's instructions, inspects and services it before delivery. In such a marketing milieu his remedies and those of persons who properly claim through him should not depend upon the intricacies of the law of sales. The obligation of the manufacturer should not be based alone on privity of contract. It should rest, as was once said, upon "the demands of social justice."

Accordingly, we hold that under modern marketing conditions, when a manufacturer puts a new automobile in the stream of trade and promotes its purchase by the public, an implied warranty that it is reasonably suitable for use as such accompanies it into the hands of the ultimate purchaser. Absence of agency between the manufacturer and the dealer who makes the ultimate sale is immaterial.

Judgments affirmed.

Notes

1. *Floodgates.* Formerly the courts had been concerned to adhere to the doctrine of privity in order to avoid one of the floodgates problems. It is interesting to note that the court in *Henningsen* found that the propensity of the automobile to cause serious harm to a far greater number of individuals than a food product was actually a factor in favor of the court's abolition of the requirement of privity in a products liability claim.

2. *Contracts or torts?* Prosser wrote that *Henningsen* "was unquestionably the most sudden and spectacular overturn of a well-established rule of law in the entire history of the law of torts." Yet Judge Francis clearly treated the case as one concerned with the law of contracts: "this [suit] is in contract." (161 A.2d at 100). Indeed, the case on breach of warranty had been pleaded only in contract. So is a third party warranty a matter of contract law or of torts?

3. *Collateral contract.* Analysis of *Henningsen* within a contractual matrix depends on identifying not one contract involved in the case, but two. One was the contract to sell and purchase the car between the dealer and Mr. Henningsen. We may call this the "main" contract. But there was also a second, or "collateral," contract between Chrysler and Mr. Henningsen for the provision of a warranty. Yet this raises the question of what consideration is provided by the buyer, since he paid no money to, or at the request of, the manufacturer. (Without consideration, the buyer would need to prove reliance on a statement by the manufacturer, so as to invoke promissory estoppel.) Judge Francis's answer was that: "The consideration for this warranty is the purchase of the manufacturer's product from the dealer by the ultimate buyer." This analysis is represented in graphic form in Figure 3.3.

4. *Collateral versus main contract.* The distinction between a "main" and a "collateral" contract is crucial. A "main" contract is capable of independent existence: it is perfectly possible to sell a car with no warranty at all (at least, it is if the car is old, or if the seller is a private owner). But a "collateral" contract cannot exist without another contract to which it is collateral: a warranty cannot be provided without a product to warrant. A collateral contract is therefore effectively parasitic on a main contract. To paraphrase Judge Francis, without Mr. Henningsen's purchase of the car, there could be no collateral contract of warranty with the manufacturer; but once the purchase is made, the contract of warranty also comes into existence.

Figure 3.3 Third Party Warranties in Contracts

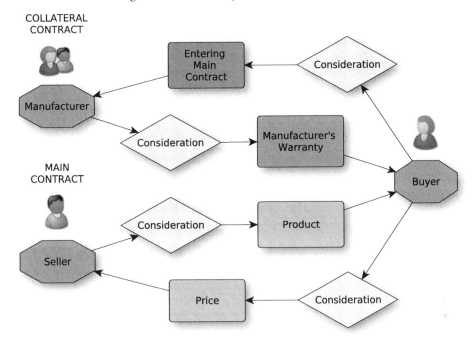

5. *Vertical privity.* The effect of third-party warranties via collateral contracts is thus to circumvent what is sometimes called "vertical" privity: see Figure 3.4. It involves one of the (typically) three potential transactions in the chain of distribution: first, between manufacturer and wholesaler; secondly, between wholesaler and retailer; and thirdly, between retailer and retail purchaser. A strict requirement to prove vertical privity would mean that the victim could bring an action for breach of warranty only against the retailer from whom she purchased the product in question, whereas the device of the collateral contract circumvents this requirement and permits a claim for breach of warranty to be brought against the manufacturer directly.

6. *Vertical privity and express warranties: proposed revisions to UCC § 2-313.* This ability to circumvent the strict requirements of vertical privity was recognized by abortive proposals in 2003 to amend Article 2 of the UCC. These would have seen two new sections, covering express warranties, added to follow § 2-313. Section 2-313 would have been retained to apply to express warranties made by the seller to the "immediate buyer," while a new § 2-313A was designed to recognize that a manufacturer (or other seller) who packages a warranty with the goods provides the "remote purchaser" with the benefit of the express warranty, even though the goods pass through the ownership of intermediaries before reaching the "remote purchaser." A new § 2-313B would have applied where an express warranty was provided through "an advertisement or a similar communication to the public," provided that the "remote purchaser" knew of the warranty at the time of purchase. A manufacturer whose advertising tempts a consumer to buy a product could thus have been bound by the contractual law of warranty by its claims of quality. Since these proposed revisions have now been abandoned, however, it remains the case that any consumer claiming to have been misled in this fashion must seek recourse through the law of misrepresentation in torts.

7. "Lemon" laws. Many states have now introduced their own "lemon" laws which provide the consumer with even greater protection. These laws typically apply to new or demonstrator motor vehicles which become defective over the first two years of ownership. If, after a reasonable number of attempts to repair such defects, the manufacturer still fails to conform the vehicle to the warranty, the manufacturer is then required either to refund the purchase price or provide a replacement vehicle. Note that "lemon" laws "piggy-back" on the idea of a third-party or collateral warranty, since the relevant warranty is provided by the manufacturer, not the seller.

Figure 3.4 Vertical and Horizontal Privity

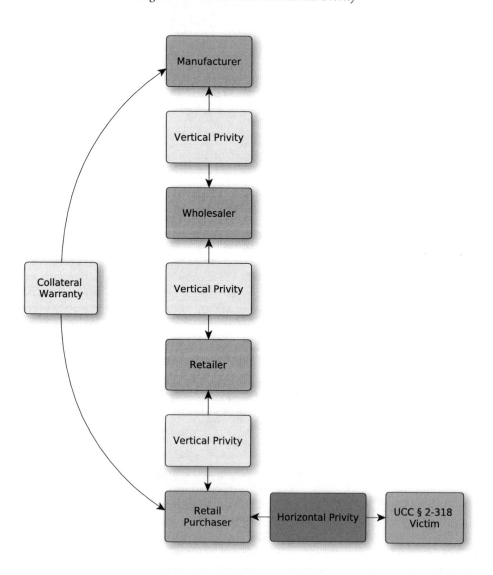

8. *Horizontal privity.* Although the notion of a third-party warranty in contract may seem to provide an effective means for circumventing the privity rule, in reality it merely shifts the problem one stage along. A third-party or collateral warranty remains a viable theory only if there is a main purchase contract to which the warranty can be collateral. In other words, the victim still has to be in privity with the seller of the goods. This is problematic if the victim was not herself the purchaser of the goods, a position which concerns what is sometimes known as "horizontal" privity. The distinction between vertical and horizontal privity, and the ability of a collateral warranty to circumvent the former, is depicted in graphic form in Figure 3.4. A victim must *either* be the retail purchaser *or* a § 2-318 victim (discussed in more detail below), *AND* have *either* vertical privity *or* a collateral warranty with the defendant.

9. *Horizontal privity and agency.* *Henningsen* seemed to demonstrate that the only way around this requirement was by showing that the actual purchaser had been acting as the victim's agent (as could be said of Mr. Henningsen for his wife). The drafters of the UCC recognized the problem, and attempted to address it essentially by widening the scope of agency in this context. They could not, however, agree on one definitive solution, and instead proposed, in § 2-318, that each state should adopt one of the following three alternative provisions. Alternative A, the most restrictive of the options, has been the one most commonly adopted by the states.

Uniform Commercial Code — Article 2 — Sales (1966)

§ 2-318. *Third Party Beneficiaries of Warranties Express or Implied.*

Alternative A

A seller's warranty whether express or implied extends to any natural person who is in the family or household of his buyer or who is a guest in his home if it is reasonable to expect that such person may use, consume or be affected by the goods and who is injured in person by breach of the warranty. A seller may not exclude or limit the operation of this section.

Alternative B

A seller's warranty whether express or implied extends to any natural person who may reasonably be expected to use, consume or be affected by the goods and who is injured in person by breach of the warranty. A seller may not exclude or limit the operation of this section.

Alternative C

A seller's warranty whether express or implied extends to any person who may reasonably be expected to use, consume or be affected by the goods and who is injured by breach of the warranty. A seller may not exclude or limit the operation of this section with respect to injury to the person of an individual to whom the warranty extends.

Notes

1. ***The continuing problem of horizontal privity.*** The text of the most commonly adopted option, Alternative A, is evidently of no assistance to an employee who is injured when using defective equipment provided by her employer. While she will usually have a worker's compensation claim against the employer, she will be unable to bring a breach of warranty suit against the manufacturer, since not only did she not purchase the equipment herself, but she is also clearly not a member of the employer's family or household, nor a house-guest. In other words, she lacks the necessary horizontal privity.

2. ***Employees and expansive interpretations of horizontal privity.*** Some states have, however, been prepared to stretch the interpretation of Alternative A. In *McNally v.*

Nicholson Mfg. Co., 313 A.2d 913, 921 (Me. 1973), for example, an employee was struck on the head by a piece of wood that was expelled from the side of a chipping machine, which had been purchased by his employer. The Supreme Court of Maine held that the employee came "within the policy scope of Section 2-318 since plaintiff may be regarded as a member of such 'family' as a corporation may reasonably be said to have." The Supreme Court of Pennsylvania took a similar view in *Salvador v. Atlantic Steel Boiler Co.*, 319 A.2d 903 (1974), as did the First District Appellate Court of Illinois in *Boddie v. Litton Unit Handling Systems*, 455 N.E.2d 142, 151 (1983), which agreed with the plaintiff's contention that:

> [I]t would be illogical to extend warranty protection to guests of the buyer's household who are only remotely connected with the product and refuse protection to employees of a purchaser of a machine intended for industrial use.

3. *Strict liability in contracts and torts.* The decisions in *McNally*, *Salvador*, and *Boddie* might be thought to have broadened the category of compensable victim to such an extent that claims of strict liability for breach of warranty in contracts would have eclipsed any need to create a new form of strict liability for defective products in torts. That would, however, be to get things back to front. In fact, much of the reason for the expansive interpretation of §2-318 of the UCC was driven by the fact that strict liability for defective products in torts had been established and codified as §402A of the Restatement (Second) of Torts (1965) (discussed in more depth in Chapter 6), which imposed such liability regardless of the lack of contractual privity between the seller and the victim. The court in *Salvador*, 319 A.2d 903, 907 (1974), noted that the "anomalous situation is certainly to be avoided" where a plaintiff's claim is permitted if his complaint is made in torts, but rejected on identical facts if the pleading is in contracts.

4. *Is there a need for strict products liability in torts?* Cases like *McNally*, *Salvador*, and *Boddie* nowadays represent the exception rather than the rule. In most states, there is now considered to be no anomaly in having different rules for, on the one hand, cases of breach of warranty in contracts and, on the other, claims of strict products liability in torts. Thus it is more typical to treat the language of §2-318 of the UCC more literally, so as to restrict the class of victims with sufficient horizontal privity to be able to make a successful claim for breach of warranty. Only when a claim is brought as a matter of strict liability in torts is there no need to prove privity at all. In *Kramer v. Piper Aircraft Corp.*, 520 So.2d 37, 39 (Fla. 1988), for example, the Supreme Court of Florida approved the view of the Third Florida District Court of Appeal in *Affiliates for Evaluation and Therapy, Inc. v. Viasyn Corp.*, 500 So.2d 688, 692 (1987), which had remarked that:

> [T]he doctrine of strict liability in tort supplants all no-privity, breach of implied warranty cases, because it was, in effect, created out of these cases. This ... did not result in the demise of the contract action of breach of implied warranty, as that action remains ... where privity of contract is shown.

5. *The practical difference between strict liability in contracts and strict liability in torts.* Even if the more expansive reading of §2-318 of the UCC is adopted, *Boddie* itself demonstrates that there is still a significant difference between strict liability for breach of warranty in contracts and strict products liability in torts. In that case, a post office employee brought an action against a general contractor and its subcontractor for injuries she suffered when her hand was caught in a partially exposed chain and gear drive mechanism of a conveyor, which had been designed and manufactured by the subcontractor before being provided by the defendants to her employer. As the court recognized, the claim for breach of warranty could not succeed, even if the employee were considered to be a member of her employer's "family," since the subcontractor manufacturer only had a contract with the main contractor, and not with the victim's employer. In other words, even if the notion of horizontal privity were extended to include her, the claim for breach of warranty failed because of her *employer's* lack of vertical privity with the supplier. The victim's claim for strict products liability was, however, allowed to proceed, as was her claim of negligence, since these claims do not require any form of privity between plaintiff and defendant.

6. *The elements of a prima facie case of breach of warranty.* The elements for a prima facie case of breach of warranty are set out in the flowchart in Figure 3.5.

Figure 3.5 The Elements of a Prima Facie Case of Breach of Warranty

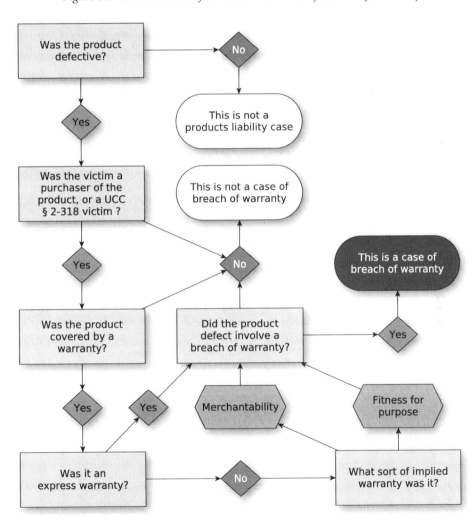

Questions

1. Can the idea of a warranty owed to a third party avoid the problems associated with both floods of claims and floods of trials?

2. Can the idea of a strict products liability claim in torts, which does not require proof of either vertical or horizontal privity, avoid the problems associated with both floods of claims and floods of trials?

3. Would the amount of damages awarded for a strict products liability claim in torts necessarily be different from that awarded for a breach of a contractual warranty?

Exclusions and Limitations

As it became more difficult for sellers to avoid being deemed to have provided either express or implied warranties (or both), businesses began to turn away from attempting to deny that any warranties had been provided, and instead focused on how to make the best of the fact that such warranties would inevitably be found to exist. It then became normal practice to draft standard express warranties designed to try to limit—or to take away altogether—the rights of the buyer.

Henningsen v. Bloomfield Motors, Inc.
161 A.2d 69 (1960) (Supreme Court of New Jersey)

[See above for the facts of this case.] FRANCIS, J. The terms of the warranty are a sad commentary upon the automobile manufacturers' marketing practices. Warranties developed in the law in the interest of and to protect the ordinary consumer who cannot be expected to have the knowledge or capacity or even the opportunity to make adequate inspection of mechanical instrumentalities, like automobiles, and to decide for himself whether they are reasonably fit for the designed purpose. But the ingenuity of the Automobile Manufacturers Association, by means of its standardized form, has metamorphosed the warranty into a device to limit the maker's liability. To call it an "equivocal" agreement, as the Minnesota Supreme Court did, is the least that can be said in criticism of it.

The manufacturer agrees to replace defective parts for 90 days after the sale or until the car has been driven 4,000 miles, whichever is first to occur, if the part is sent to the factory, transportation charges prepaid, and if examination discloses to its satisfaction that the part is defective. It is difficult to imagine a greater burden on the consumer, or less satisfactory remedy. Aside from imposing on the buyer the trouble of removing and shipping the part, the maker has sought to retain the uncontrolled discretion to decide the issue of defectiveness. Some courts have removed much of the force of that reservation by declaring that the purchaser is not bound by the manufacturer's decision. *Mills v. Maxwell Motor Sales Corporation*, 105 Neb. 465,181 N.W. 152, 22 A.L.R. 130 (Sup.Ct.1920); *Cannon v. Pulliam Motor Company*, 230 S.C. 131, 94 S.E.2d 397 (Sup.Ct.1956). In the *Mills* case, the court said:

> It would nevertheless be repugnant to every conception of justice to hold that, if the parts thus returned for examination were, in point of fact, so defective as to constitute a breach of warranty, the appellee's right of action could be defeated by the appellant's arbitrary refusal to recognize that fact. Such an interpretation would substitute the appellant for the courts in passing upon the question of fact, and would be unreasonable. *Supra*, 181 N.W. at page 154.

Also suppose, as in this case, a defective part or parts caused an accident and that the car was so damaged as to render it impossible to discover the precise part or parts responsible, although the circumstances clearly pointed to such fact as the cause of the mishap. Can it be said that the impossibility of performance deprived the buyer of the benefit of the warranty?

Moreover, the guaranty is against defective workmanship. That condition may arise from good parts improperly assembled. There being no defective parts to return to the maker, is all remedy to be denied? One court met that type of problem by holding that where the purchaser does not know the precise cause of inoperability, calling a car a "vibrator" would be sufficient to state a claim for relief. It said that such a car is not an uncommon one in the industry. The general cause of the vibration is not known. Some part or parts have been either defectively manufactured or improperly assembled in the construction and manufacture of the automobile. In the operation of the car, these parts give rise to vibrations. The difficulty lies in locating the precise spot and cause. But the warranty does not specify what the purchaser must do to obtain relief in such case, if a remedy is intended to be provided. Must the purchaser return the car, transportation charges prepaid, over a great distance to the factory? It may be said that in the usual case the dealer also gives the same warranty and that as a matter of expediency the purchaser should turn to him. But under the law the buyer is entitled to proceed against the manufacturer. Further, dealers' franchises are precarious. For example, Bloomfield Motors' franchise may be cancelled by Chrysler on 90 days' notice. And obviously dealers' facilities and capacity, financial and otherwise, are not as sufficient as those of the primarily responsible manufacturer in his distant factory.

The matters referred to represent only a small part of the illusory character of the security presented by the warranty. Thus far the analysis has dealt only with the remedy provided in the case of a defective part. What relief is provided when the breach of the warranty results in personal injury to the buyer? (Injury to third persons using the car in the purchaser's right will be treated hereafter.) As we have said above, the law is clear that such damages are recoverable under an ordinary warranty. The right exists whether the warranty sued on is express or implied. And, of course, it has long since been settled that where the buyer or a member of his family driving with his permission suffers injuries because of negligent manufacture or construction of the manufacturer's liability exists. But in this instance, after reciting that defective parts will be replaced at the factory, the alleged agreement relied upon by Chrysler provides that the manufacturer's "obligation under this warranty" is limited to that undertaking; further, that such remedy is "in lieu of all other warranties, express or implied, and all other obligations or liabilities on its part." The contention has been raised that such language bars any claim for personal injuries which may emanate from a breach of the warranty....

Although the courts, with few exceptions, have been most sensitive to problems presented by contracts resulting from gross disparity in buyer-seller bargaining positions, they have not articulated a general principle condemning, as opposed to public policy, the imposition on the buyer of a skeleton warranty as a means of limiting the responsibility of the manufacturer. They have endeavored thus far to avoid a drastic departure from age-old tenets of freedom of contract by adopting doctrines of strict construction, and notice and knowledgeable assent by the buyer to the attempted exculpation of the seller....

The task of the judiciary is to administer the spirit as well as the letter of the law. On issues such as the present one, part of that burden is to protect the ordinary man against the loss of important rights through what, in effect, is the unilateral act of the manufacturer. The status of the automobile industry is unique. Manufacturers are few in number and strong in bargaining position. In the matter of warranties on the sale of their products, the Automotive Manufacturers Association has enabled them to present a united front. From the standpoint of the purchaser, there can be no arms length negotiating on the subject. Because his capacity for bargaining is so grossly unequal, the inexorable conclusion which follows is that he is not permitted to bargain at all. He must take or leave the automobile on the warranty terms dictated by the maker. He cannot turn to a competitor for better security....

The judicial process has recognized a right to recover damages for personal injuries arising from a breach of that warranty. The disclaimer of the implied warranty and exclusion of all obligations except those specifically assumed by the express warranty signify a studied effort to frustrate that protection. True, the Sales Act authorizes agreements between buyer and seller qualifying the warranty obligations. But quite obviously the Legislature contemplated lawful stipulations (which are determined by the circumstances of a particular case) arrived at freely by parties of relatively equal bargaining strength. The lawmakers did not authorize the automobile manufacturer to use its grossly disproportionate bargaining power to relieve itself from liability and to impose on the ordinary buyer, who in effect has no real freedom of choice, the grave danger of injury to himself and others that attends the sale of such a dangerous instrumentality as a defectively made automobile. In the framework of this case, illuminated as it is by the facts and the many decisions noted, we are of the opinion that Chrysler's attempted disclaimer of an implied warranty of merchantability and of the obligations arising therefrom is so inimical to the public good as to compel an adjudication of its invalidity.

Note

Reasonableness. The UCC subjects attempts to limit or exclude the scope of warranties to a collection of tests for reasonableness, so that what reasonableness means—as well as who has the onus of proof on the issue—varies according to the type of injury sustained.

Uniform Commercial Code—Article 2—Sales (1952)

§ 2-316. *Exclusion or Modification of Warranties.*

(1) Words or conduct relevant to the creation of an express warranty and words or conduct tending to negate or limit warranty shall be construed wherever reasonable as consistent with each other; but subject to the provisions of this Article on parol or extrinsic evidence (Section 2-202) negation or limitation is inoperative to the extent that such construction is unreasonable.

(2) Subject to subsection (3), to exclude or modify the implied warranty of merchantability or any part of it the language must mention merchantability and in case of a writing must be conspicuous, and to exclude or modify any implied warranty of fitness the exclusion must be by a writing and conspicuous. Language to exclude all implied warranties of fitness is sufficient if it states, for example, that "There are no warranties which extend beyond the description on the face hereof."

(3) Notwithstanding subsection (2)

(a) unless the circumstances indicate otherwise, all implied warranties are excluded by expressions like "as is", "with all faults" or other language which in common understanding calls the buyer's attention to the exclusion of warranties and makes plain that there is no implied warranty; and

(b) when the buyer before entering into the contract has examined the goods or the sample or model as fully as he desired or has refused to examine the goods there is no implied warranty with regard to defects which an examination ought in the circumstances to have revealed to him; and

(c) an implied warranty can also be excluded or modified by course of dealing or course of performance or usage of trade.

(4) Remedies for breach of warranty can be limited in accordance with the provisions of this Article on liquidation or limitation of damages and on contractual modification of remedy (Sections 2-718 and 2-719).

§ 2-718. Liquidation or Limitation of Damages; Deposits.

(1) Damages for breach by either party may be liquidated in the agreement but only at an amount which is reasonable in the light of the anticipated or actual harm caused by the breach, the difficulties of proof of loss, and the inconvenience or nonfeasibility of otherwise obtaining an adequate remedy....

§ 2-719. Contractual Modification or Limitation of Remedy.

(3) Consequential damages may be limited or excluded unless the limitation or exclusion is unconscionable. Limitation of consequential damages for injury to the person in the case of consumer goods is prima facie unconscionable but limitation of damages where the loss is commercial is not.

§ 2-302. Unconscionable Contract or Clause.

(1) If the court as a matter of law finds the contract or any clause of the contract to have been unconscionable at the time it was made the court may refuse to enforce the contract, or it may enforce the remainder of the contract without the unconscionable clause, or it may so limit the application of any unconscionable clause as to avoid any unconscionable result.

(2) When it is claimed or appears to the court that the contract or any clause thereof may be unconscionable the parties shall be afforded a reasonable opportunity to present evidence as to its commercial setting, purpose and effect to aid the court in making the determination.

Notes

1. *Limited warranties.* To ensure that they do not run afoul of the requirement of "conspicuousness" in § 2-316 of the UCC, businesses typically no longer give apparently "blanket" warranties to consumers, but instead provide what they call "limited warranties," whose very name implies some degree of limitation, and whose terms then spell out precisely what is warranted, in what manner, and for how long.

2. *Proposed revisions to § 2-316(2).* Revisions to Article 2 of the UCC, agreed in 2003 by NCCUSL (now often called instead the Uniform Law Commission, or ULC) in conjunction with the American Law Institute (ALI), would have seen the introduction of a new rule regarding disclaimers in consumer contracts, while leaving the law relating to other contracts substantively untouched. So far as consumer contracts are concerned, the revised § 2-316(2) would have required that any exclusion or modification of the implied warranty of merchantability (or any part of it):

> must be in a record, be conspicuous, and state "The seller undertakes no responsibility for the quality of the goods except as otherwise provided in this contract" ... Language to exclude all implied warranties of fitness in a consumer contract must state "The seller assumes no responsibility that the goods will be fit for any particular purpose for which you may be buying these goods, except as otherwise provided in the contract" ...

The idea of replacing "writing" by "record" was designed to accommodate the use of electronic communications. However, following an unsuccessful attempt to persuade the legislature in Oklahoma to adopt the revisions to Article 2, NCCUSL effectively decided in 2010 to abandon the proposals, at least for the time being.

3. *Exclusions by means of "as is" terminology: the Magnuson-Moss Warranty Act of 1975 (15 U.S.C. § 2301 et seq.).* In *Ismael v. Goodman Toyota*, 106 N.C.App. 421, 417 S.E.2d 290 (1992), the plaintiff had bought a Ford Tempo "as is" for $5,054.00 (plus financing charges) from the defendant dealership, but had also purchased for an additional $695.00 a Vehicle Service Agreement, which was to cover the car for 24 months or 24,000 miles, whichever occurred first. However, the vehicle's engine was in such a bad state that it cut out the very next day and, despite repeated repairs by the dealership, the plaintiff never enjoyed more than three days' use of the car at any one time. It was finally declared irreparable by the dealership and, although the plaintiff did attempt to have the car repaired at his own expense by Ford dealerships, it remained unusable. The Court of Appeals of North Carolina noted that the buyer was a "consumer," the car was a "product," and the seller was a "merchant" under the UCC. It then remarked:

> Defendant contends that since the uncontradicted evidence proved the car was sold "as is," all express and implied warranties were effectively disclaimed pursuant to our Uniform Commercial Code..., and therefore plaintiff had no claim for breach of an implied warranty. Defendant also contends that since no express or implied warranties were given, the Act does not apply in this case. We disagree.

> "Implied warranty" as defined by the Act is "an implied warranty arising under State law ... in connection with the sale by a supplier of a consumer product." Under our Uniform Commercial Code, an implied warranty of merchantability arises in a contract for the sale of goods by a merchant unless excluded or modified.

> Defendant correctly contends that, as a general rule, the implied warranty of merchantability is excluded by an "as is" sale. However, the Act significantly limits a supplier's ability to modify or disclaim implied warranties. 15 U.S.C.A. § 2308(a). If, at the time of sale or within 90 days thereafter, a supplier enters into a service contract with the consumer which applies to such consumer product, the supplier may not disclaim or modify any implied warranty with respect to that product. Furthermore, a disclaimer made in violation of § 2308(a) is ineffective for purposes of the Act and State law.

The Court therefore held that the "as is" sale was ineffective as a disclaimer of the implied warranty of merchantability. Since that implied warranty had clearly been breached, the plaintiff was entitled to have judgment entered, subject to a new trial on the issue of damages.

4. *Prima facie unconscionable.* Although § 2-719 talks of limitations of damages for personal injury being "prima facie unconscionable," it is difficult to see what sort of evidence could rebut this presumption. Accordingly, it seems that such limitations are prohibited absolutely. However, this prohibition does not prevent a warranty from being excluded altogether under § 2-316. Such an effective exclusion would then render a limitation on damages completely unnecessary. The complexity of the current position regarding the enforceability of disclaimers and limitations can be seen from the flowchart in Figure 3.6.

Figure 3.6 The Effectiveness of Exclusion and Limitation Clauses

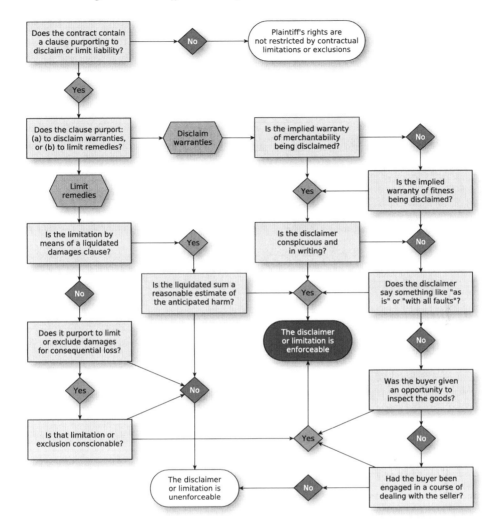

5. *Disclaiming liability versus not providing warranties.* The combined effect of the various UCC provisions on express and implied warranties and exclusions and limitations is essentially as follows:

(a) It is permissible, through appropriate language, to avoid providing any express or implied warranties; but

(b) Where such warranties are provided, it is not possible to exclude or limit liability for their breach if such breach causes personal injury.

6. *Europe, exclusions and torts.* Throughout the European Union (EU), there is a complete prohibition on "unfair terms" in consumer contracts which have been drafted in advance. Under Annex 1(a) of the Unfair Terms in Consumer Contracts Directive 93/13/EEC (1993), such unfair terms include terms "which have the object *or effect* of excluding or limiting the legal liability of a seller or supplier in the event of the death of a consumer or personal injury to the latter resulting from an act or omission of that seller or supplier" (emphasis added).

This provision therefore goes somewhat further than American law. It means that, so far as consumer contracts made within the EU are concerned, not only are attempts to limit or exclude liability for personal injury ineffective, as in note 5(b) above; but also that any attempts to avoid providing the implied terms of merchantability and fitness for purpose, as in note 5(a), are also ineffective. In other words, the European approach is concerned to ensure that liability for death and personal injury can never be avoided, no matter by what means the seller or supplier might choose to do so.

It is arguable that the continuing ability of businesses within the United States to effectively exclude any potential liability for death and personal injury in contracts (by ensuring that no implied warranties are provided) has been one of the major driving factors behind the creation of a field of strict products liability in torts. The effectiveness (or otherwise) of attempts to exclude or limit products liability in torts is considered in Chapter 13.

Questions

1. Is it appropriate that a seller or distributor can avoid providing any implied warranties in a consumer transaction, and so draft the contract to have the *effect* of excluding or limiting liability for death or personal injury?

2. Is it better for businesses to potentially face *both* claims for death or personal injury for breach of non-excludable implied terms of merchantability or fitness for purpose in contracts *and* claims of negligence in torts (the European position), *or both* claims for effectively excludable liability for death or personal injury in contracts *and* claims for strict products liability for death or personal injury in torts (the American position)?

3. Would the suggested revision to § 2-316(2) of the UCC have improved the law?

Hypothetical

Two years ago, Mr. and Mrs. Jones decided that they should purchase a new queen-size bed. Mr. Jones said to his wife: "You choose what you want, honey." Mrs. Jones went to the local Mattressco store and, without trying out the bed by lying on it, selected a bed manufactured by SlumberBed, on which a notice was placed which said that the bed was "backed with a limited five-year warranty." Included in the packaging, when the bed is delivered to the Jones's home, is a packet titled "Warranty," which says that SlumberBed "warrants that the mattress will be free of manufacturing defects for five years," and that "any defects that appear within that period will be repaired or replaced free of charge at SlumberBed's option. Any and all implied warranties of merchantability are hereby excluded." After two years' use, Mr. Jones has developed a severe, chronic back problem, which an orthopedic specialist has diagnosed as being caused by what he terms the "wholly inadequate" support provided by the SlumberBed mattress. What is Mr. Jones's legal position?

Chapter 4

Misrepresentation

Introduction

As we saw in Chapter 2, there were historically two means of circumventing the doctrine of *caveat emptor*. One involved claiming a breach of warranty; the other required proof of misrepresentation. Indeed, claims for misrepresentation are highly analogous — and often closely linked — to claims for breach of express warranty. In *Baxter v. Ford Motor Co.* 168 Wash. 456, 12 P.2d 409 (1932), the plaintiff Baxter lost his left eye and suffered a loss of sight in his right eye when his car windshield shattered. Ford had provided an express warranty that the windshield would be "shatterproof." If Baxter had bought the car from Ford, he would have had a legitimate claim for breach of an express warranty. Yet, as is the norm, Baxter had bought the car from a retail dealership, and so had no privity of contract with Ford. Since this was before the landmark decision in *Henningsen v. Bloomfield Motors Inc.*, 32 N.J. 358, 161 A.2d 69 (1960) — discussed in Chapter 3 — this appeared to rule out any claim for breach of warranty because Baxter lacked vertical privity with Ford.

Instead, Baxter sued for misrepresentation. The Supreme Court of Washington allowed the claim to proceed because it held (168 Wash. at 463) that:

> It would be unjust to recognize a rule that would permit manufacturers of goods to create a demand for their products by representing that they possess qualities which they, in fact, do not possess, and then, because there is no privity of contract existing between the consumer and the manufacturer, deny the consumer the right to recover if damages result from the absence of those qualities ...

This was much the same reasoning that led to the drafting of the now-abandoned §§ 2-313A and 2-313B of the UCC (see Chapter 3), which would have allowed a remote purchaser to bring a claim for breach of express warranty against a manufacturer. Nevertheless, warranties have traditionally been seen as part of the law of contracts, while misrepresentation has traditionally been regarded as part of the law of torts. The Products Liability Restatement, adopted by the American Law Institute in 1998, includes just one section on misrepresentation. This is § 9, which states:

> One engaged in the business of selling or otherwise distributing products who, in connection with the sale of a product, makes a fraudulent, negligent, or innocent misrepresentation of material fact concerning the product is subject to liability for harm to persons or property caused by the misrepresentation.

In other words, § 9 seeks to apply the regular law of misrepresentation to cases involving defective products, but with the addition of some tweaks. Indeed, the Reporters' Comments to § 9 make it clear that they intend simply to incorporate by reference §§ 310, 311 and 402B of the Restatement (Second) of Torts. Figure 4.1 sets out the various routes

Figure 4.1 Restatement Routes to Misrepresentation Claims about Defective Products

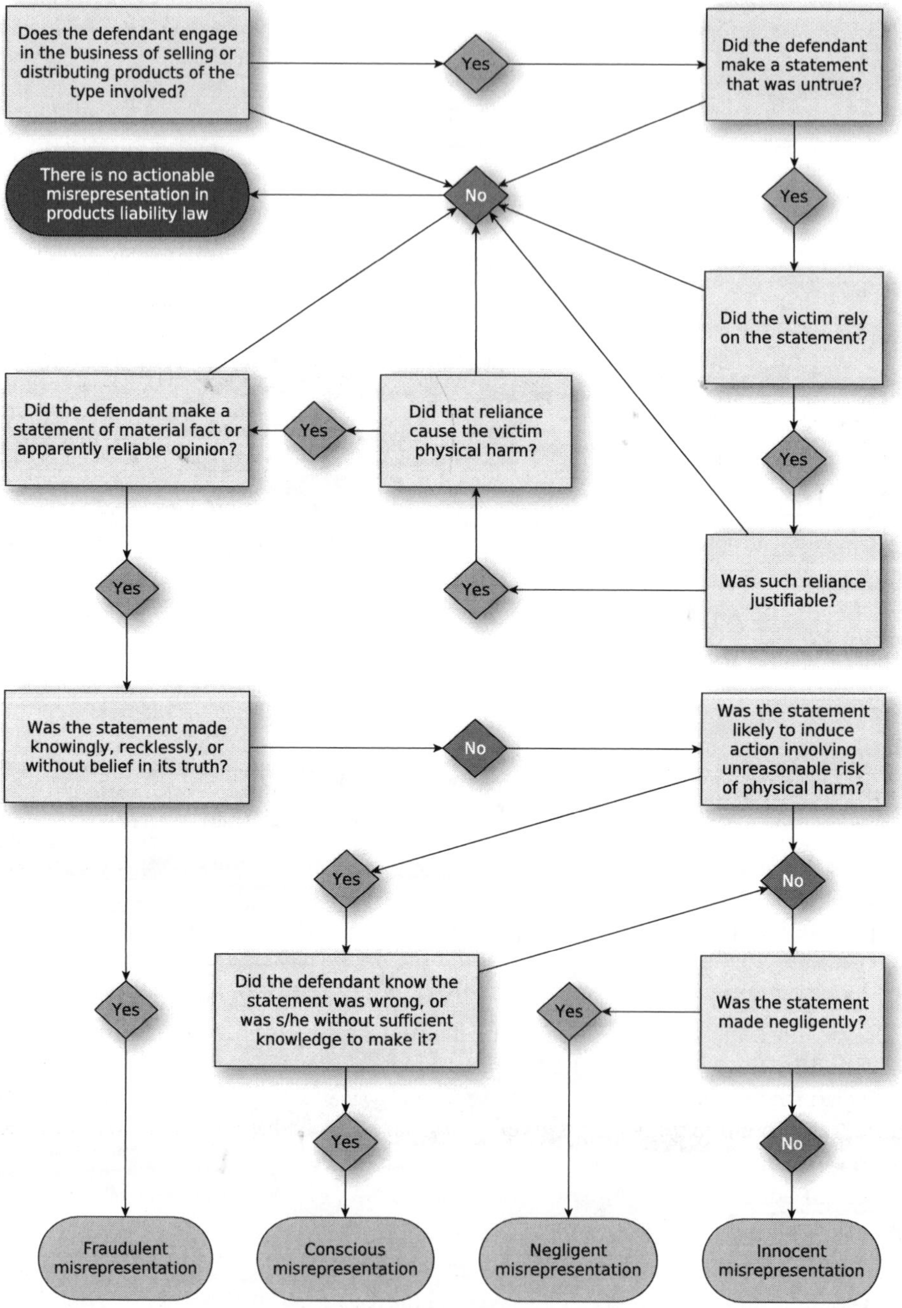

for a claim of misrepresentation concerning defective products according to the Second Restatement.

It is important to note, however, each of the relevant sections in the Second Restatement recognizes as actionable not just misrepresentations of material facts, but also misrepresentations of opinions (including opinions on law and possible future events). This is something discussed in more detail below. According to § 538 of the Second Restatement, "material" facts are those upon which the representee can reasonably be expected to rely or, according to *Boulden v. Stillwell*, 60 A. 609, 610 (Md. 1905), without which "the transaction would not have been made."

Section 9 suggests that there are three forms of misrepresentation, namely fraudulent, negligent, and innocent. However, the Second Restatement actually recognizes a fourth variant (in § 310), which it styles "conscious" misrepresentation. This seems to be a hybrid of fraudulent and negligent misrepresentation; it will be discussed further below.

One significant tweak to the regular law of misrepresentation is introduced by the requirement that, so far as product liability law is concerned, it be applied only to "[o]ne engaged in the business of selling or otherwise distributing products ..." This is the same language as that we saw (in Chapter 1) used in § 1 of the Products Liability Restatement. It seems likely, therefore, that this phrase is intended to be interpreted in the same way. It will be recalled that *Comment c* to § 1 says: "The rule stated in this Section applies only to manufacturers and other commercial sellers and distributors who are *engaged in the business of selling or otherwise distributing the type of product* that harmed the plaintiff" (emphasis added.) Once again, it is suggested that the use of the more precise terminology of "merchant" in the UCC would not only have aided consistency between commercial law on the one hand and products liability law on the other but would also have avoided any doubt.

Fraudulent Misrepresentation (Deceit)

Although actions for misrepresentation historically offered a means of circumventing the doctrine of *caveat emptor*, this was originally of limited benefit to representee victims, since the only form of misrepresentation that the law recognized as the basis for a claim for damages was fraudulent misrepresentation, usually known as the tort of deceit. As Kevin M. Teeven, A History of the Anglo-American Common Law of Contract 139 (1990), has said, this "left misrepresentations short of fraud to fall through the cracks without any clear rule of liability until quite recently." Moreover, although the representee did not need to show that she had been in privity of contract with the representor defendant at the time that the representation had been made, she did need to prove that she had relied upon the misrepresentation to her detriment. This usually meant showing that the misrepresentation had caused her to *enter into* an unprofitable contract, albeit not necessarily with the defendant.

This changed with the case of *Pasley v. Freeman*, 100 Eng. Rep. 450 (K.B. 1789), which concerned the defendant's intentional misrepresentation of a third party's creditworthiness. Although Mr. Justice Gross dissented from the majority's holding on the grounds that this was not actionable precisely because it had not induced the plaintiff to enter into a contract, the majority held, in the words of Mr. Justice Ashhurst that "the gist of the action is the injury done to the plaintiff, and not whether the defendant was or was not to gain by it."

Pasley established definitively that fraudulent misrepresentation involved a *tort* of deceit, which was completely independent of the law of contracts. This meant that the plaintiff did not need to show require privity of contract with the defendant in order to succeed with such a claim. Nevertheless, the following century saw the courts reach inconsistent conclusions as to what a plaintiff did need to prove in order to establish fraud. The required elements were finally settled by the House of Lords (the final court of appeal in England until the recent establishment of a Supreme Court in its stead) in the case of *Derry v. Peek*.

Derry v. Peek

(1889) LR 14 App. Cas. 337 (House of Lords)

LORD HERSCHELL. My Lords, in the statement of claim in this action the respondent, who is the plaintiff, alleges that the appellants made in a prospectus issued by them certain statements which were untrue, that they well knew that the facts were not as stated in the prospectus, and made the representations fraudulently, and with the view to induce the plaintiff to take shares in the company.

"This action is one which is commonly called an action of deceit, a mere common law action." This is the description of it given by Cotton L.J. in delivering judgment. I think it important that it should be borne in mind that such an action differs essentially from one brought to obtain rescission of a contract on the ground of misrepresentation of a material fact. The principles which govern the two actions differ widely. Where rescission is claimed it is only necessary to prove that there was misrepresentation; then, however honestly it may have been made, however free from blame the person who made it, the contract, having been obtained by misrepresentation, cannot stand. In an action of deceit, on the contrary, it is not enough to establish misrepresentation alone; it is conceded on all hands that something more must be proved to cast liability upon the defendant, though it has been a matter of controversy what additional elements are requisite....

Having now drawn attention, I believe, to all the cases having a material bearing upon the question under consideration, I proceed to state briefly the conclusions to which I have been led. I think the authorities establish the following propositions: First, in order to sustain an action of deceit, there must be proof of fraud, and nothing short of that will suffice. Secondly, fraud is proved when it is shewn that a false representation has been made (1) knowingly, or (2) without belief in its truth, or (3) recklessly, careless whether it be true or false. Although I have treated the second and third as distinct cases, I think the third is but an instance of the second, for one who makes a statement under such circumstances can have no real belief in the truth of what he states. To prevent a false statement being fraudulent, there must, I think, always be an honest belief in its truth. And this probably covers the whole ground, for one who knowingly alleges that which is false, has obviously no such honest belief. Thirdly, if fraud be proved, the motive of the person guilty of it is immaterial. It matters not that there was no intention to cheat or injure the person to whom the statement was made.

In my opinion making a false statement through want of care falls far short of, and is a very different thing from, fraud, and the same may be said of a false representation honestly believed though on insufficient grounds....

At the same time I desire to say distinctly that when a false statement has been made the questions whether there were reasonable grounds for believing it, and what were the means of knowledge in the possession of the person making it, are most weighty matters for consideration. The ground upon which an alleged belief was founded is a most important test of its reality. I can conceive many cases where the fact that an alleged belief was destitute of all reasonable foundation would suffice of itself to convince the Court that it was not really entertained, and that the representation was a fraudulent one. So, too, although means of knowledge are, as was pointed out by Lord Blackburn in *Brownlie v. Campbell*, a very different thing from knowledge, if I thought that a person making a false statement had shut his eyes to the facts, or purposely abstained from inquiring into them, I should hold that honest belief was absent, and that he was just as fraudulent as if he had knowingly stated that which was false.

I have arrived with some reluctance at the conclusion to which I have felt myself compelled, for I think those who put before the public a prospectus to induce them to embark their money in a commercial enterprise ought to be vigilant to see that it contains such representations only as are in strict accordance with fact, and I should be very unwilling to give any countenance to the contrary idea. I think there is much to be said for the view that this moral duty ought to some extent to be converted into a legal obligation, and that the want of reasonable care to see that statements, made under such circumstances, are true, should be made an actionable wrong. But this is not a matter fit for discussion on the present occasion. If it is to be done the legislature must intervene and expressly give a right of action in respect of such a departure from duty. It ought not, I think, to be done by straining the law, and holding that to be fraudulent which the tribunal feels cannot properly be so described. I think mischief is likely to result from blurring the distinction between carelessness and fraud, and equally holding a man fraudulent whether his acts can or cannot be justly so designated.

Judgment of the Court of Appeal reversed.

Note

Incorporation into U.S. law. Lord Herschell's definition of "fraudulent" in the context of misrepresentation was adopted in § 526 of the Second Restatement, albeit with the regrettable addition of the Latinism *scienter*, which obscures more than it explains. *Scienter* actually means "knowing" rather than fraudulent.

Restatement (Second) Torts (1977)

§ 526. Conditions Under Which Misrepresentation is Fraudulent (Scienter)

A misrepresentation is fraudulent if the maker

(a) knows or believes that the matter is not as he represents it to be,

(b) does not have the confidence in the accuracy of his representation that he states or implies, or

(c) knows that he does not have the basis for his representation that he states or implies.

§ 557A. Fraudulent Misrepresentations Causing Physical Harm

One who by a fraudulent misrepresentation or nondisclosure of a fact that it is his duty to disclose causes physical harm to the person or to the land or chattel of another who justifiably relies upon the misrepresentation, is subject to liability to the other.

Reporter's Illustration

1. A, seeking to sell B a shotgun, fraudulently tells B that it is in good condition, although he knows that there is an obstruction in the barrel. B, in reliance on the misrepresentation, buys the gun from A, and discharges it. The gun explodes and B is injured. A is subject to liability to B in an action for deceit.

Notes

1. *Procedural requirements.* Making a claim of fraudulent misrepresentation is not something to be undertaken lightly. Since what is being alleged is tantamount to a criminal offense, both state and federal courts impose heightened pleading requirements. An allegation of fraud is very grave, and the defendant must be given sufficient opportunity to prepare an adequate defense. The rules of procedure therefore require that the circumstances constituting a fraud should be stated in detail. Rule 9(b) of the Federal Rules of Civil Procedure (2007) provides: "In alleging fraud or mistake, a party must state with particularity the circumstances constituting fraud or mistake. Malice, intent, knowledge, and other conditions of a person's mind may be alleged generally." See further *In Re: Methyl Tertiary Butyl Ether (MTBE) Products Liability Litigation*, 379 F.Supp.2d 348 (2005), in Chapter 15.

2. *Misrepresentations of fact and opinion.* The decision in *Derry v. Peek* concerned only misleading statements of material fact. Erroneous statements of opinion were not actionable at the time, as the following extract explains.

Dee Pridgen & Ivan L. Preston, Enhancing the Flow of Information in the Marketplace: From Caveat Emptor to Virginia Pharmacy and Beyond at the Federal Trade Commission
14 Ga. L. Rev. 635 (1979–80)

The most significant consumerist development of misrepresentation law, however, was its transformation into statutory law by virtue of the [Federal Trade Commission] F.T.C. Act of 1914....

Early English cases refused to recognize a cause of action for misrepresentation based on a subjective claim because opinions were not deemed to be subject to truth or falsity. A seller's assessment of value, such as "this property is worth 150 dollars," was not subject to legal review because it was the type of statement of which men will be of many minds, and which is often governed by whim and caprice. Judgment or opinion, in such cases, implies no knowledge.

The law presumed there was no way of determining whether the differing opinions of buyers and sellers were other than equally correct.

Opinion statements were deemed legally nonfraudulent even when spoken with conscious intent to deceive. Thus a seller could, without danger of legal redress, tell a buyer that he (seller) thought a piece of property was worth so much, knowing full well that he had paid much less. Or, knowing that a number of established experts had decided an object was worth $100, a seller could fearlessly express an opinion to a potential buyer that the buyer value was $200. Because such statements were "merely" opinions, the intent to deceive was irrelevant, and the claim was legally untouchable.

When a seller expresses an opinion on value, however, there may be an implied factual claim. It could be assumed by a reasonable buyer, for instance, that the seller based his opinion of value on specific offers by others to buy the product, on a consensus of expert opinion, or on the going market price. If the seller knows that the implied factual basis (e.g., the offers to buy, expert consensus or going price) contradicts his proffered opinion, then there is a conscious intent to deceive on the facts, and not simply an exaggerated opinion. Yet the opinion rule, as applied by the courts, did not consider the possibility of such implied factual claims.

The opinion rule defied even the logic of *caveat emptor*, which was based on the assumed opportunity of the buyer to inspect. With opinion statements, the courts came to assume as a matter of law that the reasonable behavior of a buyer would be to discount and ignore such statements entirely. The courts made this assumption with no empirical basis whatever for the expectation that buyers would behave this way. Advertisers, on the other hand, could simply examine their sales figures to reach the opposite conclusion that buyers are indeed paying attention to the persuasive appeal of opinion.

The F.T.C. continues to assume that many opinion claims, in the form of exaggerations or "dealer's talk" known as "puffery," have no capacity to deceive. In its early years the Commission showed a strong inclination toward regulating such claims, but the courts of appeal reversed on several occasions, citing in puffery's favor the early English cases that distinguished opinions from facts. Since the 1940's the F.T.C. has abandoned any attempt to challenge systematically that ancient doctrine, but has examined puffing defenses on a case-by-case basis, rejecting the defense for claims that imply that they are capable of objective measurement, or which appear particularly credible to consumers.

) puffing

Recent empirical evidence has shown, however, that advertisements normally characterized as harmless puffery may in fact have a significant potential for serious deception. While the use of Commission resources to police false claims believed only by a credulous few would be questionable, the Commission and the academic community should conduct research to determine whether apparently innocuous puffing has the capacity to deceive substantial numbers of consumers to their detriment.

Puffery and opinion statements are not the only types of sellers' claims that avoid the literal expression of facts. Prominent in the advertising of the 1970's are at least two other types of expression that are nonfactual: social-psychological claims and nonverbal images. Both are modern creations. Although conveyable by other media, they have increased tremendously in scope and volume because of the development of television. These forms were not dealt with explicitly in early law, but the justification for the Commission's "hands-off" approach appears to stem from the same rationale that was developed to protect opinion claims in an earlier era.

"We don't sell lipstick," cosmetic tycoon Charles Revlon is reported to have said, "we sell hope." Such intangible qualities (e.g., "Coke adds life") constitute "social-psychological" claims because the advertised quality (the "life" in Coke) is not a physical property of the product but must be supplied by the consumer (e.g., by drinking Coke at a lively party). Cigarette ads may imply that the user will feel as macho as the Marlboro man or as attractive and independent as the Virginia Slims woman, but of course such feelings exist only within the individual's psychological makeup and are not inherent in the product. On the other hand, the consumer who feels more virile from smoking Marlboros or more attractive and independent by purchasing Virginia Slims has received some value from the advertisement. By the same token, however, a purported but worthless cancer cure may have the valuable effect of relieving the user's anxiety about the disease, but could seriously mislead a consumer who relies on it to the exclusion of other more effective treatments.

Advertisers assert that their social/psychological associations are not meant to be factual and that no one would take them as being literally true....

Many social/psychological and other advertising claims are made strictly without words—the pictorial elements, music, graphics or general "vibes," convey the desired image. These non-verbal advertising messages may be absorbed by consumers in a different manner than verbal messages, however, and thus bypass the normal rational evaluation of more explicit advertising claims. No one has yet developed a method for proving whether nonverbal images are deceptive or unfair. Only when the pictures misrepresent literal facts (e.g., a faked demonstration, or a man in a white coat who is not really a doctor) or depict children engaging in unsafe conduct has the Commission acted based on nonverbal content. Further research and study to understand nonverbal forms of communication might be well advised given the apparently increasing prevalence of nonverbal claims. Otherwise, they will effectively remain in the realm of *caveat emptor*.

Questions

1. What exactly is "puffery"?

2. If "puffing defenses" are examined "on a case-by-case basis," how could those investigating determine whether a particular claim was "puffery" or not?

3. Can images be puffery?

4. Are images more persuasive than words?

5. Are "social/psychological" claims effectively immune from an action for misrepresentation?

Notes

1. *Closing the opinion loophole.* The distinction drawn by the law between a false statement of fact (which was actionable) and a false statement of opinion (which was not) was, according to Judge Learned Hand in *Vulcan Metals Co. v. Simmons Mfg. Co.*, 248 F. 853, 856 (1918), a distinction that:

> has not escaped the criticism it deserves. An opinion is a fact, and it may be a very relevant fact; the expression of an opinion is the assertion of a belief, and any rule which condones the expression of a consciously false opinion condones a consciously false statement of fact. When the parties are so situated that the buyer may reasonably rely upon the expression of the seller's opinion, it is no excuse to give a false one.

Section 539 of the Second Restatement represents an attempt to address the loophole which prevented misrepresentations of opinion from becoming actionable. It states:

> (1) A statement of opinion as to facts not disclosed and not otherwise known to the recipient may, if it is reasonable to do so, be interpreted by him as an implied statement
>
> (a) that the facts known to the maker are not incompatible with his opinion; or
>
> (b) that he knows facts sufficient to justify him in forming it.
>
> (2) In determining whether a statement of opinion may reasonably be so interpreted, the recipient's belief as to whether the maker has an adverse interest is important.

Section 539 is bolstered by § 542, which provides that:

> The recipient of a fraudulent misrepresentation solely of the maker's opinion is not justified in relying upon it in a transaction with the maker, unless the fact to which the opinion relates is material, and the maker
>
> (a) purports to have special knowledge of the matter that the recipient does not have, or

(b) stands in a fiduciary or other similar relation of trust and confidence to the recipient, or

(c) has successfully endeavored to secure the confidence of the recipient, or

(d) has some other special reason to expect that the recipient will rely on his opinion.

The suggestion in §9 of the Products Liability Restatement that cases of misrepresentation can be brought only for misrepresentations of material fact is therefore really a sort of legal shorthand; for the true position is that false statements of apparently reliable opinion are also actionable. Nevertheless, the burden of showing that an opinion was indeed one on which the victim could reasonably have been expected to rely is generally heavier than that of establishing that a statement of fact was material, as is demonstrated by the case of *Tietsworth v. Harley Davidson*, below.

2. *Physical harm or economic loss?* Section 531 of the Second Restatement purports to lay down a general rule that:

> One who makes a fraudulent misrepresentation is subject to liability to the persons or class of persons whom he intends or has reason to expect to act or to refrain from action in reliance upon the misrepresentation, for pecuniary loss suffered by them through their justifiable reliance in the type of transaction in which he intends or has reason to expect their conduct to be influenced.

As with the approach to misrepresentations of opinion, this is not, however, a view which has been accepted in every state, as *Tietsworth v. Harley*, below, also demonstrates. In addition, *Tietsworth* deals with the issue of whether silence can amount to a misrepresentation.

Tietsworth v. Harley Davidson
677 N.W.2d 233 (2004) (Supreme Court of Wisconsin)

SYKES, J. This is an appeal of a motion to dismiss for failure to state a claim, and therefore we accept as true, for purposes of this review, the following facts from the amended class action complaint. Plaintiff Steven C. Tietsworth and the members of the proposed class own or lease 1999 or early-2000 model year Harley motorcycles equipped with Twin Cam 88 or Twin Cam 88B engines. Harley's marketing and advertising literature contained the following statement about the TC-88 engines:

> Developing [the TC-88s] was a six-year process.... The result is a masterpiece. We studied everything from the way oil moves through the inside, to the way a rocker cover does its job of staying oil-tight. Only 21 functional parts carry over into the new design. What does carry over is the power of a Harley-Davidson engine, only more so.

Harley also stated that the motorcycles were "premium" quality, and described the TC-88 engine as "[e]ighty-eight cubic inches filled to the brim with torque and ready to take you thundering down the road."

On January 22, 2001, Harley sent a letter to Tietsworth and other owners of Harley motorcycles informing them that "the rear cam bearing in a *small number* of Harley-Davidson's Twin Cam 88 engines has failed. While it is unlikely that you will ever have to worry about this situation, you have our assurance that Harley-Davidson is committed to your satisfaction" (emphasis added in amended complaint). The letter went on to explain that the company was extending the warranty on the cam bearing from the standard one-year/unlimited mileage warranty, to a five-year/50,000 mile warranty. Separately, Harley developed a $495 "cam bearing repair kit" and made the kit available to its dealers and service departments, "to expedite rear cam bearing repair."

On June 28, 2001, Tietsworth, a California resident, filed this proposed class action lawsuit against Harley in Milwaukee County Circuit Court, alleging four claims: (1) negligence; (2) strict products liability; (3) common-law fraudulent concealment; and (4) deceptive trade practices contrary to Wis. Stat. § 100.18(1) (the Wisconsin Deceptive Trade Practices Act or "DTPA"). Tietsworth later amended the complaint to name as representative plaintiffs four Wisconsin owners of motorcycles equipped with TC-88 engines.

The amended complaint alleges that the cam bearing mechanism in the 1999 and early-2000 model year TC-88 engines is inherently defective, causing an unreasonably dangerous propensity for premature engine failure. As is pertinent to the common-law fraud and statutory D.T.P.A. claims, the amended complaint alleged that Harley's failure to disclose the cam bearing defect induced the plaintiffs to purchase their motorcycles by causing them to reasonably rely upon Harley's representations regarding the "premium" quality of the motorcycles.

The amended complaint further alleges that if the plaintiffs had known of the engine defect, they either would not have purchased the product or would have paid less for it. The amended complaint does not allege that the plaintiffs' motorcycles have actually suffered engine failure, have malfunctioned in any way, or are reasonably certain to fail or malfunction. Nor does the amended complaint allege any property damage or personal injury arising out of the engine defect. Rather, the amended complaint alleges that the plaintiffs' motorcycles have diminished value, including diminished resale value, because Harley motorcycles equipped with TC-88 engines have demonstrated a "propensity" for premature engine failure and/or fail prematurely.

Harley moved to dismiss the complaint. The Milwaukee County Circuit Court, the Honorable William J. Haese, granted Harley's motion, dismissing the complaint in its entirety for failure to state a claim. The plaintiffs appealed the dismissal of their common-law fraud and DTPA claims only, and the court of appeals reinstated both....

The plaintiffs' common-law fraud claim is premised on the allegation that Harley failed to disclose or concealed the existence of the cam bearing defect prior to the plaintiffs' purchases of their motorcycles. It is well-established that a nondisclosure is not actionable as a misrepresentation tort unless there is a duty to disclose. Our decision in *Ollerman [v. O'Rourke Co., Inc.*, 288 N.W.2d 95 (1980)] outlined the three categories outlined the three categories of misrepresentation in Wisconsin law—intentional misrepresentation, negligent misrepresentation, and strict responsibility misrepresentation—and described the common and distinct elements of the three torts.

All misrepresentation claims share the following required elements: 1) the defendant must have made a representation of fact to the plaintiff; 2) the representation of fact must be false; and 3) the plaintiff must have believed and relied on the misrepresentation to his detriment or damage. The plaintiffs here allege intentional misrepresentation, which carries the following additional elements: 4) the defendant must have made the misrepresentation with knowledge that it was false or recklessly without caring whether it was true or false; and 5) the defendant must have made the misrepresentation with intent to deceive and to induce the plaintiff to act on it to his detriment or damage.

Ollerman reiterated the general rule that in a sales or business transaction, "silence, a failure to disclose a fact, is not an intentional misrepresentation unless the seller has a duty to disclose." The existence and scope of a duty to disclose are questions of law for the court. *Ollerman* held that

> a subdivider-vendor of a residential lot has a duty to a "non-commercial" purchaser to disclose facts which are known to the vendor, which are material to the transaction, and which are not readily discernible to the purchaser.

We specified that this was a "narrow holding," premised on certain policy considerations present in non-commercial real estate transactions.

The transactions at issue here, however, are motorcycle purchases, not residential real estate purchases, and it is an open question whether the duty to disclose recognized in *Ollerman* extends more broadly to sales of consumer goods. This is a significant common-law policy issue. But the parties did not brief it, and therefore we do not decide it.

Ollerman also held that damages in intentional misrepresentation cases are measured according to the "benefit of the bargain" rule, "typically stated as the difference between the value of the property as represented and its actual value as purchased." "Benefit of the bargain" damages in fraud cases "depend on the nature of the bargain and the circumstances of each case."

In the context of deciding when a claim accrues for purposes of the statute of limitations, we have generally held that a tort claim is not capable of present enforcement (and therefore does not accrue) unless the plaintiff has suffered actual damage. Actual damage is harm that has already occurred or is "reasonably certain" to occur in the future. Actual damage is not the mere possibility of future harm. By statute, a fraud claim accrues when the aggrieved party discovers the facts constituting the fraud. Although we are not confronted here with a question of when this claim accrued for purposes of a statute of limitations defense, the amended complaint must adequately plead an actual injury—a loss or damage that has already occurred or is reasonably certain to occur—in order to state an actionable fraud claim. In addition, fraud claims must be pleaded with particularity. The statute modifies the older cases cited by the plaintiffs.

The injury complained of here is diminution in value only—the plaintiffs allege that their motorcycles are worth less than they paid for them. However, the amended complaint does not allege that the plaintiffs' motorcycles have diminished value because their engines have failed, will fail, or are reasonably certain to fail as a result of the TC-88 cam bearing defect. The amended complaint does not allege that the plaintiffs have sold their motorcycles at a loss because of the alleged engine defect. The amended complaint alleges only that the motorcycles have diminished value—primarily diminished potential resale value—because Harley motorcycles equipped with TC-88 engines have demonstrated a "propensity" for premature engine failure and/or will fail as a result of the cam bearing defect. This is insufficient to state a legally cognizable injury for purposes of a fraud claim.

Diminished value premised upon a mere possibility of future product failure is too speculative and uncertain to support a fraud claim. The plaintiffs do not specifically allege that their particular motorcycles will fail prematurely, only that the Harley product line that consists of motorcycles with TC-88 engines has demonstrated a propensity for premature engine failure. An allegation that a particular product line fails prematurely does not constitute an allegation that the plaintiffs' particular motorcycles will do so, only that there is a possibility that they will do so.

We certainly agree with the court of appeals that the damages allegations in a fraud complaint are not evaluated against a standard of "absolute certainty" for purposes of a motion to dismiss for failure to state a claim. But an allegation that a product is diminished in value because of an event or circumstance that might—or might not—occur in the future is inherently conjectural and does not allege actual benefit-of-the-bargain damages with the "reasonable certainty" required to state a fraud claim.

This conclusion is consistent with many federal and state court decisions that have affirmed the dismissal of claims brought under fraud, strict products liability, and other tort theories where the allegedly defective product has not actually malfunctioned. These "no injury" cases are too numerous to list, but for a representative sample, see, e.g., *Angus v. Shiley Inc.*, 989 F.2d 142, 147–48 (3d Cir.1993) (affirming dismissal of a claim for intentional infliction of emotional distress based on allegedly defective heart valve that was functioning properly); *Carlson v. General Motors Corp.*, 883 F.2d 287, 297 (4th Cir.1989) (affirming dismissal of a claim for diminished resale value of diesel cars due to "poor reputation" rather than actual damage or loss resulting from vehicle defect); *Briehl v. General Motors Corp.*, 172 F.3d 623, 627–29 (8th Cir.1999) (affirming dismissal of class action lawsuit for fraud and breach of warranty where the only alleged damage from vehicles' defective brake system was overpayment and diminished resale value); *Jarman v. United Industries Corp.*, 98 F.Supp.2d 757, 767 (S.D.Miss.2000) (dismissing fraud, warranty, and various statutory claims for purchase of allegedly ineffective pesticide where there is no allegation of actual product failure); *Weaver v. Chrysler Corp.*, 172 F.R.D. 96, 99–100 (S.D.N.Y.1997) (dismissing class action fraud and warranty lawsuit for allegedly defective integrated child seats where there is no allegation that the product has malfunctioned or the defect manifested itself); *Yost v. General Motors Corp.*, 651 F.Supp. 656, 657–58 (D.N.J.1986) (dismissing fraud and warranty claim for alleged engine defect where engine has not malfunctioned and plaintiff alleges diminished value only); *Ziegelmann v. DaimlerChrysler Corp.*, 649 N.W.2d 556, 559–65 (N.D.2002) (collecting cases and dismissing class action fraud and negligence lawsuit for alleged brake system defect where damages were premised only on diminution in value); *Frank v. DaimlerChrysler Corp.*, 292 A.D.2d 118, 741 N.Y.S.2d 9, 17 (N.Y.App.Div.2002) (dismissing class action fraud, negligence, and products liability lawsuit for alleged seat backrest defect in the absence of allegation of actual product failure); *Yu v. Int'l Bus. Mach. Corp.*, 732 N.E.2d 1173, 1177–78 (2000) (affirming dismissal of class action fraud, negligence, and deceptive trade practices lawsuit for allegedly defective computer software where there was no allegation of actual product failure); *Ford Motor Co. v. Rice*, 726 So.2d 626, 631 (Ala.1998) (affirming dismissal of class action fraud lawsuit for SUV design defect alleged to cause rollover tendency where defect did not manifest itself and vehicles did not roll over).

We note, however, that the amended complaint does contain one allegation that is arguably sufficient to state a more particularized injury to these plaintiffs: at paragraph 35 of the amended complaint the plaintiffs allege that Harley knew that "all of the motorcycles with the TC-88s are defective and will prematurely fail." This reference to "all" motorcycles with TC-88 engines includes the plaintiffs' motorcycles, and therefore can be read as the equivalent of a more particularized allegation that the plaintiffs' motorcycles will fail prematurely. Accordingly, we address the application of the economic loss doctrine to this claim.

ii. Economic Loss Doctrine

Apart from the generally insufficient damages allegations in the fraud cause of action, the economic loss doctrine bars this claim. The economic loss doctrine is a judicially-created remedies principle that operates generally to preclude contracting parties from pursuing tort recovery for purely economic or commercial losses associated with the contract relationship.

Adopted by this court in *Sunnyslope Grading, Inc. v. Miller, Bradford & Risberg, Inc.*, 148 Wis.2d 910, 921, 437 N.W.2d 213 (1989), the economic loss doctrine precludes recovery in tort for economic losses resulting from the failure of a product to live up to a contracting party's expectations. The doctrine generally "requires transacting parties in Wisconsin to pursue only their contractual remedies when asserting an economic loss claim."

"Economic loss" for purposes of the doctrine includes the diminution in the value of the product because it is inferior and does not work for the general purposes for which it was manufactured and sold. It includes both direct economic loss and consequential economic loss. The economic loss doctrine has been extended to consumer transactions as well as transactions between commercial contracting parties.

The economic loss doctrine is "based on an understanding that contract law and the law of warranty, in particular, is better suited than tort law for dealing with purely economic loss in the commercial arena." "If a [contracting party] is permitted to sue in tort when a transaction does not work out as expected, that party is in effect rewriting the agreement to obtain a benefit that was not part of the bargain." ...

As we have noted, the plaintiffs' case is premised primarily on the allegation that Harley failed to disclose the alleged motorcycle engine defect. A nondisclosure is not an "assertion, representation or statement of fact" under Wis. Stat. § 100.18(1). Silence—an omission to speak—is insufficient to support a claim under Wis. Stat. § 100.18(1). The DTPA does not purport to impose a duty to disclose, but, rather, prohibits only affirmative assertions, representations, or statements of fact that are false, deceptive, or misleading. To permit a nondisclosure to qualify as an actionable "assertion, representation or statement of fact" under Wis. Stat. § 100.18(1) would expand the statute far beyond its terms.

To the extent that the amended complaint alleges any affirmative assertions, they are mere commercial "puffery" and hence legally insufficient to support a claim under the statute. Puffery has been defined as "the exaggerations reasonably to be expected of a seller as to the degree of quality of his product, the truth or falsity of which cannot be precisely determined." *State v. American TV*, 146 Wis.2d 292, 301–02, 430 N.W.2d 709 (1988).

In *American TV*, we held that "[a] general statement that one's products are best is not actionable as a misrepresentation of fact" and could not support a claim under Wis. Stat. § 100.18. We also concluded that the characterization of a product as "the finest" and a sale as a "clearance" or "closeout" were "merely examples of hyperbole and puffery," insufficient to state a claim under the D.T.P.A.

Similarly here, the affirmative statements identified in the amended complaint constitute fairly obvious examples of puffery. Harley is alleged to have advertised the TC-88 as "a masterpiece," of "premium quality," and "filled to the brim with torque and ready to take you thundering down the road."

"Premium quality" equates to "the best," and is squarely within the puffery definition of *American TV*. The term "masterpiece" is arguably more precise than "the best," insofar as it connotes a specific engineering achievement, but this does not move the term out of the domain of puffery. One reason for excluding commercial puffs from the scope of actionable misrepresentations is that they are "not capable of being substantiated or refuted," and a factfinder would have as little hope of determining whether the TC-88 was indeed "a masterpiece" as it would of determining whether it was simply "the best." Harley's statement that the TC-88 is "filled to the brim with torque and ready to take you thundering down the road" lacks even the minimal linguistic specificity required to make it amenable to proof or refutation, however entertaining the attempt might prove to be.

Accordingly, because a nondisclosure is not an "assertion, representation or statement of fact" for purposes of the D.T.P.A., and because the only affirmative assertions alleged in the amended complaint are mere puffery, the plaintiffs have failed to state a claim under Wis. Stat. § 100.18.

ABRAHAMSON, C.J. (dissenting). [M]any courts "recognize that fraud [in the inducement of a contract] can be an exception to the economic loss rule." The theory behind a fraud in the inducement exception to the economic loss rule is that contracts entered into under false pretenses cannot promote the proper ordering of risks and responsibilities between parties. One court articulated this reasoning as follows:

> [C]ontract negotiations that begin with the assumption that the other party is lying will hardly encourage free and open bargaining. The specific duty encompassed by fraud in the inducement is the duty of the parties entering into the contract to speak honestly regarding negotiated terms. How can parties freely allocate risk if they cannot rely on the opposite party to speak truthfully during negotiations regarding the subject matter of the contract — if they cannot tell what is a lie and what is not? *Budgetel Inns, Inc. v. Micros Sys., Inc.*, 8 F.Supp.2d 1137, 1148 (E.D.Wis., 1998).

Relying on this analysis, a number of jurisdictions, such as California, Illinois, and Texas, have recognized a fraud in the inducement exception to the economic loss rule. The Wisconsin Court of Appeals adopted such an exception..., holding that "the economic loss doctrine does not preclude a plaintiff's claim for intentional misrepresentation when the misrepresentation fraudulently induces a plaintiff to enter into the contract." According to the court of appeals, a fraud in the inducement exception to the economic loss rule is appropriate for a number of reasons. Intentional misrepresentations undermine the ability of parties to negotiate freely. Sound public policy supports placing the burden of loss resulting from a misrepresentation on the seller, who caused the loss and is best situated to assess and allocate the risk, rather than upon the buyer.... I agree with this approach....

What kind of "freedom of contract" and "ability to assess and insure against the risk" is being fostered or protected when a party to a contract commits an intentional tort in inducing a contract that causes monetary loss to another party? On what basis can we say that an individual consumer does not need the tort remedy of intentional misrepresentation against a manufacturer? The answer to both questions is none.

Decision of the Court of Appeals reversed.

Questions

1. The majority in *Tietsworth* held that the claims that the motorcycles were of "premium" quality, and that the TC-88 engine was "[e]ighty-eight cubic inches filled to the brim with torque and ready to take you thundering down the road" were examples of puffery, which it defined as "exaggerations reasonably to be expected of a seller as to the degree of quality of his product, the truth or falsity of which cannot be precisely determined." But if a rear cam fails, does this not suggest a level of quality below "premium" level (whatever that level is)? In other words, is it not possible to recognize different "levels" of quality without having to determine precisely what is expected at each level? Moreover, since the rider will not be able to go "thundering down the road" at all, does this not suggest that this particular claim is capable of being "precisely determined"?

2. Should claims of fraudulent misrepresentation be treated as exceptions to the economic loss rule?

3. Why did the plaintiff in *Tietsworth* not bring a claim for breach of warranty?

4. In motorbikes where the rear cam did actually fail, would an owner have had an arguable claim and, if so, would that be for a breach of warranty or a misrepresentation (or both)?

5. Does the answer to the previous question depend on how long after the sale the rear cam had failed?

6. Would it make any difference if, when it failed, the rear cam caused no other damage? What if it caused damage to other parts of the engine? What if the consequential sudden loss of power caused the rider to crash and be injured?

Notes

1. *Alternative theory: strict products liability in torts.* An alternative theory of liability in *Tietsworth* might have been strict products liability in torts but, as will be seen in Chapter 6, such a claim is likewise normally subject to the economic loss rule, and so would not have assisted the plaintiff in *Tietsworth*.

2. *Fraudulent or conscious misrepresentation?* As its enumeration perhaps suggests, §557A was not part of the original text of the Second Restatement. The original Reporter, Professor Prosser, had instead drafted §310, which involves what he termed "conscious" misrepresentation, on which his Comment (b) makes clear that liability can arise not just from misrepresentations of fact, but also from those of opinion, prediction and law.

Restatement (Second) Torts (1977)

§310. Conscious Misrepresentation Involving Risk of Physical Harm

An actor who makes a misrepresentation is subject to liability to another for physical harm which results from an act done by the other or a third person in reliance upon the truth of the representation, if the actor

(a) intends his statement to induce or should realize that it is likely to induce action by the other, or a third person, which involves an unreasonable risk of physical harm to the other, and

(b) knows

(i) that the statement is false, or

(ii) that he has not the knowledge which he professes.

Reporter's Illustration

2. A offers B a drink from a bottle of whiskey, telling him that he has himself imported it from Canada, although he knows that he has bought it for a very cheap price from an unidentified bootlegger. B drinks the whiskey, which turns out to be compounded of denatured alcohol, from which the poison has not been completely eliminated. B becomes ill. A is negligent toward B.

Notes

1. *Fraudulent and conscious misrepresentations revisited: gross negligence?* Section 310 does not entirely track *Derry v. Peek*, but instead combines the making of an inten-

tionally misleading (i.e. fraudulent) statement with an *absence* of any intention to cause the physical harm to which it unreasonably risks exposing the victim. The Reporter's Notes explicitly acknowledge the confusion that this juxtaposition of requirements might generate: "In the situations covered by this Section, the liability usually is put on the basis of deceit.... It may, however, be rested upon negligence."

In fact, even the Reporters for the American Law Institute have failed to agree on the appropriate characterization of § 310. A subsequent Reporter for the Second Restatement argued, in Comment (a) to § 557A, that: "The liability there stated is *negligence liability* and is enforced in an *ordinary negligence* action" (emphasis added), which is why it was thought necessary subsequently to add § 557A. Yet, in Comment (a) to § 9, the Reporters for the Products Liability Restatement, Professors Twerski and Henderson, treat § 310 as dealing with fraudulent misrepresentation! Perhaps the best way to conceptualize the scenario envisioned by § 310 is as a form of gross negligence, enforced by an ordinary negligence action while offering an enhanced likelihood of an award of punitive damages.

2. Lessons from the history of § 310. Above all else, this episode demonstrates the pitfalls of trying to encapsulate in one document a set of rules that accurately represent the law in a nation of many jurisdictions, and is a useful reminder that (no matter how strongly their adherents would like them to be) the Restatements are not themselves legally binding.

Questions

1. Is the Reporter's illustration of § 310 regarding the "whiskey" that is unfit for human consumption better conceived as a case falling within § 557A?

2. If so, does § 310 now have anything meaningful to say?

Negligent Misrepresentation

At the time that *Derry v. Peek* was decided, the common law recognized only two forms of misrepresentation: fraudulent and non-fraudulent (which, at the time, was often called "innocent misrepresentation"). If the misrepresentation was not fraudulent, then there was only one remedy available, and it did not include the payment of damages. Instead, plaintiffs were restricted to being able to rescind any contract into which they had entered with the representor in reliance on the latter's misrepresentation. This often left plaintiffs out of pocket: if they had entered into a contract with a third party, for example, rescission was not available. Moreover, the only financial payment they could claim was for any payments made according to the terms of the now-rescinded contract. This was called an "indemnity." Any other harm they had suffered as a result of their reliance on the non-fraudulent misrepresentation remained uncompensated.

It became clear that that state of affairs was unfair to many innocent representees. Accordingly, non-fraudulent misrepresentations eventually came to be subdivided into two categories: negligent and innocent. (Note that this means that what is called an "innocent" misrepresentation today is often not identical to what was called an "innocent" misrepresentation in decades past.) Nowadays, a claim for negligent misrepresentation essentially involves a standard negligence claim, applied to the context of a statement whose inaccuracy is due to the representor's negligence.

Restatement (Second) Torts (1977)

§ 311. Negligent Misrepresentation Involving Risk of Physical Harm

(1) One who negligently gives false information to another is subject to liability for physical harm caused by action taken by the other in reasonable reliance upon such information, where such harm results

    (a) to the other, or

    (b) to such third persons as the actor should expect to be put in peril by the action taken.

(2) Such negligence may consist of failure to exercise reasonable care

    (a) in ascertaining the accuracy of the information, or

    (b) in the manner in which it is communicated.

Hanberry v. Hearst Corporation

39 A.L.R.3d 173 (1969) (Fourth DCA, California)

AULT, J. The basic facts upon which appellant relies are repleaded in each of the causes of action under consideration. She alleges she purchased a pair of shoes on March 30, 1966 at a retail store owned and operated by the defendant Akron; the shoes had been imported and distributed to Akron by the defendant Victor B. Handal & Bros., Inc.; the shoes were defective in manufacture and design and had a low co-efficient of friction on vinyl and certain other floor coverings commonly used in this area and were slippery and unsafe when worn on such floor coverings; she was unaware of the defect and in wearing the shoes on the same day she purchased them, she stepped on the vinyl floor of her kitchen, slipped, fell and sustained severe personal injuries.

Appellant further alleges respondent Hearst publishes a monthly magazine known as Good Housekeeping in which products, including the shoes she purchased, were advertised as meeting the "Good Housekeeping's Consumers' Guaranty Seal." With respect to this seal the magazine stated: "This is Good Housekeeping's Consumers' Guaranty" and "We satisfy ourselves that products advertised in Good Housekeeping are good ones and that the advertising claims made for them in our magazine are truthful." The seal itself contained the promise, "If the product or performance is defective, Good Housekeeping guarantees replacement or refund to consumer."

Appellant alleges further she had frequently read Good Housekeeping Magazine "and believed the products bearing the seal had been examined, tested and inspected by defendant and were good and safe for the use intended"; prior to purchasing the shoes she had seen an advertisement of them, either in Good Housekeeping Magazine or in a newspaper ... which incorporated the contents of the Good Housekeeping endorsement; Good Housekeeping seal was affixed to the shoes and the container for the shoes with Hearst's consent; Hearst was paid for the advertising of the shoes which appeared it its magazine and for the use of its seal; appellant relied upon respondent's representation and seal and purchased the shoes because of them. Appellant further alleges Hearst made no examination, test or investigation of the shoes, or a sample thereof, or if such tests were made they were done in a careless and negligent manner and that Hearst's issuance of its seal and certification as to the shoes was not warranted by the information it possessed.

In the second and eighth causes of action, appellant seeks to recover on the theory of negligent misrepresentation....

The basic question presented on this appeal is whether one who endorses a product for his own economic gain, and for the purpose of encouraging and inducing the public to buy it, may be liable to a purchaser who, relying on the endorsement, buys the product and is injured because it is defective and not as represented in the endorsement. We conclude such liability may exist and a cause of action has been pleaded in the instant case. In arriving at this conclusion, we are influenced more by public policy than by whether such cause of action can be comfortably fitted into one of the law's traditional categories of liability....

Respondent's endorsement and approval of a product is not confined to the pages of its own magazine. It permits the manufacturer or retailer of a product which has been approved by Good Housekeeping Magazine to advertise that fact in other advertising media and permits its seal to appear in such ads and to be attached to the product itself. While the device used by respondent enhances the value of Good Housekeeping Magazine for advertising purposes, it does so because its seal and certification tend to induce and encourage consumers to purchase products advertised in the magazine and which bear that seal and certification. Implicit in the seal and certification is the representation respondent has taken reasonable steps to make an independent examination of the product endorsed, with some degree of expertise, and found it satisfactory. Since the very purpose of respondent's seal and certification is to induce consumers to purchase products so endorsed, it is foreseeable certain consumers will do so, relying upon respondent's representations concerning them, in some instances, even more than upon statements made by the retailer, manufacturer or distributor.

Having voluntarily involved itself into the marketing process, having in effect loaned its reputation to promote and induce the sale of a given product, the question arises whether respondent can escape liability for injury which results when the product is defective and not as represented by its endorsement. In voluntarily assuming this business relationship, we think respondent Hearst has placed itself in the position where public policy imposes upon it the duty to use ordinary care in the issuance of its seal and certification of quality so that members of the consuming public who rely on its endorsement are not unreasonably exposed to the risk of harm.

The fact Hearst is not in privity of contract with those who, relying on its endorsement, purchase the products it endorses, does not mean it is relieved from the responsibility to exercise ordinary care toward them....

In both the second and eighth cause of action of the complaint under consideration, appellant has alleged respondent extended its certification and permitted the use of its seal in connection with the shoes, she purchased without test, inspection or examination of the shoes, or a sample thereof, or if it tested, inspected or examined, it did so in a careless and negligent manner which did not reveal their dangerous and defective condition. If either of the alternative allegations is true, respondent violated its duty of care to the appellant and the issuance of its seal and certification with respect to the shoes under that circumstance would amount to a negligent misrepresentation. (See Restatement of the Law of Torts, Second Edition, vol. 2, section 311, p. 106.) ...

Hearst urges its representation the shoes were "good ones" was a mere statement of opinion, not a statement of a material fact, and therefore not actionable. Since the very purpose of the seal and its certification the shoes were "good ones" was to induce and encourage members of the public to buy the shoes, respondent is in poor position to argue its endorsement cannot legally be considered as the inducing factor in bringing about their sale. Respondent was not the seller or manufacturer of the shoes; it held itself out as a disinterested third party which had examined the shoes, found them satisfactory, and gave its endorsement. By the very procedure and method it used, respondent represented to the public it possessed superior knowledge and special information concerning the product it endorsed. Under such circumstance, respondent may be liable for negligent representations of either fact or opinion. (See Restatement of the Law of Torts, vol. 3, section 543, p. 100) …

Respondent argues no basis for liability has been shown because, "It is a matter of common knowledge that brand new soles on brand new shoes have a tendency of being slick and slippery until the shoes have been worn sufficiently long thereafter." The argument may well have merit but it is one addressed properly to the trier of fact. The case is presented to us in the pleading context. We are unwilling to hold as a matter of law that liability will not attach under any circumstance based upon a defectively designed shoe. Whether a material used in the soles of shoes is so slick and slippery as to create an unreasonable and foreseeable risk of injury, and whether the buyer of such a shoe who is injured should anticipate the condition under existing circumstances are questions of fact which cannot be decided at the pleading stage.

While we have held appellant has stated a cause of action for negligent misrepresentation against Hearst, we reject her contention she may also proceed in warranty or on the theory of strict liability in tort. She has cited no authority, and we have found none, which has extended either theory of recovery to one not directly involved in manufacturing products for, or supplying products to, the consuming public. To invoke either theory of recovery here would subject respondent to liability not warranted by the circumstances. Appellant does not contend, nor do respondent's representations permit the interpretation, it examined or tested the particular pair of shoes involved. The most that can be implied from respondent's representation is that it has examined or tested samples of the product and found the general design and materials used to be satisfactory. Application of either warranty or strict liability in tort would subject respondent to liability even if the general design and material used in making this brand of shoe were good, but the particular pair became defective through some mishap in the manufacturing process. We believe this kind of liability for individually defective items should be limited to those directly involved in the manufacturing and supplying process, and should not be extended through warranty or strict liability to a general endorser who makes no representation it has examined or tested each item marketed.

Judgment of dismissal is affirmed as to warranty; reversed as to negligent misrepresentation.

Question

Why was this not simply a case of puffery?

Reliance on Misrepresentation

As we have seen, one of the tests for determining whether an inaccurate statement is actionable in principle is whether the statement was one of material fact or opinion on which the victim representee could reasonably have been expected to rely. But while that is a necessary element of a *prima facie* case, it is not sufficient, for the plaintiff must also prove that she did, in fact rely on the statement and suffer personal injury or damage to her property as a consequence.

In *Stanley v. Wyeth, Inc.*, 991 So.2d 31 (2008), the victim's cardiologist wrote her a prescription for Cordarone, the brand name of a drug developed and manufactured by Wyeth. The pharmacist, however, filled the prescription with the generic version of amiodarone made by another manufacturer, Sandoz, Inc. Mrs. Stanley took the medication as prescribed, but developed severe liver complications, allegedly a side-effect from the drug, underwent two liver transplants, and ultimately died. A Louisiana court of appeal sustained the trial court's entering judgment for Wyeth on a preemptory motion that the victim's family had failed to state a cause of action. It held that, while Wyeth might have made representations about its product to the medical community, it had made no such representations to the victim, and she had therefore not relied upon them. The court declined to extend the notion of reliance so as to impose a duty on a drug manufacturer towards someone who does not ingest its products.

As *Stanley* demonstrates, reliance is effectively the way in which causation in fact is proved in misrepresentation cases. Without reliance by the victim, there can be no causal link between the defendant's representation and the victim's injury.

But the victim must also address an additional burden. S/he must also show that such reliance was justifiable. In effect, this is the equivalent of demonstrating the absence of what, in other torts, would be called contributory negligence by the plaintiff (with the identical effect that failure to do so completely shields the defendant from liability). Examples of unjustified reliance are where the statement involved mere puffery, or where the plaintiff had ample opportunity to investigate the veracity of a claim but failed to take it up.

However, as § 545A of the Second Restatement makes clear, a defendant who attempts to rebut a *prima facie* case of fraudulent misrepresentation by arguing that the plaintiff's reliance was unjustifiable will normally be denied the ability to utilize defenses that imply negligence on the part of the plaintiff. This is because, in such circumstances, the degree of the defendant's culpability is considered to outweigh the plaintiff's lesser fault. It is only where the defendant's culpability is considered to be no greater than that of the plaintiff that it will be permitted to avail itself of defenses that imply the negligence of the plaintiff.

Restatement (Second) Torts (1977)

§ 540. Duty to Investigate

The recipient of a fraudulent misrepresentation of fact is justified in relying upon its truth, although he might have ascertained the falsity of the representation had he made an investigation.

§ 542. Opinion of Adverse Party

The recipient of a fraudulent misrepresentation solely of the maker's opinion is not justified in relying upon it in a transaction with the maker, unless the fact to which the opinion relates is material, and the maker

(a) purports to have special knowledge of the matter that the recipient does not have, or

(b) stands in a fiduciary or other similar relation of trust and confidence to the recipient, or

(c) has successfully endeavored to secure the confidence of the recipient, or

(d) has some other special reason to expect that the recipient will rely on his opinion.

§ 545A. Contributory Negligence

One who justifiably relies upon a fraudulent misrepresentation is not barred from recovery by his contributory negligence in doing so.

Wennerholm v. Stanford University School of Medicine

128 P.2d 522 (1942) (Supreme Court of California)

GIBSON, C.J. Plaintiffs appeal from a judgment entered in favor of defendants after an order sustaining defendants' demurrers to the fifth amended complaint without leave to amend. Plaintiffs' original and first four amended complaints charged the defendants with negligence. In these complaints it was alleged that the plaintiff, Cecilia Wennerholm, consulted her family physician in regard to her obesity and that he prescribed dinitrophenol for her on a written prescription which was filled by a pharmacy. While under the care of her physician, plaintiff took the drug, which was manufactured by one of the defendants. As a result thereof, it was alleged, she lost her sight. Plaintiffs charged that the defendants published statements in medical journals and elsewhere that dinitrophenol was harmless; that these statements were read and relied upon by plaintiff and her physician; that defendants knew or should have known of the dangerous character of the drug but negligently failed to disclose that fact; and that, by reason of the negligence, fault and want of care of defendants, plaintiff suffered the loss of sight of both her eyes.

The fifth amended complaint charges the defendants with fraud. It is alleged, in substance, that the defendants are in the business of manufacturing, distributing, selling and dispensing drugs and medicines for human use; that by means of articles in newspapers, medical journals, pamphlets and circulars disseminated to the public, these defendants falsely represented that the drug would relieve obesity, was harmless and could be taken internally by human beings, and that defendants knew that the drug was inherently dangerous to human life and liable to cause blindness. It is further alleged that defendants manufactured, sold and dispensed the drug throughout the state; that the plaintiff Cecilia Wennerholm read, believed and relied on the false representations; and that, in reliance thereon, she purchased and took the drug internally....

Defendants ... argue that the allegation in the earlier complaints that the drug had been taken on prescription of a physician, which was omitted from the fifth amended complaint, must be read into the latter complaint. If this allegation is read into the complaint, defendants urge, it shows conclusively that plaintiff did not act in reliance upon the representations of defendants. If any verified pleading contains an allegation which renders a complaint vulnerable, the defect cannot be cured simply by omitting the allegation, without explanation, in a later pleading. If, however, the allegation that plaintiff took the drug on advice of her physician be read into the fifth amended complaint, it sufficiently alleges reliance by plaintiff upon defendants' representations. In actions for fraud it is not required that a defendant's representations be the sole cause of the damage. If they are a substantial factor in inducing the plaintiff to act, even though he also relies in part upon the advice of others, reliance is sufficiently shown.... In this case there was no allegation in the earlier complaints that plaintiff relied solely upon the advice of her physician; in fact, it is alleged in the second amended complaint that "plaintiff and her said physician believed and accepted the recommendations of defendants ... and relied upon the same and the said physician in reliance thereon, prescribed for plaintiff, and the said plaintiff in reliance thereon and upon the advice of her physician, formed upon such recommendation of the defendants, used said dinitrophenol." In the fifth amended complaint it is alleged that plaintiff "relying upon ... the aforesaid representations of said defendants, and not otherwise, purchased and took internally" the said drug. Accepting this statement as qualified by the allegations with respect to the physician in the earlier complaints, it sufficiently alleges that plaintiff relied, at least in substantial part, on the representations of defendants. The mere fact that a physician prescribed the drug does not establish, as a matter of law, a lack of reliance on the part of the plaintiff which would absolve the defendants from liability. No cases have been cited to us which support the proposition advanced by defendants that in circumstances such as those alleged here a prescribing physician must accept sole responsibility for the treatment which he chooses for his patients. It seems to us a more reasonable view that one who manufactures and sells a drug dangerous to life and health, knowing it to be dangerous, should be liable where, as here alleged, both physician and patient rely upon the representations made concerning the drug.

Judgment reversed.

Notes

1. *Multiple reliance and causation. Wennerholm* reiterates the standard rule of causation that a defendant needs only to be *a* cause of the plaintiff's injuries in order to be liable for them; the defendant does not need to be *the* sole cause.

2. *Reliance on representations to the public.* The plaintiff in *Wennerholm* had read statements about the drug, dinitrophenol, that were not directed toward her specifically, but were "published ... in medical journals and elsewhere." Nowadays, of course, the advertising of many pharmaceuticals is not restricted to specialist journals, but is targeted (especially on billboards, television, and the internet) directly at the general public, in the same way that any other product is promoted. The following case addresses the question of whether a consumer's reliance on the claims made in such promotional material is justifiable.

Williams v. Philip Morris
48 P.3d 824 (2002) (Court of Appeals of Oregon)

EDMONDS, P.J. Defendant Phillip Morris, Inc., is this country's largest manufacturer of cigarettes. Plaintiff is the widow and personal representative of the estate of Jesse Williams (Williams), who began smoking defendant's cigarettes in the early 1950s and continued until his death from a smoking-related lung cancer in 1997. Plaintiff brought this action to recover compensatory and punitive damages for Williams' death. The jury found for plaintiff on her claims of negligence and fraud, awarding economic damages of $21,485.80 and noneconomic damages of $800,000 on each claim. On the negligence claim, it found that Williams' negligence was 50 percent of the cause of his harm and declined to award punitive damages. It awarded punitive damages of $79.5 million on the fraud claim. The trial court reduced the punitive damages award to $32 million, on the ground that the jury's award was excessive under the United States Constitution, and reduced the award of noneconomic damages to $500,000 in accordance with ORS 18.560(1). It then entered judgment on the fraud claim as modified. Plaintiff appeals, assigning error to the reduction of the punitive damages award. Defendant cross-appeals, assigning error to a number of rulings relating to both the fraud and negligence claims. We reverse on the appeal, affirm on the cross-appeal, and remand for the trial court to enter judgment accordingly....

Williams began smoking Phillip Morris cigarettes while he was in the Army in Korea in the early 1950s. The Army provided the cigarettes, and other soldiers told him that the smoke would help keep mosquitoes away. He smoked them until the mid 1950s, when he switched to Marlboros, another Phillip Morris brand. He made the switch about the time that defendant repositioned the Marlboro brand from one that was oriented toward women to one of the first male-oriented filter cigarettes. Williams continued to smoke Marlboros or Marlboro Lights for the rest of his life, ultimately increasing to three packs a day. At that point he was spending half of his waking hours smoking.

Both Williams' wife and their children encouraged him to stop smoking, telling him that cigarettes were dangerous to his health. In response, he insisted that the cigarette companies would not sell cigarettes if they were as dangerous as his family claimed, and he stated that he had heard on television that cigarettes do not cause cancer. He quoted to them from what he said he had heard about why cigarette smoking was not harmful to a smoker's health. He also told his wife, "the tobacco company, they never said that anything like this is going to harm you. They never said there was anything wrong with the tobacco." When one of his sons would try to get him to read articles about the dangers of smoking, Williams would respond by finding published assertions showing that cigarette smoking is not dangerous....

According to an expert witness, Williams was highly addicted to cigarettes, and that addiction was physiological as well as psychological.

Williams was generally in good health and rarely saw a physician. However, in late 1995 and early 1996, he developed a cough and began, at times, to spit up blood. A radiologist interpreted chest X-rays taken at that time as normal. The problem recurred a few months later, and he began losing weight. X-rays and other tests in September and October led to a diagnosis of an inoperable poorly differentiated adenosquamous carcinoma in Williams' right lung. According to expert testimony, the primary cause of that kind of cancer is cigarette smoking. When Williams learned of the diagnosis, he expressed a feeling of betrayal. He said, "those darn cigarette people finally did it. They were lying all the time." He wanted to let other people know that they were being deceived about the harm that cigarettes could do to them. Williams received chemical and radiation therapy that provided only temporary benefits, and he died in March 1997....

Defendant's primary argument on cross-appeal focuses on the first, seventh, and eighth elements of fraud, involving the alleged representations and Williams' reliance on them. Defendant asserts that there is no evidence that it made any representation to Williams or that Williams relied on any representation that it may have made. Defendant asserts, "The essence of a claim of fraud is a communication by the defendant which is received and relied upon by the plaintiff. As Plaintiff acknowledged, she could not prove any such communication by Phillip Morris to Williams. Therefore her fraud claim fails."

Defendant interprets the requirement that plaintiff rely on a misrepresentation as meaning that "an alleged false representation must be identified specifically so that it can be critically examined." According to defendant, plaintiff cannot prove her claim without proof that defendant made a specific misrepresentation to Williams....

As we discuss below, a defendant may be liable for fraud for a misrepresentation that creates a false impression even though it is impossible to identify the specific misrepresentation on which a person relied.

Defendant's argument goes to the heart of plaintiff's theory of fraud. In contrast to most fraud cases, plaintiff does not rely on one or a few fraudulent statements made to one or a few identifiable individuals. Rather, her theory is that defendant, in concert with other tobacco companies, engaged in a decades-long public-relations effort to create the impression in the public that there was a legitimate controversy about the health effects of smoking, even though defendant knew that such an impression was false. . . .

[P]laintiff's theory fits comfortably within traditional common-law principles. Liability for fraud is not limited to those who deal directly with the injured party. Rather, a person who makes a misrepresentation may be liable to the intended recipients of a misrepresentation without regard to whether the person making the representation intends to defraud a particular person. As the Supreme Court said over 75 years ago, quoting a legal encyclopedia, it is a general rule of law in this country that:

> Where misrepresentations are made to the public at large, or to a particular class of persons, with the intention of influencing any member of the public, or of the class, to whom they may be communicated, any one injured through proper reliance thereon may secure redress. In such a case it is not necessary that there should be an intent to defraud any particular person; but the representation must of course have been intended for the public, or for a particular class of persons to which the complainant belonged. *Coughlin v. State Bank of Portland*, 117 Or. 83, 96, 243 P. 78 (1926), quoting 26 CJ 1121–23, §48bb.

In *Coughlin*, the plaintiff alleged that the defendants published misleading statements of a bank's financial condition and that the plaintiff relied on those statements in deciding to purchase stock in the bank. The Supreme Court held that the plaintiff's complaint stated a claim for fraud and entitled him to present his supporting evidence.

In addition, under Oregon law, a defendant may make misrepresentations in many different ways.

> To communicate a representation it is not necessary that the party should speak words, or write a message. The desired result may be accomplished ofttimes by conduct. Indeed, the tongue and the pen are only two of the numerous means of transmitting messages. . . . Indeed, the action for deceit . . . had its origins in false impersonation. *Pennebaker v. Kimble et al.*, 126 Or. 317, 322–23, 269 P. 981 (1928). . . .

Thus, under Oregon law, plaintiff does not need to prove that defendant expressly directed its misrepresentations to Williams or even knew of his existence, so long as plaintiff can show that Williams was within a class of people whom defendant intended to be recipients of and to rely on the message that it conveyed. In addition, the fundamental character of fraud is the communication of a misimpression to induce another to rely on it. That is something that a defendant may do by a variety of actions as well as by specific statements. Plaintiff alleges that the message that defendant intended to convey was that there was a legitimate controversy about whether there was a connection between cigarette smoking and human health and that it intended to encourage smokers to continue to smoke and not to make the necessary effort to stop smoking. As a smoker, Williams was an intended recipient of defendant's message.

The evidence would permit the jury to find that defendant conveyed the message that plaintiff describes over many years and in many ways, intentionally creating an impression on which it intended Williams and other smokers to rely. The length of the time over which defendant conveyed the message, and the nature of the misrepresentations on which Williams relied, make it unlikely that plaintiff could single out a specific instance from all of the representations that Williams received. Defendant's purpose was to create an impression in the public's mind—including smokers like Williams—that the health issue remained undecided. In late 1953, after the early studies linking cigarette smoking with cancer and the apparently connected fall in cigarette sales, a number of tobacco companies, including defendant, joined to hire a leading public relations firm to find a way to counter their effect. The first step in their subsequent campaign was the publication in January 1954 of "A Frank Statement to Cigarette Smokers." Defendant and the other leading tobacco companies, together with several associations of tobacco growers and marketers, signed the statement, which appeared in 448 newspapers. The publicity covered the great majority of the country's population. In the "Frank Statement," the signatories stated that they believed that their products were not injurious to health and announced the establishment of the Tobacco Industry Research Committee (TIRC) to conduct research into "all phases of tobacco use and health." In 1964, the TIRC was divided into the Tobacco Institute, which focussed on public relations and lobbying, and the Council on Tobacco Research (CTR), which supported scientific research.

According to plaintiff's evidence, the "Frank Statement" was the beginning of a "common front" approach among tobacco companies on the health issue, with all companies expressing essentially the same message and using the TIRC and its successors to speak for the industry as a whole. Their original position was to deny that there was a problem; thus in the 1950s and early 1960s Phillip Morris officials represented publicly that the company would "stop business tomorrow" if it thought that its products were harmful. However, as evidence of the harmful effects of tobacco increased, the industry took a different approach. Particularly after the 1964 Surgeon General's report, which emphasized the connection between smoking and lung cancer, the industry focussed on keeping the "controversy" alive and calling for "more research" for the purpose of suggesting that the health question about cigarette smoking was not yet clear. In an internal memorandum shortly after the 1964 report, a Phillip Morris vice president explained that it was necessary to "provide some answers which will give smokers a psychological crutch and a self-rationale to continue smoking." From the evidence in this case, the jury could properly infer that Williams was one of those smokers to whom defendant was referring.

Defendant and the industry continued throughout the 1970s, 1980s, and 1990s to encourage the impression that there was a genuine and continuing controversy. They did not expressly deny that cigarettes caused cancer but instead provided smokers what a Tobacco Institute memorandum described as "ready-made credible alternatives" to that conclusion by suggesting that there were other factors involved in the diseases of which smokers died and by emphasizing that there was "no proof that smoking causes cancer." The jury in this case could find from the evidence that, in making those statements, they relied on criteria for proof of causation that the scientific community generally either had never accepted or had since discarded. Although defendant and the industry emphasized the need for research, and although it is inferable from the evidence that defendant and other tobacco companies conducted a great deal of research into tobacco themselves and sponsored other researchers, they consciously avoided research in the United States that might indicate the biological effects of tobacco use and thus resolve the question that, they claimed, most needed further research. In particular, defendant conducted all sensitive research in a laboratory that it purchased in Europe, taking care to avoid preserving records of the results in this country. The person who was defendant's director of research in the late 1970s and 1980s told a subordinate that one of the director's functions was to "fuel the controversy" as to whether cigarettes cause disease. The director explained that it was his job

> to attack outside reports of links between smoking and cancer or smoking and emphysema or things of that sort by maintaining that there's a controversy and providing the information that would discredit or somehow cast [doubt] on the outside research.

Defendant and the tobacco industry promoted their message through a large number of press releases and statements and through less obvious methods, including influencing the content of apparently neutral articles and cultivating "opinion leaders" who would convey their message. They attempted to used the power of their advertising to procure favorable treatment from the print media. Industry spokespersons appeared on news shows on commercial and public television to state their position on smoking and health issues. The theme of their statements was that the evidence concerning the health effects of tobacco was based primarily on statistical relationships and that there was no proof that a specific tobacco component caused a specific disease. In addition, they suggested that there could be other causes, not connected to tobacco use, for the various diseases attributed to smoking. Although by the early 1990s the industry was forced to agree that tobacco could be a risk factor associated with a number of diseases, its spokesmen still publicly asserted that there was a long chain of intervening events involved before a disease arose from cigarette smoking. Defendant also stated publicly that it did not believe that cigarette smoking was addictive.

There is evidence that Williams received the message that defendant intended to communicate and that the message affected his decision to continue smoking and not to make more serious efforts to overcome his addiction to cigarettes. Williams read the Oregonian, other newspapers and magazines, and watched television, all of which were media through which defendant conveyed its message. The evidence includes examples of newspaper stories describing the dangers of tobacco that also contain statements from industry spokespersons insisting that the dangers were not proved and at times attacking the validity of the research suggesting harmful effects. Industry newspaper advertisements conveyed the same message. For instance, in an article published in the Oregonian in 1991, an industry spokesman said that the dangers were not proven and argued that the money that the CTR spent on research showed how open-minded the industry was.

Williams' own statements show that he received and relied on defendant's misrepresentations. When Williams' family urged him to stop smoking, he responded that what he had seen on television demonstrated that smoking did not cause cancer. When his son gave him articles on the subject, he responded by finding his own articles that countered the dangers of smoking. After his diagnosis, he told his wife that the "cigarette people" had deceived him, that he had been betrayed, and that "they were lying all of the time." The jury could find from the evidence that no one other than defendant and the rest of the tobacco industry promoted the message to which Williams referred. Because of his exclusive use of Phillip Morris products, the jury could also conclude that he meant defendant when he referred to the "cigarette people." Thus, the evidence supports a reasonable inference that Williams purchased cigarettes after September 1, 1988, in reliance on defendant's previous and continuing representations and that those cigarettes were a substantial factor in causing his lung cancer. Consequently, the trial court did not err in denying the motion for a directed verdict on the fraud claim.

Reversed and remanded with instructions to enter judgment on jury verdict.

Notes

1. *Never-ending story.* Although this represented the end of Mrs. Williams's litigation against Philip Morris over the question of fraudulent misrepresentation, the case has continued to run over the question of punitive damages. We shall return to that subject — and to this litigation — in Chapter 18.

2. *Relaxing reliance.* In another case that also stemmed from Philip Morris's repeated fraudulent misrepresentations that its cigarettes were safe, namely *Bullock v. Philip Morris USA, Inc.,* 159 Cal.App.4th 655, 676 (2008), the plaintiff was apparently unable to establish that she had heard and actually relied on any of Morris's false statements. Rejecting Morris's contentions that this meant that it could not be held liable to the plaintiff for its misrepresentations, a court of appeal in California held that:

> A plaintiff need not prove that he or she directly heard a specific misrepresentation or false promise to establish actual reliance. Rather, actual reliance is established if the defendant made a misrepresentation to a third party, the defendant intended or had reason to expect that the substance of the communication would be repeated to the plaintiff and would induce the plaintiff's reliance, and the plaintiff was misled when the substance of the communication was repeated to the plaintiff.

3. *Fraud on federal agency claims.* Many products must be approved by a federal agency in order to be available for consumer use in the United States. Tobacco is not something requiring federal approval, but pharmaceuticals, medical devices, aircraft, and aviation equipment are examples of things that are. Individuals who have been injured as a result of a defect in such products allegedly known to its manufacturers and/or sellers have sometimes alleged that they have been harmed as a result of justifiable reliance on claims made fraudulently to a federal agency.

Buckman v. Plaintiffs' Legal Committee
531 U.S. 341, 121 S.Ct. 1012 (2001) (SCOTUS)

REHNQUIST, C.J. Respondent represents plaintiffs who claim injuries resulting from the use of orthopedic bone screws in the pedicles of their spines. Petitioner is a consulting company that assisted the screws' manufacturer, AcroMed Corporation, in navigating the federal regulatory process for these devices. Plaintiffs say petitioner made fraudulent representations to the Food and Drug Administration (FDA or Administration) in the course of obtaining approval to market the screws. Plaintiffs further claim that such representations were at least a "but for" cause of injuries that plaintiffs sustained from the implantation of these devices: Had the representations not been made, the FDA would not have approved the devices, and plaintiffs would not have been injured. Plaintiffs sought damages from petitioner under state tort law. We hold that such claims are pre-empted by the Federal Food, Drug, and Cosmetic Act (FDCA), 52 Stat. 1040, as amended by the Medical Device Amendments of 1976 (MDA), 90 Stat. 539, 21 U.S.C. §301 (1994 ed. and Supp. V)....

Policing fraud against federal agencies is hardly "a field which the States have traditionally occupied," such as to warrant a presumption against finding federal pre-emption of a state-law cause of action. To the contrary, the relationship between a federal agency and the entity it regulates is inherently federal in character because the relationship originates from, is governed by, and terminates according to federal law. Here, petitioner's dealings with the FDA were prompted by the MDA, and the very subject matter of petitioner's statements were dictated by that statute's provisions. Accordingly—and in contrast to situations implicating "federalism concerns and the historic primacy of state regulation of matters of health and safety,"—no presumption against pre-emption obtains in this case.

Given this analytical framework, we hold that the plaintiffs' state-law fraud-on-the-FDA claims conflict with, and are therefore impliedly pre-empted by, federal law. The conflict stems from the fact that the federal statutory scheme amply empowers the FDA to punish and deter fraud against the Administration, and that this authority is used by the Administration to achieve a somewhat delicate balance of statutory objectives. The balance sought by the Administration can be skewed by allowing fraud-on-the-FDA claims under state tort law.…

STEVENS, J., with whom THOMAS J. joins (concurring in the judgment). As the Court points out, an essential link in the chain of causation that respondent must prove in order to prevail is that, but for petitioner's fraud, the allegedly defective orthopedic bone screws would not have reached the market. The fact that the Food and Drug Administration (FDA) has done nothing to remove the devices from the market, even though it is aware of the basis for the fraud allegations, convinces me that this essential element of the claim cannot be proved. I therefore agree that the case should not proceed.

This would be a different case if, prior to the instant litigation, the FDA had determined that petitioner had committed fraud during the § 510(k) process and had then taken the necessary steps to remove the harm-causing product from the market. Under those circumstances, respondent's state-law fraud claim would not depend upon speculation as to the FDA's behavior in a counterfactual situation but would be grounded in the agency's explicit actions. In such a case, a plaintiff would be able to establish causation without second-guessing the FDA's decisionmaking or overburdening its personnel, thereby alleviating the Government's central concerns regarding fraud-on-the-agency claims.

If the FDA determines both that fraud has occurred and that such fraud requires the removal of a product from the market, state damages remedies would not encroach upon, but rather would supplement and facilitate, the federal enforcement scheme.…

Under the pre-emption analysis the Court offers today, however, parties injured by fraudulent representations to federal agencies would have no remedy even if recognizing such a remedy would have no adverse consequences upon the operation or integrity of the regulatory process. I do not believe the reasons advanced in the Court's opinion support the conclusion that Congress intended such a harsh result. For that reason, although I concur in the Court's disposition of this case, I do not join its opinion.

Judgment of the Court of Appeals reversed.

Notes

1. *Indirect reliance.* One way to characterize the basis of the plaintiff's claim in *Buckman* is as a theory of indirect reliance. The argument effectively runs like this. The plaintiff relied on the FDA's approval, and the FDA in turn relied on the manufacturer's statements; so the plaintiff effectively relied on the manufacturer's statements. Such a claim is, perhaps, analogous to the notion of a collateral warranty in contracts which, as we saw in Chapter 3, is often provided by a manufacturer to a consumer, even though the two may have no direct relationship.

2. *The learned intermediary.* The plaintiffs in *Buckman* were unsuccessful because they could not establish that their injuries had been caused by any misrepresentation. On the one hand, they had not themselves been misled by any representations made by the screws' manufacturer. On the other, they could not establish that the physicians who then recommended the use of the screws had done so because of any representations made to them. Moreover, doctors are independent actors who are taken not simply to believe what they are told, but professionals who will use their own expertise to evaluate a product's advantages and disadvantages.

For this reason, unless it can be established that a patient's doctor has been fraudulently misled, the physician's recommendation that a particular product be used is normally taken to have broken the chain of causation between the manufacturer's representations and any subsequent harm that the patient suffers. Manufacturers argue that their advertisements do not — indeed, cannot — cause the use of products which are available only by prescription, but simply encourage patients to ask their doctors for their own, professional views on the advertised products. If these products are then prescribed, it is argued, it is because of the independent judgment of the physician as a "learned intermediary," and not because of any allegedly misleading advertising by the manufacturer. This is commonly known as the "learned intermediary" defense.

Although this makes the doctor's prescription or recommendation the proximate cause of the patient's injury, there will be no grounds for bringing any claim against the doctor unless it can be shown that his prescription was written negligently or fraudulently.

It also effectively means that, as was recognized in *Stanley v. Wyeth, Inc.*, 991 So.2d 31 (La.2008), above, a drug manufacturer normally has no duty to warn the consumer directly of any potential problems or side-effects of its drugs; its duty, rather, is to provide doctors with the relevant information.

3. *The shrinking scope of the learned intermediary defense?* Manufacturers of drugs and medical devices increasingly advertise their products direct to potential patients in the manner of regular consumer goods. The idea is that patients will then ask their doctors to prescribe the use of the manufacturers' products at a greater rate than before. It might also suggest, however, that the scope of the learned intermediary defense is likely to shrink if it can be shown that, in such circumstances, the patient has acted directly on the manufacturers' own claims.

Conte v. Wyeth
168 Cal.App.4th 89 (2008) (First DCA, California)

SIGGINS, J. Plaintiff Elizabeth Conte developed a serious and irreversible neurological condition. She alleges her condition is due to her long-term consumption of a generic prescription drug, and that the warnings provided by the manufacturers of the drug failed to adequately warn of known dangers resulting from its long-term use. The trial court granted summary judgment in favor of all the manufacturers. Judgment was entered in favor of Wyeth, Inc. (Wyeth), the name-brand manufacturer of the drug, on two grounds: (1) Conte could not show that she or her physician relied upon warnings or product labeling disseminated by Wyeth; and (2) a name-brand pharmaceutical manufacturer owes no duty to individuals who take only generic versions of its product. The court granted summary judgment in favor of three generic manufacturers on grounds of federal preemption and Conte's lack of reliance on their warnings or product labeling.

We hold that the common law duty to use due care owed by a name-brand prescription drug manufacturer when providing product warnings extends not only to consumers of its own product, but also to those whose doctors foreseeably rely on the name-brand manufacturer's product information when prescribing a medication, even if the prescription is filled with the generic version of the prescribed drug. We further conclude that Conte has shown there is a material factual dispute as to whether her doctor relied on Wyeth's product information, but that she is unable to show he relied on any information supplied by the generic manufacturer defendants. Accordingly, we reverse the judgment in favor of Wyeth and affirm the summary judgment in favor of each of the three generic manufacturers....

The defendants in these consolidated appeals manufacture and market metoclopramide, which Conte's physician prescribed in its generic and name-brand form, Reglan, to treat her gastroesophageal reflux disease. Wyeth manufactures and markets Reglan. Defendants Purepac Pharmaceutical Company (Purepac), Teva Pharmaceutical USA, Inc. (Teva), and Pliva, Inc. (Pliva) manufacture generic versions of metoclopramide.

Conte developed tardive dyskinesia, a debilitating and incurable neurological disorder. She alleges she developed her condition as a result of taking metoclopramide for almost four years between August 2000 and April 2004. It is undisputed that Conte took only the generic version of the medication, not Reglan. She claims that defendants knew or should have known of a widespread tendency among physicians to misprescribe Reglan and generic metoclopramide for periods of 12 months or longer, even though the medication is only approved for 12 weeks of use, because the drugs labeling substantially understates the risks of serious side-effects from extended use.

Her complaint, after various pretrial amendments, asserts claims for fraud, fraud by concealment and negligent misrepresentation against Wyeth; negligence, strict products liability, negligence per se, and breach of express and implied warranties against the generic manufacturers; and medical negligence against her doctor, Robert Elsen, M.D. The crux of Conte's claims against all of the drug company defendants is that she was injuriously overexposed to metoclopramide due to their dissemination of false, misleading and/or incomplete warnings about the drug's side effects....

Conte's claims against Wyeth are premised on misrepresentations in Wyeth's labeling of Reglan and in a monograph on Reglan it provided for the Physician's Desk Reference (PDR). It is undisputed that Wyeth (or its predecessor in interest) prepared the PDR monograph on Reglan/metoclopramide, which is identical to the FDA-approved package insert. Wyeth contends the trial court correctly ruled that Conte cannot establish causation because she cannot show that her prescribing physician, Dr. Elsen, relied on its allegedly inadequate warnings about Reglan when he planned her treatment. The record, reviewed in accord with the standards required for summary judgment, reveals a factual dispute that refutes Wyeth's contention.

Wyeth argues it produced undisputed evidence that Dr. Elsen did not rely on its product warnings when he prescribed metoclopramide to Conte. It bases its argument on Dr. Elsen's statement in his declaration that "[a]t no time did I rely in any way on representations made in the PDR monograph, package insert, labeling materials or other information from Wyeth regarding the medication Reglan in order to formulate my course of care and treatment for Ms. Conte." Without more, we would agree that Dr. Elsen's statement would prevent Conte from proving he relied on Wyeth's alleged misrepresentations in its product information.

But, there is more. Dr. Elsen's deposition testimony submitted by Conte in opposition to Wyeth's motion raises significant questions about the import of his declaration. Dr. Elsen testified in his deposition that he "probably" read Wyeth's monograph on Reglan in the PDR during his residency training; that the PDR was one of the sources he generally refers to in his clinical practice when he considers prescribing Reglan for his patients; and that he believed the information it contained was accurate. Dr. Elsen also had no recollection of having prescribed Reglan for Ms. Conte, but his lack of recollection testimony is contradicted by pharmacy records and his secretary's testimony. Accordingly, there are disputed factual issues as to both the accuracy of Dr. Elsen's recollection and, even if he did not specifically refer to the PDR when he formulated Conte's treatment, whether information he had previously garnered from the PDR was a substantial factor in his decision to prescribe Reglan for her....

We also are unpersuaded by Wyeth's contention that it was Conte's burden to also demonstrate that a stronger warning in the PDR would have affected Dr. Elsen's decision to prescribe the drug to her. The premise of Wyeth's causation argument was that Dr. Elsen never read Wyeth's disclosures, so any allegedly inadequate information they contained could not have affected his decision. Wyeth did not seek summary judgment on the ground that Elsen would have made the same treatment decision even if Wyeth had disclosed a higher risk of adverse side effects. Conte was not required to demonstrate a dispute over a factual issue not raised by Wyeth's summary judgment motion....

[W]e reject Wyeth's syllogism premised upon product liability doctrine that (1) this is merely a products liability lawsuit disguised as an action for fraud and misrepresentation; and (2) Conte cannot prevail on a strict products liability claim because Wyeth did not manufacture or sell the product that allegedly caused her injury; so (3) Conte loses. The conclusion would be sound were Conte in fact pursuing a cause of action against Wyeth for strict products liability. But she is not. The complaint alleges that Wyeth made intentional and/or negligent misrepresentations about the safety of metoclopramide, the risks of its long-term use, and the likelihood of its serious side effects. She does not allege that Wyeth is strictly liable because inadequate warnings rendered its product unreasonably dangerous. Rather, she charges that Wyeth failed to use due care when disseminating its product information.

Our decision today is rooted in common sense and California common law. We are not marking out new territory by recognizing that a defendant that authors and disseminates information about a product manufactured and sold by another may be liable for negligent misrepresentation where the defendant should reasonably expect others to rely on that information and the product causes injury, even though the defendant would not be liable in strict products liability because it did not manufacture or sell the product. (See *Hanberry v. Hearst Corp.*) We perceive no logical or legal inconsistency between allowing the suit for negligence and disallowing the suit for strict products liability.

Section 310 of the Restatement addresses intentional misrepresentations, and states that

> [a]n actor who makes a misrepresentation is subject to liability to another for physical harm which results from an act done by the other or a third person in reliance upon the truth of the representation, if the actor (a) intends his statement to induce or *should realize that it is likely to induce action by the other, or a third person,* which involves an unreasonable risk of physical harm to the other, and (b) knows (i) that the statement is false, or (ii) that he has not the knowledge which he professes. (Italics added.)

Section 311 provides that, "[o]ne who negligently gives false information to another is subject to liability for physical harm caused by action taken by the other in reasonable reliance upon such information, where such harm results (a) to the other, or (b) *to such third persons as the actor should expect to be put in peril by the action taken.*" (Italics added.)

> In this context, "duty" and "reasonable reliance" are closely connected. The likelihood that one's statements about personal safety will be taken seriously is a primary factor in determining whether one has a duty to exercise care in making such statements. As the Restatement puts it, such a duty "extends to any person who, in the course of an activity which is in furtherance of his own interests, undertakes to give information to another, and knows or should realize that the safety of the person or others may depend on the accuracy of the information. (*Garcia* [*v. Superior Court* (1990) 50 Cal.3d 728] at pp. 728, 735, ... quoting Rest.2d Torts, § 311, com. b, at p. 106.) ...

"Although foreseeability is most often a question of fact for the jury, when there is no room for a reasonable difference of opinion it may be decided as a matter of law." (*Hedlund v. Superior Court* (1983) 34 Cal.3d 695, 705, 194 Cal.Rptr. 805, 669 P.2d 41.) This is such a case. In California, as in most states, pharmacists have long been authorized by statute to fill prescriptions for name-brand drugs with their generic equivalents unless the prescribing physician expressly forbids such a substitution. (Bus. & Prof. Code, § 4073; *Inwood Laboratories v. Ives Laboratories* (1982) 456 U.S. 844, 847–848, fn. 4, 102 S.Ct. 2182.) It is therefore highly likely that a prescription for Reglan written in reliance on Wyeth's product information will be filled with generic metoclopramide. And, because by law the generic and name-brand versions of drugs are biologically equivalent (21 U.S.C. § 355(j)(1)(A), (B)), it is also eminently foreseeable that a physician might prescribe generic metoclopramide in reliance on Wyeth's representations about Reglan. In this context, we have no difficulty concluding that Wyeth should reasonably perceive that there could be injurious reliance on its product information by a patient taking generic metoclopramide....

In addition to foreseeability, California law also identifies various policy factors courts are to consider when they determine whether a duty of care exists in a novel situation. These ... are: the foreseeability of harm to the plaintiff; the degree of certainty that the plaintiff suffered injury; the closeness of the connection between the defendant's conduct and the plaintiff's injury; the moral blame attached to the defendant's conduct; the policy goal of preventing future harm; the burden to the defendant and consequences to the community of imposing a duty of care; and broader consequences including the availability, cost, and prevalence of insurance for the risk involved....

On the record that is before us, we find the conclusion inescapable that Wyeth knows or should know that a significant number of patients whose doctors rely on its product information for Reglan are likely to have generic metoclopramide prescribed or dispensed to them.

> In the absence of "overriding policy considerations ... foreseeability of risk [is] of ... primary importance in establishing the element of duty." ... As a classic opinion states: "The risk reasonably to be perceived defines the duty to be obeyed." (*Dillon v. Legg*, 68 Cal.2d at p. 739, quoting *Palsgraf v. Long Island R.R. Co.*, 248 N.Y. at p. 344.)

As the foreseeable risk of physical harm runs to users of both name-brand and generic drugs, so too runs the duty of care, and Wyeth has not persuaded us that consideration of other factors requires a different conclusion. We hold that Wyeth's duty of care in disseminating product information extends to those patients who are injured by generic metoclopramide as a result of prescriptions written in reliance on Wyeth's product information for Reglan.

Judgment in favor of Wyeth reversed.

Notes

1. *Generic versus brand-name drugs.* Under the Drug Price Competition and Patent Term Restoration Act of 1984, manufacturers seeking approval to market a generic drug do not have to submit their products to the same types of pre-clinical and clinical testing as manufacturers seeking to market an original product. Instead, they can make use of what is known as the Abbreviated New Drug Application (ANDA) Process. This requires that they submit evidence to the FDA, showing that the generic in question is bioequiv-

alent to its original, brand-name counterpart. This means not only that it must contain the same active ingredient, but also that it is absorbed into the body at the same rate and amount. (Note that other ingredients, such as the coating, are permitted to differ.) Evidence of bioequivalence is gathered in a specific trial designed for the purpose, typically involving between 24 and 36 adult volunteers. Results are expected to reflect those for the original, brand-name product, subject to a statistical tolerance level which permits the tested generic to yield results between 80% and 125% of the average response to the original. In addition, the FDA also requires that generics be of the same strength and dosage form (whether tablet, capsule, etc.), and have the same means of administration (whether oral, topical, injectable, etc.). These requirements enable the FDA to rely on the tests conducted regarding the original so far as efficacy and side-effects are concerned.

2. *When can a generic be manufactured?* Manufacturers who develop a new drug take out a patents on it in order to maintain an exclusive right to manufacture the drug over the lifetime of the patent which, in the United States, lasts twenty years. In practice, however, manufacturers file patents before testing has been completed and the drug is commercially available, so that the effective useful life of the patent to the manufacturer is usually significantly shorter (usually around eleven or twelve years). Generics can be manufactured once a brand-name product's patent expires.

3. *Conte versus Foster.* The Supreme Court of California declined to entertain an appeal, and so the decision in *Conte* stands. As the Court of Appeal itself realized, however, its decision departed from the majority of courts that have wrestled with this particular issue. In *Foster v. American Home Products Corp.*, 29 F.3d 165 (1994), for example, the Fourth Circuit, applying Maryland law, and reached the conclusion that the manufacturer of a name-brand prescription drug cannot be held liable under a theory of negligent misrepresentation for an injury arising from the use of a generic version of the drug. The *Conte* court considered *Foster* at length but rejected it, essentially for presuming the very things that had to be proved.

4. *Three controversies.* There are essentially three controversies here. First, *Foster* held a manufacturer could owe no duty of care in relation to a product that it had not manufactured. The *Conte* court considered that an accurate statement of the law of strict products liability (discussed in Part II) but irrelevant to a claim of misrepresentation. Second, the *Foster* court considered the claim of misrepresentation to be an impermissible attempt to get around the law of strict products liability, whereas the *Conte* court considered an action for misrepresentation to be entirely distinct from an action for strict products liability, so that a plaintiff is free to pursue either or both as she sees fit. Third, the two courts clearly have different conceptions of what is fair. As Siggins J. put it (168 Cal.App.4th 89, 109):

> *Foster* … reasons it would be unfair to allow misrepresentation actions against name-brand manufacturers for injuries caused by generic drugs because name-brand makers bear the expense of developing, testing, and formulating labeling information for new medications, while generic manufacturers merely "rid[e their] coattails" by duplicating the innovator's successful drugs and labels. (*Foster, supra*, 29 F.3d at p. 170.) The trial court here agreed: "[i]t also seems unfair to hold the pioneer manufacturer liable as insurer for not only its own production but also its generic competitors, especially when the latter enjoys the full financial benefits but no risk regarding the product." But we do not. We find the reasoning problematic. As Conte asks, what is unfair about requiring a defendant to shoulder its share of responsibility for injuries caused, at least in part, by its negligent or intentional dissemination of inaccurate information?

5. *Subsequent treatment of Conte.* In November 2009 the US Court of Appeals for the Eighth Circuit became the first appellate court to reject *Conte.* In a case with facts virtually identical to those in *Conte, Mensing v. Wyeth,* 588 F.3d 603, 613 (2009) (reversed and remanded on other grounds by *PLIVA, Inc. v. Mensing,* 131 S.Ct. 2567 (2011)), it held, applying Minnesota law, that:

> regardless of whether her doctor relied upon the Reglan label, Mensing must show that the name brand manufacturers owed *her* a duty of care. Duty is a threshold requirement for all of the tort claims Mensing asserts. See, e.g., *Noble Systems Corp. v. Alorica Central, LLC,* 543 F.3d 978, 985 (8th Cir.2008) (finding that under Minnesota law negligent misrepresentation requires the plaintiff to "prove some relationship that is sufficient to create a duty owed by the defendant to the plaintiff").
>
> Such a duty of care does not extend to all potential Reglan consumers. "Minnesota common law … requires a stronger relationship and a direct communication." *Flynn* [*v. American Home Products Corp.,* 627 N.W.2d 342, 350 (Minn.App.2001)]. Since Mensing "did not purchase or use [the name brand defendants'] product, … there was no direct relationship between them, let alone a fiduciary relationship that gave rise to a duty." *Id.* at 350. Mensing focuses on the foreseeability of harm from the defendants' action. Like the Fourth Circuit, we conclude that holding name brand manufacturers liable for harm caused by generic manufacturers "stretch[es] the concept of foreseeability too far." *Foster,* 29 F.3d at 171. As for Mensing's negligent misrepresentation claim, "the Minnesota Supreme Court has recognized negligent misrepresentation involving damages only for pecuniary loss[.]" *Flynn,* 627 N.W.2d at 350, citing *Smith v. Brutger Cos.,* 569 N.W.2d 408, 414 (Minn.1997). We find it unlikely the Minnesota Supreme Court would extend the doctrine to misrepresentation involving the risk of physical harm in these circumstances. We conclude that under Minnesota law Mensing has not shown that the name brand manufacturers owed her a duty of care necessary to trigger liability.

The Supreme Court has since held, in *PLIVA, Inc. v. Mensing,* 131 S.Ct. 2567 (2011), that such lawsuits against drug manufacturers are preempted by federal law: see Chapter 17. The wafer-thin majority in that case suggests, however, that that decision may not stand the test of time as Justices die or retire, in which case the misrepresentation issues raised in *Foster* and *Conte* will no doubt be revisited. These issues also have an impact on the courts' treatment of design defects in drugs: see Chapter 7.

6. *Implied misrepresentations?* It might be thought that, if the brand-name manufacturer can be held liable for a misrepresentation regarding its product, as in *Conte,* then the generic manufacturer should also be at risk for its implicit endorsement of the product through its manufacturing of the generic drug. There are, however, at least two problems with that theory. The first is that the notion of an "implicit misrepresentation" is not one that has found favor in the courts. In this respect, there is a clear difference between misrepresentations and warranties.

7. *Medicare and Medicaid.* The second reason is a matter of policy. It has been estimated that generics make up around 60% of all drugs dispensed through Medicare and Medicaid, and that the cost of each such prescription is over 60% less than it would be if the corresponding brand-name product were prescribed. If generic manufacturers were laid open to suits for misrepresentation despite their having made no explicit claims for their products other than that they are bioequivalent to the brand-name alternative, they would need to accumulate the resources to defend such claims, and the prices of generics would skyrocket. This would have dramatic ramifications for the financial viability of the Medicare and Medicaid programs.

Questions

1. Where do you stand on each of the three areas of controversy between *Foster* and *Conte*?

2. Would it be true to say that underlying these three areas of controversy is a focus on different parties, and that *Foster* focuses on the comparative positions of name-brand and generic manufacturers, while *Conte* focuses on the comparative positions of victim and manufacturers? If so, which is the relationship on which the courts should focus, or is it possible to consider both?

3. Is the fundamental distinction between *Conte* and *Mensing* that, in the latter, it is considered that the plaintiff has the burden of proving that she was owed a duty of care, whereas in the former it is presumed that we all owe a duty to one another unless very good reason can be found for rebutting this presumption?

4. Some critics of the decision in *Conte* have argued that, because such claims of misrepresentation will never be possible against manufacturers of generics, it effectively imposes what they have labeled "innovator liability." Is that a fair characterization or just a sound-bite political slogan?

5. Should plaintiffs be free to choose the branch of law—in this case, misrepresentation, rather than "regular" products liability law—according to what suits their case better, or should the courts insist that all cases based on injuries from defective products be decided in the same way, no matter what nomenclature the plaintiff has chosen to give the claim?

Innocent Misrepresentation

It is possible to make erroneous representations without either fraud or negligence. The law takes the view that, so long as reliance on such statements was justifiable, the representee will still be entitled to a remedy. In other words, liability for an innocent misrepresentation is strict, just as it is for a breach of warranty. However, reflecting the fact that the representor is scarcely blameworthy, both the precise circumstances in which a remedy will be available to the representee and the nature of that remedy are more limited than those afforded to victims of negligence or fraud. There will, in particular, be no chance of succeeding in a claim for punitive damages.

Restatement (Second) Torts (1977)

§ 402B. *Misrepresentation by Seller of Chattels to Consumer*

One engaged in the business of selling chattels who, by advertising, labels, or otherwise, makes to the public a misrepresentation of a material fact concerning the character or quality of a chattel sold by him is subject to liability for physical harm to a consumer of the chattel caused by justifiable reliance upon the misrepresentation, even though

(a) it is not made fraudulently or negligently, and

(b) the consumer has not bought the chattel from or entered into any contractual relation with the seller.

Caveat

The Institute expresses no opinion as to whether the rule stated in this Section may apply

(1) where the representation is not made to the public, but to an individual, or

(2) where physical harm is caused to one who is not a consumer of the chattel.

Crocker v. Winthrop Laboratories
514 S.W.2d 429 (1974) (Supreme Court of Texas)

REAVLEY, J. Glenn E. Crocker became addicted to a new drug produced by Winthrop Laboratories and known as "talwin" which had been previously thought to be non-addictive. When he was in a weakened condition and his tolerance to drugs very low because of a period of detoxification, Crocker obtained an injection of a narcotic and died soon thereafter. His widow and representative, Clarissa Crocker, brought this action for damages due to his suffering while alive as well as for his wrongful death. She recovered judgment against Winthrop Laboratories in the trial court. The Court of Civil Appeals reversed and rendered judgment for the drug company, holding that while some of the facts found by the jury (including the positive misrepresentation by the drug company that talwin was non-addictive) would warrant the recovery, the additional finding that the drug company could not reasonably have foreseen Crocker's addiction (because of his unusual susceptibility and the state of medical knowledge when the drug was marketed), constituted a complete defense. We hold that the latter finding does not bar the recovery, and we affirm the judgment of the trial court.

In July of 1967 Glenn Crocker suffered a double hernia, as well as frostbite of two fingers, while working as a carpenter in a cold storage vault. He was then 49 years old and was not a user of drugs or alcohol. His hernia was successfully repaired. The circulation of blood in his fingers, however, was not restored. Skin grafts were done on the fingers in October, but it was necessary to amputate part of his thumb in November and part of his middle finger the following January (1968). Prior to November 23, 1967, when Dr. Mario Palafox amputated part of his thumb, the several doctors who had treated him had prescribed both demerol (a narcotic) and talwin for relief of pain without observing any cause to believe him to be then addicted to any drug. Crocker told Dr. Palafox that he liked the relief he received from talwin, and Dr. Palafox responded that this was fortunate because talwin had no addicting side effect.

Crocker did develop an addiction to talwin, however, and was able to obtain prescriptions from several doctors as well as to cross the Mexican border to Juarez and acquire the same drug without a prescription under the name of "sosigon." He was hospitalized on June 3, 1968 by a psychiatrist, Dr. J. Edward Stern, for a process of detoxification (to remove the toxic agents in his body) and treatment of his drug dependency. After six days in the hospital being withdrawn from talwin as well as all narcotics, and at a time when his tolerance for potent drugs was very low, Crocker walked out of the hospital and went to his home. Because of his agitated condition and the threats he made against his wife, he was finally successful in having her call Dr. Eugene Engel who, on June 10, 1968, came to the Crocker home and gave Mr. Crocker an injection of demerol. Crocker went to his bed for the last time.

Winthrop Laboratories first put talwin on the market in July of 1967 after extensive testing and approval by the Federal Drug Administration. The descriptive material on the new drug circulated by Winthrop Laboratories in 1967 gives no warning of the possibilities of addiction. There is a heading of a paragraph in the product information of the 1967 edition of Physicians' Desk Reference Book which reads: "Absence of addiction liability." This might be considered misleading, but in view of the evidence of verbal assurances as to the properties of talwin by the drug company's representative, there is no need to deal further with the printed materials. Dr. Palafox, a prominent orthopedic surgeon in El Paso, allowed Crocker to have liberal use of talwin and assured him that it was non-addictive because of the assurance by a representative of the drug company who had detailed the doctor on the nature of the drug. There had been an extended and specific conversation between the drug company representative and Dr. Palafox about talwin, and Dr. Palafox was told that talwin was as harmless as aspirin and could be given as long as desired. Dr. Palafox testified that the representative of the defendant insisted that talwin could have no addicting effect.

Subsequent experience has proved that talwin is an extremely useful drug for the relief of pain but that it cannot be regarded as non-addictive. Doctors Palafox and Stern had seen other patients dependent upon talwin. Dr. Arthur S. Keats, chairman of the Department of Anesthesiology at Baylor School of Medicine in Houston, who did original work on the drug and who testified during this trial on the call of the drug company, agreed with the attorney for Mrs. Crocker that "there are a tremendous number of people that do develop a talwin addiction."

Dr. Palafox was of the opinion that if he had not been assured of the non-addictive character of talwin, he could probably have avoided addiction or dependence by Crocker upon any drug.

Plaintiff's medical testimony depicted the addiction to talwin as a producing cause of the death of Crocker when taken together with the chain of events including the detoxification process and the injection of demerol.

The findings of the jury included the following: ...

9. That Crocker's addiction or dependency upon talwin was an abreaction. Abreaction was defined as

> an unusual reaction resulting from a person's unusual susceptibility to the product or intended effect of the product in question; that is, such person's reaction is different in the presence of the drug in question from that in the usual person. An abreaction is one in which an unusual result is produced by a known or theoretical mechanism of action. An abreaction is one which could not have been reasonably foreseen in an appreciable class or number of potential users prior to the time Glenn E. Crocker became addicted or dependent on Talwin.

10. That at the time Crocker was taking talwin under doctors' prescriptions, the state of medical knowledge was such that Winthrop Laboratories could not have reasonably foreseen, in the exercise of ordinary care, that talwin would cause an addiction in an appreciable number of persons.

The Court of Civil Appeals held that there should be no liability on the part of the drug manufacturer because the harm to Glenn Crocker could not have been reasonably foreseen in an appreciable number of persons. Since the drug was not unreasonably dangerous to the ordinary user, the Court saw no basis for liability ...

Liability of Winthrop Laboratories will be predicated upon the finding of misrepresentation that the drug would not cause physical dependence, a fact conceded by the attorney for the company in his jury argument, and upon the findings of reliance and causation. Whatever the danger and state of medical knowledge, and however rare the susceptibility of the user, when the drug company positively and specifically represents its product to be free and safe from all dangers of addiction, and when the treating physician relies upon that representation, the drug company is liable when the representation proves to be false and harm results.

Judgment of the Court of Civil Appeals reversed and judgment of trial court affirmed.

Notes

1. *Misrepresentation, warranty, and failure to warn.* It should, by now, be apparent that there is a close relationship between some claims for breach of warranty, and those for misrepresentation. It will also become apparent in Chapter 8 that both of these types of claims bear a striking resemblance to claims of a failure to warn of the potential risks in using a particular product. Sometimes two (or even all three) of these causes of action can be maintained in the same case. In others, however—as we have seen—only one such claim may be sustainable.

2. *Rarity of innocent misrepresentation claims.* It is quite rare for a claim of innocent misrepresentation to be brought when the plaintiff has suffered physical injury. The availability in such circumstances of many other claims often renders it superfluous, so that it tends to be used much more frequently when the victim has suffered purely economic loss as a result of entering into an unprofitable contract because of the misrepresentation. Such claims are, of course, beyond the scope of this book.

Question

When is it better to sue for misrepresentation, and when is it better to sue for breach of warranty?

Hypothetical

TopMart runs a large chain of supermarkets throughout the nation. In addition to selling well-known, branded processed foods, it also sells its own-brand range under the name of GoodStuff. Contracts for the production of items for the GoodStuff range are placed with a number of different manufacturers in different states. Some of these manufacturers are those responsible for the well-known brands which TopMart stocks alongside its own-brand goods; other manufacturers do not produce items under their own name, but do make products for other supermarket chains.

A particularly popular item in the bakery section is GoodStuff Sticky Toffee Pudding, on which the packaging states: "Does not contain nuts." TopMart demands that this product is made only in facilities where the manufacturer can guarantee that no nuts are used in the production of any foods, irrespective of whether those foods will be sold under its own label or any other. TopMart's inspectors visit each of its manufacturers' premises several times a week to ensure good quality control.

A few months ago, one such manufacturer, Southern Foods, developed a fault with one of its manufacturing plants which is used to make products which contain nuts. While the fault was being repaired, Southern decided to switch such production to another of its facilities, which also makes GoodStuff Sticky Toffee Pudding. It did not inform TopMart of this change, and TopMart did not become aware of it until four days later, when one of its inspectors visited. He had been due to visit three days earlier, but illness had forced him to postpone. Southern informed the TopMart inspector that the fault in its other production facility would be repaired in two days' time, and TopMart therefore decided to do nothing about it.

Five days later Sarah, who is allergic to nuts, was rushed to hospital with anaphylactic shock after eating a GoodStuff Sticky Toffee Pudding contaminated with traces of nuts. She had already disposed of both her receipt from TopMart and the pudding's packaging. What legal advice would you give her?

Chapter 5

Negligence

Overview

We have now seen that, by the late nineteenth century, a person injured by a defective product had the following four avenues by which to bring a claim, and thus circumvent the maxim of *caveat emptor*:

1. Breach of express warranty;
2. Breach of implied warranty;
3. Fraudulent misrepresentation (deceit), or
4. Non-fraudulent misrepresentation.

Both types of warranty claim sounded in contract law. An express warranty was either a term of the contract or formed the basis of a collateral contract running alongside the main contract involving the defective product. An implied warranty was deemed by statute or by common law to be a term of the contract. Misrepresentations, however, were part of the law of torts, since, in order to be actionable, they had to induce the representee to enter into a contract—and thus had to be made before any contract was agreed. Yet, irrespective of whether the specific action contemplated sounded in contracts or torts, each of these avenues remained confined by the doctrine of privity. Without a contract with the representor, there could be no more an actionable misrepresentation than there could be a case of breach of an express or implied warranty. The difference was simply that the contractual actions required privity of contract *before* a breach of warranty, whereas those for misrepresentation in torts required proof that such privity had occurred *after*—and in reliance upon—the representation in question.

With the continuing dominance of what Professor Prosser, *Strict Liability to the Consumer in California*, 18 Hastings L.J. 9, 14 (1966–67), called this "citadel of privity," it followed that cases like *Winterbottom v. Wright* (discussed in Chapter 2) remained good law. Manufacturers and distributors of defective products essentially only had a duty not to injure a person with whom they had a contract. However, the late nineteenth century and—especially—the twentieth century saw that position change according to a sequence of events that has been described as having six phases.

Denis W. Boivin, Strict Products Liability Revisited
33 Osgoode Hall L.J. 487 (1995)

As will be shown, history reveals an ever-unfolding relationship between the concept of manufacturer negligence, on the one hand, and the manner in which courts deal with losses caused by defective products, on the other. For our purposes, this development began in the nineteenth century, where reasonable care played second fiddle to privity of contract, and is currently moving towards the view that negligence is somehow relevant when dealing with products containing defective designs or warnings, but not when dealing with manufacturing defects. More specifically, this development may be described by referring to six phases, characterized chiefly by the following events: first, the outright denial of liability in the absence of contractual privity, regardless of the presence of manufacturer negligence; second, the creation of exceptions to the privity rule for certain products and unsanctioned trading practices; third, the recognition of a general duty of care owed by the manufacturer directly to its consumers, irrespective of privity of contract, allowing an action for damages in the case of negligence; fourth, the relaxation of the negligence standard of liability in specified circumstances through a number of evidential devices such as *res ipsa loquitur*; fifth, the open adoption of a general alternative basis of liability, independent of manufacturer's fault, that is, all-encompassing strict products liability; and finally, the recognition of the limits of this new standard of liability by the application of negligence concepts in specified circumstances.

Note

We have already discussed the first two of Boivin's phases. We shall therefore now move on to the third and fourth. (Phase five will be discussed in Chapter 6; phase six in Chapters 7 and 8.)

The Duty of Care to Consumers

As is well known, the notion of products liability as a discrete area of law really stems from the judgment of Justice Cardozo (as he then was) in *MacPherson v. Buick Motor Co.* 217 N.Y. 382, 111 N.E. 1050 (1916). Buick made and sold a car to a retail dealership, which resold it to the plaintiff. While the plaintiff was in the car, it suddenly collapsed. He was thrown out and injured when the spokes of one of the wheels "crumbled into fragments" (217 N.Y. 312, 385) because it was made of defective wood. Justice Cardozo reasoned (217 N.Y. 312, 389):

> If the nature of a thing is such that it is reasonably certain to place life and limb in peril when negligently made, it is then a thing of danger. Its nature gives warning of the consequences to be expected. If to the element of danger there is added knowledge that the thing will be used by persons other than the purchaser, and used without new tests then, irrespective of contract, the manufacturer of this thing of danger is under a duty to make it carefully.

Thus Justice Cardozo eliminated the requirement, originating from the English case of *Winterbottom v. Wright*, that only those in privity of contract with the party responsible could bring a successful suit for physical injury. But while he liberated claims relating to defective products from the confines of the law of contracts, Justice Cardozo certainly did not replace them with strict liability in torts. On the contrary, he contained such claims four square within the developing law of negligence. As other states followed this line of reasoning, manufacturers throughout the nation were placed under an obligation to make products carefully—that is, with reasonable care. Lack of reasonable care in manufacture rendered products defective.

It is, however, easy to overlook the fact that not everyone injured by products which were defective because of a lack of reasonable care on the part of the manufacturer would then be successful in claiming damages. That would be to "spin" the case. The court in *MacPherson* actually spent virtually no time discussing the standard of care for manufacturers. Instead, as Justice Cardozo made clear expressly, what it was concerned with in reality was the notion of duty. He held (217 N.Y. 312, 393) that:

> There is nothing anomalous in a rule which imposes upon A, who has contracted with B, a duty to C and D and others according as he knows or does not know that the subject matter of the contract is intended for their use.

In other words, just because the privity requirement had been eliminated, it did not mean that any injured person would be able to claim if injured as a result of a manufacturer's negligence. It meant only that the source of any duty on the manufacturer arose in torts and not in contracts. As Justice Cardozo himself put it (217 N.Y. 312, 390):

> We have put aside the notion that the duty to safeguard life and limb, when the consequences of negligence may be foreseen, grows out of contract and nothing else. We have put the source of the obligation where it ought not be. We have put its source in the law.

But whether a victim was owed a duty was something that had to be proved, not taken for granted. Thus *MacPherson* established (a) that a plaintiff allegedly injured by a defective product must prove the standard litany of the elements of negligence: duty, breach, causation and damage; and (b) that whether a manufacturer owed a duty or not is determined by the foreseeability of harm to either the particular plaintiff or the class of persons of which the plaintiff was a member. These elements were subsequently encapsulated in § 395 of the Restatement (Second) of Torts.

Restatement (Second) of Torts (1965)

§ 395. Negligent Manufacture of Chattel Dangerous Unless Carefully Made

A manufacturer who fails to exercise reasonable care in the manufacture of a chattel which, unless carefully made, he should recognize as involving an unreasonable risk of causing physical harm to those who use it for a purpose for which the manufacturer should expect it to be used and to those whom he should expect to be endangered by its probable use, is subject to liability for physical harm caused to them by its lawful use in a manner and for a purpose for which it is supplied.

Notes

1. *MacPherson and Palsgraf.* It is important to note that, according to both *MacPherson* and § 395, a duty is not owed automatically by a manufacturer to anyone who happens to use or come into contact with the product concerned. On the contrary, duty is really tort law's substitute for the contractual concept of privity: there must be something about the circumstances of the case that placed the plaintiff and defendant in a legally-significant relationship with each other. As Cardozo himself put it in the famous case of *Palsgraf v. Long Island Railroad Co.*, 248 N.Y. 339, 345; 162 N.E. 99, 101 (1928), "Negligence, like risk, is thus a term of relation. Negligence in the abstract, apart from things related, is surely not a tort, if indeed it is understandable at all."

2. *Duty and breach.* Duty and breach are often confused. In fact, duty is *not* concerned with the quality of behavior of the defendant; it is, as Cardozo made clear, simply concerned with *whether* the defendant owed the plaintiff a legally-relevant obligation at all. Only if that is established does it become necessary to work out what the substantive con-

tent of that duty is or was. However, working out the *content* of the duty is not a matter of duty at all, but a question of the *standard* of care. This distinction is not just of analytical significance; it also has major practical implications. For whereas the question of whether a duty was owed is a matter of law for the court (as in *MacPherson*), the issue of the appropriate standard of conduct is typically a matter for case-by-case determination by a jury.

Standard of Care and Breach of Duty

Standard of care and breach of duty are really two sides of the same coin. While the standard of care purports to state the level of care required by the defendant in the instant case, a finding of breach of duty indicates that the appropriate standard was not, in fact, met. In other words, a plaintiff needs to assert what the defendant's appropriate standard of care was in the circumstances, and then go on to show how the defendant failed to meet it.

Restatement (Second) of Torts (1965)

§291. Unreasonableness; How Determined; Magnitude of Risk and Utility of Conduct

Where an act is one which a reasonable man would recognize as involving a risk of harm to another, the risk is unreasonable and the act is negligent if the risk is of such magnitude as to outweigh what the law regards as the utility of the act or of the particular manner in which it is done.

Notes

1. *Law and economics.* The fact that §291 is phrased in terms of balancing risk and utility has led some to assert that it embodies a test based purely on the economic implications of the conduct in question. In fact, however, nothing could be further from the truth. In *Comment a*, the Reporter, Professor Prosser, suggested that: "The problem involved may be expressed in homely terms by asking whether 'the game is worth the candle.'" It would therefore be much more accurate to say that the notion of "utility" in §291 is a much broader concept than one of economics, and that (like the Declaration of Independence) it embraces the original utilitarian appeal to what John Stuart Mill called "the greatest amount of happiness altogether." Thus the test of unreasonableness is really designed to be one that asks whether the act done was likely to increase or decrease the sum total of human happiness.

2. *Elements of negligence.* Every 1L Torts student learns that a *prima facie* case of negligence requires proof of the following four elements: duty, breach, causation, and damage. In fact, however, this obscures almost as much as it reveals, since many of these "elements" are really compound doctrines with a number of aspects to them. As we have already seen, for example, proof of breach is actually a two-stage process, which first requires identification of the appropriate standard of care before it can then be established whether or not the defendant complied with it. Similarly, causation also has two parts to it, and the second part itself has two elements.

The first part of causation, often called "factual causation," requires proof that the defendant actually caused the plaintiff's injury. The second requires that this injury was of the sort that could reasonably have been expected in the circumstances. This has generally been called "proximate causation," but this is highly misleading since, although there are really two issues here, neither is about proximity and only one concerns causation. For this reason, the Restatement of Torts (Third): Liability for Physical and Emotional Harm (2010) has, like its predecessor, eschewed the term "proximate cause." It has also rejected the Restatement (Second)'s preference for the term "legal cause," since that was equally opaque and never really caught on.

What is at stake at this stage of the forensic inquiry is whether the harm sustained by the victim was of the sort that could reasonably have been expected. (Note that the *extent* of the harm is irrelevant if the *type* of harm could reasonably have been foreseen.) The Restatement (Third) therefore talks of the "scope" of liability. This suffices so long as it is remembered that this idea encompasses another element, namely that the chain of causation must not have been interrupted by the actions of an independent third party or an unforeseeable act of nature. This is known as a superseding cause. By definition, harm resulting from such a cause could not reasonably have been foreseen. Figure 5.1 demonstrates how these more subtle elements in a *prima facie* case of negligence work together.

Figure 5.1 Proving a Prima Facie Case of Negligence

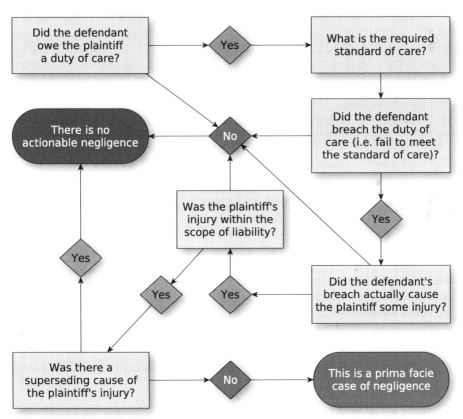

3. *Further refinements of the law of negligence.* Even with these refinements, Figure 5.1 really depicts only what may be called "garden variety" negligence suits. Many products liability cases are far from that, so that the picture so far presented may still need further augmentation. It will be seen in Chapter 9, for example, that factual causation itself has two constituent elements, namely general causation and specific causation. Moreover, both factual causation and breach may be inferred through a doctrine known as *res ipsa loquitur*, while breach may be determined as a matter of law through negligence *per se*. It is to those two doctrines that we now turn.

Res ipsa loquitur and the Fault Requirement

Nearly thirty years after *MacPherson*, the baton for leadership in the development of the law of products liability had passed to the Supreme Court of California. In *Escola v. Coca Cola Bottling Co.*, 24 Cal.2d 453, 456 (1944), a waitress in a restaurant was injured when a bottle of Coca Cola broke in her hand, apparently because of "excessive pressure of gas or by reason of some defect in the bottle". Giving the judgment of the court, Gibson C.J. affirmed judgment for the plaintiff by combining standard negligence theory (in accordance with *MacPherson*) with the use of inference. However, the degree of inference permitted was such as to relieve the plaintiff of having to prove anything beyond the obvious facts that the bottle had broken and she had been injured. Translating the phrase *res ipsa loquitur*, "the thing speaks for itself" so, as Gibson C.J. said (24 Cal.2d 453, 457):

> Plaintiff then rested her case, having announced to the court that being unable to show any specific acts of negligence she relied completely on the doctrine of *res ipsa loquitur*.

He continued (24 Cal.2d 453, 461):

> Although it is not clear in this case whether the explosion was caused by an excessive charge or a defect in the glass, there is a sufficient showing that neither cause would ordinarily have been present if due care had been used. Further, defendant had exclusive control over both the charging and inspection of the bottles. Accordingly, all the requirements necessary to entitle plaintiff to rely on the doctrine of *res ipsa loquitur* to supply an inference of negligence are present.

This is not quite strict liability, which is not interested at all in the culpability or otherwise of the defendant's conduct; proof of the defendant's reasonable conduct is no defense to a strict liability tort. By contrast, *res ipsa loquitur* is still focused on whether the defendant has behaved unreasonably. Its significance lies in the fact that it permits inferences to be drawn about the defendant's conduct from known, primary facts in circumstances where it is difficult to explain how the plaintiff could have been injured without the defendant's somehow being negligent. In practice, this has the effect of relaxing the requirement that the plaintiff should prove fault. *Res ipsa loquitur* thus permits the jury to attribute fault to the manufacturer without there being any direct proof.

Restatement (Second) of Torts (1965)

§ 328(D). Res Ipsa Loquitur

(1) It may be inferred that harm suffered by the plaintiff is caused by negligence of the defendant when

  (a) the event is of a kind which ordinarily does not occur in the absence of negligence;

(b) other responsible causes, including the conduct of the plaintiff and third persons, are sufficiently eliminated by the evidence; and

(c) the indicated negligence is within the scope of defendant's duty to the plaintiff.

(2) It is the function of the court to determine whether the inference may reasonably be drawn by the jury, or whether it must necessarily be drawn.

(3) It is the function of the jury to determine whether the inference is to be drawn in any case where different conclusions may reasonably be reached.

Notes

1. *Two types of inferences: breach and causation.* Despite the unfortunate wording, which sees "negligence" used instead of "breach," § 328(D) signals that, just as in *Escola*, *res ipsa loquitur* enables a jury to draw inferences with regard to both breach and causation (provided that the court has first determined that determined that such inferences are permissible in the circumstances of the instant case). In § 328(D), "negligence" is not intended to mean the tort of the same name (which also requires proof of duty, causation and damage) but is really deployed simply as a synonym for "unreasonableness".

2. *Modification.* The American Law Institute has since modified its approach to *res ipsa loquitur* (see below) although, as noted before, the Restatements are not law. It is, accordingly, open to debate whether the approach of the Second or Third Restatement represents a more accurate reflection of the law.

Rizzo v. Corning, Inc.
105 F.3d 338 (7th Cir. 1997)

POSNER, C.J. Joseph Rizzo and his wife Margaret brought a products liability suit in federal district court under the diversity jurisdiction against the manufacturer of the "Mr. Coffee" coffeemaker and the manufacturer of the glass portion of the coffeemaker's carafe. A jury awarded damages of $182,000 to the plaintiffs (a part of the award was to Mrs. Rizzo, for loss of consortium), and the defendants appeal. The accident giving rise to the suit came about as follows. About five months after the purchase of the coffeemaker, while the Rizzos were having breakfast in their kitchen, Mr. Rizzo reached behind him for the carafe full of hot coffee to pour his wife a cup. He lifted the carafe from its perch on the warmer plate in the coffeemaker and at the exact moment when the carafe, in its journey toward his wife's cup, was directly over his lap, it broke in two, spilling the coffee (which was heated to between 170 and 180 degrees Fahrenheit) into Mr. Rizzo's lap and causing second-degree burns.

The plaintiffs tried to show that the carafe was defective. The defendants presented contrary evidence through their expert, a materials engineer employed by one of the defendants. They argued, and their expert testified, that Rizzo must have struck the wall with the carafe, weakening the carafe, which broke a moment later as a result.... The expert also testified that the Rizzos might have weakened the carafe by using abrasive cleansers to clean it; the Rizzos denied having used abrasive cleansers.

The plaintiffs tried to prove their case by two alternative routes. The first, and thoroughly conventional, was to show that the carafe had in fact a specific, demonstrable manufacturing defect. There was a small bump in the glass wall of the carafe where it had broken. The bump was a defect, and the plaintiffs tried to show that it had been the cause of the break. Alternatively, they relied on a form or variant of res ipsa loquitur that the Illinois courts recognize in products liability cases. Under this second approach, if the plaintiff can show that the product failed at a time or in a manner it would not be expected to fail merely through normal wear and tear, and can also show that the plaintiff did not misuse the product and that no "third force" (for example, a fire, an earthquake, or the mishandling of the product by a carrier or dealer, or by a house guest) — what the Illinois courts mysteriously refer to as a "secondary cause" — was present, the jury is allowed to infer, despite the absence of evidence of a specific defect, that the accident was indeed the result of a product defect for which the manufacturer is liable. See, e.g., *Tweedy v. Wright Ford Sales, Inc.*, 357 N.E.2d 449 (1976); *Welge v. Planters Lifesavers Co.*, 17 F.3d 209, 211, 213 (7th Cir.1994)....

The defendants raise other issues, but only one has sufficient merit to warrant discussion, and that is whether the case fits the *Tweedy* doctrine. They say that the doctrine was never intended for so fragile a product as a glass carafe, the breaking of which is likely to occur without any defect. What is true but off the point is that most carafes break not because they are defectively designed or manufactured but because, being indeed fragile, they are dropped or banged against something in shipment or use or are otherwise mishandled. When that happens, however, it happens because someone has dropped or banged or otherwise abused the carafe, which the jury was entitled to find had not occurred here, though there was some evidence that it had. The very fragility of the glass, so emphasized by the defendants, works against their argument by underscoring the unusual character of the product failure in this case. A carafe designed to be used for years, not months, breaks in half without being dropped or banged or cleaned with abrasive cleansers or damaged in a flood or fire. In these unusual circumstances the accident itself is sufficient evidence of a defect to permit, though of course not compel, the jury to infer a defect. Whether these were the circumstances of the accident was a jury question. The jury was not, as the defendants argue, required to disregard the Rizzos' testimony that they didn't bang the carafe against the wall or otherwise abuse it, merely because the testimony was self-serving. Self-serving it was; but the testimony of the defendants' expert, an employee of one of the defendants, could be considered equally self-serving.

Judgment for the plaintiffs affirmed.

Restatement (Third) of Torts: Products Liability (1998)

§ 3. Circumstantial Evidence Supporting Inference of Product Defect

It may be inferred that the harm sustained by the plaintiff was caused by a product defect existing at the time of sale or distribution, without proof of a specific defect, when the incident that harmed the plaintiff:

(a) was of a kind that ordinarily occurs as a result of product defect; and

(b) was not, in the particular case, solely the result of causes other than product defect existing at the time of sale or distribution.

Questions

1. In what ways does § 3 of the Restatement (Third) modify the test for the drawing of an inference in comparison to § 328(D) of the Restatement (Second)?

2. Are those changes significant or merely cosmetic?

3. Do those changes favor plaintiffs or defendants?

Negligence *per se*

Sometimes the law goes further than permitting the fact-finder—normally the jury—to draw inferences from known primary facts. It may instead mandate a finding of breach of duty in negligence as a matter of law because of a breach of a legislative or regulatory requirement laid down by the criminal or administrative law. This is known as "negligence *per se*": negligence in itself.

The idea of negligence *per se* is controversial in a number of respects. One is that it involves creating a rule of torts out of a provision originally found in criminal or administrative law. It is not a matter of the legislature or regulatory agency expressly attempting to create a new form of tort. Quite the reverse: the point of negligence *per se* is that it involves the courts' developing a rule of torts where the original criminal or legislative provision was silent. As § 285(b) of the Restatement (Second) of Torts (1965) puts it: "The standard of conduct of a reasonable man may be … adopted by the court from a legislative enactment or an administrative regulation which does not so provide." This is done by means of a four-step process, which asks:

1. Was the plaintiff in the instant case a member of the class of persons whom the original provision was designed to protect?

2. Was the harm suffered by the plaintiff of the type that the original provision was designed to prevent or deter?

3. Would the policy behind the original provision be appropriately served by using it to impose civil liability? (See *Frederick L. v. Thomas*, 578 F.2d 513, 517 (1978)).

4. Is it possible to make the rule sufficiently precise?

Unfortunately, § 14 of the Restatement (Third) of Torts: Liability for Physical and Emotional Harm (2010) is defective in that it mentions only the first two issues. In fact, all four of these questions must be answered in the affirmative in order for a form of negligence *per se* to be recognized. The first two are clearly substitutes for the regular common law rules in negligence regarding duty of care and proximate cause respectively. Duty is always a matter for the judge in any event, so the first test is quite uncontroversial in principle (although it is often difficult to identify the relevant class in practice). Conversely, while proximate cause is theoretically a matter for the jury, it is actually often amenable to summary judgment because the courts are keen to establish boundaries beyond which liability will not be found, and so the notion embodied by the second test is also relatively unproblematic in principle.

In *Stanton by Brooks v. Astra Pharmaceutical Products, Inc.*, 718 F.2d 553 (1983), for example, Harrikah Stanton, an eight-month-old infant, had a bone-marrow test in December 1971 to determine the cause of the hemolytic anemia from which she had suffered since birth. In performing the test, the hematologist injected a two-percent solution of Xylocaine into Harrikah's right posterior iliac crest to anesthetize the area from which he would aspirate bone marrow. Shortly after the procedure, Harrikah began convulsing and experienced cardiac and respiratory arrest. Attempts to resuscitate her had little effect. The cardiac arrest resulted in severe and irreversible brain damage, so that she was rendered unable to walk, talk, or stand and requiring constant care for the rest of her life. It subsequently became apparent that Astra, the manufacturer of Xylocaine, had failed to file with the Food and Drug Administration (the "FDA") certain reports about the drug, as required by federal statutes and regulations. In the United States Court of Appeals for the Third Circuit, Becker J. commented:

Under Pennsylvania law, the violation of a governmental safety regulation constitutes negligence per se if the regulation "was, in part, intended to protect the
interest of another as an individual [and] the interest of the plaintiff which was
invaded ... was one which the act intended to protect." *Majors v. Brodhead Hotel*,
416 Pa. 265, 268, 205 A.2d 873, 875 (1965). Astra cannot seriously dispute that
section 130.35 was promulgated to protect individuals such as Harrikah Stanton from precisely the type of harm that here occurred—an unexpected adverse
reaction to Xylocaine. It thus would appear that Astra's failure to file the reports
constituted negligence per se.

The third test, however, effectively sees the jury's ability to infer matters of fact being replaced by the court's inferring the policy behind the original criminal or administrative
provision, and then deciding whether that policy is furthered or hindered by the development of a new rule in torts. As was said in *Gorton v. J.W. Mashburn*, 995 P.2d 1114, 1117
(Okla.1999), it cannot "affront the Legislature's declared intent." Nevertheless, negligence
per se is still a form of common law negligence, for it is the courts who decide to develop
the law in this matter. This can, however, be problematic when the original criminal or
administrative provision is part of federal law. Since tort law is a matter for the states individually, the invocation of negligence *per se* in respect of a federal provision seems to
some commentators to involve an improper usurpation of state sovereignty. However,
this is hardly a usurpation by the federal government, since it is the judiciary of each state
who decide whether or not to recognize negligence *per se* in respect of particular enactments or regulations. On this basis, if there is a usurpation of a state's sovereignty, it can
only be carried out by the judicial branch of that state's own government. Perhaps, rather,
it involves an improper infringement of federal power by the state. In *In re Bendectin Litigation*, 857 F.2d 290, 313–14 (1988), before the United States Court of Appeals for the
Sixth Circuit, Engel C.J. commented:

An additional issue that arises in considering the negligence per se argument,
but which we do not address here, concerns whether Congress intended the
[Food, Drug and Cosmetic Act (FDCA), 21 U.S.C. § 301 *et seq.*] to be used as a
behaviorial standard in such cases. It is clear that whether a state chooses to recognize violations of its own statutes as negligence per se is purely a question of
state law. Therefore, states like Ohio are perfectly free to apply the negligence
per se doctrine to violations of its own pure food and drug law, Ohio Revised Code
sections 3715.52 and 3715.64. However, the determination that a violation of a
federal statute such as the FDCA will create state tort liability is not a matter
solely of state law. A state's ability to use a federal statute violation as a basis for
state tort liability and negligence per se depends on the intent of Congress, and
not merely on the intent of the state. Thus, the congressional decision not to
provide a private cause of action under the FDCA becomes quite important in
considering the propriety of a state negligence per se action for violation of the
FDCA. "It may be that a decision by Congress not to create a private remedy is
intended to preclude all private enforcement. If that is so, then a state cause of
action that makes relief available to private individuals for violations of the FDCA
is pre-empted." *Merrell Dow v. Thompson*, 106 S.Ct. at 3245 (Brennan, J., dissenting).... We recognize that a mere congressional intent to preclude a private
right of action at the federal level for violations of the FDCA would not necessarily indicate that Congress intended to preclude a state remedy under a theory
of negligence per se. We only observe that preemption could be yet another obstacle to plaintiffs' reliance on a theory of negligence per se.

The fourth test relates to the question of breach, which is normally a matter for case-by-case determination by a jury. Yet the idea of negligence *per se* is that breach ceases to be amenable to such fact-finding and is determined instead by a systemic rule of law which is to be applied by the court. Thus a standard that is vague or confused cannot form the basis of negligence *per se*.

Dougherty v. Santa Fe Marine, Inc.

698 F.2d 232 (5th Cir. 1983)

PER CURIAM. This case arises out of an accident on the *Bluewater II*, a mobile offshore drilling barge owned by Santa Fe Marine, Inc. The accident involved a lifeboat manufactured by Watercraft America, Inc. Four of the men who were injured brought this action against Santa Fe Marine and Watercraft alleging a negligent failure to warn. All claims brought against Santa Fe were settled before trial. After the trial, the jury returned a verdict in favor of Watercraft and against all the plaintiffs. Plaintiffs argue that the district court erred in failing to instruct the jury that Watercraft was negligent per se. They also argue that the jury's verdict was contrary to the weight of the evidence. We reject both these arguments and affirm the judgment of the district court.

The lifeboats on the *Bluewater II* were suspended sixty feet above the water from davits extending over the side of the rig. There are two ways to place one of the lifeboats into the water. The first way is to pull on a white cable which hangs from the ceiling of the boat. This procedure allows the boat to descend at a controlled rate of speed. The second way is to pull a release lever located near the boat operator's station. When this lever is pulled, the boat is immediately disconnected from the cables that support it. This causes the boat to drop into the water.

During the course of a weekly emergency drill, part of the crew on *Bluewater II* gathered around to view a demonstration on how to lower one of the vessel's lifeboats into the water. Five men, including the plaintiffs, entered the lifeboat. In attempting to lower the boat a few feet, Howard Smith, one of the plaintiffs, pulled the wrong lever. The boat plummeted sixty feet into the water below.

The plaintiffs alleged at trial that Watercraft did not adequately warn them of the dangerous consequences that would result from pulling the release lever. They argued that Watercraft's violation of certain Coast Guard regulations constituted negligence per se.

As noted above, *Bluewater II* is a mobile offshore drilling unit. Subchapter I-A of Title 46 of the Code of Federal Regulations is entitled "Mobile Offshore Drilling Units." The purpose of this subchapter is to prescribe "rules for the design, construction, equipment, inspection and operation of mobile offshore drilling units operating under the U.S. flag." 46 C.F.R. § 107.01. Part 108 of the subchapter regulates the design of drilling units and the equipment that must be used on them.

Subpart B deals with equipment markings and instructions. Section 108.645(b) provides:

> Each mechanical disengaging apparatus control lever must be colored red with the following marked on or next to the lever: "DANGER—LEVER DROPS BOAT" or "DANGER—LEVER RELEASES HOOKS".

Unfortunately, § 108.645(b) is not the only regulation on point. Section 108.507(a)(1) requires all drilling units to have launching equipment for each lifeboat with mechanical disengaging apparatus "that is approved under Subpart 160.033 of this chapter." ...

There is a significant difference between the language of the two sections. While § 108.507(a)(1) and § 160.033-3(b) require the warning to be placed on the lever, § 108.645(b) allows the warning to be placed on or next to the lever. The difficulty in this case arises because Watercraft located the required warning next to the release lever rather than on it.

Faced with these conflicting regulations, the district court read both sections to the jury, but refused to instruct them that a violation of any of the relevant regulations in the context of this case would be negligence per se. The plaintiffs argue that this conclusion was in error. We disagree. Under the unique circumstances of this case, the district court's solution to the problem is an eminently reasonable one.

When the doctrine of negligence per se applies, the general standard of care of a reasonable man is replaced by a specific rule of conduct established in a statute or regulation. The failure to follow any Coast Guard regulation which is the cause of an injury establishes negligence per se.

Implicit in virtually all discussions of negligence per se is the unspoken assumption that the regulation in question establishes a clear minimum standard of care. If the regulation fails to do so, the reason for applying the doctrine fades. An ambiguous or contradictory regulatory standard defeats the certainty on which the rule of per se liability rests. Persons affected are deprived of a sure standard upon which they may fashion their affairs. See Restatement (Second) of Torts § 874A. (The specificity of a regulation is a relevant consideration in determining whether the doctrine should be applied.)

The regulations involved in this dispute do not establish a clear minimum standard of care. One regulation permitted Watercraft to locate the warning sign exactly where it did — next to the lever. The other regulation mandated that the warning be placed only on the lever. Watercraft was faced with conflicting directions. Using the illumination of reflective hindsight, we can say that a reasonable manufacturer in Watercraft's position might have complied with the stricter regulation. In that way, the company could have met the requirements of both regulations. Little or no additional cost would have been incurred. But the determination of whether Watercraft did what a reasonable manufacturer would have done when it read the regulations and made its design decision is a question for the jury. The district court committed no error in instructing the jury that a violation of § 108.507, § 160.033-3(b), or § 108.645(b) did not constitute negligence per se.

Of course, such regulations should not be ignored. In the case at bar, the jury should have considered them as illustrative of a reasonable manufacturer's conduct. The district court correctly charged the jury to this effect....

Judgment of the district court affirmed.

Comparing Three Forms of Action

It will, by now, be apparent that the development of the law in warranty, misrepresentation, and negligence over the last century or so has led to there being many overlaps between them in cases of apparently defective products. As will be seen in Part II, the distinct law of strict products liability that was born after the Second World War has created even more overlaps, perhaps because some of what is now considered to be covered by strict products liability doctrine is really much the same as the law of warranty, misrepresentation, and negligence — but with a new name. That controversy can, however, be postponed to Part II. What remains now is to compare the advantages and disadvantages to claims brought within the three branches of the law that we have already considered. These are tabulated in Figure 5.2.

Figure 5.2 Alternative Forms of Action

	Form of Action		
	Breach of Warranty	**Misrepresentation**	**Negligence**
Branch of Law	Contracts	Torts	Torts
Privity Required	Vertical privity or collateral warranty, plus horizontal privity	No longer required (but entering into privity may show reliance)	No, but duty of care required instead
Type of Liability	Strict (i.e. no fault required)	Fault typically required (i.e. fraud or negligence)	Fault required (i.e. negligence), but may be inferred
Causation of Harm	Failure of product to meet warranty must have caused harm; no reliance required	Reliance on representation must have caused harm	Product must have caused harm; may be inferred if circumstances warrant
Ease of Exclusion	High	Low (unless deemed puffery)	Medium
Punitive Damages	No	Often	Rarely

Perhaps the most important point to note is that the distinction between contracts and torts seems to matter in essentially two respects, which are undoubtedly connected. The first is that liability in contracts for breach of warranty is strict, whereas liability in torts for either misrepresentation or negligence requires proof of fault, albeit that this may be relaxed through the doctrines of *res ipsa loquitur* and/or negligence *per se*. (It is true that liability for innocent misrepresentation is strict but, as we saw in Chapter 4, it is seldom pleaded.) The second is that punitive damages are not available for contractual breaches of warranty, though they are available (according to the degree of culpability) in the torts of both misrepresentation and negligence.

As we move onto Part II, and see the development of a wholly new, discrete area of products liability law from the 1940s onwards, many of these same issues will re-appear, albeit in different form. Product manufacturers and distributors will continue to be liable only to those to whom they owe a duty of care. Similarly, the notion of product defects—whether as a result of flaws in manufacturing, design, or accompanying warnings—will take the place of the concept of breach in negligence, and there will be considerable controversy as to whether proof of such defects necessitates proof of negligence or is a matter of strict liability. In Part III, we shall see that proof of causation remains a very hot topic, and that the courts have been busy—especially in asbestos-related cases, where any injury suffered typically has a very long latency period—considering whether, when, and how to fashion special rules somewhat analogous to the notions of *res ipsa loquitur* and negligence *per se*. In Chapter 13, we shall revisit the question of whether attempts to disclaim liability may be effective; while in Chapter 18, by contrast, we shall see that many cases are less about liability, and more about whether punitive damages may be awarded (and, if so, of what amount).

Questions

1. Why is there a need to prove privity for actions for breach of warranty, and a requirement to prove duty of care for actions in negligence, but no need to prove any analogous requirement for actions in misrepresentation?

2. Is it true to say that one of these branches of the law is more favorable to victims (or to prospective defendants) than the others? If so, which is it?

Hypothetical

Dwayne bought a rocking-chair, made by Woodcraft, through the internet website WeSell.com, which had described the item as: "Perfect for sitting outside, enjoying balmy evenings (friends optional)." After it was delivered and he had unpacked it, Dwayne put the rocking-chair on his front porch and looked forward to sitting in it later that evening. Then he went out to the supermarket to buy some refreshment to enjoy while sitting in his new chair. While he was out, 13-year-old Amy came past the house as she walked her dog, Patch. Patch wanted to sniff some plants in Dawyne's front yard so, while still keeping Patch on the leash, Amy went on to Dwayne's front porch and sat in the rocking-chair. It immediately collapsed beneath her and, as she fell, she hit her head. Some neighbors, who saw what happened, called an ambulance (and held on to Patch). Subsequent inspection has shown that little or no glue had been applied to the joints in the rocking-chair. What is Amy's legal position?

Part II

Product Defects

Chapter 6

Manufacturing Defects

From Caveat Emptor in Contracts to
Strict Liability in Torts

The following extract neatly summarizes the history of the law—already discussed in Part I—before a specialist body of products liability law was developed.

Richard C. Ausness, From Caveat Emptor to Strict Liability:
A Review of Products Liability in Florida
24 U. Fla. L. Rev. 410 (1971–72)

Since the doctrine of *caveat emptor* gave way to a more enlightened response, the courts have struggled to place the law of products liability on a proper doctrinal foundation. Negligence, implied warranty, and strict liability have been used, but as yet no universally accepted theory has emerged....

During the nineteenth century the leading English Case, *Winterbottom v. Wright*, was interpreted by American courts to limit the seller's liability for defective products, even in tort, to those in privity with him. The privity requirement continued until 1916 when the celebrated opinion of Justice Cardozo in *MacPherson v. Buick Motor Co.* dismissed privity from products liability actions in negligence. The *MacPherson* decision was accorded immediate acceptance and has been universally followed. Its reasoning has been extended to members of the purchaser's family, employees, subsequent purchasers, others users of the chattel, and bystanders, as well as to property damage. Although the plaintiff's burden in negligence was eased by a constant tightening of the seller's standard of care and by liberal use of *res ipsa loquitur*, considerable pressure remained for the application of some principle of liability without fault.

In 1913, after prolonged agitation over unwholesome food, Washington, followed by Kansas, Mississippi, and other states, dispensed with the requirement of privity where food was involved. Numerous theories were offered to justify the imposition of liability upon sellers in the absence of both negligence and privity of contract. Finally, in 1927 the Mississippi court proposed the idea of an implied warranty running with the goods from the manufacturer to the consumer similar to a covenant running with land. This proposition was later discarded for the theory of an implied warranty made directly to the consumer, but since that time implied warranty has served as the basis of a seller's liability for food as well as other products.

A warranty, implied from the nature of the transaction or the relative situations of the parties, arises by operation of law, irrespective of the seller's intention. However, it is still associated with contract principles such as privity. Warranty, to the extent it is available to the litigant, is superior to negligence because it imposes a form of liability without fault upon the seller of goods. Defenses such as contributory negligence and assumption of risk are not entirely effective, since the defendant's standard of care is not normally at issue. The privity requirement has also been circumvented in a number of cases holding that commercial advertising and labeling techniques of manufacturers give rise to express warranties upon which the ultimate consumer is entitled to rely. Thus, the plaintiff's chances of prevailing are somewhat better when the suit proceeds under warranty theory.

A third form of products liability has rejected warranty language entirely and has predicated liability purely in tort. This was first proposed in the Restatement of Torts and was applied by the California Supreme Court in *Greenman v. Yuba Power Products, Inc.* Strict liability is regarded by some authorities as superior to implied warranty because it avoids such pitfalls as privity, disclaimers, and other unwanted legacies of the law of sales....

Strict Products Liability for Food

As Ausness suggests, strict products liability in torts for defective products was first adopted in relation to the sale and distribution of food. It has now become so entrenched in the law as to have been given its own section in the Products Liability Restatement.

Restatement (Third) of Torts: Products Liability (1998)

§ 7. Liability of Commercial Seller or Distributor for Harm Caused by Defective Food Products

One engaged in the business of selling or otherwise distributing food products who sells or distributes a food product that is defective under § 2, § 3, or § 4 is subject to liability for harm to persons or property caused by the defect. Under § 2(a), a harm-causing ingredient of the food product constitutes a defect if a reasonable consumer would not expect the food product to contain that ingredient.

Notes

"Consumer expectations" or "foreign objects" in food? The main question regarding liability for defective food has concerned how to determine whether food is defective. Jurisdictions have been split between the so-called "consumer expectations" and "foreign objects" tests. In *Zabner v. Howard Johnson's Inc*, 201 So.2d 824 (1967), the Fourth District Court of Appeal in Florida held that the question for the jury was whether a restaurant patron, who suffered punctured upper gums and fracture of teeth as result of the presence of a piece of walnut shell concealed in a walnut ice cream, might have reasonably expected to find a piece of shell in the food served. The matter was revisited in the more recent case below.

Schafer v. J.L.C. Food Systems, Inc.

695 N.W.2d 570 (2005) (Supreme Court of Minnesota)

PAGE, J. The underlying facts of this case are relatively simple and straightforward. On January 27, 2001, Karen Schafer went to a Perkins Restaurant in St. Cloud, Minnesota, with a friend and their daughters. At the restaurant, Schafer ordered a pumpkin muffin. She unwrapped the muffin and, using her fork, placed a piece of the muffin in her mouth.

Upon swallowing, she immediately felt a "sharp pain" in her throat and "a choking sensation." After drinking some water and still feeling as though there was something stuck in her throat, Schafer went directly to a hospital emergency room. Before leaving the restaurant, Schafer's friend notified a Perkins employee that, as a result of swallowing a piece of the muffin, Schafer was going to the emergency room. The rest of the muffin was not saved.

At the hospital, a doctor told Schafer that she had a cut on her throat, but the doctor did not observe any object that would have caused the cut. Schafer was prescribed a painkiller and released. Two days later, she returned to the emergency room where she was diagnosed with a throat infection and was hospitalized for three days. According to Schafer, it took her about three months to fully recover. Although Schafer is not able to identify what was in the muffin that caused the problems with her throat, she speculated in her deposition that "it had to have been something sharp and hard."

Schafer sued Perkins, alleging that the pumpkin muffin was in a defective condition unreasonably dangerous to consumers, the defective condition was a direct cause of the injury to her throat, and, as a result of the injury, she suffered damages in the form of medical expenses, loss of earnings, pain, disability, and emotional distress. Perkins, in turn, asserted a third-party claim for contribution against Foxtail Foods, the company that manufactured the muffin mix Perkins used to make the pumpkin muffin.

After some discovery, Perkins and Foxtail moved for summary judgment, arguing that Schafer had failed to establish a prima facie case of negligence because she could not identify the object in the muffin that caused her injury. The district court granted summary judgment on that basis and the court of appeals affirmed. In affirming, the court of appeals relied on *Kneibel v. RRM Enterprises*, 506 N.W.2d 664 (Minn.App.1993). *Kneibel* involved a case in which the plaintiff had eaten barbecued spareribs served by a restaurant. At some point, while chewing on meat from the ribs, the plaintiff heard and felt a "crack" in his mouth and reflexively swallowed the food. It was eventually determined that the plaintiff had cracked an otherwise healthy tooth all the way to the jaw. The plaintiff was unable to determine what object, if any, caused the cracking sensation that resulted in the broken tooth. The plaintiff sued the restaurant and others. The defendants moved for summary judgment, which was granted, and the court of appeals affirmed on the basis that the plaintiff's failure to present evidence identifying the object that caused the alleged harm precluded him from establishing negligence.

On an appeal from summary judgment, we ask two questions: (1) whether there are any genuine issues of material fact; and (2) whether the lower courts erred in their application of the law. In a negligence action, the defendant is entitled to summary judgment when the record reflects a complete lack of proof on any of the four essential elements of the claim: (1) the existence of a duty of care; (2) a breach of that duty; (3) an injury; and (4) the breach of the duty being the proximate cause of the injury. The elements most relevant in this case are proximate cause and breach....

To determine the viability of Schafer's claim, we must first establish the proper standard for assessing whether a food product is defective. We note that courts across the country have diverged on the proper test to apply in determining whether food containing an injurious object is actionable. Some courts follow what has been referred to as the "foreign-natural" test, while others have adopted what has become known as the "reasonable expectation" test....

The foreign-natural test draws a distinction between the "foreign" and "natural" characteristics of a food product ingredient. Under the test, if an object or substance in a food

product is natural to any of the ingredients of the product, there is no liability for injuries caused; if the object or substance is foreign to any of the ingredients, the seller or
manufacturer of the product may be liable for any injury caused.

The bright-line rule set out in the foreign-natural test, which assumes that all substances that are natural to the food in one stage or another of preparation are in fact anticipated by the ordinary consumer in the final product served, has been called into
question. For example, in *Betehia v. Cape Cod Corp.*, 10 Wis.2d 323, 103 N.W.2d 64
(1960), a restaurant patron was injured by a chicken bone in a chicken sandwich and
sued the restaurant for breach of implied warranty of fitness and for negligence. The
court concluded that it did not logically follow that consumers should expect that every
product containing some chicken must as a matter of law occasionally or frequently contain chicken bones or chicken-bone slivers simply because chicken bones were natural to
chicken meat. Thus, the court concluded that categorizing a substance as foreign or natural might have some importance in determining the degree of negligence of the proces-
sor of food, but it was not determinative of what was unfit or harmful for human
consumption. The court further concluded that the naturalness of a substance to a food
served was important only in determining whether the consumer might reasonably expect to find such substance in the particular type of food served.

Comparatively, the reasonable expectation test focuses on what is reasonably expected
by the consumer in the food product as served, not what might be foreign or natural to
the ingredients of that product before preparation. As applied to common-law negligence, the reasonable expectation test is related to the foreseeability of harm on the part
of the defendant; that is, the defendant has the duty of ordinary care to eliminate or remove in the preparation of the food served such harmful substance as the consumer of
the food, as served, would not ordinarily anticipate and guard against. The majority of
jurisdictions that have dealt with the defective food products issue have adopted some
formulation of the reasonable expectation test....

Under the Restatement approach, consumer expectations are based on culturally defined, widely shared standards allowing a seller's liability to be resolved by judges and triers of fact based on their assessment of what consumers have a right to expect from
preparation of the food in question. The Reporters to the Restatement note that the majority view is unanimously favored by law review commentators.

Having considered the two tests and the approach taken by the Restatement, we conclude that the reasonable expectation test is the more appropriate test to follow. Instead
of drawing arbitrary distinctions between foreign and natural substances that caused
harm, relying on consumers' reasonable expectations is likely to yield a more equitable
result. After all, an unexpected natural object or substance contained in a food product,
such as a chicken bone in chicken soup, can cause as much harm as a foreign object or
substance, such as a piece of glass in the same soup. Therefore, we agree with the majority
view and expressly adopt the reasonable expectation test as the standard for determining
defective food products liability claims in Minnesota. Accordingly, when a person suffers
injury from consuming a food product, the manufacturer, seller, or distributor of the
food product is liable to the extent that the injury-causing object or substance in the food
product would not be reasonably expected by an ordinary consumer. Whether the injury-causing object or substance in the food product is reasonably expected by an ordinary consumer presents a jury question in most cases.

Having identified the test to be applied for determining liability in defective food products cases, we now turn to the primary question presented by this case: whether circum-

stantial evidence may be used to establish a prima facie defective food products claim in cases in which the specific harm-causing object or substance cannot be identified. At oral argument, Schafer argued and Perkins and Foxtail conceded that circumstantial evidence should be available for such purposes. Perkins and Foxtail argued, however, that the circumstantial evidence available in this case was insufficient to permit Schafer's claim to go forward.

As noted, the court of appeals relied on *Kneibel* in affirming the dismissal of Schafer's lawsuit. In *Kneibel*, the court of appeals held that the claim of a plaintiff in a defective food products case could not withstand summary judgment because he failed to present sufficient evidence identifying the harm-causing object. It has been observed that this bright-line rule "[r]equiring the plaintiff to prove a 'clear defect' seemed unduly harsh under the circumstances" in *Kneibel*. Mike Steenson, *A Comparative Analysis of Minnesota Products Liability Law and the Restatement (Third) of Torts: Products Liability*, 24 Wm. Mitchell L. Rev. 1, 50 (1998). As Professor Steenson noted, the issue in cases such as *Kneibel* is "not whether the plaintiff is able to prove that a harmful agent is 'clearly defective,' but rather whether the facts justify an inference that the product is defective." In our view, the *Kneibel* rule is unduly restrictive.

We agree with the parties that when the specific harm-causing object is not known circumstantial evidence should be available, if such evidence is sufficient and other causes are adequately eliminated, for purposes of submitting the issue of liability to the jury in defective food products cases. Permitting the use of circumstantial evidence in such cases is consistent with our jurisprudence on the use of circumstantial evidence to infer negligence in other contexts. For example, in a case involving an exploding soft drink bottle, we observed that circumstantial evidence was sufficient to take the case to the jury even though the plaintiff was not able to establish a specific defect in the bottle.

The use of circumstantial evidence, however, is not without limits, nor should it be. In order to address defendants' legitimate concerns about a lack of boundaries for such claims, we hold that in defective food products cases a plaintiff may reach the jury, without direct proof of the specific injury-causing object or substance, when the plaintiff establishes by reasonable inference from circumstantial evidence that: (1) the injury-causing event was of a kind that would ordinarily only occur as a result of a defective condition in the food product; (2) the defendant was responsible for a condition that was the cause of the injury; and (3) the injury-causing event was not caused by anything other than a food product defect existing at the time of the food product's sale. In order to forestall summary judgment, each of the three elements must be met.

Finally, we must apply the test set out above to the facts presented in this case to determine whether Schafer's claim can withstand summary judgment. The record presented here establishes that Schafer purchased a pumpkin muffin at a Perkins restaurant, began eating the muffin while at the restaurant, and experienced a sharp pain and choking sensation immediately after swallowing her first bite of the muffin. According to Schafer, the pain must have been caused by a hard, sharp object. Such an occurrence is not the kind of event that an ordinary consumer would anticipate and guard against. Although the harm-causing object was never identified, Schafer immediately reported her experience to a Perkins employee and went directly to a hospital emergency room. Moreover, the events leading to Schafer's injury occurred in the presence of witnesses, Schafer's friend and their daughters. At the hospital, the doctor who examined Schafer found a cut on her throat. There is no allegation that Schafer had any throat-related ailment immediately preceding her swallowing the first bite of the muffin.

Viewing the circumstantial evidence in the record before us in the light most favorable to Schafer, we conclude that a jury could reasonably infer that Schafer's alleged injury is of a kind that would ordinarily only occur as a result of a defective condition in the pumpkin muffin served by Perkins, that Perkins was responsible for making the pumpkin muffin that caused Schafer's throat injury, and that Schafer's injury was not caused by anything other than a defect in the pumpkin muffin existing at the time of the muffin's sale. Although there may be other evidence available bearing on the severity of Schafer's injury or on Perkins' possible negligence or on Foxtail's potential responsibility, those facts are not in the record. Indeed, the lawyer for one of the respondents conceded at oral argument that summary judgment may have been premature given the record. Thus, we conclude, based on the evidence presented, that there is sufficient evidence for Schafer's claim to go forward and therefore remand to the district court for further proceedings consistent with this opinion.

Reversed and remanded to the district court.

Notes

1. *Role of inference in proving defect and causation.* As an appeal from summary judgment, the evidence must be viewed in the light most favorable to the appellant. Even so, it is striking that the Supreme Court's ruling expressly permits a plaintiff to rely on a jury's drawing reasonable inferences from the proven facts, as in the cases of *res ipsa loquitur* discussed in Chapter 5 in relation to claims of negligence. The absence of the alleged "harm-causing object" is thus not necessarily considered fatal to the plaintiff's case in relation to proof either of product defect, or of causation of harm.

2. *Systemic problem of proving specific causation.* Note, however, that even if the plaintiff had been able to produce the alleged "harm-causing object," this still would not have provided any direct proof that it had caused the harm. What it would have done, instead, is to increase the plausibility of such an inference. As we shall see in Chapter 9, proving that a specific agent caused a specific harm is a generic problem in products liability cases. Even if there is clear proof both of product defect and of harm to the user or consumer (and/or his or her property), the mechanism of causation is seldom self-evident. Thus it is frequently necessary to consider what inferences can appropriately be drawn from the known evidence.

3. *Duty and strict liability.* Although the Supreme Court of Minnesota in *Schafer* noted that "[t]he elements most relevant in this case are proximate cause and breach," this was because there was no doubt both that Perkins owed Schafer a duty and that Schafer suffered an injury. While the move from negligence to strict liability effectively means that a plaintiff no longer has any need to prove breach, all the other elements from the law of negligence remain in place for a claim of strict products liability.

We have already seen in Chapter 1, for example, that any liability of a seller or distributor of a defective product is restricted to injuries suffered by foreseeable individuals. While it is clear that the user/consumer has a right to compensation for any injury caused by a defective product, others will have a similar claim only if they could "reasonably be expected to be in the vicinity of the product during its reasonably expected use." See *Stegemoller v. ACandS, Inc.*, 767 N.E.2d 974, 975 (Ind.2002), discussed in Chapter 1.

Strict Products Liability at Large

We saw in Chapter 5 how, in *Escola v. Coca Cola Bottling Co.*, 24 Cal.2d 453 (1944), Chief Justice Gibson was prepared to relax both the fault and causation requirements of the tort of negligence by drawing inferences from known primary facts. Nevertheless, this did not go far enough for his colleague, Justice Traynor, whose concurrence provided the original justification for the development of a discrete body of no-fault products liability law.

Escola v. Coca Cola Bottling Co.

150 P.2d 436 (1944) (Supreme Court of California)

[For the facts, see Chapter 5.] TRAYNOR J. I concur in the judgment, but I believe the manufacturer's negligence should no longer be singled out as the basis of a plaintiff's right to recover in cases like the present one. In my opinion it should now be recognized that a manufacturer incurs an absolute liability when an article that he has placed on the market, knowing that it is to be used without inspection, proves to have a defect that causes injury to human beings. *McPherson v. Buick Motor Co.*, established the principle, recognized by this court, that irrespective of privity of contract, the manufacturer is responsible for an injury caused by such an article to any person who comes in lawful contact with it. In these cases the source of the manufacturer's liability was his negligence in the manufacturing process or in the inspection of component parts supplied by others. Even if there is no negligence, however, public policy demands that responsibility be fixed wherever it will most effectively reduce the hazards to life and health inherent in defective products that reach the market. It is evident that the manufacturer can anticipate some hazards and guard against the recurrence of others, as the public cannot. Those who suffer injury from defective products are unprepared to meet its consequences. The cost of an injury and the loss of time or health may be an overwhelming misfortune to the person injured, and a needless one, for the risk of injury can be insured by the manufacturer and distributed among the public as a cost of doing business. It is to the public interest to discourage the marketing of products having defects that are a menace to the public. If such products nevertheless find their way into the market it is to the public interest to place the responsibility for whatever injury they may cause upon the manufacturer, who, even if he is not negligent in the manufacture of the product, is responsible for its reaching the market. However intermittently such injuries may occur and however haphazardly they may strike, the risk of their occurrence is a constant risk and a general one. Against such a risk there should be general and constant protection and the manufacturer is best situated to afford such protection.

The injury from a defective product does not become a matter of indifference because the defect arises from causes other than the negligence of the manufacturer, such as negligence of a submanufacturer of a component part whose defects could not be revealed by inspection ... or unknown causes that even by the device of res ipsa loquitur cannot be classified as negligence of the manufacturer. The inference of negligence may be dispelled by an affirmative showing of proper care.... An injured person, however, is not ordinarily in a position to refute such evidence or identify the cause of the defect, for he can hardly be familiar with the manufacturing process as the manufacturer himself is. In leaving it to the jury to decide whether the inference has been dispelled, regardless of the evidence against it, the negligence rule approaches the rule of strict liability. It is needlessly circuitous to make negligence the basis of recovery and impose what is in reality liability without negligence. If public policy demands that a manufacturer of goods be responsible for their quality regardless of negligence there is no reason not to fix that responsibility openly.

Notes

1. *Defect and negligence.* The first point of significance in Justice Traynor's judgment is that he noted—contrary to the apparent assumption of Cardozo J. in *MacPherson*—that the finding of a defect in a product is not necessarily synonymous with a finding of negligence by its manufacturer. Some defects may arise without any fault on the part of the manufacturer, whether caused by others or by unknown factors of which the manufacturer cannot be expected to be aware. It is therefore important to distinguish the *quality of the product* from *the conduct of its manufacturer.*

2. *Two innocent parties.* Because he recognized this distinction, Justice Traynor was alive to the likelihood that individuals will be injured by products that are defective through no fault of the manufacturer. If there is to be liability only where negligence can be proved (or inferred by means of the doctrine of *res ipsa loquitur*), then any such victims will be unable to obtain compensation. This left the courts with a choice as to which of the two (both essentially innocent) parties—consumer or manufacturer—should bear the financial burden of such harm. He reasoned that a manufacturer would be more easily able to bear such losses, so that public policy required that the law be amended to achieve precisely that result.

3. *Contracts and torts revisited.* Justice Traynor argued (150 P.2d 436, 466) that the appropriate means of doing so was to transform the hitherto contractual notion of warranty—which already rested on strict liability—into a doctrine applicable within the law of torts. Thus he proposed (150 P.2d 436, 467) that liability should rest on a theory analogous—but not identical—to the notion of an implied term of merchantability:

> The manufacturer's liability should, of course, be defined in terms of the safety of the product in normal and proper use, and should not extend to injuries that cannot be traced to the product as it reached the market.

4. *Patent and latent defects.* Thus, even according to Justice Traynor's view, the plaintiff is required to prove that the alleged defect in the product was present at the time of sale or distribution. If the defect was patently obvious at that time (or when subsequently used), then the defendant may have at least a partial defense of the victim's comparative fault. In practice, most litigated cases of product defect occur because a defect was latent and thus not easily discoverable.

Such defects may sometimes take a long time to manifest themselves. One study, B.P. Lanphear & C.R. Buncher, *Latent Period for Malignant Mesothelioma of Occupational Origin*, 34 J. Occup. Med. 718 (1992), found that the latency period in 96% of cases of the asbestos-related disease, mesothelioma, was over twenty years. Such delay does not, of itself, immunize a defendant from liability; but the plaintiff will be required to show that the defect did indeed exist at the time of sale or distribution by the defendant rather than developing subsequently, and this may be very hard to do so long after the event.

5. *From concurrence to orthodoxy.* Twenty years after *Escola*, Justice Traynor's idea of no-fault products liability in torts finally became orthodoxy in California.

Greenman v. Yuba Power Products, Inc.

377 P.2d 897 (1963) (Supreme Court of California)

TRAYNOR J. Plaintiff brought this action for damages against the retailer and the manufacturer of a Shopsmith, a combination power tool that could be used as a saw, drill, and wood lathe. He saw a Shopsmith demonstrated by the retailer and studied a brochure prepared by the manufacturer. He decided he wanted a Shopsmith for his home workshop, and his wife bought and gave him one for Christmas in 1955. In 1957 he bought the necessary attachments to use the Shopsmith as a lathe for turning a large piece of wood he wished to make into a chalice. After he had worked on the piece of wood several times without difficulty, it suddenly flew out of the machine and struck him on the forehead, inflicting serious injuries. About 10½ months later, he gave the retailer and the manufacturer written notice of claimed breaches of warranties and filed a complaint against them alleging such breaches and negligence.

After a trial before a jury, the court ruled that there was no evidence that the retailer was negligent or had breached any express warranty and that the manufacturer was not liable for the breach of any implied warranty. Accordingly, it submitted to the jury only the cause of action alleging breach of implied warranties against the retailer and the causes of action alleging negligence and breach of express warranties against the manufacturer. The jury returned a verdict for the retailer against plaintiff and for plaintiff against the manufacturer in the amount of $65,000. The trial court denied the manufacturer's motion for a new trial and entered judgment on the verdict. The manufacturer and plaintiff appeal. Plaintiff seeks a reversal of the part of the judgment in favor of the retailer, however, only in the event that the part of the judgment against the manufacturer is reversed.

Plaintiff introduced substantial evidence that his injuries were caused by defective design and construction of the Shopsmith. His expert witnesses testified that inadequate set screws were used to hold parts of the machine together so that normal vibration caused the tailstock of the lathe to move away from the piece of wood being turned permitting it to fly out of the lathe. They also testified that there were other more positive ways of fastening the parts of the machine together, the use of which would have prevented the accident. The jury could therefore reasonably have concluded that the manufacturer negligently constructed the Shopsmith. The jury could also reasonably have concluded that statements in the manufacturer's brochure were untrue, that they constituted express warranties, and that plaintiff's injuries were caused by their breach....

Moreover, to impose strict liability on the manufacturer under the circumstances of this case, it was not necessary for plaintiff to establish an express warranty ... A manufacturer is strictly liable in tort when an article he places on the market, knowing that it is to be used without inspection for defects, proves to have a defect that causes injury to a human being. Recognized first in the case of unwholesome food products, such liability has now been extended to a variety of other products that create as great or greater hazards if defective.

Although in these cases strict liability has usually been based on the theory of an express or implied warranty running from the manufacturer to the plaintiff, the abandonment of the requirement of a contract between them, the recognition that the liability is not assumed by agreement but imposed by law, and the refusal to permit the manufacturer to define the scope of its own responsibility for defective products make clear that the liability is not one governed by the law of contract warranties but by the law of strict liability in tort.

The judgment is affirmed.

Notes

1. *Strict and absolute liability.* Note that, in *Greenman*, Justice Traynor abandoned both the idea and the language of absolute liability, noting that: "Plaintiff introduced substantial evidence that his injuries were caused by defective design and construction of the Shopsmith." It was now established that products liability was not absolute (which implies an inability to plead an affirmative defense) but strict, a view confirmed the following year in *Vandermark v. Ford Motor Co.*, 61 Cal.2d 256, 261; 391 P.2d 168, 37 Cal.Rptr. 896 (1964), where Justice Traynor—again giving the judgment of a unanimous Supreme Court—extended such liability to retailers.

2. *Significance of Greenman.* It is hard to overstate the importance of *Greenman* in establishing, once and for all, a discrete body of strict liability law in torts for product defects. In 1996, the Association of Trial Lawyers of America celebrated its 50th anniversary by asking tort lawyers and law professors to nominate their top ten developments in tort law during the Association's existence, and *Greenman* headed the list. See Robert Jeffrey White, *Top 10 in Torts: Evolution in the Common Law*, 32 Trial 50 (1996). *MacPherson v. Buick Motor Co.*, 217 N.Y. 382, 111 N.E. 1050 (1916), had already established that manufacturers of defective products owe a duty of care in tort. Since the relevant tort was clearly that of negligence, this meant that a plaintiff had to prove a *prima facie* case involving duty, breach, causation, and damage. *Greenman*, however, eliminated the requirement to prove breach. It substituted instead a requirement to prove defect. Strict products liability in tort law had come of age.

3. *In his own words.* Roger Traynor, the judge who had not only started the ball rolling, but who had stayed on to see his views become accepted as orthodoxy, explained matters in his own words in a lecture given at the University of Tennessee in 1965, *The Ways and Meanings of Defective Products and Strict Liability*, 32 Tenn. L. Rev. 363, 364 (1964–65). By this time he had become Chief Justice of the Supreme Court of California:

> The *Winterbottom* rationale assumed that industry could not grow and prosper if it had to pay for any and all injuries its defective products caused.... It took time, a long stretch of it from 1842's *Winterbottom v. Wright* to 1916's *MacPherson v. Buick Motor Company*, for the courts to articulate their disquiet over the ever-widening zones in which the defective products of enterprise were set loose. Disquiet there was as injuries mounted and often went uncompensated in the wake of mass production and distribution. In many an opinion the question festered without satisfactory answer: Can enterprise hew to the line of the profit margin only by letting its victims fall where they may, redressing no more than the privity-privileged?

> When Judge Cardozo rejected so narrow a view, he raised the standard of care to normal by reasoning from what had long been obvious but unheeded. The manufacturer of automobiles often deals only with dealers, and the dealer resells the product to the consumer....

> With the manufacturer's liability thus expanded, courts soon progressed to a realization that it was not enough to raise to normal the manufacturer's standard of care in the making of the product. The safety of the product was also of primary concern. This insight led to the invocation of res ipsa loquitur to permit an inference of negligence from the presence of a defect in cases where there

was hardly a basis in common experience for concluding that a defect was probably caused by negligence. With more directness, though at first solely in food cases, the courts began to impose liability on the manufacturer without negligence when his defective product injured the consumer.

Restatement (Second) of Torts (1965)

§ 402A. Special Liability of Seller of Product for Physical Harm to User or Consumer

(1) One who sells any product in a defective condition unreasonably dangerous to the user or consumer or to his property is subject to liability for physical harm thereby caused to the ultimate user or consumer, or to his property, if

(a) the seller is engaged in the business of selling such a product, and

(b) it is expected to and does reach the user or consumer without substantial change in the condition in which it is sold.

(2) The rule stated in Subsection (1) applies although

(a) the seller has exercised all possible care in the preparation and sale of his product, and

(b) the user or consumer has not bought the product from or entered into any contractual relation with the seller.

Caveat

The Institute expresses no opinion as to whether the rules stated in this Section may not apply

(1) to harm to persons other than users or consumers;

(2) to the seller of a product expected to be processed or otherwise substantially changed before it reaches the user or consumer; or

(3) to the seller of a component part of a product to be assembled.

Notes

1. *Product defect and wrongful conduct.* Subsection (2)(a) plainly followed the California approach in making it clear that products liability does not require proof of negligence. It stated expressly that a defendant manufacturer or retailer cannot avoid liability by proving that it had taken reasonable care. As *Comment a* puts it: "The rule is one of strict liability, making the seller subject to liability to the user or consumer even though he has exercised all possible care in the preparation and sale of the product." Similarly, subsection (1) recognizes that any discrete body of products liability law must focus on the defectiveness of the product rather than on the potentially wrongful behavior of the defendant manufacturer or retailer.

2. *Unreasonable danger and consumer expectations.* Yet, rather than talking simply of a product's being in a "defective condition"—as Justice Traynor and the Supreme Court of California had laid down in *Greenman*—§ 402A declares that the plaintiff must prove an additional element: that the defect was "unreasonably dangerous." This suggests that, where a product is either "merely" defective or "only" dangerous to a "reasonable" degree, that will not be enough to found a claim of product liability. At the very least, this idea seems somewhat quaint. The Reporter, Professor Prosser, attempted to justify the addition of the requirement of "unreasonable danger" in Comment *i*, which explains:

[handwritten margin note:] Req. of the 2nd rest. Not req. in 3rd rstmt

"unreasonably dangerous"

> Many products cannot possibly be made entirely safe for all consumption, and any food or drug necessarily involves some risk of harm, if only from over-consumption. Ordinary sugar is a deadly poison to diabetics, and castor oil found use under Mussolini as an instrument of torture. That is not what is meant by "unreasonably dangerous" in this Section. The article sold must be dangerous to an extent beyond that which would be contemplated by the ordinary consumer who purchases it, with the ordinary knowledge common to the community as to its characteristics.

Prosser thus envisioned that the concept of "unreasonable danger" would encapsulate what is now known as the "Consumer Expectations Test."

3. *Unreasonable danger and floodgates. Comment i* continues:

> Good whiskey is not unreasonably dangerous merely because it will make some people drunk, and is especially dangerous to alcoholics; but bad whiskey, containing a dangerous amount of fuel oil, is unreasonably dangerous. Good tobacco is not unreasonably dangerous merely because the effects of smoking may be harmful; but tobacco containing something like marijuana may be unreasonably dangerous. Good butter is not unreasonably dangerous merely because, if such be the case, it deposits cholesterol in the arteries and leads to heart attacks; but bad butter, contaminated with poisonous fish oil, is unreasonably dangerous.

Thus it appears that Prosser was concerned that there was the potential for a floodgates problem for some hapless manufacturers. On further reflection, however, the justification in *Comment i* is simply trite. Of course whiskey contaminated with something dangerous is dangerous. Anything contaminated with something dangerous is dangerous! The statement is not so much an explanation as a tautology.

4. *Defect and proximate causation.* If the objective had been simply to reflect California jurisprudence up to that point, subsection (1) should have said something like: "One who sells a defective product is subject to liability for physical harm thereby caused to the ultimate user or consumer, or to his property ..." Requiring proof only of causation and defect would still have required proof that the harm sustained fell within the doctrine of scope of liability or, to put this in more old-fashioned language, it would still have required proof that the defect was the proximate cause of the harm. *Comment h* was uncontroversial in its recognition that the concept of "cause" in subsection (1) embraced the scope of liability as well as the factual cause of harm:

> A product is not in a defective condition when it is safe for normal handling and consumption. If the injury results from abnormal handling, as where a bottled beverage is knocked against a radiator to remove the cap, or from abnormal preparation for use, as where too much salt is added to food, or from abnormal consumption, as where a child eats too much candy and is made ill, the seller is not liable.

In such cases, there would clearly be a superseding cause which, as was seen in Chapter 5, is one of the two elements comprised in the scope of liability. The existence of such a superseding cause would eliminate the liability of the seller. See *e.g., Galbreath v. Engineering Construction Corp.*, 273 N.E.2d 121 (1971); *Straley v. Kimberly*, 687 N.E.2d 360 (1997); *Erkson v. Sears, Roebuck & Co.*, 841 S.W.2d 207 (1992); *Port Authority of New York & New Jersey v. Arcadian Corp.*, 189 F.3d 305 (1999). Omission of a requirement of "unreasonable danger" would not have altered that fact because "unreasonable danger" purports to be part of the test for defect, not part of the test of causation.

5. *Comparison with California jurisprudence.* For Justice Traynor and his colleagues, it had been axiomatic that, if normal use of the product had caused harm of a type that could have been reasonably envisaged, then the product must have been defective. In *Escola*, for example, Justice Traynor had dealt with defect and danger by assuming that the former automatically implied the latter. He asserted (150 P.2d 436, 464) that: "It is to the public interest to prevent injury to the public from any defective goods by the imposition of civil liability generally." In *Greenman*, moreover, the concept of danger was never even discussed. The issue in question there was simply that of defect. Which, of course, is entirely consistent with what Justice Traynor had said in *Escola*. If a defect automatically renders a product unsafe, any discussion of a notion of danger is clearly redundant.

Questions

1. Does the California position inevitably lead to a "floodgates" problem?

2. If you think that it does, which sort of floodgates problem is it?

3. Is the floodgates problem appropriately addressed by the notion of "unreasonable danger"?

4. In the lecture quoted above, Chief Justice Traynor went on to wonder (at p. 372) whether "[t]he complications surrounding the definition of a defect suggest inquiry as to whether defectiveness is the appropriate touchstone of liability." If defectiveness is not the "appropriate touchstone of liability," what should be?

Cronin v. J.B.E. Olson Corp.

501 P.2d 1153 (1972) (Supreme Court of California)

SULLIVAN J. In this products liability case, the principal question which we face is whether the injured plaintiff seeking recovery upon the theory of strict liability in tort must establish, among other facts, not only that the product contained a defect which proximately caused his injuries but also that such defective condition made the product unreasonably dangerous to the user or consumer. We have concluded that he need not do so. Accordingly, we find no error in the trial court's refusal to so instruct the jury. Rejecting as without merit various challenges to the sufficiency of the evidence, we affirm the judgment.

On October 3, 1966, plaintiff, a route salesman for Gravem-Inglis Bakery Co. (Gravem) of Stockton, was driving a bread delivery truck along a rural road in San Joaquin County. While plaintiff was attempting to pass a pick-up truck ahead of him, its driver made a sudden left turn, causing the pick-up to collide with the plaintiff's truck and forcing the latter off the road and into a ditch. As a result, plaintiff was propelled through the windshield and landed on the ground. The impact broke an aluminum safety hasp which was located just behind the driver's seat and designed to hold the bread trays in place. The loaded trays, driven forward by the abrupt stop and impact of the truck, struck plaintiff in the back and hurled him through the windshield. He sustained serious personal injuries....

At the trial, plaintiff's expert testified, in substance, that the metal hasp broke, releasing the bread trays, because it was extremely porous and had a significantly lower tolerance to force than a non-flawed aluminum hasp would have had. The jury returned a verdict in favor of plaintiff and against Olson in the sum of $45,000 ... Judgment was entered accordingly. This appeal by Olson followed....

The history of strict liability in California indicates that the requirement that the defect made the product "unreasonably dangerous" crept into our jurisprudence without fanfare after its inclusion in section 402A of the Restatement Second of Torts in 1965. The question raised in the instant matter as to whether the requirement is an essential part of the plaintiff's case is one of first impression.

Until our decision in *Greenman v. Yuba Power Products, Inc.*, strict liability for defective products was, in effect, imposed *sub silentio* by extension of the warranty doctrine. As early as 1944, Justice Traynor, concurring in *Escola v. Coca Cola Bottling Co.* (1944) 24 Cal.2d 453, 462, 150 P.2d 436, 440, urged this court to dispense with negligence as the basis of recovery in defective products cases, to discard the fictions of warranty, and to replace them with absolute liability. "(P)ublic policy demands that responsibility be fixed wherever it will most effectively reduce the hazards to life and health inherent in defective products that reach the market." But the pronouncement of such a rule had to await the *Greenman* case in 1963 in which Justice Traynor wrote for a unanimous court: "A manufacturer is strictly liable in tort when an article he places on the market, knowing that it is to be used without inspection for defects, proves to have a defect that causes injury to a human being.... (T)he liability is not one governed by the law of contract warranties but by the law of strict liability in tort." (59 Cal.2d at pp. 62–63, 27 Cal.Rptr. at pp. 700–701, 377 P.2d at pp. 900–901.) ...

The almost inextricable intertwining of the *Greenman* and Restatement standards in our jurisprudence was inevitable, considering the simplicity of *Greenman* and the fuller guidance for many situations offered by the Restatement and its commentary. Nevertheless, the issue now raised requires us to examine and resolve an apparent divergence in the two formulations.

We begin with section 402A itself. According to the official comment to the section, a "defective condition" is one "not contemplated by the ultimate consumer, which will be unreasonably dangerous to him." (Rest.2d Torts, s 402A, com. *g.*) Comment *i*, defining "unreasonably dangerous," states,

> The article sold must be dangerous to an extent beyond that which would be contemplated by the ordinary consumer who purchases it, with the ordinary knowledge common to the community as to its characteristics.

Examples given in comment *i* make it clear that such innocuous products as sugar and butter, unless contaminated, would not give rise to a strict liability claim merely because the former may be harmful to a diabetic or the latter may aggravate the blood cholesterol level of a person with heart disease. Presumably such dangers are squarely within the contemplation of the ordinary consumer. Prosser, the reporter for the Restatement, suggests that the "unreasonably dangerous" qualification was added to foreclose the possibility that the manufacturer of a product with inherent possibilities for harm (for example, butter, drugs, whiskey and automobiles) would become "automatically responsible for all the harm that such things do in the world." (Prosser, *Strict Liability to the Consumer in California* (1966) 18 Hastings L.J. 9, 23.)

The result of the limitation, however, has not been merely to prevent the seller from becoming an insurer of his products with respect to all harm generated by their use. Rather, it has burdened the injured plaintiff with proof of an element which rings of negligence. As a result, if, in the view of the trier of fact, the "ordinary consumer" would have expected the defective condition of a product, the seller is not strictly liable regardless of the expectations of the injured plaintiff. If, for example, the "ordinary consumer" would have contemplated that Shopsmiths posed a risk of loosening their grip and letting the wood strike the operator, another *Greenman* might be denied recovery. In fact, it has been observed that the Restatement formulation of strict liability in practice rarely leads to a different conclusion than would have been reached under laws of negligence. Yet the very purpose of our pioneering efforts in this field was to relieve the plaintiff from problems of proof inherent in pursuing negligence (*Escola v. Coca Cola Bottling Co., supra,* 24 Cal.2d 453, 461–462, 150 P.2d 436) (Traynor, J., concurring) and warranty (*Greenman v. Yuba Power Products, Inc., supra,* 59 Cal.2d 57, 63, 27 Cal.Rptr. 697, 701, 377 P.2d 897, 901) remedies, and thereby "to insure that the costs of injuries resulting from defective products are borne by the manufacturers …"

Of particular concern is the susceptibility of Restatement section 402A to a literal reading which would require the finder of fact to conclude that the product is, first, defective and, second, unreasonably dangerous. A bifurcated standard is of necessity more difficult to prove than a unitary one. But merely proclaiming that the phrase "defective condition unreasonably dangerous" requires only a single finding would not purge that phrase of its negligence complexion. We think that a requirement that a plaintiff also prove that the defect made the product "unreasonably dangerous" places upon him a significantly increased burden and represents a step backward in the area pioneered by this court.

We recognize that the words "unreasonably dangerous" may also serve the beneficial purpose of preventing the seller from being treated as the insurer of its products. However, we think that such protective end is attained by the necessity of proving that there was a defect in the manufacture or design of the product and that such defect was a proximate cause of the injuries. Although the seller should not be responsible for all injuries involving the use of its products, it should be liable for all injuries proximately caused by any of its products which are adjudged "defective."

We can see no difficulty in applying the *Greenman* formulation to the full range of products liability situations, including those involving "design defects." A defect may emerge from the mind of the designer as well as from the hand of the workman.

The *Greenman* case itself indicated that

> (t)o establish the manufacturer's liability it was sufficient that plaintiff proved that he was injured while using the Shopsmith in a way it was intended to be used as a result of a defect in Design and manufacture, …

thereby suggesting the difficulty inherent in distinguishing between types of defects. Although it is easier to see the "defect" in a single imperfectly fashioned product than in an entire line badly conceived, a distinction between manufacture and design defects is not tenable.

The most obvious problem we perceive in creating any such distinction is that thereafter it would be advantageous to characterize a defect in one rather than the other category. It is difficult to prove that a product ultimately caused injury because a widget was poorly welded—a defect in manufacture—rather than because it was made of inexpensive metal difficult to weld, chosen by a designer concerned with economy—a defect in design. The proof problem would, of course, be magnified when the article in question was either old or unique, with no easily available basis for comparison. We wish to avoid providing such a battleground for clever counsel. Furthermore, we find no reason why a different standard, and one harder to meet, should apply to defects which plague entire product lines. We recognize that it is more damaging to a manufacturer to have an entire line condemned, so to speak, for a defect in design, than a single product for a defect in manufacture. But the potential economic loss to a manufacturer should not be reflected in a different standard of proof for an injured consumer.

In summary, we have concluded that to require an injured plaintiff to prove not only that the product contained a defect but also that such defect made the product unreasonably dangerous to the user or consumer would place a considerably greater burden upon him than that articulated in *Greenman*. We believe the *Greenman* formulation is consonant with the rationale and development of products liability law in California because it provides a clear and simple test for determining whether the injured plaintiff is entitled to recovery. We are not persuaded to the contrary by the formulation of section 402A which inserts the factor of an "unreasonably dangerous" condition into the equation of products liability.

We conclude that the trial court did not err by refusing to instruct the jury that plaintiff must establish that the defective condition of the product made it unreasonably dangerous to the user or consumer.

The judgment is affirmed.

Questions

1. Is the test set out in §402A simply the tortious version of the contractual test for breach of warranty?

2. Is the test of product defect best formulated to include the notion of "unreasonable danger" or without it?

3. Do you agree with Justice Sullivan that "a distinction between manufacture and design defects is not tenable"?

Strict Products Liability and Breach of Warranty

The creation of strict products liability in torts inevitably leads to the question of the nature of the relationship between that type of claim and an action for breach of warranty. For procedural reasons—typically concerned with different periods of limitation and/or repose (see Chapter 12)—it is clear that, on occasion, a plaintiff may benefit from having both types of claim available. But there are also substantive differences between an action for strict products liability in torts and an action for breach of warranty.

Seely v. White Motor Co.

63 Cal.2d 9 (1965) (Supreme Court of California)

TRAYNOR, C.J. In October 1959 plaintiff entered into a conditional sales contract with Southern Truck Sales for the purchase of a truck manufactured by defendant, White Motor Company. Plaintiff purchased the truck for use in his business of heavy-duty hauling. Upon taking possession of the truck, plaintiff found that it bounced violently, an action known as "galloping." For 11 months after the purchase, Southern, with guidance from White's representatives, made many unsuccessful attempts to correct the galloping. On July 22, 1960, when slowing down for a turn, plaintiff found that the brakes did not work. The truck overturned, and plaintiff, who was not personally injured, had the damage repaired for $5,466.09. In September 1960, after paying $11,659.44 of the purchase price of $22,041.76, plaintiff served notice that he would make no more payments. Southern thereafter repossessed the truck and resold it for $13,000.

Plaintiff brought this action against Southern and White seeking (1) damages, related to the accident, for the repair of the truck, and (2) damages, unrelated to the accident, for the money he had paid on the purchase price and for the profits lost in his business because he was unable to make normal use of the truck. During the trial plaintiff dismissed the action against Southern without prejudice. The court found that White breached its warranty to plaintiff and entered judgment for plaintiff for $20,899.84, consisting of $11,659.44 for payments on the purchase price and $9,240.40 for lost profits. It found that plaintiff had not proved that the galloping caused the accident and therefore denied his claim for $5,466.09 for the repair of the truck. Both plaintiff and White appeal from the judgment.

(1) Defendant contends that the trial court erred in awarding damages for lost profits and for the money paid on the purchase price of the truck. We do not agree with this contention. The award was proper on the basis of a breach of express warranty.

Defendant included the following promise in the printed form of the purchase order signed by plaintiff:

> The White Motor Company hereby warrants each new motor vehicle sold by it to be free from defects in material and workmanship under normal use and service, its obligation under the warranty being limited to making good at its factory any part or parts thereof.

This promise meets the statutory requirement for an express warranty:

> Any affirmation of fact or any promise by the seller relating to the goods is an express warranty if the natural tendency of such affirmation or promise is to induce the buyer to purchase the goods, and if the buyer purchases the goods relying thereon. (Civ. Code, § 1732; cf. Com. Code, §§ 2313, 2314.)

[margin note: express warranty]

The natural tendency of White's promise was to induce buyers to rely on it, and plaintiff did so rely in purchasing the goods. The reliance on the warranty, and the warranty itself, are manifested by plaintiff's continued efforts to have the truck repaired, and by defendant's acceptance of the responsibility to correct the galloping. (2) The statute requires only that plaintiff rely on the warranty. It does not additionally require that he be aware that it was made by the manufacturer instead of the dealer to reach the one who in fact made it. Surely if plaintiff sought to have a part replaced that was covered by the warranty, White could not escape its obligation by showing that plaintiff thought the warranty White made was made by the dealer.

[margin note: reliance]

Defendant contends that its limitation of its obligation to repair and replacement, and its statement that its warranty "is expressly in lieu of all other warranties, expressed or implied," are sufficient to operate as a disclaimer of responsibility in damages for breach of warranty. This contention is untenable. (3) When, as here, the warrantor repeatedly fails to correct the defect as promised, it is liable for the breach of that promise as a breach of warranty. (4) Since there was an express warranty to plaintiff in the purchase order, no privity of contract was required. Plaintiff also gave reasonable notice of the defect. (Civ. Code, § 1769; cf. Com. Code, § 2607.)

(5) The damages awarded by the trial court, "the loss directly and naturally resulting in the ordinary course of events from the breach of warranty" (Civ. Code, § 1789, subd. 6; cf. Com. Code, § 2714), can properly include lost profits as well as the amount paid on the purchase price....

It is contended that the foregoing legislative scheme of recovery has been superseded by the doctrine of strict liability in tort set forth in *Greenman v. Yuba Power Products, Inc.,* 59 Cal.2d 57, 63, and *Vandermark v. Ford Motor Co.,* 61 Cal.2d 256, 261. We cannot agree with this contention. The law of sales has been carefully articulated to govern the economic relations between suppliers and consumers of goods. (9) The history of the doctrine of strict liability in tort indicates that it was designed, not to undermine the warranty provisions of the sales act or of the Uniform Commercial Code but, rather, to govern the distinct problem of physical injuries....

The fact that the warranty theory was not suited to the field of liability for personal injuries, however, does not mean that it has no function at all. In *Greenman* we recognized only that

> rules defining and governing warranties that were developed to meet the needs of commercial transactions cannot properly be invoked to govern the manufacturer's liability to those injured by its defective products unless those rules also serve the purposes for which such liability is imposed (*Greenman v. Yuba Power Products, Inc., supra,* 59 Cal.2d 57, 63.)

Although the rules governing warranties complicated resolution of the problems of personal injuries, there is no reason to conclude that they do not meet the "needs of commercial transactions." ...

Although the rules of warranty frustrate rational compensation for physical injury, they function well in a commercial setting. (See Com. Code, § 2719; Prosser, *supra,* 69 Yale L.J. 1099, 1130, 1133.) (11) These rules determine the quality of the product the manufacturer promises and thereby determine the quality he must deliver. In this case, the truck plaintiff purchased did not function properly in his business. Plaintiff therefore seeks to recover his commercial losses: lost profits and the refund of the money he paid on the truck. White is responsible for these losses only because it warranted the truck to be "free from defects in material and workmanship under normal use and service." The practical construction of this language by both parties during the 11 months that repairs were attempted establishes that plaintiff's use of the truck was a normal use within the meaning of the warranty. White's failure to comply with its obligation to make "good at its factory any part or parts" of the truck after ample opportunity was given it to do so, entitles plaintiff to recover damages resulting from such breach. Had defendant not warranted the truck, but sold it "as is," it should not be liable for the failure of the truck to serve plaintiff's business needs.

Under the doctrine of strict liability in tort, however, the manufacturer would be liable even though it did not agree that the truck would perform as plaintiff wished or expected it to do. In this case, after plaintiff returned the truck, Southern resold it to Mr. Jack Barefield, an experienced trucker. Mr. Barefield used the truck "to pull a 40-foot band" over state highways. After driving the truck 82,000 miles, he testified that he had no unusual difficulty with it. Southern replaced two tires, added a new fifth wheel, and made minor alterations to the truck before reselling it to Mr. Barefield, so that it is possible that it found a cure for the galloping. Southern, however, replaced the tires five times, adjusted the fifth wheel, and made many other changes on the truck during the 11 months plaintiff drove it. Thus, it is more likely that the truck functioned normally when put to use in Mr. Barefield's business because his use made demands upon it different from those made by plaintiff's use. If under these circumstances defendant is strictly liable in tort for the commercial loss suffered by plaintiff, then it would be liable for business losses of other truckers caused by the failure of its trucks to meet the specific needs of their businesses, even though those needs were communicated only to the dealer. Moreover, this liability could not be disclaimed, for one purpose of strict liability in tort is to prevent a manufacturer from defining the scope of his responsibility for harm caused by his products. (*Greenman v. Yuba Power Products, Inc.,* 59 Cal.2d 57, 63.) The manufacturer would be liable for damages of unknown and unlimited scope. Application of the rules of warranty prevents this result. Defendant is liable only because of its agreement as defined by its continuing practice over 11 months. Without an agreement, defined by practice or otherwise, defendant should not be liable for these commercial losses....

The distinction that the law has drawn between tort recovery for physical injuries and warranty recovery for economic loss is not arbitrary and does not rest on the "luck" of one plaintiff in having an accident causing physical injury. The distinction rests, rather, on an understanding of the nature of the responsibility a manufacturer must undertake in distributing his products. He can appropriately be held liable for physical injuries caused by defects by requiring his goods to match a standard of safety defined in terms of conditions that create unreasonable risks of harm. He cannot be held for the level of performance of his products in the consumer's business unless he agrees that the product was designed to meet the consumer's demands. A consumer should not be charged at the will of the manufacturer with bearing the risk of physical injury when he buys a product on the market. He can, however, be fairly charged with the risk that the product will not match his economic expectations unless the manufacturer agrees that it will. Even in actions for negligence, a manufacturer's liability is limited to damages for physical injuries and there is no recovery for economic loss alone....

Plaintiff contends that, even though the law of warranty governs the economic relations between the parties, the doctrine of strict liability in tort should be extended to govern physical injury to plaintiff's property, as well as personal injury. We agree with this contention. Physical injury to property is so akin to personal injury that there is no reason to distinguish them. (See Prosser, *supra,* 69 Yale L.J. 1099, 1143; Rest. 2d Torts (Tent. Draft No. 10), § 402 A; cf. *Greenman v. Yuba Power Products, Inc.,* 59 Cal.2d 57, 62.) In this case, however, the trial court found that there was no proof that the defect caused the physical damage to the truck. The finding of no causation, although ambiguous, was sufficient absent a request by plaintiff for a specific finding.... Since the testimony on causation was in conflict, the trial court's resolution of the conflict is controlling.

The judgment is affirmed, each side to bear its own costs on these appeals.

Denny v. Ford Motor Co.

662 N.E.2d 730 (1995) (Court of Appeals of New York)

TITONE, J. As stated by the Second Circuit, this action arises out of a June 9, 1986 accident in which plaintiff Nancy Denny was severely injured when the Ford Bronco II that she was driving rolled over. The rollover accident occurred when Denny slammed on her brakes in an effort to avoid a deer that had walked directly into her motor vehicle's path. Denny and her spouse sued Ford Motor Co., the vehicle's manufacturer, asserting claims for negligence, strict products liability and breach of implied warranty of merchantability (see UCC-[2][c]; 2-318). The case went to trial in the District Court for the Northern District of New York in October of 1992.

The trial evidence centered on the particular characteristics of utility vehicles, which are generally made for off-road use on unpaved and often rugged terrain. Such use sometimes necessitates climbing over obstacles such as fallen logs and rocks. While utility vehicles are traditionally considerably larger than passenger cars, some manufacturers have created a category of down-sized "small" utility vehicles, which are designed to be lighter, to achieve better fuel economy and, presumably, to appeal to a wider consumer market. The Bronco II in which Denny was injured falls into this category. Plaintiffs introduced evidence at trial to show that small utility vehicles in general, and the Bronco II in particular, present a significantly higher risk of rollover accidents than do ordinary passenger automobiles. Plaintiffs' evidence also showed that the Bronco II had a low stability index attributable to its high center of gravity and relatively narrow track width. The vehicle's shorter wheel base and suspension system were additional factors contributing to its instability. Ford had made minor design changes in an effort to achieve a higher stability index, but, according to plaintiffs' proof, none of the changes produced a significant improvement in the vehicle's stability.

Ford argued at trial that the design features of which plaintiffs complained were necessary to the vehicle's off-road capabilities. According to Ford, the vehicle had been intended to be used as an off-road vehicle and had not been designed to be sold as a conventional passenger automobile. Ford's own engineer stated that he would not recommend the Bronco II to someone whose primary interest was to use it as a passenger car, since the features of a four-wheel-drive utility vehicle were not helpful for that purpose and the vehicle's design made it inherently less stable.

Despite the engineer's testimony, plaintiffs introduced a Ford marketing manual which predicted that many buyers would be attracted to the Bronco II because utility vehicles were "suitable to contemporary life styles" and were "considered fashionable" in some suburban areas. According to this manual, the sales presentation of the Bronco II should take into account the vehicle's "suitab[ility] for commuting and for suburban and city driving." Additionally, the vehicle's ability to switch between two-wheel and four-wheel drive would "be particularly appealing to women who may be concerned about driving in snow and ice with their children." Plaintiffs both testified that the perceived safety benefits of its four-wheel-drive capacity were what attracted them to the Bronco II. They were not at all interested in its off-road use.

At the close of the evidence, the District Court Judge submitted both the strict products liability claim and the breach of implied warranty claim, despite Ford's objection that the two causes of action were identical. With respect to the strict products liability claim the court told the jury that

> [a] manufacturer who places a product on the market in a defective condition is liable for injury which results from use of the product when the product is used for its intended or reasonably foreseeable purpose.

Further, the court stated:

> A product is defective if it is not reasonably safe.... It is not necessary for the plaintiffs to prove that the defendant knew or should have known of the product[']s potential for causing injury to establish that the product was not reasonably safe. Rather, the plaintiffs must prove by a preponderance of the evidence that a reasonable person ... who knew of the product's potential for causing injury and the existence of available alternative designs ... would have concluded that such a product should not have been marketed in that condition. Such a conclusion should be reached after balancing the risks involved in using the product against the product[']s usefulness and its costs against the risks, usefulness and costs of the alternative design as compared to the product defendant did market.

With respect to the breach of implied warranty claim, the court told the jury:

> The law implies a warranty by a manufacturer which places its product on the market that the product is reasonably fit for the ordinary purpose for which it was intended. If it is, in fact, defective and not reasonably fit to be used for its intended purpose, the warranty is breached. The plaintiffs claim that the Bronco II was not fit for its ordinary purpose because of its alleged propensity to rollover and lack of warnings to the consumer of this propensity.

Neither party objected to the content of these charges.

In response to interrogatories, the jury found that the Bronco II was not defective and that defendant was therefore not liable under plaintiffs' strict products liability cause of action. However, the jury also found that defendant had breached its implied warranty of merchantability and that the breach was the proximate cause of Nancy Denny's injuries. Following apportionment of damages, plaintiff was awarded judgment in the amount of $1.2 million. Ford subsequently moved for a new trial under rule 59(a) of the Federal Rules of Civil Procedure, arguing that the jury's finding on the breach of implied warranty cause of action was irreconcilable with its finding on the strict products liability claim. The trial court rejected this argument, holding that it had been waived and that, in any event, the verdict was not inconsistent.

On defendant's appeal, a majority at the Second Circuit held that defendant's trial conduct had not resulted in a waiver of the inconsistency issue. Reasoning that the outcome of the appeal depended upon the proper application of New York law, the court certified the following questions for consideration by this Court pursuant to article VI, §3(b)(9) of the State Constitution and rule 500.17 of the Rules of the Court of Appeals (22 NYCRR 500.17): (1) whether the strict products liability claim and the breach of implied warranty claim are identical; (2) whether, if the claims are different, the strict products liability claim is broader than the implied warranty claim and encompasses the latter; and (3) whether, if the claims are different and a strict liability claim may fail while an implied warranty claim succeeds, the jury's finding of no product defect is reconcilable with its finding of a breach of warranty.

In this proceeding, Ford's sole argument is that plaintiffs' strict products liability and breach of implied warranty causes of action were identical and that, accordingly, a defendant's verdict on the former cannot be reconciled with a plaintiff's verdict on the latter. This argument is, in turn, premised on both the intertwined history of the two doctrines and the close similarity in their elements and legal functions. Although Ford recognizes that New York has previously permitted personal injury plaintiffs to simultaneously assert different products liability theories in support of their claims, it contends that the breach of implied warranty cause of action, which sounds in contract, has been subsumed by the more recently adopted, and more highly evolved, strict products liability theory, which sounds in tort. Ford's argument has much to commend it. However, in the final analysis, the argument is flawed because it overlooks the continued existence of a separate statutory predicate for the breach of warranty theory and the subtle but important distinction between the two theories that arises from their different historical and doctrinal root.

When products liability litigation was in its infancy, the courts relied upon contractual warranty theories as the only existing means of facilitating economic recovery for personal injuries arising from the use of defective goods ...

Eventually, the contractually based implied warranty theory came to be perceived as inadequate in an economic universe that was dominated by mass-produced products and an impersonal marketplace. Its primary weakness was, of course, its rigid requirement of a relationship of privity between the seller and the injured consumer—a requirement that often could not be satisfied. Some courts (including ours) recognized certain narrow exceptions to the privity requirement in an effort to avoid the doctrine's harsher effects. However, the warranty approach remained unsatisfactory, and the courts shifted their focus to the development of a new, more flexible tort cause of action: the doctrine of strict products liability.

The establishment of this tort remedy has, as this Court has recognized, significantly diminished the need to rely on the contractually based breach of implied warranty remedy as a means of compensating individuals injured because of defective products.

Further, although the available defenses and applicable limitations principles may differ, there is a high degree of overlap between the substantive aspects of the two causes of action. Indeed, on an earlier occasion, this Court observed, in dictum, that "strict liability in tort and implied warranty in the absence of privity are merely different ways of describing the very same cause of action"....

Although the products liability theory sounding in tort and the breach of implied warranty theory authorized by the UCC coexist and are often invoked in tandem, the core element of "defect" is subtly different in the two causes of action. Under New York law, a design defect may be actionable under a strict products liability theory if the product is not reasonably safe. Since this Court's decision in *Voss v. Black & Decker Mfg. Co.*, 59 N.Y.2d 102, 108, 463 N.Y.S.2d 398, 450 N.E.2d 204, the New York standard for determining the existence of a design defect has required an assessment of whether "if the design defect were known at the time of manufacture, a reasonable person would conclude that the utility of the product did not outweigh the risk inherent in marketing a product designed in that manner." This standard demands an inquiry into such factors as (1) the product's utility to the public as a whole, (2) its utility to the individual user, (3) the likelihood that the product will cause injury, (4) the availability of a safer design, (5) the possibility of designing and manufacturing the product so that it is safer but remains functional and reasonably priced, (6) the degree of awareness of the product's potential danger that can reasonably be attributed to the injured user, and (7) the manufacturer's ability to spread the cost of any safety-related design changes (*Voss v. Black & Decker Mfg. Co.*, *supra*, at 109). The above-described analysis is rooted in a recognition that there are both risks and benefits associated with many products and that there are instances in which a product's inherent dangers cannot be eliminated without simultaneously compromising or completely nullifying its benefits. In such circumstances, a weighing of the product's benefits against its risks is an appropriate and necessary component of the liability assessment under the policy-based principles associated with tort law.

The adoption of this risk/utility balance as a component of the "defectiveness" element has brought the inquiry in design defect cases closer to that used in traditional negligence cases, where the reasonableness of an actor's conduct is considered in light of a number of situational and policy-driven factors. While efforts have been made to steer away from the fault-oriented negligence principles by characterizing the design defect cause of action in terms of a product-based rather than a conduct-based analysis, the reality is that the risk/utility balancing test is a "negligence-inspired" approach, since it invites the parties to adduce proof about the manufacturer's choices and ultimately requires the fact finder to make "a judgment about [the manufacturer's] judgment". In other words, an assessment of the manufacturer's conduct is virtually inevitable, and, as one commentator observed, "[i]n general, ... the strict liability concept of 'defective design' [is] functionally synonymous with the earlier negligence concept of unreasonable designing".

It is this negligence-like risk/benefit component of the defect element that differentiates strict products liability claims from UCC-based breach of implied warranty claims in cases involving design defects. While the strict products concept of a product that is "not reasonably safe" requires a weighing of the product's dangers against its over-all advantages, the UCC's concept of a "defective" product requires an inquiry only into whether the product in question was "fit for the ordinary purposes for which such goods are used" (UCC 2-314[2][c]). The latter inquiry focuses on the expectations for the performance of the product when used in the customary, usual and reasonably foreseeable manners. The cause of action is one involving true "strict" liability, since recovery may be had upon a showing that the product was not minimally safe for its expected purpose—without regard to the feasibility of alternative designs or the manufacturer's "reasonableness" in marketing it in that unsafe condition....

foreseeability?

As a practical matter, the distinction between the defect concepts in tort law and in implied warranty theory may have little or no effect in most cases. In this case, however, the nature of the proof and the way in which the fact issues were litigated demonstrates how the two causes of action can diverge. In the trial court, Ford took the position that the design features of which plaintiffs complain, i.e., the Bronco II's high center of gravity, narrow track width, short wheel base and specially tailored suspension system, were important to preserving the vehicle's ability to drive over the highly irregular terrain that typifies off-road travel. Ford's proof in this regard was relevant to the strict products liability risk/utility equation, which required the fact finder to determine whether the Bronco II's value as an off-road vehicle outweighed the risk of the rollover accidents that could occur when the vehicle was used for other driving tasks.

On the other hand, plaintiffs' proof focused, in part, on the sale of the Bronco II for suburban driving and everyday road travel. Plaintiffs also adduced proof that the Bronco's design characteristics made it unusually susceptible to rollover accidents when used on paved roads. All of this evidence was useful in showing that routine highway and street driving was the "ordinary purpose" for which the Bronco II was sold and that it was not "fit"—or safe—for that purpose.

Thus, under the evidence in this case, a rational fact finder could have simultaneously concluded that the Bronco II's utility as an off-road vehicle outweighed the risk of injury resulting from rollover accidents and that the vehicle was not safe for the "ordinary purpose" of daily driving for which it was marketed and sold. Under the law of this State such a set of factual judgments would lead to the concomitant legal conclusion that plaintiffs' strict products liability cause of action was not viable but that defendant should nevertheless be held liable for breach of its implied promise that the Bronco II was "merchantable" or "fit" for its "ordinary purpose." Importantly, what makes this case distinctive is that the "ordinary purpose" for which the product was marketed and sold to the plaintiff was not the same as the utility against which the risk was to be weighed. It is these unusual circumstances that give practical significance to the ordinarily theoretical difference between the defect concepts in tort and statutory breach of implied warranty causes of action.

From the foregoing it is apparent that the causes of action for strict products liability and breach of implied warranty of merchantability are not identical in New York and that the latter is not necessarily subsumed by the former. It follows that, under the circumstances presented, a verdict such as the one occurring here—in which the manufacturer was found liable under an implied warranty cause of action and not liable under a strict products cause of action—is theoretically reconcilable under New York law. Whether the particular verdict produced by the jury in this case was reconcilable in light of the charge and in accordance with case law applying rule 59(a) of the Federal Rules of Civil Procedure is a question of Federal procedure which we are not well positioned to resolve. Hence, we construe the third certified question as posing only the theoretical question of whether this jury's verdict is hypothetically possible under New York's governing legal principles.

KAYE, C.J., and BELLACOSA, SMITH, LEVINE and CIPARICK, JJ., concurred with TITONE, J.

SIMONS, J. (dissenting.) I agree with the majority that causes of action in strict products liability and breach of implied warranty are not identical. In my view, however, the strict products liability claim is substantively broader than and encompasses the implied warranty claim and, thus, the jury's verdict of no defect in the products liability cause of action is not reconcilable with its finding of breach of implied warranty....

The warranty claim in this case was for tortious personal injury and rests on the underlying "social concern [for] the protection of human life and property, not regularity in commercial exchange" (see, Restatement [Third] of Torts, § 2, comment q, at 46). As such, it should be governed by tort rules, not contract rules. Nothing has prevented us in the past from construing and applying the provisions of the Uniform Commercial Code to supplement and advance the policy concerns underlying strict products liability generally, and we should not construe the statute now to establish a standard for determining defectiveness which is inconsistent with the present law in this area (see generally, UCC 1-103). Accordingly, I dissent.

Notes

1. *Strict liability and negligence revisited.* As we saw earlier, the significance of *Greenman* was that it established the concept of strict (i.e. no fault) liability in torts for injuries caused by defective products. In *Denny*, however, strict products liability in torts is distinguished from breach of warranty liability in contracts at least partly on the grounds that the former sometimes involves a "risk/utility balancing test" that is really a "negligence-inspired approach".

2. *Terminology.* Other courts have adopted the *Denny* view. An unfortunate side-effect of this has been that the meaning of the term "strict liability" when used in the context of products liability law is now ambiguous, so that it may be used differently by different people and in different circumstances. Sometimes it is still used to mean what it has always meant: liability without fault. On other occasions, however, it is used simply as a synonym for products liability, without indicating whether fault need be proved or not.

3. *Different types of product defect.* Nevertheless, it is important not to overstate the *Denny* point. The Court of Appeals of New York did *not* say that all products liability law involves the use of a "negligence-inspired" risk/utility balancing test. What it did assert was that product defects are of different types and that, while liability for manufacturing defects remains strict in the traditional (no-fault) sense, liability for *design* defects involves this risk/utility balancing test. This distinction between manufacturing and design defects had, of course, previously been rejected as "untenable" by the Supreme Court of California in *Seely*.

Question

The dissent in *Denny* was clearly concerned that the majority was tolerating the use of contract law by the plaintiff to enable her to find a way around an inconvenient (risk-utility) test in the law of products liability in torts. We have seen plaintiffs make similar attempts before. In Chapter 4, for example, we saw plaintiffs attempt to use the law of misrepresentation to hold developers of brand-name drugs responsible for the side-effects of generics manufactured by a different corporation. In that context the courts have been split on whether such an "end-around" should be tolerated, but most (following *Foster v. American Home Products Corp.*, 29 F.3d 165 (1994) in preference to *Conte v. Wyeth*, 168 Cal.App.4th 89 (2008)) have taken the view that it should not be. Should the courts take a consistent view of attempts to circumvent regular products liability law (whether that be to permit or prohibit them) irrespective of the type of products involved, or is there something so different about automobiles as compared with drugs that it is appropriate for the courts to adopt a different approach in each context?

Manufacturing Defects

The text of § 402A of the Second Restatement mirrors *Seely* on this point, and clearly draws no express distinction between any potentially different types of product defect. However, as will be explored more fully in Chapter 7, the approach of the Products Liability Restatement mirrors the view taken in *Denny*. In fact, it purports to identify three different categories of product defect, though only the first—that of manufacturing defects—will be addressed in the rest of this Chapter. Note that liability for manufacturing defects is also applicable to used products.

Restatement (Third) of Torts: Products Liability (1998)

§ 2(a). Categories of Product Defect

A product is defective when, at the time of sale or distribution, it contains a manufacturing defect, is defective in design, or is defective because of inadequate instructions or warnings. A product ... contains a manufacturing defect when the product departs from its intended design even though all possible care was exercised in the preparation and marketing of the product.

Notes

1. *Food and drugs.* Under § 6(b)(1), § 2(a) applies to defective manufacture of prescription drugs and medical devices. As seen earlier in this Chapter, § 7 stipulates that § 2(a) applies to food products if a reasonable consumer would not expect the food product in question to contain the harm-causing ingredient.

2. *The disappearance of unreasonable danger.* One interesting consequence of the division of product defects into three categories is the re-definition of what constitutes a defect. So far as manufacturing defects are concerned, the Products Liability Restatement has abandoned the Second Restatement's terminology in § 402A of unreasonable danger, and has instead asserted that what is required is that the product in question has deviated from the manufacturer's intended design. This significant in at least two respects. The

first is that this means that a product may be defective without being dangerous. This is surely correct, and effectively vindicates the Supreme Court of California's position in *Cronin*.

3. *The disappearance of unreasonable danger (again).* A second significance is that the intent of the defendant manufacturer can, according to the Products Liability Restatement, effectively dictate whether the issue at stake is one of manufacturing defect or design defect. This seems bizarre. If a manufacturer, without any fault on its part, produces an item which does not correspond with its design and that product causes harm, then the manufacturer will be liable (because liability for manufacturing defects is strict). But if the manufacturer deliberately designs the product to be as it is, and that product causes the very same harm, then on this occasion any potential liability of the manufacturer is supposed—according to the Products Liability Restatement—to be judged according to a risk/utility balancing test. This means that intentionally designing a product to be dangerous puts a manufacturer in a better position than if it had developed a safer design but suffered an unexpected error during manufacture.

Restatement (Third) of Torts: Products Liability (1998)

§ 8. Liability of Commercial Seller or Distributor of Defective Used Products

One engaged in the business of selling or otherwise distributing used products who sells or distributes a defective used product is subject to liability for harm to persons or property caused by the defect if the defect: ...

(b) is a manufacturing defect under § 2(a) ... and the seller's marketing of the product would cause a reasonable person in the position of the buyer to expect the used product to present no greater risk of defect than if the product were new ...

A used product is a product that, prior to the time of sale or other distribution referred to in this Section, is commercially sold or otherwise distributed to a buyer not in the commercial chain of distribution and used for some period of time.

Allenberg v. Bentley Hedges Travel Serv., Inc.

22 P.3d 223 (2001) (Supreme Court of Oklahoma)

KAUGER, J. 2 On July 16, 1997, Bentley Hedges Travel arranged transportation to the airport for Ava Pattee Allenberg and her daughter, Gwinn Norman (passengers), in a used shuttle bus which it had purchased from the appellee, Arkansas Bus Exchange (Arkansas Bus). While en route to the airport, the driver of the bus ran a red light causing the bus to collide with other vehicles in an intersection. Both passengers were seated on the left side of the bus facing the center aisle. The bus was not equipped with seat belts, and the passengers were flung from their seats and injured in the collision. Ava Allenberg died a few days after the accident.

On February 19, 1998, Gwinn Norman, filed a lawsuit on her own behalf and another lawsuit as the personal representative of her mother's estate. She sued Bentley Hedges Travel and the driver of the bus alleging that they were negligent. She also sued Arkansas Bus alleging that it had distributed and sold a defective, unreasonably dangerous shuttle bus because the bus was not equipped with seat belts, adequate handholds, or secured luggage compartments....

Arkansas Bus filed answers in both causes, denying the allegations and asserting that it could not be liable because it did not manufacture, design, or produce the bus, nor did it alter, change or modify the bus in any way from its original condition....

We note at the outset that the basis of the estate representatives' lawsuits was that the shuttle bus was defective because it "had no seat belts, no protection from hard rails and surfaces, and that seats and luggage came loose in the collision" causing the passengers severe injuries. We have not previously addressed whether, under these circumstances, the bus may be defective, and we need not decide the issue today. The only issue presented is the question of law regarding whether the commercial seller of a used product can be subjected to manufacturers' products liability for alleged defects not created by the seller, and if the product is sold in essentially the same condition as when it was acquired for resale.

Arkansas Bus contends that the undisputed facts reveal that any defects were created by the manufacturer and that it purchased the shuttle bus in a used condition and, other than changing the oil and/or tires, it did not warrant, recondition, change, alter, modify, or rebuild the bus before it sold it to Bentley Hedges. It argues that, under these circumstances, commercial sellers of used goods are not subject to strict liability for injuries caused by defects which were present at the time of original distribution....

In *Moss v. Polyco*, 522 P.2d 622, we explained the rationale for holding non-manufacturer-suppliers to the same liability standard as manufacturers. Relying on cases from other jurisdictions, we noted that: 1) retailers like manufacturers, are engaged in the business of distributing goods to the public; 2) because they are an integral part of the overall producing and marketing enterprise, they should bear the cost of injuries resulting from defective products; 3) in some cases the retailer may be the only member of the marketing chain reasonably available to the public; and 4) in other cases the retailer may play a substantial part in insuring that the product is safe or may be in a position to exert pressure on the manufacturer to make the product safer.

Following the trend of other jurisdictions, in *Dewberry v. LaFollette*, 598 P.2d 241, we expanded strict liability to include lessors engaged in the business of leasing chattels even when no sale is involved on the basis that such persons put products into the stream of commerce in a fashion not unlike a manufacturer or retailer. Adopting the reasoning of the Pennsylvania Supreme Court in *Francioni v. Gibsonia Truck Corp.*, 372 A.2d 736, we noted that: 1) in some instances the lessor, like the commercial seller, may be the only member of the marketing chain available to the injured plaintiff for redress; 2) as in the case of the commercial seller, imposition of strict liability upon the lessor serves as an incentive to safety; 3) the lessor is in a better position than the consumer to prevent circulation of defective products; and 4) the lessor can distribute the cost of compensation for injuries resulting from defects by adjusting the rental terms. The estate representatives now ask that the same liability be imposed upon the commercial seller of used shuttle buses.

For three decades, courts from other jurisdictions have struggled with the question of whether or under what circumstances the commercial seller of used products should be liable for a defect attributable to the initial design or manufacturing of a used product. Their answers are as varied as the many different fact situations involved, resulting in a split in authority. Despite conflicting results reached by these jurisdictions, the courts generally agree that resolution of the question hinges upon the policies which underpin strict liability and whether those policies are promoted by applying the doctrine to commercial sellers of used products if the alleged defect was not created by the seller, and if the product is sold in essentially the same condition as when it was acquired for resale.

Some courts have imposed strict liability on commercial sellers of used products because they conclude that the Restatement (Second) of Torts, § 402A is not limited by its terms to commercial sellers of new products. These courts have found that the same policy reasons for which we previously applied strict liability to manufacturers, retailers, dealers or distributors, importers and lessors, should also apply to dealers in used goods.

In contrast, courts which have declined to extend the strict liability to commercial sellers of used products have noted that the policy reasons which underlie strict liability are not fully applicable to commercial sellers of used products. For instance, in *Tillman v. Vance Equipment Co.*, 596 P.2d 1299, 1301 (1979), the Oregon Supreme Court held that a commercial seller of a used crane was not strictly liable for a defect created by the manufacturer. The court looked to the purposes behind the strict liability doctrine and found them inapplicable to used product commercial sellers — at least in the absence of some representations of quality beyond the sale itself or of a special position of the commercial seller vis-a-vis the original manufacturer or others in the chain of original distribution....

Here, the undisputed facts reveal that any alleged defects were created by the manufacturer and Arkansas Bus purchased the shuttle bus in a used condition and, other than changing the oil and/or tires, it did not warrant, recondition, change, alter, modify, or rebuild the bus the before it sold the bus to Bentley Hedges. Consequently, under the facts presented, we align ourselves with the majority view and refuse to extend manufacturers' products liability to the commercial seller of the used bus.

Affirmed.

Notes

1. *Policy reasons.* The court in *Allenberg* did a poor job in articulating how "the policy reasons which underlie strict liability are not fully applicable to commercial sellers of used products." After all, commercial sellers of new products typically have no more ability to "warrant, recondition, change, alter, modify, or rebuild" what they sell than do commercial sellers of used products. There seem, however, to be at least three respects in which the position of those selling used products may differ from that of those selling new products:

1. Commercial sellers of used products cannot specify their desired product design to the manufacturer;

2. Used products may have been non-defective when manufactured, but may have developed a defect during the course of subsequent usage;

3. There may have been a significant lapse of time since the product's original manufacture.

Whether any or all of these differences warrant a different approach to commercial sellers of used products compared to those selling used products is, however, a matter of debate.

2. *Warranty and products liability law.* It seems likely that what the court in *Allenberg* really meant to articulate was that any potential buyer of a used product will be aware of each of the three factors just outlined, and so will not normally expect a used product to be free of defects unless the seller provides some form of warranty. Presumably such expectations will also be reflected in a suitably discounted price. But this position also means that products liability in torts for defective used products will only arise if there is also a potential cause of action for a breach of warranty in contracts. This seems — albeit only for used products — to be turning the clock back, and to be quite contrary to the reasons for the development of a discrete body of products liability law.

3. *Inspection.* Moreover, the *Allenberg* approach also carries the potential drawback that it might encourage commercial sellers of used products not to inspect the products before re-selling them. Immunizing such lack of care by a commercial seller of used products might be perfectly acceptable where the buyer him or herself is later the person injured by the defective product (since that person had the opportunity to bargain for a better-quality product, or to refrain from the purchase at all), but it is difficult to see why the courts should be prepared to reach the same conclusion when those injured—as in *Allenberg*—are innocent third parties with no greater chance to bargain for their own safety than they would have had if the product had been brand new. As we have seen, one of the defining ideas of products liability law was that, in a case where both parties are innocent, the loss should be borne by the manufacturer or seller because of its likely greater capacity to do so.

Gaumer v. Rossville Truck and Tractor Co., Inc.

292 Kan. 749 (2011) (Supreme Court of Kansas)

BEIER, J. Gaumer's father purchased the used hay baler "as is" on June 3, 2003. The baler was missing a safety shield on its side, which would have been part of the baler when it was originally manufactured and sold.

A week later, the baler malfunctioned while Gaumer was using it. He parked the baler and let its engine idle while he knelt or squatted near its side to investigate the problem. Gaumer placed his right hand on the outside of the baler for support and observed its internal operation through the hole left by the missing safety shield. When he attempted to stand up straight, he slipped, and his left arm entered the same hole in the baler. Gaumer's arm became caught in the baler's internal moving parts, and he suffered an amputation just below his left elbow.

Gaumer claimed Rossville was negligent by failing to warn about the potentially dangerous condition of the baler without the safety shield, negligent by failing to inspect the baler before the sale to Gaumer's father, and strictly liable for selling a product in an unreasonably dangerous condition.

Gaumer provided an expert witness report from engineer Kevin B. Sevart. Sevart opined that Gaumer's injuries were "significantly enhanced due to the absence of a safety device designed to specifically limit injuries in an accident such as he experienced." The report also stated:

> It has long been known by engineers and the agricultural equipment industry that shields which must be removed for, or which interfere with, routine maintenance will not likely be maintained on the machine.

The district court judge granted summary judgment on the negligence and strict liability claims, holding that the expert report's failure to mention any legal duty of Rossville to warn or inspect meant that he could not simply "piggyback the opinion of defectiveness from the manufacturer to the seller." The judge also cited two cases from the federal District Court of Kansas, *Sell v. Bertsch & Co. Inc.*, 577 F.Supp. 1393 (D.Kan.1984), and *Stillie v. AM Intern., Inc.*, 850 F.Supp. 960 (D.Kan.1994), that predicted this court would not apply strict liability to sellers of used goods.

The Court of Appeals affirmed the summary judgment on the negligence claims for failure to provide expert testimony on the standard of care of a used implement dealer. The panel reversed, however, on the strict liability claim, holding that (1) the expert opinion was sufficient to establish a prima facie case for strict liability, and (2) Kansas law, as so far enunciated by this court, supports a strict liability claim against a seller of used goods. It relied on caselaw; strict liability pattern instructions; and the Restatement (Second) of Torts § 402A (1964), which make no distinction between sellers of used and new goods, declining to carve out an exception to the Restatement rule without guidance from this court....

In *Brooks v. Dietz*, 545 P.2d 1104 (1976), this court adopted the doctrine of strict liability in tort, as set out in the Restatement (Second) of Torts § 402A (1964), for the sale of a dangerously defective product.... Brooks is significant because the text of § 402A ... makes no distinction between sellers of used and new products.

In *Kennedy v. City of Sawyer*, 228 Kan. 439, 445–46, 618 P.2d 788 (1980), this court identified two purposes of strict liability: "a desire to achieve maximum protection for the injured party and [promotion of] the public interest in discouraging the marketing of products having defects that are a menace to the public." The *Kennedy* decision also went on to endorse what is known as a "chain of distribution" liability theory.

> Under the doctrine of strict liability the liability of a manufacturer and those in the chain of distribution extends to those individuals to whom injury from a defective product may reasonably be foreseen, and then only in those situations where the product is being used for the purpose for which it was intended or for which it is reasonably foreseeable it may be used. 228 Kan. at 446.

Again, in *Kennedy*, we made no distinction between sellers of used and sellers of new products....

Rossville advances two interrelated policy considerations as reasons to avoid extension of strict liability to sellers of used products: (1) The cost of used goods will increase, and therefore (2) dealers of used products will be driven out of business.

In Rossville's view, sellers of used products, often small family businesses or sole proprietorships, will be forced to forego selling "as-is" altogether for fear of future liability and high insurance costs. If not forced completely out of the used-products business, they will have to raise their prices to account for the increased risk attached to such selling. Either way, buyers are likely to seek out "as-is" products or lower priced products elsewhere. For instance, rather than buying a used piece of agricultural equipment from a dealer such as Rossville, a Kansas farmer will instead buy directly from another farmer. In the alternative, the farmer may choose to buy from a dealer in a neighboring state that has not extended strict liability to sellers of used products. Either way, Rossville reasons, at least the same number of products likely to cause injury will remain in the stream of commerce and in use in Kansas, harming both purchasers and sellers, but the rule proposed by plaintiff will offer no offsetting decrease in the social and economic cost of injuries.

Although Rossville's policy considerations appear valid, they do not account for the defense provided by [the Kansas Product Liability Act] K.S.A. 60-3306.... [I]t provides that a seller will not be liable if it can prove that it lacked knowledge of a product's defect, lacked a duty to inspect or complied with such a duty, and that the manufacturer is solvent and susceptible to jurisdiction. This statutory defense suggests no distinction between used and new sellers, and it is likely it will often be well-suited for a defendant such as Rossville, a used-products seller of farm equipment that may not know the history of an item and has no duty to inspect for defects.

At least one Missouri commentator has recognized three policy considerations other than risk reduction, i.e., the idea of shifting the costs of injuries by spreading them among all consumers equally through increased prices: (1) protection of consumer expectations,

(2) prevention of waste through secondhand markets, and (3) compensation of victims injured by product defects. See Mechum, *Strict Liability and Used Car Dealers After the Chrysler and General Motors Bankruptcies*, 66 J. Mo. B. 14, 17–18 (2010)....

We believe the weight of the most persuasive precedent from our sister states reinforces our preliminary conclusion that strict liability should be available in Kansas against a seller of a used product. Given the plain language of the KPLA and its intersection with our precedent adopting Restatement (Second) of Torts § 402A, application of strict liability against a seller of used products appears to be consonant with previously declared and implied policy. We also note that the defense provided both new and used product sellers under K.S.A. 60-3306 should prevent the sky from falling on potential defendants.

Kansas law permits pursuit of a strict liability action against the seller of a used product. The decision of the district court is therefore reversed. The Court of Appeals is affirmed. The case is remanded to the district court for further proceedings consistent with this opinion.

Notes

1. *Second Restatement or Products Liability Restatement?* Although nothing turns on it here, it is still worth noting that Kansas continues to apply the Second Restatement of Torts in preference to the Products Liability Restatement. As will be seen, especially in Chapters 7 and 8, there is considerable controversy as to whether the Products Liability Restatement represents an accurate statement of the law; Kansas is therefore not alone in preferring the approach of the Second Restatement.

2. *Prediction of law.* There is no such thing as federal tort law, and therefore no such thing as federal products liability law. This means that, when a case finds its way into federal court through diversity jurisdiction, that court is obliged to apply the law of the state most closely connected to the case. If the state courts have not rendered a dispositive decision on the issues at stake, the federal court can either adjourn the case, while it asks the state supreme court for a ruling on the relevant law, or else decide the case itself on the basis of its own prediction of what the state courts would be likely to decide if the case were to come before them. Because of the cost and delay involved in certifying questions for the state supreme court, federal courts tend to prefer to predict state law. As with all predictions, however, there is inevitably a risk of being wrong.

Questions

1. Is it acceptable for the liability of a commercial seller of used products to depend on the solvency or otherwise of the original manufacturer of those products?

2. Many products sold today are advertised as "recertified," "reconditioned," or "factory reconditioned." Can sellers and distributors of such products effectively disclaim liability for injuries caused by such products?

3. *Comment a* to § 1 of the Products Liability Restatement claims that:

> Strict liability in tort for defectively manufactured products merges the concept of implied warranty, in which negligence is not required, with the tort concept of negligence, in which contractual privity is not required.

Does this characterization accurately capture the whole point of strict products liability in torts? Does it depend on whether the meaning of strict products liability is taken from the Second, or the Products Liability, Restatement?

Economic Loss Rule

One important distinction between liability for manufacturing defects and liability for breach of warranty is that, according to the latter, a victim can obtain compensation for damage to the product itself. Under products liability in torts, however, claims for damage to the product itself are precluded by the so-called "economic loss rule," which we first met in Chapter 1, and which characterizes such loss purely as a loss of the benefit of a bargain, so that it is covered only by the law of contracts. See, *e.g.*, *Indemnity Ins. Co. of North America v. American Aviation, Inc*, 891 So.2d 532 (Fla.2004). This raises the question of how the law should deal with a complex product which is made of many different components, and which suffers damage only because one of those components is defective. Should the law treat the complex product as one entity, or as a collection of separate products?

Jimenez v. Superior Court
58 P.3d 450 (2002) (Supreme Court of California)

[For the facts of this case, see Chapter 1.] KENNARD, J., concurring. The majority opinion, which I authored, holds that the economic loss rule does not bar recovery for damages that defective windows cause to other components of mass-produced homes in which they are installed. It does not hold, however, that the economic loss rule can never bar recovery for damages that one part or element of a finished product causes to other parts or elements of the same finished product. I write separately to express and explain my view that the crucial inquiry for applying the economic loss rule in this context is whether the component part has been so integrated into the overall unit that it has lost its separate identity.

The economic loss rule limits tort recovery under strict products liability to damages for physical harm to a person or to property other than the defective product itself. To apply the economic loss rule, therefore, one must first determine what the product at issue is. Only then can one determine whether the injury is to the product itself (and therefore subject to the economic loss rule) or to property other than the defective product (and thus subject to strict products liability in tort). Here, defendant window manufacturers have argued that the "product" is the entire house in which their windows were installed, and that the damage caused to other parts of the house by the allegedly defective windows is damage to the product itself within the economic loss rule, thus precluding application of strict liability. For the reasons that follow, I conclude that the windows may be regarded as a distinct product for purposes of the economic loss rule.

The manufacturer of a component part may be strictly liable in tort for physical injuries caused by defects in the component. As the *Restatement Third of Torts* recognizes:

One engaged in the business of selling or otherwise distributing product components who sells or distributes a component is subject to liability for harm to persons or property caused by a product into which the component is integrated if: (a) the component is defective in itself ... and the defect causes the harm ...

A comment in the *Restatement Third of Torts* addresses the issue of a component causing damage to the product of which it is a part. It says:

> [W]hen a component part of a machine or a system destroys the rest of the machine or system, the characterization process becomes more difficult. When the product or system is deemed to be an integrated whole, courts treat such damage as harm to the product itself. When so characterized, the damage is excluded from the coverage of this Restatement. A contrary holding would require a finding of property damage in virtually every case in which a product harms itself and would prevent contractual rules from serving their legitimate function in governing commercial transactions. (Rest.3d Torts, Products Liability, § 21, com. e, pp. 295–296.)

Under the Restatement view, in other words, the manufacturer of component will not be strictly liable in tort for injury to other parts of the unit in which it is installed if the component has been so integrated into the overall unit that it has lost its separate identity.

Instructive here is the United States Supreme Court's decision in *East River S.S. Corp. v. Transamerica Delaval* (1986) 476 U.S. 858. There, companies that chartered oil-transporting supertankers brought an action under maritime law seeking to hold a turbine manufacturer strictly liable in tort for income losses and repair costs resulting when a defective part of the supertankers' turbines damaged other parts of the turbines. (*Id.* at pp. 859–860.) Adopting an economic loss rule similar to the one this court had articulated in *Seely v. White Motor Co.* (1965) 63 Cal.2d 9, the high court held that "a manufacturer in a commercial relationship has no duty under either a negligence or strict products-liability theory to prevent a product from injuring itself." (*East River*, at p. 871 …) The court determined that the defective part of the turbine had been so integrated into the turbine that it lost its separate identity, and thus the manufacturer was not strictly liable in tort for injury that the component part caused to the turbine. The court reasoned that "each turbine was supplied by [the turbine designer, manufacturer, and installer] as an integrated package [and] each is properly regarded as a single unit." (*Id.* at p. 867.) Thus, the high court in *East River* determined, consistent with the *Restatement Third of Torts, Products Liability*, that the defective part had been so integrated into the turbine that it could not be regarded as a separate product.

Thereafter, the United States Supreme Court in *Saratoga Fishing Co. v. J.M. Martinac & Co.* (1997) 520 U.S. 875, addressed a related, yet distinguishable, issue in the context of equipment added to a ship *after* it had been originally built and outfitted. In *Saratoga*, the court considered whether a skiff, a net, and various spare parts added to a ship after its original sale were "other property" — that is, property other than the ship itself — so as to allow a second purchaser of the ship to recover in tort from the manufacturer for the loss of these items when the ship caught fire and sank. (*Id.* at p. 877].) The court allowed recovery because the extra equipment was "other property." The court noted that the ship as originally outfitted, without the extra equipment, was the product that was "placed in the stream of commerce by the manufacturer and its distributors." (*Id.* at p. 883.) The high court's decision is consistent with the view that a nonintegrated component may be a separate product for purposes of strict products liability law. The extra equipment at issue in *Saratoga* had not been so integrated into the ship that it lost its separate identity.

I would adopt for California the interpretation of the economic loss rule articulated in these two decisions of the United States Supreme Court and in the *Restatement Third of Torts*, discussed above. Under this interpretation, in determining whether a component manufacturer is strictly liable in tort for harm that its defective product causes to a

component manufacturer

larger object of which it is a component, the pertinent inquiry is whether the component has been so integrated into the larger unit as to have lost its separate identity. If so, strict liability is improper. But if the component retains its separate identity, so that it may be readily separated from the overall unit, the component manufacturer may be strictly liable for damages to the larger unit.

Windows are not so integrated into houses as to lose their separate identity. Windows can be readily removed from houses and replaced with other windows. A window that has been removed from one house can then be installed in another house. For this reason, I conclude that a window manufacturer is strictly liable in tort for damages that defects in its windows cause to other parts of the homes, such as stucco, insulation, framing, drywall, and baseboards.

Questions

1. Are nails used in the construction of a roof integrated into the roof, or into the house, or not integrated at all?

2. Does it matter whether the nails in question are those holding together the lumber which forms the roof's structure, or those which fix the shingles in place?

3. Is the same answer true of all nails used in the construction of dwellings? Is it true of all nails used anywhere?

4. Should roofing shingles be treated in the same way as nails?

5. Does the dichotomy between "separate identity" and "integration" involve a systemic question requiring a decision as a matter of law by the court, or is it best regarded as a question of fact for juries?

Hypothetical

Greg bought a six-month-old Kamikaze motorcycle from Hillsborough Moto Specialists, having explained to Chris, the store manager, that he planned to give it to his son, Zac, who was nine years old, for motocross (a form of off-road motorbike racing). Zac, 9, had problems with the ignition, which Greg thought was caused by a malfunctioning spark plug. Nevertheless, he did not fit a new one immediately, although he did change the fuel tank to make the Kamikaze more suitable for motocross.

While practicing off-road, Zac attempted to make the Kamikaze jump over a fallen log, but crashed while so doing because the suspension was inadequate for off-road use. The fuel tank then ruptured, and the bike burst into flames. Despite wearing HeMan leathers, which are promoted to be worn by motorbike riders, Zac suffered third-degree burns to sixty percent of his body.

What are the parties' legal positions? Would it make a difference if HeMan had marketed its leathers as "fire retardant"?

Chapter 7

Design Defects

Three Categories of Product Defect

The theory of design defect rests on the idea that a victim is entitled to compensation if injured as a result of using or consuming a product that was defectively designed. Like a manufacturing defect, such defective design might manifest itself in two ways: either as causing the initial accident in which the victim was harmed, or by exacerbating the injury that would otherwise have resulted from an accident that had a different cause. Like manufacturing defects, a design defect does not have to be the only cause of the victim's injuries in order to be actionable, although this may well mean either that any award of damages should be apportioned among several defendants and/or that it should be reduced because of the victim's own comparative fault.

In *Smith v. Yamaha Motor Corp., U.S.A.*, 5 A.3d 314 (2010), for example, the Superior Court of Pennsylvania held that the manufacturer of an ATV on which the victim was severely injured was not entitled to summary judgment on a design defect claim where the fender collapsed, trapping the rider's leg between the fender and the wheel and causing him to be crushed. Although there were arguably other causes of the accident, none involved using the ATV for a purpose for which it was not designed, and so the design defect claim remained sufficiently viable to go before a jury.

The apparent similarity of approach to design defect claims compared to claims of manufacturing defect raises the question of why it might be considered necessary now to distinguish them when the Second Restatement had not done so. Comment *a* to § 1 of the Products Liability Restatement argues that:

> [I]t soon became apparent that § 402A [of the Second Restatement], created to deal with liability for manufacturing defects, could not appropriately be applied to cases of design defects or defects based on inadequate instructions or warnings. A product unit that fails to meet the manufacturer's design specifications thereby fails to perform its intended function and is, almost by definition, defective. However, when the product unit meets the manufacturer's own design specifications, it is necessary to go outside those specifications to determine whether the product is defective.

This is the rationale behind § 2 of the Products Liability Restatement which, unlike the Second Restatement, divided defects into three categories. As Denis Boivin suggested in Chapter 5, this division effectively reintroduces a requirement to prove negligence for both design defects and failures to warn.

Restatement (Third) of Torts: Products Liability (1998)

§ 2. Categories of Product Defect

A product is defective when, at the time of sale or distribution, it contains a manufacturing defect, is defective in design, or is defective because of inadequate instructions or warnings. A product:

(a) contains a manufacturing defect when the product departs from its intended design even though all possible care was exercised in the preparation and marketing of the product;

(b) is defective in design when the foreseeable risks of harm posed by the product could have been reduced or avoided by the adoption of a reasonable alternative design by the seller or other distributor, or a predecessor in the commercial chain of distribution, and the omission of the alternative design renders the product not reasonably safe;

(c) is defective because of inadequate instructions or warnings when the foreseeable risks of harm posed by the product could have been reduced or avoided by the provision of reasonable instructions or warnings by the seller or other distributor, or a predecessor in the commercial chain of distribution, and the omission of the instructions or warnings renders the product not reasonably safe.

Notes

1. *Division of chapters.* We have already addressed the first category (defective manufacture) in Chapter 6; Chapter 8 covers the third category (defective warnings); this Chapter tackles the second category (defective design).

2. *Were there really deficiencies in § 402A?* The Reporters' identification of the alleged deficiencies of § 402A of the Second Restatement is somewhat disingenuous. Indeed, if it were true that the Second Restatement "could not appropriately be applied to cases of design defects or defects based on inadequate instructions or warnings," every state in the nation would have had no choice but to embrace the Products Liability Restatement. Yet that has simply not happened. In fact—as will be seen in Chapter 8—§ 402A already took explicit account of the issue of failures to warn, while § 402A(2) dealt with so-called design defects implicitly by asserting that strict liability "applies although ... the seller has exercised all possible care in the preparation and sale of his product ..." In other words, advocates of the approach of the Second Restatement can simply deny the claim that "when the product unit meets the manufacturer's own design specifications, it is necessary to go outside those specifications to determine whether the product is defective." After all, if someone is injured through use of the product in question, why should the manufacturer potentially have a defense simply by being able to claim that the product is supposed to behave like that? Could this be the products liability equivalent of the software developer's claim that: "It's not a bug; it's a feature!"?

3. *Justification for new approach.* The justification for the approach taken in the Products Liability Restatement has been set out by David G. Owen, *Products Liability*, in The Philosophy of Law: An Encyclopedia Vol. 2 (C.B. Gray ed., 1999), pp. 690–91:

> One of the most perplexing doctrinal problem in products liability law today is the question of who should bear responsibility for risks that neither party fairly could expect. If a product's dangers are both unknown and unknowable at the time of manufacture, the manufacturer's comprehension of and ability to prevent them may be said to be beyond the "state of the art." In such cases, where

neither party has the means to possess the truth concerning the product's dangers, the law fairly may revert to a naked freedom model, since the parties are exchanging a product that they both (mistakenly) believe to be reasonably safe....

When a consumer's prior expectations concerning product safety are fractured by an accident, and the manufacturer did not affirmatively create the unmet expectations, principles of utility and efficiency should help define a moral basis for deciding liability. Unlike values such as freedom and truth that are immensely difficult to value and compare, notions of utility and efficiency reflect the equal worth of all affected parties and hence provide a principled basis for comparative analysis that informs the "defectiveness" issue in do sign and warnings cases. The principle of utility dictates that actors seek to maximize communal welfare and, commensurately, that they seek to minimize waste. If a consumer suffers injury from an inefficient product risk — one that was excessive for the benefits achieved — the manufacturer may be faulted on moral grounds for causing waste (assuming that it was feasible to reduce the risk). However, if the maker carefully and fairly determines that the benefits of a particular design exceed its inherent dangers, then consumers who suffer injury unavoidably from those dangers may not fairly challenge the manufacturer's "legislative" design decision, a decision which was proper by hypothesis.

4. *Rhetoric versus reality.* Legal scholars are fond of creating their own, idealized models of the law, and then claiming either that the law already behaves like their model or that it is striving to do so. However, asserting that something is true does not make it so. In this extract, Owen asserts a view that treats civil law as based on principles of efficiency, and he expressly says that a consumer injured by a product is not permitted to bring an action against the manufacturer if the design was efficient (because its benefits exceeded its dangers). But do not let academic idolatry of the model of efficiency blind you to the legal reality. One of the most (in)famous cases in the whole body of product liability law suggests that Owen's assertions might be somewhat overstated.

5. *The Ford Pinto case.* In *Grimshaw v. Ford Motor Co.*, 119 Cal.App.3d 757 (1981), the Court of Appeals for the Fourth Appellate District of California heard an appeal by Ford against a judgment awarding over $6.5 million in compensatory and punitive damages to 13-year-old Richard Grimshaw — a passenger in a Ford Pinto — who had suffered severe and permanently disfiguring burns on his face and entire body, and to the family of the fatally burnt Mrs. Lilly Gray — the driver of the vehicle — after the car's fuel tank ruptured when it stalled on a freeway (due to a carburetor fault) and was then rear-ended by another vehicle.

As the late Prof. Gary Schwartz later explained in his article, *The Myth of the Ford Pinto Case*, 43 Rutgers L. Rev. 1013, 1015–16, 1020 (1990–1991):

The Pinto was one or the second generation of subcompact cars designed by the American auto industry. (The Ford Falcon and the Chevrolet Corvair were part of the first generation.) Ford began planning the Pinto in the summer of 1967. A design decision was made to place the fuel tank behind the rear axle rather than above that axle. A primary reason for this decision was that if the fuel tank were located above the axle the Pinto would have been left with a very small trunk. The key problem, however, with the behind-the-axle location was that it rendered the gas tank more vulnerable in the event of a rear-end collision. The vulnerability of the gas tank was increased by other design features. One problem was that only nine inches of "crush space" separated the gas tank and the rear axle. The Pinto's bumper, moreover, was essentially ornamental. The rear structure of the Pinto was without the reinforcement provided to many cars by horizontal cross-members and longitudinal side members known as "hat sections." Several bolts protruded out of the differential housing in a way that threatened the gas tank in the event of a collision. Finally, the fuel filler pipe was designed in a way that entailed a chance of disconnecting from the gas tank in the event of rear-end collision, resulting in the spillage of gasoline....

I have suggested that the Ford Pinto case is mythical in the sense that several misconceptions burden the public's understanding of the case. What, then, are those misconceptions? One of them—indeed, a set of misconceptions—concerns the significance of what has become a much-publicized Ford report. In pre-trial discovery in *Grimshaw*, the plaintiffs secured from Ford what Stuart Speiser calls "possibly the most remarkable document ever produced in an American lawsuit." In this report, Ford compared the "costs and benefits" of reducing the chances of certain fuel-tank fires. The safety device considered by the document would have cost $11 per vehicle; multiplied by 12.5 million vehicles, the total cost would thus have been $137 million. According to the document, the added safety provided by the device would have resulted in the avoidance of 180 deaths and another 180 serious burn injuries. Setting $200,000 as the value of life and $67,000 as the value of injury avoidance, the document calculated the total safety benefit at $49.5 million, much less than its $137 million cost.

According to Owen's argument, such cost-benefit calculations are not only to be expected of manufacturers, they are to be actively encouraged, for they enable a judge and jury in any subsequent dispute to see whether the design in question was efficient (thus exonerating the manufacturer) or not. Yet the trial judge actually ruled that this memorandum was not admissible in evidence. No wonder Schwartz talked of the "myth" of the case!

6. *The systemic problem of the model of efficiency.* Even if efficiency were the criterion for a reasonable design, it would not actually be practicable. In *United States v. Carroll Towing Co.*, 159 F.2d 169, 173 (2d. Cir. 1947), as is well known, Judge Learned Hand suggested that "if the probability be called P; the injury, L; and the burden, B; liability depends upon whether B is less than L multiplied by P: i.e., whether B is less than PL." While many subsequent commentators, notably Judge Richard Posner, have taken Learned Hand's dictum as the yardstick of efficiency, they have apparently failed to appreciate that Learned Hand himself noted just a few years later, in *Moisan v. Loftus*, 178 F.2d 148, 149 (2d Cir. 1950), that his algebraic formula could never be used to resolve a case because, "of these factors care is the only one ever susceptible of quantitative estimate, and often that is not," so that "[i]t follows that all such attempts are illusory."

7. *Comparing apples and oranges: the value of a human life.* The problem is that any calculation of efficiency requires that every variable in the equation be reduced to a monetary sum. Yet not only is it often very difficult to know how much the implementation of an alternative design would have cost, it is quite impossible to put a meaningful price on a human life, or on significant injury to the human body (let alone on the emotional consequences or any pain and suffering). But without the ability to reduce every factor to one, common denominator, the courts are left trying to compare what are essentially incommensurate interests. While we are prepared to tolerate some injury to life and limb, because no product can be guaranteed never to cause injury, the question of how much such injury is tolerable cannot be reduced to some one-size-fits-all algebraic formula, but instead typically depends on the weighing of the particular circumstances of each case. That is, after all, why different states have different approaches, and why different juries within the same state will often come to different conclusions.

8. *Two innocent parties.* If something truly unexpected occurs in the usage of a product, the reality is that we are forced to choose between two innocent parties—seller or manufacturer versus consumer or foreseeable third party—as to who should bear the loss. Unfortunately, there is no objective way to decide that question in the abstract.

9. *Moral responsibility.* There is, indeed, another popular school of thought that takes a very different view from Owen's. It argues that an inescapable element of our being human is that we are expected to take responsibility for the consequences of our actions, whether we could have envisioned them or not. Since it is the manufacturer which chose to embark upon the development of the particular product in the expectation, hope or gamble that it would make a profit from so doing, it can thus be argued that it should be the manufacturer who should bear the responsibility when something unexpectedly bad happens. On this basis, it should not necessarily matter whether the allegation is of defective manufacture, defective design or failure to warn. Indeed, for anyone who takes the view—as Traynor J. did in *Escola v. Coca Cola Bottling Co.* 150 P.2d 436, 461 (Cal. 1944)— that "a manufacturer incurs an absolute liability when an article that he has placed on the market, knowing that it is to be used without inspection, proves to have a defect that causes injury to human beings," the drawing of any distinction between defective manufacture and defective design is simply irrational.

10. *A matter of perspective.* Taking the view of the injured consumer, it is immaterial whether the product in question was made in accordance with the manufacturer's design. Everyone agrees that, if the product did not comply with design, a claim for strict products liability may arise. But, looking from the consumer's perspective, it is difficult to see why the manufacturer should have a potential defense because the product in question did comply with the design. If the consumer's own behavior was not the sole cause of his or her injuries, then it seems somewhat self-serving for the defendant to be able to claim that the product that caused the injuries was meant to work that way. Why should one person's right to be free of bodily harm be sacrificed because many other users have not suffered such injuries?

On the other hand, from the perspective of business, the distinction between defective manufacture and defective design is attractive because the profits that are made on sales of products, used without difficulty by many consumers, are not then put in jeopardy because of what has happened to one other consumer. Indeed, this particular consumer (or the circumstances of this particular consumer) must, by definition, be an anomaly if the vast majority of customers have used the product without sustaining injury. Should businesses be required to build into their plans and operations the possibility of such anomalous claims?

11. *Politics.* It is therefore clear that neither the Second Restatement § 402A's "broad-brush" approach nor that of the three categorizations in § 2 of the Third Restatement represents the more "obvious," "natural," or "common sense" approach. Preferring one over the other is, in fact, a matter of political choice. The controversy over whether the approach of the Second Restatement or that of the Products Liability Restatement should be adopted has ensured that products liability continues to be a hot topic.

Consumer Expectations Test

Reflecting this controversy, many states have refused to apply the "reasonable alternative design" test of § 2(b) of the Third Restatement to every case of an alleged design defect, and have continued instead to apply the "consumer expectations" test embraced by § 402A of the Second Restatement to at least some cases of apparently defective designs.

Soule v. General Motors Corp.

882 P.2d 298 (1994) (Supreme Court of California)

BAXTER, J. [A] complex product, even when it is being used as intended, may often cause injury in a way that does not engage its ordinary consumers' reasonable minimum assumptions about safe performance. For example, the ordinary consumer of an automobile simply has "no idea" how it should perform in all foreseeable situations, or how safe it should be made against all foreseeable hazards. (*Barker*, supra, 20 Cal.3d at p. 430, 143 Cal.Rptr. 225, 573 P.2d 443.) ...

As we have seen, the consumer expectations test is reserved for cases in which the *everyday experience* of the product's users permits a conclusion that the product's design violated *minimum* safety assumptions, and is thus defective *regardless of expert opinion about the merits of the design*. It follows that where the minimum safety of a product is within the common knowledge of lay jurors, expert witnesses may not be used to demonstrate what an ordinary consumer would or should expect. Use of expert testimony for that purpose would invade the jury's function (see Evid.Code, § 801, subd. (a)), and would invite circumvention of the rule that the risks and benefits of a challenged design must be carefully balanced whenever the issue of design defect goes beyond the common experience of the product's users.

By the same token, the jury may not be left free to find a violation of ordinary consumer expectations whenever it chooses. Unless the facts actually permit an inference that the product's performance did not meet the minimum safety expectations of its ordinary users, the jury must engage in the balancing of risks and benefits ...

GM suggests that the consumer expectations test is improper whenever "crashworthiness," a complex product, or technical questions of causation are at issue. Because the variety of potential product injuries is infinite, the line cannot be drawn as clearly as GM proposes. But the fundamental distinction is not impossible to define. The crucial question in each individual case is whether the circumstances of the product's failure permit an inference that the product's design performed below the legitimate, commonly accepted minimum safety assumptions of its ordinary consumers.

GM argues at length that the consumer expectations test is an "unworkable, amorphic, fleeting standard" which should be entirely abolished as a basis for design defect. In GM's view, the test is deficient and unfair in several respects. First, it defies definition. Second, it focuses not on the objective condition of products, but on the subjective, unstable, and often unreasonable opinions of consumers. Third, it ignores the reality that ordinary consumers know little about how safe the complex products they use can or should be made. Fourth, it invites the jury to isolate the particular consumer, component, accident, and injury before it instead of considering whether the whole product fairly accommodates the competing expectations of all consumers in all situations. Fifth, it eliminates the careful balancing of risks and benefits which is essential to any design issue. ...

We fully understand the dangers of improper use of the consumer expectations test. However, we cannot accept GM's insinuation that ordinary consumers lack any legitimate expectations about the minimum safety of the products they use. In particular circumstances, a product's design may perform so unsafely that the defect is apparent to the common reason, experience, and understanding of its ordinary consumers. In such cases, a lay jury is competent to make that determination. ...

When use of the consumer expectations test is limited as *Barker* intended, the principal concerns raised by GM and the Council are met. Within these limits, the test remains a workable means of determining the existence of design defect. We therefore find no compelling reason to overrule the consumer expectations prong of *Barker* at this late date, and we decline to do so.

Applying our conclusions to the facts of this case, however, we agree that the instant jury should not have been instructed on ordinary consumer expectations. Plaintiff's theory of design defect was one of technical and mechanical detail. It sought to examine the precise behavior of several obscure components of her car under the complex circumstances of a particular accident. The collision's exact speed, angle, and point of impact were disputed. It seems settled, however, that plaintiff's Camaro received a substantial oblique blow near the left front wheel, and that the adjacent frame members and bracket assembly absorbed considerable inertial force.

An ordinary consumer of automobiles cannot reasonably expect that a car's frame, suspension, or interior will be designed to remain intact in any and all accidents. Nor would ordinary experience and understanding inform such a consumer how safely an automobile's design should perform under the esoteric circumstances of the collision at issue here. Indeed, both parties assumed that quite complicated design considerations were at issue, and that expert testimony was necessary to illuminate these matters. Therefore, injection of ordinary consumer expectations into the design defect equation was improper.

[handwritten margin note: Consumer has no expectation]

We are equally persuaded, however, that the error was harmless, because it is not reasonably probable defendant would have obtained a more favorable result in its absence. In assessing prejudice from an erroneous instruction, we consider, insofar as relevant, "(1) the degree of conflict in the evidence on critical issues; (2) whether respondent's argument to the jury may have contributed to the instruction's misleading effect; (3) whether the jury requested a rereading of the erroneous instruction or of related evidence; (4) the closeness of the jury's verdict; and (5) the effect of other instructions in remedying the error."

Here there were no instructions which specifically remedied the erroneous placement of the consumer expectations alternative before the jury. Moreover, plaintiff's counsel briefly reminded the jury that the instructions allowed it to find a design defect under either the consumer expectations or risk-benefit tests. However, the consumer expectations theory was never emphasized at any point. As previously noted, the case was tried on the assumption that the alleged design defect was a matter of technical debate. Virtually all the evidence and argument on design defect focused on expert evaluation of the strengths, shortcomings, risks, and benefits of the challenged design, as compared with a competitor's approach.

Neither plaintiff's counsel nor any expert witness on her behalf told the jury that the Camaro's design violated the safety expectations of the ordinary consumer. Nor did they suggest the jury should find such a violation regardless of its assessment of such competing design considerations as risk, benefit, feasibility, and cost. The jury never made any requests which hinted it was inclined to apply the consumer expectations test without regard to a weighing of risks and benefits.

Under these circumstances, we find it highly unlikely that a reasonable jury took that path. We see no reasonable probability that the jury disregarded the voluminous evidence on the risks and benefits of the Camaro's design, and instead rested its verdict on its independent assessment of what an ordinary consumer would expect. Accordingly, we conclude, the error in presenting that theory to the jury provides no basis for disturbing the trial judgment.

Judgment of the Court of Appeal affirmed.

Green v. Smith & Nephew A.H.P., Inc.

629 N.W.2d 727 (2001) (Supreme Court of Wisconsin)

WILCOX, J. Green is a health care worker. She began employment at St. Joseph's Hospital in Milwaukee in 1978 where, prior to the commencement of this action, she worked as a radiology technologist and, beginning in 1986, as a CT scan technologist. During the course of this employment, hospital rules required Green to wear protective latex gloves while attending patients. Initially, Green used one or two pairs of gloves per shift. However, upon her promotion to the CT department, this use began increasing and, by about 1987 or 1988, Green's job required her to don up to approximately forty pairs of gloves per shift.

Prior to 1989, Green never had experienced allergies; however, in 1989 Green began suffering various health problems. Early that year, Green's hands became red, cracked, and sore, and began peeling. In response to this condition, she applied hand lotion, changed the soap she used, changed the type of hand towels she used, and tried various other remedies. Nevertheless, the rash continued.

By September 1989, Green's condition deteriorated. Her rash spread to her upper trunk and neck, and she began experiencing chronic cold-like symptoms such as a runny nose and watery eyes. Green's symptoms grew increasingly severe, eventually culminating in an acute shortness of breath, coughing, and tightening of the throat. As a result, Green spent significant time in the hospital: approximately one day in September 1989; approximately five days beginning in late March 1990; approximately five days in February 1991; and approximately three days beginning in late April 1991.

After undergoing various treatments and tests, Green was diagnosed in May 1991 with latex allergy. This allergy has compelled Green to avoid contact with latex, thus causing her to change jobs and limit the items she purchases, things she eats, and activities in which she participates. Moreover, Green's latex allergy caused her to develop asthma, thereby further limiting her lifestyle.

In 1994 Green commenced the present products liability action against S & N. Green alleged that the S & N gloves which she had used at St. Joseph's Hospital were defective in two respects: (1) the gloves contained excessive levels of allergy-causing latex proteins; and (2) the cornstarch with which S & N powdered its gloves increased the likelihood that persons would inhale the latex proteins. Green conceded that the proteins in S & N's gloves naturally occur in the rubber-tree latex from which they are produced. Green also conceded that S & N did not add any proteins to its gloves. However, Green argued that although S & N could have significantly reduced the protein levels in and discontinued powdering its gloves by adjusting its production process, S & N nonetheless utilized a production process that maintained these defects in the gloves. These defects, Green alleged, created the unreasonable danger that S & N's gloves would cause consumers to develop latex allergy and suffer allergy-related conditions. Moreover, Green alleged that as a result of these unreasonably dangerous defects, S & N's gloves caused her to develop latex allergy and allergy-related conditions and, therefore, suffer injuries. Consequently, Green claimed, S & N should be held strictly liable for these injuries.

At the subsequent trial on Green's claim, the parties presented in pertinent part the following evidence to the jury. Latex allergy is caused by exposure to latex proteins. Upon exposure to latex proteins, some persons' immune systems produce antibodies to expel those proteins. The likelihood that such a person's immune system will produce antibodies in response to latex proteins increases in relation to the person's exposure to the proteins. Once a person's immune system produces these antibodies, he or she is "sensitized" to latex. Subsequent exposure to latex then may cause that person to develop progressively worse allergic reactions including irreversible asthma and even anaphylaxis, a hypersensitivity which, upon exposure to even a small amount of latex proteins, may trigger a life-threatening allergic reaction—anaphylactic shock. However, at the time Green began experiencing her injuries, the health care community generally was unaware that persons could develop latex allergy.

The primary cause of latex allergy is latex gloves and, for this reason, latex allergy disproportionately affects members of the health care profession. According to Green's medical experts, the vast majority of people with latex allergy—up to 90 percent—are health care workers. And while latex allergy is not common among the general population, Green's medical experts testified that it affects between 5 and 17 percent of all health care workers in the United States.

Green further presented evidence that high-protein, powdered latex gloves are more dangerous than low-protein, powderless gloves....

At the close of the case, the circuit court instructed the jury on the law surrounding Green's claim for strict liability. The court explained:

> A manufacturer of a product who sells or places on the market a defective product which is unreasonably dangerous to the ordinary user or consumer and which is expected and does reach the consumer without substantial change in the condition in which it is sold is regarded by law as responsible for harm caused by the product even though he or she has exercised all possible care in the preparation and sale of the product provided the product was being used for the purposes for which it was designed and intended to be used. A product is said to be defective when it is in a condition not contemplated by the ordinary user or consumer which is unreasonably dangerous to the ordinary user or consumer, and the defect arose out of design, manufacture or inspection while the article was in the control of the manufacturer. A defective product is unreasonably dangerous to the ordinary user or consumer when it is dangerous to an extent beyond that which would be contemplated by the ordinary user or consumer possessing the knowledge of the product's characteristics which were common to the community. A product is not defective if it is safe for normal use.
>
> A manufacturer is not under a duty to manufacture a product which is absolutely free from all possible harm to every individual. It is the duty of the manufacturer not to place upon the market a defective product which is unreasonably dangerous to the ordinary user or consumer....

Strict products liability holds manufacturers and other sellers of products accountable for selling defective and unreasonably dangerous products that cause injuries to consumers. Since 1967, Wisconsin has adhered to the rule of strict products liability set forth in the *Restatement (Second) of Torts* 402A (1965) ...

To prevail on a claim under this rule, a plaintiff must prove all of the following five elements: (1) that the product was in defective condition when it left the possession or control of the seller, (2) that it was unreasonably dangerous to the user or consumer, (3) that the defect was a cause ... of the plaintiff's injuries or damages, (4) that the seller engaged in the business of selling such product or, put negatively, that this is not an isolated or infrequent transaction not related to the principal business of the seller, and (5) that the product was one which the seller expected to and did reach the user or consumer without substantial change in the condition it was when he [or she] sold it.

In the case at hand, S & N initially contends that the circuit court incorrectly instructed the jury regarding the first two elements of this standard. Specifically, S & N argues that the circuit court erroneously instructed the jury that: (1) a product can be deemed defective and unreasonably dangerous based solely on consumer expectations about that product ... Accordingly, S & N asks us to review the circuit court's jury instructions.

On review, this court will affirm a circuit court's choice of jury instructions so long as the selected instructions fully and fairly inform the jury of the relevant law. The issue of whether the jury instructions fully and fairly explained the relevant law is a question of law, which this court reviews *de novo*....

S & N maintains that the consumer-contemplation standard enunciated in the jury instructions is at odds with current Wisconsin law. According to S & N, this court has recognized that the consumer-contemplation test is not appropriate in all strict products liability cases. S & N observes that in *Sumnicht v. Toyota Motor Sales, U.S.A., Inc.*, 121 Wis.2d 338, 360 N.W.2d 2 (1984), we cited a list of five permissive factors that may be beneficial to plaintiffs in proving their case[s]: 1) [C]onformity of defendant's design to the practices of other manufacturers in its industry at the time of manufacture; 2) the open and obvious nature of the alleged danger;.... extent of the claimant's use of the very product alleged to have caused the injury and the period of time involved in such use by the claimant and others prior to the injury without any harmful incident ... ; 4) the ability of the manufacturer to eliminate danger without impairing the product's usefulness or making it unduly expensive; and 5) the relative likelihood of injury resulting from the product's present design.... Accordingly, S & N concludes, pursuant to *Sumnicht*, Wisconsin applies a hybrid consumer expectation risk-benefit test.

Based on its reading of *Sumnicht*, S & N argues that the court of appeals erred in affirming the circuit court's deviation from the pattern jury instruction. S & N contends that had the circuit court instructed the jury about the defect element of Green's claim according to the pattern jury instruction (i.e., in terms of whether the gloves were reasonably fit for their intended purpose), the jury could have considered the Sumnicht factors set out above. This, S & N asserts, would have allowed the jury to consider not only consumer expectations about S & N's gloves, but also facts such as: the gloves' effectiveness in preventing the spread of disease; the gloves' potential danger to only 5 to 17 percent of consumers; and S & N's inability to know of and, therefore, to eliminate the danger presented by the gloves' alleged design defects. But by instructing the jury solely in terms of consumer contemplation, S & N argues, the circuit court prevented the jury from considering the Sumnicht factors, including the risks and benefits of its gloves. S & N thus concludes that the circuit court's jury instruction erroneously incorporated a products liability standard that conflicts with Sumnicht.

We disagree. In *Vincer v. Esther Williams All-Aluminum Swimming Pool Co.*, 69 Wis.2d 326, 230 N.W.2d 794 (1975), this court adopted Comment g to 402A, which provides that a product is defective where the product is, at the time it leaves the seller's hands, *in a condition not contemplated by the ultimate consumer*, which will be unreasonably dangerous to him [or her]. *Id.* at 330, 230 N.W.2d 794 (quoting *Restatement (Second) of Torts* 402A (1965)) (emphasis added). Similarly, in the same case, this court adopted Comment i to 402A, which provides in pertinent part that a defective product is unreasonably dangerous where it is *dangerous to an extent beyond that which would be contemplated by the ordinary consumer* who purchases it, with the ordinary knowledge common to the community as to its characteristics. *Id.* at 331,230 N.W.2d 794 (quoting *Restatement (Second) of Torts* 402A (1965)) (emphasis added). These Comments provide that although defect and unreasonable danger are distinct elements to a claim in strict products liability, both elements are based on consumer expectations. See *Sumnicht*, 121 Wis.2d at 367–70, 360 N.W.2d 2. Accordingly, based on our adoption of the definitions set out in these Comments, we concluded in *Vincer*:

> [T]he test in Wisconsin of whether a product contains an unreasonably dangerous defect depends upon the reasonable expectations of the ordinary consumer concerning the characteristics of this type of product. If the average consumer would reasonably anticipate the dangerous condition of the product and fully appreciate the attendant risk of injury, it would not be unreasonably dangerous and defective. This is an objective test and is not dependent upon the knowledge of the particular injured consumer....

In Sumnicht ... *we explained:*

> Two separate approaches have emerged to evaluate design defect—a consumer-contemplation test and a danger-utility [i.e., risk-benefit] test....
>
> Under the consumer-contemplation test, ... a product is defectively dangerous if it is dangerous to an extent beyond that which would be contemplated by the ordinary consumer who purchased it with the ordinary knowledge common to the community as to the product's characteristics.
>
> Under [the danger-utility test] approach, a product is defective as designed if, but only if, the magnitude of the danger outweighs the utility of the product. The theory underlying this approach is that virtually all products have both risks and benefits and that there is no way to go about evaluating design hazards intelligently without weighing danger against utility. There have been somewhat different ways of articulating this ... test. But in essence, the danger-utility test directs attention of attorneys, trial judges, and juries to the necessity for weighing the danger-in-fact of a particular feature of a product against its utility.

Id. at 367–68, 360 N.W.2d 2 (quoting *Prosser & Keeton on the Law of Torts* 99 at 698–99 (W. Page Keeton et al. eds., 5th ed.1984)) (footnotes and quotations omitted). We then unequivocally held that "Wisconsin is committed to the consumer-contemplation test for determining whether a product is defective." *Id.* at 368, 360 N.W.2d 2.

After reaffirming Wisconsin's legal standard for products liability, we examined what evidence was necessary to support Sumnicht's claim. The defendants argued that we could not sustain the jury verdict that their automobiles were defective and unreasonably dangerous because there was no proof of "an alternative, safer design, practicable under the circumstances." *Id.* at 370, 360 N.W.2d 2 (quotation omitted). In rejecting this argument, we explained that we have "refrained from adopting mandatory factors that must be weighed when determining if a product is defective and unreasonably dangerous." *Id.* at 371, 360 N.W.2d 2. We did, however, suggest that the set of five permissive factors cited by S & N "may be beneficial to plaintiffs in proving their case[s]." *Id.* at 372, 360 N.W.2d 2.

But contrary to S & N's contentions, the *Sumnicht* factors did not change the nature of Wisconsin's consumer-contemplation test. In listing the *Sumnicht* factors, this court merely recognized that consumer expectations about products may vary depending on the nature of and consumer familiarity with those products. These factors are not supplements to the consumer-contemplation test, to be considered in addition to consumer expectations. Nor are these factors independent legal tests.

Rather, the *Sumnicht* factors are considerations that may be relevant to determining whether the ordinary consumer could anticipate and, hence, contemplate an alleged unreasonably dangerous defect. For example, one of the *Sumnicht* factors is "[c]onformity of the defendant's design to the practices of other manufacturers in the industry at the time of manufacture." *Id.* at 372, 360 N.W.2d 2. This factor does not allow a plaintiff to prove that a manufacturer's design is defective simply by proving that the design did not conform with other manufacturers' designs for similar products. *Id.* at 371, 360 N.W.2d 2 ("The question is not whether any other manufacturer has produced a safer design, but whether the specific product in question is defective and unreasonably dangerous."). Instead, this factor may allow a plaintiff to show that because the defendant manufacturer's design differed from other contemporary manufacturers' designs, an ordinary consumer familiar with the other manufacturers' designs may not be able to contemplate the potential danger presented by the relevant aspect of the defendant manufacturer's design. To further illustrate, another *Sumnicht* factor is "the ability of the manufacturer to eliminate danger without impairing the product's usefulness or making it unduly expensive." *Id.* at 372, 360 N.W.2d 2. This factor does not imply that in determining a manufacturer's liability, a trier of fact must balance the danger that the manufacturer's product presents to consumers with the benefits or cost-value of the product; *Sumnicht* expressly rejected such a risk-benefit analysis. *Id.* at 368, 360 N.W.2d 2; see also *id.* at 371, 360 N.W.2d 2 ("A product may be defective and unreasonably dangerous even though there are no alternative, safer designs available."). To the contrary, this factor allows parties to show that due to the inherent nature or cost of a particular product, the ordinary consumer may expect, for example, the product to include more or less safety devices.

In sum, the *Sumnicht* factors must be understood and applied in light of the consumer-contemplation test. Instead of abrogating or redefining Wisconsin's products liability standard, *Sumnicht* reiterated this state's devotion to the consumer-contemplation test: Wisconsin strict products liability law applies the consumer-contemplation test and only the consumer-contemplation test in all strict products liability cases.

In the present case, the circuit court properly instructed the jury on this standard. As the court of appeals aptly noted, the circuit court's instruction was "essentially a clone of Comment g to 402A, which was adopted by *Vincer.*" And as explained above, in products liability cases, this state adheres solely to the consumer-contemplation test delineated in 402A, ... further defined in *Vincer.* Therefore, we hold that based on our prior products liability caselaw, the circuit court did not erroneously exercise its discretion in instructing the jury that it could find S & N's gloves to be defective and unreasonably dangerous based solely on consumer expectations about those gloves....

We fail to see that any of these policy considerations advanced by S & N warrant this court to overrule *Sumnicht, Vincer,* ... and the rest of Wisconsin products liability law. First, we do not agree with S & N that the consumer-contemplation test is inappropriate in cases involving complex products. The consumer-contemplation test imposes liability where a product is: (1) "in a condition not contemplated by the ultimate consumer"; and (2) "dangerous to an extent beyond that which would be contemplated by the ordinary consumer." *Vincer*, 69 Wis.2d at 330–31, 230 N.W.2d 794 (quoting *Restatement (Second) of Torts* 402A cmts. g and i). Neither of these elements necessarily require proof that at the time of injury, the plaintiff pursuing a claim in products liability knew of or understood the defective or unreasonably dangerous condition of the product that caused his or her injury.

We agree with S & N that in many instances, ordinary consumers may not know of or fully understand the technical or mechanical design aspects of the product at issue. In such instances, the technical or mechanical product design features of the product will comprise "condition[s] not contemplated by the ultimate consumer." Thus, the inquiry in those cases must focus on whether the design features present an unreasonable danger to the ordinary consumer.

unreasonable danger

A determination of "unreasonable danger," like a determination that a product is in a condition not contemplated by the ordinary consumer, does not inevitably require any degree of scientific understanding about the product itself. Rather, it requires understanding of how safely the ordinary consumer would expect the product to serve its intended purpose. If the product falls below such minimum consumer expectations, the product is unreasonably dangerous.

These standards are straightforward and may be applied even in "complex" cases.

Decision of the court of appeals affirmed.

This ct used consumer expectation test

Questions

1. Is the "consumer expectations" test more appropriate to be decided by a judge or by a jury?

2. How consistent are the applications of such a test likely to be? Does this matter?

3. Are there other considerations that might be just as—or even more—important than consistency?

Note

Influence of U.S. law abroad. It is not only states like Wisconsin which have retained the "consumer expectations" test from the Second Restatement. Many other countries (as well as the European Union) have followed the lead of the United States in developing a discrete body of products liability law. But they have modeled their own law on the approach of the Second Restatement. Thus they typically do not distinguish design defects from defects in manufacturing, nor do they adopt the "risk-utility" test favored by the Reporters of the Products Liability Restatement. Instead, such legislation continues to require that all alleged defects be evaluated according to the "consumer expectations" test.

Consumer Protection Act 1987 (United Kingdom)

3.—(1) Subject to the following provisions of this section, there is a defect in a product for the purposes of this Part if the safety of the product is not such as persons generally are entitled to expect; and for those purposes "safety", in relation to a product, shall include safety with respect to products comprised in that product and safety in the context of risks of damage to property, as well as in the context of risks of death or personal injury.

(2) In determining for the purposes of subsection (1) above what persons generally are entitled to expect in relation to a product all the circumstances shall be taken into account, including—

(a) the manner in which, and purposes for which, the product has been marketed, its get-up, the use of any mark in relation to the product and any instructions for, or warnings with respect to, doing or refraining from doing anything with or in relation to the product;

(b) what might reasonably be expected to be done with or in relation to the product; and

(c) the time when the product was supplied by its producer to another;

and nothing in this section shall require a defect to be inferred from the fact alone that the safety of a product which is supplied after that time is greater than the safety of the product in question.

Notes

1. *Surrogate for welfare state?* In their article, *Is European Products Liability More Protective than the Restatement (Third) of Torts: Products Liability?*, 65 Tenn. L. Rev. 985, 1028, 1029 (1997–98), Geraint G. Howells & Mark Mildred argue that:

> [I]n the American products liability sphere, the plaintiff and defendant lobbies appear more polarized than their European counterparts. This polarization may be because of the greater role products liability law is expected to play in the United States as a surrogate for both a social security and health service and as a vehicle through which political action can be achieved....
>
> [T]he growth of liability laws may be viewed as a reaction to the retreat of the welfare state. In part, liability suits are viewed as necessary to control the safety of products in an era when regulation is becoming more complex and enforcement less evident.

2. *Confusion or deliberate obfuscation?* Howells and Mildred also suggest that the focus of so-called "tort reform" has been somewhat inaccurate, and that, if there are problems with American products liability laws, these might be the inevitable product of much more fundamental, structural elements that are not present—or not present to the same extent—in European legal systems:

> Legislatures in the United States are reforming substantive law and making it more defendant-friendly, but instability seems to persist. This instability does not arise from the legal definition of "defect" but stems from the structural questions relating to jury trials, lawyers' fees, lack of liability for the prevailing party's costs, and high damage awards, particularly punitive damages. There may be good reasons for including some of these elements in the American legal system. It is unfortunate, however, if instead of discussing the need for these elements, attention is focused on substantive law reform in a way that undermines the original grand theory of products liability as a means to spread the impact of dangerous products among all product users rather than to let the loss fall at random on unfortunate victims. (65 Tenn. L. Rev. 985, 1029–30.)

Questions

1. Is the point of products liability law to be economically efficient, or is it to promote corrective justice, or distributive justice, or a combination of these, or something else?

2. To what extent is it true that products liability law performs the same role as that of the welfare state in other industrialized countries?

3. Does this suggest that the creation of a universal health care system as part of a more developed welfare state would render much product liability law unnecessary?

4. The nations that make up the European Union do not use juries in products liability cases. Does this suggest that their adoption of the "consumer expectations" test is inappropriate?

Risk-Utility and Reasonable Alternative Design

At a symposium at Brooklyn Law School on November 13, 2008, entitled *The Products Liability Restatement: Was It a Success?*, one of the Reporters for the Products Liability Restatement, Professor Aaron D. Twerksi, argued that the risk-utility-based "reasonable alternative design" (RAD) test for design defect is not only superior to the "consumer expectations" test but is actually the *only* meaningful test. "There is no alternative" to the RAD test, he asserted.

This extraordinarily sweeping assertion can be justified, however, only if we take the view that the proper test for ascertaining design defectiveness is to be found in the law of negligence rather than strict liability. By definition, defendants fail to discharge their standard of care if they fail to do what is reasonable — and what is reasonable can only be ascertained by comparing the defendant's conduct with other possible course of action. So the Twerski defense of the RAD test is both trite and question-begging. It is completely misguided if the governing law is held to be some form of strict liability, as in the law of warranty, where the "consumer expectations" test has, historically, clearly held sway. Perhaps it is no wonder, then, that the RAD test remains highly controversial.

Roach v. Kononen
525 P.2d 125 (1974) (Supreme Court of Oregon)

HOWELL, J. Professor Wade in his articles, *Strict Tort Liability of Manufacturers*, 19 Sw. L.J. 5 (1965), and *On the Nature of Strict Tort Liability for Products*, 44 Miss. L.J. 825 (1973), suggests that, at least in the context of an alleged defect in the design, a product can be defectively designed only if it is unreasonably dangerous. He posits the test that a manufacturer should be held strictly liable if the product is "not duly safe"; or, stated in a test which looks to the manufacturer's conduct, the test would be, "assuming that the defendant had knowledge of the condition of the product, would he then have been acting unreasonably in placing it on the market?" This test is characterized as similar to negligence, except that the element of *scienter* is missing. Factors which should be considered by the court in balancing the utility of the risk against the magnitude of the risk are:

1. The usefulness and desirability of the product — its utility to the user and to the public as a whole.

2. The safety aspects of the product — the likelihood that it will cause injury, and the probable seriousness of the injury.

3. The availability of a substitute product which would meet the same need and not be as unsafe.

4. The manufacturer's ability to eliminate the unsafe character of the product without impairing its usefulness or making it too expensive to maintain its utility.

5. The user's ability to avoid danger by the exercise of care in the use of the product.

6. The user's anticipated awareness of the dangers inherent in the product and their avoidability, because of general public knowledge of the obvious condition of the product, or of the existence of suitable warnings or instructions.

7. The feasibility, on the part of the manufacturer, of spreading the loss by setting the price of the product or carrying liability insurance. (44 Miss. L.J. at 837–38.)

We agree that these factors should be considered by a court before submitting a design defect case to the jury. Also, proof of these factors bears on the jury's determination of whether or not a given design is defective.

However, be all this as it may, it is generally recognized that the basic difference between negligence on the one hand and strict liability for a design defect on the other, is that in strict liability we are talking about the condition (dangerousness) of an article which is designed in a particular way, while in negligence we are talking about the reasonableness of the manufacturer's actions in designing and selling the article as he did. The article can have a degree of dangerousness which the law of strict liability will not tolerate even though the actions of the designer were entirely reasonable in view of what he knew at the time he planned and sold the manufactured article. As Professor Wade points out, a way of determining whether the condition of the article is of the requisite degree of dangerousness to be defective (unreasonably dangerous; greater degree of danger than a consumer has a right to expect; not duly safe) is to assume that the manufacturer knew of the product's propensity to injure as it did, and then to ask whether, with such knowledge, something should have been done about the danger before the product was sold. In other words, a greater burden is placed on the manufacturer than is the case in negligence because the law assumes he has knowledge of the article's dangerous propensity which he may not reasonably be expected to have, had he been charged with negligence.

In determining whether the evidence of dangerous defectiveness is sufficient to make a jury question, the court considers those tests previously set forth.

It is generally recognized that in the vast majority of cases, the application of either the theory of strict liability or of negligence seldom leads to different conclusions. We find this to be particularly true when considering whether a product which is allegedly defectively designed is in a "defective condition unreasonably dangerous."

But in any case, whether a court characterizes the cause of action as arising in negligence or strict liability, the proof of a defect which must be marshalled (*sic*) in support of the plaintiff's case usually takes the same form and usually what proves one proves the other. As the Court of Appeals for the Eighth Circuit held:

> The comparative design with similar and competing machinery in the field, alternate designs and post accident modification of the machine, the frequency or infrequency of use of the same product with or without mishap, and the relative cost and feasibility in adopting other design (*sic*) are all relevant to proof of defective design. *Hoppe v. Midwest Conveyor Company, Inc.*, 485 F.2d 1196, 1202 (8th Cir. 1973).

Judgment affirmed.

Notes

1. *Risk assessment.* What the law effectively requires of manufacturers is that they carry out an assessment of the risks involved in distributing the product in question. Many businesses use a matrix similar to the one in Figure 7.1. At one corner of the matrix, if both the likelihood and likely severity of harm involved in using the product are high, that will normally suggest that the product's design should be modified (or, perhaps, supplemented with an appropriate warning or instructions, which we shall tackle in Chapter 8). An unmodified product embodying these levels of risk which then injures someone will typically leave its manufacturer liable for a design defect. At the other corner of the chart, if both likelihood and likely severity of harm are low, then there would seem to be absolutely no need for the manufacture to adopt an alternative design. So far as the other seven combinations are concerned, however, it is impossible to be categorical. Reasonable people can — and do — disagree over when, in these circumstances, the manufacturer should be expected to adopt an alternative design.

Figure 7.1 A Risk Assessment Matrix

Likelihood of Harm	Likely Severity of Harm		
	HIGH	MEDIUM	LOW
HIGH	Very high risk: design modification required		
MEDIUM			
LOW			Minimal risk: no design modification required

2. *Accurate information and its limits.* Conducting effective risk assessment naturally requires that a manufacture have good information both about the product and the way in which it is likely to be used. However, even the best information about the past will not necessarily prove an accurate guide to what happens in the future, so risk assessment can never be a perfect science. Moreover, it is apparent that the assessment of risk — and whether design modifications are advisable — involves an element of judgment; a manufacturer can never guarantee that its judgement will be echoed in court, even if the judge or jury attempts to embark on a roughly similar form of risk assessment.

3. *"Consumer expectations" versus "reasonable alternative design."* Moreover, coming to the view that a design modification would be desirable does not necessarily mean that an alternative design is reasonably practicable. It may, for example, be very expensive to implement an alternative design. In products liability litigation, the extent to which such a factor should be taken into account is highly controversial: is the jury to be allowed to decide — simply as a matter of robust common sense in its role as arbiter of community standards — whether consumers expect to tolerate such risks, or is it to be told to focus on whether there was an alternative design that any reasonable manufacturer would have adopted?

4. *Proving a negative.* It is often said that it is impossible to prove a negative. This is, of course, just hyperbole — especially where the civil standard of proof is involved — but it is certainly often harder to prove a negative than show that something really did happen. It is therefore clearly significant that the "reasonable alternative design" test requires plaintiffs to prove a negative: they must establish that an alternative design was available to the defendant that *would not have resulted in injury to the victim.*

5. *Mutually exclusive, or alternative tests?* Many states have chosen to treat the "consumer expectations" and "reasonable alternative design" not as mutually exclusive, but as alternatives to be invoked as appropriate. Note that, despite the requirement to prove a negative for the "reasonable alternative design" test, the "consumer expectations" test is not always the more plaintiff-friendly.

Ray v. BIC Corp.

925 S.W.2d 527 (1996) (Supreme Court of Tennessee)

WHITE, J. In this Rule 23 case we are called upon to address whether our products liability statute, codified at Tennessee Code Annotated Section 29-28-101 to -108, provides for a risk-utility test in addition to the consumer expectation test for determining whether a product is unreasonably dangerous. For the reasons set forth below, we hold that our present statute provides for two tests: the consumer expectation test and the prudent manufacturer test. The latter requires risk-utility balancing in its application.

On September 3, 1982, the Memphis apartment building in which Erma Holman and her two minor sons, Frederick and Donnie Ray, were residing was destroyed by fire. A cigarette lighter, manufactured by the BIC Corporation, had been left in the apartment by a friend of Holman's. When Holman left to walk her oldest son, Donnie, to the bus stop, four-year old Frederick was left alone in the apartment. When Holman returned, the apartment was ablaze. Young Frederick sustained serious injuries, including incapacitating brain damage.

Ten years later, on September 3, 1992, Holman filed a lawsuit against BIC Corporation on behalf of her minor son, Frederick. In her complaint, she alleged that the source of the fire, the BIC cigarette lighter, was an "unreasonably dangerous" product within the meaning of Tennessee Code Annotated Section 29-(8) because it was not child-resistant. Specifically, plaintiff alleged that "[d]efendant ... manufactured an unreasonably dangerous disposable cigarette lighter which was unreasonably dangerous at the time it left the control of the Defendant." Additionally, plaintiff contended that defendant was liable because the lighter "would not be put on the market by a reasonably prudent manufacturer or seller assuming that [the manufacturer or seller] knew of its dangerous condition."

BIC Corporation moved for summary judgment on the basis that the product was not unreasonably dangerous. Plaintiff countered with the affidavit of an engineer whose opinion was that the lighter could have been manufactured without significantly increasing the cost to include child-resistant features which would more likely than not have prevented the injuries.

The federal district court granted summary judgment to defendant. Plaintiff appealed to the Sixth Circuit Court of Appeals which has certified this question for our consideration: whether Tenn.Code Ann. § 29-28-102(8), in addition to the "consumer expectation" test, provides for another separate and distinct test for determining whether a product is "unreasonably dangerous," i.e., the "risk-utility" test.

The Tennessee Products Liability Act provides that a manufacturer or seller may be liable for injuries caused by a product that is determined to be in a "defective condition or unreasonably dangerous at the time it left the control of the manufacturer or seller." Tenn.Code Ann. § 29-28-105(a) (1980 Repl.). In this case, plaintiff alleges that the BIC cigarette lighter was an unreasonably dangerous product. The Act defines an unreasonably dangerous product as a product [that] is dangerous to an extent beyond that which would be contemplated by the ordinary consumer who purchases it, or a product [that] because of its dangerous condition would not be put on the market by a reasonably prudent manufacturer or seller assuming that [the manufacturer or seller] knew of its dangerous condition. Tenn.Code Ann. § 29-28-102(8) (1980 Repl.).

Unquestionably, the first clause of the definition establishes a "consumer expectation" test for determining whether a product is unreasonably dangerous. That test, defined generally as, whether the product's condition poses a danger beyond that expected by an ordinary consumer with reasonable knowledge, has been employed by many states....

It is also unquestionable that defendant in this case would be entitled to summary judgment if the consumer expectation test is the only applicable standard for determining unreasonable dangerousness. An ordinary consumer would expect that a cigarette lighter, left in the hands of a young child, could cause danger and injury concomitant to that occurring in this case. The more difficult question is whether that conclusion ends the inquiry. Again, unquestionably, it does not.

In addition to the consumer expectation test clearly set forth in the first clause of the statutory definition, the second clause, joined disjunctively with the first, establishes a second test. That clause provides that a product is unreasonably dangerous if a reasonably prudent manufacturer or seller, aware of the product's dangerous condition, would not put the product on the market. (Tenn.Code Ann. §29-28-102(8) (1980 Repl.). We must determine whether that test, which we will refer to as the "prudent manufacturer" test, is a separate, distinct test from the consumer expectation test found exclusive by the district court or the risk-utility test urged by the plaintiff.

The consumer expectation test, clearly set forth in the first clause of the definition section, derives from the *Restatement (Second) of Torts*, Section 402A. Comment (i) to that section states that before a product is deemed unreasonably dangerous it must be "dangerous to an extent beyond that which would be contemplated by the ordinary consumer who purchases it, with the ordinary knowledge common to the community as to its characteristics." ... Under this test, a product is not unreasonably dangerous if the ordinary consumer would appreciate the condition of the product and the risk of injury.

By contrast, the prudent manufacturer test imputes knowledge of the condition of the product to the manufacturer. The test is whether, given that knowledge, a prudent manufacturer would market the product....

Some jurisdictions—notably Washington and Oregon—have, at times, concluded that the two approaches are really one, representing "two sides of the same coin." ... In explaining this conclusion these courts have suggested that "a manufacturer who would be negligent in marketing a given product..., would necessarily be marketing a product which fell below the reasonable expectations of consumers who purchase it." ...

Clearly, however, as the courts combining the tests have come to realize, the focus of the two tests is entirely different. The consumer expectation test is, by definition, buyer oriented; the prudent manufacturer test, seller oriented. Notwithstanding the difference in focus, these courts predict that the tests "should produce similar results." ...

[W]e see distinct and important differences in the consumer expectation and the prudent manufacturer tests under our statute. First, the former requires the consumer to establish what an ordinary consumer purchasing the product would expect. The manufacturer or seller's conduct, knowledge, or intention is irrelevant. What is determinative is what an ordinary purchaser would have expected. Obviously, this test can only be applied to products about which an ordinary consumer would have knowledge. By definition, it could be applied only to those products in which "everyday experience of the product's users permits a conclusion...." ... For example, ordinary consumers would have a basis for expectations about the safety of a can opener or coffee pot, but, perhaps, not about the safety of a fuel-injection engine or an air bag.

Alternatively, the prudent manufacturer test requires proof about the reasonableness of the manufacturer or seller's decision to market a product assuming knowledge of its dangerous condition. What the buyer expects is irrelevant under this test. In contrast to the consumer expectation test, the prudent manufacturer test is more applicable to those circumstances in which an ordinary consumer would have no reasonable basis for expectations. Accordingly, expert testimony about the prudence of the decision to market would be essential.

The straight-forward, unambiguous language of our statute establishes two distinct tests for ascertaining whether a product is unreasonably dangerous: the consumer expectation test and the prudent manufacturer test. In addition to having completely different focuses, the two tests have different elements which require different types of proof. The two tests are neither mutually exclusive nor mutually inclusive. While the statute does not limit applicability of the tests, the prudent manufacturer test will often be the only appropriate means for establishing the unreasonable dangerousness of a complex product about which an ordinary consumer has no reasonable expectation. Likewise, it may form the sole basis for establishing liability for a product whose dangerousness is the result of a latent defect.

We decline to weave the two tests into one. As the Oregon courts noted after revising their previous combined approach:

> [T]he distinction between the [two] tests is not merely academic. The result in some, perhaps most, product liability cases might be the same regardless of which test the jury applies; nonetheless, in some cases, the difference in the test can affect the outcome. A jury might well conclude that a product is not unreasonably dangerous under the cost/benefit calculus of an omniscient reasonable manufacturer but is still unsafe in a manner, or to an extent, not expected by an ordinary consumer.... The difference in perspective — "reasonable manufacturer" versus "ordinary consumer" — can, as a practical matter, make all the difference.

Having concluded that our statute incorporates a test other than the consumer expectation test for proving the unreasonable dangerousness of a product, we turn now to the issue of the relationship, if any, between that test and the risk-utility test urged by plaintiff.

Our research has revealed that, in reality, what plaintiff refers to as the risk-utility test is more correctly an analysis which involves the balancing of numerous factors. Under the approach, the court balances the usefulness of the product against the magnitude of risk or danger likely to be caused by the product....

In order to determine whether the second test in our statute, which we have called the prudent manufacturer test, anticipates a risk-utility analysis, we turn to the most commonly used description of both. Generally stated, the prudent manufacturer test imposes liability in circumstances in which a reasonably prudent manufacturer with knowledge of a product's dangerousness would not place the product in the stream of commerce. As expanded by Dean Wade, the test has evolved into a consideration of various factors which must be weighed to determine whether the manufacturer was reasonably prudent. The factors include the usefulness and desirability of the product, the safety aspects of the product, the availability of a substitute product which would meet the same need, the manufacturer's ability to eliminate the unsafe character, the user's ability to avoid danger, the user's awareness of the danger, and the feasibility of spreading the loss....

In effect, the prudent manufacturer test, by definition, requires a risk-utility analysis. The determination of whether a product is unreasonably dangerous turns on whether, balancing all the relevant factors, a prudent manufacturer would market the product despite its dangerous condition. Naturally, a prudent manufacturer would consider usefulness, costs, seriousness and likelihood of potential harm, and the myriad of other factors often lumped into what plaintiff called a risk-utility test . . .

The test under our statute does not include a shifting of the burden of proof to defendant. Rather, the burden remains on plaintiff in a products liability action to establish injury as a result of an unreasonably dangerous product. Plaintiff may meet this burden either by establishing that the product was dangerous beyond that contemplated by an ordinary consumer (consumer expectation test) or by establishing that a reasonably prudent manufacturer, assumed to know the product's dangerous condition, would not have marketed the product (prudent manufacturer test employing risk-benefit analysis).

Our statute does not limit the application of either test to only certain types of actions. Nonetheless, the consumer expectation test will be inapplicable, by definition, to certain products about which an ordinary consumer can have no expectation. Despite the potentially overlapping nature of the tests, plaintiff here relied only on the second test, which we have defined as requiring consideration of numerous factors. Our statute clearly authorizes plaintiff to attempt to establish the unreasonable dangerousness of a product by employing a prudent manufacturer test which includes a risk-utility balancing approach.

BIRCH, C.J., and DROWOTA, ANDERSON and REID, JJ., concurred.

Vautour v. Body Masters Sports Industries, Inc.

784 A.2d 1178 (2001) (Supreme Court of New Hampshire)

DUGGAN, J. The plaintiffs in this products liability action, David S. Vautour and Susan Vautour, appeal an order of the Superior Court (Fitzgerald, J.) granting a motion for directed verdict to the defendant, Body Masters Sports Industries, Inc. We reverse and remand. Mr. Vautour was injured while using a leg press machine manufactured by the defendant. . . .

Mr. Vautour's injury occurred while moving his feet down to do calf raises. Although he was aware of the machine's warning label, Mr. Vautour did not have the upper stops engaged at the time of his accident. As a result, the sled and his knees fell rapidly toward his chest, injuring his feet. Mr. Vautour brought suit against the defendant under the theories of strict liability, negligence, and breach of warranty. Mr. Vautour contends that the location of the safety stops "exposed users to an unreasonable risk of harm and that this design defect" caused his injuries. . . .

After the plaintiffs withdrew their claim for breach of warranty, the superior court granted the defendant's motion for directed verdict on the strict liability and negligence claims, concluding that:

> The point at which safety stops could be placed along the sled carriage without interfering with the muscle-strengthening function of the machine, the point at which stops must be placed to ensure that users are reasonably safe from physical injury, and the degree of risk to which users might reasonably be exposed when engaging in such leg strengthening exercises are each factual questions which appear, by their nature, to require specialized knowledge in the areas of design engineering, physiognomy, bio-mechanics, and safety standards in the field of athletic training.

Because the average juror could not be expected to know about these topics and because the plaintiffs' expert failed to offer any testimony regarding the acceptable risk of injury, where the safety stops should be located, or how his proposed alternative design would prevent the type of injuries suffered by Mr. Vautour, the superior court concluded that the plaintiffs failed to introduce evidence sufficient to support their strict liability and negligence claims. . . .

A product is defectively designed when it "is manufactured in conformity with the intended design but the design itself poses unreasonable dangers to consumers." To prevail on a defective design products liability claim, a plaintiff must prove the following four elements: (1) the design of the product created a defective condition unreasonably dangerous to the user; (2) the condition existed when the product was sold by a seller in the business of selling such products; (3) the use of the product was reasonably foreseeable by the manufacturer; and (4) the condition caused injury to the user or the user's property.

To determine whether a product is unreasonably dangerous, we explained in *Bellotte v. Zayre Corp.*, 116 N.H. 52, 54, 352 A.2d 723 (1976), that a product "must be dangerous to an extent beyond that which would be contemplated by the ordinary consumer who purchases it, with the ordinary knowledge common to the community as to its characteristics." In *Price v. BIC Corp.*, 142 N.H. 386, 389, 702 A.2d 330 (1997), we further explained that whether a product is unreasonably dangerous to an extent beyond that which would be contemplated by the ordinary consumer is determined by the jury using a risk-utility balancing test.

Under a risk-utility approach, a product is defective as designed "if the magnitude of the danger outweighs the utility of the product." We have articulated the risk-utility test as requiring a "multifaceted balancing process involving evaluation of many conflicting factors." In order to determine whether the risks outweigh the benefits of the product design, a jury must evaluate many possible factors including the usefulness and desirability of the product to the public as a whole, whether the risk of danger could have been reduced without significantly affecting either the product's effectiveness or manufacturing cost, and the presence and efficacy of a warning to avoid an unreasonable risk of harm from hidden dangers or from foreseeable uses. "Reasonableness, foreseeability, utility, and similar factors are questions of fact for the jury."

The defendant contends that the risk-utility test, as articulated in *Thibault*, implicitly requires a plaintiff to offer evidence of a reasonable alternative design. Because the jury is instructed to consider whether the risk of danger could have been reduced without significantly affecting the effectiveness of the product and the cost of manufacturing, the defendant contends that evidence of a reasonable alternative design is required. The defendant urges us to adopt the *Restatement (Third) of Torts* § 2(b) (1998), which requires a plaintiff in a design defect case to prove that the risks of harm posed by the product could have been reduced or avoided by a reasonable alternative design. *Restatement (Third) of Torts* § 2(b) provides that:

> [A product] ... is defective in design when the foreseeable risks of harm posed by the product could have been reduced or avoided by the adoption of a reasonable alternative design by the seller or other distributor, or a predecessor in the commercial chain of distribution, and the omission of the alternative design renders the product not reasonably safe. By requiring a plaintiff to present evidence of a safer alternative design, section 2(b) of the *Restatement* thus elevates the availability of a reasonable alternative design from merely "a factor to be considered in the risk-utility analysis to a requisite element of a cause of action for defective design." *Hernandez v. Tokai Corp.*, 2 S.W.3d 251, 256 (Tex.1999).

There has been considerable controversy surrounding the adoption of *Restatement (Third) of Torts* § 2(b). Most of the controversy stems from the concern that a reasonable alternative design requirement would impose an undue burden on plaintiffs because it places

a "potentially insurmountable stumbling block in the way of those injured by badly designed products." Commentators have noted that for suits against manufacturers who
produce highly complex products, the reasonable alternative design requirement will
deter the complainant from filing suit because of the enormous costs involved in obtaining expert testimony. Thus, because of the increased costs to plaintiffs of bringing
actions based on defective product design, commentators fear that an alternative design
requirement presents the possibility that substantial litigation expenses may effectively
eliminate recourse, especially in cases in which the plaintiff has suffered little damage.

On a practical level, the *Restatement*'s requirement of proof of an alternative design may
be difficult for courts and juries to apply. To determine whether the manufacturer is liable for a design defect, the jury must currently decide whether the plaintiff has proven
the four essential elements of a design defect case. As part of this analysis, the jury must
determine whether the design of the product created a defective condition unreasonably
dangerous to the user. In order to prove this element under the *Restatement*, a plaintiff
must meet the requirement of proving the "availability of a technologically feasible and
practical alternative design that would have reduced or prevented the plaintiff's harm."
Restatement (Third) of Torts § 2 comment *f* at 24 (1998). The *Restatement*, however, contains far-reaching exceptions. According to the *Restatement*, the reasonable alternative
design requirement does not apply when the product design is "manifestly unreasonable."
Id. comment *e* at 21–22. Plaintiffs are additionally not required to produce expert testimony in cases in which the feasibility of a reasonable alternative design is obvious and understandable to laypersons. Consequently, a requirement of proving a reasonable alternative
design coupled with these broad exceptions will introduce even more complex issues for
judges and juries to unravel.

A more important consideration is that while proof of an alternative design is relevant in a design defect case, it should be neither a controlling factor nor an essential element that must be proved in every case. As articulated in *Thibault*, the risk-utility test
requires a jury to consider a number of factors when deciding whether a product is unreasonably dangerous. This list is not meant to be exclusive, but merely illustrative. "Depending on the circumstances of each case, flexibility is necessary to decide which factors"
may be relevant. Thus, the rigid prerequisite of a reason able alternative design places
too much emphasis on one of many possible factors that could potentially affect the risk-
utility analysis. We are therefore satisfied that the risk-utility test as currently applied protects the interests of both consumers and manufacturers in design defect cases, and we
decline to adopt section 2(b) of the *Restatement*.

The defendant argues that even if we do not adopt the reasonable alternative design
requirement, the superior court's decision should still be affirmed because the plaintiffs
chose to proceed on that theory. The defendant argues that by electing to proceed solely
on the theory that the leg press was unreasonably dangerous because of the improper design of the sled and handles, the plaintiffs had an obligation to present sufficient evidence
on the feasibility of a safer, alternative design. We disagree. The plaintiffs' burden was to
present evidence regarding the risk-utility factors; they did not have the duty of proving
a safer, alternative design.

Here, the plaintiffs presented sufficient evidence that the leg press machine was unreasonably dangerous pursuant to the risk-utility balancing test. The plaintiffs' expert testified that the defendant's design was "dangerous to the user, from an injury perspective,"
and his proposed design was safer than the defendant's current design. Although he did not
specify exactly where the safety stops should have been placed to prevent Mr. Vautour's
injuries, he did testify that his design was mechanically feasible and, under similar cir-

cumstances, machines with such a design would be, overall, less dangerous. It was up to the jury to assess the weight to be given this testimony. "Weighing of substantive evidence is the very essence of the jury's function. Consequently the trial judge has been granted little discretion to withdraw questions of substantive fact from a jury's consideration." While certainly a reasonable jury could have found this evidence insufficient to establish that the leg press design was unreasonably dangerous, we cannot say that no reasonable jury could have found otherwise. Nor can we say, when viewing the evidence in the light most favorable to the plaintiffs, that the sole reasonable inference from this testimony is so overwhelmingly in favor of the defendant that no contrary verdict could stand. Thus, we hold that the trial court erroneously granted the defendant's motion for directed verdict upon the plaintiffs' strict liability, design defect claim. Under New Hampshire law, the plaintiffs' evidence was sufficient to establish a *prima facie* case.

Finally we note that because the plaintiffs did not appeal the trial court's decision to dismiss their negligence claim, they have waived that issue.

Reversed and remanded.

Notes

1. *Most common approach.* One state that has recently decided to adopt the risk-utility test as its exclusive means of deciding cases of allegedly defective design is South Carolina. The state's Supreme Court adopted this approach in *Branham v. Ford Motor Co.*, 701 S.E.2d 5 (2010), although, far from believing that it had no choice, the court noted:

> Some form of a risk-utility test is employed by an overwhelming majority of the jurisdictions in this country. Some of these jurisdictions exclusively employ a risk-utility test, while others do so with a hybrid of the risk-utility and the consumer expectations test, or an explicit either-or option. States that exclusively employ the consumer expectations test are a decided minority.

The most common approach among the various US jurisdictions to addressing the question of design defects is set out graphically in Figure 7.2.

2. *Economic loss rule (again).* Another South Carolina case demonstrates how even the risk-utility test may be irrelevant where the economic loss rule is applied. In *Sapp v. Ford Motor Co.*, 687 S.E.2d 47 (2009), two independent buyers of the same make, model, and year of truck each brought a products liability action against Ford, seeking damages for the damage to, or destruction of, their vehicles when faulty cruise control switches caused the trucks to catch fire. Neither plaintiff suffered personal injury or damage to other property. They alleged, however, that Ford knew of a design defect in the cruise control switch, which would short circuit and cause a fire in the engine compartment.

Both actions were dismissed on the grounds that the economic loss rule precluded their tort claims. Their appeals were consolidated for review. The state's Supreme Court affirmed the rulings of the trial courts, reasoning as follows:

> In *Kennedy* [v. *Columbia Lumber & Mfg. Co.*, 384 S.E.2d 730, 734 (1989)], we held the economic loss rule does not preclude a homebuyer from recovering in tort against the developer or builder where the builder violates an applicable building code, deviates from industry standards, or constructs a house that he knows or should know will pose a serious risk of physical harm. Such an exception was and still remains necessary to protect homeowners. As explained in *Kennedy*, the mechanics of home purchasing have evolved and drastically changed over the past two hundred years and, accordingly, courts have shifted from following the

Figure 7.2 Tests for Design Defect

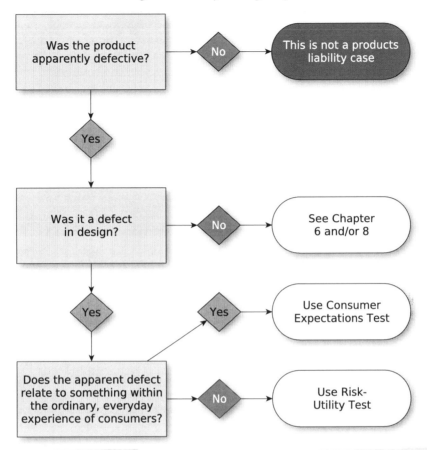

doctrine of *caveat emptor* ("let the buyer beware") to the doctrine of *caveat ven-ditor* ("let the seller beware"). A home is typically an individual's single largest investment and is a completely different type of manufactured good than any other type of product that a consumer will buy. Moreover, courts have recognized that the transaction between a builder and a buyer for the sale of a home largely involves inherently unequal bargaining power between the parties. For these reasons, we created this narrow exception to the economic loss rule to apply solely in the residential home context.

The rule announced in *Kennedy* followed a long line of South Carolina cases directed toward protecting consumers only in the residential home building context, and we noted that this holding followed cases from around the country expanding protections afforded to homebuyers and imposing tort liability on residential homebuilders.

In *Colleton Preparatory Academy, Inc. v. Hoover Universal, Inc.*, 666 S.E.2d 247 (2008), this Court was faced with the issue of whether to expand the *Kennedy* exception to the economic loss rule beyond the residential home building context to all manufacturers. The majority held that the economic loss rule will not preclude a plaintiff from filing a products liability suit in tort where only the product itself is injured when the plaintiff alleges breach of duty accompanied by a clear, serious, and unreasonable risk of bodily injury or death. The dissent argued that this decision not only broadly expanded the exception to the economic loss rule, but also completely altered the law on products liability in South Carolina. In our view, the traditional economic loss rule provides a more stable framework and results in a more just and predictable outcome in products liability cases. Accordingly, we overrule *Colleton Prep.* to the extent it expands the narrow exception to the economic loss rule beyond the residential builder context.

Questions

1. Apart from the "reasonable alternative design" test, which other (related) doctrine of products liability law—indeed, of tort law in general—typically requires a plaintiff to prove a negative?

2. Does the South Carolina's homebuyer exception to the economic loss "rule" make sense?

3. Are there any other circumstances in which an exception should be made to the economic loss "rule," or has the "rule" simply outlived any useful purpose that it might once have had?

Roles of Judge and Jury

Arguably the true significance of the RAD standard in the Third Restatement lies less in the precise formulation of the test for design defect, and more in the question as to who should be the arbiter of the test. Professor James A. Henderson, Jr., the other Reporter for the Products Liability Restatement, made it clear at the 2008 Brooklyn symposium that he considered the RAD standard to be more relevant not so much as a direction to triers of fact, but as a standard for motions for summary judgment. Indeed, he remarked that his view of the Products Liability Restatement as a whole was to provide a degree of clarity to the law sufficient for what he called a "robust motions practice," and took the view that, if a case could survive a motion for summary judgment, he did not think that the Products Liability Restatement should be used as a method for fettering the discretion of the jury.

It is submitted that Professor Henderson's view has much to recommend it. It means that, whereas the standard of reasonable care in a negligence case is set and applied by the jury—subject, of course, to the court's inherent jurisdiction to rule that there is insufficient evidence supporting one party's case to allow the case to go to the jury—the RAD test is essentially one to be applied at an earlier stage by the judge. The reason for this is that the determination of whether a particular, alternative design is "reasonable" depends on the weighing of a number of factors of risk and utility, and such a task is, according to some commentators, beyond the competence of the jury.

The case below is concerned with the law in Pennsylvania, where the courts have attempted to draw an analogous—but not identical—distinction between the roles of judge and jury.

Moyer v. United Dominion Industries, Inc.
473 F.3d 532 (3rd Cir. 2007)

FUENTES, J. Plaintiffs are five factory workers who allege serious and permanent hand injuries after years of using defendant's swager, a machine used to form metal. Plaintiffs claim that the swager was defectively designed because it emitted excessive vibration, and that the defendant failed to warn them of the vibration risk. Before trial, and in accordance with Pennsylvania law, the District Court conducted a risk-utility analysis and determined, as a threshold matter, that the swager was "unreasonably dangerous." After a two-week jury trial on the design defect and failure to warn claims, a jury awarded plaintiffs and their wives approximately $13.5 million. On appeal, we consider several evidentiary issues, as well as whether plaintiffs' claims are barred by the applicable statute of limitations. For the reasons that follow, we will affirm in part, reverse in part, and remand for further proceedings....

Under Pennsylvania law, strict liability allows recovery when a defective product that is "unreasonably dangerous" causes harm to a user or consumer. See *Phillips v. A-Best Prod. Co.*, 542 Pa. 124, 665 A.2d 1167, 1170 (1995) (quoting *Restatement (Second) of Torts* §402A). Yet, in *Azzarello v. Black Bros. Co.*, 480 Pa. 547, 391 A.2d 1020, 1026 (1978), the Pennsylvania Supreme Court rejected the use of the "unreasonably dangerous" formulation as part of the jury instructions in products liability cases. In *Azzarello*, the Court was concerned that, although a jury is obviously competent to resolve disputes about the condition of a product, whether that condition justifies placing liability upon the supplier presents an entirely different question. Because the Supreme Court believed the "unreasonably dangerous" decision to be a question of law, the resolution of which depends upon social policy considerations, it concluded that the judge must make that decision.

In *Surace v. Caterpillar, Inc.*, 111 F.3d 1039 (3d Cir.1997), we considered how the trial judge should make the threshold unreasonably dangerous determination. Applying Pennsylvania law, we held that the judge should "engage in a risk-utility analysis, weighing a product's harms against its social utility." We identified some of the factors relevant to this analysis:

1. The usefulness and desirability of the product—its utility to the user and to the public as a whole;

2. The safety aspects of the product—the likelihood that it will cause injury, and the probable seriousness of the injury;

3. The availability of a substitute product which would meet the same need and not be as unsafe;

4. The manufacturer's ability to eliminate the unsafe character of the product without impairing its usefulness or making it too expensive to maintain its utility;

5. The user's ability to avoid danger by the exercise of care in the use of the product;

6. The user's anticipated awareness of the dangers inherent in the product and their avoidability, because of general public knowledge of the obvious condition of the product, or of the existence of suitable warnings or instruction; and

7. The feasibility, on the part of the manufacturer, of spreading the loss of [sic] setting the price of the product or carrying liability insurance.

Relying on these factors, the judge makes the pre-trial determination as a matter of law.

If the judge concludes that a product is "unreasonably dangerous" the case is submitted to the jury, which then decides, based on all the evidence presented, "whether the facts of the case support the averments of the complaint." In making this determination, however, the jury does not balance the risk-utility factors, even though the judge has only done so as a threshold matter. Instead, the jury considers whether the product "left the supplier's control lacking any element necessary to make it safe for its intended use or possessing any feature that renders it unsafe for the intended use."

The Pennsylvania Supreme Court intends that this division of labor between judge and jury will preserve the substantive distinction between strict liability and negligence causes of action. The Court has explained that the jury's focus should be on the condition of the product, not on the conduct of the supplier.

The two-step process adopted in *Azzarello* is not without controversy. Soon after the case was decided, one commentator noted that *Azzarello's* limitation of the jury's role was "a matter of concern since the jury has traditionally played an important role in the expansion of the law of products liability." Aaron D. Twerski, *From Risk-Utility to Consumer Expectation: Enhancing the Role of Judicial Screening in Product Liability Litigation,* 11 Hofstra L. Rev. 861, 926 (1983). Another writer more recently noted that "*Azzarello* remains to this day one of the most controversial opinions ever issued on the subject of strict products liability for alleged design defects." John M. Thomas, *Defining "Design Defect" in Pennsylvania: Reconciling Azzarello and the Restatement (Third) of Torts,* 71 Temp. L. Rev. 217, 217 (1998). Furthermore, the latest *Restatement of Torts* has called Pennsylvania's products liability law "sometimes difficult to decipher." See *Restatement (Third) of Torts: Products Liability* § 2, Reporters' Note, *cmt. d,* at 54. Even a member of Pennsylvania's Supreme Court recently criticized *Azzarello's* controversial approach.

Our own review of products liability law reveals that most other jurisdictions give the jury a central role in making the strict liability determination and regard juries as capable of balancing risk-utility factors, even though some of those factors may touch on matters of social policy. Indeed, our research fails to disclose any other jurisdiction that has adopted the two-step approach or denies the jury a chance to apply the risk-utility test. Nevertheless, the *Azzarello* framework represents the Pennsylvania Supreme Court's decision about the proper adjudication of the substantive rights of litigants in the products liability context, and, as a federal court sitting in diversity, "we are bound to adjudicate the case in accordance with applicable state law." *Nationwide Mut. Ins. Co. v. Cosenza,* 258 F.3d 197, 202 (3d Cir.2001)....

As discussed, *Azzarello* reserves a screening function for the judge who makes the "unreasonably dangerous" determination before the jury considers the case. If the judge concludes that the product is unreasonably dangerous under the facts as alleged by the plaintiff, the jury makes factual determinations regarding liability. Specifically, the jury is required, under *Azzarello,* to consider whether a product "lack[s] any element necessary to make it safe for its intended use." We do not believe that, under this approach, the Pennsylvania Supreme Court expects that a judge will prevent all evidence considered in the risk-utility analysis from reaching the jury. Nor do we believe that, when the *Azzarello* Court adopted its own strict liability standard, it intended to deprive the jury of its significant fact-finding responsibilities. Indeed, comparing the "intended use" standard with the risk-utility standard, we observe that evidence pertinent to one will often be relevant to the other.

For one thing, just as the judge has considered "safety" under the second risk-utility factor, the jury will also have to consider evidence relevant to whether the product is "safe." Moreover, just as the judge has evaluated feasible alternatives to a product under the fourth risk-utility factor, the jury will also have to evaluate them to assess the "condition" of a product. And, as discussed below, to assess other factual issues, such as causation or lack of defect, the jury will have to consider evidence relied on by the judge. In other words, evidence should not be excluded from the jury simply because it was relevant to the judge's threshold risk-utility analysis. Such a relevance determination must be made on its own merits, even though the jury's consideration of this evidence provides the defendant an opportunity to contest certain facts relevant to the judge's analysis.

Affirmed in part, reversed in part, and remanded.

Notes

1. *Judge and jury.* Throughout the law of torts, the division of labor between judge and jury is crucial. The trial judge's role is not just to see "fair play" in the pleadings and courtroom, but also to decide systemic questions. The jury, on the other hand, is charged not only with making findings of fact specific to the case at hand, but also with applying the standards of the community and acting as its conscience. Pennsylvania's division of labor requires judges to make systemic findings of "unreasonable danger" regarding a particular product. Only if the judge finds that the product was unreasonably dangerous does the jury then get to decide the other material issues of fact.

2. *Unreasonable danger.* The Pennsylvania approach is, however, striking for two reasons. First, it is difficult to see how a finding that a product was unreasonably dangerous can be said to be a systemic matter. On the contrary, it seems to represent a specific finding in a specific case. On this basis, the expression of concern by Professor Twerski to which Judge Fuentes refers, seems apposite. Secondly, it also creates an oddity that, once the judge has found that the product was potentially unreasonably dangerous according to one test, the jury is then asked to decide the matter definitively according to a different test.

3. *Distinguishing issues in causation.* There is, however, an alternative reading of Pennsylvania law. As will be seen in Chapter 9, factual causation in more complex cases has two elements: general causation and specific causation. Factual causation requires the plaintiff to show that the alleged causative agent is capable of causing the *type* of harm which the plaintiff is alleged to have sustained. Only once that has been established is the plaintiff then in a position to attempt to prove specific causation, i.e. that the specific acts of the defendant caused the *specific* harm suffered by the plaintiff. Since general causation is clearly a systemic matter, it is one for the court to determine, while specific causation is for the jury.

4. *Idiosyncratic or wise?* While Judge Fuentes suggests that Pennsylvania law has reached an idiosyncratic position in the determination of product defect, it is arguable that, in fact, Pennsylvania law has been more perspicacious than other jurisdictions in realizing that the concept of "unreasonable danger" has little or nothing at all to do with product defect. It is, in fact, concerned with establishing one of the elements of factual causation. Thus expecting the court to rule that that the product was potentially "unreasonably dangerous" so as to allow the case to proceed to the jury means nothing other than requiring the judge to see that the plaintiff has proved general causation: that it was reasonably foreseeable that the design of the product could cause the type of harm alleged. It is then for the jury to determine whether the product was actually defective.

5. *Pennsylvania vs. Products Liability Restatement.* Seen in this light, Professor Twerski's concern seems misplaced, for the Pennsylvania Supreme Court is simply being rigorous in its application of the normal rules of factual causation. Instead, what the Pennsylvania approach really calls into question is the language of the Products Liability Restatement. For arguably what the Restatement ostensibly includes as a test of defect — "the foreseeable risks of harm posed by the product could have been reduced or avoided by the adoption of a reasonable alternative design" — is better seen as a test of general causation. No wonder there has been so much confusion in its interpretation!

Substantial Modification

We saw when we looked at warranties (in Chapter 3) that the law divides implied warranties into those concerning merchantability (where the product is to be used for its ordinary purpose) and those concerning fitness for purpose (where the product is to be used for a specific, non-standard purpose of which the seller is aware). A similar concept applies in the context of design defects, but this time it refers to what the product manufacturer can expect of the user or consumer. Thus the manufacturer can only be liable for a design defect where the product's use was "reasonably anticipated." To put this another way, a product cannot be said to suffer from a design defect after it has undergone a substantial modification since it was initially sold or distributed, because it is no longer the product that it was originally designed to be.

Matthews v. Remington Arms Co., Inc.
641 F.3d 635 (5th Cir. 2011)

BARKSDALE, J. Following a bench trial, judgment was rendered against Jerry Matthews' claim under the Louisiana Products Liability Act (LPLA) for his injuries that resulted from his firing a Remington Model 710 rifle. When Matthews fired it, the bolt head, which was designed to be connected to the bolt body by a bolt-assembly pin, did not lock with the barrel, allowing an uncontained explosion.

At issue are the district court's findings that ... pursuant to LPLA, manufacturer Remington Arms Company, Inc., did not "reasonably anticipate" a user would fire its rifle after someone had removed, but failed to reinstall, that pin. Concerning that reasonably-anticipated-use finding, primarily at issue is whether the district court erred by concluding that, for purposes of LPLA, the scope of Matthews' "use" of the rifle included such removal and failure to reinstall; that is, whether his "use" was firing the rifle with the bolt-assembly pin missing, as opposed to only firing it....

In 2000, Remington introduced its Model 710 bolt-action rifle. Instead of using a solid bolt, that model was manufactured with a two-piece bolt assembly: the bolt head is attached to the bolt body with a bolt-assembly pin. The bolt handle is attached to the bolt body. When the bolt handle and, therefore, the bolt body, is rotated downward, the bolt head (if the bolt-assembly pin is installed) simultaneously rotates downward and locks the "lugs" on the bolt head into the mating locking recesses in the receiving barrel interface (rifle receiver): the firing position. In such an instance, the rifle is "in battery". Only when the rifle is in battery will it fire properly.

The bolt-assembly pin, a cylinder, is not of insignificant size; it is .685# long and .247# in diameter. It is made from low-strength, unhardened steel. The pin is essential to the simultaneous downward rotation of the bolt head and body. If the bolt-assembly pin is missing or malfunctioning, it is possible for the bolt handle and body to be rotated into locked position without the bolt head also rotating into locked position. In that situation, the lugs on the bolt head will not lock into the mating locking recesses in the rifle receiver, resulting in inadequate engagement between the bolt-head lugs and their locking recesses. In this situation, the rifle is "out of battery". If the trigger is pulled while a round is chambered and the rifle is out of battery, the rifle will either misfire or, as happened to Matthews, have an uncontained explosion.

Under normal conditions (in battery), the bolt-assembly pin does not contain the pressure from the cartridge's being fired; the bolt head contains the pressure with the seal that is created when the locking lugs are engaged with their mating recesses in the rifle receiver—that engagement is critical to pressure containment. Accordingly, the rifle can be fired without the pin in place if the bolt head is locked in place—the pin is not the critical pressure containment device.

The Model 710's owner's manual instructs users to disassemble the bolt assembly, including removing the bolt-assembly pin, for cleaning; and to reassemble the bolt assembly, by reinserting the bolt-assembly pin. Remington also instructs its factory assembly workers to keep a finger beneath the bolt-assembly-pin hole on the bolt body to prevent the bolt-assembly pin from falling out during assembly; however, this instruction is not included in the owner's manual. The owner's manual does not include any warnings of potential hazards if the bolt-assembly pin is not properly installed. Matthews, who borrowed, instead of owned, the rifle, testified he neither received, nor read, the owner's manual prior to the accident....

When the rifle fired by Matthews left Remington's control in 2001, it contained a bolt-assembly pin manufactured to specifications. Matthews' mother-in-law, Margaret Minchew, purchased the rifle from her nephew in 2006. It had been owned by several persons before she purchased it; but, when she acquired it, she did not receive the owner's manual.

Before the date of the accident, Matthews and others fired the rifle without incident; but, prior to Matthews' accident, someone disassembled the rifle and the bolt assembly and failed to reinstall the bolt-assembly pin....

[A]t issue is whether it was "reasonably anticipated" by Remington that someone would fail to reinstall the bolt-assembly pin and that the rifle would be fired in that condition. As discussed, the establishment of each LPLA element is a question of fact, reviewed for clear error....

Under LPLA, whether a use is reasonably anticipated is an objective standard ascertained from the manufacturer's viewpoint at the time of manufacture....

We can not say that the district court clearly erred in finding that Remington should not have reasonably anticipated (reasonably expected) the rifle to be fired after someone had removed, but failed to reinstall, the bolt-assembly pin. This is evidenced by the instructions in Remington's Model 710 owner's manual to reinstall the bolt-assembly pin when reassembling the bolt assembly. Of course, it was "reasonably foreseeable" that a user might drop the bolt-assembly pin during reassembly, as evidenced by the instruction from Remington to its assembly workers to keep a finger beneath the bolt-assembly-pin hole during the initial assembly; however, that is *not* the LPLA standard. The standard is: at the time of manufacture, how did the manufacturer reasonably expect its product to be used by an ordinary person....

Matthews failed to prove Remington, at the time of manufacture of the rifle at issue, was aware of a single other incident where a Model 710 rifle, or any rifle using a similar two-piece bolt assembly, was fired without a properly installed and functioning bolt-assembly pin.

DENNIS, J. (dissenting). I respectfully dissent. The undisputed, concrete facts of this fully tried case show that the damage to the claimant, Jerry Matthews, arose from his own use of the rifle to shoot at a target, a use that an objective rifle manufacturer should reasonably expect of an ordinary person in the same or similar circumstances as Matthews'. Matthews did not allege or attempt to show that his damage arose from the use of the rifle by another person or entity. Thus, both the district court and the majority of this panel erred in misinterpreting and misapplying the Louisiana Products Liability Act (LPLA or "the Act") as if it required Matthews to show that his damage arose from a reasonably expected use of the rifle by another person or entity. The LPLA does not place such an additional and greater burden upon a claimant at the threshold reasonably-anticipated-use stage of a products liability case. Therefore, their dismissal of Matthews' claim on the ground that he failed to demonstrate that his damages arose from his reasonably anticipated use of the rifle was legal error. It may be that Matthews' case ultimately might have failed on the merits of his design and warning claims, but under the LPLA he should not have been poured out of court at the threshold reasonably-anticipated-use stage, because he obviously used the rifle as a manufacturer should reasonably have anticipated, and did not use the rifle in an irrational or abnormal way.

Judgment affirmed.

Notes

1. *Design and foreseeable use.* It is surely arguable—and Judge Dennis did indeed argue in the rest of his dissent—that Matthews's "unexpected use" of the rifle came about because of a design specification by Remington that made it foreseeable that a substantial modification—the removal of the bolt-pin assembly—would at some time occur. Automobiles and airplanes too are made in such a way that parts will be regularly disassembled, making it foreseeable that one or more parts may not be replaced correctly before use, but that does not make their design defective. Perhaps the true issue in *Matthews* is that the victim acquired the rifle from another, non-expert individual rather than from a professional gunsmith, and so found himself in the same position as someone who acquires a used vehicle from another private motorist rather than from a dealership.

2. *Design, misuse, and modifications.* Part of the point of good product design is to guard against possible misuse. Sometimes the only sensible way to achieve this objective is by means of appropriate warnings (which will be addressed in Chapter 8). But it may also be possible—and even quite simple—to design a product so as to make it inoperable without appropriate safety features in place. Power tools, for example, are often designed so that they can be operated only if the user has two hands on the equipment. Similarly, they usually feature a cut-out device, which will render the machine inoperable if safety guards are removed. Of course, it is always possible for someone to get around these features (which is why they usually need to be accompanied with appropriate warnings about the possible consequences of doing so), but the idea is to make such dangerous modifications possible to achieve only by someone who is clearly intent on overriding all safety precautions. Such modifications are then treated by the courts as a superseding cause of the victim's injuries, thus immunizing the original manufacturer from a claim for a design defect.

The problem that *Matthews* illustrates is that it may be that the person who suffers the serious consequences of operating an unsafe product may well be someone (who may never be identified) other than the person who carried out the dangerous modification. The victim will then be left with no recourse against the modifier, and in search of an alternative—often equally innocent—defendant who might be held responsible to pay compensation, but will often be thwarted by an inability to demonstrate proximate causation because of the superseding act of a third party. The dominant view was expressed by Chief Judge Cooke in the Court of Appeals of New York in *Robinson v. Reed-Prentice Division of Package Machinery Co.*, 403 N.E.2d 440, 444 (1980):

Many products may safely and reasonably be used for purposes other than the one for which they were specifically designed. For example, the manufacturer of a screwdriver must foresee that a consumer will use his product to pry open the lid of a can and is thus under a corresponding duty to design the shank of the product with sufficient strength to accomplish that task. In such a situation, the manufacturer is in a superior position to anticipate the reasonable use to which his product may be put and is obliged to assure that no harm will befall those who use the product in such a manner. It is the manufacturer who must bear the responsibility if its purposeful design choice presents an unreasonable danger to users. A cause of action in negligence will lie where it can be shown that a manufacturer was responsible for a defect that caused injury, and that the manufacturer could have foreseen the injury. Control of the instrumentality at the time of the accident in such a case is irrelevant since the defect arose while the product was in the possession of the manufacturer.

The manufacturer's duty, however, does not extend to designing a product that is impossible to abuse or one whose safety features may not be circumvented. A manufacturer need not incorporate safety features into its product so as to guarantee that no harm will come to every user no matter how careless or even reckless. Nor must he trace his product through every link in the chain of distribution to insure that users will not adapt the product to suit their own unique purposes. The duty of a manufacturer, therefore, is not an open-ended one. It extends to the design and manufacture of a finished product which is safe at the time of sale. Material alterations at the hands of a third party which work a substantial change in the condition in which the product was sold by destroying the functional utility of a key safety feature, however foreseeable that modification may have been, are not within the ambit of a manufacturer's responsibility. Acceptance of plaintiff's concept of duty would expand the scope of a manufacturer's duty beyond all reasonable bounds and would be tantamount to imposing absolute liability on manufacturers for all product-related injuries.

3. *An innocent victim.* On the facts as found by the trial court, at least as interpreted by Judge Dennis, *Matthews* is a case — the more cynical might say "yet another case" — where the victim is an innocent party but is still denied recovery from the defendant. As we saw in Chapter 6, when Justice Roger Traynor was developing a new, discrete body of strict liability law for product defects, the precise point of doing so was to enable such innocent victims to be compensated, irrespective of whether the manufacturer was at fault or not. It seems that Traynor's view no longer holds sway, at least not in every case.

4. *Substantial modification and comparative fault.* Just as the development of products liability law had been about moving towards protecting innocent victims, even at the expense of innocent manufacturers or distributors, there was also (as is discussed more fully in Chapter 11) a move away from applying doctrines that provide a complete affirmative defense in favor of utilizing the concept of comparative fault. This then enables the burden of any injury to be shared between the parties in proportions appropriate to the circumstances of each particular case.

If the doctrine of comparative fault had been applied in *Matthews*, it would have required the fact-finder to examine to what degree (if any) Matthews himself was at fault for firing the rifle without the bolt-pin assembly and, if he was, to reduce his damages to an appropriate degree. As Judge Dennis pointed out:

Matthews
case

The district court specifically found that Matthews' use of the rifle was not obviously dangerous; that Matthews was able to rotate the bolt handle into what
appeared to be the closed position prior to pulling the trigger; and *that both he
and an ordinary user would have assumed that the rifle was safe to fire at that point*
(emphasis in original).

5. *Questions of fact and law.* The bigger problem, then, with the majority's decision
in *Matthews* is that it has the effect of taking a question of fact away from the fact-finder
(typically, a jury) and turning it into a question of law for the court. This seems problematic
not only because it seems to be a usurpation of the power of the jury, but also because it
turns a nuanced question about comparative fault in the circumstances of the case into
a bright-line, systemic issue which leads to an all-or-nothing result.

Questions

1. Is the majority's decision in *Matthews* really predicated on the expectation that any
maintenance on the rifle—like any maintenance on an automobile or airplane—would
be carried out with reasonable skill and care?

2. If so, is this a reasonable expectation when so many rifles are maintained by their
owners or users rather than by professional gunsmiths?

3. Does this effectively operate as an equivalent of the pharmaceutical manufacturer's
learned intermediary defense and, if so, is that appropriate?

4. What would be the effect of avoiding talking about what the manufacturer might
reasonably have anticipated when it designed and manufactured the product, and instead
focusing on whether any subsequent modification made to the product was so substantial as to effectively render it a different product (or, at least, a product sufficiently different as to turn it into something for which the original manufacturer could not be held
responsible)? Would this approach be (a) more consistent with the general approach of
products liability law, and (b) preferable to the approach of focusing on the "reasonable
expectations" of the manufacturer?

Prescription Drugs and Medical Devices

*3rd
Rest.*

The test of "reasonable alternative design" inevitably presupposes that an alternative design for the product in question is viable, so that the relevant question becomes whether
it was reasonable to expect the manufacturer to adopt it. However, the Reporters for the
Third Restatement took the view that the assumption that there is a feasible alternative
design is inappropriate where prescription drugs and medical devices are concerned. They
took this view for two main reasons. First, prescription drugs and medical devices become available to the general public only after they have been subjected to extensive clinical trials, which have themselves been reviewed by the Food and Drug Administration
(FDA). Permitting a finding that an alternative formulation or specification should have
been adopted would imply that a judge and/or jury could predict the outcome of clinical trials on a drug or device which might not yet even exist. Secondly, even after clinical trials have been conducted, a drug or device cannot be made generally available unless
it has first been formally approved and licensed by the FDA. Thus allowing a judge and/or
jury to find that an alternative formulation or specification should have been used might

involve a ruling that the manufacturer should have been making a drug or device that has not been licensed by the FDA. The Reporters therefore chose to a adopt a much tougher standard for defect than §2(b) which, accordingly, does not apply to prescription drugs and medical devices.

Restatement (Third) of Torts: Products Liability (1998)

§6. *Liability of Commercial Seller or Distributor for Harm Caused by Defective Prescription Drugs and Medical Devices*

(a) A manufacturer of a prescription drug or medical device who sells or otherwise distributes a defective drug or medical device is subject to liability for harm to persons caused by the defect. A prescription drug or medical device is one that may be legally sold or otherwise distributed only pursuant to a health-care provider's prescription.

(b) For purposes of liability under Subsection (a), a prescription drug or medical device is defective if at the time of sale or other distribution the drug or medical device:

(1) contains a manufacturing defect as defined in §2(a); or

(2) is not reasonably safe due to defective design as defined in Subsection (c); or

(3) is not reasonably safe due to inadequate instructions or warnings as defined in Subsection (d).

(c) A prescription drug or medical device is not reasonably safe due to defective design if the foreseeable risks of harm posed by the drug or medical device are sufficiently great in relation to its foreseeable therapeutic benefits that reasonable health-care providers, knowing of such foreseeable risks and therapeutic benefits, would not prescribe the drug or medical device for any class of patients....

(e) A retail seller or other distributor of a prescription drug or medical device is subject to liability for harm caused by the drug or device if:

(1) at the time of sale or other distribution the drug or medical device contains a manufacturing defect as defined in §2(a); or

(2) at or before the time of sale or other distribution of the drug or medical device the retail seller or other distributor fails to exercise reasonable care and such failure causes harm to persons.

Notes

1. *Criticism of §6(c).* In *Freeman v. Hoffman-LaRoche, Inc.* 260 Neb. 552, 566; 618 N.W.2d 827, 839 (2000), the Supreme Court of Nebraska was blunt in its criticism of §6(c):

> There are several criticisms of §6(c), which will be briefly summarized. First, it does not accurately restate the law. It has been repeatedly stated that there is no support in the case law for the application of a reasonable physician standard in which strict liability for a design defect will apply only when a product is not useful for any class of persons. Rather, as illustrated by the discussion of the treatment of comment *k* under the Second Restatement in other jurisdictions, the majority of courts apply some form of risk-utility balancing that focuses on a variety of factors, including the existence of a reasonable alternative design. The few cases that the Third Restatement cites to as support for the reasonable physician test also apply a risk-utility test. Thus, §6(c) does not re-

state the law and instead seeks to formulate new law with no precedential support. See, e.g., George W. Conk, *Is There a Design Defect in the Restatement (Third) of Torts: Products Liability?* 109 Yale L.J. 1087 (2000); Richard L. Cupp, Jr., *The Continuing Search for Proper Perspective: Whose Reasonableness Should Be At Issue in a Product Design Defect Analysis? Seventh Annual Health Law Symposium Proving Product Defect After the Restatement (Third) of Torts: Product Liability,* 30 Seton Hall L. Rev. 233(1999); Richard L. Cupp, Jr., *Rethinking Conscious Design Liability for Prescription Drugs: The Restatement (Third) Standard Versus a Negligence Approach,* 63 Geo. Wash. L. Rev. 76 (1994); Teresa Moran Schwartz, *Prescription Products and the Proposed Restatement (Third),* 61 Tenn. L. Rev. 1357 (1994); Michael J. Wagner and Laura L. Peterson, *The New Restatement (Third) of Torts—Shelter From the Product Liability Storm for Pharmaceutical Companies and Medical Device Manufacturers?* 53 Food & Drug L.J. 225 (1998).

2. *Prescription drugs and medical devices.* The approval process for medical devices is governed by the Medical Device Amendments of 1976 (MDA), 21 U.S.C. § 360(c) *et seq.,* and is not the same as that for prescription drugs. One difference is that not all new medical devices—unlike all new pharmaceuticals—are required to be submitted to the same approval process. Some devices can, for example, be approved under an abbreviated process under § 510(k), which simply requires the manufacturer to show that the new device is "substantially equivalent" to a device that has already been approved. A fuller discussion of the process for medical devices may be found in the judgment of Justice Scalia in *Riegel v. Medtronic, Inc.,* 128 S.Ct. 999 (2008), which is extracted in Chapter 17.

Questions

1. The test for a manufacturing defect of a prescription drug or medical device remains the same as that for any other product, while that for design defect is different for prescription drugs and medical devices as compared with other products. Is this difference justifiable?

2. Is it appropriate to have prescription drugs and medical devices governed by the same test for design defect?

3. How is a "class of patients" in § 6(c) to be defined? Is it possible to have a "class" of one?

4. Dolly M. Trompeter, *Sex, Drugs, and the Restatement (Third) of Torts, Section 6(c): Why Comment e is the Answer to the Woman Question,* 48 Am. U.L. Rev. 1139, 1142 (1999), asserted that "if every user suffered harm, and no one derived benefit from a medical product, only then could a victim bring a successful claim for design defect." Is she correct?

5. Since women consume a greater share of medical products than men, and it is difficult to see how any regulatory system can test products for pregnant women, does § 6(c) have the effect of discriminating against women?

6. Many brand-name pharmaceuticals are lawfully copied and sold more cheaply as so-called "generic" drugs. If someone is injured after lawfully taking a generic drug, can the manufacturer of the original, brand-name pharmaceutical be liable for the victim's injuries under a theory of design defect?

7. If a significant number of a particular type of heart valve implants have been found to fail without warning, does anyone currently fitted with such an implant, but which has not failed, have any claim either against the manufacturer or against the surgeon who fitted it?

The "State of the Art"

So far we have seen that a design's alleged defectiveness may be judged against either a consumer expectations test, or according to an evaluation of the risks and utility of the product so as to determine whether the manufacturer should have adopted a reasonable alternative design. We have also seen that whether the courts choose to apply one test or the other—or somehow to combine them, as in Pennsylvania—has significant implications for the outcome of the case. One of those implications concerns a defendant's plea that the design amounted to the best possible at the time: it was, as the phrase goes, the "state of the art". Such a plea is essentially inapplicable to cases where the consumer expectations test should be applied, since that test is concerned solely with whether such expectations were met; it is not interested in hearing any explanation as to why they were not. But the notion of "state of the art" is effectively a trump card when the risk-utility test is implicated. If the design truly reflected the state of the art at the time when the product was made, then by definition no reasonable alternative design was available, and so the plaintiff's claim must be denied. The normal weighing of various factors to assess the competing risks and utility of the design is thus abandoned in favor of judgment as a matter of law for the defendant.

As is explained in the following case, a plea that the design represented the state of the art is therefore very different from a representation that it reflected industry custom. A custom can still be evaluated to see whether a reasonable alternative design was available, whereas an effective plea that the design in question reflected the state of the art simply denies the validity of any such evaluation. It is, therefore, potentially very powerful. This means, of course, that any such plea is typically bitterly contested.

Boatland of Houston, Inc. v. Valerie Bailey

609 S.W.2d 743 (1980) (Supreme Court of Texas)

McGEE, J. The admissibility and effect of "state of the art" evidence has been a subject of controversy in both negligence and strict product liability cases. In negligence cases, the reasonableness of the defendant's conduct in placing the product on the market is in issue. Evidence of industry customs at the time of manufacture may be offered by either party for the purpose of comparing the defendant's conduct with industry customs. An offer of evidence of the defendant's compliance with custom to rebut evidence of its negligence has been described as the "state of the art defense." See generally L. Frumer & M. Friedman, *Products Liability* s 16A(4)(i) (1980). In this connection, it is argued that the state of the art is equivalent to industry custom and is relevant only to the issue of the defendant's negligence and irrelevant to a strict liability theory of recovery.

In our view, "custom" is distinguishable from "state of the art." The state of the art with respect to a particular product refers to the technological environment at the time of its manufacture. This technological environment includes the scientific knowledge, economic feasibility, and the practicalities of implementation when the product was manufactured. Evidence of this nature is important in determining whether a safer design was feasible. The limitations imposed by the state of the art at the time of manufacture may affect the feasibility of a safer design....

Logically, the plaintiff's strongest evidence of feasibility of an alternative design is its actual use by the defendant or others at the time of manufacture. Even if a safer alternative was not being used, evidence that it was available, known about, or capable of being developed is relevant in determining its feasibility. In contrast, the defendant's strongest rebuttal evidence is that a particular design alternative was impossible due to the state of the art. Yet the defendant's ability to rebut the plaintiff's evidence is not limited to showing that a particular alternative was impossible; it is entitled to rebut the plaintiff's evidence of feasibility with evidence of limitations on feasibility. A suggested alternative may be invented or discovered but not be feasible for use because of the time necessary for its application and implementation. Also, a suggested alternative may be available, but impractical for reasons such as greatly increased cost or impairment of the product's usefulness. When the plaintiff has introduced evidence that a safer alternative was feasible because it was used, the defendant may then introduce contradictory evidence that it was not used.

Thus in response to the Baileys' evidence of kill switch use in 1978, the time of trial, Boatland was properly allowed to show that they were not used when the boat was sold in 1973. To rebut proof that safety switches were possible and feasible when Bailey's boat was sold because the underlying concept was known and the "Quick Kill," a simple, inexpensive device had been invented, Boatland was properly allowed to show that neither the "Quick Kill" nor any other kill switch was available at that time.

It could reasonably be inferred from this evidence that although the underlying concept of automatic motor cut-off devices was not new, kill switches were not as feasible an alternative as the Baileys' evidence implied. Boatland did not offer evidence of technological impossibility or absolute nonfeasibility; its evidence was offered to show limited availability when the boat was sold. Once the jury was informed of the state of the art, it was able to consider the extent to which it was feasible to incorporate an automatic cut-off device or similar design characteristic into Bailey's boat. The feasibility and effectiveness of a safer design and other factors such as utility and risk, were properly considered by the jury before it ultimately concluded that the boat sold to Bailey was not defectively designed.

In cases involving strict liability for defective design, liability is determined by the product's defective condition; there is no need to prove that the defendant's conduct was negligent. Considerations such as the utility and risk of the product in question and the feasibility of safer alternatives are presented according to the facts as they are proved to be, not according to the defendant's perceptions. Thus, even though the defendant has exercised due care his product may be found defective. When the Baileys introduced evidence of the use of kill switches, Boatland was entitled to introduce rebuttal evidence of nonuse at the time of manufacture due to limitations imposed by the state of the art. Evidence offered under these circumstances is offered to rebut plaintiff's evidence that a safer alternative was feasible and is relevant to defectiveness. It was not offered to show that a custom existed or to infer the defendant's compliance therewith. We would be presented with a different question if the state of the art in 1973 with respect to kill switches had not been disputed and Boatland had attempted to avoid liability by offering proof that Bailey's boat complied with industry custom.

CAMPBELL, J. (dissenting, joined by RAY, J.). I dissent.

"State of the art" does not mean "the state of industry practice." "State of the art" means "state of industry knowledge." At the time of the manufacture of the boat in question, the device and concept of a circuit breaker, as is at issue in this case, was simple, mechanical, cheap, practical, possible, economically feasible and a concept seventy years old, which required no engineering or technical breakthrough. The concept was known by the industry. This fact removes it from "state of the art."

Boatland is a retail seller. It is not the manufacturer. From the adoption of strict liability in this case, and consideration of public policy, each entity involved in the chain of commercial distribution of a defective product has been subject to strict liability for injuries thereby caused, even though it is in no way responsible for the creation of a defective product or could not cure the defect. The remedy for a faultless retail seller is an action for indemnity against the manufacturer.

In products liability, the measure is the dangerously defective quality of the specific product in litigation. The focus is on the product, not the reasoning behind the manufacturer's option of design or the care exercised in making such decisions. Commercial availability or defectiveness as to Boatland is not the test. Defectiveness as to the product is the test. If commercial unavailability is not a defense or limitation on feasibility to the manufacturer, it cannot be a defense to the seller.

The manufacturer of the boat, Mr. Hudson, testified as follows as concerns the concept of a "kill switch." It is practically without dispute that this is one of the simplest mechanical devices and concepts known to man. Its function is, can be, and was performed by many and varied simple constructions. It is more a concept than an invention. The concept has been around most of this century. It is admittedly an easily incorporated concept. Was an invention required in order to incorporate a circuit breaker on a bass boat? Absolutely not! Did the manufacturer have to wait until George Horton invented his specific "Quick Kill" switch before it could incorporate a kill switch of some sort on its bass boats? Absolutely not! Mr. Hudson uses an even simpler electrical circuit breaker on his boats.

Mr. Hudson testified he could have made a kill switch himself, of his own, and of many possible designs, but simply did not do it. Why didn't he do it? He didn't think about it. He never had any safety engineer examine his boats. He hadn't heard of such, he puts them on now, but still thinks people won't use them.

Was the manufacturer faced with a limitation or state of the art due to commercial unavailability? No. If the manufacturer of this boat were the defendant in this case, would the majority hold under this evidence that the commercial unavailability of someone else's simple product is a limitation on the manufacturer's capability (feasibility) to incorporate a device performing the same safety function on its boat? Not if any semblance of strict product liability is to be preserved.

The test for defectiveness of a given product is the same, whether the defendant is the manufacturer, wholesaler or retail seller. The focus is upon the product and not the care or conduct of the particular defendant. The majority opinion has made a new test for each.

The next critical point that the majority fails to take cognizance of is that the factors held by this Court in *Turner v. General Motors Corp.*, 584 S.W.2d 844, 848 (Tex.1979), to apply as to a manufacturer, in its design of a product, have absolutely no relevance or relation to the reasons for holding the mere retail supplier strictly liable to a consumer. The *Turner* decision and its departure from the Restatement definition of the term "unreasonably dangerous," was limited solely to the liability of a manufacturer in its design of products. The definition of "unreasonably dangerous" in the Restatement (2d) of Torts, s 402A, Comment (i) remains applicable to a retail supplier who did not participate in the product design. The focus is thus upon the expectation of an ordinary consumer instead of the propriety of the manufacturer's decision as to design. The harm to the plaintiff in the admission of evidence of commercial unavailability to a retail seller lies in the certainty of such evidence to divert the jury's thought to the reasonableness of the supplier's conduct instead of the true issue; whether the danger was beyond the contemplation of the ordinary use.

What is this Court faced with in this case? Nothing more than a defendant seller attempting to avoid liability by offering proof that Bailey's boat complied with industry practice (which it did at that time) but not because of any limitations on manufacturing feasibility at that time. This is an industry practice case. The evidence does not involve "technological feasibility." The law of the majority opinion is that a simple device, not supplied by the manufacturer, is a defense in a strict liability suit, against a retailer, even though the industry practice was created by the manufacturing industry.

There is no dispute that commercially marketed "kill switches" for bass boats were unavailable to Boatland at the time it sold the boat. Horton's "Quick Kill" was unavailable. The important point is that there is no dispute that at the time of the manufacture of Mr. Bailey's boat, a circuit breaker, whether electrical or mechanical could have easily and cheaply been incorporated into the boat.

Evidence of commercial unavailability to this retail seller should not be admissible. If it is, the majority opinion has created a new and separate test for defectiveness for a retail seller in a strict liability case. The type of commercial unavailability evidence offered here is not true limitation on feasibility to the manufacturer and therefore relevant to the existing state of the art, rather, it is the result of practice in the bass boat manufacturing industry. Subjective commercial unavailability to a retail seller does not operate as a limitation on objective state of the art.

Feasibility as to Boatland is not the test. In a design case, the test is one of feasibility, or a limitation on feasibility as to the manufacturer. If, as to the manufacturer, unavailability to a retail seller is due to the manufacturer's custom or standard, then such evidence should not be admitted because this would allow the manufacturer to set its own standards for liability. I would hold that the trial court erred in permitting such evidence by Boatland to go to the jury, and would affirm the judgment of the Court of Civil Appeals.

Judgment of the court of civil appeals reversed.

Notes

1. *Defense?* Although Justice McGhee observed that the notion of a "state of the art" design has been said to be a defense, that epithet is actually a little misleading. Indeed, the learned judge certainly did not treat the plea in this way. On the contrary, he approved the fact that the jury had been asked to use the evidence regarding the state of the art to consider the extent to which the plaintiff's proposed alternative design (incorporating an automatic cut-off device) was feasible. The plea that a design met the state of the art is not an affirmative defense. It is not used to rebut a plaintiff's *prima facie* case. It is, rather, a means of denying an essential element in the plaintiff's attempt to build that *prima facie* case in the first place: it argues that the design was simply not defective at all. If the plaintiff cannot prove that the product was defective, then clearly there is nothing on which a claim can be based.

2. *Lead-based paint. Smith v. 2328 University Ave. Corp.*, 52 A.D.3d 216 (2008), is a case in point. It involved an action for damages for injuries sustained by the infant plaintiffs as the result of their exposure to lead-based paint in the apartment where they resided between 1995 and 2001. While the litigation was pending, NL Industries was identified as the manufacturer of the paint pigments containing the lead used to make the paint that allegedly poisoned the infants, and so a second amended complaint alleged causes of action against NL for negligence and strict products liability. An appellate court in New

York denied the claim, however, because any interior lead paint present in the plaintiffs' home was applied before 1960, when the manufacture, sale, and distribution of lead-based pigments and/or paint, and its use in residential units, was outlawed. Since the paint pigments manufactured by NL were not defective at the time they were created, nor was distribution thereof prohibited until 1960, there was no question of finding the manufacturer liable. Indeed, any injury that had arisen would have been due to poor maintenance of the property in failing to prevent the paint from peeling and flaking, at which point it would have become hazardous through possible ingestion or inhalation.

3. *Affirmative defenses.* Affirmative defenses are used very differently. Their point is to enable defendants to argue that, *despite* the plaintiff's having been able to prove every element of her claim, she should nevertheless not obtain judgment against the defendant for some or all of her injuries. Such a defense is clearly not as powerful as pleading that a central element in the plaintiff's case has never been proved. Affirmative defenses are discussed in more detail in Part IV.

Questions

1. How far afield is it permissible to go to establish the "state of the art"? Are we necessarily to stop at municipal, state, or national boundaries? Are Americans entitled to expect the best products in the world?

2. Is "state of the art" a term that refers to the best design known, the best design currently in mass production, or the best design currently considered to be economically viable? What are the dangers inherent in taking each of these approaches?

Subsequent Remedial Measures

The law regarding subsequent remedial measures is closely related to that of state of the art. Now codified for federal courts in Federal Rule of Evidence 407, it provides that:

> When, after an injury or harm allegedly caused by an event, measures are taken that, if taken previously, would have made the injury or harm less likely to occur, evidence of the subsequent measures is not admissible to prove negligence, culpable conduct, a defect in a product, a defect in a product's design, or a need for a warning or instruction. This rule does not require the exclusion of evidence of subsequent measures when offered for another purpose, such as proving ownership, control, or feasibility of precautionary measures, if controverted, or impeachment.

The purpose of Rule 407 is clear. If the design would not have been considered defective at the time the product was made, then hindsight cannot retrospectively make it defective. Certainly, a design that reflected the state of the art at the time cannot subsequently be impugned because of later developments. As was said in *Morse v. Minneapolis & St. Louis Ry. Co.*, 16 N.W. 358, 359 (Minn. 1883):

> A person may have exercised all the care which the law required, and yet in the light of his new experience, after an unexpected accident has occurred, and as a measure of extreme caution, he may adopt additional safeguards. The more careful a person is, the more regard he has for the lives of others, the more likely he would be to do so, and it would seem unjust that he could not do so without

being liable to have such acts construed as an admission of prior negligence. We think such a rule puts an unfair interpretation upon human conduct, and virtually holds out an inducement for continued negligence.

Any attempt to refer to such developments to provide the basis for a case of product liability must therefore normally be brought as a post-sale failure to warn claim (for which see Chapter 8), although it should be noted (as it is in Chapter 8) that many states are also reluctant to recognize such claims.

However, the policy underlying Rule 407 is inapplicable to subsequent remedial measures taken by a non-party, because they will not expose the non-party to liability. Admitting evidence of such measures will therefore not act as "an inducement for continued negligence" or, to put this another way, as a perverse incentive to refrain from making products safe. For this reason, the Third Circuit held in *Diehl v. Blaw-Knox*, 360 F.3d 426, 430 (2004), that Rule 407 did not call for the exclusion of evidence of subsequent remedial measures taken by a non-party. As the court said, "it hardly makes sense to speak of a party's fault being 'admitted' by someone other than the party". The District Court's decision to exclude such evidence was therefore reversible error.

In its application to subsequent remedial measures taken by the product manufacturer, however, Rule 407 seems quite categorical. Indeed, the Rule was amended in 1997 to make clear that it applies not only to cases of product defect where fault is alleged, but also to cases of strict liability. Yet there remain at least three controversial issues. First, although the states all have some version of a rule barring evidence of subsequent remedial measure, they do not all mirror Rule 407 precisely. In particular, some states have continued with a rule which is more like the pre-1997 version, so that it does not apply to claims of strict liability. The reasons for this were explained by the Supreme Court of California in *Ault v. International Harvester Co.*, 13 Cal.3d 113 (1974):

> When the context is transformed from a typical negligence setting to the modern products liability field, however, the "public policy" assumptions justifying this evidentiary rule are no longer valid. The contemporary corporate mass producer of goods, the normal products liability defendant, manufactures tens of thousands of units of goods; it is manifestly unrealistic to suggest that such a producer will forego making improvements in its product, and risk innumerable additional lawsuits and the attendant adverse effect upon its public image, simply because evidence of adoption of such improvement may be admitted in an action founded on strict liability for recovery on an injury that preceded the improvement. In the products liability area, the exclusionary rule ... does not affect the primary conduct of the mass producer of goods, but serves merely as a shield against potential liability. In short, the purpose ... is not applicable to a strict liability case and hence its exclusionary rule should not be gratuitously extended to that field.

Yet even in those states where strict products liability claims are held to be outside the subsequent remedial measures rule, it remains to be determined exactly what that means in practice since the promulgation of the Products Liability Restatement. While manufacturing defects certainly involve strict liability, they simply involve a departure from the intended design. Accordingly, the rule seems quite irrelevant in such cases. The only strict products liability claims to which this could be relevant therefore seem to be (a) cases of alleged manufacturing defects in states that continue to apply § 402A of the Second Restatement, and (b) design defect cases which fall to be decided under the consumer expectations test.

This seems to be the implicit explanation for cases such as *Forma Scientific, Inc., v. Biosera Inc.*, 960 P.2d 108 (1998), where the Supreme Court of Colorado held that a manufacturer of ultra-cold freezers was strictly liable for a design defect after a freezer failed and the plaintiff's store of blood cell antibodies, which were sold for use in the health care industry, was destroyed. Evidence of post-accident changes in the design of the freezers was held admissible because the feasibility of the alternative design was not in doubt, and such evidence did help to establish the appropriate level of expectations for the consumer (albeit that the "consumer" here was actually another business).

This brings us to the second controversial issue, which was highlighted by the Supreme Court of Pennsylvania in *Duchess v. Langston Corp.*, 769 A.2d 1131, 1142, 1143 (2001), namely that products are supposed to be judged defective (or not) "at the time of distribution" and not at some point thereafter. On this basis it should be irrelevant whether the claim implicates fault or not. It was striking, indeed, that the Court was

> More fundamentally ... unable to meaningfully distinguish claims asserting negligent design from those asserting a design defect in terms of their effect on the implementation of remedial measures and/or design.

The Court therefore held that evidence of subsequent remedial measures is normally admissible in all products liability claims, whether they are framed in negligence or strict liability.

On the facts of *Duchess*, however, the Court held that one of the exceptions in the rule applied. The plaintiff, Mr. Duchess, had been injured while cleaning one of his employer's machines, which had been manufactured by the defendant, Langton. He wished to introduce evidence of the subsequent fitting of an additional safety device, known as an interlock, to assist in his claim of a design defect. For the reasons already stated, the Court would not have permitted him to do so, but for the fact that the defendant's expert witness (and counsel) both asserted that the alternative design proposed by the plaintiff was impractical. Such assertions amounted, said the Court, to controverting the feasibility of precautionary measures, so that the plaintiff was entitled to introduce evidence of subsequent remedial measures to challenge the defendant's assertions. It concluded (769 A.2d, at 1149–50):

> We recognize the difficulties in defending against a claim of an alternative, safer design, while at the same maintaining the advantage of the rule excluding evidence that an alternative design was later employed. Significantly, however, the rule does not require the surrender of a vigorous defense — presently, Langston was free to fully develop and advance the position that, in the time frame in which the Saturn III was delivered to Duchess's employer, its design was both acceptable and safe. To this end, Langston's presentation of evidence concerning the restricted access to the print shield location during normal operations, the ready availability and ease of application of safety precautions, and the training and experience of operators was both relevant and consistent with maintenance of the evidentiary exclusion. Langston also could have addressed the trade-offs associated with the design process on such terms, for example, by pointing out that an interlock would require substantial adjustments to the set-up process for printing that were not warranted given the safety of the existing design. Langston's evidence and arguments, however, went further, advancing the position that visual observation of the anilox/wiper rolls in operation was essential to the performance of the machine's function, and thus proper printing would be precluded by introduction of an interlock.

In such circumstances, we find that the exceptions in Rule 407 (and its common law counterpart) were implicated, both to permit the Duchesses to establish the feasibility of the alternate design and to impeach Langston's essential assertion that it could not practically be done. The trial court, then, should have determined whether the probative value of the evidence (in terms of feasibility and impeachment) exceeded its prejudicial impact, and whether some lesser restorative measure would have sufficed. Here, however, the trial court did not perform such task or otherwise undertake an appropriate exercise of its discretion. Rather, it excluded the evidence of the design change to the Saturn III based upon the erroneous conclusion that Langston had never placed feasibility in issue or implicated impeachment concerns.

Since we are unable to conclude that the advantage gained by Langston in these circumstances was insubstantial, we hold that the Superior Court's decision to award a new trial was correct.

This takes us to the third issue, which concerns the precise determination of the time after which remedial measures may be implemented without their being used in evidence. A literal reading of Rule 407 suggests that the relevant time is that of the plaintiff's injury. This is problematic for two reasons. First, product liability is concerned with products that are found to have been defective at the time of sale or distribution. If the subsequent remedial measures rule is supposed to be designed to avoid the benefits of hindsight being retrospectively applied to evaluate the safety or otherwise of a product, then the rule should logically run from the date of sale or distribution and not from the date of any subsequent injury.

This was, indeed, the view taken by the Supreme Court of South Carolina in *Branham v. Ford Motor Co.*, 701 S.E.2d 5, 17–18 (2010), even though the evidence in question did not relate to subsequent remedial measures, but to subsequent admissions of the product's defectiveness. In *Branham*, the plaintiff had been injured when the Bronco II vehicle in which he was a passenger rolled over. A memorandum and a tape-recording from three years after the year of manufacture (but twelve years before the accident) were admitted into evidence at trial. They contained admissions by Ford engineers that: "Our data are not terribly favorable. Our rollover rate is three times higher than the Chevy S-10 Blazer," while commenting that they had nevertheless succeeded in "cloud[ing the] minds" of representatives of *Consumers Report*. The Supreme Court held that admission of what it called this "post-distribution evidence" was prejudicial error and ordered a new trial.

There is, however, the question of whether such evidence should be barred in cases where the manufacturer had already decided to implement the remedial measures before either the injury or the sale or distribution, but had not yet implemented that decision. Mark Boyco and Ryan Vacca, *Who Knew? The Admissibility of Subsequent Remedial Measures When Defendants Are Without Knowledge of the Injuries*, 38 McGeorge L. Rev. 653, 662 (2007) have commented:

Admitting such evidence is far less likely to discourage safety improvements because the person making the improvement does not know of the plaintiff's injuries, and therefore, is unlikely to anticipate a lawsuit at all. Although after making the improvement the prospective defendant believes the chances of an accident are reduced, it still appreciates the potential for litigation as preventative measures are not infallible. However, as far as the potential defendant knows, no accidents have taken place yet, and therefore, it believes that any improvements it takes will only be seen as prudent and cautious. In this scenario, there is no risk of discouraging safety improvements. Still, a literal reading of Rule 407 suggests the doctrine of subsequent remedial measures would bar the admissibility of the improvement.

But that is not the last of it. Certainly, evidence that a defendant was considering making an improvement before gaining knowledge of a plaintiff's injury is relevant to show whether the failure to make the improvement earlier was reasonable. Indeed, can a defendant's improvement be "remedial" at all if not made with the intent to remedy the conditions which led to a plaintiff's harm?

This was indeed the approach that the Seventh Circuit took in *Kaczmarek v. Allied Chemical Corp.*, 836 F.2d 1055, 1060 (1987). Writing for the court, Judge Posner observed that:

> Once the decision to adopt the safety measure has been taken, presumably on sufficient grounds, the fact that an accident occurred can only strengthen them. And since the decision itself will be admissible, the incremental evidentiary impact of the fact that the decision was carried out is unlikely to be great. Indeed, if after an accident the injurer rescinded a decision for safety made before the accident occurred, his conduct would strike the average jury as perverse. So the injurer is unlikely to rescind merely to keep from the jury evidence that the remedial measure was implemented.

On the facts of *Kacmarek* itself, however, Judge Posner ruled that "the considerations pro and con the exception sought in this case are too closely balanced for us to want to complicate the administration of Rule 407 by creating ... an exception" so that the trial judge's decision, to refuse to allow the jury to hear of the implementation of the design change after the accident, was affirmed. This approach of allowing the jury to hear of the decision to change the design before the victim had been injured, but refusing to allow it to hear of the actual implementation, was subsequently followed in *Dewick v. Maytag Corporation*, 296 F.Supp.2d 905 (N.D. Ill. 2003).

Questions

1. Are the problems associated with the application of Rule 407 (and its state equivalents) evidence of a defect in the drafting of the rule, or evidence of confusion as to what constitutes a design defect?

2. What is the appropriate time after which remedial measures may be implemented without their being used in evidence? Should it reflect more what the defendant knew than what it did?

3. If the rule may not apply when the defendant seeks to challenge the feasibility of the plaintiff's proposed alternative design, would the defendant actually do better to concede the design's feasibility and so challenge the plaintiff's claim on other grounds?

Ultrahazardous Products

Since the English case of *Rylands v. Fletcher*, (1868) L.R. 3 H.L. 330, involving the bursting of a reservoir, became assimilated into American law, it has been established that liability for injuring someone when engaged in an ultrahazardous activity is strict (i.e. it requires no proof of fault). It has sometimes been suggested that a manufacturer's liability for injuries sustained as a result of the use of an ultrahazardous product should be similarly strict. The issue raised by such products is quite simple. If they are so dangerous, it is often suggested that this must automatically mean that they suffer from a design defect, on the grounds that they possess insufficient utility to outweigh the high risks involved. Thus a person injured as a result of the use or consumption of one of these products should be able to claim compensation from the manufacturer and/or distributor. Although others are sometimes included, four products tend to be identified as ultrahazardous: alcohol, asbestos, tobacco, and handguns.

Paul R. Bonney, Manufacturers' Strict Liability for Handgun Injuries: An Economic Analysis
73 Geo. L.J. 1437 (1984–85)

As this note has demonstrated, handgun purchasers both underestimate the injury costs of handguns and fail to account fully for third party handgun injuries. The current rule of no handgun manufacturer liability produces an inefficient result. People purchase too many handguns because they base their purchasing decisions on an artificially low price—a price that does not reflect the full costs of handguns. Thus, economic analysis dictates that a strict liability rule be applied to handgun manufacturers. Only by holding manufacturers strictly liable will an efficient level of handgun sales be realized.

Handgun victims or their survivors generally should be able to recover from manufacturers for all handgun injuries. This rule of strict liability for handgun manufacturers, however, must be refined in several ways because of the unique nature of handgun sales, use, and injury. The economic analysis presented in Part II indicates that a defense of contributory negligence should be added to the strict liability rule in order to encourage product users to exercise appropriate care. In the case of handguns, the defense should apply to two classes of plaintiffs—users and victims. When handgun users act negligently and injure themselves, they should be barred from recovering against the manufacturer. When handgun victims act negligently in causing themselves to be injured by another, they should be barred from recovering against the manufacturer. The victim, if not negligent, should always be able to sue the manufacturer directly. The victim should not first have to attempt to recover from the handgun user. A corollary to this point is that the manufacturer who pays for a victim's injuries should be able to sue the handgun user for negligence in use. In effect, the manufacturer should be subrogated to the rights of the victim. This refinement would allow full recovery to innocent victims and would permit a reduction in manufacturer liability in those cases in which the manufacturer could find a user who is not judgment proof.

Victims of accidental, nonnegligent discharging of handguns should also be permitted to recover from handgun manufacturers. Victims now can recover from manufacturers under traditional products liability doctrine for injuries that result from gun malfunction or the absence of safety devices. Yet where the gun functions properly, the victim should still be able to recover against the manufacturer when the handgun is used in such a manner that the victim is accidently, but nonnegligently, injured. Of course, victims should recover from manufacturers when the victims are injured intentionally by users....

Judge Mentz stressed in *Richman* that "it hardly seems unfair to require manufacturers and purchasers, rather than innocent victims, to pay for the risks [of handguns]" 571

F. Supp. at 203. Judge Mentz also emphasized that "both fairness and efficiency" suggest that the handgun manufacturer be held liable. *Id.* at 203–04. And as Justice Traynor stated:

> The purpose of [strict] liability is to insure that the costs of injuries resulting from defective products are borne by the manufacturers that put such products on the market rather than by the injured persons who are powerless to protect themselves. *Greenman*, 59 Cal. 2d at 63, 377 P.2d at 901, 27 Cal. Rptr. at 701.

Notes

1. *Pre-emption.* As we saw in Chapter 6, *Greenman* is the case that established the law of strict products liability. However, the arguments advanced by Bonney have not generally found favor with the courts, who have generally avoided addressing the question head-on. Instead, they have tended to take the view that such cases have effectively been pre-empted by the political process, reasoning that Congress has decided to permit the widespread sale and use of these products—albeit sometimes under certain restrictions—and that it is not for the courts to usurp the legislative function. The issue of pre-emption is considered at greater length in Chapter 17.

2. *Negligence without* res ipsa loquitur. In the few cases that have allowed a plaintiff's claim to proceed, the courts have insisted on applying the ordinary law of negligence, albeit often with a more relaxed standard for proof of duty. But just because a duty may be held to have been owed to the plaintiff does not necessarily mean, of course, that it has been breached, nor that any such breach was a cause of the plaintiff's injuries. Claims that the requirements of *res ipsa loquitur* have been satisfied because the product in question is ultrahazardous have not generally been entertained.

USA v. Stevens, 994 So.2d 1062 (2008), is a case in point. A laboratory had some anthrax stolen, and a man to whom some of this anthrax was then apparently mailed died after inhaling it. The question for the Supreme Court of Florida was whether any potential liability of the laboratory should be determined according to the law of negligence, or by a theory of strict liability for engaging in an ultrahazardous activity in working with or designing an ultrahazardous product. A majority held that the undoubted fact that anthrax is ultrahazardous did not mean that this was a case of strict liability but simply went to the question of the degree of care which the laboratory should have taken in ensuring that its anthrax remained secure from theft or other escape: "where the risk of injury is great[, …] the corresponding duty of the lab is heightened." The case was therefore to be determined in accordance with the ordinary law of negligence.

Questions

1. Does *Stevens* imply that a manufacturer of an ultrahazardous product is in a better position to defend a products liability lawsuit than the manufacturer of a "regular" product, because the latter can be held liable for a manufacturing defect, whereas any defect in an ultrahazardous product might actually render the product less dangerous? If so, is this an anomaly that needs to be rectified?

2. If working with anthrax is not to be considered an ultrahazardous activity, is no activity now to be considered under that rubric?

3. If a handgun is discharged in a manner that causes a nonnegligent injury, where is the product defect?

4. Some jurisdictions recognize "social host" and/or "dram shop" liability, where the provider (whether for money or otherwise) of alcohol to someone who is already (or who, as a result, becomes) intoxicated can be held liable to the victim of an accident caused by the intoxicated person. In those jurisdictions that do recognize this form of liability, would it make sense to recognize analogous liability for those who provide handguns which are subsequently used to cause injury to an innocent third party?

5. Can someone who suffers cancer or other injury as a result of passive smoking recover for that injury from tobacco manufacturers?

Hypothetical

Since the early 1960s, air in passenger jets has typically combined re-circulated existing cabin air with air "bled" off the engines. This "bleed air" is sucked into the engines before being cooled and compressed, and is then pumped into the plane. However, the new Boeing 787 Dreamliner does not use bleed air and instead compresses atmospheric air from outside the plane. Boeing says that the change in design is because of advances in electrical systems and not concerns over bleed air.

In the 1980s, new planes began to be fitted with air filters, designed to filter contaminants out of air pumped through the cabin. The manufacturers' instructions were that these filters should be replaced every 25,000 miles. It is known, however, that many filters have been left in place for considerably longer, even up to 75,000 miles and beyond.

Faye White, a flight attendant with Tampania Airlines for ten years, flew regularly on planes built in the 1980s until she retired due to ill health. She has a documented medical history of chronic migraines, tremors and vision loss, which symptoms started to appear only after she had been flying with Tampania for five years. A former colleague has suggested that these symptoms might have been brought on by Faye's ingestion of bleed air contaminated by oil and toxic fuel residues from the aircraft engines.

If she approached you to represent her as her attorney, how would you tackle this case?

Chapter 8

Failures to Warn

Is There a Duty to Warn at All?

While a product may have been appropriately designed and correctly manufactured, it is still possible that it may present certain hazards when used as intended. A knife is clearly one example; a lawnmower another. If both work as intended, then neither suffers from either of the types of product defect that have been considered so far. On the other hand, both products are still dangerous pieces of equipment that could do very real harm while in use. For that reason, the courts have held that, in order to make a product *reasonably* safe, it is sometimes necessary for the manufacturer or distributor to provide one or more warnings as to how the product should (or should not) be used. A failure to provide a reasonable instruction or warning may then render the manufacturer or distributor liable for harm that ensues when the product is used.

Failure-to-warn claims are similar to claims of misrepresentation, so that there is often significant overlap between the two theories in a given case. There are, however, two differences. First, whereas misrepresentations can occur with or without fault on the part of the representor, a claim for failure to warn will succeed, as we shall see, only where the defendant can be shown to have been at fault. In other words, this is another area in which it is misleading to talk of products liability law as being "strict" liability, since fault must always be shown (irrespective of whether a state follows the Second or Products Liability Restatement).

The second distinction between misrepresentation claims and those for failure to warn is that the former concerns *mis*feasance. It applies only to statements that have actually been made, reflecting the law's normal position that, on the one hand, there is no duty to act, but, on the other, that any act actually performed must be performed to an appropriate standard. Claims of failure-to-warn, however, are essentially about *non*feasance: the law in this area goes beyond the common law's default position and does impose a duty to act — and such actions must, of course, be reasonable.

While it is common to focus upon warnings as another theory of product defect that a victim might seek to utilize, it should also be noted that providing an appropriate warning will not only be a good defense to a failure-to-warn claim, but may be used too as part of the defendant's case to show that the product's *design* was not defective. This means that a defendant may seek to utilize any warning given as a defense, even where the plaintiff makes no allegation that it was itself somehow defective.

In Chapter 7, we saw that there is a very real controversy over the appropriate approach to questions of alleged design defects. So far as the duty to warn is concerned — and despite the fact that there is no controversy as to whether fault must be shown or not—there are also two different approaches to be found in the Restatements. However, neither Restatement requires a manufacturer to warn of an obvious risk.

Restatement (Second) of Torts (1965)

§ 388. Chattel Known to be Dangerous for Intended Use

One who supplies directly or through a third person a chattel for another to use is subject to liability to those whom the supplier should expect to use the chattel with the consent of the other or to be endangered by its probable use, for physical harm caused by the use of the chattel in the manner for which and by a person for whose use it is supplied, if the supplier

(a) knows or has reason to know that the chattel is or is likely to be dangerous for the use for which it is supplied, and

(b) has no reason to believe that those for whose use the chattel is supplied will realize its dangerous condition, and

(c) fails to exercise reasonable care to inform them of its dangerous condition or of the facts which make it likely to be dangerous.

Restatement (Third) of Torts: Products Liability (1998)

§ 2(c). Categories of Product Defect

A product ... is defective because of inadequate instructions or warnings when the foreseeable risks of harm posed by the product could have been reduced or avoided by the provision of reasonable instructions or warnings by the seller or other distributor, or a predecessor in the commercial chain of distribution, and the omission of the instructions or warnings renders the product not reasonably safe.

Notes

1. *The "sophisticated user."* In *Johnson v. American Standard, Inc.*, 43 Cal.4th 56 (2008), the Supreme Court of California considered a complaint brought by a trained HVAC technician, who claimed that the maintenance and repairs he performed on air conditioning units in the normal course of his job created and exposed him to phosgene gas, causing him to develop pulmonary fibrosis. He sued various chemical manufacturers, chemical suppliers, and manufacturers of air conditioning equipment, including American Standard.

Large air conditioning systems commonly use R-22, a hydrochlorofluorocarbon refrigerant. The refrigerant can decompose into phosgene gas when exposed to flame or high heat, as could happen while a technician is brazing air conditioner pipes containing residual refrigerant. Exposure to phosgene gas may cause numerous health problems, and manufacturers and HVAC technicians have generally known of the dangers this exposure could cause since as early as 1931. The dangers and risks associated with R-22 are noted on Material Safety Data Sheets (MSDS's). Applying § 388 of the Second Restatement, it was plain that the plaintiff was among those who should have been aware of these risks at the time of his injury, so that he was a "sophisticated user" and could not succeed with his failure to warn claim.

2. *Second or Products Liability Restatement?* Note how, in *Johnson*, the Supreme Court of California employed the terminology of the Products Liability Restatement to identify the complaint as being about a "failure to warn," but applied a test from the Second Restatement to decide on the substantive legal position in California.

Mills v. Giant of Maryland, LLC
441 F.Supp.2d 104 (2006) (US District Court, District of Columbia)

KENNEDY, J. Plaintiffs—Milton Mills, Rashid Gholson, Hua-Wei Cherng, Norma Humphries, Lynette Garner, Darrell Bransome, Paul Miller, Glenda Costner, Sybil Harold, and Elizabeth Russell—bring this putative class action on behalf of "all those lactose intolerant persons who, unaware of their condition, have purchased milk in Washington, D.C., and suffered the consequences of their condition." Plaintiffs seek injunctive relief and an award of damages as a result of what they allege was the defendants'—Giant of Maryland, LLC; Safeway, Inc.; Horizon Organic; Dean Foods Co.; Nestle Holdings, Inc.; Farmland Dairies, LLC; Shenandoah's Pride, LLC; Stonyfield Farm, Inc.; and Cloverland Farms Dairy, Inc.—"negligent failure to warn causing personal injury." Plaintiffs additionally assert a products liability claim premised on defendants' sale of milk without proper warning labels. Before the court are defendants' motions to dismiss. Upon consideration of the motions, the oppositions thereto, the record of this case, and the argument of counsel at a hearing, the court concludes that plaintiffs' claims must be dismissed.

Plaintiffs seek to focus attention on what is purported to be a widespread, but largely unrecognized, health problem—lactose intolerance. This condition results from the absence of lactase enzymes that facilitate the digestion of lactose, the sugar found in milk. Following the consumption of milk and milk-products, those who suffer from lactose intolerance exhibit symptoms including "flatulence, bloating, cramps, and diarrhea."

According to plaintiffs, while nearly all infants and young children are able to digest lactose, lactose intolerance is pervasive among adults. Plaintiffs assert that "75% of the world's population, including 90% of Asian Americans, 90% of Native Americans, 60% to 80% of African Americans, 50% to 80% of Latinos, and 6% to 22% of Caucasians are lactose intolerant."

Notwithstanding the vast number of people allegedly afflicted with lactose intolerance, plaintiffs insist that the extent to which people suffer from this condition has been minimized by the milk industry and "the government's marketing efforts." Plaintiffs maintain that defendants, with the aid of the government, have propagated the myth that milk is a necessary part of a healthy diet while simultaneously stifling information about the incidence of lactose intolerance.

Because of the limited dissemination of information about the scope of lactose intolerance, plaintiffs contend that many individuals remain unaware that they suffer from this illness. Plaintiffs, for example, are all individuals who, "unaware of their lactose intolerance, have unwittingly been subjected to gastrointestinal pain and discomfort by purchasing and consuming milk sold by defendants."

In order to address the public's ignorance of what plaintiffs allege is a common malady, plaintiffs request that defendants be enjoined from marketing their products in the District of Columbia until they adopt a warning label that alerts consumers about the possible risks of lactose intolerance. Plaintiffs suggest two possible warning labels:

> WARNING—IF YOU EXPERIENCE DIARRHEA OR STOMACH CRAMPS AFTER CONSUMING MILK, YOU MAY BE LACTOSE INTOLERANT. CHECK WITH YOUR PHYSICIAN.

> WARNING—LACTOSE INTOLERANT INDIVIDUALS MAY EXPERIENCE BLOATING, DIARRHEA, OR OTHER GASTROINTESTINAL DISCOMFORT FROM CONSUMING MILK. CHECK WITH YOUR PHYSICIAN.

In addition, the named plaintiffs seek money damages for the injuries they have suffered as a result of milk consumption....

Plaintiffs assert two claims, both premised on defendants' failure to include a warning on milk. Plaintiffs' first claim relies on a negligence theory, the second on a theory of strict liability. Under either theory, the manufacturer or seller's duty to warn remains the same, "essentially one of ordinary care." *East Penn Mfg. Co. v. Pineda*, 578 A.2d 1113, 1118 (D.C.1990). "The seller or manufacturer of a product whose use could result in foreseeable harm has a duty to give a warning which adequately advises the user of attendant risks and which provides specific directions for safe use."

The court agrees with defendants that, in the case before the court, no such duty exists. The *Restatement (Second) of Torts* § 402A *cmt. j*, states that a "seller may reasonably assume that those with common allergies, as for example to eggs or strawberries, will be aware of them, and he is not required to warn against them." If no duty exists to warn consumers that they may be allergic to common food items, then *a fortiori*, no duty exists to warn those that consume dairy products of the potential dangers of lactose intolerance. Although hospitalization or fatalities are possible when an individual has a severe allergic reaction, see, e.g., *Bruse v. Holiday*, 16 A.D.3d 785, 790 N.Y.S.2d 765, 767 (N.Y.App.Div.2005) (plaintiff hospitalized for anaphylactic shock caused by contact with shellfish); *St. Luke's Midland Reg'l Med. Ctr. v. Kennedy*, 653 N.W.2d 880, 882 (S.D.2002) (claimant suffered anaphylactic shock following contact with latex), nowhere do plaintiffs allege that any such danger exists for the lactose intolerant. At worst, someone that suffers from lactose intolerance can expect to suffer gastrointestinal discomfort of the nature previously discussed.

Plaintiffs have not cited, nor has the court been able to otherwise find, any case in which a duty to warn has been imposed under similar circumstances. As defendants correctly identify, in every case relied upon by plaintiffs the duty to warn arose when the allergen contained in the food was not an obvious ingredient. See *Edwards v. Hop Sin, Inc.*, 140 S.W.3d 13, 16–17 (Ky.Ct.App.2003) (addressing oysters that were contaminated by bacteria); *Livingston v. Marie Callender's Inc.*, 72 Cal.App.4th 830, 85 Cal.Rptr.2d 528, 533–34 (1999) (soup that professed to be "made from the freshest ingredients" contained monosodium glutamate); *Brown v. McDonald's Corp.*, 101 Ohio App.3d 294, 655 N.E.2d 440, 443–44 (1995) (addressing a failure to warn consumers that a hamburger contained an ingredient derived from seaweed). Here, the only alleged danger is purportedly posed by the inherent qualities of milk, hence, defendants have no duty to warn consumers about lactose intolerance.

For the reasons set forth above, the defendants' motions to dismiss are granted.

Notes

1. *Interactions with other potentially harmful causes. Mills* is essentially a case where the plaintiffs alleged that the manufacturers of a product should warn about its potential for harmful interactions with something else, specifically lactose intolerance. In such cases, neither the product that is the subject of the complaint (milk) nor the other potentially harmful cause (lactose intolerance) will cause harm in isolation; it is only in combination that there is the risk of harm.

2. *Warnings about potentially harmful interactions.* As we shall see later in this Chapter, drug manufacturers are often placed under a duty to warn about potentially harmful interactions with other substances. However, the wording of § 2(c), which talks of

"the foreseeable risks of harm posed by the product," means that there can also be a duty to warn of foreseeably harmful interactions with other substances or conditions when other types of products are involved (although not, as in *Mills*, when those risks are obvious). In the following case, however, the plaintiffs evidently attempted to take this principle a little too far.

O'Neil v. Crane Co.

266 P.3d 987 (2012) (Supreme Court of California)

CORRIGAN, J. This case involves the limits of a manufacturer's duty to prevent foreseeable harm related to its product: When is a product manufacturer liable for injuries caused by adjacent products or replacement parts that were made by others and used in conjunction with the defendant's product? We hold that a product manufacturer may not be held liable in strict liability or negligence for harm caused by another manufacturer's product unless the defendant's own product contributed substantially to the harm, or the defendant participated substantially in creating a harmful combined use of the products.

Defendants Crane Co.... and Warren Pumps LLC ... made valves and pumps used in Navy warships. They were sued here for a wrongful death allegedly caused by asbestos released from external insulation and internal gaskets and packing, all of which were made by third parties and added to the pumps and valves post sale. It is undisputed that defendants never manufactured or sold any of the asbestos-containing materials to which plaintiffs' decedent was exposed. Nevertheless, plaintiffs claim defendants should be held strictly liable and negligent because it was foreseeable workers would be exposed to and harmed by the asbestos in replacement parts and products used in conjunction with their pumps and valves.

Recognizing plaintiffs' claims would represent an unprecedented expansion of strict products liability. We decline to do so. California law has long provided that manufacturers, distributors, and retailers have a duty to ensure the safety of their products, and will be held strictly liable for injuries caused by a defect in their products. Yet, we have never held that these responsibilities extend to preventing injuries caused by other products that might foreseeably be used in conjunction with a defendant's product. Nor have we held that manufacturers must warn about potential hazards in replacement parts made by others when, as here, the dangerous feature of these parts was not integral to the product's design. The broad rule plaintiffs urge would not further the purposes of strict liability. Nor would public policy be served by requiring manufacturers to warn about the dangerous propensities of products they do not design, make, or sell.

BACKGROUND

During World War II, defendants sold parts to the United States Navy for use in the steam propulsion systems of warships. These propulsion systems were vast and complex. Massive boilers generated steam from seawater. The steam flowed through a maze of interconnected pipes to power the ship's engines and provide energy for use throughout the vessel. A single ship contained several miles of piping. Because the steam flowing through this system was extremely hot and highly pressurized, the pipes and attached components required insulation to prevent heat loss and protect against accidental burns. Navy specifications required the use of asbestos-containing insulation on all external surfaces of the steam propulsion systems. Asbestos insulation was also used as an internal sealant

within gaskets and other components of the propulsion system. The Navy preferred asbestos over other types of insulating materials because it was lightweight, strong, and effective. Indeed, asbestos was considered to be such an important resource that a 1942
federal regulation ordered its conservation for the war effort. Plaintiffs' expert admitted
there was no acceptable substitute for asbestos until at least the late 1960's. Warships could
not have been built without it.

The Navy's Bureau of Ships oversaw the design and construction of warships. Naval
engineers created specifications that provided detailed design, material, and performance
requirements for equipment to be used on board. Equipment that did not conform with
the Navy's specifications was rejected. Product manufacturers were required to comply with
naval specifications, including those mandating the use of asbestos.

Reversed and remanded.

Questions

1. Did the Court in *O'Neil* hold that the defendants owed no duty to the plaintiff, or
that they did not breach their duty?

2. Could the defendants also have argued that their parts had become integrated into
a larger system over which they had no control?

3. Why did the plaintiffs not argue that the defendants' products suffered from a design defect?

Notes

1. *"Reasonable instructions or warnings"*. The phrase "reasonable instructions or warnings" in §2(c) of the Products Liability Restatement encapsulates the three issues spelled
out separately in subsections (a) to (c) in §388 of the Second Restatement. In principle,
it ought to be possible to think of the issues as essentially twofold, with the first concerned with whether there is a duty to provide any instruction or warning at all, and the
second with what such a warning should say. This might suggest that the question of how
to word a warning becomes germane only if it has first been established that there is, indeed, a duty to warn. In practice, however, the order in which these issues are addressed
will normally be reversed since, without having first established what the warning might
say, it will frequently be difficult to decide whether there is indeed a duty to say it.

2. *What should a warning or instruction say?* Some products—for example, tobacco
and pharmaceuticals—must carry warnings whose wording is either specified or approved by a federal law or agency.

Restatement (Third) of Torts: Products Liability (1998)

§4. Noncompliance and Compliance with Product Safety Statutes or Regulations

In connection with liability for defective design or inadequate instructions or warnings:

(a) a product's noncompliance with an applicable product safety statute or administrative regulation renders the product defective with respect to the risks sought to be reduced by the statute or regulation; and

(b) a product's compliance with an applicable product safety statute or regulation is
properly considered in determining whether the product is defective with respect to the

risks sought to be reduced by the statute or regulation, but such compliance does not preclude as a matter of law a finding of product defect.

Notes

1. *Negligence and strict liability.* As *Comment a* to § 4 points out, § 4 cannot be applicable to cases falling within §§ 1 and 2(a) because the latter both deal with cases where liability is strict (i.e. without fault). In such cases, compliance (or otherwise) with any statute or regulation will be irrelevant. Section 4 is therefore relevant only to cases of alleged defects associated with negligence, typically defects of design and failures to warn.

2. *Floodgates revisited.* While, as was seen in Chapter 7, there has been considerable controversy as to whether defective design should be assessed on the basis of negligence or strict liability, there is really no such controversy about alleged failures to warn. These must be judged by a negligence or reasonableness standard, because of a potential floods of claims problem. Strict liability would mean that *any* failure to provide a warning—or a warning with the specific wording preferred by a judge or jury—with *any* product which subsequently does harm would fix the manufacturer and/or distributor with liability, even if the product itself was not only free of both design and manufacturing defects but the lack of warning was perfectly reasonable in the circumstances.

3. *Negligence per se and proximate cause.* The two paragraphs of § 4 are clearly related, and in some ways are almost the obverse of each other. As matters of law, however, paragraphs (a) and (b) tackle two, very different issues. Paragraph (a) performs two functions. It acts like the doctrine of negligence *per se* in establishing that a failure to meet the requirements of a particular statute or regulation also automatically establishes that the product suffers from a defect (whether concerned with design or warning). But it also fulfils the function of proximate cause, because it restricts the damage or injuries, for which the seller or distributor might be liable, to those which were within the scope of the risk that the statute or regulation sought to address.

4. *Federalism.* Paragraph (b) of § 4, however, has a very different role. It implicitly recognizes that tort law is traditionally a matter for the individual states. The Commerce Clause (Article I, Section 8, Clause 3) of the Constitution of the United States grants the federal government the power to regulate "commerce … among the several states." The Supremacy Clause (Article VI, paragraph 2) of the federal Constitution makes clear that "the Judges in every State shall be bound thereby, any Thing in the Constitution or Laws of any State to the contrary notwithstanding."

But this does not necessarily mean that compliance with a federal statute or regulation will render a seller or distributor immune from liability on that issue. The federal government may set minimum standards with which everyone is expected to comply, but that does not prevent each state's judiciary from enforcing greater standards. In principle, such latter standards would not conflict with, but would merely build on, the federal standards. There is, however, a limit beyond which the states' imposition of greater standards cannot go: they cannot (whether through the legislature, administrative agency or judiciary) impose such higher standards if these would have a significant impact on interstate commerce, because that is an area of law over which sole jurisdiction is vested in the federal government.

5. *What should a warning or instruction say (again)?* For most products, where a warning is not mandated by legislation or regulation, things are not clear-cut. Different states

can, and do, take different approaches to the wording of warnings on such products. As *Comment i* to § 2 of the Products Liability Restatement notes:

> In evaluating the adequacy of product warnings and instructions, courts must be sensitive to many factors. It is impossible to identify anything approaching a perfect level of detail that should be communicated in product disclosures. For example, educated or experienced product users and consumers may benefit from inclusion of more information about the full spectrum of product risks, whereas less-educated or unskilled users may benefit from more concise warnings and instructions stressing only the most crucial risks and safe-handling practices. In some contexts, products intended for special categories of users, such as children, may require more vivid and unambiguous warnings. In some cases, excessive detail may detract from the ability of typical users and consumers to focus on the important aspects of the warnings, whereas in others reasonably full disclosure will be necessary to enable informed, efficient choices by product users. Product warnings and instructions can rarely communicate all potentially relevant information, and the ability of a plaintiff to imagine a hypothetical better warning in the aftermath of an accident does not establish that the warning actually accompanying the product was inadequate. No easy guideline exists for courts to adopt in assessing the adequacy of product warnings and instructions. In making their assessments, courts must focus on various factors, such as content and comprehensibility, intensity of expression, and the characteristics of expected user groups.

6. *Is there a duty to provide a warning or instruction?* This is usually addressed by first considering the two issues in subsections (a) and (b) of § 388 of the Second Restatement: what risks are foreseeable to the manufacturer or distributor, and are they also obvious to the consumer? If the consumer is aware of the risks involved, no warning could convey any useful information to the consumer. Thus—because the hazard is obvious—it would not be necessary to warn that users of a knife might cut themselves. On the other hand, the precise workings of a lawnmower (such as how soon the blade will stop spinning after the power is turned off), while familiar to many, are not obvious to every reasonable user. Providing instructions for use and warnings as to certain dangers is therefore likely to make the lawnmower appreciably safer for some consumers than if they had been provided with no such information.

But that does not completely resolve the matter, for there is still the matter of working out what level of care is reasonable for the manufacturer to take, in accordance with § 388(c) of the Second Restatement. The real question is whether these customers' need for information should outweigh the manufacturer or distributor's burden of having to provide such information, when it may be both expensive and of little use to many other consumers. The needs of (some) consumers and the potential consequences of a failure to warn must therefore be weighed against the additional burden imposed upon the manufacturer or distributor before it will be possible to conclude whether the warnings provided were inadequate under § 2(c) of the Products Liability Restatement. Moreover, Comment *i* to § 2 points out that:

> Depending on the circumstances, Subsection (c) may require that instructions and warnings be given not only to purchasers, users, and consumers, but also to others who a reasonable seller should know will be in a position to reduce or avoid the risk of harm. There is no general rule as to whether one supplying a product for the use of others through an intermediary has a duty to warn the ultimate product user directly or may rely on the intermediary to relay warn-

ings. The standard is one of reasonableness in the circumstances. Among the factors to be considered are the gravity of the risks posed by the product, the likelihood that the intermediary will convey the information to the ultimate user, and the feasibility and effectiveness of giving a warning directly to the user. Thus, when the purchaser of machinery is the owner of a workplace who provides the machinery to employees for their use, and there is reason to doubt that the employer will pass warnings on to employees, the seller is required to reach the employees directly with necessary instructions and warnings if doing so is reasonably feasible.

The interplay of the different issues involved in a failure to warn claim are set out in Figure 8.1.

7. *Two hidden issues.* Arguably, however, the questions of what a warning might say and whether there is a duty to provide it elicit answers that are less important than the issues of (a) who gets to make these decisions, and (b) according to which test of reasonableness. In other words, the central controversies regarding failure to warn claims seem to cover the same ground already trodden by the disputes over claims of design defects.

8. *Who decides?* Since the question of whether to provide a warning is one of duty, this should be a question for the court. This would make it readily amenable to applications for summary judgment. However, since it is difficult to decide whether or not there was a duty to warn without knowing what such a warning might look like, having a judge give summary judgment on the duty issue effectively requires that he or she has also determined what the warning might say. Yet, as the Supreme Court of North Dakota pointed out in *Crowston v. Goodyear Tire & Rubber Company*, 521 N.W.2d 401 (1994), since the latter determination implicates the issue of reasonable care, it should normally be a matter for the jury. So having the court decide whether or not there was a duty to warn seems to require that it trespass on the jury's territory. On the other hand, the only way to allow the jury to work out what a warning might have said (and thus enable it to decide whether the defendant's conduct was reasonable or inadequate) is to allow it to also determine whether there was indeed a duty to warn at all, so this requires the court to abdicate its normal responsibility. In practice, as the judgments in the cases below demonstrate, the courts have not taken a consistent approach to this dilemma; indeed, they seem sometimes to behave as if it did not exist. Yet who gets to decide these questions is frequently of even more significance than the criteria which they are supposed to apply.

9. *Consumer expectations or risk-utility test?* In fact, one of the reasons why the identity of the decisionmaker is so important is that it may actually dictate the appropriate criteria. The differences between § 402A (already discussed in Chapters 6 and 7) and § 388 of the Second Restatement, on the one hand, and § 2(c) of the Products Liability Restatement, on the other, are admittedly slight on their face. Yet the ideological baggage carried by each Restatement are such that, whatever the semantics of the words employed, the implications of adopting one or other Restatement can be very different. We are back, once again, to the controversy between the consumer expectations test—held, for example, by the Tenth Circuit in *Ahrens v. Ford Motor Co.*, 340 F.3d 1142, 1146 (2003), to be mandated by Oklahoma law—and the risk-utility test. But even if the judiciary of a particular state can agree on the test to be employed, they may still differ as to its application.

Figure 8.1 Failure to Warn

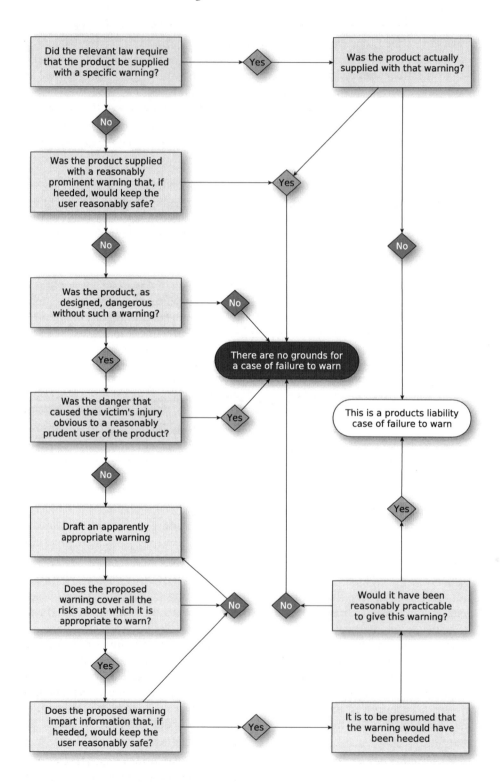

Greene v. A.P. Products Ltd.
717 N.W.2d 855 (2006) (Supreme Court of Michigan)

CORRIGAN, J. In this case we consider the scope of a manufacturer's or seller's duty to warn of product risks under MCL 600.2948(2). We conclude that the statute imposes a duty to warn that extends only to material risks not obvious to a reasonably prudent product user, and to material risks that are not, or should not be, a matter of common knowledge to persons in the same or a similar position as the person who suffered the injury in question. Because the material risk associated with ingesting and inhaling Wonder 8 Hair Oil, as occurred here, would have been obvious to a reasonably prudent product user, the failure to warn against the risk is not actionable. The Court of Appeals misunderstood this duty and held that a duty also existed to warn of the kind of injuries that were suffered. The Court of Appeals also incorrectly allowed various warranty claims to proceed on the basis that the warning was inadequate. Because no warning was required, these holdings were in error. Accordingly, we reverse the judgment of the Court of Appeals and reinstate the trial court's order granting summary disposition to all defendants.

I. Underlying Facts and Procedural History

In April 1999, plaintiff purchased a spray bottle of African Pride Ginseng Miracle Wonder 8 Oil, Hair and Body Mist-Captivate (Wonder 8 Hair Oil) from defendant Pro Care Beauty Supply, which is currently known as Super 7 Beauty Supply, Inc. Defendant A.P. Products, which was subsequently acquired by Revlon Consumer Products Corporation, packaged and labeled Wonder 8 Hair Oil. Wonder 8 Hair Oil was marketed principally to African-Americans as a new type of spray-on body and hair moisturizer containing eight natural oils. Plaintiff decided to try the oil after reading the ingredients on the label, some of which were familiar to her and some of which were not. Although the bottle's label cautioned the user never to spray the oil near sparks or an open flame, it did not warn that the hair oil should be kept out of reach of children or that it was potentially harmful or fatal if swallowed. Plaintiff's 11-month-old son, Keimer Easley, had been left unattended. Somehow he obtained the bottle of hair oil, which had been left within his reach. He ingested and inhaled the hair oil. The child died about one month later from multisystem organ failure secondary to chemical pneumonitis, secondary to hydrocarbon ingestion. In other words, the mineral oil clogged the child's lungs, causing inflammatory respiratory failure.

Plaintiff filed this products-liability action, alleging that defendants breached their duty to warn that the product could be harmful if ingested and that it should be kept out of reach of small children. Plaintiff further claimed that defendants breached an implied warranty by failing adequately to label the product as toxic.

Defendants moved for summary disposition. A.P. Products and Revlon argued that they had no duty to warn because the material risks associated with ingesting Wonder 8 Hair Oil were obvious to a reasonably prudent product user. They further argued that the lack of warning was not the proximate cause of the injury and that the product had been misused in a way that was not reasonably foreseeable. Super 7 Beauty Supply argued that plaintiff failed to establish that it, as a nonmanufacturing seller, had independently breached an express or implied warranty or was independently negligent. It further argued that plaintiff failed to show that the product was not fit for its ordinary uses or for a particular purpose.

The trial court granted defendants' motions for summary disposition. The Court of Appeals reversed and remanded, concluding that the questions whether the Wonder 8

Hair Oil required a warning label, whether defendants breached an implied warranty, and whether plaintiff established proximate cause should have been submitted to a jury.

Defendants sought leave to appeal in this Court. We granted defendants' applications for leave to appeal.

II. Standard of Review

This case requires us to determine whether the Court of Appeals erred in reversing the trial court's grant of summary disposition in favor of defendants under MCR 2.116(C)(10). We review this issue de novo. "In reviewing such a decision, we consider the affidavits, pleadings, depositions, admissions, and other documentary evidence submitted by the parties in the light most favorable to the party opposing the motion." "Summary disposition under MCR 2.116(C)(10) is appropriately granted if there is no genuine issue regarding any material fact and the moving party is entitled to judgment as a matter of law."

III. Analysis

Before 1995, a manufacturer's or seller's duty to warn of material risks in a products-liability action was governed by common-law principles. Tort reform legislation enacted in 1995, however, displaced the common law. MCL 600.2948, in chapter 29 of the Revised Judicature Act, now governs a defendant's duty to warn of an obvious danger in a products-liability action. It states, in relevant part:

> A defendant is not liable for failure to warn of a material risk that is or should be obvious to a reasonably prudent product user or a material risk that is or should be a matter of common knowledge to persons in the same or similar position as the person upon whose injury or death the claim is based in a product liability action.

Under the plain language of MCL 600.2948(2), a manufacturer has no duty to warn of a material risk associated with the use of a product if the risk: (1) is obvious, or should be obvious, to a reasonably prudent product user, or (2) is or should be a matter of common knowledge to a person in the same or a similar position as the person upon whose injury or death the claim is based. Accordingly, this statute, by looking to the reasonably prudent product user, or persons in the same or a similar position as the injured person, establishes an objective standard.

In determining what constitutes a material risk, we are mindful that the statutes governing statutory construction direct us to construe "all words and phrases ... according to the common and approved usage of the language," but construe "technical words and phrases, and such as may have acquired a peculiar and appropriate meaning in the law" according to such peculiar and appropriate meaning. Our research reveals that the term "material risk" has no prior "peculiar and appropriate meaning in the law." It is thus not a term of art. When considering a word or phrase that has not been given prior legal meaning, resort to a lay dictionary such as Webster's is appropriate. *Random House Webster's College Dictionary* (1997) defines "material," in relevant part, as "important: to make a material difference; pertinent: a material question." *Random House Webster's College Dictionary* (1997) defines "risk" as "exposure to the chance of injury or loss." We thus conclude that a "material risk" is an important or significant exposure to the chance of injury or loss.

Finally, regarding the meaning of the statute, we conclude that the Legislature has imposed no duty to warn beyond obvious material risks. The statute does not impose a duty to warn of a specific type of injury that could result from a risk. The Court of Appeals, however, mistakenly held that warnings must cover not only material risks, as described, but must also cover potential injuries that could result....

Here, tragically, plaintiff's 11-month-old son died after ingesting and inhaling Wonder 8 Hair Oil. Under the law, however, defendants owed no duty to warn of specific injuries or losses, no matter how severe, if it is or should have been obvious to a reasonably prudent product user that ingesting or inhaling Wonder 8 Hair Oil involved a material risk. We conclude that it is obvious to a reasonably prudent product user that a material risk is involved with ingesting and inhaling Wonder 8 Hair Oil.

The product, as plaintiff concedes, was not marketed as safe for human consumption or ingestion. Rather, the label clearly states that the product is intended for use as a hair and body oil. Although subjective awareness is not the standard, we find it noteworthy that plaintiff herself demonstrated an understanding that Wonder 8 Hair Oil posed a material risk if ingested. We believe it would also be obvious to a reasonably prudent user that ingestion and inhalation of the product poses a material risk. The ingredient label's inclusion of eight natural oils has no bearing on our conclusion. Many, if not all, oils are natural. It should be obvious to a reasonably prudent product user that many oils, although natural, pose a material risk if ingested or inhaled. For instance, the reasonably prudent product user would know that breathing oil would be harmful. A reasonably prudent product user would also know that ingesting such things as crude oil or linseed oil poses a material risk although such oils are natural and pose no immediate danger from contact with hair or skin. In fact, paraffin oil is listed as one of the ingredients in Wonder 8 Hair Oil. It should be obvious to a reasonably prudent product user that ingesting paraffin oil poses a material risk since paraffin is commonly associated with such things as wax.

Additionally, the product label on Wonder 8 Hair Oil does not state that it contains only natural oils. Indeed, it lists numerous other ingredients, many of which would be unfamiliar to the average product user, such as isopropryl myristate, fragrance, and azulene. Given such unfamiliar ingredients, a reasonably prudent product user would be, or should be, loath to ingest it.

Accordingly, we hold that defendants owed no duty to warn plaintiff that her son's ingestion and inhalation of the Wonder 8 Hair Oil posed a material risk. Moreover, defendants owed no duty to warn of the potential injuries that could arise from ingesting and inhaling the product.

The plaintiff also pleaded breach of implied warranty under MCL 600.2947(6)(a) and breach of implied warranty of merchantability under MCL 440.2314(2)(e) with respect to the nonmanufacturing seller, Super 7 Beauty Supply. Plaintiff claimed that, in the absence of a warning, the oil was not properly labeled. Because no warning was required, however, these claims are without merit. Defendants are therefore entitled to judgment as a matter of law.

IV. Response to Justice Cavanagh's Dissent

The crux of Justice Cavanagh's dissent is that we erroneously conclude that the obviousness of one risk means the obviousness of all risks. This contention, however, is a gross mischaracterization of our holding and can be found nowhere in our opinion. Rather, we hold that a defendant has no duty to warn of a material risk that is or should be obvious to a reasonably prudent product user. We further hold that the material risk associated with the ingestion and inhalation of hair oil is or should be obvious to a reasonably prudent product user. This conclusion is entirely consistent with the plain language of the statute and focuses on the obviousness of the material risk in question. It does not charge Michigan consumers with "knowledge of hidden dangers" as suggested by Justice Cavanagh.

Justice Cavanagh also contends that we fail to identify the material risk in question and mislabel the risk as "ingesting or inhaling" the hair oil. Contrary to his contention, we have clearly identified the material risk in this case. To the contrary, Justice Cavanagh has mislabeled the risk as the "consequence" that results from the misuse of the product.

The material risk in this case is neither the misuse of the product (the inhalation or ingestion) nor the consequence of the misuse (injury or death). Rather the material risk is the important or significant exposure to the chance of loss or injury stemming from certain behavior, in this case, the ingestion and inhalation of hair oil. In simple terms, the material risk is the chance that injury could result from drinking or inhaling hair oil. Because a reasonable person knows or should know that ingesting or inhaling hair oil would expose that person to the chance of injury or loss, a defendant has no duty to warn that ingesting or inhaling hair oil could result in exposure to injury or loss. Furthermore, the statute does not require that a person be aware of the worst injury or loss (death) that could possibly result from the misuse of the product.

TAYLOR, C.J., and YOUNG and MARKMAN, JJ., concurred.

WEAVER, J. (concurring). I concur in the majority's result and analysis, except for part IV, the majority's response to Justice CAVANAGH's dissent.

CAVANAGH, J. (dissenting). Michigan consumers beware: If you know or should know that there is any material risk from using or accidentally misusing the product you buy, then the manufacturer of that product now has no duty to warn you of any risk at all, even when the potential harm you knew of is not the harm you ultimately suffer. Stated differently, if you know or should know that if, for example, you accidentally drink or inhale a product, you may become ill, then you are charged with knowing that if you accidentally drink or inhale that product, you could die. And the manufacturer need not warn you of either of those risks—illness or death. According to the majority, the obviousness of any material risk, such as that of illness, is identical to and has the same effect on your behavior as the obviousness of all risks, including death.

To cut right to the core of the majority's faulty reasoning, the majority completely misreads MCL 600.2948(2), and, in doing so, reaches the erroneous conclusion that obviousness of one risk means obviousness of all risks. The governing statute states:

> A defendant is not liable for failure to warn of a material risk that is or should be obvious to a reasonably prudent product user or a material risk that is or should be a matter of common knowledge to persons in the same or similar position as the person upon whose injury or death the claim is based in a product liability action.

The majority ignores key words and basic grammatical structure. Specifically, the Legislature used the word "a" in the phrase "a material risk," thus directing its mandate toward that particular risk. "A" is an "[i]ndefinite article functioning as an adjective" and is "[u]sed before nouns and noun phrases that denote a single, but unspecified, person or thing [.]" The *American Heritage Dictionary*, New College Edition (1981). Notably, then, the word that "a" precedes is limited to "a single" noun. Thus, in this case, "a material risk" refers to "a single," or one, material risk. As a result, the otherwise unspecified single material risk to which the statute refers must be identified before it can be determined whether that risk was common knowledge or obvious to a reasonably prudent product user.

But the majority ignores the word "a," fails to correctly identify the material risk at issue, and writes the word "obvious" completely out of the statute. In doing so, the majority erroneously concludes that all risks are obvious as long as some risk is obvious. Accordingly, the majority holds that the alleged obviousness of "any" material risk absolves a manufacturer from warning about "all" material risks, even if other material risks are not obvious. The effect on this case is the result that because a reasonably prudent product user would have purportedly known that there was a risk of illness from misusing the Wonder 8 Hair Oil, plaintiff should have known there was a risk of death. Therefore, defendants had no duty to warn their consumers about any risk at all.

By concluding this way, the majority rewrites the statute and, consequently, fails to effectuate the protections the Legislature intended. Had the Legislature intended what the majority holds, it would have written the statute as follows: "A defendant is not liable for failure to warn of any material risk when a material risk should be obvious to a reasonably prudent product user ..." Or it would have stated, "A defendant need not warn about all material risks if one material risk should be obvious to a reasonably prudent product user ..." Plainly, it did not write the statute that way, and the majority errs by ignoring the unambiguous language.

To determine in what instances a manufacturer will have no duty to place a warning on its product and what exactly it must warn about, it must first be determined what the "material risk" is alleged to be. By the majority's own proffered definition, "material" means "important: to make a material difference; pertinent: a material question." The first question, then, is "In what must the material difference be made?" According the word its common meaning in the context in which it is used, for the risk to be "material," it must make an important or pertinent difference in the consumer's actions with respect to the product. For instance, the risk would be material if it would bear on whether the consumer purchases the product or how the user deals with the product after purchasing it. Thus, if, to require a warning, the risk must be an important one that makes a material difference in the user's actions, and it must be obvious as well, then the risk involved must be identified. Otherwise, there is no way to determine whether the risk is obvious and no way to determine whether it would make some "material difference."

So it is clear from the statutory language that all risks are not equal, for one is likely to act differently depending on the risk involved. Simply stated, even assuming that a reasonably prudent product user would know that there was a risk of becoming ill from a product, this same consumer does not necessarily know that there is a risk of death. It is not enough to equate two different risks and charge the consumer with knowledge of the more serious one if he has knowledge of the one less serious because it is unreasonable to assume that a reasonably prudent product user would act the same in both circumstances. Thus, the risk of illness, if found to be "a" material risk, must be considered separately from other material risks, such as death. In other words, because the statute states that a manufacturer has no duty "to warn of a material risk that is or should be obvious to a reasonably prudent product user or a material risk that is or should be a matter of common knowledge to persons in the same or similar position," MCL 600.2948(2), the question becomes whether knowledge of the risk of death would have caused the person to act differently, making it a "material" risk, and, if so, whether that risk was or should have been "obvious." We can determine neither whether a risk was "material" nor whether it was obvious unless we know what the risk is alleged to be.

By alternatively failing to identify the material risk at issue in this case and mislabeling the risk as "ingesting or inhaling" the oil, the majority prevents the statute from operating as the Legislature intended and deprives Michigan consumers of their right to assess levels of risk when making purchasing decisions....

KELLY, J. (dissenting). The majority dismisses the product label's inclusion of "eight natural oils" and simply asserts that "[i]t should be obvious to a reasonably prudent product user that many oils, although natural, pose a material risk if ingested or inhaled." It also concludes that, "[g]iven such unfamiliar ingredients, a reasonably prudent product user would be, or should be, loath to ingest it."

I disagree. The vast majority of the ingredients listed on the label are seemingly edible food products. They include avocado oil, coconut oil, and wheat germ oil. Also, the label contains a number of safely ingestible herbs: rosemary, sage, angelica root, licorice root, Job's tears, cedar, clove, lemon balm, and chamomile. In addition, the product label announces that it contains Vitamins E, A, and D. None of these ingredients alerts a reasonably prudent product user to the fatal result of ingesting them. On the contrary, they seem harmless and inviting.

Conclusion

Here, the majority improperly holds as a matter of law that Wonder 8 Hair Oil's material fatal risk was open and obvious. It finds that all reasonable users of this product should be aware that swallowing or inhaling it can result in death. Like the Court of Appeals, I do not believe that is true. The question whether the material risk is open and obvious is for the jury to decide. I would reverse the trial court's grant of summary disposition to defendants and remand the case to the trial court for further proceedings.

Notes

1. *Lack of congeniality.* For some time the Supreme Court of Michigan was known as a place where many of the judges did not get along, as exemplified by part IV of the majority judgment. Justice Weaver regularly deplored this behavior from her colleagues and thus did not join in that part of the majority judgment, despite concurring with its holding. After Chief Justice Taylor failed to be re-elected—a surprise since sitting judges are normally re-elected—Justice Weaver became the Chief Justice for Michigan.

2. *Summary of Different Approaches.* We are now in a position to summarize the respective approaches of the Second and Products Liability Restatements to the different types of product defect. These approaches are tabulated in Figure 8.2.

Figure 8.2 The Different Tests for Product Defects

Type of Defect	Second Restatement	Products Liability Restatement
Manufacturing	Unreasonably dangerous, as judged according to consumer expectations	Departed from intended design
Design	Unreasonably dangerous, as judged according to consumer expectations	Failed to adhere to a reasonable alternative design, which a weighing of the relevant risks and utility shows would have been more appropriate
Failure to Warn	Failed to provide the warning that a reasonable consumer would have expected to help avoid injury	Failed to provide the warning that a weighing of the relevant risks and utility shows would have been appropriate to help avoid injury

3. *Would the user or consumer have taken any notice?* The discussion of warnings hitherto makes an assumption—noted expressly in *Comment j* to §402A of the Second Restatement—which may not always be true. It takes for granted that, if an instruction or warning is provided, the user or consumer will take note of it. This is what is sometimes known as the "heeding presumption." In practice, of course, many users will either not read such warnings or will ignore them, thinking "it will never happen to me." The law deals with this practical reality by bifurcating the matter of whether the warning would have been effective. Thus whether *reasonable people* would change their behavior, if warned, goes to the question of whether the seller's or distributor's failure to warn amounted to inadequate warnings or instructions. However, whether *the plaintiff* would have changed his or her behavior, if warned, is a question of cause in fact because it is a form of the so-called "but-for" test: if the warning had been provided, the accident would not have happened. Causation in fact will be addressed more fully in Chapter 9.

Questions

1. An inaccurately labeled product—for example, an item of processed food that fails to indicate that it contains nuts—may be just at least as dangerous as one that carries an inadequate warning. Is a failure to warn, or an inadequate warning, therefore simply an alternative form of making a misrepresentation, and/or a form of breach of an implied warranty?

2. Is there any need for the law to recognize failure-to-warn claims? Should we instead rely on the law of misrepresentation and/or warranty?

3. According to an illustration to §389 of the Second Restatement, a business that manufactures and sells combs for use in permanent wave treatment in beauty shops will be liable to D in the circumstances outlined below:

> Heat treatment of the hair is normal and customary in such shops. A's combs are highly inflammable, and dangerous in the presence of heat. A sells a quantity of the combs to B, a dealer, accompanying them with a warning that they are to be used for cold treatment only. B sells some of the combs to C, a beauty shop operator, but neglects to pass on the warning. C uses the combs in heat treatment of D's hair. They catch fire, and D is burned.

Is this also the position under the Products Liability Restatement?

4. A sixteen-year-old girl at a party consumes a tablet of ecstasy, which she has never taken before, and then dies because she proceeds to drink a copious amount of water. Should her parents be able to bring a civil claim against the manufacturer and/or distributor of the ecstasy tablet on the grounds that they failed to warn against this danger?

Restatement (Third) of Torts: Products Liability (1998)

§6. *Liability of Commercial Seller or Distributor for Harm Caused by Defective Prescription Drugs and Medical Devices*

(a) A manufacturer of a prescription drug or medical device who sells or otherwise distributes a defective drug or medical device is subject to liability for harm to persons caused by the defect. A prescription drug or medical device is one that may be legally sold or otherwise distributed only pursuant to a health-care provider's prescription.

(b) For purposes of liability under Subsection (a), a prescription drug or medical device is defective if at the time of sale or other distribution the drug or medical device ...

(3) is not reasonably safe due to inadequate instructions or warnings as defined in Subsection (d)....

(d) A prescription drug or medical device is not reasonably safe due to inadequate instructions or warnings if reasonable instructions or warnings regarding foreseeable risks of harm are not provided to:

(1) prescribing and other health-care providers who are in a position to reduce the risks of harm in accordance with the instructions or warnings; or

(2) the patient when the manufacturer knows or has reason to know that health-care providers will not be in a position to reduce the risks of harm in accordance with the instructions or warnings....

Comment b. Rationale.

The obligation of a manufacturer to warn about risks attendant to the use of drugs and medical devices that may be sold only pursuant to a health-care provider's prescription traditionally has required warnings directed to health-care providers and not to patients. The rationale supporting this "learned intermediary" rule is that only health-care professionals are in a position to understand the significance of the risks involved and to assess the relative advantages and disadvantages of a given form of prescription-based therapy. The duty then devolves on the health-care provider to supply to the patient such information as is deemed appropriate under the circumstances so that the patient can make an informed choice as to therapy. Subsection (d)(1) retains the "learned intermediary" rule. However, in certain limited therapeutic relationships the physician or other health-care provider has a much-diminished role as an evaluator or decisionmaker. In these instances it may be appropriate to impose on the manufacturer the duty to warn the patient directly. See Subsection (d)(2).

Comment d. Manufacturers' liability for failure adequately to instruct or warn prescribing and other health-care providers.

Failure to instruct or warn is the major basis of liability for manufacturers of prescription drugs and medical devices. When prescribing health-care providers are adequately informed of the relevant benefits and risks associated with various prescription drugs and medical devices, they can reach appropriate decisions regarding which drug or device is best for specific patients. Sometimes a warning serves to inform health-care providers of unavoidable risks that inhere in the drug or medical device. By definition, such a warning would not aid the health-care provider in reducing the risk of injury to the patient by taking precautions in how the drug is administered or the medical for device is used. However, warnings of unavoidable risks allow the health-care provider, and thereby the patient, to make an informed choice whether to utilize the drug or medical device. Beyond informing prescribing health-care providers, a drug or device manufacturer may have a duty under the law of negligence to use reasonable measures to supply instructions or warnings to nonprescribing health-care providers who are in positions to act on such information so as to reduce or prevent injury to patients.

Notes

1. *Design defects and failures to warn.* As we saw in Chapter 7, § 6(c) of the Products Liability Restatement considers such products to have been defectively designed only if "rea-

sonable health-care providers … would not prescribe the drug or medical device for *any* class of patients" (emphasis added). Since that is an extremely heavy burden to discharge, the Reporters are right to recognize that, under the Products Liability Restatement: "Failure to instruct or warn is the major basis of liability for manufacturers of prescription drugs and medical devices."

2. *The significance of the "learned intermediary".* As we saw in Chapter 4, the "learned intermediary" defense works to shield manufacturers of drugs and medical devices from liability where the latter have been prescribed by a qualified physician. In Chapter 4, the doctrine operated as a defense to claims of misleading advertising by manufacturers. In the context of failures to warn, the defense immunizes manufacturers who fail to warn patients directly about possible dangers that the drug or device might carry. The explanation for the application of the defense in this context is provided in the next case. It also points out that the defense remains applicable even if the manufacturer had failed to provide appropriate warnings to the doctor, if those warnings would have made no difference to the doctor's decision to prescribe the treatment concerned.

Dietz v. Smithkline Beecham Corp.
598 F.3d 812 (11th Cir. 2010)

BARZILAY, J. Plaintiff-Appellant Donna Dietz ("Appellant") appeals the district court's grant of summary judgment for Defendant-Appellee Smithkline Beecham Corp. ("SBC") in her wrongful death suit, which arose out of her husband's suicide while taking Paxil, a drug manufactured by SBC. For the reasons stated below, the district court's decision is affirmed.

On April 3, 2002, the 33 year-old Garrison David Dietz ("Dietz"), Appellant's late husband, met with his family practitioner, James Zuppa, M.D. Dietz presented with anxiety, depression, insomnia, and stress, but expressed that he had no suicidal ideation and disclosed no history of psychological illness. Dr. Zuppa diagnosed Dietz with major depression and offered him hospitalization for psychiatric treatment, which Dietz declined. Consequently, Dr. Zuppa prescribed him Paxil, a selective serotonin reuptake inhibitor ("SSRI") antidepressant manufactured by SBC, and Ambien, a sleep aid. He then instructed Dietz to schedule a follow-up visit in three weeks and to contact him in the event of an "acute crisis." He also referred him to a nearby psychologist. Eight days after having filled and begun his Paxil prescription, Dietz committed suicide by throwing himself in front of a train.

Appellant filed a diversity suit in the Northern District of Georgia on April 24, 2007, alleging that under Georgia law SBC was (1) strictly liable as "a manufacturer of a defective and unreasonably dangerous product, and for marketing defects and misrepresentations, which proximately caused Gary Dietz's injuries and death," (2) "unreasonable, or negligent, and was a proximate cause of Garry Deitz's injuries and death," and (3) "liable under a breach of warranty." SBC filed two motions for summary judgment, the first of which raised Georgia's learned intermediary doctrine as an affirmative defense and is at issue in the present opinion….

In standard products liability cases premised on a failure to warn, Georgia law insists that a plaintiff show that the defendant had a duty to warn, that the defendant breached that duty, and that the breach proximately caused the plaintiff's injury. *Wheat v. Sofamor, S.N.C.,* 46 F.Supp.2d 1351, 1362 (N.D.Ga.1999) (holding that proximate cause is necessary element of plaintiff's case whether proceeding under strict liability or negligence theory). Within the context of prescription drugs, however, Georgia employs the learned intermediary doctrine, which alters the general rule that imposes liability on a manufacturer for failing to warn an end user of the known risks or hazards of its products. According to the doctrine, the manufacturer of

> a prescription drug ... does not have a duty to warn the patient of the dangers involved with the product, but instead has a duty to warn the patient's doctor, who acts as a learned intermediary between the patient and the manufacturer. The rationale for the doctrine is that the treating physician is in a better position to warn the patient than the manufacturer, in that the decision to employ prescription medication ... involves professional assessment of medical risks in light of the physician's knowledge of a patient's particular need and susceptibilities. *McCombs v. Synthes (U.S.A.)*, 587 S.E.2d 594, 594 (2003).

In most cases, a court begins its inquiry under this doctrine by determining whether the manufacturer provided the learned intermediary with an adequate warning. If the warning was adequate, the inquiry ends, and the plaintiff cannot recover. If the warning is inadequate, or merely presumed to be, the plaintiff must demonstrate that the deficient warning proximately caused the alleged injury to prevail. Therefore, in cases where

> a learned intermediary has actual knowledge of the substance of the alleged warning and would have taken the same course of action even with the information the plaintiff contends should have been provided, courts typically conclude that ... the causal link is broken and the plaintiff cannot recover. *Ellis* [*v. C.R. Bard, Inc.*], 311 F.3d 1272, 1283 n. 8 (11th Cir.2002).

Appellant cannot demonstrate that SBC's alleged failure to warn Dr. Zuppa about increased suicide risks associated with Paxil proximately caused Dietz to commit suicide. The doctor provided explicit, uncontroverted testimony that, even when provided with the most current research and FDA mandated warnings, he still would have prescribed Paxil for Dietz's depression. Pursuant to Georgia's learned intermediary doctrine, this assertion severs any potential chain of causation through which Appellant could seek relief, and Appellant's claims thus fail.

Affirmed.

Notes

1. *Devices and drugs.* In *O'Connell v. Biomet, Inc.*, 250 P.3d 1278 (2010), the Colorado Court of Appeals was persuaded by § 6(d) of the Products Liability Restatement to apply the learned intermediary defense to manufacturers of medical devices (in that case, a fixator for repairing a fractured elbow). It reasoned:

> the learned intermediary doctrine should apply to failure to warn claims in the context of a medical device installed operatively when it is available only to physicians and obtained by prescription, and the doctor is in a position to reduce the risks of harm in accordance with the instructions or warnings.

2. *Failure to warn or misrepresentation?* In the consolidated case of *Beale v. Biomet, Inc.*, 492 F.Supp.2d 1360 (2007), moreover, a federal district court in Florida refused to allow two plaintiffs (who each suffered severe pain after the surgical implantation of a partial knee prosthetic device known as a Biomet Repicci II Unicondylar Knee, and who eventually needed revision surgery on their knees) to circumvent the learned intermediary defense to a failure to warn claim by pleading misrepresentations in the products advertising instead. The judge held:

While Plaintiffs have provided various names for their claims against Biomet, the claims are all ultimately based upon Biomet's alleged failure to warn of the risks of the device. Because Florida has adopted the learned intermediary doctrine, I conclude that … the doctrine bars the Plaintiffs' claims in this case.

holding

3. *Inapplicability of learned intermediary defense.* In some circumstances, however, it may not be appropriate to instruct the jury on the learned intermediary defense.

Hyman & Armstrong, P.S.C. v. Gunderson

279 S.W.3d 93 (2008) (Supreme Court of Kentucky)

SCHRODER, J. On September 28, 1993, Mary Gunderson, age thirty-two, gave birth by cesarean section to her second child, Wesley Gunderson. Because Mary did not want to breastfeed, Mary's obstetrician, Dr. Lyman Armstrong, prescribed the drug Parlodel (bromocriptine mesylate) to stop lactation. Mary began taking Parlodel on September 29, and was discharged from the hospital on October 1 to recover at home. Mary's recovery was uneventful until October 4, when Mary complained of a severe headache and pain between her shoulder blades radiating down her back. Mary went to bed that night at around 11:30 p.m. The next morning Mary's mother discovered Mary dead in her bed. Authorities were called and Detective David Burks of the Jeffersontown Police Department began a death scene investigation. Mary was found in bed lying on her back with her arms bent backwards by her head in a gravity-defying position. Mary was also found to have voided from her bladder….

On September 8, 1994, Mary's Estate, her husband, Ronald Gunderson, and her two minor children … filed suit against Sandoz Pharmaceutical Corporation, … the maker of Parlodel, and … Dr. Armstrong, alleging products liability and medical malpractice in causing Mary's death. The case was tried from February 2, 2004, to February 28, 2004, and resulted in a judgment for the Plaintiffs totaling $19,098,263. Apportioning 90% liability to Sandoz and 10% to Dr. Armstrong, the jury awarded $7,848,263 in compensatory damages ($6,000,000 for loss of parental consortium and $1,848,263 for loss of services and earning power). $11,250,000 in punitive damages was assessed against Sandoz.

On appeal to the Court of Appeals, the court vacated the portion of the judgment awarding punitive damages because the trial court failed to instruct the jury that punitive damages could not be based on conduct that occurred outside of Kentucky. The court thus remanded the action for a new trial "on the amount of Sandoz's punitive damages liability." The judgment was affirmed in all other respects. Sandoz and Dr. Armstrong filed separate motions for discretionary review, which were granted and consolidated for review before this Court….

[A new] warning was approved by the FDA in 1987. In conjunction with the new warning, the FDA required Sandoz to send a "Dear Doctor" letter to obstetricians noting the changes in the package insert and specifically calling attention to the adverse reactions. At trial, the Gundersons presented evidence that Sandoz failed to send the "Dear Doctor" letter to more than a small fraction of the doctors registered in the college of obstetricians and gynecologists. Because of the FDA's concern that so few doctors had received the letter, in 1988, the FDA required Sandoz to send the letter again to a wider audience and decided to reconsider Parlodel's indication for use as a lactation suppressant at a 1988 FDA advisory committee meeting. Upon reviewing the available data on Parlodel's use for PPLS during that meeting, including the results of the ERI study and ADRs, the advisory committee recommended that Parlodel's indication for PPLS should be withdrawn. The committee concluded that risks of potentially serious side effects from Parlodel use outweighed the relatively minor discomfort of postpartum lactation. The committee recommended that the condition be treated conservatively as it had traditionally been, with breast binding and analgesics. The FDA adopted the committee's recommendation in 1989 and asked manufacturers of bromocriptine to voluntarily withdraw their drug's lactation suppression indications. With the exception of Sandoz, all manufacturers complied with the FDA's request. Sandoz, however, continued to market Parlodel for PPLS. In fact, in the second "Dear Doctor" letter sent by Sandoz dated May 3, 1990, Sandoz wrote:

> The results of the epidemiologic study, conducted by Epidemiology Resources, Incorporated, were presented [to the FDA Fertility and Maternal Health Advisory Committee] showing no causal relationship between reported seizures and the use of Parlodel.... Subsequently, the FDA requested Sandoz to voluntarily withdraw this [PPLS] indication for Parlodel. Sandoz considers this request inappropriate for the following reasons:
>
> The question of need is one that should be determined between an informed patient and her physician and not by a governmental agency.
>
> There is strong disagreement with the conclusion that there is no need for a drug to prevent lactation in the postpartum period. Although not all women who elect not to breast feed may require therapy to prevent lactation, a significant number will benefit from such therapy.
>
> As demonstrated in controlled trials, the use of Parlodel therapy to prevent the engorgement and pain that occur in many women who elect not to breast feed is a more effective approach than treating the engorgement and pain once they occur with analgesics and ice packs....

Further, the Gundersons presented evidence that before Mrs. Gunderson's death in 1993, Sandoz knew of additional adverse reactions to Parlodel and misrepresented them or failed to report them to the FDA as required by law. In particular, there was evidence that prior to 1993, Sandoz knew of at least ninety-eight cases of hypertension, eighty-six cases of seizure, and thirty-three cases of stroke associated with Parlodel, but made no effort to provide doctors with these updated figures after the 1987 package insert. It was not until 1994, after the FDA had initiated procedures to withdraw its approval for the PPLS indication for Parlodel, that Sandoz voluntarily withdrew that indication.

In his deposition read at trial, Dr. Armstrong admitted that he had not read the 1987 updated package insert for Parlodel. Dr. Armstrong testified that he did not receive either "Dear Doctor" letter sent by Sandoz regarding Parlodel, and that if he had, he would not have prescribed Parlodel for Mrs. Gunderson.

From our review of the record, we conclude that Sandoz failed to present sufficient evidence of an adequate warning to Dr. Armstrong of the risks of Parlodel, thus it was not error for the trial court to fail to give the jury instruction on the learned intermediary doctrine. While the package insert and PDR entry for Parlodel contained warnings of the risks of seizure and hypertension for postpartum patients, other evidence undermined the effectiveness of these warnings....

This evidence showed that Sandoz repeatedly attempted to downplay or conceal the risks of Parlodel and intentionally undermined any existing warnings. This systematic approach to minimizing the risk posed by Parlodel rendered the various warnings that were available inadequate under the learned-intermediary doctrine. Thus, we conclude that the trial court did not err in failing to instruct the jury as to the learned-intermediary defense.

Affirmed.

Questions

1. Prescription-only pharmaceuticals are increasingly advertised direct to patients (or prospective patients), routinely accompanied by a long list of warnings of side-effects and complications, and a comment that patients should consult their doctor. In such circumstances is a patient less likely to heed warnings passed on by their physician? Does this matter?

2. It is also well known that the longer the list of such warnings, the less likely they are to be heeded. Does this mean that only certain warnings should be given and, if so, how is the decision to be made as to which ones?

3. Does it matter if the warnings provided by the physician are not identical to any issued in the advertisements?

4. Would a failure to provide warnings in the advertisements implicate § 6(d)(2) of the Products Liability Restatement?

5. Should plaintiffs be allowed to choose the theory on which they bring their case and, if so take advantage of any ability that that affords them to circumvent defenses available to the defendant if the suit had been brought according to a different theory?

6. Is *Gunderson* a case of misrepresentation or of a failure to warn?

Is There a Post-Sale Duty to Warn?

If all liability for defective products were strict, there would be no need for any law on post-sale warnings, since any user or consumer injured by a defective product would automatically have a valid claim against the manufacturer and/or distributor. Indeed, it is for this reason that there is little need for the law to recognize a post-sale duty to warn when the product in question suffers from a manufacturing defect. Instead, the question of post-sale duties to warn arises when it is alleged that a manufacturer or distributor subsequently learns (or should have become aware) that an apparently acceptable product design contains a latent defect.

The debate over post-sale duties to warn raises the following issues. From the perspective of the consumer, it is likely to be hazardous to continue using the product in question (or to continue using it without taking additional precautions), so the consumer or user would clearly be in a safer position if the manufacturer or distributor passed on new information which has come to light since the sale or distribution.

From the point of view of those on whom such a duty might be imposed, however, there are two countervailing considerations. First, if the design was apparently sound at the time of sale or distribution, why should new liability be imposed simply with the benefit of hindsight? As the Arizona Court of Appeals put it in *Wilson v. United States Elevator Corp.*, 972 P.2d 235, 241 (1998) (quoting *Lynch v. McStome & Lincoln Plaza Assoc.*, 548 A.2d 1276 (Pa. Super. Ct, 1988)):

> The clear effect of imposing a [continuing] duty ... would be to inhibit manufacturers from developing improved designs that in any way affect the safety of

their products, since the manufacturer would then be subject to the onerous, and oftentimes impossible, duty of notifying each owner of the previously sold product that the new design is available for installation, despite the fact that the already sold products are, to the manufacturer's knowledge, safe and functioning properly.

Secondly, even if public policy considerations of promoting public safety can sometimes be held to trump the fear of inhibiting innovation, manufacturers and distributors may face the significant practical problem noted by the Georgia Court of Appeals in *Johnson v. Ford Motor Company*, 637 S.E. 2d 202, 207 (2006), where it pointed out that a "negligent failure to warn claim may arise from a manufacturer's post-sale knowledge acquired months, years, or even decades after the date of the first sale of the product." Apart from the obvious problem of never-ending liability going well beyond statutes of limitation and repose that would apply to other types of product defect, this also creates the significant practical difficulty of finding out who still uses or operates the product in question in order to pass on the necessary warnings.

Recognizing that there is no uniformity of approach among the states to this issue, § 10 of the Products Liability Restatement avoids attempting to lay down a clear rule as to when a post-sale duty may be imposed, and instead lists the following factors as among those which the courts may take into account:

- whether the seller or distributor knows or ought to know that the product poses a risk to persons or property
- the degree of that risk
- whether it is possible to identify those at risk
- whether it is practicable to communicate the warning to those at risk.

In addition, although the Products Liability Restatement does not mention it as a factor to be taken into account, courts may consider the prior conduct of the defendant as a relevant matter when deciding whether, on the facts of a particular case, it would be appropriate to impose a post-sale duty to warn.

About half the states have adopted the theory of a post-sale duty to warn. See, for example, *Lewis v. Ariens Co.*, 751 N.E.2d 862, 867 (Mass.2001), *Densberger v. United Techs. Corp.*, 297 F.3d 66, 71 (2d Cir.2002) (applying Connecticut law). In *Sherlock v. Quality Control Equipment Co.*, 79 F. 3d 731 (1996), the Eighth Circuit, applying Missouri law, held that a successor corporation has a post-sale duty to warn customers of dangers that existed in its predecessor's product. In this case, the successor corporation had both actual knowledge of a defect and received an actual economic benefit because it had sold replacement parts for the machine to its predecessor's customers.

Some states, on the other hand, have refused to adopt the Product Liability Restatement's approach of weighing a number of factors in favor of a more "bright-line rule" concerning the applicability or otherwise of a post-sale failure to warn. In *Bryant v. Giacomini*, 391 F.Supp.2d 495, 503 (2005), a federal district court in Texas ruled that:

> Under Texas products liability law, a manufacturer has no duty to warn about a product after it has been manufactured and sold. Instead, a manufacturer's duty to warn is determined at the time the product leaves the manufacturer.
>
> There are two possible exceptions to this general rule. The first exception is where the manufacturer regains some significant control over the product. The second is where a manufacturer assumed a post-sale duty and then did not use

reasonable means to discharge that duty. In that instance, it must also be established that the plaintiff's injury was a proximate result of the breach of that assumed duty.

Question

Section 10(b)(4) of the Products Liability Restatement was originally drafted to provide that a post-sale warning was required "only if the risk of harm outweighs the costs of providing a post sale warning." Is the final version, which simply provides a list of factors to be taken into account, preferable to the original draft? Why (not)?

Northstar & Assoc. v. W.R. Grace & Co.
66 F.3d 173 (8th Cir. 1995)

LOKEN, J. In 1986, T.H.S. Northstar Associates ("THS") purchased the Northstar Center in downtown Minneapolis. After completing the purchase, THS discovered ceiling tiles and other surfaces contaminated with asbestos fibers. THS sued W.R. Grace & Co., the manufacturer of Monokote 3, an asbestos-laden material used in fireproofing the Northstar Center, to recover the costs of asbestos abatement and removal. After a six-week trial, the jury awarded THS $6,240,000 in compensatory damages. Both sides appeal. We conclude that the district court properly applied Minnesota law in submitting THS's claims to the jury but erred in later submitting an interrogatory to clarify the jury's facially valid verdict. We remand for recalculation of damages but otherwise affirm. . . .

In this case, Grace contends that THS, a purchaser with notice of a risk, may not sue Grace, the third party who tortiously created that risk. . . . [T]ort law takes this type of notice into account through the doctrine of assumption of risk. Grace asserts, in essence, that THS assumed the risk of asbestos contamination when it purchased the Northstar Center knowing that its fireproofing contained asbestos. Assumption of risk was historically a complete defense, but Minnesota law has for the most part replaced the traditional defense with a statutory comparative fault regime. The district court submitted comparative fault to the jury, expressly defining THS's fault to include its pre-purchase knowledge of the risk. Thus, Grace's subsequent-purchaser-with-notice theory is nothing more than an attack on the district court's application of the Minnesota comparative fault statute. Unless THS's alleged notice is a form of assumption of risk excluded from the comparative fault statute, that attack must fail.

Grace next challenges the district court's jury instruction and special interrogatory on THS's failure to warn claim. The instruction stated in relevant part:

> [I]f a manufacturer learns that a previously distributed product poses a danger to users, it must give additional warnings or instructions that will enable users to make informed decisions and use the product safely. . . . A manufacturer has no duty to warn, however, if the user is or should be fully aware of all of the dangers inherent in the product, but past experience or familiarity with a product does not necessarily alert a user to all of the dangers associated with the product.

The special interrogatory asked the jury, "Did Grace both have and breach a duty to adequately warn or instruct Northstar about the hazards associated with Monokote 3? "

Grace first argues that the special interrogatory, by asking if Grace had a duty to warn, violated the principle that the existence of that duty is a question of law for the court. However, Grace waived this issue by urging at the instruction conference:

> Grace believes that there should be an interrogatory that inquires whether or not there was a duty, specifically whether or not [THS] was a knowledgeable user.... [T]he jury has to find that there was a duty. And if there was a duty, whether or not it was breached.

Moreover, the court's instruction properly resolved the legal question by defining when a manufacturer has a continuing duty to warn. Consistent with Minnesota law, it left fact issues for the jury, such as breach of the duty and whether THS was a user who "knew or should have known" of the danger.

Grace next argues that the evidence in this case does not establish "special circumstances" imposing a continuing duty to warn under Minnesota law. In *Hodder*, the Minnesota Supreme Court imposed such a duty based upon the following facts: (1) the manufacturer insisted its product was safe if used properly; (2) it became evident to the manufacturer over time that great care was required in the handling and servicing of the product, or serious injury would occur; and (3) the manufacturer continued in the business of selling related products and undertook a duty to warn users of post-sale hazards. We agree with the district court that the evidence in this case justified submitting the continuing-duty-to-warn issue to the jury. In particular, Grace's pamphlets, letters, and extensive publicity discussing the risks of asbestos-containing materials and purporting to advise building owners on how to manage that risk raise a jury issue under *Hodder* whether to impose a continuing legal duty to warn.

Vacated and remanded for recalculation of damages; otherwise affirmed.

Patton v. Hutchinson Wil-Rich Manufacturing Co.

861 P.2d 1299 (1993) (Supreme Court of Kansas)

SIX, J. This is a first impression products liability case. Four questions concerning a manufacturer's post-sale duties to warn of danger incident to use of its product have been certified by the United States District Court for the District of Kansas....

The Certified Questions

The four certified questions are:

I. Whether Kansas products liability law recognizes a continuing duty to warn theory of liability requiring manufacturers who learn of a danger incident to the use of their products after the sale of those products to warn ultimate consumers who purchased the products prior to the time the manufacturers learned of the potential danger through warnings disseminated to the manufacturers' retailers who have continuing contact with the consumers.

II. Whether Kansas products liability law recognizes a continuing duty to warn theory of liability requiring manufacturers who learn of a danger incident to the use of their products after the sale of those products to directly warn ultimate consumers who purchased the products prior to the time the manufacturers learned of the potential danger.

III. Whether Kansas products liability law places a duty to retrofit upon manufacturers who learn of a potential danger incident to the use of their products after the products have been sold.

IV. Whether Kansas products liability law places a duty to recall upon manufacturers who learn of a potential danger incident to the use of their products after the products have been sold.

Answers to the Certified Questions

Because of the infinite variety of products marketed in this state, the following answers are inexorably linked to and amplified by the corresponding portions of the opinion.

We answer the four certified questions as follows:

A qualified yes.

A qualified yes.

No.

No....

Plaintiff Ryan Patton's father purchased the cultivator from a Wil-Rich dealer in 1977. The cultivator is 28 feet wide and consists of a main body and two "wings." The wings are raised and lowered hydraulically by the use of cylinders attached to each wing and controlled from the cab of the tractor. When fully raised the wings are approximately at a 90 degree angle. When raised, the wings are held up by hydraulic pressure if the cylinders are correctly attached and fully charged. The wings can also be held up by a lock pin which is inserted manually. If the hydraulic cylinders are not properly attached and fully charged, the wing will fall rapidly when the lock pin is removed.

On April 21, 1990, Ryan Patton was changing a hydraulic wing lift cylinder on the cultivator. The wings were fully raised and pinned up by the lock pin. Patton finished changing the cylinder and proceeded to remove the lock pin on the right wing. He did so by standing directly under the raised right wing of the cultivator and pushing up the wing. This relieved pressure on the lock pin and Patton proceeded to pull it out. When he did so the wing fell on him, causing him serious injury....

Several other individuals have been injured in accidents connected with vertical fold cultivator wings manufactured by HWR. These accidents appear to have occurred as early as 1983. HWR was aware of these accidents. Patton admits that prior to 1977, HWR had no notice of accidents involving cultivator wings falling when the mechanical lock pin on the wing was removed. A secondary safety wing latch which was developed in 1983 by Deere & Company, one of HWR's competitors, was unknown to cultivator manufacturers in 1976. Similarly, the other safety devices which Patton alleges should have been on the cultivator were unknown to the industry in 1976. Deere & Company instituted a mandatory safety improvement program for all vertical fold 90°field cultivators in October 1983. The Deere retrofit program became known to John Kehrwald, Vice President of Engineering and Manufacturing at HWR, at some point four or five years after it was initiated. Kehrwald recognized his company had problems with the cultivator wings in 1983. Kehrwald indicated that he believed it was an acceptable risk to choose not to retrofit the HWR cultivators.

Patton stated that there was no way to know whether the hydraulic cylinders are fully charged. Consequently, he believed that after installing a new cylinder, it was safe to remove the lockpin on the wings without doing anything more.

There are no warning labels or decals on the wings of the cultivator. The instruction manual neither details the method by which a cylinder should be changed nor mentions hazards. Patton did not receive any warning concerning hazards or safety modifications from either the dealership or HWR....

In considering whether HWR may have a duty to warn of product hazards after the point of sale, we choose the label "post-sale" rather than "continuing". The post-sale claim is separate from the warning claim asserted with respect to the point of sale. See *Jones v. Hit-*

tle Service, Inc., 219 Kan. at 634, 549 P.2d 1383 (duty to warn arises only when the supplier "knows or has reason to know that the chattle is or is likely to be dangerous for the use for which it is supplied"); *Restatement (Second) of Torts* § 388[a] (1964). A post-sale warning could not be given at the point of sale because a manufacturer would not have knowledge to give it.

A variety of courts have found that a manufacturer does not have a post-sale duty to notify product purchasers or users of changes in the state of the art concerning the safe use of the product. *Collins v. Hyster Co.*, 174 Ill.App.3d 972, 977, 124 Ill.Dec. 483, 529 N.E.2d 303 (1988), lv. to app. denied 124 Ill.2d 554, 129 Ill.Dec. 148, 535 N.E.2d 913 (1989) (forklift products liability case), recognized the duty to warn distinction in the defect at sale and new design improvement contexts: "Certainly the law does not contemplate placing the onerous duty on manufacturers to subsequently warn all foreseeable users of products based on increased design or manufacture expertise that was not present at the time the product left its control." *Lynch v. McStome & Lincoln Plaza*, 378 Pa.Super. at 440–42, 548 A.2d 1276, considered a manufacturer's duty to retrofit an escalator with a new braking system or to warn the owners of the new design. The court determined that no such duty existed.

The state of the art may be altered by the development of a more effective safety device. For business reasons, a manufacturer may seek to bring product improvement to the attention of its past customers, and it should be encouraged to do so in a manner that does not underplay important safety developments. Patton neither requests nor do we impose a requirement that a manufacturer seek out past customers and notify them of changes in the state of the art....

Comstock v. General Motors Corp., 358 Mich. 163, 99 N.W.2d 627 (1959), the seminal case upon which Patton relies, held that a manufacturer's duty to warn of a known latent defect exists not only at the time of sale but also when such a defect becomes known to the manufacturer. The *Comstock* facts presented a situation where the defective automobile brake was present at the time of manufacture. The Michigan court limited its holding by observing that: (1) the brake hazard became known to General Motors "shortly after" the car had been put on the market, and (2) the defect was life threatening. 358 Mich. at 177–78, 99 N.W.2d 627.

The post-sale duty to warn varies among jurisdictions. In *Cover v. Cohen*, 61 N.Y.2d 261, 275, 473 N.Y.S.2d 378, 461 N.E.2d 864 (Ct.App.1984), a duty to warn product users of discovered dangers was imposed. See *Hodder v. Goodyear Tire & Rubber Co.*, 426 N.W.2d 826, 833 (Minn.1988), cert. denied 492 U.S. 926, 109 S.Ct. 3265, 106 L.Ed.2d 610 (1989). In *doCanto v. Ametek, Inc.*, 367 Mass. 776, 784–85, 328 N.E.2d 873 (1975) (alleged defective commercial ironer), the Supreme Court of Massachusetts stated: "When the manufacturer of such a machine learns or should have learned of the risk created by its fault, it has a duty to take reasonable steps to warn at least the purchaser of the risk." See also *Smith v. FMC Corp.*, 754 F.2d 873, 877 (10th Cir.1985) (alleged defective cranes); *Owens-Illinois v. Zenobia*, 325 Md. 420, 446, 601 A.2d 633 (Ct.App.1992) (asbestos strict products liability case); and *Harris v. Int'l. Harvester*, 127 Misc.2d 426, 429–30, 486 N.Y.S.2d 600 (S.Ct.1984) (alleged negligence in connection with design of farm tractor).

Some courts have elected to further limit the scope of the applicable duty to warn to particular contexts. For example, in *Walton v. Avco Corp.*, 530 Pa. 568, 577–78, 610 A.2d 454 (1992) (*Walton II*, a strict liability case) the court imposed on a helicopter manufacturer a duty to warn owners that a defective part had been incorporated into the helicopter. See also *Walton v. Avco Corp.*, 383 Pa.Super. 518, 531–32, 557 A.2d 372 (1989)

(*Walton I*), for the lower court's analysis which draws a distinction between household consumer goods and a manufacturer of a unique product such as the helicopter....

We recognize a manufacturer's post-sale duty to warn ultimate consumers who purchased the product who can be readily identified or traced when a defect, which originated at the time the product was manufactured and was unforeseeable at the point of sale, is discovered to present a life threatening hazard. We agree with the Wisconsin Supreme Court in *Kozlowski* when it observed, after applying a post-sale warning duty to a sausage making machine under a claim of strict liability and negligence:

> We do not in this decision hold that there is an absolute continuing duty, year after year, for all manufacturers to warn of a new safety device which eliminates potential hazards. A sausage stuffer and the nature of that industry bears no similarity to the realities of manufacturing and marketing household goods such as fans, snowblowers or lawn mowers which have become increasingly hazard proof with each succeeding model. It is beyond reason and good judgment to hold a manufacturer responsible for a duty of annually warning of safety hazards on household items, mass produced and used in every American home, when the product is 6 to 35 years old and outdated by some 20 newer models equipped with every imaginable safety innovation known in the state of the art. It would place an unreasonable duty upon these manufacturers if they were required to trace the ownership of each unit sold and warn annually of new safety improvements over a 35 year period. 87 Wis.2d at 901, 275 N.W.2d 915.

We acknowledge practical problems associated with imposing a post-sale duty to warn. The question of whether such a duty arises in a particular case will depend on the facts of that case. The passage of time from manufacture and initial sale to the discovery of previously unknown hazards may reflect that the product has changed ownership many times. The original purchaser may have moved. The length of product life will vary. What is reasonably prudent post-sale conduct for one manufacturer and one type of product may not be reasonable for another manufacturer of an entirely different type of product. The sale of the farm cultivator was made to Patton's father on a one-time basis 13 years before the injury. What sales records will be available to the manufacturer? Notification by a manufacturer to all prior purchasers of a product may be extremely burdensome, if not impossible. In the case at bar, the manufacturer's retailer has continuing contact with the consumers. We reason that a manufacturer who was unaware of a hazard at the time of sale and has since acquired knowledge of a life-threatening hazard should not be absolved of all duty to take reasonable steps to warn the ultimate consumer who purchased the product; however, the warning of unforeseeable dangers is neither required nor possible at the time of sale. A manufacturer is to be given a reasonable period of time after discovery of the life-threatening hazard in which to issue any post-sale warning that might reasonably be required.

The imposition of liability upon a manufacturer for inadequately warning an ultimate consumer who purchased the product prior to the time the manufacturer learned of the potential danger regarding the dangers of the product is dependent upon a reasonableness test and the manufacturer's actual or constructive knowledge of the risk. A post-sale duty to warn does not exist until either actual or constructive knowledge is acquired by the manufacturer concerning a later life-threatening hazard posed by a product when the product is used for its normally intended purpose. The alleged defect in the cultivator was unknown to HWR when it was initially sold. We do not apply a strict liability theory to the post-sale duty to warn. The cardinal inquiry is, was HWR's post-sale conduct reasonable? The reasonableness standard is flexible. The type of notice of a problem revealed by product use that will impose a post-sale duty to warn will be a function of the degree of danger which the problem involves and the number of instances reported. Whether a prima facie case has been made for the presence of a post-sale duty will depend on the facts of each case. Each plaintiff must make an initial showing that the manufacturer acquired knowledge of a defect present but unknown and unforeseeable at the point of sale and failed to take reasonable action to warn of the defect.

The nature of the post-sale warning and where and to whom it should be given will involve a case-by-case analysis. The analysis shall include but not be limited to the examination of such factors as: (1) the nature of the harm that may result from use without notice, (2) the likelihood that harm will occur (Does future continuing use of the product create a significant risk of serious harm which can be lessened if a post-sale warning is given?), (3) how many persons are affected, (4) the economic burden on the manufacturer of identifying and contacting current product users (Does the manufacturer have an ongoing relationship with the purchaser or other knowledge of the identity of the owner of the product which provides a practical way of providing a post-sale warning?), (5) the nature of the industry, (6) the type of product involved, (7) the number of units manufactured or sold, and (8) steps taken other than giving of notice to correct the problem. The facts may indicate that notice to all ultimate consumers who purchased the product prior to the time the manufacturer learned of a potential danger is unreasonable, if not impossible. Notice to the distributor or retail seller may, in certain contexts, meet the reasonableness standard.

The particular facts may reflect that a lack of notice was not unreasonable and that a reasonable manufacturer under the circumstances would have taken no post-sale action. Knowledge and reasonableness, as determinative factors, will provide an incentive to manufacturers to issue warnings if latent product hazards are discovered after the initial sale and a warning under the circumstances would be reasonable. We cannot fashion a "bright line" rule from a farm cultivator case that applies with interpretative ease to the infinite variety of products that inhabit the marketplace.

Each trial judge will necessarily be required to make a determination as to whether the record presents a fact question as to knowledge and reasonableness whenever a plaintiff's claim of negligent breach of a post-sale duty to warn is alleged. Generally, resolution of the issue of reasonableness, after an initial court determination that the issue is presented, will be one of fact for the jury. The trial judge, in instructing the jury on a post-sale duty to warn, shall utilize the relevant factors referenced herein, including the nature and likelihood of the injury posed by the product, the feasibility and expense of issuing a warning, whether the warning would be effective, and whether ultimate consumers who purchased the product can be identified.

The answer to certified questions three and four is "no." Patton has provided no statute or case law to support the claim that HWR is subject to a duty to retrofit or recall the cultivator. We reason that product recalls are properly the business of administrative agencies as suggested by the federal statutes that expressly delegate recall authority. Extensive federal recall legislation deals with the post sale obligations of manufacturers of products such as automobiles, consumer products, boats, and medical devices.

Notes

1. *Duty to recall?* In line with traditional tort principles, manufacturers and sellers may, by their own conduct, voluntarily assume a duty to recall. In *Blossman Gas Co. v.*

Williams, 375 S.E. 2d 117 (Ga. Ct. App. 1988) a Georgia court held that a when a vendor agreed to notify customers of a manufacturer recall and failed to do so, its negligence gave rise to a cause of action. Effectively, its undertaking to recall established a new standard of care for itself, so that its own subsequent non-compliance automatically meant that it had breached its duty.

2. *A matter for the courts, or for legislatures?* In *Modelski v. Navistar International Transportation Corp.*, 707 N.E. 2d 239, 247 (Ill. App. Ct. 1999) an Illinois court argued that legislatures are better suited to impose such a duty because they are in a better position to create statutes that take into consideration the various types of products and whether statutes of repose "should be enacted to limit the potentially indefinite duration of the duty." The *Modelski* court recognized that a court imposing a "duty to retrofit used products to incorporate post-sale state of the art designs would be the equivalent of mandating that manufacturers insure that their products will always comply with current safety standards." And, in 1992, the Tenth Circuit held in *Romero v. Int'l Harvester Co.*, 979 F.2d 1444, that if the product was not defective at the time of sale, then the manufacturer did not have a duty to retrofit the product after sale. The Supreme Court of Kentucky took a similar view in *Ostendorf v. Clark Equipment Co.*, 122 S.W.3d 530 (2003). However, as mentioned above, manufacturers of medical devices and pharmaceuticals are held to a higher standard and are expected to continue to test their products.

3. *When might there be a duty to retrofit?* The purpose of requiring manufacturers to issue post-sale warnings or recalls is either to have the product returned for a full refund before it causes any harm, or to have the product modified to avoid its causing such harm. Douglas R. Richmond, *Expanding Products Liability: Manufacturers' Post-Sale Duties to Warn, Retrofit and Recall*, 36 I.D.L.R. 7, 68 argues that the duty to retrofit should apply only when three conditions are met:

1. The danger the product poses must be so extraordinary, pronounced, or special that a post-sale warning will not protect consumers;

2. The manufacturer must be able to identify and locate product owners or users of a particular product; and

3. The manufacturer must be able to regain control of the product, as in the case of periodic service calls or regular maintenance visits, or the manufacturer must have the ability or right to compel consumers to cooperate in a retrofit program.

4. *Post-sale duty to warn, or continuing duty to warn?* Although some courts have talked of a "continuing duty to warn," this can be somewhat misleading. It suggests that a manufacturer or distributor, already aware of a defect in the product, repeatedly breaches its duty every day after sale until either the product is scrapped or it causes injury. Such an approach would have the effect of tolling any statute of limitations—i.e. preventing the time for filing suit from running—for defective design claims in circumstances which are unlikely to have been foreseen by any legislature. It is therefore preferable to avoid such language, and to talk of a post-sale duty to warn, which arises when new information comes to light after sale or distribution has already taken place.

Flax v. DaimlerChrysler Corporation

272 S.W.3d 521 (2008) (Supreme Court of Tennessee)

HOLDER, J. In their complaint, the plaintiffs asserted a claim based on DCC's failure to warn consumers that the Caravan's seatbacks posed a danger to children placed behind them. Prior to trial, the plaintiffs filed a trial brief clarifying that they were attempting to bring two separate failure to warn claims. The first claim is a traditional failure to warn claim alleging that DCC failed to provide a warning prior to or at the time the Caravan was sold. Tennessee courts have long held that a manufacturer may be held strictly liable for failing to warn consumers of the dangers of a particular product at the time of sale. The General Assembly has also acknowledged that a failure to warn claim is a valid basis for a product liability action. Accordingly, the trial court permitted the plaintiffs to proceed with the traditional failure to warn claim, and DCC has not appealed the trial court's ruling on that issue.

The plaintiffs' second failure to warn claim is more problematic. In their trial brief, the plaintiffs asserted that DCC should also be held liable for failing to warn the plaintiffs of the condition of the seatbacks after the Caravan was sold. Plaintiffs argued their second claim is what is commonly referred to as a "post-sale failure to warn" claim, a claim that has not been previously recognized in Tennessee. Under the assumption that their second claim was a post-sale failure to warn claim, the plaintiffs argued that the trial court should join the jurisdictions that recognize the post-sale failure to warn claims and adopt the post-sale failure to warn provisions of the *Restatement (Third) of Torts*. The trial court was persuaded by the plaintiffs' arguments and allowed the plaintiffs to present evidence and argument at trial in support of their second failure to warn claim. At the conclusion of the trial, the jury found the defendants liable on the plaintiffs' second failure to warn claim.

DCC contends that the trial court erred in recognizing the post-sale failure to warn claim. We agree. Although different states apply the doctrine differently, the vast majority of courts recognizing post-sale failure to warn claims agree that a claim arises when the manufacturer or seller becomes aware that a product is defective or unreasonably dangerous after the point of sale and fails to take reasonable steps to warn consumers who purchased the product. Accordingly, courts apply the traditional failure to warn claim when a manufacturer or seller had knowledge of a defect at the time of sale and apply the post-sale failure to warn claim when a manufacturer or seller learns of the defect after the time of sale.

Unlike plaintiffs in post-sale duty to warn cases, the plaintiffs in this case do not allege that DCC discovered problems with the seatbacks after the time of sale. On the contrary, the theory of the plaintiffs' case was that DCC had knowledge that the seats were defective and unreasonably dangerous as early as the 1980s. Furthermore, DCC does not deny that it had knowledge of the performance of its seats at the time of sale but argues that the seats functioned in a non-defective and reasonably safe manner. There is therefore no dispute regarding DCC's knowledge at the time of sale of the Caravan. Although the plaintiffs allege that DCC continued to receive notice that its product was dangerous after the sale, they do not allege that DCC received any new information during this period. Accordingly, this case does not present the facts necessary to allow us to consider the merits of recognizing post-sale failure to warn claims. Rather, the plaintiffs' allegation that DCC was negligent in failing to warn the plaintiffs after the sale is an attempt to impose liability a second time for what is essentially the same wrongful conduct. If a defendant negligently fails to warn at the time of sale, that defendant does not breach any new duty to the plaintiff by failing to provide a warning the day after the sale. Instead, the defendant merely remains in breach of its initial duty. For these reasons, we conclude that the trial court erred by adopting and applying the post-sale failure to warn claim in this case. We express no opinion, however, as to the merits of recognizing that cause of action in an appropriate case.

Affirmed in part; reversed in part.

Cigna Insurance Co. v. OY Saunatec, Ltd.

241 F.3d 1 (1st Cir. 2001)

LIPEZ, J. On March 18, 1997, the Waltham Racquet Club suffered severe damage from a fire that began on the sauna heater located in its men's sauna room. Its insurer, Cigna Insurance Company, later instituted this subrogation action against OY Saunatec, Ltd., the manufacturer of the sauna heater, alleging that Saunatec had negligently designed the heater, negligently failed to warn, and breached its implied warranty of merchantability. Saunatec appeals and Cigna cross-appeals from a judgment entered on a jury verdict finding in favor of Cigna on its negligence claims and in favor of Saunatec on the breach of warranty claim....

Under Massachusetts law, there is no post-sale duty to warn unless the product at issue was negligently designed as originally sold. See *Williams v. Monarch Machine Tool Co.*, 26 F.3d 228, 232 (1st Cir.1994). When the design defect is present at the time of sale, the manufacturer "has a duty to take reasonable steps to warn at least the purchaser of the risk" as soon as it "learns or should have learned of the risk created by its fault." *doCanto v. Ametek, Inc.*, 367 Mass. 776, 328 N.E.2d 873, 878 (1975) (citing *Carney v. Bereault*, 348 Mass. 502, 204 N.E.2d 448 (1965)).

There was ample evidence to support a conclusion that the heater was negligently designed. According to the UL standards in existence at the time of the sale of the heater, all heaters must include some form of guard to prevent combustible materials from coming into contact with any part of the heater that exceeded 536 degrees Fahrenheit. The "guard" could include the rocks that are normally piled on top of the heating elements in a sauna heater. If the rocks prevented contact, the industry standards at the time of sale generally did not require the addition of a separate metal grill on top of the heater. In the case of the club's heater, however, the rocks were an insufficient barrier between combustible materials and the high temperature parts of the heater. Under the UL standards then in force, Saunatec was required to modify its heater, either by adding a metal grill or by increasing the dimensions of the heater to allow for more rocks to be included on top of the elements. Without these design changes, the heater failed to adhere to the industry safety standards. The UL standards also required that heaters pass a drape test. Under this test, cloth material was draped over the heater to determine if the placement of a towel on the heater would start a fire. Evidence at trial demonstrated that the club's heater could not have passed this test. The jury was justified in concluding that the heater had been negligently designed at the time of sale, thus triggering a duty to warn of post-sale safety improvements.

B. The nature of the danger

Though a negligently designed product is an essential prerequisite for the duty to warn, the duty does not arise in every case involving a negligently designed product. Saunatec is correct in its general contention that, when the dangers associated with a defective product are open and obvious, there is usually no duty to warn "because a warning will not reduce the likelihood of injury." To fall under this rule, the dangers must have been sufficiently obvious to say that the plaintiff was "fully aware of the risks posed by the product." Saunatec unpersuasively contends that the risks posed by the heater were open and obvious from the time of sale because all people are aware that there is a remote risk of fire associated with leaving towels on sauna heaters even when those heaters are properly designed.

The knowledge of a general risk associated with an entire class of properly designed products, however, is not sufficient to allow the conclusion in this case that at the time of sale the club was "fully aware of the risks posed by the product." The evidence at trial indicated that, in contrast to properly designed heaters that will not normally cause fires even when a towel is left on them for an entire day, the club's defectively designed heater could start a fire in under ten minutes after a towel was left on it. The differing times to combustion of a properly designed heater versus the club's heater were solely the result of the defective design of the latter. Though the lack of a grill contributed to the danger posed by the club's heater, it was not a signal of a design defect. Many heaters sold at that time did not have grills and were not defective, just as the club's heater might not have been defective if the rocks on top of the heater had provided a more effective guard. In short, Saunatec cannot escape the duty to warn engendered by its negligent design because this heater posed an inordinate risk of fire that was by no means open and obvious from the time of sale.

C. Warning of design improvements

Saunatec next contends that the first fire effectively notified the club of the danger posed by its heater, making any warning that Saunatec might have given superfluous. The jury found that the first fire gave the club notice that its heater was defective. That fire may also have made the club fully aware of the danger posed by the heater. Nonetheless, it is still not sufficient to extinguish Saunatec's duty to warn. Though the duty to warn principally extends to warnings of the danger created by a design defect, it is not limited to warning solely of those dangers. Massachusetts courts have indicated that in certain cases, the manufacturer of a negligently designed product also has a duty "to warn at least the purchaser of changes which eliminate or tend to eliminate the risk created by the manufacturer's initial fault."

This is one of those cases. The jury could reasonably conclude that Saunatec should have known of the defect and that Saunatec had developed a safety improvement that would have eliminated the danger that arose from its design defect. Saunatec conducted tests upon its heaters in order to ensure that they met the UL standards. When a particular model failed to meet those standards, Saunatec would change the design. Though not all heaters that Saunatec manufactured at the time this heater was designed needed metal grills to satisfy the UL, Saunatec knew that some did. Indeed, by 1975 or 1976, Saunatec had modified its designs to include metal grills upon all heaters sold in the United States. In 1978, the UL changed its standards to require that all heaters it listed include a metal grill as shielding between combustible materials and the heating elements. Finally, the club's expert also testified at length that the addition of a metal grill was feasible and would have both cured the defect in the heater and prevented both fires.

Furthermore, the rationale that underlies the refusal to impose a duty to warn of open and obvious dangers cannot apply here to defeat Saunatec's duty to warn of design changes. Unlike warnings of open and obvious dangers, which are not required under Massachusetts law because it is unlikely that such a warning would "reduce the likelihood of injury," a warning of a design change that can eliminate the risk posed by a defect is, at least potentially, effective. In the present case, the evidence indicated that if the club had heeded a warning to install a grill on the heater, it would have completely eliminated "the risk created by [Saunatec's] initial fault." Consequently, we conclude that this issue was properly before the jury, even if the first fire fully apprised the club of the dangers associated with its heater. The district court was correct in instructing on this issue.

Judgment affirmed.

Hypothetical

Eric owned a truck which was starting to show signs of wear. He was particularly concerned about the rusty state of his fuel tank. He mentioned this to his friend, Fred, in the bar one night. Fred suggested that they use his sand-blasting equipment to clean the rust off the tank. "I bet it's only a cosmetic issue. When we've finished, it'll look like new," he said. That weekend they set up the equipment and began to sand-blast the fuel tank. At first, Fred's prediction seemed to be coming true. Then the fuel tank exploded. Expert evidence has found that the cause of the explosion was the ignition of fuel vapor by static electricity, which was itself generated by the friction of sand passing through the nylon tubing of the sand-blasting equipment. Fred died in the explosion; Eric was severely burned.

The manual that came with the sand-blasting equipment recommended the use of silicone carbide as the abrasive of choice. However, Fred had bought the equipment as a ten-year-old, reconditioned item from a business on eBay, and the manual had not been supplied with the equipment. Fred had used the equipment to clean other metal items several times before the fatal incident, and he had used regular sand each time without apparent problems. Modern sand-blasting equipment uses rubber-lined hose to reduce static.

What is the legal position both of Eric and of Fred's widow, Diane?

Part III

Causation

Chapter 9

Causation in Fact

Basic Doctrine

It should, by now, be apparent that there are effectively six different types of claim that may be brought by a plaintiff alleging that s/he was injured by a defective product. These are depicted in a Venn diagram in Figure 9.1. As this demonstrates, each form of action operates independently of all the others, but different claims often overlap.

There is, however, something that all the different types of claims have in common. Proof of one or more of the above six defects does not suffice for a successful claim. On the contrary, it must also be proved, on a preponderance of the evidence, that the defect caused the victim's injuries. We therefore need now to address the doctrine of causation.

As §§ 15–17 of the Third Restatement expressly note, the rules relating to proof of causation in fact for products liability do not differ in principle from those applied in other areas of the law of torts. It must, however, be remembered that there are two generally-accepted methods of proving cause in fact: the "but-for" test and the "substantial factor" test. Each has its own difficulties. The but-for test requires the plaintiff to prove a negative: that, but for the product defect, the injury would not have occurred. This tends to limit its utility to cases where the alleged causative mechanism appears well understood. In more complex cases, such as where there are apparently several causative agents, or where any causal relationship is not well understood, it will be much more common for the courts to adopt the substantial factor test.

["but-for"]
["substantial factor" test]

Restatement (Third) of Torts: Products Liability (1998)

§ 16. Increased Harm Due to Product Defect

(a) When a product is defective at the time of commercial sale or other distribution and the defect is a substantial factor in increasing the plaintiff's harm beyond that which would have resulted from other causes, the product seller is subject to liability for the increased harm.

(b) If proof supports a determination of the harm that would have resulted from other causes in the absence of the product defect, the product seller's liability is limited to the increased harm attributable solely to the product defect.

(c) If proof does not support a determination under Subsection (b) of the harm that would have resulted in the absence of the product defect, the product seller is liable for all of the plaintiff's harm attributable to the defect and other causes.

(d) A seller of a defective product that is held liable for part of the harm suffered by the plaintiff under Subsection (b), or all of the harm suffered by the plaintiff under Subsection (c), is jointly and severally liable or severally liable with other parties who bear legal

Figure 9.1 The Six Different Types of Claim in Products Liability

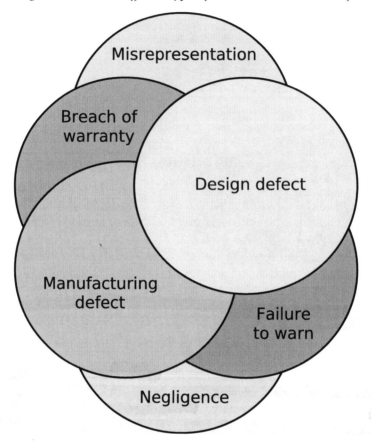

responsibility for causing the harm, determined by applicable rules of joint and several liability.

Notes

1. *Joint and several liability, or just several liability?* The rationale for the application of the doctrine of joint and several liability is simply that, since the harm sustained by the victim is one indivisible whole, it is, by definition, impossible to apportion liability according to the degree of *harm* which each party's conduct caused. Some states have, however, passed legislation abandoning this approach in favor of apportioning liability according to the degree of *fault* of each of the parties involved. In these states, therefore, liability is several but not joint, so that the victim must seek compensation from every tortfeasor in order to recover the full sum to which s/he is entitled.

2. *Comparative and contributory fault.* As in other areas of torts, the sum of compensation recoverable by victims will, in most states, be reduced by a fraction which reflects their own share of blame. In a few jurisdictions, however, the old common law defense of contributory negligence continues to apply, so that a victim who is partially to blame for his or her own injury will be entirely barred from claiming compensation from others (and some other states will also deny any compensation if the victim's fault was equal

to or greater than that of the defendant). This topic is addressed in more detail in Chapter 11.

General Causation

Although the basic doctrine of causation in torts also applies in cases of alleged product liability, the nature of the inquiry in many such cases means that several practical differences will often become manifest. The first of the characteristics peculiar to products liability law is the common—but not universal—bifurcation of proof of causation in fact. This involves drawing a distinction between so-called *general* causation on the one hand and what is known as *specific* causation on the other. General causation demands that the plaintiff prove, on a preponderance of the evidence, that the product is *capable* of causing the *type* of injury alleged. Specific causation, on the other hand, requires the plaintiff to show that the product in question *caused* the plaintiff's *actual* injuries. Both the but-for and substantial factor tests are applicable to proof of specific, rather than general, causation.

[margin note: general vs. specific causation]

While this may appear to be a major departure from the regular law of causation in torts, the reality is quite different. In a "regular" torts case, such as a car wreck caused by a negligent driver, it is simply that everyone already knows that car accidents are capable of causing a variety of physical and emotional injuries, so proof of general causation is simply assumed. Indeed, this may also be true of some products liability cases (as would be the case if the car wreck had actually been caused by a defective tire). In such a case, there would again be no need to prove general causation.

The position is, however, different when dealing with claims concerning products about which knowledge is limited. These typically involve so-called "toxic torts," where the products are either new—often pharmaceuticals or medical devices—or allegedly contain latent defects (often involving some form of carcinogen) whose effects become apparent only over a relatively long period of time. If a product is new, it will be impossible to claim complete knowledge of its potential consequences. The same will be true of knowledge of a product's long-term effects until it has been in general use for at least the period of time over which the plaintiff claims to have been exposed. So, before an alleged victim can bring evidence that s/he was harmed by the specific product in question, s/he must first demonstrate, on a preponderance of the evidence, that such products can indeed cause the sort of injury which s/he has sustained. In cases involving products about which knowledge of potential defects—or of the effects which they might bring about—is limited, the courts do not therefore assume general causation, but instead require it to be proved.

Lack of knowledge, of course, cuts both ways. We cannot be sure if a plaintiff should potentially be able to recover compensation from the manufacturer or distributor of the product in question; but neither can we be sure whether the manufacturer or distributor has a credible defense. But since the law places the burden of proof on the plaintiff, it is for him (or her) to prove general causation just as much as it is for him (or her) to prove specific causation. Indeed, it cannot be over-emphasized that a plaintiff who brings a case about such a product must prove *both* general causation *and* specific causation.

However, the nature of the question to be answered in each of these elements is very different. General causation requires a generic or systemic finding: a given product either is, or is not, capable of causing injuries of a particular type. This is therefore an issue of law for the court, which makes it particularly amenable, in appropriate cases, to summary judgment. Specific causation, on the other hand, relates to findings regarding the particular case at hand. As with "regular" torts cases, it is therefore, quite clearly, a matter for the jury. Moreover, just as the issue of causation in fact may be bifurcated as a matter of legal technicality, so too may pre-trial motions frequently ask that a court bifurcate the issue as a matter of practical convenience. If the court then finds that there is no proof of general causation, there will be no need for a full jury trial.

In Re: Meridia Products Liability Litigation
328 F.Supp.2d 791 (2004) (US District Court, N.D. Ohio)

GWIN, J. In support of their motion for summary judgment, Defendants primarily argue that the Plaintiffs have failed to come forth with any evidence that Meridia causes compensable injury. If Defendants are correct, then Plaintiffs' claims for strict liability (all theories thereof), negligence, and negligence per se must fail. After all, causation of an alleged injury is an element of each of these claims.

Toxic tort cases present a unique challenge to the classical conception of causation. Other tort cases, such as slip-and-fall or car accident cases, feature scenarios where causation is fairly obvious—if one car collides with another, common sense dictates that a range of injuries from broken limbs to internal bleeding to death can result. Toxic tort cases, however, generally involve less-common injuries that often function at the cellular level. The causation inquiry in toxic tort cases is more complicated because the injuries themselves are usually not immediately obvious and the connection between exposure and injury is not a matter of common sense or everyday experience. Moreover, a variety of exposures frequently can associate with the condition. Using one example, both smoking and exposure to asbestos increase the risk of lung cancer. When smoking and exposure to asbestos combine, the risk of cancer increases precipitously. Similarly, Meridia users are typically obese, a condition that, alone, is a risk factor for cardiovascular disease. When cardiovascular injury occurs, it is difficult to precisely identify the precipitating cause.

In toxic tort cases, the causation inquiry is two-pronged. First, a plaintiff must show that the substance to which she was exposed *can cause* the type of injury alleged. Next, a plaintiff must show that in her case, exposure to the substance *actually caused* the alleged injury. *Sterling v. Velsicol Chem.* Corp., 855 F.2d 1188 (6th Cir.1988); *Bonner v. ISP Techs. Inc.*, 259 F.3d 924, 928 (8th Cir.2001) ("[t]o prove causation in a toxic tort case, a plaintiff must show both that the alleged toxin is capable of causing injuries like that suffered by the plaintiff in human beings subjected to the same level of exposure as the plaintiff, and that the toxin was the cause of the plaintiff's injury"); *In re Breast Implant Litig.*, 11 F.Supp.2d 1217, 1224 (D.Colo.1998) (collecting cases). The first prong is called "generic" or "general" causation; the second goes by the moniker "specific" or "individual" causation. *In re Hanford Nuclear Reservation Litig.*, 292 F.3d 1124, 1129 (9th Cir.2002) ("'Generic causation' has typically been understood to mean the capacity of a toxic agent ... to cause the illnesses complained of by plaintiffs. If such capacity is established, 'individual causation' answers whether that toxic agent actually caused a particular plaintiff's illness."); *Jack v. Glaxo Wellcome, Inc.*, 239 F.Supp.2d 1308, 1320–21 (N.D.Ga.2002) ("General causation is the capacity of a product to cause injury; specific causation is proof that the product in question caused the injury of which the plaintiff complains.") (citation omitted). *See also Goebel v. Denver & Rio Grande Western Ry. Co.*, 346 F.3d 987, 990 (10th

Cir.2003) (identifying "two separate aspects of causation … in this case: (1) general causation, meaning that the particular circumstances in the tunnel *could* have caused Mr. Goebel's injury, and (2) specific causation, meaning that those circumstances *did in fact* cause Mr. Goebel's injury.") [*general vs. specific*]

With a large number of discrete clinical settings associated with each plaintiff's claims, the examination regarding individual causation is unwieldy. The more appropriate course restricts the inquiry on consolidated motions for summary judgment to the logically prior issue, general causation. Multidistrict Litigation ("MDL") seeks to promote judicial economy and litigant efficiency by allowing the transferee court to preside over matters common among all cases. Given this function, the transferee court typically does not rule on cumbersome, case specific legal issues.

By its nature, specific causation is not common to all plaintiffs. Rather, it involves a "determination [that] is highly individualistic, and depends upon the characteristics of individual plaintiffs." Therefore, the Court limits its inquiry to general causation, i.e., whether the plaintiff shows sufficient evidence that the substance in question has the capacity to cause harm. Indeed, other MDL cases have reserved specific causation questions to cases that are remanded. [*specific causation*]

The Court first turns to examining whether the Plaintiffs show sufficient evidence that Meridia is capable of causing compensable injury. Because the Court examines this case on a motion for summary judgment, the issue may be better phrased, "Have Plaintiffs offered sufficient evidence that Meridia causes the types of injuries of which they complain?" If the answer to this question is negative, it stops plaintiffs from demonstrating specific causation. *See Soldo v. Sandoz Pharm. Corp.*, 244 F.Supp.2d 434, 525 (W.D.Pa.2003) ("The issue of specific causation is material, however, only if plaintiff can demonstrate general causation …") (quoting *Brumbaugh v. Sandoz Pharm. Corp.*, 77 F.Supp.2d 1153, 1155 (D.Mont.1999)).

For Defendants, Meridia operates safely and effectively, and has few serious side effects. More critical for the issues presently before this Court, the Defendants claim that Plaintiffs show no evidence sufficient to make out a case that Meridia causes compensable injury. Supporting this conclusion, Defendants cite the opinions of numerous scientific and medical experts, as well as epidemiological studies. Restating their argument: The obese population using Meridia suffer from increased risk of cardiovascular conditions. Unless epidemiological studies show this risk increases with Meridia ingestion, there is no way to attribute the condition to the Meridia use. [*D arg*]

Defendants' motion for summary judgment granted, dismissing all of Plaintiffs' claims against the Pharmaceutical Defendants. Plaintiffs' claims against the Physician Defendants continued to pend.

Michael D. Green, D. Michal Freedman & Leon Gordis, Reference Guide on Epidemiology

Reference Manual on Scientific Evidence, 3d ed.,
Federal Judicial Center & National Academy of Sciences, 2011

Epidemiology is the field of public health and medicine that studies the incidence, distribution, and etiology of disease in human populations. The purpose of epidemiology is to better understand disease causation and to prevent disease in groups of individuals. Epidemiology assumes that disease is not distributed randomly in a group of individuals and that identifiable subgroups, including those exposed to certain agents, are at increased risk of contracting particular diseases.

Judges and juries increasingly are presented with epidemiologic evidence as the basis of an expert's opinion on causation. In the courtroom, epidemiologic research findings are offered to establish or dispute whether exposure to an agent caused a harmful effect or disease. Epidemiologic evidence identifies agents that are associated with an increased risk of disease in groups of individuals, quantifies the amount of excess disease that is associated with an agent, and provides a profile of the type of individual who is likely to contract a disease after being exposed to an agent. Epidemiology focuses on the question of general causation (i.e., is the agent capable of causing disease?) rather than that of specific causation (i.e., did it cause disease in a particular individual?). For example, in the 1950s, Doll and Hill and others published articles about the increased risk of lung cancer in cigarette smokers. Doll and Hill's studies showed that smokers who smoked 10 to 20 cigarettes a day had a lung cancer mortality rate that was about ten10 times higher than that for nonsmokers. These studies identified an association between smoking cigarettes and death from lung cancer that contributed to the determination that smoking causes lung cancer.

However, it should be emphasized that *an association is not equivalent to causation.* An association identified in an epidemiologic study may or may not be causal. Assessing whether an association is causal requires an understanding of the strengths and weaknesses of the study's design and implementation, as well as a judgment about how the study findings fit with other scientific knowledge. It is important to emphasize that all studies have "flaws" in the sense of limitations that add uncertainty about the proper interpretation of the results. Some flaws are inevitable given the limits of technology, resources, the ability and willingness of persons to participate in a study, and ethical constraints. In evaluating epidemiologic evidence, the key questions, then, are the extent to which a study's limitations compromise its findings and permit inferences about causation.

A final caveat is that employing the results of group-based studies of risk to make a causal determination for an individual plaintiff is beyond the limits of epidemiology. Nevertheless, a substantial body of legal precedent has developed that addresses the use of epidemiologic evidence to prove causation for an individual litigant through probabilistic means, and the law developed in these cases is discussed later in this reference guide.

The following sections of this reference guide address a number of critical issues that arise in considering the admissibility of, and weight to be accorded to, epidemiologic research findings. Over the past several decades, courts frequently have confronted the use of epidemiologic studies as evidence and recognized their utility in proving causation. As the Third Circuit observed in *DeLuca v. Merrell Dow Pharmaceuticals, Inc.*: "The reliability of expert testimony founded on reasoning from epidemiological data is generally a fit subject for judicial notice; epidemiology is a well-established branch of science and medicine, and epidemiological evidence has been accepted in numerous cases." Indeed, much more difficult problems arise for courts when there is a paucity of epidemiologic evidence.

Three basic issues arise when epidemiology is used in legal disputes, and the methodological soundness of a study and its implications for resolution of the question of causation must be assessed:

1. Do the results of an epidemiologic study or studies reveal an association between an agent and disease?

2. Could this association have resulted from limitations of the study (bias, confounding, or sampling error), and, if so, from which?

3.   Based on the analysis of limitations in Item 2, above, and on other evidence, how plausible is a causal interpretation of the association?

Notes

1. ***Weight to be given to epidemiological evidence.*** In 1965 Sir Austin Bradford Hill, *The Environment and Disease: Association or Causation?* 58 Proc. Royal Soc'y Med. 295 (1965), suggested factors to be taken into account in assessing evidence of causation. These are:

factors to consider for causation

A. Chronology: This is the only necessary factor. The symptom identified must occur after exposure to the potential agent (and if there is an expected delay between exposure and expected effect, then the effect must occur after that delay). If there was no exposure before disease, then the agent in question cannot be a cause.

B. Strength of Association: The higher the relative risk, the greater the likelihood that the relationship between agent and symptom is causal. However, a small association does not necessarily mean that there is no causal effect.

C. Dose-Response Relationship: Greater exposure to the agent usually leads to greater incidence of the symptom. However, in some cases, the mere presence of the agent can trigger the symptom. In other cases, an inverse proportion may be observed, so that greater exposure leads to lower incidence.

D. Degree of Replication: The more that the results of a given study can be replicated across different samples observed by different persons in different places increases the probability of a causal relationship between agent and symptom.

E. Plausibility: By definition, an explanation for a potential causal mechanism that is scientifically—normally biologically or chemically—plausible strengthens its credibility. However, the importance of this factor is diminished by the fact that epidemiological studies are utilized precisely because of a lack of knowledge about either the factor and/or the causes of the symptom.

F. Coherence: Coherence between epidemiological and laboratory findings increases the likelihood of an effect. A typical response to epidemiological studies suggesting a causal link between a factor and a symptom is to try to reproduce the symptom in a laboratory experiment. However, such experiments may necessarily be limited in scope or simply unethical to undertake (e.g. exposing individuals to potentially deadly toxins). On the other hand, laboratory experiments may be able to rule out alternative explanations.

G. Real-life Experiment: It may be instructive to discover what happens when exposure ceases, or when a hypothesis is tested as to appropriate remedial measures. However, where a disease is triggered by exposure above a particular threshold, those who have already suffered such exposure will not exhibit any reduction in symptoms; in fact, they may continue to get worse.

H. Specificity: The more specific an association between a factor and a symptom, the bigger the probability of a causal relationship.

I. Analogy, or Consistency with Other Relevant Knowledge: Hill wrote: "In some circumstances it would be fair to judge by analogy. With the effects of thalidomide and rubella before us we would surely be ready to accept slighter but similar evidence with another drug or another viral disease in pregnancy."

2. ***Inference.*** Hill emphasized that that these nine factors cannot be definitive. Since "[a]ll scientific work is incomplete—whether it be observational or experimental," these

factors can only assist in the drawing of appropriate inferences: "None of my nine view-points can bring indisputable evidence for or against the cause-and-effect hypothesis and none can be required as a *sine qua non*." The point about the drawing of such inferences is that they inevitably involve interpretation. Thus epidemiology can never directly prove cause and effect. What it demonstrates is, to some extent at least, in the eye of the beholder.

3. *General causation as an elastic concept.* Hill also emphasized that "differential standards" of proof of a causal relationship would often be appropriate:

> Thus on relatively slight evidence we might decide to restrict the use of a drug for early-morning sickness in pregnant women. If we are wrong in deducing causation from association no great harm will be done. The good lady and the pharmaceutical industry will doubtless survive.
>
> On fair evidence we might take action on what appears to be an occupational hazard, e.g. we might change from a probably carcinogenic oil to a non-carcinogenic oil in a limited environment and without too much injustice if we are wrong. But we should need very strong evidence before we made people burn a fuel in their homes that they do not like or stop smoking the cigarettes and eating the fats and sugar that they do like. In asking for very strong evidence I would, however, repeat emphatically that this does not imply crossing every "t", and swords with every critic, before we act.

4. *Risks, probabilities, and statistics.* Where science is not yet in a position to determine beyond doubt whether a particular illness or injury has been caused by a specific agent, we are inevitably left with having to uphold or reject a claim of causation on the basis of what is, by definition, inadequate information. This means that we have to ascertain the likely risks involved, and then decide whether we have sufficient knowledge about those risks to be able to say that it was more likely than not that the plaintiff was injured by the agent that s/he has identified in her complaint. This is often complicated by the fact that, where the alleged toxic agent is a pharmaceutical, it is likely that the plaintiff was already ill to begin with, for otherwise s/he would presumably not be taking the drug in question.

[handwritten margin note: Bayes' Theorem]

In statistical terms, this means that we must try to work out the probability that the victim was injured by the alleged agent rather than just by random chance, personal susceptibility, or illness over which the defendant had no control. Bayes' Theorem (BT) is often cited as the most appropriate means to accomplish this, since it uses a simple mathematical formula to calculate probabilities based on a predetermined set of conditions (such as the known characteristics of the plaintiff, and the prevalence of injury that s/he has sustained among the general population). The trouble is that it is easy to be seduced by the apparently objectively accurate expressions of probability that such statistical analysis generates. As Mike Redmayne has recognized in a book review, 63 Mod. L. Rev. 457, 458 (2000):

> [T]he concept of "accurate probabilit[ies]" is arguably meaningless: all probabilities are in some sense inaccurate because they are based on incomplete information. What is more, it looks to me as though the process of developing point-valued probabilities for the case-specific information so that we can feed them into BT will be more trouble than it is worth. We will be relying on guesswork, and different doctors will give widely varying values to the probabilities. The calculations will also be complicated by the fact that we will need to take into account the dependency relations between the different probabilities. All we will gain is false precision....

Just because we have managed to get a point-valued probability out of BT, we should be under no illusion that we will then be in a position to promote efficiency in Landes and Posner's terms. It all depends on the information we have in the first place, and in medical causation cases I cannot see that we will often have good enough information to justify using the[se] formulae ...

5. *Probability, statistics, and causation.* As a result of his skepticism of the results that statistical analysis can produce, Redmayne rejects as being "far too hard a line to take" the argument that, without epidemiological statistics demonstrating a causal link between a drug and an injury, a plaintiff should not be able to win a case. He points out, 63 Mod. L. Rev. 457, 459 (2000), that:

> Good epidemiological studies can take several years to conduct, yet before the epidemiological evidence is in we might have other evidence to suggest that a particular drug is harmful. Although I would agree that it is difficult to prove causation without epidemiological studies, it is not something we should rule out. Turning plaintiffs away because a certain type of evidence which might support their claim does not yet exist does not seem to be a justifiable course to take. It would be like deciding against the prosecution in a rape case just because the amount of semen recovered from the victim proved insufficient for DNA profiling.

Questions

1. Bradford Hill was writing not for a legal, but for a medical audience. To what extent should the law adopt an approach like Hill's in determining general causation?

2. Are the limitations of both epidemiology and statistical methodologies well understood by the legal community?

3. If we cannot rely on the use of epidemiological statistics to demonstrate a causal link between a drug and an injury, what can we rely on?

4. Would you give the same answer regarding other potential causative agents?

Troyen A. Brennan, Causal Chains and Statistical Links: The Role of Scientific Uncertainty in Hazardous-Substance Litigation
73 Cornell L. Rev. 469 (1987–88)

In the late nineteenth century, Mach outlined a corpuscularian theory of science that incorporated elements of positivism. Positivism is the belief that scientific knowledge unceasingly expands. Mach's disciple, C.G. Hempel, produced the most thorough description of this synthesis. Hempel's discussion is interesting because the positivism-corpuscularian philosophy of science outlines many of the assumptions that underlie Newtonian physics. Courts, if not scientists, use these assumptions to understand scientific evidence.

Hempel argued that a scientific theory was merely the relationship between a covering law, defined as one of a general set of deductive principles, and an explanadum, the phenomenon that the covering law was to explain. The relationship was formally logical, but Hempel expressed it in causal terms. Thus, deductive causal analysis, as defined by covering laws, connected and explained phenomena. Deductive reasoning produced logical relationships between events, essentially enrolling phenomena into causal chains.

The covering law-explanadum model leads to the following corollaries. First, science progresses as deductively derived causal chains develop from applying covering laws to more phenomena. Uncertainty results from a phenomena without applicable covering law. Second, scientific knowledge constantly expands as causal chains connect previously unexplained phenomena. Third, deductive reasoning takes precedence over inductive reasoning. The primary method of causal explanation, and thus of knowledge, was thought to be deductive reasoning.

Hempel was criticized for failing to explain the increasing role of statistical evidence in science. Ultimately, Hempel acknowledged that inductive-statistical evidence could be used in scientific explanation, but he doubted that such evidence could provide the basis for causal reasoning and thus afforded such evidence a subsidiary status. This position proved untenable. Indeed, developments in physics called into question the entire structure of positivism-corpuscularianism. At the end of the nineteenth century, the mechanistic physics and mathematics of Newton, upon which corpuscularian notions were so dependent, were undermined by field theories supported by integro-differential equations and matrix analysis. This process continued in the twentieth century with the development of quantum mechanics and the theory of relativity. Philosophers of science simply could not ignore the expanding role of inductive reasoning and statistical evidence in physics. These developments in physics paralleled others in medicine, with epidemiologists William Farr and John Snow, among others, pioneering the use of probabilistic evidence.

In the past twenty years philosophers have come to appreciate the importance of theory and hypothesis building in the enterprise of science. The philosophy of science now recognizes that scientists consciously use hypothesis testing to confront uncertainty, often using probabilistic evidence and inductive reasoning. Moreover, scientific progress is not understood as the relentless accumulation of phenomena under covering laws, but as a succession of theories or "problem shifts." Scientists use theories to formulate hypotheses. They test these hypotheses by designing experiments that will provide anticipated results defined by the hypotheses. The whole process relies heavily on inductive reasoning. More important, scientists often based their reasoning on probabilistic evidence. Science is not simply an extension of causal chain analysis or covering law deductions.... This also means that scientific progress is not simply the expansion of covering laws; rather science develops as certain hypotheses provide better explanation when tested and refinement improves theories.

This is not to say that causal language is not scientific language. Scientists use causal concepts to set up hypotheses. The method by which they test these hypotheses often involves using inductive reasoning and probabilistic evidence. Thus a scientific explanation is framed in terms of causality, but the evidence to support that explanation need not involve a neat, deductively derived causal chain. Indeed more often than not, the evidence is summarized by a probability statement in the form of a "p" value.

In summary, scientists understand that theories define uncertainty and provide the basis for hypothesis building. The process of hypothesis building and testing depends largely on inductive reasoning. Scientists often use probabilistic evidence to test hypotheses. As a result, statistical evidence deserves the same status as any other type of evidence. Moreover, one cannot expect science to provide deductive causal chains as the basis for all knowledge. Scientists recognize that the causal concepts they use often express probabilistic reasoning as deductive reasoning....

An empiricist posture toward causation has dominated Anglo-American jurisprudence of torts. Although negligence does not result in liability unless it causes injury or damage, legal scholars have recognized that identification of a cause is seldom straightforward....

Jurists' confrontation with difficult cases can explain the law's willingness to abandon the ordinary meaning of causation ... Innocuous events producing unexpected results can be used in a casual chain analysis in such a way that liability falls in an unjust manner. Indeed, the tragic-comedy of a causal chain of events recounted in a case like *Palsgraf v. Long Island Railroad* provides the highlight of first year tort classes. The lack of an easily identifiable "cause in fact" in such cases forces a court to incorporate policy issues into causal attribution ...

The past ten to fifteen years have witnessed a great deal of ferment in tort law, especially regarding causation. Legal scholars have begun to explore the validity of causes founded on probabilistic evidence rather than deductive reasoning. Hart and Honoré have stated:

> It is easy here to be misled by the natural metaphor of a causal "chain," which may lead us to think that the causal process consists of a series of single events each of which is dependent upon (would not have occurred without) its predecessor in the "chain" and so is dependent upon the initiating action or event. In truth in any causal process we have at each phase not single events but complex sets of conditions, and among these conditions are some which are not only subsequent to, but independent of the initiating action or event.

Unlike James and Perry's complaint about the length of causal chains, Hart and Honoré's statement evinces a recognition that causation is not simply a matter of identifying causal links ...

[I]t is interesting to note that the distinctions between but for cause and probabilistic causation coincide neatly with those between Newtonian physics and modern science noted earlier. But for causation theory assumes the existence of causal chain analysis, depends on a mechanistic understanding of causation, and coincides with everyday, common sense notions of causation. The corpuscularian thinker can deductively derive a cause in fact. The only problem with but for causation concerns the reach of the deductive reasoning: selecting from the causal chain the but for cause upon which liability falls can be difficult. In contrast, probabilistic causation relies on probabilistic reasoning, and is independent of a mechanistic understanding of causation. Furthermore, probabilistic reasoning does not coincide with conventional notions of causation. Thus, but for cause or cause in fact is the concept of causation that is employed in corpuscularian science, while probabilistic cause is integral to scientific research....

probability

In summary, legal notions of causation reflect a complex interplay of several concepts. But for causation or cause in fact, which reflects commonly held assumptions about causation as well as certain moral and political notions of responsibility, tends to dominate the disposition of tort claims. Moreover, this rendition of but for causation coincides neatly with that of corpuscularian science. Probabilistic linkage is distinguished from but for cause, but has a nebulous role in Anglo-American legal reasoning. Probabilistic causal notions correspond to the causal notions that modern science employs in that they are based on probabilistic evidence rather than simple deductively derived causal chains. Legal scholars generally have not assumed the existence of a singular causal power, nor have they used probabilistic notions in analyses of causation, but rather have relied on the policy-laden concept of proximate cause to identify the bearer of liability.

proximate cause

From this discussion of competing notions of causation in law and science emerges a hypothesis that explains why courts have so much trouble with causation issues in toxic tort litigation. The scientific association between a toxic substance and injury to a person relies on probabilistic evidence: epidemiological studies and statistical associations. Philosophers of science readily accept such evidence and, indeed, acknowledge that probabilistic reasoning dominates much of physics and medicine. In corpuscularian writing, probabilistic evidence is second best, if acceptable at all, and corpuscularian notions of causation coincide with but for concepts of causation in tort law. Both rely heavily on causal chain analyses and individual actions. Corrective justice aspects of tort law assume the existence of traceable causal chains leading from actor to harm. As a result, tort law tends to induce a corpuscularian approach to scientific evidence. Litigants bringing scientific issues to court are expected to show causes in fact or but for causes, with minimal support from the policies of proximate cause.

A corpuscularian judge would not want to deal with probabilistic notions, as he would regard these as inferior methods of reasoning. Rather than accept probabilistic statements, a corpuscularian judge would delay a decision until deductive, mechanistic, but for causes are available. Nor would a corpuscularian judge welcome uncertainty in a scientific issue- uncertainty will be overcome according to positivism, and it is best to wait until this occurs. In addition, tort law's corrective justice aspects would not permit uncertainty in the causal assignment of responsibility.

In this regard, common law courts are neither unscientific nor ignorant. Rather, they cling to conceptions of individual responsibility that coincide neatly with eighteenth century science's notions of causation. Thus, it is not enough simply to say that courts should adopt probabilistic reasoning. They must be instructed. But given the importance of the moral concept of individual responsibility in tort law, we can expect courts to accommodate only so much probabilistic reasoning.

Unfortunately, toxic substance injury cases cannot produce mechanistic, deductively- derived causal evidence, and a corpuscularian judge cannot process the available probabilistic evidence. Thus, the causation problem in toxic tort litigation could result from an epistemological quandary. Judges, using but for causation when analyzing tort claims, may slip into corpuscularian reasoning about scientific evidence, even when that evidence is primarily probabilistic....

Unfortunately, even ... intensely litigated issues have not produced adequate discussions of causation. When a rare tumor is closely associated with a toxic substance, courts generally take the causation issue as a given. This is the case in the asbestos litigation as well as in the diethylstilbestrol/vaginal adenocarcinoma cases.

Courts are troubled by the probabilistic evidence of causation with regard to hazardous substance injury. In this section I have outlined some theoretical explanations for these difficulties. Courts rely on mechanistic notions of causation and are confused by probabilistic ones. This reliance on mechanistic causes reflects the notions of responsibility inherent in liberalism. Moreover, courts assume that when mechanistic causes are not yet available, it is best to procrastinate, as science is constantly producing new mechanistic causes. As a result, courts are both corpuscularian and positivistic....

The difficulty that judges and lawyers, as well as juries, have with statistical and epidemiological evidence arises from the uncertainty involved in this kind of evidence, uncertainty that conflicts with causal chain analysis paradigms. A scientist develops hypotheses and then tests them by designing studies that indicate the strength of the underlying reasoning. When that test involves statistics, as it often does in biomedical science, the result is consciously hedged with uncertainty. Before courts can use probabilistic evidence to resolve legal problems raised by toxic substances, courts must understand the nature of the uncertainty in toxicological evidence.

Question

Science is concerned with identifying biochemical mechanisms in order to understand and treat various human pathologies. The law of products liability is concerned with attributing responsibility for harm suffered by a particular person. Should the latter's conception of causation necessarily mirror the former's? Why (not)?

Specific Causation

As we have seen, there is considerable debate as to how the law should seek to make judgments on issues of general causation when the science involved is fraught with uncertainty. There is also reason to be concerned about lawyers' ability to translate accurately the precise message of any scientific evidence into something legally meaningful. The problem there is particularly acute because resolution of issues of general causation is treated as a matter of law for the court. This means that any holding by an appellate court that a particular product cannot cause a certain type of harm has the effect of preventing any alleged victim of that very type of harm from being able to argue, within the same jurisdiction, that his or her injuries were actually caused by that product.

Critics have argued that this involves an underhand usurpation by the bench of the jury's function to hear and try the evidence, so that a victim may often be deprived of his or her constitutional right to trial by jury. Like Redmayne, above, they have argued that we cannot deny victims a right to have the evidence in their case heard simply because years of painstaking trials and research has not yet been conducted, since this simply means that we do not know whether a specific product can cause a certain type of harm, not that we know that it cannot.

The next two extracts, by Walker and McGarity, highlight the problems caused by strict adherence to the requirements of proof of general causation in the face of scientific uncertainty. Walker argues that a better way to approach such cases is to deal with them at the level of specific causation. In other words, his proposal would permit individuals to try to prove, before a jury, that they were, in fact, injured by the product in question and that, since "proof" in the context of a civil trial sets the standard at the level of a preponderance of the evidence rather than 100% certainty, there are statistically sound ways of adjudicating upon the evidence in such cases. Of course, since such issues would be judged on a case-by-case basis, a verdict on one plaintiff's claim would have no bearing on the outcome of another claim brought by another plaintiff. McGarity argues that, unless we are prepared to relax the rules on causation, we risk precipitating an "accountability crisis."

Vern R. Walker, Restoring the Individual Plaintiff to Tort Law by Rejecting "Junk Logic" about Specific Causation
56 Ala. L. Rev. 381 (2004)

Judges have been removing the individual plaintiff from torts cases, often as a byproduct of a campaign against "junk science." In place of the individual plaintiff, they have been installing an abstract "statistical individual," and adopting rules that decide cases on statistical grounds. This Article argues that, ironically, the reasoning behind these decisions and rules is too often an example of the "junk logic" that judges should be avoiding. The Article analyzes the logical warrant for findings of fact about specific causation, and uses that analysis to critique such rules as (1) a "0.5 inference rule" for factfinding, (2) a "greater-than-50%" rule for evaluating the legal sufficiency of evidence, and (3) certain rules of admissibility following the Supreme Court's decisions in *Daubert* and *Kumho Tire*. Judges are using such rules to wrongly decide a wide variety of tort cases, from products liability cases to medical malpractice and toxic exposure cases.

This Article demonstrates that the many kinds of uncertainty inherent in warranted findings about specific causation require the factfinder to make decisions that are necessarily pragmatic, non-scientific, and non-statistical in nature. Such uncertainties are inherent in the logic of specific causation, and are not peculiar to toxic tort cases, or to epidemiologic evidence, or even to scientific evidence. The presence of significant degrees of such uncertainties make it impossible to prove specific causation in any factual or scientific sense. Warranted findings must rest upon the common sense, practical fairness, and rough justice of the factfinder, except in categories of cases where tort policies can justify the adoption of decision rules for the entire category. Such rules, however, should not rest on the misguided statistical reasoning of past cases, but on proper policy foundations. If this Article can clear away the logical misunderstandings, perhaps judges will provide better policy justifications and develop better rules.

Tort law uses the term "specific causation," sometimes called "individual causation," to refer to the factual issue of which particular events caused or will cause a particular injury in a specific plaintiff. Specific causation is distinguished from "general causation," also called "generic causation," which addresses whether there is any causal relationship at all between types of events and types of injuries. Specific causation is whether a specific event caused or will cause a specific injury, while general causation is whether such events can (ever) cause such injuries. Usually, for a plaintiff to win damages in a torts case, the plaintiff must prove both general and specific causation.

A finding about specific causation can be prospective and predictive, as in: "It is unlikely that the defendant's negligent conduct, which resulted in the exposure of Jessica Jones to benzene, will cause her to develop lung cancer." Or a finding might be retrospective and explanatory, as in: "It is unlikely that the defendant's negligent conduct and Jessica Jones's resulting exposure to benzene caused her lung cancer." This Article argues that both versions, despite their temporal differences, have a similar logical structure in their warrant. Therefore, the analysis provided here applies to both prospective and retrospective findings of specific causation.

The central epistemic problem posed by specific causation is justifying how a less-than-universal generalization about causation in groups can ever warrant a probabilistic finding about causation in a specific case. When and why does statistical evidence about causation in a group warrant a finding of causation in a specific member of the group? For example, if 10% of people who experience a certain type of chemical exposure later develop cancer as a result of that exposure, what is the probability that the exposure of a specific person (for example, Jessica Jones) will cause (or did cause) her to develop cancer? What reason is there to place her in the 10% category, as opposed to the 90% category? The problem of justification exists regardless of the magnitude of the statistics. If 75% of certain types of patients at a certain stage of a disease die within 5 years from the normal progression of the disease, despite the best treatment, then what is the probability that a specific individual with the disease, who was misdiagnosed when her disease was at the relevant stage and who subsequently died within 5 years, would have died from the disease in any case, despite the misdiagnosis? Warranted findings about such questions depend upon inferences from what typically (or statistically) happens in groups of which the specific individual is a member.

This Article shows that every warranted finding about specific causation possesses certain types of uncertainty or potential for error. Part I of the Article examines uncertainties about general causation that decrease the warrant or evidentiary support for a conclusion about specific causation. It demonstrates that there are four logically distinct types of uncertainty that are necessarily present: measurement uncertainty, sampling uncertainty, modeling uncertainty, and causal uncertainty. For each type of uncertainty, there are techniques for reducing and characterizing the extent or degree of uncertainty. In the end, however, a reasonable factfinder must decide whether the residual uncertainty of each type is acceptable or not for purposes of the tort case—that is, for warranting a conclusion of specific causation in the context of tort law.

Part II of the Article analyzes two additional uncertainties involved in drawing a conclusion about a specific individual. The first section addresses the problem of identifying the appropriate group to serve as a reference group for that individual. It examines the warrant for finding that a reference group adequately represents the specific individual—that is, that it adequately matches the plaintiff in all causally relevant variables, such as being a woman, being age 40, having no history of cancer in the immediate family, and so forth. The second section of Part II discusses the uncertainty in assigning a particular probability to the individual case, even when the reference group adequately represents the specific individual. These two major sources of uncertainty can be called, respectively, uncertainty about plaintiff representativeness and uncertainty about assigning a probability to the individual plaintiff.

Part III of the Article summarizes all of these uncertainties into a coherent factfinding approach. It then uses this logical analysis to critique certain judicial rules that are threatening individualized factfinding in tort law. The argument is that for each type of uncertainty, as well as for the overall uncertainty, someone must decide whether the residual uncertainty is acceptable for purposes of tort law. Such decisions cannot be purely epistemic or scientific in nature, because they involve balancing the expected risks and benefits of making findings in the face of uncertainty, as well as weighing the equitable treatment of the parties and other non-epistemic considerations. While expertise can inform certain aspects of those decisions, there is no reason to think that experts are the optimal decision-makers. Policy-based rules are needed about who is the best decider of such questions (the jury or the judge) and whether such decisions should be made on case-specific factors or on rules governing categories of cases.

Unfortunately, instead of facing such non-epistemic issues squarely, and developing policies and rules to address them, many judges have relied on faulty reasoning to adopt unjustified rules that appear to be logically compelling. The second section of Part III examines a variety of cases in which judges have relied on such fallacious reasoning—cases involving judicial factfinding about liability for oral contraceptives, judicial rulings on sufficiency of evidence in medical malpractice cases, and judicial decisions on admissibility of expert testimony in toxic-exposure cases. Specific causation in such cases cannot be a scientific issue, however, and any decisions should be justified on substantive policy grounds, not statistical grounds. It is reasonable to hope that once such judges better understand the warrant for finding specific causation, they will rest their rulings on a proper policy basis, and restore the individual plaintiff to tort law.

Note

The Supreme Court's decisions in *Daubert* and *Kumho Tire* will be discussed at greater length in Chapter 14.

Questions

1. Is it appropriate to use evidence of statistical probabilities to try to prove specific, rather than general, causation?

2. If it is appropriate, does that necessarily render proof of general causation redundant?

3. If Walker's proposal is feasible, should it be adopted only in cases where the scientific evidence is uncertain, or should it be permitted in every case?

4. Would Walker's proposal be more persuasive if the damages available to the plaintiffs under his analysis were restricted to cover payment for medical monitoring so as to ensure early detection of any illness or injury caused by exposure to the toxic agent? (The topic of medical monitoring is discussed later in this Chapter.)

Thomas O. McGarity, Proposal for Linking Culpability and Causation to Ensure Corporate Accountability for Toxic Risks
26 Wm. & Mary Envtl. L. & Pol'y Rev. 1 (2001)

Less than a week before this Symposium convened, *The Washington Post* reported that a prominent international drug company had arranged during the late 1990s to test an exceedingly profitable drug in human beings for effectiveness in treating Hepatitis B. Although the initial results were promising, the principle investigator, Hong Kong virologist Dr. Nancy Leung, discovered that patients taking the drug for more than one year became infected by a highly pathogenic mutant virus that appeared to cause liver failure. She reported that the treatment may have resulted in the death of one subject. The company, however, belittled her concerns and continued to publish over her name an "upbeat" scientific abstract that did not mention her concerns. The company also provided Dr. Leung with slides for a presentation at an international scientific meeting that portrayed her research in a misleading fashion. The Food and Drug Administration ("FDA") approved the drug in 1998 based upon one-year's worth of results from research conducted by Leung and others. When an FDA investigator visited Dr. Leung's laboratory during a pre-approval investigation, the company provided a report that contained no reference to the dead patient that Dr. Leung had mentioned in her original report, an omission that was later discovered only because Dr. Leung's hospital provided the investigator with an unaltered version of her full report.

Although it is too early to gauge the FDA's reaction to this very recent revelation, it is entirely possible, indeed probable, that the drug will remain on the market (perhaps with an additional side-effect warning) and that many cases of fatal liver failure will result from the mutant viruses. Should the heirs of one of the victims sue the company responsible for marketing the drug, their attorneys will face an uphill battle in proving that the victim's liver failure was caused by a mutant virus that resulted from the plaintiff's treatment with the defendant's drug. After all, persons suffering from Hepatitis B frequently suffer liver failure, and no one knows for sure whether the mutant virus actually causes liver failure. The most that some future epidemiological study can say with confidence is that it appears that more patients with Hepatitis B who take the drug suffer from liver failure than similarly situated patients who do not take the drug. Depending upon the power of the statistical analysis suggesting an association between the drug and the increased incidence of liver failure, it may be difficult for a plaintiff to find an attorney willing to invest the considerable time and resources required to bring such a lawsuit against a drug company anxious to protect its hundred-million-dollar-a-year product. If attempts to sue the manufacturer therefore fail and if, as is likely, the FDA does not take any punitive action against the company, then the company will have avoided all responsibility for reprehensible conduct that at the very least put patients at risk. The company might be held accountable in corporate heaven, but not down here on earth.

Let me begin with a controversial assessment and a debatable prediction, neither of which will I attempt to support empirically in this article. My assessment of the past twenty years of developing toxic tort law is that any realistic threat of a "liability crisis" ended years ago with the widespread adoption of tort reform legislation in state legislatures, careful screening by White House and Justice Department officials of prospective federal judges for their views on "judicial activism" with respect to judicially imposed constraints on business enterprises, and the pervasive airing of tort liability "horror stories" in the media. Highly publicized, but largely unwarranted claims that the common law courts and federal regulatory agencies (the two primary governmental institutions for ensuring corporate accountability for health and environmental risks) were relying too heavily upon "junk science" brought about changes in both of those institutions that have caused them to be far more cautious about regulating and imposing liability upon business entities. This reticence on the part of existing constraining institutions came at a time of booming economic expansion and rapid technological developments (especially in the areas of pharmaceutical and agricultural technologies) that had a significant potential to do great harm to human health and the environment. My prediction is that these developments will precipitate an "accountability crisis" that will begin to intrude upon the public consciousness in the coming years as stories of unpunished corporate malfeasance, like the one above, appear in the media on a regular basis....

The political momentum appears at the moment to be moving rather powerfully in the opposite direction. But the momentum will shift in the not-too-distant future as we realize that a global economy with few effective health and environmental protections is a frightening place. If I am correct in predicting that an impending accountability crisis will provide a political setting in which far-reaching changes in the existing tort regime are legitimately on the table, the relatively modest changes suggested here may forestall more aggressive changes aimed at shifting the burden of proof altogether, or replacing the common law with a full-fledged administrative reparations regime.

Fifteen years ago, as the phrase "toxic tort" was first entering the trial lawyers' lexicon, they were optimistic that the common law would prove an effective vehicle for compensating persons injured by exposure to toxic substances, for exacting retribution against those who callously exposed innocent people to toxic risks, and for sending a message to companies that pollution had a steep price that could be avoided only by limiting polluting activities. One of the earliest practitioners of the newly emerging discipline predicted that "[c]hanges in laws to lessen the victim's causation burden are making it easier for plaintiffs to recover in toxic-tort cases." Another pioneer of toxic tort litigation argued that judicial recognition of claims based upon the new science of "clinical ecology" would "substantially increase opportunities for victims to recover for their injuries."

Time has not borne out those rosy projections.... In retrospect, causation has proven a very effective stumbling block that has not only precluded compensation for all but the most clearly understood environmentally caused diseases, but has also stood in the way of ambitious attempts to protect the public health generally through toxic tort litigation.

Questions

1. Do we face a choice between a "liability crisis" and an "accountability crisis," or is it possible to avoid both?

2. If we do face such a choice, which is it preferable to tolerate?

Note

In a toxic tort case, establishing specific causation will often require some exploration of the victim's medical history, perhaps to ascertain the chronology of the pathology or to rule out other possible causative agents. Such inquiry is normally restricted to the victim's physical condition. In the following failure-to-warn case, however, the determination of specific causation rested on the nature of the victim's mental state.

Crowston v. Goodyear Tire & Rubber Company

521 N.W.2d 401 (1994) (Supreme Court of North Dakota)

VANDE WALLE, C.J. On June 4, 1986, Crowston, a 20 year old employee on the night shift at a Fargo service station, was seriously injured while inflating a 16 inch light truck tire on a mismatched 16.5 inch wheel. Crowston had worked at the service station for only a few weeks and had limited experience repairing tires and operating a tire changing machine. According to Crowston's employer, night shift employees were not authorized to do any repair work. According to Crowston, a customer asked him to repair the tubes in four light truck tire/wheel assemblies, and he repaired two of the tires without incident.

The third tire/wheel assembly was a mismatched 16.5 inch wheel manufactured by Kelsey-Hayes in 1973 and 16 inch tube-type tire manufactured by Goodyear in 1977. According to Crowston, he locked the assembly into a tire changing machine, and removed the tube without taking the tire off the wheel. After repairing the tube and reinserting it into the tire, he inserted the tire bead over the flange of the rim and lubricated the bead area while the assembly remained locked into the tire changing machine. However, as he had with the first two tires, he then removed the assembly from the tire changing machine and began inflating the tire on the floor. According to Crowston, he had inflated the tire to 28 pounds per square inch (psi) when he was interrupted by a customer. Crowston testified that, after helping that customer, he resumed inflating the tire when it exploded, seriously injuring him. Crowston sued Goodyear and Kelsey-Hayes, alleging negligence and strict liability in tort in the design, manufacture, and sale of their component parts of the tire/wheel assembly.

Crowston alleged that, when the component parts of the tire/wheel assembly were sold, they were defective and unreasonably dangerous and failed to include adequate warnings. He also alleged that after the manufacture and sale of the component parts of the assembly, both defendants received knowledge that mismatching 16 inch tires and 16.5 inch wheels created a dangerous condition which could result in explosions during inflation of the tire and that both defendants negligently failed to give adequate post-sale warnings about those mismatching dangers....

The defendants moved for partial summary judgment on Crowston's claim that the defendants negligently failed to give appropriate post-sale warnings about the dangers associated with mismatching 16 inch tires and 16.5 inch wheels. They asserted that they had no post-sale duty to warn about the dangers associated with mismatching. The district court granted the defendants' motion for summary judgment on that claim....

Crowston asserts that the district court erred in granting summary judgment dismissal of his claim that the defendants negligently failed to provide appropriate post-sale warnings about the dangers of mismatching 16 inch tires and 16.5 inch wheels.

Crowston alleged that, after the defendants manufactured and sold the component parts of this tire/wheel assembly, they learned that users were mismatching the parts, thereby creating a dangerous situation which could result in explosions during inflation of the tire. He argues that the defendants had a post-sale duty to warn the public and the individual purchasers of this tire and this wheel about the dangers of mismatching. He contends that summary judgment was inappropriate because there are genuine issues of material fact about whether the defendants performed their post-sale duty in a reasonable manner. The defendants respond that they did not have a post-sale duty to warn because, under North Dakota law, products liability is determined by the condition of the product at the time it is sold. Alternatively they assert that, assuming a post-sale duty to warn may exist in some circumstances, it does not apply to these products....

We hold that, under negligence failure to warn principles, the defendants had a post-sale duty to warn about dangers associated with the use of their products. In those situations, manufacturers can satisfy that duty by taking reasonable steps to warn foreseeable users about the dangers associated with their product. The reasonableness of the post-sale warnings depend on the facts of each particular case....

Accepting, as we must for purposes of summary judgment, that these defendants became aware of the dangers of mismatching after their respective manufacture and sale of the parts of the tire/wheel assembly, we cannot say, as a matter of law, that their post-sale warnings of the dangers of mismatching in this case met the reasonableness standard. Rather, the issue of the reasonableness of their warnings is a fact question which is inappropriate for summary judgment. We therefore conclude the district court erred in granting summary judgment on Crowston's claim that the defendants negligently breached their post-sale duty to warn. We reverse the summary judgment and remand for further proceedings on that claim. However, our decision does not necessarily require a retrial on Crowston's other claims. Instead, we separately analyze the issues involved with those claims to determine whether or not reversible error occurred.

Crowston raises several issues pertaining to the admission of evidence at the trial of his other claims....

In *Butz v. Werner*, 438 N.W.2d 509, 517 (N.D.1989), this court held that "when no warning is given the plaintiff is entitled to the benefit of a presumption that an adequate warning, if given, would have been read and heeded." See *Restatement (Second) of Torts* 402A, Comment j (1965). The *Butz* presumption applies only to strict liability failure to warn claims, not to negligent failure to warn claims. *Jacobs v. Anderson Bldg. Co.*, 459 N.W.2d 384 (N.D.1990). "A party against whom a presumption is directed has the burden of proving that the nonexistence of the presumed fact is more probable than its existence." N.D.R.Evid. 301. See *Butz, supra*. Absent the introduction of evidence to rebut the *Butz* presumption, the proximate cause element of a strict liability failure to warn claim is presumptively established.

In this case, Dr. Richard Harper, a psychiatrist, reviewed Crowston's medical and social records and testified at trial that Crowston had an anti-social personality disorder which made it highly unlikely he would have read or followed any additional warnings on the tire or the wheel. Harper testified that Crowston's anti-social personality disorder would cause him to act on his own internal impulses, have poor judgment, act impulsively, and do the opposite of directions or warnings.

Crowston argues that Dr. Harper's testimony was inadmissible to show his character for the purpose of proving he acted in conformity therewith. The defendants respond that Dr. Harper's testimony was relevant and necessary to rebut the *Butz* presumption.

In *Technical Chemical Co. v. Jacobs*, 480 S.W.2d 602, 606 (1972), the Texas Supreme Court described evidence that could be used to rebut the presumption that a warning would have been read:

> Depending upon the individual facts, this may be accomplished by the manufacturer's producing evidence that the user was blind, illiterate, intoxicated at the time of the use, irresponsible or lax in judgment or by some other circumstance tending to show that the improper use was or would have been made regardless of the warning....

Dr. Harper's testimony was offered for the purpose of rebutting the *Butz* presumption. His testimony was probative of the issue of whether Crowston would have read or heeded any warnings that might have been on the tire or the wheel and was relevant and necessary to rebut the *Butz* presumption. The trial court carefully limited the evidence to Crowston's personality disorder and excluded other character evidence after concluding that its probative value was substantially outweighed by its prejudicial effect. The trial court did not abuse its discretion in admitting Dr. Harper's testimony....

Summary judgment dismissal of Crowston's post-sale duty to warn claim reversed and remanded. Dismissal of other claims affirmed.

Question

Why could the evidence regarding Crowston's mental state not be applied so as to enable the Court to affirm the dismissal of his post-sale (negligent) failure-to-warn claim as well as what the court characterized as the strict liability failure-to-warn claim?

Donald G. Gifford, The Challenge to the Individual Causation Requirement in Mass Products Torts
62 Wash. & Lee L. Rev. 873 (2005)

The signature torts of our time are no longer motor vehicle accidents in which an individual plaintiff sues an individual defendant whose actions can be causally connected with a specific victim's harm. Claims against manufacturers of tobacco products, handguns, lead pigment, and many other mass products are generally brought on behalf of collective plaintiffs—usually either class action representatives or states or municipalities seeking reimbursement of amounts paid to Medicaid recipients as a result of the harms caused. In these actions and other cases against manufacturers of mass products, the identity of the party that manufactured the product that caused any individual victim's harm frequently is unknown. Instead, plaintiffs seek to impose liability on defendant-manufacturers collectively, through various legal theories including civil conspiracy or concert of action, alternative liability, and market share liability.

Operating together, the collective plaintiff and the collective or indeterminate defendant fundamentally challenge the traditional requirement of individualized causation in tort law. No longer, at least in the important subset of tort liability known as mass products torts, is tort law focused on the costs of an accident, that is, seeking compensation for an individual victim from an identified wrongdoer for harm caused during a discrete event. Today, tort litigation is often explicitly intended as the chosen vehicle to address social problems such as handgun violence, tobacco-related diseases, and childhood lead poisoning. Control of the litigation in these high profile mass torts cases has shifted from an individual wronged party and her counsel to lawyers representing governmental or other collective entities suing in relation to harms suffered by thousands or even hundreds of thousands of victims.

The challenge to the traditional requirement of individual causation also has been at the core of the revitalized debate among tort scholars during the past generation as to what constitutes the fundamental essence of tort law. Two very different conceptions of the theory of torts have emerged. Law and economics and other instrumental conceptions of tort law—most often identified with the views of Guido Calabresi and Richard Posner—posit that tort law pursues policy objectives derived from the needs of the society external to the legal system, such as wealth maximization, accident prevention, or the goal of distributing losses on a widespread basis. Instrumental theorists typically do not believe that it is necessary for a particular victim of harm to identify the particular injurer who caused her specific harm in order to recover. William Landes and Richard Posner, who share an instrumental conception of tort law, have virtually mocked any requirement of individual causation: "[C]ausation in the law is an inarticulate groping for economically sound solutions...." In short, those with an instrumental conception of tort law generally view any requirement of particularity in causation as "old fashioned" and likely to impede their goals.

The instrumental assault on traditional tort law causation principles, however, has provoked a strong response from those scholars who view the tort system as pursuing corrective justice; that is, as a means of requiring the injuring party to repair the losses caused by his or her wrongful conduct. Ernest Weinrib and other corrective justice scholars argue that intrinsic to the entire notion of tort liability is the idea that a particular victim must prove that his harm was caused by a particular injurer.

This Article begins, in Part II, with a brief summary of the debate between the proponents of the instrumental and the proponents of the corrective justice theories of tort. This debate addresses such overarching issues as the goals of tort law and the justification for tort liability. Perhaps more than on any other concrete issue, however, the proponents of the two approaches divide on the question whether a particular victim must prove that a particular injurer caused her injury as a prerequisite for recovery.

During the same decades that this debate over the grand theory of tort law has raged, courts have encountered mass products torts cases in which the existence of a continuing requirement of individual causation, if left intact, would prove decisive in denying liability for the victims' losses. The attack upon the particular victim/particular injurer paradigm of tort liability first reached a critical threshold in the 1970s and the 1980s when victims of asbestos-related diseases joined in class actions and consolidated cases to sue asbestos products manufacturers and often were unable to identify the specific manufacturers whose products caused their illnesses. Similarly, the individual causation requirement also posed an insurmountable barrier to lead-poisoned children and Vietnam veterans suffering from diseases caused by the defoliant Agent Orange and seeking compensation from product manufacturers.

Sindell v. Abbott Laboratories, probably the classic causation case of that era, was the unusual exception in which plaintiffs recovered. The facts in *Sindell* illustrate the causation problem faced by victims of mass products torts. The plaintiff sued on behalf of herself and other similarly situated women suffering from cancerous and pre-cancerous growths that allegedly resulted from their mothers' consumption, at least ten or twelve years earlier, of diethylstilbestrol (DES), a synthetic compound of estrogen intended to prevent miscarriages in pregnant women. She lacked the means to identify which pharmaceutical company manufactured the DES consumed by her mother because the eleven drug companies named in the complaint and scores of additional drug companies used an identical chemical formula for the drug, which was approved by the federal Food and Drug Administration. The plaintiff admitted that she could not identify which company had manufactured the drug responsible for her injury, and accordingly, the trial court dismissed the complaint. The California Supreme Court, however, reversed the case on appeal and introduced the concept of market share liability, a form of causation that dispensed with the individual causation requirement.

Part III analyzes how victims of latent diseases caused by exposure to mass products and the victims' attorneys, during the 1980s, tried to combine procedural devices such as class actions and consolidations—that in effect created "collective plaintiffs"—with new "collective defendant" theories of causation. These theories, such as market share liability and alternative liability, would enable courts to hold multiple and indeterminate manufacturers of products liable without proof of individual causation. By the late 1980s, with rare exceptions, it was clear that these challenges to the principle of individual causation were unsuccessful. For the most part, the tort system had rejected this first wave of the instrumentalist challenge to the traditional requirement of individual causation.

The problems caused by the inability of victims of latent diseases and their attorneys to prove individual causation have not disappeared, however. A "second wave" of challenges to the individual causation requirement was launched during the mid-1990s when state governments sued tobacco manufacturers to "recoup" the financial losses they had experienced as a result of tobacco-related illnesses, consisting largely of medical assistance (Medicaid) payments to victims of such diseases. The new form of the "collective plaintiff" in the late 1990s and early years of the twenty-first century was the state, municipality, health insurer, union health and welfare fund, or hospitalize suing to recover the collective entity's financial losses resulting from harms experienced by individual victims, such as those resulting from tobacco-related illnesses, handgun violence, and childhood lead poisoning. When the states, municipalities, and other organizational litigants tried to overcome causation requirements using those substantive law approaches that generally had been rejected by the courts during the 1980s, such as market share liability, they were usually—as would be expected—unsuccessful. The states and other new collective plaintiffs, however, arguably have experienced somewhat greater success in using substantive tort claims, such as fraud and public nuisance, in new and novel ways that enable them to recover their financial losses without proving an individual causation link between any particular manufacturer and any specific victim.

Today the fate of the individual causation requirement in mass products tort law hangs in the balance. It is difficult to predict whether the second wave challenges to the individual causation requirement that are inherent in the state and municipal recoupment actions will be any more successful in overturning the particular injurer/particular victim causation paradigm than were the class actions and consolidated mass torts claims of the 1980s. What is clear, however, is that these novel forms of tort litigation provide an unusual testing ground for the most fundamental theories of the nature of tort liability, as well as having important "real world" consequences for the economic and social problems resulting from tobacco-related illnesses, handgun violence, and childhood lead poisoning.

Notes

1. *Sindell v. Abbott Laboratories.* We shall revisit the *Sindell* case in Chapter 15.

2. *Latency and medical monitoring.* Gifford refers to some of the problems faced by victims of latent diseases. Another issue is that an individual may become aware of having been exposed to a toxic substance, but be unable to make a claim for physical injury at that point because the diseases with which that toxic agent is associated have long latency periods. Some courts have been prepared to ameliorate this situation by recognizing a claim for the expenses of appropriate medical monitoring. In *Hansen v. Mountain Fuel Supply Co.*, 858 P.2d 970, 979 (1993), a case concerning exposure to asbestos, the Supreme Court of Utah laid out a set of eight requirements for such a claim to succeed:

1. exposure

2. to a toxic substance,

3. which exposure was caused by the defendant's negligence,

4. resulting in an increased risk

5. of a serious disease, illness, or injury

6. for which a medical test for early detection exists

7. and for which early detection is beneficial, meaning that a treatment exists that can alter the course of the illness,

8. and which test has been prescribed by a qualified physician according to contemporary scientific principles.

8 req.

The Supreme Court of Louisiana adopted a similar checklist in *Bourgeois v. A.P. Green Indus., Inc.*, 716 So. 2d 335 (1998).

3. *A legally recognized injury?* Many other states have taken the view, however, that demonstrating a good medical case for monitoring does not constitute a legally-recognized form of harm, so that the costs of such monitoring are not compensable. See, for example, *Badillo v. Am. Brands, Inc.*, 16 P.3d 435 (Nev. 2001); *Mergenthaler v. Asbestos Corp.*, 480 A.2d 647 (Del. 1984). In *Henry v. Dow Chemical Co.*, 701 N.W.2d 684, 691–92 (2005), the Supreme Court of Michigan ruled that individuals exposed to dioxins that had been negligently released into the Tittabawassee flood plain failed to state a valid claim because no physical injuries had manifested themselves. Justice Corrigan, writing for the majority, declared that any injury that the plaintiffs had suffered was best characterized either as one of pure economic loss (*i.e.*, payment for the medical monitoring), which would be precluded by the economic loss rule; or was one for the *fear* of suffering some dreadful disease in the future, which was also not recoverable without any current manifestation of physical harm.

prohibit party from recovering in tort when the tort results in purely economic loss

4. *Michigan split.* It was noted in Chapter 8 that the Michigan Supreme Court has been deeply fractured on a number of issues. In *Henry*, Justice Weaver concurred in the majority's judgment except for its citation of a law review article that she deplored, 701 N.W.2d at 705, as "clumsy and crude." The article had been written by a fellow Justice on the same court!

5. *Policy split.* Justice Cavanagh dissented, 701 N.W.2d at 706, on policy grounds:

At its core, this case is about rights and responsibilities. Defendant is undeniably responsible for years of actively contaminating the air, water, and soil that surrounds plaintiffs' homes. Defendant is undeniably responsible for the suffering that plaintiffs must endure as they face years of wondering if the contamination that they and their children have been exposed to will result in devastating illnesses and their untimely deaths. Thus, the issue is who should pay for plaintiffs' medical monitoring costs under the unique circumstances of this case when it is clear that defendant is responsible for the wrong that prompted the need for plaintiffs to be medically monitored. Stated differently, where defendant has contaminated the environment, should plaintiffs, defendant, or the taxpayers of the state of Michigan pay plaintiffs' medical monitoring costs? Whatever the majority's intent, the result of disregarding the only question properly posed in this case is that plaintiffs' physical health is inexcusably deemed secondary to defendant's economic health.

Questions

1. What is/are the purpose(s) of products liability law?

2. Is this purpose, or are these purposes, best served by strict adherence to requirements to prove (a) both general and specific causation; (b) general causation only; (c) specific causation only; or (d) neither type of causation?

3. Alternatively, would it be better to require proof of either or both types of causation, but to operate a more relaxed test or tests for each? If so, how should the courts "relax" the test(s)?

4. Is it accurate to say that proof of causation on the basis of a preponderance of the evidence is really a matter, first, of assessing the risks to which a defendant exposed the plaintiff, and then drawing inferences from such exposure(s)?

5. In the same vein, is it more accurate to say that apportioning responsibility for a specific injury among several defendants is really based, not on the increased harm that each one caused the victim (as § 16 of the Products Liability Restatement suggests), but according to the enhanced *risk* of harm to which each defendant exposed the victim?

6. If your answer to either (or both) of questions 4 and 5 is "yes," does this lend support to the arguments of any of the commentators quoted in this Chapter regarding proof of causation?

James v. Bessemer Processing Co., Inc.

714 A.2d 898 (1998) (Supreme Court of New Jersey)

STEIN, J. The critical issue presented by this appeal concerns the specificity of proofs required to entitle plaintiff to a jury trial on the question whether decedent's stomach and liver cancer was proximately caused by prolonged, frequent and repetitive exposure to defendants' petroleum and chemical products that contained no warning of their hazardous propensities. Defendants contend that the lack of proof of the specific content of their individual products and lack of proof of specific exposure to each product justified the Law Division's grant of summary judgment.

Over the course of his twenty-six years of employment with Bessemer Processing Company, Inc. (Bessemer), decedent Walter James (James) was exposed on a daily basis to a wide array of residues of petroleum products and other chemical substances, many allegedly containing benzene, polycyclic aromatic hydrocarbons and other human carcinogens. On February 8, 1990, at the age of fifty-two, James died of stomach and liver cancer. James's widow, plaintiff Ida James, brought this survivorship and wrongful death action against multiple defendants, alleging that they failed to warn of the dangerous propensities of the substances they shipped to Bessemer and that James's continuous exposure to those substances was the cause of his illness and death.

The Law Division granted summary judgment to all defendants on the ground that plaintiff would be unable to establish that James's cancer was caused by specific products manufactured by specific defendants. That court issued separate orders dismissing plaintiff's complaint against various defendants on procedural grounds. The Appellate Division reversed the summary judgment order dismissing plaintiff's complaint against all named defendants....

The primary issue posed by this appeal is whether a plaintiff in a toxic-tort, failure-to-warn case can establish a prima facie case on the element of "medical causation" by satisfying the "frequency, regularity and proximity" test pronounced by the Appellate Division in *Sholtis v. American Cyanamid Co.*, 238 N.J. Super. 8, 568 A.2d 1196 (1989), absent evidence that the illness was caused by specific products manufactured by specific defendants....

As this appeal arises from the Law Division's order of summary judgment in favor of defendants, we review the evidentiary record in a light most favorable to plaintiff. James began his employment with Bessemer in September 1963 at the age of twenty-five and worked as a general laborer at Bessemer's Newark facility for twenty-six years until his illness forced his retirement in October 1989. Bessemer, a wholly-owned subsidiary of Kingsland Drum and Barrel (Kingsland), was engaged in the cleaning and reconditioning of used and empty fifty-five-gallon drums for further use by the petroleum industry and certain other chemical manufacturers. Generally, Kingsland would retain those drums that could be cleaned through a hot water and caustic washing process, and would forward to Bessemer those drums that either contained stickier and more viscous residues requiring incineration and blasting, or those drums that needed to be recontoured because of physical damage. In all, Kingsland forwarded to Bessemer approximately thirty percent of the drums it received from its customers. The entities supplying drums to Kingsland for reconditioning had no direct contact with Bessemer, because all drums were originally sent to Kingsland and Kingsland billed the entities who supplied the drums for the reconditioning services performed by Bessemer....

During his employment with Bessemer, James functioned predominantly as a "utility man," available to fill in for absent workers at any position in the plant as required by his employer. Daniel Stewart, who worked for Bessemer from 1949 until 1984, indicated that he saw defendant perform every job required at the Bessemer plant, including cutting the heads off drums; operating the incinerator, sand blaster, rolling machines, and heading machines; welding and painting drums; and, as previously described, cleaning the slop hole. James was diagnosed with stomach cancer in October 1989. He died at the age of fifty-two on February 8, 1990. The cause of his death was "carcinoma with metastasis to the liver and peritoneum."

Due to a lack of business, Kingsland and Bessemer ceased operations in June 1992. The business records that had been kept at Bessemer throughout the period of James's employment were "production documents" that indicated the number of drums that had been reconditioned. However, they did not indicate the name of the corporate customer that had provided to Kingsland the drums that were reconditioned at Bessemer, nor did they indicate the specific chemical residue contained in any particular drum. All other records were kept at Kingsland, including bills of lading and billing invoices indicating the number of drums picked up by Kingsland drivers from a specific customer, but not reflecting the content of the empty drums. Pursuant to the requirements of the Resource Conservation Recovery Act (RCRA), 42 U.S.C.A. §6901, et seq., each shipment of drums picked up by Kingsland contained a certification from the supplier of the drums attesting that the supplier used its best efforts to remove the residue in the drums. However, the RCRA certifications did not indicate the nature of the residue in the drums.

Beginning some time in the late 1980s, around the time that James was diagnosed with cancer, Kingsland began receiving Material Safety Data Sheets (MSDSs) from both the companies supplying drums for reconditioning and the companies supplying various products used in the reconditioning process. The MSDSs contained warnings of and safety instructions regarding the hazards of the residues and products received. However, although such MSDSs were provided for each substance that Kingsland potentially might receive, they did not necessarily indicate which specific products or residues a supplier had provided to Kingsland or in what quantities drums containing such residues may have been supplied. Kingsland officials indicated that all records generally were kept for three years and then destroyed. At some time within a few months after the cessation of operations at Kingsland and Bessemer in June 1992, Kingsland representatives destroyed all of the existing records that may have been pertinent to this litigation. Those defendant suppliers and manufacturers that responded to plaintiff's interrogatories all indicated that they knew of no records kept by their companies indicating the quantities, trade names or chemical compositions of any of the residues contained in drums sent to Bessemer by Kingsland for reconditioning.

Many of the drums that arrived at Bessemer had labels that listed the contents of the drum, displayed the name of the manufacturer of the contents, and contained some general health warnings that became more specific around the late 1980s. Those labels were removed as part of the incineration process. In November 1989, Kingsland received a citation from the Occupational Safety and Health Administration (OSHA) for failure to have a hazardous communication plan describing to its workers the hazards of residues contained in the drums with which they worked daily.

Because of the lack of documentation concerning the identity of the suppliers of the drums that were reconditioned at Bessemer and the identity of the material in those drums, plaintiff was required to rely predominantly on the memory of Bessemer employees and executives in her efforts to obtain discovery regarding that information. Before joining Bessemer as a defendant in this action, plaintiff served interrogatories on Bessemer, one of which asked for the identity of the chemical compositions and trade names of all of the substances to which James was exposed during his employment with Bessemer. Bessemer answered by explaining that James was subject to exposure from any type of material that might be shipped in 55 gallon steel drums, except herbicides, pesticides and hazardous materials described in 49 C.F.R. §261.33(e) (acutely hazardous materials). Empty drums whose previous contents held the aforementioned material were not accepted at Bessemer. The majority of the empty drums, from 1960 to the mid eighties would have contained petroleum based products. From the early eighties to 1989, the mixture of the drum residues became highly varied, and included but [was] not limited to: resins, dyes, paints, solvents, fragrances and unknown substances....

In addition to the information elicited during discovery from lay witnesses, the record before the Law Division on defendants' motion for summary judgment included the reports of plaintiff's toxicological, medical and economic experts. Plaintiff's expert in toxicology, Dr. Myron Mehlman, reviewed summaries of James's medical records, summaries of deposition transcripts and witness statements, as well as scientific, governmental and medical literature on the carcinogenicity of various chemicals to which James was exposed during his employment at Bessemer. Dr. Mehlman cites several studies dating back as far as 1928 indicating the health risks of benzene exposure and describes decades-old epidemiological studies revealing a causative link between cancer and exposure to benzene and polycyclic aromatic hydrocarbons (PAHs) found in gasoline and petroleum products.

The toxicologist's report explains that "[b]enzene is present in many petroleum products, petroleum distillates, jet fuels, diesel fuels, crude oil, and is a significant component of gasoline (up to 6%)," and that "[b]enzene is currently classified by the Environmental Protection Agency (EPA), the American Conference of Governmental Industrial Hygienists (ACGIH), and IARC [the International Agency for Research on Cancers] as a human carcinogen." The report adds that "[a]nimal studies ... have clearly and without question demonstrated the carcinogenic effects of benzene...."

Dr. Mehlman indicated that "PAHs are a group of chemicals that are present in oil, petroleum products, and tobacco smoke. There are more than 100 different PAH compounds. Usually humans are not exposed to an individual PAH alone, but to a mixture of PAHs." The report indicates PAHs can enter the body through inhalation or skin contact, and that the primary exposure to PAHs occurs in the workplace. Many of the PAHs have been found to cause cancer in animals, and "[r]eports on humans show that individuals exposed to PAHs by inhalation or skin contact for long periods [or] to mixtures that contain PAHs and other compounds can also develop cancer." The Department of Health and Human Services has determined that six PAH compounds are carcinogens. IARC classifies thirteen PAH compounds as "having sufficient evidence for carcinogenicity (meaning they are human carcinogens)." The EPA has also determined that those thirteen PAH compounds are "probable human carcinogens," meaning that they more likely than not cause cancer.

Based on the testimony of Bessemer workers and the MSDSs provided in discovery by Shell and Exxon, Dr. Mehlman determined that the chemicals and products to which James was exposed included black oils, motor oils, PAHs, solvents and formaldehydes. He noted that many of the MSDSs provided by Exxon "indicate that numerous products contained extremely high levels of benzene and PAHs." Based on the evidence obtained by plaintiff during discovery and on numerous epidemiological and animal studies, Dr. Mehlman concluded that

> workplace exposures to various petroleum products (i.e., benzene, gasoline, mineral spirits, mineral oils) and chemicals, which contain gasoline, aromatic hydrocarbons, such as benzene, toluene, xylene, ethyl benzene, naphtha, acrylonitrile, formaldehyde, polycyclic aromatic hydrocarbons (i.e., benzo-alpha-pyrene), light cat-cracked naphtha ("LCCN") and other chemicals caused Mr. James to suffer from stomach and liver cancer.

Plaintiff also presented two reports of her medical expert, Dr. Rowland Goodman. Relying on the evidence obtained during discovery and on the report of the toxicological expert, Dr. Goodman concluded that

> the patient absorbed one or more of these carcinogens through his gastrointestinal tract and through his lungs. These chemicals then spread to his stomach causing a derangement of the DNA mechanism such that one or more of the cells grew in an uncontrolled fashion clinically known as cancer....

This Court set forth the elements of a cause of action for strict liability in the context of a products-liability, failure-to-warn claim in *Coffman v. Keene Corp.*, 133 N.J. 581, 593–95, 628 A.2d 710 (1993). We explained that

> [t]o establish a cause of action in strict liability for a defective product, a plaintiff must prove that the defect existed when the product left the defendant's con-

trol and that the defect caused injury to a reasonably foreseeable user. In a failure-to-warn case, the alleged product defect is not a flaw in the structure or design of the product itself. Rather, the defect is the absence of a warning to unsuspecting users that the product can potentially cause injury. Nevertheless, the same elements to establish a cause of action apply when a plaintiff's claim concerning a defective product is based on a failure to warn.

Just as in this case, the failure-to-warn claim in *Coffman* arose from an occupational exposure over many years to the products of multiple manufacturers, in that case asbestos products, that led to the plaintiff's illness. As in most toxic or environmental tort actions, the predominant issue was whether the plaintiff could satisfy the element of causation. The Court stated that [c]ausation is a fundamental requisite for establishing any product-liability action. The plaintiff must demonstrate so-called product-defect causation — that the defect in the product was a proximate cause of the injury. When the alleged defect is the failure to provide warnings, a plaintiff is required to prove that the absence of a warning was a proximate cause of his harm.

However, we also adopted in *Coffman* a rebuttable "heeding presumption" in products-liability, failure-to-warn cases. We held that

> with respect to the issue of product-defect causation in a product-liability case based on a failure to warn, the plaintiff should be afforded the use of the presumption that he or she would have followed an adequate warning had one been provided, and that the defendant in order to rebut that presumption must produce evidence that such a warning would not have been heeded.

We stressed that the effect of the heeding presumption would be to "direct factual inquiries to the real causes of injury in a failure-to-warn case." In other words, it would shift the plaintiff's burden on the element of causation away from proof that the defendant's failure to warn caused the plaintiff's exposure to the defendant's product (product-defect causation), and toward proof that the defendant's product caused the plaintiff's injury or illness (medical causation).

As a result of the heeding presumption, the burden on a plaintiff to establish product-defect causation in the failure-to-warn context is not an onerous one. Initially, the plaintiff must establish that the defendant had a duty to warn. To establish such a duty, the plaintiff must satisfy "a very low threshold of proof in order to impute to a manufacturer sufficient knowledge to trigger the duty to provide a warning of the harmful effects of its product." In cases proceeding under a theory of strict liability, knowledge of the harmful effects of a product will be imputed to a manufacturer on a showing that "knowledge of the defect existed within the relevant industry." Once proof of such knowledge in the industry has been established, triggering the duty to warn, the plaintiff must show that an adequate warning was not provided. When proceeding under a theory of negligence, the plaintiff must demonstrate that the specific defendant knew or should have known of the potential hazards of the product. Then, assuming that the heeding presumption is unrebutted, it may be presumed that the defendant's failure to warn caused the plaintiff's harmful exposure to the product. Thus, "product-defect causation" in the failure-to-warn context is presumed upon proof that the defendant had a duty to warn and does not require proof of actual causation to satisfy the plaintiff's burden on that element. A plaintiff must introduce evidence that the defendant's failure to warn of the hazards of its product led to plaintiff's exposure only if it becomes necessary to defeat a defendant's attempt to rebut the heeding presumption with its own proofs.

As noted by the court below, the fact that Bessemer may have failed its employees by not warning or instructing them regarding the hazards of toxic exposure in the workplace does not necessarily relieve defendants from liability for failure to warn. In the employment context, a manufacturer's duty to warn of the dangers posed by its products extends to both the employer and the employees of the recipient entity. The heeding presumption also applies to both the employer and the employee. Again, that heeding presumption is rebuttable with respect to either the employer or the employee. We held in *Coffman* that to overcome the heeding presumption in a failure-to-warn case involving a product used in the workplace, the manufacturer must prove that had an adequate warning been provided, the plaintiff-employee with meaningful choice would not have heeded the warning. Alternatively, to overcome the heeding presumption, the manufacturer must show that had an adequate warning been provided, the employer itself would not have heeded the warning by taking reasonable precautions for the safety of its employees to take measures to avoid or minimize the harm from their use or exposure to the dangerous product.

Whether either James or his superiors at Bessemer would have heeded warnings from defendant manufacturers had adequate warnings been provided over the course of James's employment and exposure is a question for the jury, and the burden of proof on that issue lies with defendants.

In a toxic-tort action, in addition to product-defect causation a plaintiff must prove what is known as "medical causation" — that the plaintiff's injuries were proximately caused by exposure to the defendant's product. As recognized by the Appellate Division below, the requirement set forth in *Coffman* that a plaintiff prove both product-defect and medical causation applies not only to asbestos cases, but also to other cases involving occupational exposure to toxic materials. To prove medical causation, a plaintiff must show "that the exposure [to each defendant's product] was a substantial factor in causing or exacerbating the disease."

This Court has emphasized for over a decade the "extraordinary and unique burdens facing plaintiffs who seek to prove causation in toxic-tort litigation." *Rubanick v. Witco Chem. Corp.*, 125 N.J. 421, 433, 593 A.2d 733 (1991); see also *Landrigan v. Celotex Corp.*, 127 N.J. 404, 413, 605 A.2d 1079 (1992) (noting that in toxic-tort context "proof that a defendant's conduct caused decedent's injuries is more subtle and sophisticated than proof in cases concerned with more traditional torts"); *Ayers v. Jackson Township*, 106 N.J. 557, 585–87, 525 A.2d 287. In *Ayers*, we elaborated on the unique difficulties facing toxic-tort plaintiffs:

> By far the most difficult problem for plaintiffs to overcome in toxic tort litigation is the burden of proving causation. In the typical tort case, the plaintiff must prove tortious conduct, injury and proximate cause. Ordinarily, proof of causation requires the establishment of a sufficient nexus between the defendant's conduct and the plaintiff's injury. In toxic tort cases, the task of proving causation is invariably made more complex because of the long latency period of illnesses caused by carcinogens or other toxic chemicals. The fact that ten or twenty years or more may intervene between the exposure and the manifestation of disease highlights the practical difficulties encountered in the effort to prove causation.

Legal scholars have long struggled with the problem of adapting traditional legal doctrines of causation to the difficulties of proving medical causation in the toxic-tort context, but courts have been resistant to novel models of causation. In our toxic-tort precedents, this Court has tried to strike a balance with regard to proof of causation that is fair to both plaintiffs and defendants in view of the almost certain lack of direct scientific proof in such cases.

The problem of proving medical causation with respect to a specific defendant's products is further compounded where, as here, a plaintiff has been exposed to multiple products of multiple defendants over an extended period of time. In such a case, the burden of proving that the plaintiff's exposure to the products of any single defendant was a "substantial factor" causing or exacerbating the plaintiff's illness is a formidable one. The Appellate Division panel in *Sholtis* relied on a Fifth Circuit decision that had addressed a similar issue in determining causation in a multiple-defendant, asbestos-exposure context.

> In the instant case, it is impossible, as a practical matter, to determine with absolute certainty which particular exposure to asbestos dust resulted in injury to Borel. It is undisputed, however, that Borel contracted asbestosis from inhaling asbestos dust and that he was exposed to the products of all the defendants on many occasions. It was also established that the effect of asbestos dust is cumulative, that is, each exposure may result in an additional and separate injury. We think, therefore, that on the basis of strong circumstantial evidence the jury could find that each defendant was the cause in fact of some injury to Borel.

Consistent with the reasoning of the court in *Borel*, and borrowing language from the Fourth Circuit's opinion in *Lohrmann v. Pittsburgh Corning Corp.*, 782 F.3d 1156, 1162–63 (4th Cir.1986), the court in *Sholtis* adopted a "frequency, regularity and proximity" test to establish liability in the multiple-defendant, asbestos-exposure context. Under that test, in order to prove that exposure to a specific defendant's product was a substantial factor in causing or exacerbating the plaintiff's disease, the plaintiff is required to prove "an exposure of sufficient frequency, with a regularity of contact, and with the product in close proximity" to the plaintiff. The court reemphasized that its adoption of such a standard was required by the unique difficulties faced by a plaintiff attempting to establish causation in the toxic-tort context: "Since proof of direct contact is almost always lacking ... courts must rely upon circumstantial proof of sufficiently intense exposure to warrant liability." Id. at 29, 568 A.2d 1196 (footnote omitted). In the context of occupational asbestos-exposure cases, the "frequency, regularity and proximity test" first pronounced in *Lohrmann* has often been applied in other jurisdictions. See, e.g., *Shetterly v. Raymark Indus., Inc.*, 117 F.3d 776, 780 (4th Cir.1997) (applying Maryland law); *Jackson v. Anchor Packing Co.*, 994 F.2d 1295, 1301 (8th Cir.1993) (applying Arkansas law and noting that "a majority of courts have adopted the 'frequency, regularity and proximity' standard"); *Tragarz v. Keene Corp.*, 980 F.2d 411, 420 (7th Cir.1992) (indicating that Illinois has adopted frequency, regularity and proximity test, but noting "it is not a rigid test with an absolute threshold level necessary to support a jury verdict"); *Slaughter v. Southern Talc Co.*, 949 F.2d 167, 171 & n.3 (5th Cir.1991) (adopting frequency-regularity-proximity test for causation in asbestos cases and noting that "[c]ourts in every circuit but the D.C. Circuit, and the First, Second and Fifth Circuits have adopted the *Lohrmann* test. In addition, Michigan, Massachusetts, New Jersey, Illinois, Pennsylvania, Maryland, Nebraska, and Oklahoma have adopted the test."); *Robertson v. Allied Signal, Inc.*, 914 F.2d 360, 380 (3d Cir.1990) (applying Pennsylvania law and noting that frequency, regularity and proximity analysis applies to expert scientific testimony as well as to co-worker testimony of exposure). Cf. *Ingram v. ACandS, Inc.*, 977 F.2d 1332, 1343–44 (9th Cir. 1992) (rejecting frequency, regularity and proximity test where Oregon law applied because causation burden under Oregon law is less stringent, requiring only evidence that defendant's asbestos was present in workplace to create jury question).

We stress that the "frequency, regularity and proximity" test bears no relationship to theories of collective liability that some courts have adopted in contexts where the specific tortfeasor or tortfeasors that caused the plaintiff's injury cannot be identified. The "frequency, regularity and proximity" test assigns liability only to those defendants to whose products the plaintiff can demonstrate he or she was intensely exposed. The court in *Sholtis* invoked the apt analogy of a multi-vehicle accident ...

The court below rejected defendants' contention that the "frequency, regularity and proximity" test pronounced in *Sholtis* should be limited to cases involving asbestos exposure, holding that

> at least for summary judgment purposes, we are convinced that the *Sholtis* analysis is relevant to the "medical causation" issue in a toxic-tort case, such as this, involving occupational exposure to cancer-causing substances manufactured by a determinant number of defendants, all of whom, it is alleged, acted tortiously by failing to warn of the dangerous propensities of their products.
>
> We recognize that the dynamics and causative effects of exposure to asbestos dust may differ from the disease process resulting from exposure to chemicals containing known carcinogens. However, these differences should not cause rejection of the "frequency, regularity and proximity" model. Based on circumstantial evidence, the jury may find in any toxic-tort case, that a plaintiff in the workplace was exposed to the cancer-causing products of defendant-manufacturers on many occasions, and that the exposures were a substantial factor in causing plaintiff's cancer. Application of the "frequency, regularity and proximity" test necessarily focuses on the cumulative effects of exposure to the carcinogen over a prolonged period of time, the dosage of exposure and mode of absorption into the human body. Whether the claim is asbestosis or stomach cancer, the frequency, regularity and proximity of exposure will be an important and fundamental factual link in plaintiff's experts' analysis and methodology in reaching an ultimate theory of causation.

The court further noted a Pennsylvania appellate court decision in which a "frequency and regularity" of exposure standard was applied to the determination of the sufficiency of a complaint seeking damages for workplace exposure to carcinogens (cadmium). *Jobe v. W.P. Metz Refining*, 445 Pa. Super. 76, 664 A.2d 1015, 1020 (1995), appeal denied, 544 Pa. 659, 676 A.2d 1199 (1996)). We agree with the reasoning and conclusion of the Appellate Division, and hold that a plaintiff in an occupational-exposure, toxic-tort case may demonstrate medical causation by establishing: (1) factual proof of the plaintiff's frequent, regular and proximate exposure to a defendant's products; and (2) medical and/or scientific proof of a nexus between the exposure and the plaintiff's condition.

Judgment of Appellate Division affirmed. Case remanded for further proceedings.

Hypothetical

On January 18, Dr. George, a surgeon, advised his patient, Miss Lester, that the best way to treat her condition involved surgery to insert a special medical device. However, he failed to warn Miss Lester of a small (1–2 per cent) but unavoidable risk that the device might lead to partial paralysis of the lower body if, no matter how expertly it had been inserted, it moved and pressed against her spinal cord. Three days later, the surgery was skillfully performed by Dr. George, but the implant nevertheless led to Miss Lester suffering this syndrome. The trial judge gave summary judgment for the defendants (the manufacturer of the implant and Dr. George) on the grounds that the failure to warn was not a cause of Miss Lester's injury because while, if duly warned, Miss Lester would have carried out some further research of her own and so would not have undergone surgery on January 21, she would still have agreed to the surgery at a later date. Does Miss Lester have good grounds for an appeal?

Chapter 10

Asbestos-Related Claims

Signature Diseases

As we all now know, asbestos is a very dangerous product. Yet because of its resistance to chemicals, its properties as an excellent insulator against heat and fire, and its being quite hard-wearing, it was formerly often mixed with cement to form fire-resistant mats to be incorporated into the design of buildings and ovens to act as a flame-retardant barrier, or to be used as brake pads in automotive vehicles. These uses have all now been banned, as it has become known that inhalation of asbestos fibers can cause a number of very serious diseases, including lung cancer.

There has been a huge amount of asbestos litigation throughout the USA, and it shows little sign of abating. The major reason for this is that, despite the bans, asbestos causes two signature diseases—asbestosis (a form of pneumoconiosis) and mesothelioma (a particularly virulent and painful form of lung cancer, and which is always terminal)—whose latency periods are quite long. Moreover, it will often be impossible to deal with claims relating to both diseases at the same time, since the latency period for mesothelioma is much longer than that for asbestosis. In addition, we still know very little about the causal mechanism for either disease. These facts create problems in ascertaining both when a victim suffered (or should have realized that he or she had suffered) injury, and what exposure(s) caused that injury. We saw in Chapter 9 the problems involved in proving causation if the traditional rules are adhered to strictly in cases where the scientific evidence is uncertain.

One response to these issues would have been simply to apply the standard rules of causation and injury. As we saw in Chapter 9, this is the courts' default response. Yet, so far as exposure to asbestos and asbestos products is concerned, the law has developed a number of rules that relax the regular requirements to prove causation.

As you read the following materials, ask yourself the following sets of questions:

1. Why has the law developed special rules for asbestos? Is it simply because the law of torts just cannot ignore the severity of the diseases which asbestos can cause? Is it because exposure of individuals to asbestos "was not merely the product of misjudgment, but rather a conspiracy on the part of asbestos manufacturers," as suggested by David Rosenberg, *The Dusting of America: A Story of Asbestos—Carnage, Cover-up, and Litigation*, 99 Harv. L. Rev. 1693 (1986), reviewing Paul Brodeur, Outrageous Misconduct: The Asbestos Industry On Trial (1985). Or is it because, although we know little about the causal mechanisms of the diseases which are triggered by asbestos, we are certain that both asbestosis and mesothelioma are always caused by exposure to asbestos and nothing else?

2. Are the special rules employed in proving asbestos-related injury appropriate? If they are, could they be usefully applied to cases involving toxic agents other than asbestos?

We begin with the ground-breaking decision of the Fifth Circuit Court of Appeals, which signaled the courts' rejection of the asbestos industry's generic attempts to rely on a state-of-the-art defense.

Borel v. Fibreboard Paper Products Corp.
493 F.2d 1076 (5th Cir. 1973)

WISDOM J. Clarence Borel began working as an industrial insulation worker in 1936. During his career, he was employed at numerous places, usually in Texas, until disabled by the disease of asbestosis in 1969. Borel's employment necessarily exposed him to heavy concentrations of asbestos dust generated by insulation materials. In his pre-trial deposition, Borel testified that at the end of a day working with insulation material containing asbestos his clothes were usually so dusty he could "just barely pick them up without shaking them." Borel stated:

> You just move them just a little and there is going to be dust, and I blowed this dust out of my nostrils by handfuls at the end of the day, trying to use water too, I even used Mentholatum in my nostrils to keep some of the dust from going down in my throat, but it is impossible to get rid of all of it. Even your clothes just stay dusty continually unless you blow it off with an air hose.

Borel said that he had known for years that inhaling asbestos dust "was bad for me" and that it was vexatious and bothersome, but that he never realized that it could cause any serious or terminal illness. Borel emphasized that he and his fellow insulation workers thought that the dust "dissolves as it hits your lungs"....

On January 19, 1969, Borel was hospitalized and a lung biopsy performed. Borel's condition was diagnosed as pulmonary asbestosis. Since the disease was considered irreversible, Borel was sent home. Borel testified in his deposition that this was the first time he knew that he had asbestosis.

Borel's condition gradually worsened during the remainder of 1969. On February 11, 1970, Borel underwent surgery for the removal of his right lung. The examining doctors determined that Borel had a form of lung cancer known as mesothelioma, which had been caused by asbestosis. As a result of these diseases, Borel later died before the district case reached the trial stage.

The medical testimony adduced at trial indicates that inhaling asbestos dust in industrial conditions, even with relatively light exposure, can produce the disease of asbestosis. The disease is difficult to diagnose in its early stages because there is a long latent period between initial exposure and apparent effect. This latent period may vary according to individual idiosyncrasy, duration and intensity of exposure, and the type of asbestos used. In some cases, the disease may manifest itself in less than ten years after initial exposure. In general, however, it does not manifest itself until ten to twenty-five or more years after initial exposure. This latent period is explained by the fact that asbestos fibers, once inhaled, remain in place in the lung, causing a tissue reaction that is slowly progressive and apparently irreversible. Even if no additional asbestos fibers are inhaled, tissue changes may continue undetected for decades. By the time the disease is diagnosable, a considerable period of time has elapsed since the date of the injurious exposure. Furthermore, the effect of the disease may be cumulative since each exposure to asbestos dust can result in additional tissue changes. A worker's present condition is the biological product of many years of exposure to asbestos dust, with both past and recent exposures contributing to the overall effect. All of these factors combine to make it impossible, as a practical matter, to determine which exposure or exposures to asbestos dust caused the disease.

A second disease, mesothelioma, is a form of lung cancer caused by exposure to asbestos. It affects the pleural and peritoneal cavities, and there is a similarly long period between initial contact and apparent effect. As with asbestosis, it is difficult to determine which exposure to asbestos dust is responsible for the disease....

The plaintiff introduced evidence tending to establish that the defendant manufacturers either were, or should have been, fully aware of the many articles and studies on asbestosis. The evidence also indicated, however, that during Borel's working career no manufacturer ever warned contractors or insulation workers, including Borel, of the dangers associated with inhaling asbestos dust or informed them of the ACGIH's threshold limit values for exposure to asbestos dust. Furthermore, no manufacturer ever tested the effect of their products on the workers using them or attempted to discover whether the exposure of insulation workers to asbestos dust exceeded the suggested threshold limits.

The plaintiff sought to hold the defendants liable for negligence, gross negligence, and breach of warranty or strict liability. The negligent acts alleged in the complaint were: (1) failure to take reasonable precautions or to exercise reasonable care to warn Borel of the danger to which he was exposed as a worker when using the defendant's asbestos insulation products; (2) failure to inform Borel as to what would be safe and sufficient wearing apparel and proper protective equipment and appliances or method of handling and using the various products; (3) failure to test the asbestos products in order to ascertain the dangers involved in their use; and (4) failure to remove the products from the market upon ascertaining that such products would cause asbestosis. The plaintiff also alleged that the defendants should be strictly liable in warranty and tort. The plaintiff contended that the defendants' products were unreasonably dangerous because of the failure to provide adequate warnings of the foreseeable dangers associated with them....

[I]n cases such as the instant case, the manufacturer is held to the knowledge and skill of an expert. This is relevant in determining (1) whether the manufacturer knew or should have known the danger, and (2) whether the manufacturer was negligent in failing to communicate this superior knowledge to the user or consumer of its product. *Wright v. Carter Products, Inc.*, 2 Cir. 1957, 244 F.2d 53. The manufacturer's status as expert means that at a minimum he must keep abreast of scientific knowledge, discoveries, and advances and is presumed to know what is imparted thereby. But even more importantly, a manufacturer has a duty to test and inspect his product. The extent of research and experiment must be commensurate with the dangers involved. A product must not be made available to the public without disclosure of those dangers that the application of reasonable foresight would reveal. Nor may a manufacturer rely unquestioningly on others to sound the hue and cry concerning a danger in its product. Rather, each manufacturer must bear the burden of showing that its own conduct was proportionate to the scope of its duty....

The defendants' position is that they did not breach their duty to warn because the danger from inhaling asbestos was not foreseeable until about 1968 and that, in view of the long latent period of the disease, Borel must have contracted asbestosis well before that date....

As stated in our recital of the facts, several studies published during the 1930's and 1940's reported the danger to asbestos plant workers and others exposed to asbestos dust and urged precautionary measures to eliminate hazardous concentrations. The American Conference of Governmental Industrial Hygienists, beginning in 1947, issued guidelines suggesting threshold limit values for exposure to asbestos dust. Even the Fleischer-Drinker report in 1945, relied on by the defendants, cautioned that exposure to high concentrations of asbestos dust could cause asbestosis and recommended the use of ventilation and respiratory protection devices.

The evidence also tended to establish that none of the defendants ever tested its product to determine its effect on industrial insulation workers. Nor did any defendant ever attempt to determine whether the exposure of insulation workers or others to asbestos dust exceeded the A.C.G.I.H.'s recommended threshold limit values, or indeed, whether those standards were accurate or reliable.

As previously mentioned, the foreseeability of the danger must be measured in light of the manufacturer's status as an expert and the manufacturer's duty to test its product. In these circumstances, we think the jury was entitled to find that the danger to Borel and other insulation workers from inhaling asbestos dust was foreseeable to the defendants at the time the products causing Borel's injuries were sold.

The defendants next challenge the jury's finding that their products were unreasonably dangerous for failure to give warnings. They cannot deny, however, that once the danger became foreseeable, the duty to warn attached. Here, the defendants gave no warning at all. They attempt to circumvent this finding by arguing, disingenuously, that the danger was obvious.

Decision of the district court affirmed.

Questions

1. Why did Judge Wisdom describe the defendants as arguing "disingenuously" that the danger to the insulation workers was obvious?

2. Could the manufacturers have meaningfully tested their products when the latency period for both asbestosis and mesothelioma is so long? Does it matter?

Market Share Liability

In *Borel*, the plaintiff clearly established general causation of both asbestosis and mesothelioma by exposure to asbestos fibers. Since general causation involves a matter of law, it is a question that does not need to be revisited in the courts (unless, presumably, some unforeseen new evidence comes to light).

The plaintiff in *Borel* was also able to establish specific causation of the victim's own asbestosis and mesothelioma. However, the long latency periods of both these diseases, coupled with the likelihood that any victim will have been exposed to asbestos products made by different manufacturers, means that many other victims will struggle to establish specific causation by specified defendants. In order to avoid such victims going uncompensated, one suggestion was that liability for causation of the signature asbestos diseases should simply be apportioned among all manufacturers of asbestos products according to their respective market shares. However, while applied by some states to some other defective products (see Chapter 15), this idea has not found favor with the courts in asbestos-related cases.

Black v. Abex Corporation

603 N.W.2d 182 (1999) (Supreme Court of North Dakota)

KAPSNER, J. Rochelle Black appeals from a summary judgment dismissing her wrongful death and survival claims premised upon market share or alternative liability against numerous asbestos manufacturers. Concluding Black has failed to raise a genuine issue of material fact which would preclude summary judgment, we affirm.

Rochelle Black's husband, Markus, served in the Air Force as an auto mechanic from 1971 to 1986. He died of lung cancer in 1991. Black sued forty-eight asbestos manufacturers, alleging her husband's death had been caused by his occupational exposure to asbestos-containing products. Included in her complaint were claims based upon market share and alternative liability.

The defendants moved for partial summary judgment requesting dismissal of the market share and alternative liability claims. The court granted the motion for partial summary judgment and dismissed those claims in its Pretrial Order dated August 29, 1995.

Subsequently, all remaining claims against the defendants were either settled or voluntarily dismissed prior to the scheduled trial. On February 25, 1999, the court entered a "Concluding Order" covering this and several other consolidated asbestos cases, indicating all of the cases had been "fully and finally disposed of and the time for all appeals of this Court's orders and judgments in those cases has run." Black filed a notice of appeal from the Concluding Order and from the 1995 Pretrial Order granting the motion for summary judgment....

The genesis of market share liability lies in the California Supreme Court's decision in *Sindell v. Abbott Laboratories*, 26 Cal.3d 588, 163 Cal.Rptr. 132, 607 P.2d 924 (1980). In *Sindell*, the court held that women who suffered injuries resulting from their mothers' ingestion of the drug DES during pregnancy could sue DES manufacturers, even though the plaintiffs could not identify the specific manufacturer of the DES each of their respective mothers had taken. The court fashioned a new form of liability which relaxed traditional causation requirements, allowing a plaintiff to recover upon showing that she could not identify the specific manufacturer of the DES which caused her injury, that the defendants produced DES from an identical formula, and that the defendants manufactured a "substantial share" of the DES the plaintiff's mother might have taken. Id. at 936–37. The court held each defendant would be liable for a proportionate share of the judgment based upon its share of the relevant market, unless it demonstrated it could not have made the product which caused the plaintiff's injury.

The essential elements of market share liability are summarized in W. Page Keeton et al., Prosser and Keeton on the Law of Torts, § 103, at 714 (5th ed.1984):

> The requirements for market-share liability seem to be: (1) injury or illness occasioned by a fungible product (identical-type product) made by all of the defendants joined in the lawsuit; (2) injury or illness due to a design hazard, with each having been found to have sold the same type product in a manner that made it unreasonably dangerous; (3) inability to identify the specific manufacturer of the product or products that brought about the plaintiff's injury or illness; and (4) joinder of enough of the manufacturers of the fungible or identical product to represent a substantial share of the market.

The overwhelming majority of courts which have addressed the issue have held market share liability is inappropriate in cases alleging injury from exposure to asbestos. The most oft-cited rationale is that asbestos is not a fungible product, as evidenced by the wide variety of asbestos-containing products, the varying types and amounts of asbestos in those products, and the varying degrees of risk posed by those products. The leading treatise recognizes:

> [I]t can reasonably be argued that it would not be appropriate to apply this fungible product concept to asbestos-containing products because they are by no means identical since they contain widely varying amounts of asbestos. (Prosser, *supra*, § 103, at 714.)

Black essentially concedes market share liability is inappropriate in a "shotgun" asbestos case, where the plaintiff is alleging injury from exposure to many different types of asbestos products. Black asserts, however, market share liability may be appropriate when the plaintiff seeks to hold liable only manufacturers of one type of asbestos-containing product. Relying upon *Wheeler v. Raybestos-Manhattan*, 8 Cal.App.4th 1152, 11 Cal.Rptr.2d 109 (1992), Black asserts she should be allowed to proceed in her market share claims against the manufacturers of asbestos-containing "friction products," including brake and clutch products. In *Wheeler*, the California Court of Appeal held a plaintiff could proceed on a market share theory against manufacturers of asbestos-containing brake pads. The court overturned the trial court's order granting a nonsuit in favor of the manufacturers, concluding the plaintiff's offer of proof sufficiently alleged that the brake pads, although not identical, were "fungible" because they contained percentages of asbestos within a "restricted range" of between forty and sixty percent and posed nearly equivalent risks of harm.

Black requests that we recognize market share liability as a viable tort theory under North Dakota law. Black further requests that we follow *Wheeler* and hold that automotive "friction products," including asbestos-containing brake and clutch products, are sufficiently fungible to support a market share claim....

This Court has never addressed whether market share liability is recognized under North Dakota tort law. Other courts faced with the question have reached varying conclusions on the general availability of this novel remedy. We find it unnecessary to resolve this general issue because we conclude, assuming market share liability were recognized in this state, summary judgment was still appropriate based upon the record in this case.

The dispositive question presented is whether Black has raised a genuine issue of material fact on the issue of fungibility. Market share liability is premised upon the fact that the defendants have produced identical (or virtually identical) defective products which carry equivalent risks of harm. Accordingly, under the market share theory, it is considered equitable to apportion liability based upon the percentage of products each defendant contributed to the entire relevant market.

This reasoning hinges, however, upon each defendant's product carrying an equal degree of risk. As the Supreme Court of Oklahoma explained in *Case*, 743 P.2d at 1066:

> In the *Sindell* case, and those following it, it was determined that public policy considerations supporting recovery in favor of an innocent plaintiff against negligent defendants would allow the application of a theory of liability which shifted the burden of proof of causation from plaintiff to defendants. However, as previously stated, that theory was crafted in a situation where each potential defendant shared responsibility for producing a product which carried with it a singular risk factor. The theory further provided that each potential defendant's liability would be proportional to that defendant's contribution of risk to the market in which the plaintiff was injured. This situation thus provided a balance between the rights of the defendants and the rights of the plaintiffs. A bal-

ance being achieved, public policy considerations were sufficient to justify the application of the market share theory of liability.

Similar reasoning was employed by the Supreme Court of Ohio in *Goldman*, 514 N.E.2d at 701:

> Crucial to the *Sindell* court's reasoning was this fact: there was no difference between the risks associated with the drug as marketed by one company or another, and as all DES sold presented the same risk of harm, there was no inherent unfairness in holding the companies accountable based on their share of the DES market. Numerous other courts have stressed the importance of a singular risk factor in market share cases.

Unless the plaintiff can demonstrate that the defendants' products created a "singular risk factor," the balance between the rights of plaintiffs and defendants evaporates and it is no longer fair nor equitable to base liability upon each defendant's share of the relevant market. The rationale underlying market share liability, as developed in *Sindell*, is that it did not matter which manufacturer's product the plaintiff's mother actually ingested; because all DES was chemically identical, the same harm would have occurred. Thus, any individual manufacturer's product would have caused the identical injury, and it was through mere fortuity that any one manufacturer did not produce the actual product ingested. Under these circumstances, viewing the overall DES market and all injuries caused thereby, it may be presumed each manufacturer's products will produce a percentage of those injuries roughly equivalent to its percentage of the total DES market. As the *Sindell* court recognized, "[u]nder this approach, each manufacturer's liability would approximate its responsibility for the injuries caused by its own products."

In order to prevail on its market share claims, Black would therefore have to demonstrate that the asbestos-containing "friction products" her husband was exposed to carried equivalent degrees of risk. Black asserts this problem has been "disposed of" by the holding in *Wheeler*. Although *Wheeler* recognized that non-identical products may give rise to market share liability if they contain roughly equivalent quantities of a single type of asbestos fiber, the court did not hold that all asbestos-containing friction brake products in all cases will be considered fungible. In fact, the court in *Wheeler* indicated that such products must carry a nearly equivalent risk of harm to support market share liability. Furthermore, *Wheeler* was a reversal of a nonsuit based upon an offer of proof made by the plaintiff. The court stressed its holding was narrow: the plaintiffs had not proven the elements of a market share case, but were merely being afforded the opportunity to prove it. Clearly, *Wheeler* does not serve as evidence of fungibility and equivalent risks of harm of the products in this case.

Black points to uncontroverted evidence in this record that the four remaining defendants produced friction products which contained between seven and seventy-five percent asbestos fibers. This is a far greater range than the forty to sixty percent the *Wheeler* court considered "roughly comparable" for purposes of fungibility under *Sindell*. It is closer to the fifteen to one-hundred percent range which the Supreme Court of Ohio held precluded market share liability as a matter of law. It seems obvious that a product which contains seventy-five percent asbestos would create a greater risk of harm than one which contains only seven percent. Absent introduction of expert evidence demonstrating that in spite of the differences the products would produce equivalent risks of harm, application of market share liability would be inappropriate.

Black failed to present competent, admissible evidence from which a fact finder could determine the "friction products" her husband was exposed to carried equivalent risks of harm and were fungible under *Sindell*. Accordingly, summary judgment was appropriate.

Questions

1. Does this suggest that market share liability can be applicable only to pharmaceuticals, where the active ingredient of the various products on the market can be determined to be bioequivalent?

2. If the category of products to which market share liability can be applied is so strictly limited, is it appropriate even to have such a doctrine at all?

Relaxing Rules of Causation in Other Ways

Although market share liability has been rejected as inapplicable to cases of asbestosis and mesothelioma, the plight of the victim in establishing specific causation so long after the exposure to asbestos has led the courts to relax the standard rules of causation in other respects.

Jane Stapleton, Two Causal Fictions at the Heart of U.S. Asbestos Doctrine
122 L.Q. Rev. 189 (2006)

Asbestos litigation is the longest-running mass tort litigation in U.S. history. By 2002 approximately 730,000 individuals had brought claims against some 8,400 business entities, and defendants and insurers have spent a total of $70 billion on litigation (Carroll et al., Asbestos Litigation (2005)). By 2000 there were "virtually no first-line asbestos manufacturers (and few of their insurers) left standing …": S. Issacharoff, "*Shocked*": *Mass Torts and Aggregate Asbestos Litigation after Amchem and Orbitz* (2000) 80 Tex. L.Rev. 1925 at 1931. Today 73 corporate asbestos defendants have dissolved or filed for reorganisation under Ch.11 (protective bankruptcy), 37 doing so since January 2000. The resulting stays in litigation against those first-line entities have driven U.S. claimants increasingly to target "peripheral" solvent defendants.

It is clear that such an "elephantine mass of asbestos cases … defies customary judicial administration" (*Ortiz v. Fibreboard Corp* (1999) 527 U.S. 815 at 821) and U.S. courts have been forced to create novel handling techniques. This note deals with the two little appreciated but dramatic accommodations U.S. courts have made to causation doctrine in the asbestos area. Both these legal fictions stem from the decision in *Borel v. Fibreboard Paper Prods Corp*, 493 F.2d 1076 (5th Cir. 1973), cert. denied, 419 U.S. 869 (1974).

Until the *Borel* case, asbestos-related injuries were overwhelmingly seen by the general public as an issue confined to the employees of asbestos miners and manufacturers. Since such employees, like most U.S. employees, are barred from suing their employers in tort by the "sole remedy" rule of workers' compensation legislation, successful asbestos claims had been confined before *Borel* to the realm of workers' compensation, where the legislation channelled all the liability to the last employment in which the employee suffered exposure to asbestos.

But Clarence Borel was not employed by an asbestos miner or manufacturer: he worked for a company that installed insulation. He was exposed to asbestos from 1936 until January 1969 when he was diagnosed with asbestosis. In October 1969 Borel filed a tort claim using the recently recognised common law "products liability" doctrine reflected in s.402A of the *Restatement (Second) of Torts* (1965) against all 11 asbestos manufacturers with whose products he had been required to work. In February 1970 Borel underwent surgery whereupon it was discovered that he "had a form of lung cancer known as mesothelioma, which had been caused [sic] by asbestosis" (at 1083). Borel died before the case reached trial. At trial each defendant to whose asbestos Borel had been exposed was held to have been a "substantial factor" of some injury to Borel and each was held jointly and severally liable for Borel's total condition. In September 1973 the trial verdict in Borel's favour was upheld by the Fifth Circuit: *Borel v. Fibreboard Paper Prods Corp*, 493 F.2d 1076 (5th Cir. 1973), *cert. denied*, 419 U.S. 869 (1974). It is highly significant that the Fifth Circuit was under the impression that there was no rational way to apportion injury for the cumulative disease asbestosis, a view not shared by U.K. courts (see, e.g. *Holtby v. Brigham & Cowan (Hull) Ltd.*, [2000] 3 All E.R. 421, CA). It also believed that it had been established that Borel's mesothelioma had been caused by his asbestosis: a connection that has no valid medical basis.

The "substantial factor" approach: fiction of a threshold contraction mechanism for cancers

Under orthodox doctrine an asbestos defendant can only be liable to the claimant if it can be shown that there was some actual factual causal link between its wrongful dose of asbestos and the contraction of the claimant's condition or part thereof.

There are three possible mechanisms by which a disease may be contracted. First, the disease may occur via a single-hit mechanism where a single "insult" such as the inhalation of a single fibre of a mineral results in the total injury suffered. Infectious diseases are typically caused in this way. A well-known nondisease example of a single "insult" mechanism is *Cook v. Lewis* [1952] 1 D.L.R. 1. Secondly, the mechanism may be cumulative. Here each exposure, including the first, results in some actual injury. Each exposure is by itself a but-for factor to some actual injury even though it is not a but-for factor to the entire condition. Asbestosis is caused by such a mechanism: *Holtby v. Brigham & Cowan (Hull) Ltd.*, above. Thirdly, a disease may operate by a threshold mechanism where there is no injury at all until the accumulated dose exceeds some threshold. Here a pre- and less-than-threshold dose is not by itself a but-for factor to any actual injury. Where the threshold is passed, any pre-threshold dose is a cause of the entire injury which is triggered. Noise-induced deafness seems to be caused by such a mechanism: *Thompson v. Smith Shiprepairers (North Shields) Ltd.*, [1984] Q.B. 405.

In *Borel* the court held that a plaintiff was entitled to get to the jury on the issue of factual cause against an individual defendant merely by showing exposure (that was not *de minimis*) to that defendant's product. Subsequent U.S. courts have described this approach as the "substantial factor test of causation rather than the but-for test" (*Mavroudis v. Pittsburgh-Corning Corp*, 935 P.2d 684 at 689 (1997)). There would be nothing unorthodox about this, nor would it rest on a fiction, where it is known that the relevant injury is contracted by a cumulative mechanism as in the case of asbestosis or by a threshold mechanism. Under such mechanisms the fact that the exposure by one defendant was not a but-for factor in relation to the entire condition is irrelevant.

But being entitled to get to the jury on the issue of factual cause merely by showing exposure is a radical doctrine when applied to mesothelioma. The severity of mesothelioma is not dose-related: it is an "indivisible" disease. The method by which it is contracted cannot therefore be a cumulative mechanism. But beyond this medical science has not determined its mechanism: it may be by a single "insult" or it may be by a threshold mechanism. All we know is that the risk of mesothelioma is related to the degree of exposure so that each exposure to asbestos contributes to the risk. If the contraction mechanism were by a single "insult", the fibres of any one defendant may have played no role at all in any injury to the claimant: scientifically it cannot be said that all of the asbestos products to which the plaintiff was exposed contributed to the mesothelioma. It follows that if the *Borel* approach, of being entitled to show the defendant was a "substantial factor" in the contraction of the condition on the basis of mere exposure, is applied to mesothelioma cases it rests on the fiction that mesothelioma is known to be contracted by a threshold mechanism.

This is exactly what happened after *Borel*. Though it is extraordinary to foreign eyes, U.S. courts since *Borel* have not generally made any distinction between the causal issue in asbestosis and mesothelioma claims: regardless of which condition has been contracted, a U.S. asbestos plaintiff is entitled to get to the jury on the issue of factual cause merely by showing a non-*de minimis* exposure by the defendant. Specifically, the radical nature of the "substantial factor" fiction as applied to mesothelioma has gone virtually unremarked. Even in cases where the fiction is acknowledged such as *Rutherford v. Owens-Illinois, Inc*, 941 P.2d 1203 (Cal. 1997), little if any rationale for its adoption is provided. Indeed, the exasperated court in the mesothelioma case of *Mavroudis* (at p.687) noted that:

> Although we are aware that substantial factor causation instructions are commonly given in asbestos-injury cases tried in Washington, no published Washington case cited by the parties or found by this court through independent research directly addresses the propriety of substantial factor instructions in asbestos-injury cases (emphasis added).

The *Restatement (Third) of Torts: Liability for Physical Harm (Basic Principles), Proposed Final Draft No.1* (ALI, April 6, 2005) recognises that U.S. courts treat all asbestos cases as if the contraction mechanism was via a threshold mechanism, so that each exposure can be a factual cause:

> courts have assumed, without much discussion, that the model for disease causation, even for progressive disease like asbestosis, is the one contained in this Comment [i.e. the threshold mechanism]. Since the first asbestos case in which a plaintiff was successful, courts have allowed plaintiffs to recover from all defendants to whose asbestos products the plaintiff was exposed.

For example, in the mesothelioma case of *Eagle-Picher Industries, Inc v. Balbos*, 604 A.2d 445 (Md. 1992) the defendant did not even dispute that

> the principle of proximate causation by which the evidence concerning causation in fact is to be determined is the substantial factor rule, and not the "but-for" rule (at 459).

Courts have even extended the "substantial factor" approach and threshold mechanism fiction to cases of multiple exposures to different toxic agents, cigarette smoke and asbestos, each of which is a risk factor for the plaintiff's disease, namely lung cancer: *Manguno v. Babcock & Wilcox*, 961 F.2d 533 (5th Cir. 1992, applying Louisiana law).

The "indivisibility-of-injury" fiction for cumulative disease of asbestosis

Under orthodox doctrine, once it has been shown that a defendant did contribute to the contraction of at least some of the claimant's disease, because it is known that the disease mechanism is cumulative or by a threshold, the extent to which the defendant can be liable to the claimant will turn on the medical question of whether the *severity* of the disease is dose-related. By definition a condition caused by a cumulative mechanism is dose-related in its severity. But we have just seen that in the U.S. all asbestos cases are treated as if the contraction mechanism was via a threshold mechanism. Where the mechanism is, or is deemed to be, a threshold mechanism, the disease severity might be dose-independent. For example, the disease is not contracted until there have been four hits but the severity of the resulting disease is independent of whether the total exposure was 4 or 40 hits. Conversely, where the mechanism is, or is deemed to be, a threshold mechanism, the disease severity might be dose-dependent. For example, the disease is not contracted until there have been four hits and thereafter the severity of disease is dependent on total exposure, being more severe for 40 than 4 hits.

The court in *Borel* held the asbestos manufacturers to be liable *in solidum*, each thereby being liable to Mr Borel for the full amount of his injury. This approach, thereafter followed in U.S. asbestos cases, treats the asbestos disease as if the severity of the disease was dose-independent, in other words, as if it were an indivisible injury. While this "indivisible injury" treatment accords with the scientific reality of mesothelioma it involves a dramatic "fiction" when applied to asbestosis. For example, in *Norfolk & Western Ry. Co. v. Ayers*, 538 U.S. 135 at 143 (2003) one asbestosis plaintiff had been exposed by the defendant for only three months and had worked with asbestos elsewhere as a pipe fitter for 33 years. The defendant was held liable for his total condition. This is in stark contrast to the approach of the United Kingdom: see *Holtby v. Brigham & Cowan (Hull) Ltd.*, above.

Comment

It is true that a striking difference between the approach of courts in the United States and other common law courts is that in the U.S. "the general tendency of courts in tort cases, once negligence is established, is to resolve doubts about causation, within reason, in the plaintiff's favor": *Kwasny v. United States*, 823 F.2d 194 (7th Cir. 1987). But, even so, the twin asbestos fictions stand out as extreme departures from orthodoxy. What might explain their creation, their apparent continuing acceptance even by beleaguered defendants, the uncertainty of their boundaries and their general neglect by academic commentators?

The answer would seem to lie in a combination of structural features of the U.S. common law system. First, there is a multiplicity of jurisdictions. Tort law is a state matter, so there are 51 separate tort law regimes in the United States (including the federal jurisdiction). Moreover, in nearly all of these jurisdictions there has been modern statutory intervention affecting liability in the asbestos area with the result that there are nearly 100 different primary sources of relevant law. By accepting the *Borel* holdings, all parties could see efficiencies. Secondly, since most U.S. employees are barred from suing their employer in tort, injured workers were forced to sue other parties in order to access tort-level damages. But targets included not only those who had been personally careless in their mining, manufacture and supply of the asbestos to which the plaintiff was exposed, but also, thanks to s.402A of the *Restatement (Second) of Torts* (1965), innocent downstream "mere suppliers" of the relevant asbestos containing products. This results in the notorious phenomenon of the typical U.S. asbestos claim naming dozens of defendants. Rationalisation by the market-share device (see *Sindell v. Abbott Labs*, 607 P.2d 924 (Cal. 1980)) was rejected for asbestos claims: unlike the pharmaceutical involved in *Sindell*, asbestos products are not identical and, since they do not pose similar risks, the problems involved in defining the relevant "asbestos market" were insuperable.

Next, the medical testimony about asbestos diseases has often been confused: see, for example, in *Eagle-Picher Industries, Inc v. Balbos*, 604 A.2d 445 at p.459 (Md. 1992). Trial court nervousness about the basis for division has also been cited as a reason for the "indivisibility-of-injury" fiction by the *Restatement (Third) of Torts: Liability for Physical*

Harm (Basic Principles), Proposed Final Draft No.1 (at p. 472). But by far the most powerful force behind the meek acquiescence of defendants and trial courts in the two asbestos fictions seems to have been the operation of the U.S. costs rule in the context of a litigation phenomenon, the scale of which was quickly recognised to be uniquely threatening to the civil justice system. Under the U.S. costs rule defendants pay their own costs even if they prevail at trial. In the context of mammoth volume of asbestos claims, this has, oddly, produced a great deal of common interest between plaintiffs' lawyers, defendants and trial courts: a unique interest in managing and processing claims as cheaply as possible. Taking fine doctrinal points about causation and division does not easily fit within this agenda. In the context of other well known broad-brush, plaintiff-friendly causation rules such as that in *Summers v. Tice*, 33 Cal.2d 80; 199 P.2d 1 (Cal. 1948), the market-share approach, and the heeding presumption in the area of products liability, the two asbestos fictions may not even seem all that remarkable to U.S. practitioners. (The indifference of the legal academy is harder to fathom. Astonishingly, even the Reporters of *Restatement (Third) of Torts: Products Liability* (1998) sanguinely state, with no reference to *Borel*'s case, that "traditional notions of causation retain their vitality in products liability": Henderson and Twerski, *Intuition and Technology in Product Design Litigation: an Essay on Proximate Causation* (2000) 88 Geo. L.J. 659 (at 660).)

Nevertheless and finally, it should be noted that a parallel development has dramatically affected the operation of the two asbestos fictions. It was not until the 1960s and 1970s that most U.S. states replaced the traditional rule that contributory negligence was a full defence with systems of comparative fault. This led in the 1980s to attacks on the doctrine of *in solidum* (joint and several) liability; and by 2000 a majority of states had, to some extent at least, abandoned that doctrine for independent tortfeasors even in relation to unequivocally indivisible injuries: *Restatement (Third) of Torts: Apportionment of Liability* (American Law Institute, 2000) at p.164. When, in the 1990s, first-line asbestos defendants began to become unavailable and peripheral parties came to be the targets of litigation, the sweep of the liability imposed on peripherals by the two fictions prompted even further abrogation of *in solidum* liability. For example, until 2004 in Texas a toxic tort defendant could only escape *in solidum* liability if it were less than 15 per cent responsible. The threshold before *in solidum* liability bites was then raised to 50 per cent: Tex. Civ. Prac. & Rem. Code Ann. §33.013(c).

Figure 10.1 Causation in Asbestos Cases: Law vs. Medical Science

	Mesothelioma	Asbestosis
Medical Science	Severity is dose-independent. Causation must be either by: (a) One "insult"; or (b) A threshold mechanism	Causation is cumulative. Severity may be: (a) Dose-dependent; or (b) Dose-independent
Law	Presumes threshold mechanism of causation, which implies: (a) an indivisible injury; and (b) joint and several liability (or apportionment by fault in states where that has been abolished)	Presumes severity is dose-independent, which implies: (a) an indivisible injury; and (b) joint and several liability (or apportionment by fault in states where that has been abolished)
Nature of Legal Fiction	Assumes knowledge of causation of disease	Assumes knowledge of causation of severity of disease

Notes

1. *Summary.* The differences between the law's approach to causation of the signature asbestos diseases and that of medical science are tabulated in Figure 10.1.

2. *The initial English approach.* Stapleton argues that the US approach to signature asbestos diseases is out of step with the rest of the common law world. It is worth considering what can be learned from the approach favored elsewhere, which has taken its lead from England. *Fairchild v. Glenhaven Funeral Services Ltd.*, [2002] UKHL 22, was the first significant decision as to the approach to be taken in English law to the causation of signature asbestos diseases. In *Fairchild* the House of Lords (since re-named the Supreme Court) held that, where a claimant could establish that he had contracted mesothelioma as the result of being tortiously exposed to asbestos by two or more defendants, but could not establish on a preponderance of the evidence which one of them had caused the disease, he nevertheless had a good cause of action against both defendants, on the grounds that each had materially increased his risk of contracting the disease.

In *Barker v. Corus (UK) PLC*, [2006] UKHL 20, two new issues arose. The first was whether liability under *Fairchild* should be proportionate to the risk to which each defendant had exposed the victim, or whether—since mesothelioma is an indivisible disease—each defendant should be held jointly and severally liable for the whole. Lord Roger took the view, in his dissent, that since the liability under *Fairchild* was not for the risk of harm but for making a material contribution to causing the disease, each defendant must be jointly and severally liable as would be any other tortfeasor in respect of an indivisible injury. The majority of the House of Lords held, however, that liability for mesothelioma under *Fairchild* is for exposing the victim to the *risk* of harm, and therefore a defendant's liability should be in proportion to the contribution he has made to that risk. Whilst mesothelioma is indivisible, the risk of it can and should be divided.

The second issue in *Barker* arose because Mr. Barker had been self-employed on some (but certainly not all) of the occasions of his exposure to asbestos, and so had effectively put himself at risk on those occasions. This led to the question of whether there should be apportionment where some exposures to asbestos have been tortious and some non-tortious. The majority held that, since *Fairchild* provided a cause of action where there was a material increase in the risk of harm, it was irrelevant that some of the exposure was non-tortious. Apportionment was therefore appropriate between tortfeasors.

Lord Roger agreed that that is the correct implication of the majority's approach to the first issue. He noted, however, that his own approach to the first issue would mean that none of the defendants could be liable to the victim for, if liability is truly joint and several, that would make the claimant wholly liable for his own injury, and would thus bar his claim against anyone else.

3. *Joint and several liability.* The original common law rule, which still applies in England, is that multiple defendants who each contributed to an indivisible injury are jointly and severally liable for it. In other words, each of them is liable to compensate for the full extent of the victim's loss. This is extremely helpful for a plaintiff where one (or more) of the potential defendants has gone bankrupt or is untraceable, because full compensation can still be obtained from the tortfeasor who remains in business. However, many American states have now abandoned that rule in favor of apportioning liability according to the degree of fault of each of the parties involved, including the victim. This may mean that defendants (or their insurers) pay less but, where one or more defendant is untraceable or bankrupt, it also means that the victim(s) will be under-compensated.

Question

Is it possible for a sufferer of either asbestosis or mesothelioma to succeed in a claim for compensation without the courts' operating some sort of causal fiction (whether of the types that Stapleton has identified or otherwise)?

Contribution to Risk

As *Barker* demonstrates, an issue closely linked to that of causation is that of apportionment of damages. The reason for this is fairly obvious: only those defendants (and their insurers) who have been held to have contributed to the harm suffered by the victim are expected to pay for the compensation that s/he is awarded. As a matter of principle, those who have contributed to the victim's injury are identified first; only then can the proportion of the compensation that should be met by each of them be determined. One method of apportionment depends on the amount of harm that each defendant has caused the victim. But that approach is, by definition, inapplicable to cases of indivisible harm, which the causal fictions presuppose to be true of the signature asbestos diseases. The other method of apportionment—which, therefore, seems at first glance to be the only possibility here—reflects the comparative responsibility of each of the parties. But that raises the question of how comparative fault of the parties is to be measured.

So yet another possibility may be considered. Since we do not really know how mesothelioma and asbestosis are caused, might it make more sense to deal with the questions of causation and apportionment together? This could be achieved according to the degree of risk to which the victim was being exposed, and would be assessed according to the length and intensity of each exposure. That is essentially the theory underlying the House of Lords' approach in *Barker v. Corus*.

Indeed, while the standard approach of tort law has, of course, been based on causation of harm, and not contribution to the risk of harm, Lord Reid noted in the House of Lords around forty years ago, in *McGhee v. National Coal Board*, [1973] 1 W.L.R. 1, 5, that:

> I can see no substantial difference between saying that what the [defendants] did materially increased the risk of injury to the [plaintiff] and saying that what the [defendants] did made a material contribution to his injury.

While it is easy to take this statement as suggesting that increasing the risk of someone's being injured equates to causation of harm—an approach which was advocated (for some cases at least) by the late Gerald Boston, *Toxic Apportionment: A Causation and Risk Contribution Model*, 25 Envtl. L. 549 (1995)—that is not at all what Lord Reid had in mind. Instead, his argument "[f]rom a broad and practical viewpoint" was that, if the plaintiff can establish on a preponderance of the evidence both that s/he has suffered harm and that the defendant materially increased (i.e. contributed to) the risk of that harm to the plaintiff, we can then infer that the defendant made a material contribution to (i.e. was a cause of) the plaintiff's injury.

To the extent that this theory is based on the calculation of probabilities rather than regular proof of causation of harm, it is somewhat analogous to the recognition of claims for the loss of a chance to avoid death that have been recognized elsewhere in the law of torts. But that also means that it faces the same obstacle of finding meaningful statistics about the relevant risks, so that the probabilities may be calculated on a rational basis. This might be less of a problem in asbestos cases than with other products, since asbestos has been so heavily studied; but it might, conversely, prove to be an even bigger problem if a case were to call for the risks associated with one specific product to be compared with the risks associated with a wholly different product or form of activity.

This leads on to the next issue, which asks how this approach (if adopted) should deal with a plaintiff who is partially to blame for his or her own injuries. One option would be to continue to approach the matter as one of relative contribution (including by the plaintiff) to the risk; the other would be to retreat back to the doctrine of comparative responsibility—which takes us back to where we began. Both approaches could mean requiring the courts to compare the incomparable.

Another question raised by the "contribution to risk" approach is whether non-tortious conduct which exposed the plaintiff to a risk of the very type of harm that s/he suffered should be included in the calculations. As Michael D. Green, *Second Thoughts about Apportionment in Asbestos Litigation*, 37 Sw. U.L. Rev 531, 545 (2008) has said:

> [I]f exposure to non-tortious sources of asbestos also create *(sic)* a risk of harm, there is no conceptual or practical reason why those exposures could not be apportioned along with the tortious causes, with the plaintiff bearing the share of risk attributed to non-tortious causes. We all, after all, "assume the risk" of non-tortiously caused harm, and this is just one more risk to which we are all subject without tort law providing compensation.

It is surely clear that, whatever approach is taken to proving causation and apportioning damages, it will inevitably be complicated and hard to administer in practice. This has led Green to conclude:

> [T]he most sensible way to address apportionment would be by enacting an administrative compensation scheme that would render apportionment moot. That recommendation [i]s based on recognition of the tremendous toll of litigation in this massest of mass torts. If we are going to continue the unfortunate path of litigating asbestos cases, let's recognize the ways in which it is different and make necessary adjustments. (37 Sw. U.L. Rev 531, 552.)

Interestingly, both the majority and minority views expressed in the House of Lords in *Barker* were considered unacceptable to the British Parliament, which promptly passed what is now § 3 of the Compensation Act 2006. This provides that a victim who can establish causation against any defendant using the principle in *Fairchild* is now entitled to claim compensation for the full extent of his injury from that defendant (even if it might have arisen from other, non-tortious, exposure). That defendant is, however, able to claim contributions from others who tortiously exposed the victim to asbestos. This effectively puts the burden of untraceable or impecunious defendants on the solvent defendants (and their insurers) rather than on the victim (or, in the case of the victim's inevitable death, the victim's family).

Questions

1. Since we do not yet fully understand the causal mechanisms by which asbestosis and mesothelioma are contracted, is it even meaningful to talk about either establishing causation of, or contribution to the risk of causing, either disease? Does Lord Reid's view make sense?

2. Because litigating asbestos cases is "unfortunate," should we "recognize the ways in which it is different and make necessary adjustments"?

3. If the answer to question (2) is in the affirmative, should such adjustments apply to every disease known to be caused by asbestos, or only to its signature diseases?

4. Does it make sense to distinguish requirements for proof of causation from those concerning apportionment of damages?

5. What are the differences in practice between apportioning responsibility for causing an injury according to (a) the degree of harm caused, (b) the degree of risk of harm to which each party contributed, (c) the degree of exposure to the causative agent, and (d) the degree of fault by each party?

6. Which is the preferable approach and why? Does it make a difference whether the injury sustained is a "regular" injury, or one of the signature asbestos diseases?

7. Whenever one of the approaches (a), (b), or (c) in question (5) above is adopted to apportion liability, should innocent (i.e. non-tortious) conduct which contributed to the harm, risk of harm, or exposure be included in, or excluded from, the relevant calculation?

Herber v. Johns-Manville Corp.

785 F.2d 79 (3rd Cir. 1986)

STAPLETON, J. In the course of his employment as a pipefitter, Mr. Herber was exposed to asbestos products. In 1978, he was diagnosed as having pleural thickening, a condition associated with exposure to asbestos. He brought a products liability action against appellees in the district court claiming damages under a strict liability theory. The court denied Herber's proffer of evidence that his exposure to appellees' asbestos had increased the risk of his developing a cancer. The court did so on the alternative bases of insufficiency under New Jersey tort law and undue prejudice under Federal Rule of Evidence 403. This ruling prevented Herber from seeking damages from the jury for the increased risk of developing a future cancer, the future cancer itself, the cost of medical monitoring for signs of cancer, and fear of the future cancer.

A jury, in special interrogatories, found that Herber's lungs manifested exposure to appellees' asbestos products, that appellees were liable for any harm caused by this exposure, that Herber had suffered a physical injury (apparently the pleural thickening), but that Herber had suffered no loss for which compensation should be paid. Specifically, the jury found that the plaintiff had experienced an "injury to his lungs," that exposure to appellees' "asbestos containing products" was the proximate cause of plaintiff's injury, and that the "sum of money [that] would fairly, reasonably, and adequately compensate plaintiff for injuries attributable to defendants' products" was "none." The trial court entered a judgment in favor of appellant in the amount of zero dollars. This timely appeal followed.

II. THE FUTURE CANCER CLAIM

Under *Erie R.R. Co. v. Tompkins*, 304 U.S. 64, 58 S.Ct. 817 (1938), we are required to apply the law of the state in which the district court sat. When the state law is unclear, we are required to predict what the state's highest court would rule. *Commission v. Estate of Bosch*, 387 U.S. 456, 87 S.Ct. 1776, 18 L.Ed.2d 886 (1967). Decisions of lower state courts are not controlling upon us but we acknowledge their expertise in analyzing the law of their state and give appropriate deference.

Noting that Mr. Herber had proffered no expert opinion or other evidence that would permit a factual finding that he will more likely than not experience cancer in the future, the district court held that New Jersey law does not provide compensation for an increased risk of a future injury that remains a possibility rather than a probability. As a result, the district court refused to permit the existence of this element of alleged damage to be litigated. We hold that the court did not err in this regard.

New Jersey law clearly recognizes a cause of action for anticipated future harm. In *Coll v. Sherry*, 29 N.J. 166, 175, 148 A.2d 481, 486 (1959), the New Jersey Supreme Court set out the general rule that "[i]f the prospective consequences may, in reasonable probability be expected to flow from the past harm, plaintiff is entitled to be indemnified for them." The New Jersey Supreme Court has applied this rule to a claim for prospective cancer. In *Lorenc v. Chemirad Corp.*, 37 N.J. 56, 76, 179 A.2d 401, 411 (1962), defendant's negligence caused plaintiff to burn his hand with a liquid of defendant's manufacture. Plaintiff sought compensation for the burn's effects, both present and future, including a probable malignancy. The New Jersey Supreme Court found no error in the trial court's instruction to the jury that "in order to make an award ... [as compensation for the malignancy, the jury] must find, by the greater weight of the believable evidence, that plaintiff has shown 'he will probably develop malignancy because of this injury.'"

Herber has thus alleged an injury, a future cancer, cognizable under New Jersey law. However, he did not proffer evidence of a probable future cancer as required by both *Lorenc* and *Coll*. Recognizing this fact, Herber argues that he should nevertheless be compensated for the present increased risk of the future cancer attributable to appellees' asbestos. That is, Herber urges that he should be allowed to introduce evidence that, because of his exposure to asbestos, the chance that he will develop a cancer has significantly increased. This increase in risk, says Herber, is an element of the damage he has actually suffered and should be considered in the calculation of his damage award. In his view, he should thus receive an amount equal to the amount one having an asbestos-caused cancer would receive, proportionately reduced to reflect the probability that he will not contract cancer.

We view Herber's argument as fundamentally at odds with New Jersey's approach to compensable injury. *Coll* and *Lorenc* stand for the proposition that a future injury, to be compensable, must be shown to be a reasonable medical probability. The objective of this approach is not only to provide compensation for harm that is likely to occur but also to ensure that an award of damages is not made for an injury that probably will not be suffered. Since this is venerable and well settled New Jersey policy, we are not disposed to predict a departure from this case law in the absence of signposts pointing clearly in that direction. We find none.

The New Jersey Supreme Court has expressly reserved decision on the issue of "[w]hether 'increased risk,' standing alone, is an actionable element of damage...," and we have been referred to no opinion of that Court which suggests to us that it is prepared to recognize increased risk as an independent injury. Nor has Herber's argument found favor in the lower courts of New Jersey. We have found no reported opinion endorsing it and there are two well-reasoned opinions rejecting it. *Devlin v. Johns-Manville Corp.*, 202 N.J.Super. 556, 495 A.2d 495 (Law Div.1985); *Ayers v. Jackson Twp.*, 189 N.J.Super. 561, 461 A.2d 184 (Law Div.1983), vacated on other grounds, 202 N.J.Super. 106, 493 A.2d 1314 (App.Div.1985).

In addition to the absence of supporting authority, we perceive no practical or policy grounds which might move the New Jersey Supreme Court to fashion new doctrine in this area. As both the *Ayers* and *Devlin* courts noted, for example, New Jersey recognizes cancer as an injury separate and distinct from asbestosis and, accordingly, recognizes a cause of action for cancer which does not accrue until one has discovered, or should have discovered, that one has such an injury. See *Ross v. Johns-Manville Corp.*, 766 F.2d 823 (3d Cir.1985) (discussing New Jersey law). Thus, in New Jersey, Mr. Herber and others similarly situated run no risk that judicial relief will be unavailable should they hereafter contract cancer.

Herber finds in New Jersey Supreme Court's recognition of a "lost chance" cause of action in *Evers v. Dollinger, supra*, some intimation that it might be willing to embrace recovery for increased risk. We, however, find no such intimation.

Under the lost chance doctrine, a plaintiff can recover for damage suffered as the result of nonfeasance that reduced the probability of avoiding an injury actually sustained. The degree of causation required under the lost chance doctrine is lower than that traditionally required. Rather than requiring "but for" causation, the lost chance doctrine requires only a showing that the defendant's negligence was a "substantial factor" in the causation of the injury. Thus, where a physician negligently fails to diagnose breast cancer that subsequent to his nonfeasance becomes malignant, New Jersey law permits the plaintiff to recover upon showing that the physician's failure was a "substantial factor" in the development of the malignancy....

But the change in the degree of causation accompanying the adoption of the lost chance doctrine does not imply a change in New Jersey's view of cognizable injury. Moreover, the lost chance rule only applies to injuries already incurred....

IV. THE EMOTIONAL DISTRESS CLAIM

The district court ruled that appellant could not present to the jury evidence of the emotional anguish he has allegedly suffered as a result of his fear of cancer. This ruling was based on the view that New Jersey law did not permit recovery for such distress absent evidence that it has resulted in physical injury or sickness. In reaching this conclusion, the district court relied upon a decision of the New Jersey Superior Court which states that " ... proof of substantial bodily injury or sickness as a result of the emotional trauma remains as an essential element of proof." *Ayers* 461 A.2d at 189.

We conclude that the *Ayers* case is inapposite in the situation before us and that the trial court erred in refusing to entertain Herber's claim for emotional distress.

In *Evers*, 471 A.2d 405, the Supreme Court of New Jersey expressly recognized a claim for emotional harm based on a fear of future cancer. In this malpractice action, the defendant physician had negligently failed to diagnose and treat a cancer in the plaintiff's breast that ultimately had to be removed in a radical mastectomy. The plaintiff had been prepared to show in the trial court that "she suffered anxiety, emotional anguish and mental distress" resulting in part "from the realization, following the confirmation of her malignancy, that defendant's delay in her treatment had increased the risk that she would again fall victim, perhaps fatally, to the disease." *Evers*, 471 A.2d at 409. The Supreme Court held that this was a viable claim ...

The defendants in *Devlin*, like the district court in this case, relied heavily on the *Ayers* case. We find the *Devlin* court's distinction between our situation and that before the court in *Ayers* to be persuasive:

> The recent case of *Ayers v. Jackson Twp.*, 189 N.J.Super. 561, 461 A.2d 184 (Law Div.1983) in which plaintiffs were denied recovery for their fear of future cancer is clearly distinguishable from the case at bar. None of the plaintiffs in *Ayers* were presently suffering from physical illness as a result of their ingestion of pollutants. The experts in that case conceded that there was no way to ascertain if any of the plaintiffs would in fact ever suffer from any illness in the future. The

emotional injury of which plaintiffs in this case complain stems from the substantial bodily harm they have already suffered as a result of ingesting asbestos over an extended period of time. In this case there has been "[i]mmediate and direct physical impact and injury" which was non existent in factual situations presented in *Ayers*.

In New Jersey, as in most states, the law of damages in cases involving no physical impact and injury has had a development largely independent of the law of damages in physical impact and injury cases. While there are signs of a possible confluence and there has been some recent movement in the New Jersey law governing situations like the one in *Ayers*, we believe the New Jersey law in physical impact and injury cases is well settled. Because the jury in this case found that exposure to the defendants' asbestos had caused pleural thickening, we are confident that the Supreme Court of New Jersey would treat Mr. Herber's emotional distress claim no differently than a pain and suffering claim in a slip and fall case. While the appellees' intimate that the infiltration of Mr. Herber's lungs may be characterized as involving little impact and the pleural thickening as involving insubstantial injury, only slight impact and injury have been found by the New Jersey courts to warrant recovery for emotional distress caused by fear. See, e.g., *Porter v. Delaware L. & W.R.R. Co.*, 73 N.J.L. 405, 63 A. 860 (1906) (plaintiff hit by dust and light debris from falling bridge entitled to recover in claim for fright).

In short, Herber's failure to proffer evidence of a consequential physical manifestation of his fear of cancer does not mean that he has no compensable claim for emotional distress under New Jersey law. The district court therefore erred in holding otherwise.

The district court held, in the alternative, that evidence of fear of cancer was unduly prejudicial and would be excludable under Rule of Evidence 403. Since barring mention of the future harm that a plaintiff presently fears effectively precludes proof of a claim based on that fear, we hold that the court's ruling under Rule 403 was abusive of discretion. We believe a properly instructed jury can responsibly distinguish between a claim for a future cancer and a claim for present anxiety about a possible future cancer....

The new trial should thus focus on whether Herber suffers from emotional distress caused by exposure to the defendants' products and whether he requires medical monitoring for signs of cancer as a result of that exposure.

Vacated and remanded.

Notes

1. ***Stapletons.*** Judge Stapleton and Professor Jane Stapleton are *not* the same person!

2. ***Medical monitoring.*** In *Simmons v. Pacor, Inc.*, 674 A.2d 232 (1996), a case along the same lines as *Herber*, the Supreme Court of Pennsylvania held that: (1) asymptomatic pleural thickening, *i.e.*, unaccompanied by disabling consequences or physical impairment, is not compensable injury, so that (2) plaintiffs could not recover for emotional distress, but that (3) those with asbestos-related asymptomatic pleural thickening can recover for the costs of medical monitoring.

3. ***The English approach (again).*** The House of Lords in England took a rather different approach in *Rothwell v. Chemical & Insulating Co. Ltd.*, [2007] UKHL 39. There the claimants had been negligently exposed to asbestos dust with the foreseeable consequences that they had developed pleural plaques (areas of fibrous thickening of the pleural membrane which surrounds the lungs), were at risk of developing one or more long-term as-

bestos-related diseases, and now suffered anxiety at that prospect. Giving judgment for the House, Lord Hoffmann said:

> Save in very exceptional cases, [the pleural plaques] cause no symptoms. Nor do they cause other asbestos-related diseases. But they signal the presence in the lungs and pleura of asbestos fibres which may independently cause life-threatening or fatal diseases such as asbestosis or mesothelioma. In consequence, a diagnosis of pleural plaques may cause the patient to contemplate his future with anxiety or even suffer clinical depression.
>
> Proof of damage is an essential element in a claim in negligence and in my opinion the symptomless plaques are not compensatable damage. Neither do the risk of future illness or anxiety about the possibility of that risk materialising amount to damage for the purpose of creating a cause of action, although the law allows both to be taken into account in computing the loss suffered by someone who has actually suffered some compensatable physical injury and therefore has a cause of action. In the absence of such compensatable injury, however, there is no cause of action under which damages may be claimed and therefore no computation of loss in which the risk and anxiety may be taken into account.

4. *What counts as harm?* In *Herber*, *Simmons*, and *Rothwell* the courts recognized that pleural thickening typically produces no symptoms and that, in such cases, there is therefore no harm for which compensation can be awarded. Where they differ is that, while the House of Lords was prepared to consider only physical injury as compensable harm, the American courts were prepared to contemplate other types of harm. For the House of Lords, therefore, evidence of pleural thickening without more meant that the claimant failed to establish one of the required elements of the tort of negligence. For the American courts, however, the presence of pleural thickening was clear *evidence* of a different kind of legally-recognized harm.

Questions

1. Why do courts insist that victims must establish that they have suffered physical harm in order to be able to claim compensation for their emotional distress?

2. Do you prefer the American or English approach to identifying physical harm?

3. What are the implications of the two approaches so far as the application of a statute of limitations is concerned?

4. *Herber* and *Simmons* do differ in one significant respect, for the former considered a claim for emotional distress permissible, while the latter did not. Which is the better view?

Pustejovsky v. Rapid-American Corporation
35 S.W.3d 643 (2000) (Supreme Court of Texas)

GONZALES J. This case raises the question whether a plaintiff may bring separate actions for separate latent occupational diseases caused by exposure to asbestos. Specifically, we must decide whether the single action rule or the statute of limitations bars Henry Pustejovsky, who settled an asbestosis suit with one defendant in 1982, from bringing suit against different defendants twelve years later for asbestos-related cancer. The trial court granted summary judgment for the defendants based on limitations. The court of appeals affirmed, holding that under the single action rule, Pustejovsky's cause of action for cancer accrued, and limitations began to run, when he knew of the asbestosis. We conclude, however, that neither the single action rule nor the statute of limitations bars Pustejovsky's later claim for asbestos-related cancer. Accordingly, we reverse the court of appeals' judgment and remand this case to the trial court for further proceedings consistent with this opinion....

As Dr. Robb testified, asbestosis is a non-malignant disease caused by inhaling asbestos dust. When inhaled, asbestos fibers may begin a scarring process that destroys air sacs in the lung where oxygen is transferred into the blood. The condition is marked by decreased pulmonary function and lung capacity. Symptoms include shortness of breath, a dry and unproductive cough, and in some cases, weight loss and chest pain. The scarring is progressive and incurable, but it is not always fatal. According to Dr. Robb, the latency period between toxic exposure and manifestation of asbestosis is typically fifteen to twenty-five years.

Dr. Robb testified further that mesothelioma is a malignant tumor in the membranes lining the lungs, abdomen, and chest. The cancer is a very painful and severely debilitating disease that almost always causes the victim's death within seven to fifteen months of diagnosis. The latency period for mesothelioma is generally over fifteen years, averages thirty to forty years, and in some cases can extend as long as seventy years.

Dr. Robb explained that mesothelioma does not have any causal connection to asbestosis. While both diseases are associated with exposure to asbestos, mesothelioma is not dependant on a precondition of asbestosis, and asbestosis does not necessarily develop into, or cause the development of, mesothelioma. According to Dr. Robb, approximately fifteen percent of asbestosis victims also contract mesothelioma....

In his summary judgment response, Pustejovsky argued that because the diseases are separate, distinct conditions, his asbestosis diagnosis could not trigger limitations for a disease that would not manifest for another twelve years. Because he brought suit for mesothelioma in less than a year of its diagnosis, Pustejovsky contends that limitations does not bar his present suit.

The defendants did not offer medical evidence controverting Dr. Robb's testimony. Rather, Rapid American argues that the fact that asbestosis and mesothelioma are distinct diseases does not matter because both diseases were caused by the same course of exposure to asbestos. Rapid American contends that the single action rule requires that the statute of limitations for all causes of action based on asbestos exposure began to run from the 1982 diagnosis of asbestosis. Therefore, it argues, Pustejovsky's present claim for mesothelioma is time-barred as a matter of law....

For several decades, courts have grappled with the problem of applying limitations to toxic exposure diseases with protracted latency periods, particularly when the exposure can cause more than one disease with different latency periods.... [S]ome courts consider the single action rule to be unmalleable and have applied the rule to different diseases caused by the same exposure. But other courts and commentators have recognized that the single action rule is a catch 22 for victims of multiple latent diseases, if applied to them the same as traditionally applied to victims of traumatic injuries. A plaintiff who sues for asbestosis is precluded from any recovery for a later-developing lethal mesothelioma. But the discovery rule would preclude a plaintiff with asbestosis from waiting to see if an asbestosis-related cancer later develops if, as Rapid American contends, all damages for exposure to asbestosis must be brought in a single suit.

A plaintiff suing for asbestosis could join that claim with a claim for the prospect of developing cancer in the future. But the plaintiff can only recover future damages for injury that the plaintiff has a reasonable medical probability of developing. According to the expert testimony here, only fifteen percent of asbestosis victims ever develop mesothelioma. If so, then no asbestosis plaintiff could establish future damages with the requisite certainty. Rapid American's position means for the asbestosis victim that any later-developing terminal condition must go un-redressed....

Most jurisdictions that have considered the question, however, allow separate actions for separate diseases arising from the same exposure to asbestos. An early case to treat distinct asbestos diseases separately is *Wilson v. Johns-Manville Sales Corp.*, 684 F.2d 111 (D.C.Cir.1982). In that case, an employee who developed mesothelioma several years after being diagnosed with asbestosis died without ever filing suit. When his widow sued, his employer asserted that the suit was untimely because limitations began to run upon the asbestosis diagnosis. The controlling issue was whether manifestation of any asbestos-related disease triggered limitations for all separate and district diseases. Speaking for the court, Judge Ruth Bader Ginsberg commented:

> In latent disease cases, [the] community interest would be significantly undermined by a judge-made rule that upon manifestation of any harm, the injured party must then, if ever, sue for all harms the same exposure may (or may not) occasion some time in the future.

The court concluded in that case that the plaintiff's asbestosis diagnosis did not start limitations to run on later developing mesothelioma....

In the typical case involving progressive injuries, the single action rule may occasionally result in uncompensated damages, in order to vindicate other competing interests. But in asbestos-related cases, in which multiple, latent injuries may manifest years or even decades apart, the rule would produce much more erratic results. The summary judgment record reveals that no amount of due diligence would have allowed Pustejovsky to recover for mesothelioma when he brought his suit for asbestosis. It is our long-established rule that a plaintiff may recover damages for a disease that may develop in future years only if the person establishes that there is a reasonable medical probability that the disease will appear. Courts have interpreted this test to mean that the plaintiff must demonstrate a greater than fifty percent chance of incurring the future damages. Under this rule, a plaintiff who has been injured by exposure to asbestos must demonstrate a greater than fifty percent chance of developing cancer to recover future damages related to the cancer. As one court noted in an asbestos case:

> Texas would permit a plaintiff to recover damages for a disease that may develop in future years only if he introduces expert testimony establishing that there is a reasonable medical probability that the disease will appear. "Possibility alone cannot serve as the basis for recovery, for mere possibility does not meet the preponderance of the evidence standard. Certainty, however, is not required: the plaintiff need demonstrate only that the event is more likely to occur than not."

Dartez, 765 F.2d at 466 (quoting *Gideon*, 761 F.2d at 1137) (holding the proof adduced did not establish a reasonable probability of developing cancer). But nothing in this record demonstrates that Pustejovsky had a greater than fifty percent chance of developing cancer at the time of his first suit. As with many similarly situated asbestosis sufferers, it is unlikely that Pustejovsky could have adduced evidence at the time of his first suit that would have allowed him to recover for his future risk of cancer. We conclude that applying a single accrual rule under these circumstances would be inconsistent with the transactional approach to res judicata, further supporting Pustejovsky's argument that we should adopt a separate accrual rule in this case....

Allowing separate limitations for separate disease processes does not betray the purposes that limitations and the single action rule serve. Like statutes of limitations, the single action rule is intended to discourage stale and fraudulent claims. But evidence about the litigation's crucial issue, whether the plaintiff actually has mesothelioma, only improves as the disease progresses from asymptomatic to diagnosable. If limitations for an asbestos-related malignancy runs from the discovery of the cancer then damages are tried for an existing, diagnosable disease instead of for the risk or fear of cancer.

The single action rule, like limitations and res judicata, serves the purpose of giving defendants a point of repose. However, a defendant is in no different position with respect to an asbestosis plaintiff who may develop mesothelioma in the future than with an individual who contracts mesothelioma without ever suffering asbestosis. And the defendant's need for repose must be balanced against the plaintiff's need of an opportunity to seek redress for the gravest injuries, those culminating in wrongful death.

An additional policy reason for the single action rule is the need to protect defendants from vexatious, piecemeal litigation and provide judicial economy. But having to defend against the potential for cancer in every asbestosis case, if we were to allow such a claim, is arguably more vexatious and judicially inefficient than allowing a separate action for actual cancer cases.

After considering the interests underlying the statute of limitations, the discovery rule, and the single action rule, we conclude that the prior asbestosis settlement does not bar Pustejovsky's suit for mesothelioma. We hold that a person who sues on or settles a claim for a non-malignant asbestos-related disease with one defendant is not precluded from a subsequent action against another defendant for a distinct malignant asbestos-related condition. The diagnosis of a malignant asbestos-related condition creates a new cause of action, and the statute of limitations governing the malignant asbestos-related condition begins when a plaintiff's symptoms manifest themselves to a degree or for a duration that would put a reasonable person on notice that he or she suffers from some injury and he or she knows, or with reasonable diligence should know, that the malignant asbestos-related condition is likely work-related....

We limit our holding to asbestos-related diseases resulting from workplace exposure ... We have considered on other occasions arguments that established doctrine and procedures must change to accommodate asbestos litigation, and on some occasions made those changes. The judicial system has had extensive experience dealing with the issues, and the relevant medical science is advanced. We are unaware of any other toxic-exposure torts currently in litigation that present these circumstances.

Reversed and remanded.

Questions

1. Mesothelioma is a form of lung cancer. If Mr. Pustejovsky had suffered a different form of lung cancer, instead of mesothelioma, would the result in this case have been the same?

2. Would the result have been the same if Mr. Pustejovsky had first developed not asbestosis, but a type of lung cancer other than mesothelioma, and then gone on to develop mesothelioma too?

3. Does the judgment in *Pustejovsky* effectively mean that defendants in toxic torts cases are unable to rely on the double jeopardy rule, because the victim may be suffering from a latent disease at the time of the initial litigation which manifests itself only some time later?

Stiffening the Rules of Causation

Although the rules regarding proof of causation have typically been relaxed where the plaintiff has suffered one of the signature asbestos diseases, some courts have recently become more reluctant to adopt this more relaxed approach. The Supreme Court of Texas is a leading example.

Borg-Warner Corporation v. Flores

232 S.W.3d 765 (2007) (Supreme Court of Texas)

JEFFERSON CJ. Sixty-six-year-old Arturo Flores is a retired brake mechanic. Flores spent much of his working life—from 1966 until his retirement in 2001—in the automotive department at Sears in Corpus Christi. While there, Flores handled several brands of brake pads, including those manufactured by Borg-Warner. Flores used Borg-Warner pads from 1972–75, on five to seven of the roughly twenty brake jobs he performed each week. Borg-Warner disk brake pads contained chrysotile asbestos fibers, fibers that comprised seven to twenty-eight percent of the pad's weight, depending on the particular type of pad. Flores's job involved grinding the pads so that they would not squeal. The grinding generated clouds of dust that Flores inhaled while working in a room that measured roughly eight by ten feet.

Flores sued Borg-Warner and others, alleging that he suffered from asbestosis caused by working with brakes for more than three decades. At the week-long trial, Flores presented the testimony of two experts, Dr. Dinah Bukowski, a board-certified pulmonologist, and Dr. Barry Castleman, Ph.D., an "independent consultant in . . . the field of toxic substance control." Dr. Bukowski examined Flores on a single occasion in May 2001. She reviewed Flores's x-rays, which revealed interstitial lung disease. Although there are more than 100 causes (including smoking) of such disease, Dr. Bukowski diagnosed Flores with asbestosis, based on his work as a brake mechanic coupled with an adequate latency period. According to Dr. Bukowski, asbestosis is "a form of interstitial lung disease, one of the scarring processes of the lungs caused from the inhalation of asbestos and found on biopsy to show areas of scarring in association with actual asbestos bodies or asbestos fibers." Dr. Bukowski noted that asbestosis can be fatal and is progressive, meaning that the scar tissue increases over time. Once inhaled, the fibers cannot be expelled, and there is no known cure for asbestosis. She asserted that Flores's asbestosis could worsen; that he could suffer stiffening of his lungs, loss of lung volume, and difficulty with oxygenation. She acknowledged that everyone is exposed to asbestos in the ambient air; "it's very plentiful in the environment, if you're a typical urban dweller." She conceded that Flores's pulmonary function tests showed mild obstructive lung disease, which was unrelated to asbestos exposure. . . .

Borg-Warner's expert, pulmonologist Dr. Kathryn Hale, examined Flores and testified that, in her opinion, he did not have asbestosis and that his x-rays did not show "any asbestos disease." She also testified that she had reviewed the literature, including epidemiological studies involving brake mechanics, and had not seen any articles indicating that auto mechanics suffered an increased risk of lung cancer or mesothelioma. She acknowledged that Flores's medical records included an x-ray report from a NIOSH certified B-reader physician who opined that Flores had "bilateral interstitial fibrotic changes consistent with asbestosis in a patient who has had an adequate exposure history and latency period," but Hale testified that she relied on criteria promulgated by the American Thoracic Society, and under those criteria, Flores did not have asbestosis.

The jury found that (1) Flores sustained an asbestos-related injury or disease; (2) Borg-Warner's negligence (as well as that of three other settling defendants) proximately caused Flores's asbestos-related injury or disease; (3) all four defendants were "engaged in the business of selling brake products"; and (4) the brake products had marketing, manufacturing, and design defects, each of which was a producing cause of Flores's injury. The jury apportioned to Borg-Warner 37% of the causation and 21% to each of the other three defendants. The jury awarded Flores $34,000 for future physical impairment, $34,000 for future medical care, $12,000 for past physical pain and mental anguish, and $34,000 for future physical pain and mental anguish....

The court of appeals affirmed....

Asbestosis appears to be dose-related, "so that the more one is exposed, the more likely the disease is to occur, and the higher the exposure the more severe the disease is likely to be." See 3 David L. Faigman et al., Modern Scientific Evidence: The Law And Science Of Expert Testimony § 28:22, at 447 (2007); cf. id. § 28:5, at 416 (noting that "it is generally accepted that one may develop mesothelioma from low levels of asbestos exposure"). While "[s]evere cases [of asbestosis] are usually the result of long-term, high-level exposure to asbestos, ... '[e]vidence of asbestosis has been found many years after relatively brief but extremely heavy exposure.'" Stephen J. Carroll et al., Rand Institute For Civil Justice, Asbestos Litigation 13 (2005) (citing American Thoracic Society, *The Diagnosis of Nonmalignant Diseases Related to Asbestos: 1996 Update: Official Statement of the American Thoracic Society*, 134 Am. Rev. Respiratory Disease 363, 363–68 (1996)). One text notes that:

> There is general agreement from epidemiologic studies that the development of asbestosis requires heavy exposure to asbestos ... in the range of 25 to 100 fibers per cubic centimeter year. Accordingly, asbestosis is usually observed in individuals who have had many years of high-level exposure, typically asbestos miners and millers, asbestos textile workers, and asbestos insulators. Andrew Churg, Nonneoplastic Disease Caused by Asbestos, in Pathology of Occupational Lung Disease 277, 313 (Andrew Churg & Francis H.Y. Green eds., Williams & Wilkins 1998) (1988).

This record, however, reveals nothing about how much asbestos Flores might have inhaled. He performed about fifteen to twenty brake jobs a week for over thirty years, and was therefore exposed to "some asbestos" on a fairly regular basis for an extended period of time. Nevertheless, absent any evidence of dose, the jury could not evaluate the quantity of respirable asbestos to which Flores might have been exposed or whether those amounts were sufficient to cause asbestosis. Nor did Flores introduce evidence regarding what percentage of that indeterminate amount may have originated in Borg-Warner products. We do not know the asbestos content of other brands of brake pads or how much of Flores's exposure came from grinding new pads as opposed to blowing out old ones. There were no epidemiological studies showing that brake mechanics face at least a doubled risk of asbestosis. See *Merrell Dow Pharms., Inc. v. Havner*, 953 S.W.2d 706, 715

(Tex.1997). While such studies are not necessary to prove causation, we have recognized that "properly designed and executed epidemiological studies may be part of the evidence supporting causation in a toxic tort case," and "the requirement of more than a doubling of the risk strikes a balance between the needs of our legal system and the limits of science." *Id.* at 717–18. Thus, while some respirable fibers may be released upon grinding some brake pads, the sparse record here contains no evidence of the approximate quantum of Borg-Warner fibers to which Flores was exposed, and whether this sufficiently contributed to the aggregate dose of asbestos Flores inhaled, such that it could be considered a substantial factor in causing his asbestosis. *Union Pump*, 898 S.W.2d at 775; *see also Rutherford v. Owens-Illinois, Inc.*, 16 Cal.4th 953, 67 Cal.Rptr.2d 16, 941 P.2d 1203, 1219 (Cal.1997)....

We recognize the proof difficulties accompanying asbestos claims. The long latency period for asbestos-related diseases, coupled with the inability to trace precisely which fibers caused disease and from whose product they emanated, make this process inexact. The Supreme Court of California has grappled with the appropriate causation standard in a case involving alleged asbestos-related cancer and acknowledged the difficulties in proof accompanying such claims:

> Plaintiffs cannot be expected to prove the scientifically unknown details of carcinogenesis, or trace the unknowable path of a given asbestos fiber.... [W]e can bridge this gap in the humanly knowable by holding that plaintiffs may prove causation in asbestos-related cancer cases by demonstrating that the plaintiff's exposure to defendant's asbestos-containing product in reasonable medical probability was a substantial factor in contributing to the aggregate dose of asbestos the plaintiff or decedent inhaled or ingested, and hence to the risk of developing asbestos-related cancer, without the need to demonstrate that fibers from the defendant's particular product were the ones, or among the ones, that actually produced the malignant growth. *Rutherford*, 67 Cal.Rptr.2d 16, 941 P.2d at 1219.

Thus, substantial-factor causation, which separates the speculative from the probable, need not be reduced to mathematical precision. Defendant-specific evidence relating to the approximate dose to which the plaintiff was exposed, coupled with evidence that the dose was a substantial factor in causing the asbestos-related disease, will suffice. As one commentator notes,

> [i]t is not adequate to simply establish that "some" exposure occurred. Because most chemically induced adverse health effects clearly demonstrate "thresholds," there must be reasonable evidence that the exposure was of sufficient magnitude to exceed the threshold before a likelihood of "causation" can be inferred. Eaton, 12 J.L. & Pol'y at 39.

Dr. Bukowski acknowledged that asbestos is "plentiful" in the ambient air and that "everyone" is exposed to it. If a single fiber could cause asbestosis, however, "everyone" would be susceptible. No one suggests this is the case. Given asbestos's prevalence, therefore, some exposure "threshold" must be demonstrated before a claimant can prove his asbestosis was caused by a particular product.

In analyzing the legal sufficiency of Flores's negligence claim, then, the court of appeals erred in holding that "[i]n the context of asbestos-related claims, if there is sufficient evidence that the defendant supplied *any* of the asbestos to which the plaintiff was exposed, then the plaintiff has met the burden of proof." 153 S.W.3d at 213 (emphasis added).... We note too, that proof of causation may differ depending on the product at issue; "[i]n some products, the asbestos is embedded and fibers are not likely to become loose or air-borne, [while] [i]n other products, the asbestos is friable." *In re Ethyl Corp.*, 975 S.W.2d 606, 617 (Tex.1998). We have recognized that "[t]his, of course, bears on the extent and intensity of exposure to asbestos," *Ethyl Corp.*, 975 S.W.2d at 617, two factors central to causation. We have described situations in which workers were "so covered with asbestos as to be dubbed 'the snowmen of Grand Central.'" *Temple-Inland*, 993 S.W.2d at 95. That is not the situation here, where the asbestos at issue was embedded in the brake pads. Dr. Castleman testified that brake mechanics could be exposed to "some" respirable fibers when grinding pads or blowing out housings, and Flores testified that the grinding generated dust. Without more, we do not know the contents of that dust, including the approximate quantum of fibers to which Flores was exposed, and in keeping with the *de minimis* rule espoused in *Lohrmann* and required by our precedent, we conclude the evidence of causation in this case was legally insufficient. *Lohrmann*, 782 F.2d at 1162; *Union Pump*, 898 S.W.2d at 775.

Judgment reversed, and rendered for Borg-Warner.

Questions

1. Did the Supreme Court of Texas render judgment for the defendant in *Borg-Warner* on the grounds of a lack of proof of general causation or specific causation?

2. What sort of evidence would have been sufficient to enable Mr. Flores's claim to succeed?

3. Would Mr. Flores's claim have been more likely to succeed if he had had a different occupation (but otherwise the evidence was identical)?

4. Could the decision in *Borg-Warner* be equally applicable to cases of mesothelioma?

5. Do you agree with the decision in *Borg-Warner*?

Hypothetical

George worked for six years as a delivery driver, during which time he regularly visited businesses where asbestos was used. It now turns out both that he has been continually exposed to asbestos dust and that he has contracted mesothelioma. The various parties to the case have stipulated that such exposures were negligent. The current state of medical evidence regarding mesothelioma tells us that:

1. The greater the exposure to asbestos dust, the more likely it is that the exposed person will contract mesothelioma (but we do not know whether it is contracted by one "insult" or a threshold mechanism); and

2. The degree of exposure to asbestos dust makes no difference to the severity of the disease.

George's exposure to asbestos was first to that of Business A for two years, then to that of Business B for two years, and then to that of Business C for two years. Which (if any) of these businesses is liable to compensate George for the mesothelioma that he has now contracted, and for what percentage of his injuries?

Part IV

Affirmative Defenses

Chapter 11

Defenses Based on the Victim's Own Conduct

Affirmative Defenses

An affirmative defense excuses or exonerates the defendant's conduct even though the victim may be able to establish a *prima facie* case of liability, and has the effect of reducing or eliminating entirely the defendant's liability to pay compensation for the victim's injury. In a sense, then, the defendant gets two bites at the cherry: the first involves attempting to deny one or more elements of the plaintiff's case, while the second—using an affirmative defense—involves saying that, even if the victim's allegations can be established on a preponderance of the evidence, the defendant should nevertheless still not be held liable to pay compensation.

Examples of the first category include assertions that the product in question was supplied without a warranty, or that no false representation was made, or that the product was not defective, or that the product or representation did not cause the harm of which the plaintiff complains. While these arguments, if accepted by the judge and/or jury, certainly provide the defendant with a defense to the plaintiff's claims, they are not what the law calls "affirmative defenses." The point of such pleas is simply to deny one or elements of the plaintiff's theory of the case, and so argue that the plaintiff is unable to prove, on a preponderance of the evidence, one or more of the elements necessary to establish a *prima facie* case.

Doctrines which the law labels "affirmative defenses" are, by contrast, those which deny the plaintiff the ability to recover some, or all, of the compensation claimed despite his or her already having established a *prima facie* case of liability against the defendant. Proof of a *prima facie* case creates a rebuttable presumption that the plaintiff is entitled to a remedy; an affirmative defense rebuts that presumption. A good example of the distinction is *Boatland of Houston, Inc. v. Valerie Bailey*, 609 S.W.2d 743 (1980), which was discussed in Chapter 7 (and to which we shall return later in this Chapter). There the Supreme Court of Texas held that a plea that a design met the state of the art was not an affirmative defense, but amounted to a denial of the plaintiff's claim of design defect. Unable to prove a defect, the plaintiff failed to establish a *prima facie* case.

The distinction between denying an element of the plaintiff's *prima facie* case and denying liability *despite* the plaintiff's *prima facie* case is not merely semantic. In the former, both the burden of production of the evidence and the burden of persuasion fall on the plaintiff. With the latter, although the burden of persuasion remains with the plaintiff, the burden of production shifts to the defendant. This is the reason for the label, "affirmative defenses." In order for an affirmative defense to be effective, the defendant cannot simply deny the plaintiff's allegations and leave the onus on the latter to overcome these denials, but must instead affirmatively plead a specific defense and produce evidence to support such a plea.

Affirmative defenses typically available to a defendant in a products liability case may broadly be divided into three groups. The first concerns the conduct of the victim, and implicates the defenses of assumption of risk, contributory negligence, and comparative fault. Those are the defenses that will be tackled in this Chapter.

The second group concerns defenses based on lapses of time, after which a victim may be barred from seeking compensation. Such lapses of time include defenses based on statutes of limitation and of repose. The third group involves contracts between the defendant and third parties. Instances of such defenses include contracts with other businesses in the distribution chain, contracts involving the sale or purchase of another company's assets (including the right to manufacture the defective product), and contracts to manufacture products for the federal government. Defenses based on lapse of time will be considered in Chapter 12, while those involving third party contracts will be tackled in Chapter 13.

Defenses Based on the Victim's Own Conduct

Affirmative defenses that are based on the victim's own conduct are, unfortunately, beset by four common confusions. The first confuses the entirely distinct defenses of consent and voluntary assumption of risk. The second concerns the question of whether the relevant determinations to be made are questions of law for the court, or of fact for the jury. The third relates to the interplay between assumption of risk and comparative fault. The fourth confuses comparative fault and comparative causation. Each of these issues will be considered in the course of this Chapter.

Let us tackle the first confusion first. According to the common law, "to one who consents, there can be no injury" or, as it sometimes expressed in a Latinism, *volenti non fit injuria.* In other words, a victim who consented to the harm cannot subsequently claim recompense from the person who caused it. The consent of the victim provides the person responsible for causing the harm with a complete defense. A good example is a patient's consent to surgery. Without such consent (which we consider implicit in an emergency), the surgeon would be committing a battery. Another example is sexual intercourse: without consent, such conduct would again amount to a battery (and, perhaps, assault and false imprisonment too), as well as the criminal offense of rape. Yet another example is boxing: acts that would otherwise amount to the torts of assault (apprehending an immediate battery), battery (being struck forcefully), and possibly even false imprisonment (being confined within the ring by the ropes) are transformed by the boxer's consent into entirely justifiable behavior.

The first point to be made, then, is that consent is a defense to cases of potentially *intentional* torts. This makes sense because it is very difficult to see how someone can consent to negligent conduct. A surgeon performing an operation to which the patient has consented is not absolved from blame if, for example, she negligently removes the patient's gall bladder instead of his appendix. Nor is the anesthetist immune from suit if she administers nitrous oxide instead of oxygen.

It is, of course, possible that injury—even very serious injury, or death—might result from surgery that is carried out to the highest possible standard of care, since no-one can guarantee an injury-free outcome, and those undergoing surgery are often already ill. But the fact that serious injury might result from the surgical team's entirely ethical and professional conduct does not mean that they will be excused from causing equivalent or lesser injury if they act negligently. So the second point to note is that, when the defense of consent is implicated, it relates to the type of conduct of the potential defendant, not to the injury or potential outcome of the conduct.

In other words, the defense of consent applies so as to negate the tortiousness of the defendant's conduct. The plaintiff's consent makes the defendant's otherwise tortious conduct justifiable. A boxer consents to being punched on the head and upper torso, and so transforms those blows from acts of assault and battery into legitimate sporting activity. Since consensual acts are justified and not tortious, the perpetrator cannot be held liable for any injuries that may be suffered as a consequence.

We can, thirdly, draw the conclusion that the defense of consent will ordinarily be irrelevant to potential cases of products liability. Manufacturers and distributors of defective products are not engaged in the commission of intention torts such as assault, battery, and false imprisonment. Neither do those using such products consent to the manufacturers' and distributors' conduct. Indeed, it is extremely difficult to see what such "consent" could possibly look like. The only cases where there is likely to be any discussion of consent concerns the issues of express or implied warranties, where it might be argued that the victim expressly or implicitly consented to something that the manufacturer or distributor had done. Even then, however, the issue at stake would not implicate any affirmative defense. It would simply be an instance of a defendant's arguing that there was no actionable breach of warranty: in other words, a denial of an element of the victim's *prima facie* case rather than a plea of an affirmative defense in spite of proof of the victim's *prima facie* case.

Assumption of Risk

In products liability cases, the relevant defense, with which consent is commonly confused, is that known by the somewhat misleading label of "voluntary assumption of risk." The label is misleading because it is generally agreed that this defense can be presented in either of two forms: express and implied. While express (or primary) assumption of risk is exactly what it says—and typically occurs when someone signs a waiver or disclaimer—implied (or secondary) assumption of risk does not require any conscious consideration of the matter by the plaintiff, and is simply "deemed" by the law to have been present by extrapolation from the circumstances of that person's conduct.

A conclusion that someone impliedly assumed the risk is not, therefore, the result of a painstaking attempt to ascertain the victim's attitude to the risk, but is simply a conclusion essentially foisted on the parties by the courts after the fact. That is not to say that the notion of implied assumption of risk is necessarily unjustifiable. It is, rather, to emphasize something that should really be obvious but which nevertheless gets frequently overlooked: *deeming* that a person assumed a risk is nothing like the same thing as a finding that the person actually, voluntarily, assented to it. This is amply demonstrated by the following case.

Sheehan v. The North American Marketing Corp.
610 F.3d 144 (1st Cir. 2010)

SAYLOR, J. This is an appeal of a decision granting summary judgment in a product liability action arising out of a tragic swimming pool accident. Plaintiff-appellant Jennifer

Sheehan is a resident of Rhode Island. Defendants-appellees The North American Marketing Corp. ("NAMCO") and Delair Group, LLC, are a seller and manufacturer, respectively, of swimming pools. Jurisdiction is based on diversity of citizenship.

Sheehan suffered a catastrophic injury in 2002 when she broke her neck attempting to dive into a shallow, above-ground pool. As a result of the accident, she was rendered a quadriplegic. She brought suit for negligence, strict liability, breach of express warranty, and breach of implied warranty, alleging in substance that the design of the pool was defective. The district court granted summary judgment on the grounds that Sheehan assumed the risk of serious injury when she attempted the dive and that her proof of proximate cause was unduly speculative. While we are less certain as to the causation issue, we find that the assumption of risk defense applies as a matter of law. We accordingly affirm.

Background

On August 8, 2002, at about 1:30 p.m., Sheehan and Marvin Nadiger drove to the Islander Restaurant in Warwick, Rhode Island. Sheehan was then thirty-two years old. At the restaurant, the two shared a scorpion bowl, a drink made with fruit juice and alcohol. After leaving the restaurant, they drove to the Oakland Beach Club in Warwick, where Sheehan drank two or three twelve-ounce beers and had one or two shots of tequila. They then drove to Nadiger's home in Warwick, arriving at approximately 5:30 p.m. Not long after arriving, Nadiger, Sheehan, and Nadiger's three children decided to go swimming in the pool located in his backyard.

The swimming pool was an above-ground "Johnny Weismuller Safari" model manufactured by Delair and sold by NAMCO. It was 18 feet in diameter and four feet high. At the time of the incident, the pool was filled with about three and one-half feet of water. A ladder over the edge of the pool was used for entry and exit. There was no decking or other platform next to the pool.

The top perimeter of the pool was covered by a piece known as a "coping." The coping was made of flat extruded aluminum with ridges or grooves on its surface. It was approximately six and one-half inches wide inches wide. Its function was to connect the pieces of the pool wall and prevent damage to the top surface of the wall.

It is undisputed that the coping was not intended to be stood upon or used for diving.

The pool contained at least four relevant warning labels.

First, there was a warning sign on the coping where the ladder entered the pool. That sign stated "DANGER" in bold red capital letters against a white background. That was followed by the words "NO DIVING-SHALLOW WATER-DIVING MAY CAUSE DEATH OR PERMANENT INJURY." Those words were in bold black capital letters. There was also a pictogram showing a person striking his head on the bottom of the pool, with red lines suggesting an injury to the neck; the drawing was in a red circle with a red diagonal slash across it.

Second, there was a sign stating "DANGER-NO DIVING-SHALLOW WATER" on the inside portion of the coping above the waterline, visible to persons within the pool. The warning faced the inside of the pool, approximately one-third of the way around the circumference from the ladder. The sign on the coping was approximately 1.25 inches high in bold red capital letters against a white background.

Third, there was an identical sign stating "DANGER-NO DIVING-SHALLOW WATER" approximately two-thirds of the way around the pool from the ladder.

Fourth, on each of the three slip-resistant ladder treads on the outside of the pool, there was an embossed sign that stated "DANGER-SHALLOW WATER-DO NOT DIVE OR JUMP" in capital letters.

Sheehan testified that she did not read the warnings, but even if she had, she would have dived anyway....

While playing with the children, but before attempting her first dive, Sheehan noticed that the "thin metal" coping around the top edge of the pool "wasn't springy, but it wasn't sturdy either. It was kind of loose."

After playing in the pool for about thirty minutes, Sheehan hoisted herself up into a sitting position and then to a standing position on the coping. She stood on the coping for about twenty seconds and then performed a shallow dive, during which she intentionally aimed across the pool and not down. Sheehan testified that she was aware that diving into shallow water could be dangerous because she could hit her head on the bottom of the pool. However, she also testified that the only danger she thought she was facing was that she could get scraped on the bottom of the pool, and that she had never heard of anyone getting hurt from diving into shallow water.

Sheehan successfully executed her first dive without injury. She came up out of the water in front of Nadiger, who was in the pool. According to Nadiger, at that point he said, "Can't you read? You can't dive," and pointed to the warning on the side of the pool. He testified that both of them then laughed.

Sheehan then climbed onto the same part of the coping to attempt a second dive. She again pulled herself up into a sitting and then a standing position on the coping. After standing on the coping for about ten seconds, she attempted to perform a shallow dive. As she was attempting to dive, she lost her balance and entered the pool at a steep angle, described by witnesses as a "jackknife." She struck her head on the bottom of the pool, which caused her to suffer a burst fracture of the C5 vertebra. The injury rendered her a quadriplegic.

Sheehan testified that she did not know what caused her to lose her balance or how she slipped during her second dive: "I don't know. I just lost my balance and slipped." She does not know where her arms and feet were positioned before and during her second dive, nor does she know how she entered the pool during her second dive. She could only recall looking at her feet as she stood on the coping and then entering the water.

Sheehan's blood-alcohol level, which was taken at the hospital when she arrived later that evening, was 0.16%. According to the report of the toxicologist, her blood-alcohol level at the time of the injury was likely even higher, between 0.169% and 0.178%. Individuals with this blood-alcohol level typically show outward signs of intoxication—e.g., a staggered gait, impaired vision, and decreased reaction time—though Sheehan herself denied feeling any impairment from the alcohol while diving.

Expert Evidence

All parties submitted expert reports in support of their positions in the summary judgment proceedings. There is no dispute that Sheehan's injuries were caused by the top of her head striking the bottom of the pool. One of Sheehan's experts suggested that the injury could have been avoided if she had successfully performed her second dive in the same manner as the first dive. Sheehan also offered evidence to support her allegation that the coping was defective in its design and was the proximate cause of her injury.

Her engineering expert, Gaston L. Raffaelli, opined that the coping was defective because it was unstable and narrow. He stated that it was foreseeable that pool users would use the narrow coping as a resting place and that swimmers would easily hoist themselves onto it because it was only a few inches above the water. He further opined that it was foreseeable that pool users would stand on the coping and re-enter the pool by either jumping or diving into it. He also stated that the presence of the narrow and unstable coping was a danger to pool users because they could lose their balance and topple into the pool in an uncontrolled manner. In Raffaelli's opinion, Sheehan's injury would have been avoided had the defendants designed the pool in a way to prevent pool users from standing on the coping. He suggested that this could have been accomplished by installing a design modification, such as a cap, that would prevent users from accessing the coping of the pool.

Her aquatic safety expert, Thomas C. Ebro, expressed a similar opinion. He opined that the narrow and unstable nature of the six-inch coping was inherently dangerous because pool users could easily stand on top of it, thereby subjecting them to the risk of losing their balance and falling into or out of the pool. He also suggested that the manufacturer should have incorporated a rounded cap over the coping to prevent pool users from standing on or obtaining access to it. He stated that, in his opinion, had the defendants incorporated such a design, Sheehan's injuries would have been avoided.

The District Court's Ruling and the Appeal

On April 2, 2008, the district court granted the defendants' motion for summary judgment on all counts....

Sheehan now appeals that decision. She contends that the district court (1) erroneously concluded that the expert evidence as to the proximate cause of her injuries was based on improper speculation; (2) failed to recognize that a legitimate question of fact existed as to whether she fully appreciated and understood the risk of sustaining a serious injury; and (3) failed to consider her intoxicated state as a relevant factor under the assumption of the risk doctrine.

We review the district court's grant of summary judgment de novo. Summary judgment is appropriate "if the pleadings, the discovery and disclosure materials on file, and any affidavits, show that there is no genuine issue as to any material fact and that the movant is entitled to judgment as a matter of law." Fed.R.Civ.P.56(c). We view the record in the light most favorable to the non-moving party and resolve all reasonable inferences in its favor, without weighing the evidence or evaluating the credibility of the witnesses. The district court's decision may be upheld even if we reject its rationale, provided that we find independently sufficient grounds in the record.

Nature of the Alleged Design Defects

In a products liability action under Rhode Island law, the plaintiff must prove the following five elements: (1) that there was a defect in the design or construction of the product; (2) that the defect existed at the time the product left the hands of the defendant; (3) that the defect rendered the product unreasonably dangerous; (4) that the product was being used in a way in which it was intended at the time of the accident; and (5) that the defect was the proximate cause of the accident and the plaintiff's injuries.

Sheehan alleges three different types of design defects. First, she contends that the coping was too narrow, which caused her to lose her balance when she stood on it to dive. Second, she contends that the coping was unstable, which also contributed to her loss of balance. Third, she contends that the coping design tempted her to climb on it to dive, and that it should have been designed so that it would have been difficult or impossible to stand on it at all....

We think it is a close call whether Sheehan's causation evidence is sufficient to survive summary judgment. An alleged defect in a product need not be the only cause of harm to the plaintiff; liability may be found where the defect is a "substantial factor" in bringing about the harm. See Restatement (Second) of Torts §431 (1965). It is uncontested that Sheehan lost her balance and that the coping was narrower than the length of a normal adult foot. Common sense and ordinary experience would suggest that it is more difficult to maintain one's balance on a narrow surface, or to regain balance on such a surface once it has been lost. Similarly, although the evidence of the coping's alleged unsteadiness was thin, perhaps a reasonable jury could infer from Sheehan's observation that the coping "was kind of loose" that instability was a substantial factor in causing her to fall into the pool....

Rather than deciding th[is] difficult question[], we find that Sheehan's claim should be resolved on the grounds of assumption of the risk.

Assumption of the Risk

Assumption of the risk is an affirmative defense in a products liability action in Rhode Island. A plaintiff assumes the risk of injury when she "knowingly accepts a dangerous situation." In order to establish an assumption-of-risk defense, defendants must prove that the plaintiff knew of the existence of the danger, appreciated its unreasonable character, and voluntarily exposed herself to it. The standard is ordinarily subjective, and is based upon "what the particular individual in fact saw, knew, understood, and appreciated." The district court held that NAMCO and Delair were entitled to summary judgment because Sheehan must be held to have known and appreciated the risk of diving into a shallow, above-ground pool.

Sheehan argues that genuine issues of material fact remain unresolved as to her appreciation of the risk of diving. Such disputes ordinarily involve questions of subjective knowledge and are therefore left for the trier of fact. However, if the facts "suggest only one reasonable inference," the issue becomes a question of law for the judge. Thus, the courts of Rhode Island have found on multiple occasions that a plaintiff assumed a risk as a matter of law....

The danger of diving head-first into shallow water in an above-ground swimming pool was, or should have been, obvious to a thirty-two-year-old adult woman of normal intelligence. Sheehan knew the depth of the pool, and indeed had been in it for half an hour prior to the accident. If that were not enough, there were abundant warnings against diving on and around the coping, which Sheehan testified she did not read and would have ignored had she read them.

Sheehan seeks to avoid the conclusion that she knew and accepted the risk of diving as a matter of law by parsing the risk involved. By her account, the worst possible outcome that she considered was the risk that she would scrape the bottom of the pool on a poorly executed dive. But the issue is not whether she subjectively believed that the risk could be minimized or avoided.

Under Rhode Island law, when the circumstances are such that a person is presumed to know the risks of her dangerous conduct, she is charged with knowing all the ordinary risks associated with that conduct. Thus, Sheehan cannot be said to have assumed only the risk of a perfectly executed shallow dive; the risk that she assumed included the possibility that something would go wrong and the dive would not be perfect. Put another way, the risk of a poorly executed or botched dive is subsumed within the risk of diving generally.

Sheehan's best argument, and one which gives us pause, is that she may have assumed the risk of diving but never assumed the risk of falling from the allegedly defective coping. Plainly this case would look different if Sheehan had stood on the coping to dive and fallen backwards onto the ground, or if she had stood on the coping while engaged in some activity other than diving, such as exiting the pool or cleaning it. The pool had no warning against standing on the coping—as opposed to diving or jumping from it— and the language of the warnings as given ("NO DIVING—SHALLOW WATER") at least suggests that the primary problem with diving is misjudging the depth of the water and not tumbling from the coping.

Nevertheless, we agree that summary judgment is warranted on these facts. Sheehan stood on the coping in order to dive, and the injury that occurred was the same one contemplated by the multiple warnings—including on the coping itself. The warnings made clear that no diving should be undertaken (whether from the narrow coping or from anywhere else). Under these circumstances, as a matter of law Sheehan assumed the risk of diving, including the risk that she might fall from the coping into the pool while attempting to dive.

Finally, we are unimpressed with Sheehan's fallback position that the district court failed to take proper account of her intoxication in assessing her subjective knowledge of the risk of diving. She has cited to no case, in Rhode Island or elsewhere, suggesting that voluntary intoxication weighs in her favor. The usual rule in tort is that a person who voluntarily becomes intoxicated "is held thereafter to the same standard as if he were a sober person." Charitably construed, Sheehan's argument is that assumption of risk is a subjective doctrine, unlike the usual objective standards of reasonable conduct that prevail in tort, and thus that this is one area where voluntary intoxication may be of unusual relevance.

The problem with the objection is that excuses based on drunkenness are too easy to make and too costly to permit. Those concerns have equal force when a plaintiff seeks to evade responsibility for assuming the risk of obviously dangerous conduct. We see no reason to suppose that the Supreme Court of Rhode Island, if presented with the question, would depart from the standard rule in this context.

That is not to say, of course, that Sheehan does not deserve enormous sympathy for her current tragic circumstances. Nonetheless, under Rhode Island law, there are certain risks that are so self-evident that a person will be deemed to have understood them as a matter of law. Diving head-first into a shallow, above-ground pool is such a risk, and bars recovery here.

For the foregoing reasons, we affirm the district court's decision granting defendants' motion for summary judgment.

Notes

1. *Reasonable, not voluntary.* It needs to be emphasized that the court in *Sheehan* did not find that Sheehan herself had actually, voluntarily consented to the risk of being injured while diving. Indeed, there was simply no evidence on which to base such a conclusion. Instead, the court found that, in the circumstances, she was presumed to be aware of the danger and to have decided to risk serious injury nevertheless. This presumption as to the victim's state of mind was based on an inference drawn from facts relating to her conduct and the overall context. In other words, the court employed a test of reasonableness—which is objective—to draw an inference as to the victim's state of mind—which is necessarily subjective. Moreover, even if the court had been prepared to accept Sheehan's evidence that she had not appreciated the danger, the court ruled that that would have been irrelevant—and so could not displace the inference—because such

a state of mind would, in the circumstances, have been unreasonable. In other words, the label given to this defense of *voluntary* assumption of risk is really quite inaccurate. It would be much better to call it *apparent* or *reasonable* assumption of risk.

2. *Questions of fact and law.* The relevance of Sheehan's level of intoxication played a very interesting part in the court's decision. While its role *as a matter of fact* explained how the plaintiff might have failed to appreciate the danger, the court took it instead as evidence *as a matter of law* that explained the plaintiff's apparent indifference to risk. As the court itself pointed out, this is the standard approach throughout the nation, and reflects a policy intended to prevent victims from using their voluntary intoxication as a means of denying the defendant an otherwise viable defense (in this case, assumption of risk). This treatment of what might initially appear to be a matter of fact as, instead, a matter of law again has the effect of transforming an issue that is apparently about the victim's *subjective* state of mind (*voluntary* assumption of risk) into an *objective* matter of reasonableness (*reasonable* assumption of risk).

3. *Assumption of risk per se?* The legal system's approach to victims' intoxication thus has two significant effects. Not only does it, as just noted, transform what would otherwise be a factual inquiry into a question of law for the court; it also transforms voluntary intoxication into a sort of "assumption of risk *per se*," where the very fact of the victim's being intoxicated creates a defense for the defendant. These transformations together mean that cases involving a victim's intoxication are apt for resolution by summary judgment.

4. *Defining a dive.* This approach to victim intoxication often avoids the courts' having to make difficult decisions. The court in *Sheehan* was unusually candid in expressing its relief at being able to avoid a close call on the issue of causation — and, arguably, it did not even really appreciate just how difficult that issue might have been in only slightly different circumstances. The court made it clear that assumption of risk would not have been an available defense if the plaintiff had fallen, rather than dived, into the pool. But what constitutes diving? If there had been no evidence of Sheehan's being intoxicated, and she had simply been standing on the coping, facing forward (perhaps even contemplating a dive), but fell in because the coping wobbled, would that constitute a dive or a fall? Does there need to be some knee-bend, or forward leaning, or even a jump, to constitute a dive?

What Is Assumption of Risk?

As *Sheehan* demonstrates, the affirmative defense of assumption of risk works quite differently from that of consent. Rather than applying to potentially intentional torts, assumption of risk is potentially applicable to cases where the nature of the allegation against the defendant involves either negligence or no fault at all (i.e. strict liability). This distinction leads to another: unlike sex, surgery, or boxing, the nature of non-intentional conduct is much less predictable. Accordingly, the consequences of such conduct are even harder to predict. That is why the phrase is assumption of *risk*: the plaintiff is said to have agreed to run the risk of something bad happening. In other words, the defense operates by treating the victim as having assumed the risk of suffering harmful consequences — whatever they might turn out to be — as a result of the defendant's behavior (whatever that might turn out to be).

How assumption of risk differs from consent may be easier to understand by means of an example. Say that a woman decides to have an IUD inserted. This means that she consents to a medical procedure, and so provides the nurse, midwife or OBGYN with a defense to conduct that would otherwise amount to the intentional tort of battery. By no stretch of the imagination can this be construed, however, as her agreeing to have a defective IUD inserted!

So far as the IUD itself is concerned, the only potential defense would be that of assumption of risk. This would mean that the woman had agreed to run the risks of suffering some harm as a result of being fitted with the IUD. But note carefully what this implies. Product manufacturers and distributors have no need of a defense when the potential plaintiff has no case—whether of a tort or a breach of contract—in the first place. So if the woman was warned, for example, that the IUD might cause some bleeding, which she then experiences, this is not a matter of assumption of risk. It is simply that the warning means that the potential defendants cannot be liable for a failure to warn. In other words, an essential element (failure to warn) of the woman's *prima facie* case of product defect cannot be proved. The defense of assumption of risk would thus be meaningful here only if the warning had not been given. In those circumstances, there would be a *prima facie* case of a failure to warn, for which the woman could seek compensation unless barred by an affirmative defense.

We get to the nub of the issue when we consider what the legal position would be if the complaint were that the bleeding had been caused by defective design or manufacture of the IUD. In such a case, the manufacturer would not succeed in defending itself by arguing that, when the woman agreed to have the IUD inserted, she voluntarily assumed the risk of its being defective. If she had been warned about possible bleeding, it could truthfully be said that she had agreed to assume that risk—but it was a risk she assumed *only if the product itself was not defective.*

In other words, any risk assumed by the victim is simply one that recognizes that, in our imperfect world where results cannot be guaranteed, even nondefective products can sometimes cause harm. Since the products involved in such cases are not defective, the victim has no basis for a claim in products liability law. But the reason for that inability to succeed in such a suit is not the result of the defendant's utilizing an affirmative defense. It is simply that, since the product in question is not defective, one of the elements that the victim is required to prove in order to establish a *prima facie* case is missing.

It now becomes apparent that the doctrine of "assumption of risk" is not really what it claims to be. In fact, the phrase "assumption of risk" typically means either that the defendant owed no duty to the victim (because s/he was unforeseeable), or that the defendant did not breach such a duty (*e.g.*, by manufacturing or distributing a defective product). *Sheehan*, for example, is a clear case of a finding of no duty (because of the victim's intoxication). As was made clear in Chapter 1, duty is unquestionably a matter of law for the court, so there seems little to be gained—other than wholesale confusion—by rendering a "no duty" verdict through the superfluous figleaf of "assumption of risk."

Thus, whatever the courts might claim, they are not really using the notion of "assumption of risk" to describe an affirmative defense at all. In fact, whether they cite this explanation as a proxy for a "no duty" or a "no breach" determination, what they are actually asserting is simply the absence of an essential element in the plaintiff's *prima facie* case.

It is no wonder that students often get confused about the distinction between the absence of an element of the plaintiff's *prima facie* case and the assertion of an affirmative defense in spite of proof of the plaintiff's *prima facie* case—because courts continue to perpetuate this confusion on a regular basis. Whether they do this intentionally or without thinking is a matter about which readers might like to ponder further.

Questions

1. Should the courts establish, for the purposes of cases involving injuries resulting from the entering of a swimming pool, a clear definition of what constitutes a dive? What might the consequences be if they did so?

2. According to the court itself in *Sheehan*, the victim "brought suit for negligence, strict liability, breach of express warranty, and breach of implied warranty, alleging in substance that the design of the pool was defective." Are pleas of "no duty" or "no breach" (whether made by means of the terminology of assumption of risk or otherwise) likely to be equally effective as a defense against each of these types of claim?

3. As we have seen, the court in *Sheehan* used the notion of "assumption of risk" as a means of denying that the pool manufacturer owed a duty to the victim. Would "assumption of risk" still have been applicable if the victim in *Sheehan* had not been intoxicated and, if so, would it still have meant "no duty" or would it have meant "no breach"?

4. In what respects do the implications of using the label of "assumption of risk" to render a holding of "no duty" differ from the implications of using the same label as a means of rendering a holding of "no breach"?

5. Is it appropriate for a judge, rather than a jury, to make a "no breach" ruling?

6. We have, in the past, abandoned other terminology in the law of torts because it was inaccurate or misleading. A recent example is the abandonment in § 29 of the Restatement (Third) of Torts: Liability for Physical and Emotional Harm of the terminology of "proximate cause" in favor of "scope of liability." Is it now time to jettison the terminology of "assumption of risk"?

Comparative Fault

Another reason why the terminology of "assumption of risk" may be superfluous is the growing importance of the doctrine of comparative fault.

The common law was traditionally a simple beast. Cases were decided entirely for the plaintiff or entirely for the defendant and, if the plaintiff was entitled to a remedy, that simply involved the payment of damages. Such simplicity did not always mesh well with the growing complexities of life, where an accident and/or injury can have more than one cause, and so the harshness and inflexibility of the common law came to be mitigated by a new body of equitable principles. Yet equity had no impact either on the position of an unsuccessful plaintiff—encapsulated by the maxim that "equity follows the law"—or on how damages for a successful plaintiff were to be quantified.

Equity therefore left untouched the traditional common law position which, in keeping with its general all-or-nothing approach, was that a plaintiff who was at least partly to blame for his or her own misfortune was not entitled to any compensation at all from anyone else, even if the fault of that other person had been far greater than that of the victim. This was known as the defense of contributory negligence. It originated, like the rest of the common law, in England, although the English abandoned it in 1945. Contributory negligence has now been largely abandoned in the United States as well, with only Alabama, Maryland, North Carolina, Virginia, and the District of Columbia retaining it as a complete defense.

All those jurisdictions that have abandoned contributory negligence have replaced it with a similar but different regime, typically known as comparative fault (but sometimes, confusingly, still called contributory negligence, which is also what it is called in England). This requires that the compensation for the plaintiff's injury must be apportioned between the parties according to their respective degrees of fault.

It is important to emphasize that the doctrine of comparative fault requires that both the defendant's and the victim's conduct must have been causes of the victim's injury. In other words, it implicitly involves the "substantial factor" test of causation, and identifies each party's behavior as *a* factor—rather than *the* sole cause—of the victim's injury.

Where the parties identified as causing the victim's injury do not include the victim, it is possible that the defendants would (as we saw in Chapter 9) be jointly and severally liable, where each defendant is liable for 100% of the victim's injuries. However, as was noted in Chapter 9, joint liability has been abolished in the majority of states (except for cases of vicarious liability), so that liability is now more typically apportioned among the defendants according to the degree of their respective fault. In cases where the victim's own conduct has been a substantial factor in the causation of his or her own injuries, the doctrine of comparative fault achieves much the same result by apportioning liability between defendant(s) and plaintiff according to their respective fault.

This provides yet another reason for rejecting the idea that "assumption of risk" is an affirmative defense. For if a victim who is partially to blame for his or her own injuries is barred only from receiving a proportion of the compensation that reflects his or her degree of fault, there seems absolutely no good reason for barring a victim from receiving *any* compensation when s/he was in no way to blame. Indeed, cases where a defendant would formerly have pleaded "assumption of risk" as an affirmative defense are now better pleaded as instances of comparative fault.

Boatland of Houston, Inc. v. Valerie Bailey
609 S.W.2d 743 (1980) (Supreme Court of Texas)

[For the facts of this case, see Chapter 7.] POPE, J., (concurring, and in which BARROW, J., joins). I also concur in its holding that state of the art may be developed by the evidence directed at the issue concerning defect, but that state of the art is not itself an issue which should be submitted to the jury. This case, however, dramatically illustrates the problems with shadowy distinctions between defenses in products cases and negligence cases, and the need to reexamine certain defenses.

Defendant Boatland asserted three defenses, each of which the court submitted to the jury, and all of which the jury answered favorably to the defendant Boatland. The jury made findings that (1) decedent misused the boat, (2) decedent failed to follow proper warnings and instructions, and (3) decedent voluntarily assumed the risk.

It is my opinion that all of those defensive issues are issues which mix and ask about the decedent's contributory negligence. The defendant alleged that the decedent misused the boat in these ways: (1) he drove the boat at an unsafe speed, (2) he failed to keep a proper lookout, (3) he permitted passengers to stand in the boat, and (4) he failed to place the motor in a tilt position. Those are traditional contributory negligence allegations even though we call them "misuse" when we move from a negligence case to a products case....

In an action in which the plaintiff pleads an action in ... negligence and alternatively as [product] liability, the defendant receives an issue on contributory negligence and another issue on misuse. The same evidence bears on both. This is, however, a double submission of the same acts or omissions. If the jury answers that there was no contributory negligence, but that there was misuse, we run into the problem of conflicts.

Misuse is really contributory negligence, and it would simplify trials if we treated it as such. We should recognize this fact and hold a plaintiff to the standard of an ordinary prudent person or of reasonableness in his use of the product. We should eliminate the confusing misuse defense and return to contributory negligence as an appropriate defense in [product] liability cases.

Voluntary assumption of risk should also be eliminated as a viable defense in [product] liability cases. There is no more reason for an all-or-nothing defense in [product] liability cases than there is in negligence cases....

The defense under the more familiar format of contributory negligence, which would subsume and supplant the confusing defenses of misuse and voluntary assumption of risk could restore simplicity to the trials of product liability cases. In such a trial, the fault of the supplier and the plaintiff should be apportioned between the product's defect and the plaintiffs' sub-par conduct....

Sooner or later, and the sooner the better, we must bring products liability cases within a manageable format. Simplicity, order and consistency can be advanced in those cases, in my opinion by:

1. The elimination of the misuse and voluntary assumption of risk issues and by substituting in their place the more familiar issue about contributory negligence on the part of the plaintiff.

2. The submission of a products liability case to determine the percentage that the defective product caused the event and the percentage that the substandard conduct of the plaintiff caused it.

Restatement (Third) of Torts: Products Liability (1998)

§ 17. Apportionment of Responsibility Between or Among Plaintiff, Sellers, and Distributors of Defective Products, and Others

(a) A plaintiff's recovery of damages for harm caused by a product defect may be reduced if the conduct of the plaintiff combines with the product defect to cause the harm and the plaintiff's conduct fails to conform to generally applicable rules establishing appropriate standards of care.

(b) The manner and extent of the reduction under Subsection (a) and the apportionment of plaintiffs recovery among multiple defendants are governed by generally applicable rules apportioning responsibility.

Notes

1. *Pure schemes.* Comparative fault in the US (though not in England) comes in two flavors, known as "pure schemes" and "modified schemes." Under a pure scheme, the plaintiff is entitled to receive damages that reflect the defendant's proportion of the fault. (This is the only approach now taken in England and most other common law jurisdictions.) So if the plaintiff is found by a jury to have been 65% to blame for her own in-

juries, she will receive 35% of the jury's assessment of the compensation to which she would have been entitled if she had been blameless. Pure schemes are in place in twelve states: Alaska, Arizona, California, Florida, Kentucky, Louisiana, Mississippi, Missouri, New Mexico, New York, Rhode Island, and Washington.

2. *Modified schemes.* Modified schemes are a sort of compromise between pure schemes and the old law of contributory negligence. They impose a threshold requirement, according to which the defendant must be found to have been—depending on the jurisdiction—at least 50%, or at least 51%, to blame for the plaintiff's injuries in order for the latter to receive anything. So long as this threshold is met, plaintiffs will again receive the damages that reflect the defendant's proportion of the fault; otherwise, they receive nothing. Arkansas, Colorado, Georgia, Idaho, Kansas, Maine, Nebraska, North Dakota, Tennessee, Utah, and West Virginia all operate a 50% threshold. All the others have set the bar at 51% except for South Dakota (which sets it much higher) and Michigan, which has its own, unique approach, which distinguishes economic from noneconomic damages.

3. *Flowchart.* The various alternative approaches concerning comparative fault are set out in the flowchart in Figure 11.1.

4. *Comparing incomparables.* The problem with comparative fault (which also applies to the apportionment of liability between defendants on the basis of fault) is that it often requires a comparison between apples and oranges. The defendant's "fault" may be in the manufacturing or designing of a product, or in failing to warn about a significant danger; the victim's "fault" may be in using the product unreasonably or in some other, unrelated conduct. There is clearly no objective metric which establishes the respective percentages of "fault" between such disparate forms of behavior: it is simply a matter for a jury to determine, in a rough, common-sense way in the light of all the evidence. While the jury's involvement is sometimes taken as signifying that the respective apportionment of fault is a matter of fact, it is plainly nothing of the sort, and is really a matter of judgment by a group of individuals who are taken as the community's appropriate representatives.

5. *Comparative fault or comparative causation?* Because of this inherent lack of precision in apportioning fault, an alternative approach is to focus on comparative (or relative) causation. It must be emphasized that the two approaches are quite different. In *Murray v. Fairbanks Morse*, 610 F. 2d 149, 159 (1979), the Court of Appeals for the Third Circuit argued:

> Although we may term a defective product "faulty," it is qualitatively different from the plaintiff's conduct that contributes to his injury. A comparison of the two is therefore inappropriate.... We believe that if the loss for a particular injury is to be apportioned between the product defect and the plaintiff's misconduct, the only conceptual basis for comparison is the causative contribution of each to the particular loss or injury. In apportioning damages we are really asking how much of the injury was caused by the defect in the product versus how much was caused by the plaintiff's own actions. We agree with the Ninth Circuit when it noted that comparative causation "is a conceptually more precise term than 'comparative fault' since fault alone without causation does not subject one to liability." *Pan-Alaska Fisheries, Inc. v. Marine Construction & Design Co.*, 565 F.2d 1129, 1139 (9th Cir. 1977).

6. *Reasserting comparative fault.* This view was, however, rejected by the Supreme Court of Oregon in *Sandford v. Chevrolet Division of General Motors*, 642 P.2d 624, 630–31 (1982), which observed:

Figure 11.1 Comparative Fault

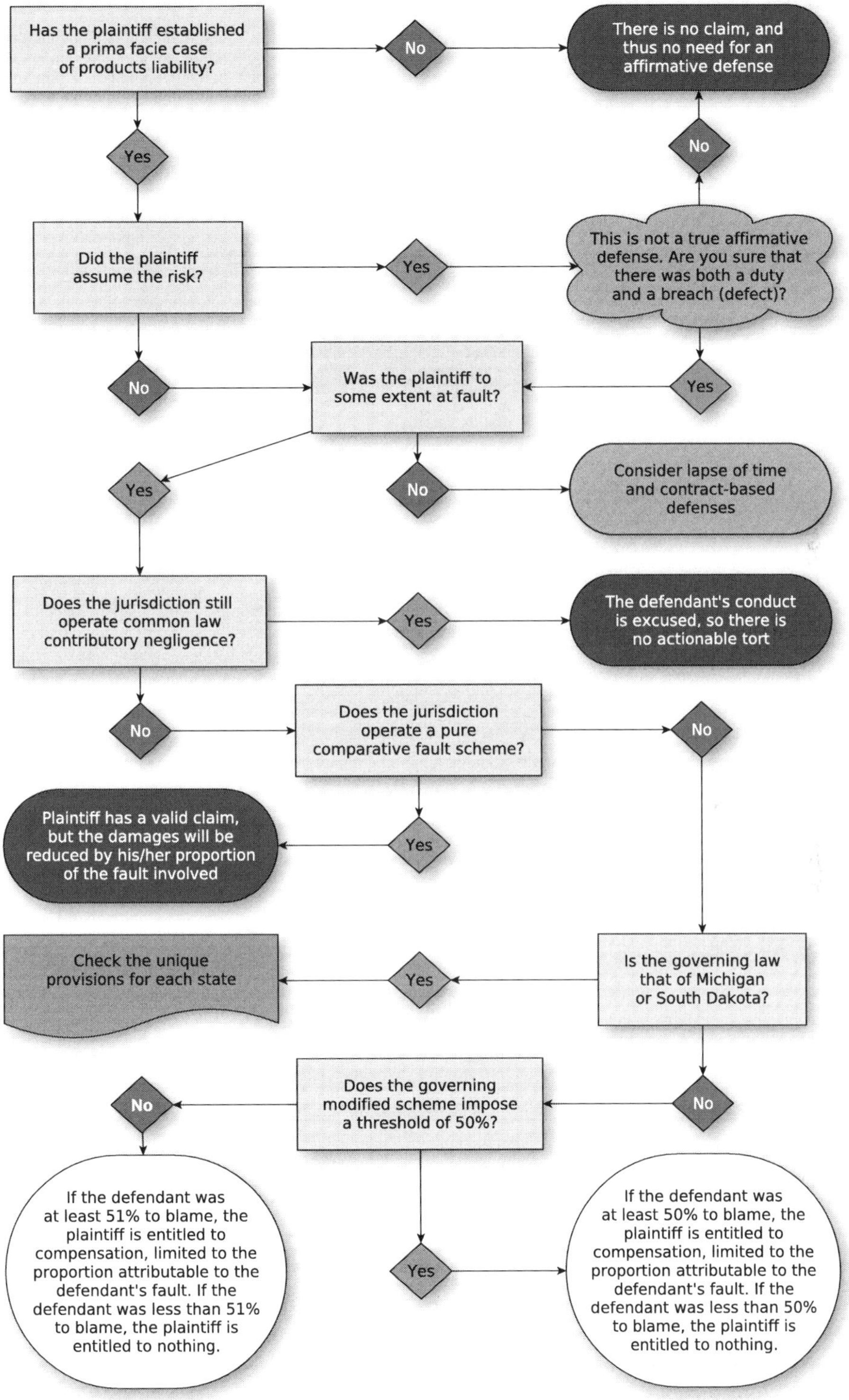

With due respect ... we are not persuaded that the concept of "comparative causation" is more cogent or meaningful than comparative fault, if by "causation" is meant some relation of cause and effect in the physical world rather than the very attribution of responsibility for which "causation" is to serve as the premise.

Both the defect and the plaintiff's fault must in fact be causes of one injury before a question of apportionment of fault arises....

The concept of apportioning causation must be tested on the assumption that both causes had to join to produce the injury for which damages are to be allocated. There are cases in which it may be possible to segregate the harm done by one cause from different or incremental harm done by a second cause, so as to apply proportional allocation to the additional harm only. This might be possible when a quantitative increase in a source of harm causes a corresponding increase in the injury, such as side effects from a negligent overdose of a dangerously defective drug, or if, for instance, Mrs. Sandford had broken a leg in an accident caused by the defective tire and thereafter had been burned by material negligently stored in her vehicle....

Once it is assumed, however, that two or more distinct causes had to occur to produce an indivisible injury, we doubt that the purpose of the proportional fault concept is to subject the combined causation to some kind of vector analysis, even in the rare case of simultaneous, physically commensurable forces. In most cases, it would be a vain exercise to search for a common physical measure for the causative effect of a product defect and of the injured party's negligent conduct.

Four Types of Comparative Fault

In products liability cases, comparative fault can come into play in four different ways. The differences matter because it will often dictate the approach to be taken. This should not be taken, however, as implying that the states always agree on which approach is to be taken when, since the ramifications of each type of case also differ from one jurisdiction to the next.

The first type of case that potentially implicates comparative fault involves the victim's misusing or unreasonably modifying what turns out to be a defective product. In such cases, the victim's comparative fault is a concurrent cause of her injuries along with the original product defect, so that both contribute to the victim's injury. An example is *Sandford v. Chevrolet Division of General Motors*, 642 P.2d 624 (1982), where the driver of a pickup truck was badly burned when the truck turned over because of a defective tire, and then caught fire. The plaintiff succeeded in her claim against the tire's manufacturer and distributor, but the Supreme Court of Oregon (which ordered a retrial on other grounds) made it clear that her damages were subject to a reduction in proportion to her own negligence concerning her manner of operation of the vehicle.

A variant of this type of case is where the victim's conduct causes the initial accident, but then the defective state of the product increases the injuries sustained by the victim. Vehicle crashworthiness cases, such as *Whitehead v. Toyota Motor Corp.*, 897 S.W.2d 684 (1995), are prime examples, although it must be noted that the product liability claim will then be restricted to the additional injury suffered by the plaintiff. This sort of comparative fault actually involves much the same as the approach of comparative causation, advocated above in *Pan-Alaska Fisheries*. In *Whitehead*, the plaintiff's own negligence in driving his pickup truck caused the initial accident, but the vehicle seatbelt system was defective and "enhanced" his injuries. The Supreme Court of Tennessee held that:

> Any claim for "enhanced injuries" is nothing more than a claim for injuries that were actually and proximately caused by the defective product. For example, suppose that a plaintiff is driving a car and is involved in a two-car accident, for which plaintiff is entirely at fault; suppose further that plaintiff incurs $100,000 in damages as a result of this accident. Even though plaintiff's fault precludes him from recovering from the other driver, plaintiff brings an action against the manufacturer of the car, alleging that the seat belt system is defective. Plaintiff alleges that if the seat belt system had been properly designed and installed, he would have only suffered $50,000 in damages.
>
> This type of claim is often characterized as one for "enhanced injuries." The name given to the action has no real significance, however, because it merely represents the portion of the total damages for which the manufacturer is potentially liable; it is the "products liability" component of the suit. (The manufacturer could not be liable for the first $50,000 in damages, which would have been incurred even if the seat belt had been properly manufactured and installed). Therefore, it is illogical to hold that comparative fault applies to products liability actions generally, but does not apply to "enhanced injury" claims. The questions are, in reality, the same.

A second type of concurrent comparative fault occurs where the victim engages in other unreasonable conduct, unrelated to the defective product, but which also contributes to the causation of the injury. *Champagne v. Raybestos-Manhattan, Inc.*, 212 Conn. 509 (1989), was just such a case. The decedent victim had been wrongfully exposed to asbestos while employed by the General Dynamics Corporation, where he was responsible for insulating various systems during the construction and overhaul of submarines—a process that often involved the handling of products containing asbestos. He subsequently contracted and died of lung cancer. However, his widow's award of damages from Raybestos, who manufactured the asbestos products to which the decedent had been exposed, was subject to a reduction for comparative fault. This was because the jury heard evidence that "the incidence of cancer in smokers exposed to asbestos is from ten to sixty times more than the incidence of cancer in nonsmokers exposed to asbestos," and so concluded that the decedent was therefore 75% at fault for his own death.

The third type of comparative fault occurs where the plaintiff fails to take reasonable steps to avoid the consequences of a product defect which has now become apparent. Here, the victim's comparative fault has nothing to do with the use or operation of the product in question. It also occurs later in the chain of events, although still before any actionable injury has been sustained. This is tantamount to an unreasonable failure to mitigate loss.

In *McDonald v. Federal Laboratories Inc.*, 724 F. 2d 243 (1984), for example, police officer McDonald brought a breach of warranty and negligent design claim for injuries he sustained when a mace cannister, manufactured by Federal, accidentally discharged when it banged against the car door while he was carrying it in a holster on his gun belt. The mace penetrated McDonald's police uniform, saturating his stomach, legs and groin area. McDonald's eyes and cheekbones were also burning. He immediately returned to the station to wash the exposed parts of his body. Though having a "funny feeling" in his pants or loin area, McDonald did not change his clothing because he believed that the mace could not have penetrated a heavy pair of police pants. The accident happened at 1:00 am. McDonald finished his duty tour at 8:00 a.m., and then went home.

Later the same day, McDonald began experiencing severe discomfort and blistering on his stomach, legs and groin area. He went to a local health center and received prescription medication from a dermatologist. Because of the severity of the blistering, McDonald was unable to return to work for twenty days. Upon his return, McDonald continued to apply medication and bandages to the inflamed areas but, after a month, the pain and itching became unbearable and McDonald discontinued work two months later. After various treatments, he returned to duty six months later but was then again exposed to mace, triggering a recurrence of the severe blistering. As a result, McDonald became unable to return to police work and was involuntarily retired approximately eighteen months after the original exposure.

The jury returned a total verdict of $929,000 in favor of McDonald, but this was reduced to $789,650 to give effect to a jury finding of 15% comparative negligence on McDonald's part. The Court of Appeals for the First Circuit affirmed.

The fourth type of comparative fault involves the plaintiff's doing something unreasonable after the product's defectiveness has manifested itself, exacerbating any injury that she has already been caused. The difference between this and the third type of occurrence is that the third is essentially concerned with a failure to take reasonable steps to prevent injury, whereas the fourth implicates conduct which adds to an injury that has already been sustained.

The distinction between the four scenarios can sometimes be crucial because, while there is no doubt that the first three involve comparative fault, the states have not taken a consistent approach to the fourth. Some see it as involving one injury (which means that damages would indeed be open to apportionment according to comparative fault), while others (like the Supreme Court of Oregon in *Sandford*, above) see it as an instance of two separate injuries. On the latter basis, responsibility for each injury may be attributed solely on the basis of factual causation rather than fault, so that the victim may recover compensation for the original but not the augmented injury; or else the comparative fault of plaintiff and defendant may become relevant only in respect of the augmented injury.

Comment *b* to § 15 of the Third Restatement expressly leaves all these possibilities open. Nevertheless, some courts have doubted whether the doctrine of comparative fault should be applicable at all to a products liability action.

Kimco Development Corp. v. Michael D's Carpet Outlets

637 A.2d 603 (1993) (Supreme Court of Pennsylvania)

[An action to recover for damage resulting from a fire was brought against the manufacturer of polyurethane foam carpet padding because of the defendant's negligence and fault under products liability theory in failing to warn of the highly flammable nature of the padding.] PAPAKADOS, J. General Foam ... contends that comparative negligence should constitute a defense to a products liability case brought under § 402A of the Restatement (Second) of Torts and specifically in the products liability case brought against it by Michael D's in this litigation. We granted allocatur here to consider this important issue which has not been previously addressed by this Court. The Superior Court thought that "logic and simple fairness" demanded that the jury's apportionment of negligence (80%

to Michael D's and 20% to General Foam) should have been applied in determining General Foam's liability for Michael D's fire loss. Nonetheless, the Superior Court concluded that the current state of the law in Pennsylvania is to the contrary. The Superior Court relied on our opinion in *McCown v. International Harvester Co.*, 463 Pa. 13, 342 A.2d 381 (1975), where we specifically rejected contributory negligence as a defense in products liability actions brought under §402A of the Restatement (Second) of Torts. *McCown* was decided prior to the enactment of Pennsylvania's Comparative Negligence Statute, 42 Pa.C.S.A. §7102 (effective June 27, 1978), and we have yet to consider the precise issue at stake here. Nonetheless, the Superior Court was persuaded to apply McCown by analogy on the theory that this Court has steadfastly refused to allow strict product liability actions to become "contaminated" by negligence principles. A similar conclusion was recently drawn about the current state of Pennsylvania law in this area by the United States Third Circuit Court of Appeals in *Dillinger v. Caterpillar, Inc.*, 959 F.2d 430 (3d Cir.1992).

The law amongst the various states is in considerable disarray on the point in question. In *Kinard v. Coats Co.*, 553 P.2d 835, 37 Colo.App. 555 (1976), the court ruled that products liability under §402A does not rest on negligence principles but on the concept of strict enterprise liability for casting a defective product into the stream of commerce. Thus, the focus is on the nature of the product and the consumer's reasonable expectations with regard to the product, rather than upon the conduct of either the manufacturer or the person injured. The Court declined to inject negligence concepts into an area of liability that they thought rests on totally different policy considerations....

We ... decline to extend negligence concepts to the area of §402A strict product liability.

In 1966, in *Webb v. Zern*, 422 Pa. 424, 220 A.2d 853 (1966), we adopted the Restatement (Second) of Torts §402A as the law of this Commonwealth. Throughout the development of §402A liability, we have been adamant that negligence concepts have no place in a strict liability action....

Our position is not based solely on the problem of the conceptual confusion that would ensue should negligence and strict liability concepts be commingled, although that concern is not negligible. Rather, we think that the underlying purpose of strict product liability is undermined by introducing negligence concepts into it. Strict product liability is premised on the concept of enterprise liability for casting a defective product into the stream of commerce.

> The development of a sophisticated and complex industrial society with its proliferation of new products and vast change in the private enterprise system has inspired a change in legal philosophy from the principle of caveat emptor which prevailed in the early nineteenth century market place to view that a supplier of products should be deemed to be 'the guarantor of his products' safety.' *Salvador v. Atlantic Steel Boiler Co.*, 457 Pa. 24, 32, 319 A.2d 903, 907 (1974). The realities of our economic society as it exists today forces the conclusion that the risk of loss for injury resulting from defective products should be borne by the suppliers, principally because they are in a position to absorb the loss by distributing it as a cost of doing business. In an era of giant corporate structures, utilizing the national media to sell their wares, the original concern for an emerging manufacturing industry has given way to the view that it is now the consumer who must be protected. Courts have increasingly adopted the position that the risk of loss must be placed upon the supplier of the defective product without regard to fault or privity of contract. *Azzarello v. Black Brothers Co.*, 480 Pa. 547, 391 A.2d 1020 (1978).

The deterrent effect of imposing strict product liability standards would be weakened were we to allow actions based upon it to be defeated, or recoveries reduced by negligence concepts. We will not countenance such a development.

For the reasons set forth above, we hereby expressly adopt the rule that comparative negligence may not be asserted as a defense in § 402A strict product liability actions.

Affirmed.

Notes

1. *Comparative fault and strict products liability.* The approach of the Supreme Court of Pennsylvania in *Kimco* has not met with unanimous approval throughout the states. One of the clearest illustrations of the level of disunity among the judiciary is *Webb v. Navistar Intern. Transp. Corp.*, 692 A.2d 343, 343–44 (1996), which concerned an appeal from a jury verdict that held the defendant liable to plaintiffs Bruce and Martha Webb for "strict products liability" for a design defect and/or failure to warn plaintiffs of dangers inherent in the design of a tractor. A majority of the Supreme Court of Vermont agreed to reverse and remand. Giving judgment for the majority, Justice Dooley declared in frustration:

> Justice Morse, Justice Peck and I hold that principles of comparative causation apply in this products liability action. We do not agree, however, to a general rule on when comparative principles apply in strict products liability actions, nor on how to implement these principles when they do apply. I believe this case must be reversed and remanded for a new trial because the trial judge failed to instruct the jury on comparative causation. Justice Morse concludes that Bruce Webb is more than fifty percent responsible, as a matter of law, and therefore, under 12 V.S.A. § 1036 (comparative negligence), he would enter judgment for defendant. Justice Peck agrees with Justice Morse that judgment should be entered for defendant but on the ground that the tractor is not defective as a matter of law. Justice Johnson and Justice Gibson would affirm the judgment for plaintiffs; they would hold that comparative principles are not applicable in products liability actions.
>
> The positions of the Justices produce no majority on the mandate. A majority of the Court agrees, however, that the judgment entered on the jury verdict cannot be affirmed....
>
> The dissent criticizes the majority for creating a rat's maze from which there is no exit. We strongly disagree with the characterization of the cause or consequence of the Court's voting. If the dissent would accept that comparative causation has now become the rule in products liability cases in Vermont, and participate in an implementation design to guide future cases, the trial judge in this case might know exactly what to do on remand. If a majority could not agree on an implementation design, the trial judge and parties would at least know the full range of options and votes in support of each on this Court. I share Justice Peck's view that we should do all in our power to avoid stalemate, if possible.

2. *A matter of semantics.* The problem at the heart of this controversy may simply be driven by the sloppy use of the terminology of "strict liability" that we noted in Chapter 6. Originally, such terminology was confined to cases—such as breach of warranty in contracts—where there was no requirement to prove that the defendant was at fault. There seems little justification for the application of comparative fault in such cases, since the whole point of these actions is to render the distributor or manufacturer liable irrespective of fault.

The problem is that, as we have seen throughout this book, the terminology of "strict liability" has been adopted by many judges and other commentators as a synonym for "products liability," even when the particular action involved requires proof of fault by the defendant. This is most clearly true of cases of defective design and failures to warn. In such cases, of which both *Webb* and *Kimco* are examples, the manufacturer and/or distributor must be shown to be at fault in a manner that is tantamount to common law negligence. For this reason, applying the doctrine of comparative fault in a manner analogous to its application in the law of negligence seems eminently justifiable.

That leaves us with the conundrum of whether the manufacture or distribution of a product with a manufacturing defect effectively constitutes a form of fault. If it does, then the approach of the Supreme Court of Tennessee in *Whitehead v. Toyota Motor Corp.* seems quite appropriate. But if it does not—and, of course, Justice Traynor's motivation for the creation of products liability actions in *Escola v. Coca Cola Bottling Co.*, 150 P.2d 436 (1944), was, as we saw in Chapter 6, to create a new form of no-fault liability—then there seems little reason to "contaminate" that concept by importing a doctrine from the law of negligence.

Questions

1. Would it have been preferable to treat *Sheehan* as a case involving comparative fault, even though the plaintiff was intoxicated?

2. What practical difference would it have made to treat *Sheehan* as a case of comparative fault?

Comparative Fault as a Sword, Not a Shield

A novel development in the law of comparative fault has played a significant role in the saga of tobacco litigation in Florida. Since the class action against Big Tobacco was prospectively decertified by the Supreme Court of Florida in *Engle v. Liggett Group, Inc.*, 945 So.2d 1246 (2006), many of the plaintiffs' attorneys have adopted the strategy of pleading their client's comparative fault in continuing to smoke as part of their client's own case. The idea is that a jury is not then presented with a victim who seeks to blame only the tobacco companies for his resultant cancer, but with a person who recognizes that s/he was to some extent also the author of his or her own misfortune. By framing the claim in this way, plaintiffs can be portrayed as reasonable individuals who made a mistake, rather than potentially as money-grabbing wastrels who have failed to take any responsibility for themselves. This approach also enables a victim's attorney to contrast the reasonableness of his or her client's position with the apparent callousness of the defendant tobacco companies, who seek to deny any responsibility at all.

While the plaintiff will obviously lose some of the compensatory damages that might otherwise be awarded in a successful suit, the chances of winning at trial are thought to be considerably enhanced in comparison to the regular all-or-nothing approach. (This way of framing the plaintiff's case might also have an effect on the likelihood of an award of punitive damages being made, as well as on the size of any such award.) Unsurprisingly, the tobacco companies have fought this strategy, but have found it accepted as legitimate by the courts. In a wrongful death suit brought in *R.J. Reynolds Tobacco Company v. Martin*, 53 So. 3d 1060 (Fla.2010), the plaintiff's attorneys adopted precisely this approach of pleading comparative fault as a sword rather than a shield, and saw their client awarded $5 million in compensatory damages, with a reduction of 34% to reflect her husband's comparative fault. A punitive damages award of $25 million was also made. (Other aspects of this case are discussed in Chapter 15.) The Supreme Court of Florida declined to entertain an appeal, so those awards stand. In fact, *Martin* simply applied the reasoning of the case below.

Philip Morris USA, Inc. v. Arnitz

933 So.2d 693 (2006) (Second DCA, Florida)

SILBERMAN, J. Arnitz began smoking cigarettes in the early 1960s, when he was fourteen or fifteen years old. Beginning in the 1970s, Arnitz made numerous unsuccessful attempts to quit smoking. In 2000, he was diagnosed with lung cancer and emphysema. He was unable to quit smoking until he began chemotherapy treatments, and he last smoked in August 2000. The medical testimony that Arnitz presented reflected that his more than thirty-five-year smoking history caused his lung cancer and emphysema.

Arnitz filed his original complaint on June 6, 2000, and filed his amended complaint on June 30, 2000, against Philip Morris and other defendants whom Arnitz subsequently dropped from the lawsuit. The amended complaint asserted claims for negligence, strict liability, and "conspiracy to commit actual fraud." At issue here is the strict liability claim, which alleged design defects in Philip Morris brand cigarettes....

In the amended complaint, Arnitz alleged as follows:

> At all times material, the ordinary consumer, including the plaintiff, did not in the exercise of ordinary diligence know of the likelihood of, the severity of, or the risks from defendants' tobacco products, which risks are outlined above. However, plaintiff admits he shares comparative fault with defendants and seeks an apportionment of damages.

Arnitz points out on appeal that this allegation reflects that "while Arnitz knew that smoking posed some health risk, he and other consumers did not know of the increased risk posed by the defects in the product." Thus, Arnitz proceeded on the theory that he was partially at fault and that the jury should apportion an appropriate percentage of responsibility to him.

On July 1, 2004, Arnitz filed his notice that he was dropping the conspiracy to defraud claims. On July 6, 2004, Philip Morris filed its notice that it was withdrawing certain affirmative defenses, including its affirmative defense of "comparative fault and/or comparative negligence." Then, on July 22, 2004, Philip Morris filed its motion to strike Arnitz's references in his pleadings to comparative negligence and apportionment of fault. Judge William P. Levens, who was not assigned to try the case, conducted a hearing on Philip Morris's motion on August 4, 2004. He granted Philip Morris's motion to strike references to comparative fault and apportionment of damages in Arnitz's reply to the affirmative defenses. Judge Levens denied Philip Morris's motion to strike Arnitz's "self-limiting admission of fault and apportionment of damages" in the amended complaint and left it to the trial judge to determine whether Arnitz should be free to raise the issue at trial.

On September 2, 2004, Philip Morris filed a motion entitled "Defendant Philip Morris USA Inc.'s Motion in Limine to Exclude Plaintiff's Argument and Evidence of Comparative Fault, and Admit Evidence Regarding Plaintiff's Awareness of the Risks of Smoking and Plaintiff's Smoking Decisions." In it, Philip Morris argued that Arnitz should not be allowed to introduce evidence of comparative fault because Philip Morris had withdrawn that affirmative defense. However, in the same motion it argued that it should be able to present evidence of Arnitz's awareness of the risks of smoking to rebut his design defect claim. Philip Morris argued that it was necessary to show that Arnitz was aware of the dangers of smoking to prove that its cigarettes were not "dangerous to the extent beyond that which would be contemplated by the ordinary consumer," citing *Cassisi v. Maytag Co.*, 396 So.2d 1140, 1144 (Fla. 1st DCA 1981). Philip Morris contended that this evidence could be introduced, subject to a limiting instruction that the jury not consider the evidence as fault on the part of Arnitz.

The trial judge, Judge Sam D. Pendino, heard this motion on October 4, 2004, two days before the beginning of jury selection. Judge Pendino denied the motion and agreed with Arnitz that because he pleaded comparative fault he could present evidence on the issue, even though Philip Morris had withdrawn that defense. Judge Pendino stated, "I can understand if you want to drop your affirmative defense of comparative fault, but to preclude them from presenting whatever case they want to present would not be equitable. They can argue comparative fault in any aspect of a case, particularly if they plead it." Further, the judge stated, "I just don't think that I can tell the plaintiff how they should present their case. They want to admit a certain amount of fault, I'm going to let them."

Later that day, while the court was considering a host of other motions in limine, Arnitz announced that he would be dropping his failure to warn claims and negligence claims entirely; thus, Arnitz was going to proceed to trial solely on the strict liability design defect claim. In light of these changed circumstances, Philip Morris moved for reconsideration of the trial court's ruling on its motion to preclude Arnitz from introducing evidence of comparative fault. The trial court stated that "if the Defense could use it [comparative fault] in a strict liability case, so can the Plaintiff." After the parties presented case law supporting the proposition that a defendant could raise comparative negligence in a strict liability case, the trial court denied Philip Morris's motion for reconsideration.

A fourteen-day trial ensued, at which both parties presented evidence regarding Arnitz's comparative fault. The trial court instructed the jury on comparative fault. The jury found that Philip Morris placed "Marlboro or Benson & Hedges cigarettes on the market with a defective design which was a legal cause of loss, injury or damage to" Arnitz. The jury awarded a gross award of $600,000 but assigned sixty percent of the responsibility for the damages to Arnitz and forty percent to Philip Morris. Thus, the trial court entered a final judgment for Arnitz in the amount of $240,000.

On appeal, Philip Morris contends that a plaintiff cannot inject comparative fault into a lawsuit and that comparative fault is strictly an affirmative defense for the defendant to raise. We recognize at the outset that comparative fault is generally raised as an affirmative defense. Furthermore, the Florida Supreme Court has recognized that a defendant is entitled to raise comparative negligence as a defense in a strict liability case alleging a design defect if based on grounds "other than failing to discover or guard against a defect" and that "lack of ordinary due care could constitute a defense to strict tort liability." Thus, comparative negligence can be raised as a defense in a case alleging a design defect in cigarettes, unless the defendant claims that the plaintiff's fault is in not discovering the alleged defects in the cigarettes. Here, the alleged defects are that the tobacco was flue cured and that the additives made the cigarettes more inhaleable and more dangerous. Although Arnitz asserted that he did not know of these alleged defects, he acknowledged some comparative fault because he knew generally of the hazards of smoking, he should have quit smoking, and perhaps he did not try hard enough to quit.

The fact that comparative negligence may be raised as an affirmative defense does not mean that a defendant can determine how a plaintiff shapes his theory of the case. Arnitz points out on appeal that even though he "acknowledged partial responsibility for his smoking-related injuries, Philip Morris claims to have had the right to censor the presentation of Arnitz' case and to suppress truthful testimony in order to prevent Arnitz' acceptance of partial responsibility from reaching the jury." ...

Here, although Philip Morris had withdrawn its affirmative defense of comparative negligence, Arnitz had pleaded comparative fault in his amended complaint. Arnitz's theory of his case was that although he was aware of health risks associated with smoking cigarettes and, therefore, was partly to blame for having smoked despite knowing those risks, he was unaware of the design defects in Philip Morris's cigarettes that made them even more dangerous.

We agree with Arnitz that if a plaintiff chooses to plead his own comparative fault, a defendant should not be able to control the plaintiff's theory of his case and preclude the plaintiff from accepting some responsibility for his injuries....

Here, Phillip Morris asserts that it must be allowed the choice in which defenses it raises. However, ... Arnitz, as plaintiff, must be allowed to choose the theory under which his case is tried. Arnitz admitted that he was partly responsible for his injuries because he continued to smoke after he became aware of the health risks associated with smoking; but he also contended that Philip Morris brand cigarettes had a design defect that made them even more dangerous and that he and other consumers were unaware of this increased health risk. We conclude that the trial court did not err in allowing Arnitz to present his theory of the case to the jury and, based on the pleadings, in instructing the jury on comparative negligence.

Judgment affirmed.

Hypothetical

The luge is a Winter Olympics event in which lugers sled down a bobsleigh run, lying face up and feet first. Steering requires flexing of the sled's runners with the calf of each leg, or exerting opposite shoulder pressure to the seat. Accomplished lugers can achieve speeds of over 85 m.p.h., and the fastest recorded speed was over 95 m.p.h.

Shawn is a luger, who was hoping to qualify for the U.S. Winter Olympic team. He accordingly took part in trials to identify the fastest lugers in the nation, at which each competitor was supplied with a new type of sled, designed and built by a brand-new corporation, Snowcraft USA.

During practice before the first officially timed run, many of the competitors complained that the sleds made bends 9 and 10 too dangerous because they were simply traveling too fast, so that many of the lugers were struggling to maintain control. Shawn and another competitor, Gene, gave an interview to a national television station, in which Shawn asked: "Are they trying to kill us?" Gene nodded, and commented: "Well, it's happened before," which was widely understood at the time to be a reference to the death of an Olympic luger in Canada in 2010.

In a public statement, the organizing body rejected the criticisms as "the expression of inevitable nerves before a big event." It said that its technical team had inspected the run before practice began, and had evaluated it according to internationally-agreed standards as "tough, but fair." It suggested that this was entirely appropriate for an Olympic qualifying competition, and noted that the sleds were doing precisely what is expected of them: go fast.

Despite their criticisms, both Gene and Shawn took part in the official competition the next day. On his first officially-timed run, Gene set a time that placed him in the top 20% of those who had competed by that stage. Shawn's run followed. He built up terrific speed through bend 9, which caused him to run so wide on bend 10 that he and his sled were launched out of the run as if fired like a human cannonball. He flew into a television crane with such force that his injuries rendered him a tetraplegic.

It has since become clear that the runners on the Snowcraft sleds are much less flexible than those on better-known brands, a fact that makes them faster in a straight line but much more difficult to steer.

The crane into which Shawn crashed was supporting a television cameraman and his equipment. The force of the impact caused the camera to collapse on the cameraman, who fell from his perch and landed on the partially snow-covered ground over twenty feet below, sustaining breaks to his wrist, both legs, and a rib. It has since been established that the camera had been fitted with the wrong tripod at manufacture, so that it was inherently unstable. It has also emerged that the cameraman had completely failed to secure the camera to the crane, despite the manufacturer's strong recommendations that this must be done when in use in such circumstances.

Advise Shawn and the cameraman. Would it make a difference if:

(a) the competitors had signed a waiver relating to the sleds?

(b) the remaining lugers refused to continue the event unless and until provided with well-known types of sled?

(c) the organizers subsequently provided the remaining lugers with different types of sleds to complete the competition, even before asked to do so by the lugers themselves?

Chapter 12

Lapse of Time

Statutes of Limitations

One of the cornerstones of the rule of law is the idea that everyone should be in a position to know his or her rights and obligations before making a decision to embark on, or refrain from, a particular course of conduct. While this notion is discussed most commonly in relation to constitutional and criminal law, it is equally applicable to matters that are the province of private, civil law. This is why, for example, those not party to a contract are immune from suit for breach of that contract. It also explains the power of the concept of foreseeability in torts. If a person had no reason to believe that someone else would be affected by his or her conduct, it would be unjustifiable to impose an obligation to take care to avoid injuring that person.

The same reasoning also means that alleged victims of someone else's unlawful conduct must bring their claims in a timely fashion. This provides a degree of predictability to potential defendants, who would otherwise be open to lawsuits into perpetuity.

The traditional means of imposing time limits on a plaintiff's right to bring a claim are known as limitations periods or—because such periods are typically established by legislation—statutes of limitations. They operate by requiring that a victim bring suit within a fixed period after s/he first becomes aware (or should have become aware) that s/he has sustained an injury. In *Griffin v. Unocal Corp.*, 990 So.2d 291 (Ala.2008), for example, the executrix of the estate of a deceased former employee of a tire-manufacturing facility brought a wrongful death action against chemical companies, alleging that the employee's acute myelogenous leukemia was caused by exposure to various chemicals during his employment. The Tuscaloosa Circuit Court held the claims to be barred by Alabama's two-year statute of limitations because the claims had been brought too late after the last date of exposure. The Supreme Court reversed and remanded because of its holding that a personal injury action based on exposure to hazardous chemicals did not accrue on the date of last exposure to those chemicals, but when injury manifested itself.

The period involved typically ranges between one and six years, depending on the precise nature of the claim (such as whether it is framed in contracts or torts) and the jurisdiction. Some statutes have set out special time limits for particular products, such as asbestos, hazardous chemical substances, and intrauterine devices.

If two different statutes of limitations appear applicable to the same case, the usual approach is to apply the stricter limit. In *Kambury v. DaimlerChrysler Corp.*, 50 P.3d 1163, 1164 (2002), for example, the Supreme Court of Oregon had to determine which limitations period applies in a civil action seeking damages for the death of a person killed by a defective product. It noted:

The trial court examined the statute specifying a three-year limitation period for wrongful death actions and the statute providing for a two-year limitation period for product liability actions, and concluded that the two-year period applied. The Court of Appeals analyzed the same statutes and concluded that the three-year period applied. We conclude that the Court of Appeals erred. Accordingly, we reverse and remand for further proceedings.

A similar conflict over the appropriate limitations period arises when a plaintiff has suffered different types of harm at different times as a result of using the same defective product.

Pooshs v. Philip Morris USA, Inc.
250 P.3d 181 (2011) (Supreme Court of California)

KENNARD, J. Plaintiff was a cigarette smoker for 35 years, from 1953 through 1987. In 1989, she was diagnosed with chronic obstructive pulmonary disease (COPD), which plaintiff knew was caused by her smoking habit. Nevertheless, she did not sue the manufacturers of the cigarettes that she had smoked, and the statutory period for doing so elapsed.

In 1990 or 1991, plaintiff was diagnosed with periodontal disease, which she knew was caused by her smoking habit. Again, she did not sue the various cigarette manufacturers, and the statutory period for doing so elapsed.

In 2003, plaintiff was diagnosed with lung cancer. This time, she sued. We must decide whether the lawsuit is barred by the statute of limitations, which requires that a suit be brought within a specified period of time after the cause of action accrues.

The matter comes to us from the United States Court of Appeals for the Ninth Circuit. The Ninth Circuit has asked us to answer two questions:

1. Under California law, when may two separate physical injuries arising out of the same wrongdoing be conceived of as invading two different primary rights?

2. Under California law, may two separate physical injuries—both caused by a plaintiff's use of tobacco—be considered "qualitatively different" for the purposes of determining when the applicable statute of limitations begins to run? (*Pooshs v. Phillip Morris USA, Inc.* (9th Cir.2009) 561 F.3d 964, 966–967.)

In granting the Ninth Circuit's request, we restated the two questions in a single question: "When multiple distinct personal injuries allegedly arise from smoking tobacco, does the earliest injury trigger the statute of limitations for all claims, including those based on the later injury? " ...

With respect to the first question, we held in *Grisham* [*v. Philip Morris U.S.A., Inc.* (2007)] 40 Cal.4th 623, 54 Cal.Rptr.3d 735, 151 P.3d 1151, that there is no special presumption that smokers are aware of the dangers of smoking. We observed, however, that there is a general, rebuttable presumption that a plaintiff has knowledge of the wrongful causes of an injury. To rebut this general presumption a plaintiff must make certain specific allegations that the plaintiff in *Grisham* had not made and, in light of her other allegations, could not plausibly make. Accordingly, in that case the plaintiff's economic injury claim was time-barred under the applicable statute of limitations....

A statute of limitations strikes a balance among conflicting interests. If it is unfair to bar a plaintiff from recovering on a meritorious claim, it is also unfair to require a defendant to defend against possibly false allegations concerning long-forgotten events, when important evidence may no longer be available. Thus, statutes of limitations are not mere technical defenses, allowing wrongdoers to avoid accountability. Rather, they mark the point where, in the judgment of the legislature, the equities tip in favor of the defendant (who may be innocent of wrongdoing) and against the plaintiff (who failed to take prompt action):

> [T]he period allowed for instituting suit inevitably reflects a value judgment concerning the point at which the interests in favor of protecting valid claims are outweighed by the interests in prohibiting the prosecution of stale ones. (*Johnson v. Railway Express Agency* (1975) 421 U.S. 454, 463–464, 95 S.Ct. 1716, 44 L.Ed.2d 295.)

Critical to applying a statute of limitations is determining the point when the limitations period begins to run. Generally, a plaintiff must file suit within a designated period after the cause of action accrues. (Code Civ. Proc., § 312.) A cause of action accrues "when [it] is complete with all of its elements"—those elements being wrongdoing, harm, and causation. (*Norgart v. Upjohn Co.*, 21 Cal.4th 383, 397.)

Application of the accrual rule becomes rather complex when, as here, a plaintiff is aware of both an injury and its wrongful cause but is uncertain as to how serious the resulting damages will be or whether additional injuries will later become manifest. Must the plaintiff sue even if doing so will require the jury to speculate regarding prospective damages? Or can the plaintiff delay suit until a more accurate assessment of damages becomes possible? Generally, we have answered those questions in favor of prompt litigation, even when the extent of damages remains speculative. Thus, we have held that "the infliction of appreciable and actual harm, however uncertain in amount, will commence the statutory period." (*Davies v. Krasna*, 14 Cal.3d 502, 514.)

The most important exception to that general rule regarding accrual of a cause of action is the "discovery rule," under which accrual is postponed until the plaintiff "discovers, or has reason to discover, the cause of action." (*Norgart v. Upjohn Co., supra*, 21 Cal.4th at p. 397.) Discovery of the cause of action occurs when the plaintiff "has reason ... to suspect a factual basis" for the action. (*Id.* at p. 398.) "The policy reason behind the discovery rule is to ameliorate a harsh rule that would allow the limitations period for filing suit to expire before a plaintiff has or should have learned of the latent injury and its cause." (*Buttram v. Owens-Corning Fiberglas Corp.* (1997) 16 Cal.4th 520, 531.) ...

As relevant here, the plaintiff in *Grisham* sued cigarette manufacturers for smoking-related injuries. She contended that the cigarette manufacturers had wrongfully induced her addiction to tobacco, and she alleged claims for economic injury (the cost of purchasing cigarettes) and personal injury (emphysema and periodontal disease). We concluded in *Grisham* that the economic injury claim was barred by the applicable statute of limitations because the plaintiff knew or should have known about her injury long before she filed suit. That conclusion raised the question whether the personal injury claims were also barred, on the theory that the plaintiff had suffered only one indivisible harm and that the physical injuries were simply another category of damages related to that single harm. In addressing this question in *Grisham*, we did not decide whether the two injuries (economic and physical) implicated two separate primary rights. Instead, we focused exclusively on the statute of limitations, and we held that appreciable harm in the form of an economic injury does not begin the running of the statute of limitations on a suit to recover damages for a physical injury. *Grisham* interpreted the "appreciable and actual harm" rule ... to be limited to cases involving a single type of injury, and we found no case applying that rule to a later-discovered injury of a different type.

In *Grisham*, we also emphasized the impractical consequences of a contrary conclusion, relying on *Fox v. Ethicon Endo-Surgery, Inc.* (2005) 35 Cal.4th 797, 27 Cal.Rptr.3d 661, 110 P.3d 914. There, the plaintiff underwent gastric bypass surgery. She later sued the surgeon and the hospital for medical malpractice. During discovery, she learned that her alleged injury might have been caused by a defective stapler manufactured by a nonparty. The plaintiff then amended her complaint to add as a defendant the stapler manufacturer, which asserted the statute of limitations as a defense. We concluded in *Fox* that knowledge of the facts supporting a medical malpractice cause of action against one defendant does not necessarily commence the running of the statute of limitations with respect to a separate products liability cause of action against a different defendant.

Grisham involved a claim against the *same* defendants alleging *different* injuries, whereas *Fox* involved a claim against *different* defendants alleging the *same* injury. Nevertheless, we held that the policy underlying our holding in *Fox* was equally applicable in *Grisham*. In *Grisham*, we quoted the following language from *Fox*:

> [I]t would be contrary to public policy to require plaintiffs to file a lawsuit "at a time when the evidence available to them failed to indicate a cause of action." Were plaintiffs required to file all causes of action when one cause of action accrued, ... they would run the risk of sanctions for filing a cause of action without any factual support. Indeed, it would be difficult to describe a cause of action filed by a plaintiff, before that plaintiff reasonably suspects that the cause of action is a meritorious one, as anything but frivolous. At best, the plaintiff's cause of action would be subject to demurrer for failure to specify supporting facts. (*Grisham*, 40 Cal.4th at pp. 644–645, quoting *Fox*, 35 Cal.4th at p. 815.)

Applying that language from *Fox* to the facts in *Grisham*, we rejected a rule that

> would compel cigarette smokers either to file groundless tort causes of action based on physical injury against tobacco companies as soon as they discovered they were addicted to cigarettes and had an unfair competition cause of action…, or risk losing their right to sue in tort for such physical injury.

Such a requirement, *Grisham* said, "would violate the essence of the discovery rule that a plaintiff need not file a cause of action before he or she 'has reason at least to suspect a factual basis for its elements.'" Furthermore, "[i]t would directly contravene 'the interest of the courts and of litigants against the filing of potentially meritless claims.'" In *Grisham*, we expressly stopped short of deciding the issue presented here, in which a single wrong gives rise to two injuries of the same general type (physical injuries), but the two injuries become manifest at different times and are alleged to be separate and distinct. Nevertheless, we see no reason not to apply to this case the logic of *Grisham*. In both cases, the injuries arose at different times and were separate from one another. In *Grisham*, the injuries were separate from one another in that one was economic and the other was physical; here, the Ninth Circuit has asked us to assume that the injuries are three separate diseases....

It is true that here plaintiff's COPD involved the same part of the body (the lungs) as her lung cancer. Nevertheless, as we noted earlier, the Ninth Circuit has asked that in deciding the statute of limitations issue we accept as true plaintiff's factual assertion "that COPD is a separate illness, which does not pre-dispose or lead to lung cancer and that it has nothing medically, biologically, or pathologically to do with lung cancer." (See 123 Cal.Rptr.3d at p. 588.) Assuming that assertion to be true, it does not matter that both diseases affect the lungs. The significant point is that the later-occurring disease (lung cancer) is, according to plaintiff's offer of proof, a disease that is separate and distinct from the earlier-occurring disease (COPD). Therefore, under the logic of our decision in *Grisham*, the statute of limitations bar can apply to one disease without applying to the other.

In response to the Ninth Circuit's inquiry, we conclude that when a later-discovered latent disease is separate and distinct from an earlier-discovered disease, the earlier disease does not trigger the statute of limitations for a lawsuit based on the later disease.

CANTIL-SAKAUYE, C.J., and BAXTER, WERDEGAR, CHIN, CORRIGAN, and SUZUKAWA, JJ. concurred.

Notes

1. *Accrual of cause of action.* It was stressed in the very first Chapter of this book that no cause of action for products liability can arise unless and until the plaintiff has suffered a physical injury. "Wrongdoing" alone, without any resultant injury, is insufficient to found a lawsuit. In many ways, all that *Pooshs* does is apply that truism.

2. *Analogy with asbestos cases.* The Ninth Circuit had expressly asked the Court to assume that all three injuries suffered by the plaintiff in *Pooshs* were separate, independent illnesses. This is analogous to the way in which cases of asbestosis and mesothelioma are handled, as we saw in Chapter 10.

3. *Tolling.* Whatever limitation period is laid down, it is extended in certain circumstances. In each case the limitation period is said to be "tolled" (i.e. suspended) until a later date, at which the statute of limitation will then start to run. What the Supreme Court of California referred to in *Pooshs* as the "discovery rule" is one example: the limitation period was tolled until the victim discovered, or ought to have discovered, her injury. Another circumstance in which the limitation period is tolled is where the victim is a minor, in which case it is tolled until the victim attains the age of majority. A limitation period will also be tolled if the defendant unlawfully conceals evidence of responsibility for the victim's injury, until such time as the latter becomes aware (or should have become aware) of the relevant information.

Questions

1. If the plaintiff in *Pooshs* had previously sued Philip Morris for her COPD and/or periodontal disease, would she still have been able to sue for the lung cancer?

2. Would it make more sense to treat all injuries to the same part of the body as one type of injury?

3. Would it be helpful to create a new rule that all injuries caused by the same defective product are treated as one type of injury?

Statutes of Repose

Cases like *Pooshs* illustrate why many manufacturers of products feel that statutes of limitations do not protect their interests sufficiently. They would prefer to have much greater certainty as to their current legal position, and so argue for clearly-defined time limits that cannot be tolled, and to which the "discovery rule" is inapplicable. Section 2-725 of the Uniform Commercial Code provides a model for such a rule, although it still permits tolling.

Uniform Commercial Code—Article 2—Sales (1952)

§ 2-725. Statute of Limitations in Contracts for Sale

(1) An action for breach of any contract for sale must be commenced within four years after the cause of action has accrued. By the original agreement the parties may reduce the period of limitation to not less than one year but may not extend it.

(2) A cause of action accrues when the breach occurs, regardless of the aggrieved party's lack of knowledge of the breach. A breach of warranty occurs when tender of delivery is made, except that where a warranty explicitly extends to future performance of the goods and discovery of the breach must await the time of such performance the cause of action accrues when the breach is or should have been discovered....

(4) This section does not alter the law on tolling of the statute of limitations ...

Notes

1. *Nomenclature.* Obviously the UCC is concerned with the law of contracts. Moreover, despite its nomenclature, § 2-725 does not (apart from subsection (4)) operate like a form of statute of limitations as traditionally conceived in the law of torts. This is because tort law has always required (a) that there be some form of harm or injury before there could be any grounds for bringing a lawsuit, and (b) that the limitation period could not start to run unless and until the victim was aware (or should have been aware) of sustaining an injury. In the law of contracts, however, the period of time in which to bring an action has traditionally run from the date of breach.

2. *Length of time.* As we saw in Chapter 3, the UCC grew out of the Uniform Sales Act of 1906 which, in turn, was modeled on England's Sale of Goods Act 1893. The limitations period in § 2-725 does not, however, directly reflect the position in England. There the equivalent period is six years from the date of breach, or three years in cases where the breach is alleged to have caused physical injury or death.

3. *Tort reform.* Over the last thirty years or so, some states have passed statutes, known as "statutes of repose," to create ultimate endpoints, beyond which no claims can be made in the law of torts (including products liability) in a manner analogous to § 2-725(a) of the UCC. As with other instances of so-called "tort reform," they are designed to limit both the availability and size of awards of damages to plaintiffs.

4. *Turning the tide.* In many ways, statutes of repose mark something of a turning of a tide in the law. The previous forty years or so had seen the law move steadily away from complete defenses such as assumption of risk and contributory negligence (and, before that, the abandonment of the "fellow servant" rule) towards a more nuanced approach typified by the doctrine of comparative fault, where a sort of "balancing of equities" can be performed by a jury that has heard all the evidence in the case. Statutes of limitation fit well with this trend since, as the Supreme Court of California noted in *Pooshs*, "they mark the point where ... the equities tip," and allow the period to be tolled in appropriate circumstances.

Statutes of repose, by contrast, introduce a new complete defense at a point in time that has nothing to do with the facts of each case. Indeed, they essentially represent a rejection of the notion of balancing the interests of plaintiff and defendant. They are instead designed to create a more predictable economic climate for product manufacturers, and they also have the effect of reducing the need to maintain records that may be required to mount an effective defense to a lawsuit (or that may be accessed by the plaintiff through discovery).

5. *Periods of repose.* Under statutes of repose, which typically impose periods of between four and twelve years (depending on jurisdiction and type of claim), the clock starts ticking at the time the product was manufactured, sold, delivered, or used, rather than at the time of any injury. As a result, plaintiffs who suffer an injury well after purchasing or using the product, or well after it was manufactured, may find that they are unable to bring a claim because the time period which their state has deemed appropriate for such claims has passed. While this probably affects relatively few cases, it can be extremely problematic for plaintiffs who have contracted a devastating disease that takes a long time to manifest itself, such as lung cancer or mesothelioma. Statutes of repose typically do not apply, however, to cases where the defendant engaged in willful, wanton, or reckless conduct.

6. *Tolling.* Just like a limitation period, periods of repose may also be tolled, albeit in much more limited circumstances. A statute of repose will normally be tolled only if the defendant unlawfully conceals evidence of its responsibility for the victim's injury, until such time as the latter becomes aware (or should have become aware) of the relevant information.

In *Stimpson v. Ford Motor Co.*, 988 So.2d 1119 (Fla.2008), for example, the buyer of an automobile brought an action against Ford, alleging that a defect caused the vehicle to unexpectedly accelerate, injuring her. The Circuit Court entered summary judgment in favor of Ford, but the Fifth District Court of Appeal for Florida noted that the plaintiff had adduced evidence that Ford had both known of this defect and concealed it for some time. The state's twelve-year statute of repose would have been tolled during any period of concealment. Accordingly, there was a genuine issue of material fact that precluded summary judgment as to whether the statute of repose governing the buyer's product liability claim was tolled, so that the case was reversed and remanded.

7. *Relationship with statutes of limitations.* Statutes of repose do not replace or preempt statutes of limitations; instead, where they overlap, a plaintiff must meet the filing requirements of the more restrictive statute. This will change according to whether the injury sustained by the plaintiff is patent—i.e., readily noticeable—or latent. If patent, the statute of limitations will normally set the more restrictive deadline, since both periods will start to run at more or less the same time, and the limitations period is typically significantly shorter. If the injury sustained is latent, however, the statute of limitations will be tolled until the injury becomes apparent. For this reason, the statute of repose will normally set the more restrictive period since, although the period involved will be longer, it will have started to run on manufacture or sale of the product, irrespective of the latency of any injury. It should also be noted that statutes of repose will often set more restrictive periods of time when the victim is a minor, regardless of whether the injury sustained is latent or patent.

8. *Post-sale duties to warn.* It appears that post-sale duties to warn are not normally subject to statutes of repose. One of the justifications for such statutes relates to evidentiary and discovery issues (specifically, that evidence may get lost or destroyed, and that manufacturers may go out of business). These same issues do not apply to the post-sale duty to warn because most of the crucial evidence—regarding the actions of the manufacturer after its learning of a latent defect—cannot come into existence until some time after the initial sale of the product.

Of course, as we saw in Chapter 8, not all states recognize post-sale duties. But where they are recognized, the application to them of a statute of repose would make very little sense. As the Supreme Court of Georgia recognized in *Chrysler v. Batten*, 450 S.E. 2d

208, 213 (1994), there is "the possibility that this duty may not emerge until long after the statute of repose has extinguished any cause of action arising out of the product's sale." That would fundamentally undermine the purpose of recognizing a post-sale duty to warn in the first place. Indeed, if a statute of repose applied to such post-sale duties, then once the period of repose expired, the manufacturer would be best advised to remain silent about any new dangers of which it subsequently learns, in case its issuing of a warning were taken to indicate that it is voluntarily assuming a new obligation. The Oregon Supreme Court thus explained in *Erickson Air Crane v. United Technologies Corp.*, 735 P.2d 614 (1987), that:

> In refusing to apply the statute of repose to the plaintiff's post-sale failure to warn claim, the court [must] carefully and rightfully distinguish[] between the timing of a defendant's conduct giving rise to a time-of-sale breach of duty and the conduct constituting a post-sale failure to warn.

Constitutionality

Having been recognized in old English common law long before their introduction stateside, there is no doubt that limitations periods are constitutional unless unreasonably short. However, since they are much more modern creations and work very differently, the same cannot be said so categorically about statutes of repose.

Heath v. Sears, Roebuck & Co.

123 N.H. 512 (1983) (Supreme Court of New Hampshire)

DOUGLAS, J. Generally, both federal and State courts recognize the power of legislative bodies to enact statutes of limitations which prescribe a reasonable time within which a party is permitted to bring suit for the recovery of his rights. The United States Supreme Court has stated:

> It may be properly conceded that all statutes of limitation[s] must proceed on the idea that the party has full opportunity afforded him to try his right in the courts. A statute could not bar the existing rights of claimants without affording this opportunity; if it should do so, it would not be a statute of limitations, but an unlawful attempt to extinguish rights arbitrarily, whatever might be the purport of its provisions. *Wilson v. Iseminger*, 185 U.S. 55, 62, 22 S.Ct. 573, 575, 46 L.Ed. 804 (1902).

The concept of allowing a reasonable period of time for suit to be brought after the cause of action arises is not new in our law, for along with "substantive rights, the first settlers brought over the incidental rights of adequate remedy and convenient procedure." *State v. Saunders*, 66 N.H. 39, 74, 25 A. 588, 589 (1889)....

Part one, article fourteen of the New Hampshire Constitution provides:

> Every subject of this state is *entitled to a certain remedy*, by having recourse to the laws, *for all injuries he may receive* in his person, property, or character; to obtain right and justice freely, without being obliged to purchase it; completely, and without any denial; promptly, and without delay; conformably to the laws (emphasis added).

In an effort to facilitate the vindication of tort victims' rights, legislatures and courts have developed the "discovery" rule, under which a cause of action does not accrue until the plaintiff discovers or, in the exercise of reasonable diligence, should have discovered both the fact of his injury and the cause thereof. *Raymond v. Eli Lilly & Co.*, 117 N.H. 164, 171, 371 A.2d 170, 174 (1977). The rule is premised on "the manifest unfairness of foreclosing an injured person's cause of action before he has had even a reasonable opportunity to discover its existence." *Brown v. Mary Hitchcock Memorial Hosp.*, 117 N.H. 739, 741–42, 378 A.2d 1138, 1139–40 (1977).

Although the legislature's power is broad in determining how long a plaintiff may have to initiate a cause of action and when that limitation period begins to run, this power may not be exercised in an unconstitutional manner. In *Carson v. Maurer*, 120 N.H. 925, 424 A.2d 825 (1980), we held that, although not a fundamental right, "the right to recover for personal injuries is ... an important substantive right." *Id.* at 931–32, 424 A.2d at 830. Thus, the classifications there at issue were required to be "reasonable" and to "rest upon some ground of difference having a fair and substantial relation to the object of the legislation ..." *Id.* at 932, 424 A.2d at 831....

The unreasonableness inherent in a statute which eliminates a plaintiff's cause of action before the wrong may reasonably be discovered was noted by Judge Frank in his dissent in *Dincher v. Marlin Firearms Co.*, 198 F.2d 821, 823 (2d Cir.1952), in which he condemned the "Alice in Wonderland" effect of such a result:

> Except in topsy-turvy land, you can't die before you are conceived, or be divorced before ever you marry, or harvest a crop never planted, or burn down a house never built, or miss a train running on a non-existent railroad. For substantially similar reasons, it has always heretofore been accepted, as a sort of logical 'axiom,' that a statute of limitations does not begin to run against a cause of action before that cause of action exists, *i.e.*, before a judicial remedy is available to a plaintiff.

Reversed and remanded.

Groch v. Gen. Motors Corp.

117 Ohio St.3d 192 (2008) (Supreme Court of Ohio)

O'CONNOR, J. The federal district court's initial certification order reads as follows: ...

> The Amended Complaint alleges the following: Plaintiff Douglas Groch ('Groch') was injured on March 3, 2005 when the trim press he was operating came down on his right arm and wrist. At the time of his injury Plaintiff Douglas Groch was acting in the course and scope of his employment with Defendant General Motors Corporation. The trim press that he was using was manufactured by Defendants Kard Corporation and Racine Federated, Inc.
>
> Groch brought an action in the Court of Common Pleas, Lucas County, Ohio seeking damages from Defendant General Motors Corporation ('GM') based on a theory of employer intentional tort and from Defendants Kard Corporation and Racine Federated, Inc. (respectively, 'Kard' and 'Racine') based on a theory of product liability. Plaintiff Chloe Groch ('Chloe') sought damages for loss of consortium.
>
> The action was removed to federal court by GM. Federal jurisdiction is based on 28 U.S.C. 1332 because there is diversity between the Plaintiffs and the Defendants, and the amount in controversy exceeds $75,000.00....

Kard and Racine assert that they are immune from liability based on the statute of repose for products liability claims provided at R.C. 2305.10. To fully adjudicate this matter and fully determine the rights and liabilities of each party, this Court needs a determination by the Ohio Supreme Court regarding the constitutionality of the statutes under the Ohio Constitution....

R.C. 2305.10(C)(1), the products-liability statute of repose, provides:

> Except as otherwise provided in divisions (C)(2), (3), (4), (5), (6), and (7) of this section or in section 2305.19 of the Revised Code, no cause of action based on a product liability claim shall accrue against the manufacturer or supplier of a product later than ten years from the date that the product was delivered to its first purchaser or first lessee who was not engaged in a business in which the product was used as a component in the production, construction, creation, assembly, or rebuilding of another product.

R.C. 2305.10(C)(2) through (7) lists six exceptions to the operation of that statute, none of which apply in this case....

A central fact in this case is that the trim press that injured Douglas Groch was "delivered" for R.C. 2305.10(C) purposes to the end user, General Motors, more than ten years prior to his injury. Another central fact is that petitioners filed suit "after the effective date of this amendment" for purposes of former R.C. 2305.10(F). Therefore, if R.C. 2305.10(C) and former 2305.10(F) are constitutional, those statutes prevent petitioners from recovering from Kard Corporation and Racine Federated.

Petitioners' arguments that R.C. 2305.10 is unconstitutional are largely based on past decisions of this court holding other statutes of repose unconstitutional. That this court has struck down statutes of repose in the past, however, does not necessarily mean that the products-liability statute of repose in this case must meet the same fate....

The first key point from *Arbino* [*v. Johnson & Johnson*, 116 Ohio St.3d 468, 880 N.E.2d 420 (2007)] is that the legislative branch of government is "the ultimate arbiter of public policy," and in fulfilling that role, the legislature continually refines Ohio's tort law to meet the needs of our citizens.

The second key point is that

> even considering the numerous opinions by this court on this issue, the basic constitutionality of tort-reform statutes is hardly settled law. Our prior review has focused on certain unconstitutional facets of the prior tort-reform laws that can be addressed to create constitutionally valid legislation. We have not dismissed all tort reform as an unconstitutional concept.

> While stare decisis applies to the rulings rendered in regard to specific statutes, it is limited to circumstances "where the facts of a subsequent case are substantially the same as a former case." *Rocky River v. State Emp. Relations Bd.* (1989), 43 Ohio St.3d 1, 5, 539 N.E.2d 103. We will not apply *stare decisis* to strike down legislation enacted by the General Assembly merely because it is similar to previous enactments that we have deemed unconstitutional. To be covered by the blanket of stare decisis, the legislation must be phrased in language that is substantially the same as that which we have previously invalidated. *Id.* at 22–23....

A. Open Courts and Right to a Remedy

Section 16, Article I of the Ohio Constitution provides,

All courts shall be open, and every person, for an injury done him in his land, goods, person, or reputation, shall have remedy by due course of law, and shall have justice administered without denial or delay.

This provision contains two distinct guarantees. First, legislative enactments may restrict individual rights only "by due course of law," a guarantee equivalent to the Due Process Clause of the Fourteenth Amendment to the United States Constitution. *Sedar v. Knowlton Constr. Co.* (1990), 49 Ohio St.3d 193, 199, 551 N.E.2d 938. That aspect of Section 16 will be addressed later in this opinion, in Part III B.

The second guarantee in Section 16 is that

all courts shall be open to every person with a right to a remedy for injury to his person, property or reputation, with the opportunity for such remedy being granted at a meaningful time and in a meaningful manner. *Sedar*, 49 Ohio St.3d at 193.

It is this second guarantee that we address at this point. In considering this aspect of Section 16, it is necessary to discuss our prior decisions in two cases that are significant here, *Sedar v. Knowlton Constr. Co.* and *Brennaman v. R.M.I. Co.* (1994), 70 Ohio St.3d 460, 639 N.E.2d 425....

In opening the analysis in *Sedar*, the court explained the key difference between a statute of repose and a statute of limitations.

Unlike a true statute of limitations, which limits the time in which a plaintiff may bring suit *after* the cause of action accrues, a statute of repose ... potentially bars a plaintiff's suit *before* the cause of action arises (emphasis sic.). *Id.*, 49 Ohio St.3d at 195, 551 N.E.2d 938....

We also observed that

[t]his court would encroach upon the Legislature's ability to guide the development of the law if we invalidated legislation simply because the rule enacted by the Legislature rejects some cause of action currently preferred by the courts.... Such a result would offend our notion of the checks and balances between the various branches of government, and the flexibility required for the healthy growth of the law. *Sedar*, 49 Ohio St.3d at 202.

Sedar ultimately concluded:

The right-to-a-remedy provision of Section 16, Article I applies only to existing, vested rights, and it is state law which determines what injuries are recognized and what remedies are available. *Sedar*, 49 Ohio St.3d at 202....

In *Brennaman v. R.M.I. Co.* (1994), 70 Ohio St.3d 460, 639 N.E.2d 425, this court entertained a constitutional challenge to the same statute, former R.C. 2305.131, that we upheld in *Sedar*....

After acknowledging that *Sedar* had recently upheld the constitutionality of that statute, the court stated, "We revisit our conclusion in *Sedar*." *Brennaman*, 70 Ohio St.3d at 466. In an abbreviated discussion devoid of any in-depth analysis, a majority of this court simply set forth the text of Section 16, Article I; cited one case, *Burgess v. Eli Lilly & Co.* (1993), 66 Ohio St.3d 59, 61, 609 N.E.2d 140, for the proposition that the General Assembly is constitutionally precluded from depriving a claimant of a right to a remedy before the claimant knew or should have known of the injury; and summarily declared that the statute, because it was a statute of repose, deprived the plaintiffs of the right to sue those who had negligently designed or constructed improvements to real property once ten years had elapsed after the negligent service, and was thus unconstitutional. *Brennaman*, 70 Ohio St.3d at 466.

The *Brennaman* court then stated that a plaintiff must have a reasonable period of time to see to seek compensation after an accident under Section 16, Article I and that former R.C. 2305.131 conflicted with this right. The court quoted the dissent in *Sedar* to make the point:

> R.C. 2305.131 effectively closes the courthouse to [Brennaman] and individuals like [her] in contravention of the express language of Section 16, Article I, thereby violating constitutionally protected rights. *Brennaman*, 70 Ohio St.3d at 466, quoting *Sedar*, 49 Ohio St.3d at 205 (Douglas, J., dissenting).

The court completed its discussion of the issue by stating:

> Today we reopen the courthouse doors by declaring that R.C. 2305.131, a statute of repose, violates the right to a remedy guaranteed by Section 16, Article I of the Ohio Constitution, and is, thus, unconstitutional. We overrule *Sedar v. Knowlton Constr. Co.* (*Brennaman*, 70 Ohio St.3d at 466–467) ...

Although R.C. 2305.10(C) is different from the statute of repose at issue in *Sedar* and *Brennaman*, it is similar in a key respect. As with the statute of repose at issue in those cases, R.C. 2305.10(C) operates to potentially bar a plaintiff's suit before a cause of action arises. Thus, the statute can prevent claims from ever vesting if the product that allegedly caused an injury was delivered to an end user more than ten years before the injury occurred. This feature of the statute triggers the portion of *Sedar*'s fundamental analysis concerning Section 16, Article I that is dispositive of our inquiry here. Because such an injured party's cause of action never accrues against the manufacturer or supplier of the product, it never becomes a vested right.

As this court stated in *Sedar*, 49 Ohio St.3d at 202:

> The right-to-a-remedy provision of Section 16, Article I applies only to existing, vested rights, and it is state law which determines what injuries are recognized and what remedies are available.

Here, the General Assembly has established through the enactment of R.C. 2305.10(C) the injuries that are recognized and the remedies that are available. As in *Sedar*, the statute at issue here does not violate Section 16, Article I of the Ohio Constitution....

We find that the interpretation of the open-courts and right-to-a-remedy provisions by this court in *Sedar* is more fully developed and appropriate than that set forth in *Brennaman*. We specifically adopt *Sedar*'s rationale here, finding that its holding is based on proper construction of the requirements of Section 16, Article I....

B. Due Process and Equal Protection

Petitioners assert that R.C. 2305.10(C) and former 2305.10(F) violate the "due course of law" guarantee of Section 16, Article I. Petitioners urge this court to apply strict scrutiny in evaluating the statutes because they restrict fundamental rights. Under such an analysis, a statute restricting fundamental rights "will be considered unconstitutional unless it is shown to be necessary to promote a compelling governmental interest." *Sorrell v. Thevenir*, 69 Ohio St.3d at 423, 633 N.E.2d 504.

As we did in *Arbino*, however, we reject a strict-scrutiny approach to the due-process challenge raised in this case. R.C. 2305.10(C) and former 2305.10(F) do not impinge upon fundamental rights....

We will instead employ a rational-basis review, under which the statute will be upheld if it is rationally related to a legitimate government purpose and is not unreasonable or arbitrary. In conducting this review, we must consider whether the General Assembly's purposes in enacting the legislation at issue provide adequate support to justify the statute's effects....

Because the due-process and equal-protection challenges both require us to review legislative purpose, we will address that issue first.

In Section 3 of S.B. 80, the General Assembly made a "statement of findings and intent" explaining certain provisions of the bill. We will concentrate here on those findings relating to the products-liability statute of repose.

Section 3(C) of S.B. 80 states:

> In enacting division (D)(2) of section 2125.02 and division (C) of section 2305.10 of the Revised Code in this act, it is the intent of the General Assembly to do all of the following: ...
>
> (3) To recognize that subsequent to the delivery of a product, the manufacturer or supplier lacks control over the product, over the uses made of the product, and over the conditions under which the product is used;
>
> (4) To recognize that under the circumstances described in division (C)(3) of this section, it is more appropriate for the party or parties who have had control over the product during the intervening time period to be responsible for any harm caused by the product;
>
> (5) To recognize that, more than ten years after a product has been delivered, it is very difficult for a manufacturer or supplier to locate reliable evidence and witnesses regarding the design, production, or marketing of the product, thus severely disadvantaging manufacturers or suppliers in their efforts to defend actions based on a product liability claim;
>
> (6) To recognize the inappropriateness of applying current legal and technological standards to products manufactured many years prior to the commencement of an action based on a product liability claim;
>
> (7) To recognize that a statute of repose for product liability claims would enhance the competitiveness of Ohio manufacturers by reducing their exposure to disruptive and protracted liability with respect to products long out of their control, by increasing finality in commercial transactions, and by allowing manufacturers to conduct their affairs with increased certainty;
>
> (8) To declare that division (D)(2) of section 2125.02 and division (C) of section 2305.10 of the Revised Code, as enacted by this act, strike a rational balance between the rights of prospective claimants and the rights of product manufacturers and suppliers and to declare that the ten-year statutes of repose prescribed in those sections are rational periods of repose intended to preclude the problems of stale litigation but not to affect civil actions against those in actual control and possession of a product at the time that the product causes an injury to real or personal property, bodily injury, or wrongful death.

For purposes of both due process and equal protection, we determine that the above findings adequately demonstrate that the statutes bear a real and substantial relation to the public health, safety, morals, or general welfare of the public and are not unreasonable or arbitrary....

[W]e uphold the statutes challenged in this case as not unreasonable or arbitrary. Although some of the legislative findings may be open to debate, we will not second-guess their validity. . . .

C. The Takings Clause

[P]etitioners argue that R.C. 2305.10(C) and former 2305.10(F) constitute an improper taking under Section 19, Article I of the Ohio Constitution. Petitioners propose that a person who has sustained bodily injury through the fault of another has a property interest in a claim for relief and that R.C. 2305.10 materially interferes with that property interest, so that a taking occurs when an injured party is "divested of his cause of action."

We reject this argument. . . . An existing, identifiable property interest was at stake in that case—a claimant's tort recovery from a third party through a trial or through a settlement. In contrast, as discussed in Part III A above, the statute of repose at issue in this case involves a cause of action that never accrues and thus is prevented from vesting once the ten-year repose period has passed. Because there is no property right, there can be no taking. Consequently, we determine that R.C. 2305.10(C) and former 2305.10(F) are constitutional on their face under Section 19, Article I.

D. The Retroactivity Clause

Section 28, Article II of the Ohio Constitution provides, "The general assembly shall have no power to pass retroactive laws."

Petitioners assert that former R.C. 2305.10(F) is unconstitutional as applied to them because it retroactively extinguishes a substantive right in violation of Section 28, Article II. Petitioner Douglas Groch was injured on March 3, 2005. The effective date of the S.B. 80 amendments to R.C. 2305.10 was April 7, 2005, after the injury. Pursuant to former R.C. 2305.10(F), R.C. 2305.10(C) applies to all actions "commenced on or after" April 7, 2005. For their suit to be timely, and to avoid the bar of R.C. 2305.10(C), petitioners had to commence their suit prior to April 7, 2005. Petitioners filed their complaint after that date. Therefore, if former R.C. 2305.10(F) and current 2305.10(C) are valid, they combine to prevent petitioners from recovering on their accrued cause of action. . . .

Both R.C. 2305.10(C)(4) and (C)(5) recognize that once a products-liability cause of action accrues, a plaintiff should have no fewer than two years in which to commence a suit. This recognition is consistent with R.C. 2305.10(A), the general products-liability statute of limitations, which states that, subject to certain exceptions (including those in R.C. 2305.10(C)), such a claim "shall be brought within two years after the cause of action accrues." . . .

We hold that former R.C. 2305.10(F) operates unreasonably as applied to petitioners because it provided them with only 34 days to commence their suit, with the consequence that they lost their cause of action if they did not file suit within 34 days. When we look to the other provisions of R.C. 2305.10 referred to above, we determine that a reasonable time to commence a suit in this situation should have been two years from the date of the injury. Under this approach, because petitioners filed their suit within two years of the date of the injury, their suit was timely. To the extent that former R.C. 2305.10(F) mandates a different result, we hold that petitioners have met their burden of demonstrating that the statute as applied to them is unconstitutional under Section 28, Article II.

In light of the foregoing, we hold that to the extent that former R.C. 2305.10(F) (now (G)) affects an accrued substantive right by providing an unreasonably short period of time in which to file suit for certain plaintiffs whose injuries occurred before the S.B. 80 amendments to R.C. 2305.10 became effective, and whose causes of action therefore accrued for purposes of R.C. 2305.10(C), former R.C. 2305.10(F) is unconstitutionally retroactive under Section 28, Article II of the Ohio Constitution.

MOYER, C.J., and LUNDBERG STRATTON and CUPP, JJ., concur.

PFEIFER, J., (concurring in part and dissenting in part). I dissent from this court's holding that R.C. 2305.10 is facially constitutional. I concur with the majority that R.C. 2305.10 is unconstitutional as applied to the appellant and that R.C. 4123.93 and 4123.931 are facially constitutional.

It is hard to decide what is more offensive about the majority opinion regarding the facial constitutionality of R.C. 2305.10: how it arrives at its decision or what the decision means for Ohioans. How the decision will affect Ohioans is speculative at this point, but how the majority reaches its decision demonstrates a continued disdain for *stare decisis* and a propensity to engage in legal mumbo jumbo to obscure that fact.

Today, the majority bases its decision on *Sedar v. Knowlton Constr. Co.*, a case that has been overruled. It remains overruled. The case that overruled *Sedar* and declared statutes of repose unconstitutional pursuant to Section 16, Article I of the Ohio Constitution, *Brennaman v. R.M.I. Co.* remains in effect. Somehow, it does not control this case. This court's decision in *State ex rel. Ohio Academy of Trial Lawyers v. Sheward* (1999), 86 Ohio St.3d 451, 715 N.E.2d 1062, which reiterated our holding in *Brennaman* when the General Assembly once again imposed statutes of repose, is ignored. What has changed since this court last overruled statutes of repose in 1994 and 1999? Not the language of the statutes in question and not the Ohio Constitution.

That this court was clear and blunt in *Brennaman* was no sin. Section 16, Article I of the Ohio Constitution is also clear and blunt:

> All courts shall be open, and every person, for an injury done him in his land, goods, person, or reputation, shall have remedy by due course of law, and shall have justice administered without denial or delay.

As we said in *Brennaman*, "This section of the Ohio Constitution protects the right to seek redress in Ohio's courts when one is injured by another." 70 Ohio St.3d at 466. *Brennaman* relied in part upon this court's decision in *Burgess v. Eli Lilly & Co.* (1993), 66 Ohio St.3d 59, 609 N.E.2d 140, in which

> this court held that the General Assembly is constitutionally precluded from depriving a claimant of a right to a remedy "before a claimant knew or should have known of her injury." *Brennaman*, 70 Ohio St.3d at 466, quoting *Burgess*, 66 Ohio St.3d at 61.

Burgess, in turn, relied upon

> a line of cases … [in which] this court established a threshold point at which government may impose a statute of limitations on a potential claimant. That line of decisions established that a statute of limitations could not begin to run before a claimant knew or should have known of her injury. *Burgess*, 66 Ohio St.3d at 60–61.

As recently as two months ago, *Brennaman* was cited as authority by this court. In *Arbino v. Johnson & Johnson*, the majority opinion cited *Brennaman* as an example of how this court has defined the rights associated with Section 16, Article I. The majority called this court's interpretation "well settled":

The definition of these rights is well settled. "When the Constitution speaks of remedy and injury to person, property, or reputation, it requires an opportunity granted at a meaningful time and in a meaningful manner." We have interpreted this provision to prohibit statutes that effectively prevent individuals from pursuing relief for their injuries. See, *e.g.*, *Brennaman v. R.M.I. Co.* (1994).

For good measure, the *Arbino* majority cited *Brennaman* yet again later in the opinion:

> This right [to a remedy in an open court] protects against laws that completely foreclose a cause of action for injured plaintiffs or otherwise eliminate the ability to receive a meaningful remedy. See *Brennaman*, 70 Ohio St.3d at 466.

The preceding paragraph should have controlled this case. But, in two months, *Brennaman* has morphed from a case worthy of citation as part of this court's well-settled jurisprudence regarding Section 16, Article I of the Ohio Constitution to an object of derision by basically the same majority that relied upon it in *Arbino*....

I do not agree that this court owes all legislation passed by the General Assembly the presumption of constitutionality. This presumption, regrettably employed even by me in a few majority opinions, has no basis in the Constitution. Our role is to determine constitutionality, and we undermine our constitutional role by accepting any impingement on that power by any other branch of government.

In *Sheward*, 86 Ohio St.3d 451, 715 N.E.2d 1062, this court held that the General Assembly's attempt to subvert this court's decision in *Brennaman* by again passing statutes of repose was unconstitutional....

Sheward's discussion on statutes of repose concluded with an admonition ignored by the majority in this case:

> While some members of this court, now and in the past, may disagree with the holding in *Brennaman*, no member of this court can, consistent with his or her oath of office, find that the General Assembly has operated within the boundaries of its constitutional authority by brushing aside a mandate of this court on constitutional issues as if it were of no consequence. Indeed, the very notion of it threatens the judiciary as an independent branch of government and tears at the fabric of our Constitution. *Sheward*, 86 Ohio St.3d at 478.

And so it goes....

Note

The applicability of the various lapse of time defenses is set out in the flowchart in Figure 12.1.

Questions

1. Does the distinction between statutes of repose that prevent the "vesting" or creation of a right to a remedy, and those that extinguish the right after it has come into existence, provide a sound basis for deciding whether such statutes are constitutional?

2. If a case can be resurrected after being overruled, can a right to seek compensation be likewise resurrected after it has apparently been extinguished?

Figure 12.1 Lapse of Time

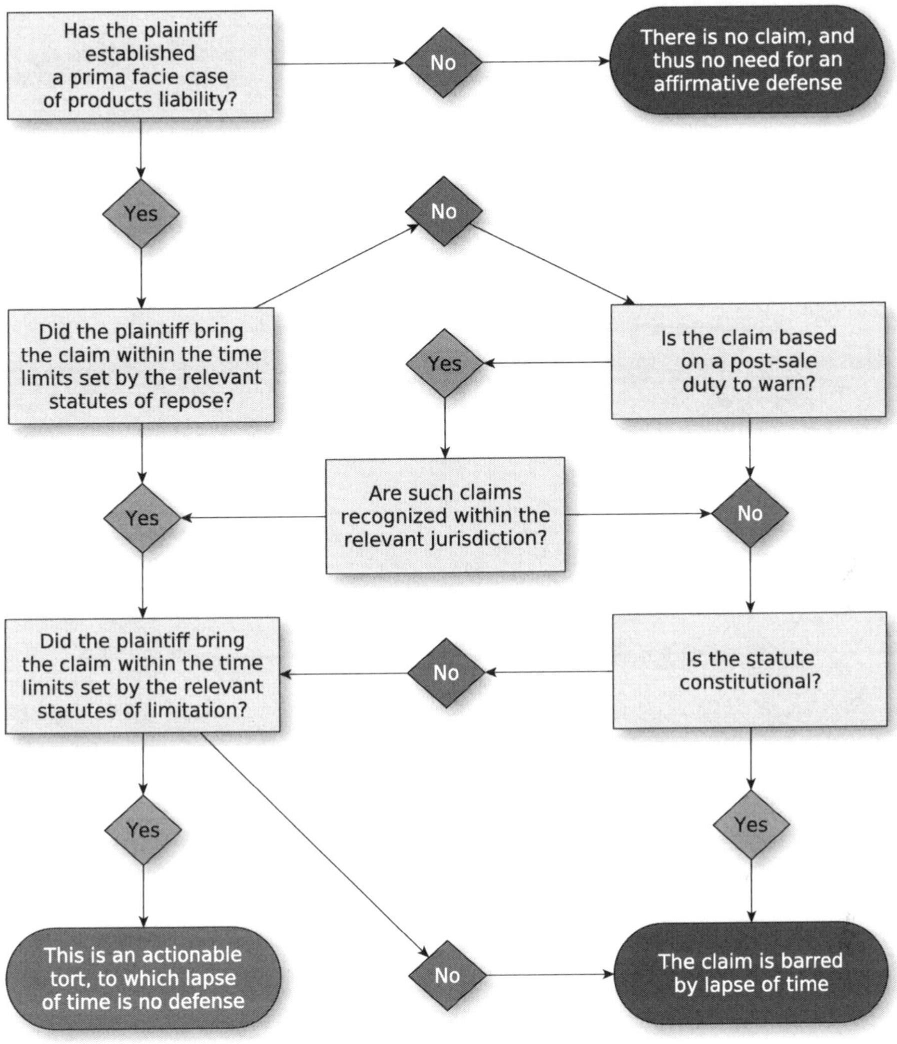

Hypothetical

Georgina used to work at a factory out of town. Her employment came to an end eleven years ago, however, when she was badly burned in a fire that gutted the whole building. After investigations by the fire department and the factory owner's insurers, the cause of the fire was thought to be the careless throwing away of a cigarette by one of Georgina's fellow employees, although the culprit was never identified. Georgina's injuries were sufficiently severe to render her permanently unfit to work, and she received a payment from her employer's workers' compensation scheme.

The owner built a more modern facility at a new location, while the burnt-out factory building has stood, derelict and open to both vagrants and the elements, ever since. Georgina has, however, just been contacted by Joe, who was the deputy chief at the fire department at the time of the original fire and subsequent investigations. It turns out that he never believed the original, official explanation for the fire and, after subsequently being promoted to chief, he took the opportunity to revisit the scene and carry out some further investigations of his own. Indeed, he has done so with six other cases too, whose official explanations he found unsatisfactory. Having recently retired, he has just signed a contract to write a book about these incidents and, in return for passing on his findings to Georgina, he is hoping that she would be able to provide a first-hand account of how fast the fire spread.

Joe says that he has found evidence that shows that the true cause of the fire was a lathe that had been wired incorrectly, causing a short that had slowly melted some cable until it became so hot that it burst into flames. Since the lathe had been delivered only two days before the fire, any such defect would seem to have been present when it was delivered.

Georgina now seeks your advice about the possibility of bringing a claim against the manufacturer of the lathe. But the state has a statute of limitations that sets a time limit of two years for products liability cases, and a statute of repose that sets the ultimate time bar at ten years from the date of delivery. How would you respond?

Chapter 13

Contract-Based Defenses

Plaintiff Waivers

We saw in Chapter 3 that opportunities for a potential defendant to modify or exclude any liability for breach of a contractual warranty are severely limited by §2-316 of the UCC. Under §2-719, moreover, "[l]imitation of consequential damages for injury to the person in the case of consumer goods is prima facie unconscionable." As was pointed out in Chapter 3, it is extremely hard for a product manufacturer to rebut this presumption.

However, it is sometimes easy to forget that there is never any requirement for a manufacturer or distributor to provide any express warranties. Moreover, as we saw in Chapter 3, §2-316(3) of the UCC provides a straightforward means of limiting liability, primarily through the use of terminology such as "goods are sold 'as is'" to prevent the implied warranties of merchantability and fitness for purpose from arising.

In fact, the bigger difficulty for manufacturers and distributors is that waivers, disclaimers, and other limitations of liability based on contracts do not normally bar claims of product defect that sound in torts.

Boles v. Sun Ergoline, Inc.

223 P.3d 724 (2010) (Supreme Court of Colorado)

COATS, J. Savannah Boles brought suit against Sun Ergoline, Inc., asserting a strict products liability claim for personal injury. Sun Ergoline moved for summary judgment, countering that Boles's claim was barred by a release she signed prior to using its product. The trial court agreed and granted Sun Ergoline's motion on the basis of the following undisputed facts.

Executive Tans operated an upright tanning booth manufactured by Sun Ergoline. Prior to using the booth, Boles signed a release form provided by Executive Tans that contained the following exculpatory agreement:

> I have read the instructions for proper use of the tanning facilities and do so at my own risk and hereby release the owners, operators, franchiser, or manufacturers, from any damage or harm that I might incur due to use of the facilities.

After entering the booth, several of Boles's fingers came in contact with an exhaust fan located at the top of the booth, partially amputating them.

On direct appeal, the court of appeals affirmed. In doing so, it found, among other things, that the language of the release was broad enough to include any damage or harm that might occur due to Boles's use of the facilities; that nothing in the law of this jurisdiction precludes a release from insulating a manufacturer from liability for a defective product; and that there existed no genuine issue of material fact suggesting willful and wanton conduct or gross negligence by the defendant. It then applied the four-part test we announced in *Jones v. Dressel*, 623 P.2d 370, 376 (1981), as the district court had also done, and found no violation of public policy.

We granted Boles's petition for a writ of certiorari challenging the court of appeals' determination that the exculpatory agreement barred her strict products liability claim.

More than a quarter century ago, this court rejected the assertion that any agreement purporting to shield a party from liability for its own tortious conduct would violate the public policy of the jurisdiction. Instead we held that although an exculpatory agreement attempting to insulate a party from liability for its own simple negligence may be disfavored, it is not necessarily void. We there delineated four factors to be considered in determining whether such a release agreement should be enforced to bar a claim for damages premised on simple negligence. *Jones*, 623 P.2d at 376

> [T]here are four factors which a court must consider: (1) the existence of a duty to the public; (2) the nature of the service performed; (3) whether the contract was fairly entered into; and (4) whether the intention of the parties is expressed in clear and unambiguous language....

We did not, however, suggest that the factors we identified in *Jones*, with regard to claims of simple negligence, would also be adequate or appropriate to determine the validity of release agreements with regard to other kinds of tort claims. Quite the contrary, at precisely the same time we made clear that in no event could public policy permit an exculpatory agreement to shield against a claim for willful and wanton conduct, regardless of the circumstances or intent of the parties. And more recently, we have identified other public policy considerations invalidating exculpatory agreements, without regard to the *Jones* factors....

"Strict products liability" has been described as a "term of art that reflects the judgment that products liability is a discrete area of tort law which borrows from both negligence and warranty" but "is not fully congruent with classical tort or contract law." Restatement (Third) of Torts: Products Liability § 1 cmt. a (1998). Rather than resting on negligence principles, it "is premised on the concept of enterprise liability for casting a defective product into the stream of commerce." *Smith v. Home Light & Power Co.*, 734 P.2d 1051, 1054 (Colo.1987) (quoting *Jackson v. Harsco Corp.*, 673 P.2d 363, 365 (Colo.1983)). In strict products liability, the focus is on the nature of the product rather than the conduct of either the manufacturer or the person injured.

As such, strict products liability evolved to accommodate, and is driven by, public policy considerations surrounding the relationship between manufacturers and consumers in general, rather than any particular transaction or contract for sale. In addition to the typical inaccessibility of information and inequality of bargaining power inherent in any disclaimer or ordinary consumer's agreement to release a manufacturer, a claim for strict products liability is also premised on a number of public policy considerations that would be flatly thwarted by legitimizing such disclaimers or exculpatory agreements. Not least among these is the deliberate provision of economic incentives for manufacturers to improve product safety and take advantage of their unique "position to spread the risk of loss among all who use the product." *Smith*, 734 P.2d at 1058.

Without fanfare or extended discussion, perhaps because it follows so inexorably from its policy justifications for recognizing this cause of action in the first place, the Second

Restatement of Torts clearly indicates that exculpatory agreements between a manufacturer and an end-user can have no effect. See Restatement (Second) of Torts § 402A cmt. m ("The consumer's cause of action ... is not affected by any disclaimer or other agreement ... attached to and accompanying the product into the consumer's hands."). And although the expanded and more sophisticated discussion of this matter in the Third Restatement distinguishes "the majority of users and consumers" from consumers "represented by informed and economically powerful consumer groups or intermediaries, with full information and sufficient bargaining power," who "contract with product sellers to accept curtailment of liability in exchange for concomitant benefits," the Third Restatement would even more emphatically prohibit "contractual exculpations" from barring or reducing otherwise valid products liability claims for personal injuries by ordinary consumers against sellers or distributors of new products.

There appears to be virtually universal agreement on this point among the other jurisdictions considering the question.

In order to resolve the case before us, we consider it unnecessary, and in fact unwise, to attempt a comprehensive description of the kind of "economically powerful consumer groups" or bargained-for consideration that might conceivably permit, consistent with public policy, a release from claims of strict products liability. It is enough here that an agreement releasing a manufacturer from strict products liability for personal injury, in exchange for nothing more than an individual consumer's right to have or use the product, necessarily violates the public policy of this jurisdiction and is void.

Because the lower courts erred in applying the four-part test of *Jones* to a strict products liability claim and in finding the exculpatory agreement in this case enforceable, the judgment of the court of appeals is reversed with directions to remand for further proceedings consistent with this opinion.

Reversed and remanded.

Note

Used products. As we saw in Chapter 6, being a seller or distributor of a used product is not, by itself, a defense to a products liability claim. This is recognized by § 8 of the Products Liability Restatement, which is quoted in that Chapter. The Restatement's Reporters had originally suggested a rule that disclaimers should be held to be effective in excluding liability for defective used products, but their suggestion was rebuffed by the membership of the American Law Institute. After a number of redrafts, the Reporters came up with a formulation that allows courts to enforce disclaimers regarding used products where it seems appropriate to do so.

Questions

1. If a product manufacturer or distributor does not provide any express warranty for its products, and effectively excludes the implied warranty of merchantability, is it appropriate for someone who suffers an injury caused by a defect in one of these products to circumvent these obstacles by pleading his or her case in another way?

2. Many products sold today are advertised as "recertified," "reconditioned," or "factory reconditioned." Can sellers and distributors of such products effectively disclaim liability for injuries caused by such products?

Government Contractors

The defense of sovereign immunity to claims for compensation is well known, but strangely anomalous in a republic. It originates from England, from a time when the monarch made the law, and the judges, as his appointees—hence the name of the Court of King's (or Queen's) Bench—refused to find against him because it was *his* laws that they were applying.

It is something of an irony that, despite the fact that the Declaration of Independence railed against "the present King of Great Britain ... [who] has made Judges dependent on his Will alone for the tenure of their offices, and the amount and payment of their salaries," the doctrine of sovereign immunity was nevertheless retained in the United States. Indeed, its retention was on much the same basis as it had been explained in England. Justice Oliver Wendell Holmes observed in *Kawananakoa v. Polyblank,* 205 U.S. 349, 353 (1907), for example, that:

> A sovereign is exempt from suit, not because of any formal conception or obsolete theory, but on the logical and practical ground that there can be no legal right as against the authority that makes the law on which the right depends.

So we face the irony that, while the federal Constitution was designed as a system of checks and balances to prevent any one branch of government effectively behaving like a British monarch, American common law permitted the government to do just that. Moreover, such immunity is enjoyed not just by the federal government, but by the states too. In *Alden v. Maine,* 527 U.S. 706 (1999), for example, the Supreme Court held that sovereign immunity was a pre-Constitutional right of the states, which they retained even after the Constitution was ratified.

Ironically, the doctrine of sovereign immunity was abolished in the United Kingdom in 1947, so that cases for compensation are now routinely brought—and won—against the British government without apparently undermining either the legal system or the government itself. In any event, if Justice Holmes's explanation for the longevity of the doctrine is accepted, it provides a justification for the immunity of only the legislature and judiciary, for it is only those branches of government that have the power to make primary law (*i.e.*, statutes and precedents respectively). By definition, the executive has no such power, and should therefore have no such immunity.

That was part of the reasoning behind the Tucker Act of 1887 (28 U.S.C. §§ 1346(a), 1491), which waived sovereign immunity for the federal government in relation to claims brought under the law of contracts (and in some other, non-tortious circumstances). So far as the law of torts is concerned, the Federal Tort Claims Act of 1946 (which was substantially repealed and reenacted as the Federal Tort Claims Act of 1948) abolished sovereign immunity for negligence and other unintentional torts. The Act was passed after an incident in 1945 in which a military pilot's negligence caused a B-25 bomber and its crew to crash into the Empire State Building, leaving the families of those on board or in the building barred from seeking vicarious redress from the federal government. Indeed, that state of affairs was considered so unacceptable that the 1946 statute was even made retroactive to 1945 so as to enable the victims of the crash to claim compensation.

United States Code—Title 28: Federal Tort Claims Act (1948)

§ 2674. Liability of United States

The United States shall be liable, respecting the provisions of this title relating to tort claims, in the same manner and to the same extent as a private individual under like circumstances, but shall not be liable for interest prior to judgment or for punitive damages.

If, however, in any case wherein death was caused, the law of the place where the act or omission complained of occurred provides, or has been construed to provide, for damages only punitive in nature, the United States shall be liable for actual or compensatory damages, measured by the pecuniary injuries resulting from such death to the persons respectively, for whose benefit the action was brought, in lieu thereof.

With respect to any claim under this chapter, the United States shall be entitled to assert any defense based upon judicial or legislative immunity which otherwise would have been available to the employee of the United States whose act or omission gave rise to the claim, as well as any other defenses to which the United States is entitled.

§ 2680. Exceptions

The provisions of this chapter ... shall not apply to—

(a) Any claim based upon an act or omission of an employee of the Government, exercising due care, in the execution of a statute or regulation, whether or not such statute or regulation be valid, or based upon the exercise or performance or the failure to exercise or perform a discretionary function or duty on the part of a federal agency or an employee of the Government, whether or not the discretion involved be abused....

(h) Any claim arising out of ... misrepresentation, deceit, or interference with contract rights ...

(j) Any claim arising out of the combatant activities of the military or naval forces, or the Coast Guard, during time of war.

(k) Any claim arising in a foreign country....

Note

Most states have now also passed legislation to waive the immunity so far as cases of negligence by their employees are concerned, although they maintain the immunity for cases of intentional wrongdoing. Yet, while the bench may no longer be populated by "agents of the king," the courts have repeatedly cut back even these limited attempts to waive sovereign immunity (see, especially, *Feres v. U.S.*, 340 U.S. 135 (1950)), and have even extended it in certain circumstances to cover contractors doing work—including manufacturing what turn out to be defective products—for the government.

Torrington Co. v. Stutzman
46 S.W. 829 (2000) (Supreme Court of Texas)

O'NEILL, J. This case arises out of a Navy helicopter crash that killed two Marines. A jury found that a defective bearing in the helicopter's tail rotor assembly caused the crash. The trial court rendered judgment for the plaintiffs against the bearing's manufacturer and the manufacturer's successor. We consider a number of issues, including ... (4) whether the trial court erred in refusing to submit a jury question on the government-contractor defense ...

On July 31, 1992, a Navy helicopter crashed, killing two Marines, Phillip D. Stutzman and James Pulaski. It is undisputed that the crash was caused by the failure of a bearing, although the parties dispute what caused the bearing to fail. The bearing was manufactured in 1984 by Fafnir Bearings, a division of Textron, Inc. Textron is also the parent company of Bell Helicopter Textron, Inc. (Bell), the company that manufactured the helicopter. Fafnir was purchased in 1985 by Torrington's parent corporation, Ingersoll-Rand Co., and became a division of Torrington. The purchase agreement requires Ingersoll-Rand to indemnify Textron for products liability claims based upon the bearing....

The trial court refused Torrington's request for a jury question on the government-contractor defense. Torrington contends that this refusal was reversible error. We disagree.

The government-contractor defense, also called the military contractor defense, is a federal common-law defense. It is based upon the premise that liability claims arising from government procurement contracts could create a significant conflict between state tort law and the federal interest in immunizing the federal government from liability for performing a "discretionary function," an act for which the government may not be sued under the Federal Tort Claims Act. See *Boyle v. United Techs. Corp.*, 487 U.S. 500, 511, 108 S.Ct. 2510, 101 L.Ed.2d 442 (1988); *Tate v. Boeing Helicopters*, 55 F.3d 1150, 1153 (6th Cir.1995); 28 U.S.C. § 2680(a). The financial burden of judgments against contractors would ultimately be passed through to the United States itself, since defense contractors will predictably raise their prices to cover, or to insure against, continued liability for government-ordered designs. See *Boyle*, 487 U.S. at 511–12. Accordingly, liability for design defects in military equipment cannot be imposed under state law when (1) the United States approved reasonably precise specifications, (2) the equipment conformed to those specifications, and (3) the supplier warned the United States about the dangers in the equipment's use that were known to the supplier but not to the United States.

As *Boyle*'s language indicates, courts have not traditionally applied this defense to manufacturing defects. That is because manufacturing defects are deviations from intended designs and therefore cannot be considered the product of an exercise of discretion. Torrington argues that the defense nevertheless shields Textron from liability based upon the bearing's alleged contamination, relying on *Harduvel v. General Dynamics Corp.*, 878 F.2d 1311 (11th Cir.1989). In *Harduvel*, an F-16 crashed, killing the pilot. The jury, applying Florida law, found manufacturing and design defects in the plane and that the government-contractor defense did not apply. The Eleventh Circuit reversed and rendered judgment for the defendant, holding that the defense applied because the defect complained of was actually a design defect and not a manufacturing defect. Thus, *Harduvel* holds that, under the government-contractor defense, federal law determines the question of whether a defect is one of manufacturing or design.

The *Harduvel* court emphasized that the defense's purpose is to protect the government's exercise of discretion. Therefore, liability for true manufacturing defects, which are deviations from intended designs, are not covered because they cannot be considered the product of an exercise of discretion. As *amicus curiae* Texas Association of Defense Counsel notes: "The government-contractor defense does not apply to manufacturing defects, but is designed to protect only those contractors that follow the government's directives."

We have already held that there is some evidence—the existence of contamination and debris—to support the jury's manufacturing defect finding. Citing *Harduvel*, Torrington argues that even this evidence does not preclude the government-contractor defense if the manufacturing defect is systemic. Again, Torrington misreads *Harduvel*. *Harduvel* holds that evidence of a systemic defect tends to show that the defect is one of design and not manufacture because, if a defect is common, it is more likely intended than unintended. But this distinction is ultimately one between an unintended configuration and an intended configuration that may produce unintended and unwanted results. No one contends, and it would be untenable to argue, that a contaminated and debris-filled bearing was the configuration either the Navy or the manufacturers it employed intended. Accordingly, we hold that the trial court did not err in refusing to submit the government-contractor defense to the jury. Torrington further argues that, as Textron's successor, the government-contractor defense protects it from liability stemming from defects in the bearing Textron manufactured. But this ignores the fact that Torrington's liability is premised not on its status as a successor, but rather on its own conduct in allegedly negligently performing an undertaking. It is difficult to imagine that Torrington's failure to list unserialized bearings was the product of the exercise of government discretion and hence within the defense's intended purview.

PHILLIPS, C.J., ENOCH, BAKER, ABBOTT, HANKINSON, and GONZALES JJ. concurred.

Affirmed in part; reversed and remanded in part.

Note

The label "military contractor defense" is something of a misnomer, since some courts have been prepared to hold that manufacturers of products that are designed, built, and used solely for civilian purposes are entitled to avail themselves of the defense.

Carley v. Wheeled Coach
991 F.2d 1117 (3rd Cir. 1993)

COWEN, J. Plaintiff Mary Carley appeals the grant of summary judgment dismissing her claim for personal injuries caused by an alleged design defect in an ambulance manufactured by defendant Wheeled Coach Industries, Inc. ("Wheeled Coach"). The issue in this appeal is whether the manufacturer of a nonmilitary product may assert the government contractor defense, recognized in *Boyle v. United Technologies Corp.*, 487 U.S. 500, 108 S.Ct. 2510, 101 L.Ed.2d 442 (1988), in a strict products liability action based on a design defect. We conclude that the government contractor defense is available to nonmilitary contractors under federal common law. However, because Wheeled Coach failed to prove that it warned the United States government of dangers in its ambulance known to Wheeled Coach but not to the government, we will reverse the grant of summary judgment and remand for trial.

Plaintiff Mary Carley is an emergency medical technician employed by the Virgin Islands Department of Health at St. Croix Hospital. On September 2, 1988, she was on duty and riding as a passenger in a 1987 Ford E-350 Type II 6.9 liter diesel-powered ambulance manufactured by Wheeled Coach, a Florida corporation. While the ambulance was en route to the scene of an emergency, an automobile failed to properly yield the right-of-way. The ambulance made an evasive maneuver and flipped over. Carley suffered injuries to her knee and back, including a herniated disk. A police officer who witnessed the accident reported that the ambulance was driven in a reasonable and safe manner for an emergency situation.

The ambulance was manufactured by Wheeled Coach pursuant to a contract ... with the United States General Services Administration ("GSA"). The GSA solicited bids for the manufacture of the ambulance in compliance with the Federal Specification for Ambulance KKK-A-1822B, dated June 1, 1985, which was incorporated into the contract. After Wheeled Coach completed the ambulance, a GSA quality assurance inspector examined it, concluded that it complied with contract specifications, and released it for shipment.

On April 4, 1989, Carley filed suit against Wheeled Coach in the District Court of the Virgin Islands..., alleging strict products liability and breach of warranty arising from the manufacture and sale of an ambulance with a design defect. Carley claimed that the ambulance was unreasonably prone to turn over during intended use because of an excessively high center of gravity. One of the affirmative defenses raised by Wheeled Coach was the government contractor defense. Wheeled Coach claimed that it was immune from liability because it built the ambulance in the performance of its obligations under a contract with the United States government....

The Court ... relied heavily on *Yearsley v. W.A. Ross Construction Co.*, 309 U.S. 18, 60 S.Ct. 413, 84 L.Ed. 554 (1940), in which [it was] held that the contractor could not be held liable for damages under state law, reasoning that "if [the] authority to carry out the project was validly conferred, that is, if what was done was within the constitutional power of Congress, there is no liability on the part of the contractor for executing its will." *Id.* at 20–21, 60 S.Ct. at 414.

This same rationale, which is equally applicable to military and nonmilitary contractors, underlies the modern government contractor defense. A private contractor who is compelled by a contract to perform an obligation for the United States should, in some circumstances, share the sovereign immunity of the United States. Though the contractor in *Yearsley* was an agent of the United States, while the contractor in *Boyle* and the present case were independent contractors, this distinction was not significant to the Court in *Boyle*. The Court regarded the federal interest in a performance contract in *Yearsley* as being essentially the same as the federal interests in procurement contracts. The imposition of liability on an independent contractor who enters into a procurement contract with the United States directly implicates the significant federal interest in the completion of the government's work. That significant federal interest exists regardless of whether the procurement contract is military or nonmilitary in nature....

The [Federal Tort Claims Act] FTCA authorizes damages suits against the United States for injuries caused by the tortious conduct of any federal employee acting within the scope of his employment, to the same extent that a private person would be liable under state law. 28 U.S.C. § 1346(b) (1988). This waiver of sovereign immunity, however, does not apply to "[a]ny claim ... based upon the exercise or performance or the failure to exercise or perform a discretionary function or duty on the part of a federal agency or an employee of the Government, whether or not the discretion involved be abused." *Id.* § 2680(a). In *Boyle*, the Court stated that the discretionary function exception of the FTCA suggests the outlines of a "significant conflict" between federal interests and state law in the procurement context which would justify displacement of state law. The Court concluded that the selection of military equipment designs by the armed forces is a discretionary function within the meaning of section 2680(a), for the following reasons:

> [Selection of military equipment designs] often involves not merely engineering analysis but judgment as to the balancing of many technical, military, and even social considerations, including specifically the trade-off between greater safety and greater combat effectiveness. And we are further of the view that permitting "second-guessing" of these judgments through state tort suits against contractors would produce the same effect sought to be avoided by the FTCA

exemption. The financial burden of judgments against the contractors would ultimately be passed through, substantially if not totally, to the United States itself, since defense contractors will predictably raise their prices to cover, or to insure against, contingent liability for the Government-ordered designs.

Id. at 511–12, 108 S.Ct. at 2518 (citation omitted). Though government contracts for nonmilitary products do not involve considerations of combat effectiveness, all of the other policy reasons cited by the Court in support of the government contractor defense are equally applicable to military and nonmilitary procurements. To determine the design of a nonmilitary product, the government sometimes may engage in complex engineering analysis and may trade off product safety in favor of other technical, economic, or social considerations. If nonmilitary contractors were not protected by a government contractor defense, their increased financial burdens would pass through to the government. Also, allowing state tort actions against nonmilitary contractors who have complied with government contracts would, in effect, empower state authorities to "second-guess" federal policy decisions respecting the design of products for use in civilian projects....

We now consider whether defendant Wheeled Coach has satisfied the three-prong test of the government contractor defense. The defendant bears the burden of proving each element of the defense. Where a defendant has moved for summary judgment, it must establish that there is no genuine issue of material fact as to each element of the defense.

The first prong of the government contractor defense requires that the United States approved reasonably precise specifications. Though it is necessary only that the government approve, rather than create, the specifications, in this case the government itself created and approved the specifications for the allegedly defective ambulance....

The second prong of the government contractor defense requires that the product manufactured by the defendant conformed to the government's specifications. In support of its motion for summary judgment, Wheeled Coach submitted the affidavits of its government sales manager Paul Holzapel and its mechanical engineering supervisor Robert Carlton. The Holzapel affidavit states that Wheeled Coach built the ambulance in absolute compliance with the GSA's specifications. The completed ambulance was inspected by a GSA quality assurance inspector, who determined that the ambulance complied with contract specifications and released it for shipment to the Virgin Islands. The Carlton affidavit states that the ambulance was manufactured according to the government's specifications, and that Carlton performed tests and measurements on the ambulance indicating that the height of its center of gravity is 36.5 inches above ground level, which meets the government's requirement that it be no higher than 43 inches.

Plaintiff Carley offered no affidavits or other evidence in opposition to Wheeled Coach's motion for summary judgment. We conclude that Wheeled Coach established as a matter of law that the ambulance conformed to the government's specifications, satisfying the second prong of the government contractor defense.

The third prong of the government contractor defense requires that the supplier warned the United States about the dangers in the use of its product that were known to the supplier but not to the United States. The district court took judicial notice "of the fact that the government conducts numerous crashworthiness tests, and the well known rollover problems of vehicles having a high center of gravity." The court concluded that the third prong therefore was satisfied because Wheeled Coach could not have been more aware than the government of the ambulance's tendency to rollover. We disagree. "A judicially noticed fact must be one not subject to reasonable dispute in that it is either (1) generally known within the territorial jurisdiction of the trial court or (2) capable of accurate and ready determination by resort to sources whose accuracy cannot reasonably be questioned." Fed.R.Evid. 201(b). The facts judicially noticed by the district court are not beyond reasonable dispute and therefore do not satisfy Rule 201(b).

The government may perform various tests on vehicles, but the quantity and nature of those tests are not matters of common knowledge, nor are they readily provable through a source whose accuracy cannot reasonably be questioned. Likewise, the district court could not have determined, beyond reasonable dispute, that the rollover propensities of vehicles with high centers of gravity are well known. Most people probably know little, if anything, about how high centers of gravity cause vehicular accidents. The facts judicially noticed by the district court are not the kind of readily ascertainable facts that satisfy Rule 201(b).

Aside from the judicially noticed facts, there is no evidence on record showing that Wheeled Coach warned the GSA about dangers in its ambulance that were known to Wheeled Coach but not to the GSA. Wheeled Coach only offered the evidence which we have deemed sufficient to satisfy the first two prongs of the three-part test. Though plaintiff Carley submitted no affidavits or other evidence in opposition to Wheeled Coach's motion for summary judgment, her failure to respond did not relieve Wheeled Coach of its burden of proving its entitlement to summary judgment. Wheeled Coach failed to meet its burden.

Wheeled Coach argues that in the absence of any evidence opposing its motion, it established the government contractor defense by showing that it built the ambulance in accordance with the government's specifications. Wheeled Coach, in effect, argues that its satisfaction of the first two prongs of the defense also satisfies the third prong. We disagree.

The third prong of the government contractor defense prevents the displacement of state law where the manufacturer has built a product according to the government's specifications but has not informed the government of known risks. The Supreme Court specifically adopted the third prong to prevent manufacturers from having an incentive to withhold knowledge of risks. A manufacturer, therefore, cannot be relieved of the responsibility of proving all three elements of the government contractor defense....

We hold that the government contractor defense is available to nonmilitary contractors under federal common law, but a genuine issue of material fact exists as to whether Wheeled Coach satisfied the third prong of that defense by warning the government of dangers known to Wheeled Coach but not to the government. We therefore will reverse the grant of summary judgment and remand the case to the district court. If Wheeled Coach establishes at trial that it satisfied the third prong of the government contractor defense, then federal common law preempts state law and Wheeled Coach is not liable for the alleged design defect in its ambulance.

If Wheeled Coach fails to establish the government contractor defense, then the district court must determine whether Wheeled Coach is liable under state law.

BECKER, J. (concurring and dissenting). Using *Boyle v. United Technologies Corp.*, 487 U.S. 500, 108 S.Ct. 2510, 101 L.Ed.2d 442 (1988), as a springboard, the majority has announced a sweeping rule of federal common law under which federal government contractors may share the government's immunity from tort liability. In my view, the majority has extended *Boyle*, which dealt only with contracts for military equipment and was premised on concerns unique to the military, far beyond its logical limits. In so doing, the majority has encroached on the domain of Congress and that of the states. I would hold the *Boyle* defense inapplicable to nonmilitary government contracts such as the one at issue....

The courts are split on the question whether *Boyle*'s federal government contractor defense can be extended to contracts for nonmilitary equipment. However, the only other federal court of appeals that has specifically addressed the issue has refused to extend the defense to contracts for nonmilitary equipment. In *Nielsen v. George Diamond Vogel Paint Co.*, 892 F.2d 1450 (9th Cir.1990), the Ninth Circuit held that the *Boyle* defense did not extend to a products liability suit brought by a civilian employee of the Army Corps of Engineers against a paint manufacturer for injuries incurred while painting a dam for the Corps. The defendants argued that they were entitled to summary judgment under *Boyle* because they manufactured the paint in accordance with government-approved specifications and did not know of any dangers that were unknown to the government. Rejecting this argument, the Ninth Circuit reasoned that, although the Supreme Court in *Boyle* based the government contractor defense in part on the policies behind the discretionary function exception to the FTCA, "the policy behind the defense remains rooted in considerations peculiar to the military." *Nielsen*, 892 F.2d at 1454....

I believe that the Ninth Circuit has adopted the sounder approach. It was the heightened federal interest in shielding government decisions involving the national security, and not merely the exercise of discretion by government officials, which justified the Supreme Court's decision in *Boyle* to take the extreme and rare step of displacing state law with a rule of federal common law. No such interest justifies the majority's decision in this case to extend the *Boyle* defense to all government contractors.

In applying the government contractor defense, courts have explained that it is simply not fair to impose tort liability on a government contractor who has merely complied with government specifications and therefore is not at fault. However, ... strict liability law in the Virgin Islands is not based on negligence or faulty conduct. In fact, strict liability for design defects applies to sellers and distributors even though they may not have actually manufactured the allegedly defective product. Thus, in my view, the fairness rationale for the government contractor defense carries little weight in the strict liability context. At all events, the notion that holding government contractors liable for designs specified by the government is unfair does not outweigh, in my view, the policies of victim compensation, cost-spreading, and deterrence that underpin § 402A.

The doctrine of sovereign immunity is also considered a rationale for application of the government contractor defense. Although the Virgin Islands Legislature has waived the government's sovereign immunity from personal injury claims alleging negligence or a wrongful act or omission, this waiver does not apply to strict liability claims. The United States government is also immune from strict liability. Some courts have explained that the government's immunity from strict liability for design defects would be meaningless if a private contractor who simply fulfills the terms of a government-approved contract cannot share the immunity.

I am not persuaded. The best explanation for the application of sovereign immunity today is that by restricting suits brought directly against the government, judicial interference with governmental policy-making is minimized. But there is a significant difference between subjecting the government directly to tort liability claims and allowing such claims against private government contractors.

Tied up with the sovereign immunity rationale for the government contractor defense is the concern that if government contractors are subject to liability for design defects, they will pass the costs on to the government, whereas if the government itself had made the product, it would be immune from such liability.... I am not persuaded that an interest in cutting government costs justifies immunizing private government contractors from liability for design defects. In my view, the strong policy interests behind the application of strict liability for design defects (compensation of injured victims, cost-spreading, and deterring unsafe products) outweigh any putative lowering of the cost of government procurement that might result from immunizing government contractors.

In short, none of the rationales for the government contractor defense outweigh the policies behind § 402A so as to convince me that the defense should be applied as a matter of Virgin Islands common law. Therefore, while I agree with the majority that the summary judgment order of the district court must be reversed and the case remanded, and to that extent concur in the judgment, I would direct the district court to conduct proceedings in the absence of either a federal or a Virgin Islands government contractor defense.

Reversed and remanded.

Notes

1. *Three-part test.* In *Russek v. Unisys Corp.*, 921 F.Supp. 1277, 1281–82 (1999), a district court, applying New Jersey law, applied the government contractor defense to shield the manufacturer of letter sorting machines from claims for repetitive stress injuries by Postal Service employees. The court set out the test for the applicability of the defense as follows:

> Under *Boyle* and *Carley*, state law causes of action against government contractors are preempted where (1) the government approves reasonably precise specifications, (2) the equipment conformed to those specifications, and (3) the contractor warned the government about all dangers in the use of the equipment that were known to the contractor but not to the government. *Boyle*, 487 U.S. at 512, 108 S.Ct. at 2518–19; *Carley*, 991 F.2d at 1119.

A similar decision had previously been reached by the United States District Court for the District of Maryland, Southern Division, in *Yeroshefsky v. Unisys*, 962 F.Supp. 710 (1997).

2. *Application.* In *Silverstein v. Northrop Grumman Corp.*, A.2d 881 (2004), the Superior Court of New Jersey held that the government contractor defense immunized General Motors against a claim for the defective design of a postal service vehicle after it had rolled over when struck by another vehicle and caused serious injuries to the driver.

3. *Flowchart.* The application of the various tests for contract-based defenses to a products liability claim is depicted in Figure 13.1.

4. *Failures to warn.* So far, we have noted that the government contractor defense is applicable to design defect claims, but not to claims arising out of manufacturing defects. In the following case, the Sixth Circuit considered the application of the defense to claims for failure to warn.

Tate v. Boeing Helicopters
55 F.3d 1150 (1995) (US Court of Appeals, Sixth Circuit)

RYAN, J. The defendants built and sold to the Army a helicopter that crashed during a training mission in July 1990. Three crew members were killed and two others were in-

Figure 13.1 Contract-Based Defenses

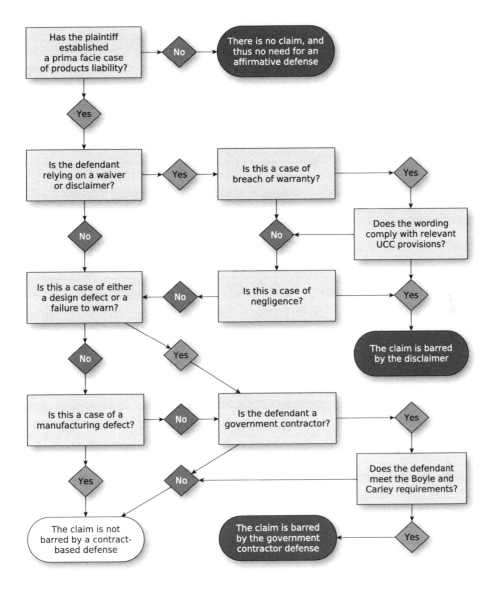

jured. One of the survivors, and family members of two soldiers who perished, brought this diversity action under Kentucky law, alleging theories of design defect and failure to warn. The district court granted summary judgment for the defendants based on the government contractor defense established in *Boyle v. United Technologies Corp.*, 487 U.S. 500, 108 S.Ct. 2510, 101 L.Ed.2d 442 (1988), and dismissed the case. We affirm summary judgment for the defendants as to the design defect claim, but vacate and remand as to the failure to warn claim....

We agree that the defendants' success in establishing the government contractor defense against the design defect claim does not by itself establish a defense to the plaintiffs' failure to warn claim. Several of our sister circuits have applied the government contractor defense against failure to warn claims; those cases do not focus on the underlying design defects, but instead focus on the warnings. Warning the government of dangers arising from a specific design—the third condition of *Boyle*—does not encompass or state a failure to warn claim; it simply encourages contractors to provide the government with all the information required to soundly exercise its discretion. "By contrast, tort law duties to warn accomplish an entirely different objective of helping those who use or otherwise come into contact with a product to protect their own safety." *In re Joint E. & S. Dist. N.Y. Asbestos Litig.*, 897 F.2d 626, 632 (2d Cir.1990). In the government contractor defense context, design defect and failure to warn claims differ practically as well as theoretically. Simply because the government exercises discretion in approving a design does not mean that the government considered the appropriate warnings, if any, that should accompany the product. This is especially true with regard to military equipment procurement where complex judgments by representatives of the Armed Forces often involve "balancing of many technical, military, and even social considerations." *Boyle*, 487 U.S. at 511, 108 S.Ct. at 2518. We hold that the government contractor defense is not necessarily established merely by satisfying the government contractor defense conditions as to design defect claims.

Although the rule announced in *Boyle* applies only to design claims, and the government contractor defense as applied against failure to warn claims is independent of design defect claims, *Boyle* provides guidance in determining when state law governing a failure to warn claim can be displaced. The *Boyle* Court explained that the government contractor defense displaces state law when imposing state tort liability "significant[ly] conflict[s]" with a federal interest. As we have seen, there is a federal interest in protecting the government's FTCA exemption for discretionary functions. When the government exercises its discretion and approves designs prepared by private contractors, it has an interest in insulating its contractors from liability for such design defects. Similarly, when the government exercises its discretion and approves warnings intended for users, it has an interest in insulating its contractors from state failure to warn tort liability.

Accordingly, the rationale for applying the government contractor defense to a failure to warn claim tracks the *Boyle* analysis closely. When state law would otherwise impose liability for a failure to warn of dangers in using military equipment, that law is displaced if the contractor can show: (1) the United States exercised its discretion and approved the warnings, if any; (2) the contractor provided warnings that conformed to the approved warnings; and (3) the contractor warned the United States of the dangers in the equipment's use about which the contractor knew, but the United States did not. As in design defect cases, in order to satisfy the first condition—government "approval"—in failure to warn cases, the government's involvement must transcend rubber stamping. And where the government goes beyond approval and actually determines for itself the warnings to be provided, the contractor has surely satisfied the first condition because the government exercised its discretion. The second condition in failure to warn cases, as in design defect cases, assures that the defense protects the government's, not the contractor's, exercise of discretion. Finally, the third condition encourages frank communication to the government of the equipment's dangers and increases the likelihood that the government will make a well-informed judgment. Since none of this analysis was undertaken by the district court, we must remand....

We reiterate that the FTCA's discretionary function exemption delineates the contours of the defense. Government *discretion* is required, not dictation or prohibition of warnings. Where a contractor proposes warnings that the government substantively approves, and satisfies the second and third conditions, the defense displaces state law—even if the government did not "prohibit" the contractor from proposing more alarming warnings.

Affirmed in part; vacated and remanded in part.

Notes

1. ***Dangerous helicopters.*** *Tate* is just one of a significant number of cases of deaths and injuries resulting from apparently defective parts in military helicopters. One of the most recent is *Getz v. Boeing Co.*, 690 F.Supp.2d 982 (2010), where an Army Report found that a helicopter with 22 military personnel on board suffered a "sudden catastrophic failure of the number two engine." The United States District Court for the Northern District of California held that the government contractor defense precluded liability of the engine, component, and helicopter manufacturers not only for design defects and failures to warn, but also (without explanation) for manufacturing defects.

2. ***Summary judgment and immunity.*** The government contractor defense might appear to offer defendants a shortcut to summary judgment in their favor, irrespective of the precise circumstances in which the plaintiff was injured or killed. That, however, was not the view of the Ninth Circuit in *Rodriguez v. Lockheed Martin Corp.*, 627 F.3d 1259 (2010). *Rodriguez* arose out of a live-fire U.S. Army training exercise in Hawaii in 2006, when an 81mm M374A3 HE (High Explosive) mortar cartridge, manufactured by General Dynamics, exploded prematurely in the barrel of a mortar. Shrapnel from the explosion killed Staff Sergeant Rodriguez and caused serious injuries to three other soldiers. The Army conducted an investigation, which identified several possible causes of the explosion including material defects in the cartridge and a "double loading" scenario in which a cartridge was already in the tube when another cartridge was loaded. The Army's report concluded that "the evidence and test data cannot identify the exact cause of the malfunction incident."

General Dynamics moved for summary judgment on the grounds of, among other things, the government contractor defense. The district court denied the motion on the grounds that there were disputed issues of fact, including whether the cartridge had been manufactured according to the government's specifications. General Dynamics filed an interlocutory appeal, reasoning that its claimed right to immunity includes the right not to proceed to trial. The Ninth Circuit held, however, that the general contractor defense does *not* confer immunity at all, reiterating its own previous statements in *United States ex rel. Ali v. Daniel, Mann, Johnson & Mendenhall*, 355 F.3d 1140, 1147 (2004) and *Del Campo v. Kennedy*, 517 F.3d 1070, 1078 n. 10 (2008). Instead, the defense

> "allows a contractor-defendant to *receive the benefits* of sovereign immunity *when a contractor complies* with the specifications of a federal government contract." *Phillips v. E.I. DuPont de Nemours & Co.* (*In re Hanford Nuclear Reservation Litigation*), 534 F.3d 986, 1000 (9th Cir.2008) (emphasis added). This wording implicitly recognizes our consistent position that the government contractor defense is not a grant of immunity but is only a corollary financial benefit flowing from the government's sovereign immunity.

627 F.3d at 1265–66. Since it was faced with an interlocutory appeal, but no immunity from trial was at stake, the Ninth Circuit dismissed the appeal for lack of jurisdiction.

Questions

1. In a nation and legal system where the federal Constitution is designed to limit the power of government, is the doctrine of sovereign immunity justifiable?

2. Does the Ninth Circuit's distinction in *Rodriguez* between sovereign immunity and "the benefits of sovereign immunity" make sense?

3. What is the best justification for extending the benefits of sovereign immunity to for-profit contractors?

4. Should it (or its benefits) be so extended?

5. In *Carley*, Judge Becker argued that "the strong policy interests behind the application of strict liability for design defects (compensation of injured victims, cost-spreading, and deterring unsafe products) outweigh any putative lowering of the cost of government procurement that might result from immunizing government contractors." Does a "weighing" of the alternatives depend on how many accidents take place, how many individuals are killed and injured, and/or how much such accidents cost in purely financial terms, or is this issue to be decided simply as a matter of principle?

6. As will be seen in Chapter 15, the Supreme Court declared in *Erie Railroad Co. v. Tompkins*, 304 U.S. 64, 58 S.Ct. 817 (1938), that there is no longer any such thing as federal tort law unless created by statute. Yet in *Torrington*, the Supreme Court of Texas referred to the "government-contractor defense, also called the military contractor defense, [as] a federal common-law defense." Are these two statements capable of reconciliation?

7. Is it true to say that, as the law currently stands, the government can choose to specify products which are cheap but unsafe, and by so doing confer immunity on the manufacturer that supplies them; whereas if the government specifies a safer, more expensive option, the supplier will lose its immunity if it supplies the cheaper version? If so, is this distinction justifiable, or does it just encourage the government to pay for low-quality or defective products with its citizens' lives?

8. Since the Tucker Act enables claims to be brought against the federal government for breach of contract, would the plaintiffs in *Tate* have been better advised to sue for breach of warranty so as to avoid the government contractor defense?

9. What is, and/or should be, the position regarding claims for post-sale failures to warn?

Part V

Procedural Issues

Chapter 14

Expert Evidence

A Question of Weight or Admissibility?

Over seventy years ago, the *doyen* of torts professors, William L. Prosser, *Joint Torts and Several Liability*, 25 Cal. L. Rev. 413, 443 (1936–1937), wrote that: "In the law of torts, substance and procedure were once husband and wife; but surely the day has come when that marriage has been dissolved." Prosser's specific complaint related to the rules of substance and procedure related to joint and several liability, but the law of products liability has arguably found itself plagued with a similarly unhappy marriage since the decision of the Supreme Court in the case of *Daubert v. Merrell Dow Pharmaceuticals*, 509 U.S. 579 (1993).

Indeed, it might fairly be contended that debate over the substantive rules of product liability law is, to some degree, a form of shadow-boxing. As we have seen on many occasions already, the real issue in many cases is who gets to make the important decisions: judge or jury. In principle, products liability cases are supposed to be tried by juries. As Judge E. Grady Jolly put it in *Viterbo v. Dow Chemical Co.*, 826 F.2d 420, 422 (5th Cir., 1987):

> The district court should, initially, approach its inquiry with the proper deference to the jury's role as the arbiter of disputes between conflicting opinions. As a general rule, questions relating to the bases and sources of an expert's opinion affect the weight to be assigned that opinion rather than its admissibility and should be left for the jury's consideration.

However, juries will only ever have a role to play if there is evidence for them to hear. The trial judge has to rule on the admissibility or otherwise of the evidence of experts — as well, of course, on whether a person can be considered to be an expert at all. The decision to admit or exclude expert evidence can make or break a case. Effectively, therefore — albeit indirectly — judges often decide the outcome of products liability cases. The rationale for this apparent usurpation of the function of juries was provided by Judge Jolly in *Viterbo*, 826 F.2d at 422, as follows:

> In some cases, however, the source upon which an expert's opinion relies is of such little weight that the jury should not be permitted to receive that opinion. Expert opinion testimony falls into this category when that testimony would not actually assist the jury in arriving at an intelligent and sound verdict. If an opinion is fundamentally unsupported, then it offers no expert assistance to the jury. Furthermore, its lack of reliable support may render it more prejudicial than probative, making it inadmissible under Fed.R.Evid. 403.

Oddly, the law regarding the admissibility of expert evidence regarding defective products was originally based on a criminal case where a defense expert claimed to be able to distinguish truthful answers from false ones by measuring the respondent's blood pressure.

Frye v. United States

293 F. 1013 (1923) (Court of Appeals, District of Columbia)

VAN ORSDEL, J. Appellant, defendant below, was convicted of the crime of murder in the second degree, and from the judgment prosecutes this appeal.

A single assignment of error is presented for our consideration. In the course of the trial counsel for defendant offered an expert witness to testify to the result of a deception test made upon defendant. The test is described as the systolic blood pressure deception test. It is asserted that blood pressure is influenced by change in the emotions of the witness, and that the systolic blood pressure rises are brought about by nervous impulses sent to the sympathetic branch of the autonomic nervous system. Scientific experiments, it is claimed, have demonstrated that fear, rage, and pain always produce a rise of systolic blood pressure, and that conscious deception or falsehood, concealment of facts, or guilt of crime, accompanied by fear of detection when the person is under examination, raises the systolic blood pressure in a curve, which corresponds exactly to the struggle going on in the subject's mind, between fear and attempted control of that fear, as the examination touches the vital points in respect of which he is attempting to deceive the examiner.

In other words, the theory seems to be that truth is spontaneous, and comes without conscious effort, while the utterance of a falsehood requires a conscious effort, which is reflected in the blood pressure. The rise thus produced is easily detected and distinguished from the rise produced by mere fear of the examination itself. In the former instance, the pressure rises higher than in the latter, and is more pronounced as the examination proceeds, while in the latter case, if the subject is telling the truth, the pressure registers highest at the beginning of the examination, and gradually diminishes as the examination proceeds.

Prior to the trial defendant was subjected to this deception test, and counsel offered the scientist who conducted the test as an expert to testify to the results obtained. The offer was objected to by counsel for the government, and the court sustained the objection. Counsel for defendant then offered to have the proffered witness conduct a test in the presence of the jury. This also was denied.

Counsel for defendant, in their able presentation of the novel question involved, correctly state in their brief that no cases directly in point have been found. The broad ground, however, upon which they plant their case, is succinctly stated in their brief as follows:

> The rule is that the opinions of experts or skilled witnesses are admissible in evidence in those cases in which the matter of inquiry is such that inexperienced persons are unlikely to prove capable of forming a correct judgment upon it, for the reason that the subject-matter so far partakes of a science, art, or trade as to require a previous habit or experience or study in it, in order to acquire a knowledge of it. When the question involved does not lie within the range of common experience or common knowledge, but requires special experience or special knowledge, then the opinions of witnesses skilled in that particular science, art, or trade to which the question relates are admissible in evidence.

Numerous cases are cited in support of this rule. Just when a scientific principle or discovery crosses the line between the experimental and demonstrable stages is difficult to define. Somewhere in this twilight zone the evidential force of the principle must be recognized, and while courts will go a long way in admitting expert testimony deduced from a well-recognized scientific principle or discovery, the thing from which the deduction is made must be sufficiently established to have gained general acceptance in the particular field in which it belongs.

We think the systolic blood pressure deception test has not yet gained such standing and scientific recognition among physiological and psychological authorities as would justify the courts in admitting expert testimony deduced from the discovery, development, and experiments thus far made.

The judgment is affirmed.

Note

Confusion of forum? It is arguable whether it has ever made much sense to apply *Frye* to products liability cases, not least for the prosaic reason that *Frye* was a criminal case which turned on the reliability of a test developed by the expert himself, whereas products liability cases are civil matters where a third party expert is called to testify as to the appropriateness or otherwise of the defendant's product or warning. Moreover, while *Frye* acted as a bulwark against parties' calling self-proclaimed experts to expound upon their own, somewhat fanciful theories, it also made it almost impossible to allege a product defect where a drug had shown no signs during testing of producing the injuries which patients had undoubtedly suffered. The case below, *Daubert v. Dow Merrell Pharmaceuticals* highlighted precisely this problem. However, the Supreme Court in *Daubert* decided to abandon the rule in *Frye* not for these—or indeed, for any—substantive reasons, but on procedural grounds.

The Current Federal Standard

Daubert v. Merrell Dow Pharmaceuticals, Inc.
509 U.S. 579, 113 S.Ct. 2786 (1993) (SCOTUS)

BLACKMUN, J. Petitioners Jason Daubert and Eric Schuller are minor children born with serious birth defects. They and their parents sued respondent in California state court, alleging that the birth defects had been caused by the mothers' ingestion of Bendectin, a prescription antinausea drug marketed by respondent. Respondent removed the suits to federal court on diversity grounds.

After extensive discovery, respondent moved for summary judgment, contending that Bendectin does not cause birth defects in humans and that petitioners would be unable to come forward with any admissible evidence that it does. In support of its motion, respondent submitted an affidavit of Steven H. Lamm, physician and epidemiologist, who is a well-credentialed expert on the risks from exposure to various chemical substances. Doctor Lamm stated that he had reviewed all the literature on Bendectin and human birth defects more than 30 published studies involving over 130,000 patients. No study had found Bendectin to be a human teratogen (i.e., a substance capable of causing malformations in fetuses). On the basis of this review, Doctor Lamm concluded that maternal use of Bendectin during the first trimester of pregnancy has not been shown to be a risk factor for human birth defects.

Petitioners did not (and do not) contest this characterization of the published record regarding Bendectin. Instead, they responded to respondent's motion with the testimony of eight experts of their own, each of whom also possessed impressive credentials. These experts had concluded that Bendectin can cause birth defects. Their conclusions were based upon "in vitro" (test tube) and "in vivo" (live) animal studies that found a link between Bendectin and malformations; pharmacological studies of the chemical structure of Bendectin that purported to show similarities between the structure of the drug and that of other substances known to cause birth defects; and the "reanalysis" of previously published epidemiological (human statistical) studies.

The District Court granted respondent's motion for summary judgment. The court stated that scientific evidence is admissible only if the principle upon which it is based is "sufficiently established to have general acceptance in the field to which it belongs." The court concluded that petitioners' evidence did not meet this standard. Given the vast body of epidemiological data concerning Bendectin, the court held, expert opinion which is not based on epidemiological evidence is not admissible to establish causation. Thus, the animal-cell studies, live-animal studies, and chemical-structure analyses on which petitioners had relied could not raise by themselves a reasonably disputable jury issue regarding causation. Petitioners' epidemiological analyses, based as they were on recalculations of data in previously published studies that had found no causal link between the drug and birth defects, were ruled to be inadmissible because they had not been published or subjected to peer review.

The United States Court of Appeals for the Ninth Circuit affirmed. Citing *Frye v. United States*, the court stated that expert opinion based on a scientific technique is inadmissible unless the technique is "generally accepted" as reliable in the relevant scientific community. The court declared that expert opinion based on a methodology that diverges "significantly from the procedures accepted by recognized authorities in the field … cannot be shown to be 'generally accepted as a reliable technique.'"

The court emphasized that other Courts of Appeals considering the risks of Bendectin had refused to admit reanalyses of epidemiological studies that had been neither published nor subjected to peer review. Those courts had found unpublished reanalyses "particularly problematic in light of the massive weight of the original published studies supporting [respondent's] position, all of which had undergone full scrutiny from the scientific community." Contending that reanalysis is generally accepted by the scientific community only when it is subjected to verification and scrutiny by others in the field, the Court of Appeals rejected petitioners' reanalyses as "unpublished, not subjected to the normal peer review process and generated solely for use in litigation." The court concluded that petitioners' evidence provided an insufficient foundation to allow admission of expert testimony that Bendectin caused their injuries and, accordingly, that petitioners could not satisfy their burden of proving causation at trial.

We granted certiorari … in light of sharp divisions among the courts regarding the proper standard for the admission of expert testimony.…

The merits of the *Frye* test have been much debated, and scholarship on its proper scope and application is legion. Petitioners' primary attack, however, is not on the content but on the continuing authority of the rule. They contend that the *Frye* test was superseded by the adoption of the Federal Rules of Evidence. We agree.

We interpret the legislatively enacted Federal Rules of Evidence as we would any statute.… Rule 402 provides the baseline:

> All relevant evidence is admissible, except as otherwise provided by the Constitution of the United States, by Act of Congress, by these rules, or by other rules prescribed by the Supreme Court pursuant to statutory authority. Evidence which is not relevant is not admissible.

"Relevant evidence" is defined as that which has "any tendency to make the existence of any fact that is of consequence to the determination of the action more probable or less probable than it would be without the evidence." Rule 401. The Rule's basic standard of relevance thus is a liberal one....

Here there is a specific Rule that speaks to the contested issue. Rule 702, governing expert testimony, provides:

> If scientific, technical, or other specialized knowledge will assist the trier of fact to understand the evidence or to determine a fact in issue, a witness qualified as an expert by knowledge, skill, experience, training, or education, may testify thereto in the form of an opinion or otherwise.

Nothing in the text of this Rule establishes "general acceptance" as an absolute prerequisite to admissibility. Nor does respondent present any clear indication that Rule 702 or the Rules as a whole were intended to incorporate a "general acceptance" standard....

That the *Frye* test was displaced by the Rules of Evidence does not mean, however, that the Rules themselves place no limits on the admissibility of purportedly scientific evidence. Nor is the trial judge disabled from screening such evidence. To the contrary, under the Rules the trial judge must ensure that any and all scientific testimony or evidence admitted is not only relevant, but reliable....

That these requirements are embodied in Rule 702 is not surprising. Unlike an ordinary witness, see Rule 701, an expert is permitted wide latitude to offer opinions, including those that are not based on firsthand knowledge or observation. See Rules 702 and 703. Presumably, this relaxation of the usual requirement of firsthand knowledge ... is premised on an assumption that the expert's opinion will have a reliable basis in the knowledge and experience of his discipline.

Faced with a proffer of expert scientific testimony, then, the trial judge must determine at the outset, pursuant to Rule 104(a), whether the expert is proposing to testify to (1) scientific knowledge that (2) will assist the trier of fact to understand or determine a fact in issue. This entails a preliminary assessment of whether the reasoning or methodology underlying the testimony is scientifically valid and of whether that reasoning or methodology properly can be applied to the facts in issue. We are confident that federal judges possess the capacity to undertake this review. Many factors will bear on the inquiry, and we do not presume to set out a definitive checklist or test. But some general observations are appropriate.

Ordinarily, a key question to be answered in determining whether a theory or technique is scientific knowledge that will assist the trier of fact will be whether it can be (and has been) tested....

Another pertinent consideration is whether the theory or technique has been subjected to peer review and publication. Publication (which is but one element of peer review) is not a *sine qua non* of admissibility; it does not necessarily correlate with reliability ... and in some instances well-grounded but innovative theories will not have been published ... Some propositions, moreover, are too particular, too new, or of too limited interest to be published. But submission to the scrutiny of the scientific community is a component of "good science," in part because it increases the likelihood that substantive flaws in methodology will be detected.... The fact of publication (or lack thereof) in a peer reviewed journal thus will be a relevant, though not dispositive, consideration in assessing the scientific validity of a particular technique or methodology on which an opinion is premised.

Additionally, in the case of a particular scientific technique, the court ordinarily should consider the known or potential rate of error ...

Finally, "general acceptance" can yet have a bearing on the inquiry.... Widespread acceptance can be an important factor in ruling particular evidence admissible, and "a known technique which has been able to attract only minimal support within the community," *Downing*, 753 F.2d, at 1238, may properly be viewed with skepticism.

The inquiry envisioned by Rule 702 is, we emphasize, a flexible one. Its overarching subject is the scientific validity and thus the evidentiary relevance and reliability of the principles that underlie a proposed submission. The focus, of course, must be solely on principles and methodology, not on the conclusions that they generate.

Throughout, a judge assessing a proffer of expert scientific testimony under Rule 702 should also be mindful of other applicable rules. Rule 703 provides that expert opinions based on otherwise inadmissible hearsay are to be admitted only if the facts or data are "of a type reasonably relied upon by experts in the particular field in forming opinions or inferences upon the subject." Rule 706 allows the court at its discretion to procure the assistance of an expert of its own choosing. Finally, Rule 403 permits the exclusion of relevant evidence "if its probative value is substantially outweighed by the danger of unfair prejudice, confusion of the issues, or misleading the jury...." Judge Weinstein has explained:

> Expert evidence can be both powerful and quite misleading because of the difficulty in evaluating it. Because of this risk, the judge in weighing possible prejudice against probative force under Rule 403 of the present rules exercises more control over experts than over lay witnesses.

We conclude by briefly addressing what appear to be two underlying concerns of the parties and *amici* in this case. Respondent expresses apprehension that abandonment of "general acceptance" as the exclusive requirement for admission will result in a "free-for-all" in which befuddled juries are confounded by absurd and irrational pseudoscientific assertions. In this regard respondent seems to us to be overly pessimistic about the capabilities of the jury and of the adversary system generally. Vigorous cross-examination, presentation of contrary evidence, and careful instruction on the burden of proof are the traditional and appropriate means of attacking shaky but admissible evidence.... Additionally, in the event the trial court concludes that the scintilla of evidence presented supporting a position is insufficient to allow a reasonable juror to conclude that the position more likely than not is true, the court remains free to direct a judgment, Fed. Rule Civ. Proc. 50(a), and likewise to grant summary judgment, Fed. Rule Civ. Proc. 56. These conventional devices, rather than wholesale exclusion under an uncompromising "general acceptance" test, are the appropriate safeguards where the basis of scientific testimony meets the standards of Rule 702.

Petitioners and, to a greater extent, their *amici* exhibit a different concern. They suggest that recognition of a screening role for the judge that allows for the exclusion of "invalid" evidence will sanction a stifling and repressive scientific orthodoxy and will be inimical to the search for truth.... It is true that open debate is an essential part of both legal and scientific analyses. Yet there are important differences between the quest for truth in the courtroom and the quest for truth in the laboratory. Scientific conclusions are subject to perpetual revision. Law, on the other hand, must resolve disputes finally and quickly. The scientific project is advanced by broad and wide-ranging consideration of a multitude of hypotheses, for those that are incorrect will eventually be shown to be so, and that in itself is an advance. Conjectures that are probably wrong are of little use, however, in the project of reaching a quick, final, and binding legal judgment—often of great consequence—about a particular set of events in the past. We recognize that, in practice, a gatekeeping role for the judge, no matter how flexible, inevitably on occasion will prevent the jury from learning of authentic insights and innovations. That, nevertheless, is the balance that is struck by Rules of Evidence designed not for the exhaustive search for cosmic understanding but for the particularized resolution of legal disputes....

Accordingly, the judgment of the Court of Appeals is vacated, and the case is remanded for further proceedings consistent with this opinion.

Notes

1. *Plaintiff- or defendant-friendly?* A major irony has resulted from the judgment in *Daubert*. The decision in the actual case was favorable to the plaintiffs, who had no realistic prospect of success under the rule in *Frye*. Yet the way in which *Daubert* has subsequently been interpreted is usually considered to be very much more favorable to defendants than to plaintiffs, because it encourages judges to scrutinize plaintiffs' claims (and the credentials of their experts) much more closely before permitting them to be heard by a jury.

2. *Relevance and reliability.* A significant problem with the majority view in *Daubert* is that, as Rehnquist CJ pointed out in his dissent, it confuses relevance with reliability. Whether an expert's evidence is credible is surely a matter of weight, not of admissibility. The majority in the Supreme Court effectively developed a standard in *Daubert* which requires trial judges instead of juries to evaluate experts' opinions. This confusion became all the more apparent when Rule 702 was subsequently revised (in 2000)—supposedly to take account of the judgment in *Daubert* and its subsequent interpretations—so that it now reads:

> *Rule 702. Testimony by Experts.* If scientific, technical, or other specialized knowledge will assist the trier of fact to understand the evidence or to determine a fact in issue, a witness qualified as an expert by knowledge, skill, experience, training, or education, may testify thereto in the form of an opinion or otherwise, if (1) the testimony is based upon sufficient facts or data, (2) the testimony is the product of reliable principles and methods, and (3) the witness has applied the principles and methods reliably to the facts of the case.

3. *Lack of sufficient facts or data.* The first factor is obviously uncontroversial: any testimony without foundation in fact is clearly not expert. In *Smith ex rel. Smith v. Clement*, 983 So.2d 285 (2008), the Supreme Court of Mississippi affirmed the trial court's striking of the summary judgment affidavit of a plaintiff school district's expert mechanical engineer. On the basis of maintenance records that went back only three years, he claimed that a school bus had caught fire because of a leak from improperly flared copper tubing in its propane fuel system, and that this was "the same copper tubing" as that fitted by the defendants fourteen years before. The Court noted, by contrast, that the defendant's expert had, from the same evidence, drawn the conclusion that:

> there are no reliable, or valid, scientific principles or methods that could be utilized by any engineer, or any other specialist, that would enable that person to give an opinion based in science regarding from what manufacturer or seller the copper tubing or brass fittings ... came, the age of the tubing and fittings, the date that the tubing and fittings were installed, or the date that the tubing was flared and by whom it was flared.

4. How to evaluate the third factor? The evaluation of factor (3) is, however, much more problematic. It is often difficult to see how it can be addressed without hearing the evidence that the expert will give (especially under cross examination). In practice, this typically leads courts to hold a so-called "*Daubert* hearing" without the jury present in order to determine the admissibility (or otherwise) of the allegedly expert testimony.

5. Judges versus juries. Perhaps more than in any other area of the law, *Daubert* and the cases which have followed it highlight the schizophrenic attitude of American jurisprudence to the jury. On the one hand, trial by jury is guaranteed by the Seventh Amendment to the Constitution, while the jury itself is venerated as the ultimate trier of fact whose verdicts cannot be overturned simply because the trial judge or appellate judges disagree with them. On the other hand, however, there is often significant apprehension about letting the jury see or hear certain evidence. So while the jury's verdicts may not be overturned, the chances of such verdicts being different from those that trial judges would have reached are limited because the very same judges restrict the evidence that the juries may hear.

It is significant that in other common law systems, where juries are rarely used, the issue of admissibility of expert evidence is much less controversial. In those jurisdictions, the trial judge will, in any event, be deciding all questions of fact. As a result, s/he will often choose to admit all the evidence proffered by the parties, and then (just as Chief Justice Rehnquist advocated in *Daubert*) decide what weight to give it.

6. Solving problems or causing them? In his dissent in *Daubert*, 509 U.S. at 600, Rehnquist CJ complained that:

> Questions arise simply from reading ... the Court's opinion, and countless more questions will surely arise when hundreds of district judges try to apply its teaching to particular offers of expert testimony.

7. Federalism. One of the obvious questions is whether *Frye* should necessarily be applied in state courts, since by definition they are not bound by the Federal Rules of Evidence. Nevada is one state where *Daubert* has not been adopted: see, e.g., *Yamaha Motor Co., U.S.A. v. Arnoult*, 955 P.2d 661 (1998). Indeed, courts in Nevada have described *Daubert* doctrine as a "work in progress," so that the "doctrine's further development in federal courts should be observed before it is adopted as law of Nevada. There is no present need to adopt *Daubert* into Nevada law." *Dow Chemical Co. v. Mahlum*, 970 P.2d 98, 108 n.3 (1998).

8. Federal law. However, whether by reason of diversity jurisdiction or because of the existence of a governing federal statute (e.g. regulating bankruptcy protection or multi-district litigation), a great deal of complex products liability litigation takes place in federal court. Thus, although tort law is said to be a matter for the states—and, since *Erie Railroad v. Tompkins*, 304 U.S. 64 (1938) (discussed further in Chapter 15), there has been no distinctive body of substantive federal tort law—the fact that the federal courts are free to adopt their own rules of procedure means effectively that federal law often "trumps" state law.

Questions

1. About which aspects of a products liability case will expert testimony be required?

2. What are the practical ramifications of using the *Daubert* test instead of the test of "general acceptance" laid down in *Frye*?

3. Which test is preferable?

4. Would it be even more preferable to admit all potentially relevant evidence, and then have the trial judge direct the jury on what weight (if any) should be assigned to such evidence?

Standard of Appellate Review

General Electric Co. v. Joiner
522 U.S. 136 (1997) (SCOTUS)

REHNQUIST, CJ. We granted certiorari in this case to determine what standard an appellate court should apply in reviewing a trial court's decision to admit or exclude expert testimony under *Daubert v. Merrell Dow Pharmaceuticals, Inc.*, 509 U.S. 579, 113 S.Ct. 2786, 125 L.Ed.2d 469 (1993). We hold that abuse of discretion is the appropriate standard. We apply this standard and conclude that the District Court in this case did not abuse its discretion when it excluded certain proffered expert testimony.

I

Respondent Robert Joiner began work as an electrician in the Water & Light Department of Thomasville, Georgia (City), in 1973. This job required him to work with and around the City's electrical transformers, which used a mineral-oil-based dielectric fluid as a coolant. Joiner often had to stick his hands and arms into the fluid to make repairs. The fluid would sometimes splash onto him, occasionally getting into his eyes and mouth. In 1983 the City discovered that the fluid in some of the transformers was contaminated with polychlorinated biphenyls (PCB's). PCB's are widely considered to be hazardous to human health. Congress, with limited exceptions, banned the production and sale of PCB's in 1978. See 90 Stat.2020, 15 U.S.C. § 2605(e)(2)(A).

Joiner was diagnosed with small-cell lung cancer in 1991. He sued petitioners in Georgia state court the following year. Petitioner Monsanto manufactured PCB's from 1935 to 1977; petitioners General Electric and Westinghouse Electric manufactured transformers and dielectric fluid. In his complaint Joiner linked his development of cancer to his exposure to PCB's and their derivatives, polychlorinated dibenzofurans (furans) and polychlorinated dibenzodioxins (dioxins). Joiner had been a smoker for approximately eight years, his parents had both been smokers, and there was a history of lung cancer in his family. He was thus perhaps already at a heightened risk of developing lung cancer eventually. The suit alleged that his exposure to PCB's "promoted" his cancer; had it not been for his exposure to these substances, his cancer would not have developed for many years, if at all.

Petitioners removed the case to federal court. Once there, they moved for summary judgment. They contended that (1) there was no evidence that Joiner suffered significant exposure to PCB's, furans, or dioxins, and (2) there was no admissible scientific evidence that PCB's promoted Joiner's cancer. Joiner responded that there were numerous disputed factual issues that required resolution by a jury. He relied largely on the testimony of expert witnesses. In depositions, his experts had testified that PCB's alone can promote cancer and that furans and dioxins can also promote cancer. They opined that since Joiner had been exposed to PCB's, furans, and dioxins, such exposure was likely responsible for Joiner's cancer.

The District Court ruled that there was a genuine issue of material fact as to whether Joiner had been exposed to PCB's. But it nevertheless granted summary judgment for petitioners because (1) there was no genuine issue as to whether Joiner had been exposed to furans and dioxins, and (2) the testimony of Joiner's experts had failed to show that there was a link between exposure to PCB's and small-cell lung cancer. The court believed that the testimony of respondent's experts to the contrary did not rise above "subjective belief or unsupported speculation." 864 F.Supp. 1310, 1326 (N.D.Ga.1994). Their testimony was therefore inadmissible.

The Court of Appeals for the Eleventh Circuit reversed. 78 F.3d 524 (1996). It held that "[b]ecause the Federal Rules of Evidence governing expert testimony display a preference for admissibility, we apply a particularly stringent standard of review to the trial judge's exclusion of expert testimony." *Id.*, at 529. Applying that standard, the Court of Appeals held that the District Court had erred in excluding the testimony of Joiner's expert witnesses. The District Court had made two fundamental errors. First, it excluded the experts' testimony because it "drew different conclusions from the research than did each of the experts." The Court of Appeals opined that a district court should limit its role to determining the "legal reliability of proffered expert testimony, leaving the jury to decide the correctness of competing expert opinions." *Id.* at 533. Second, the District Court had held that there was no genuine issue of material fact as to whether Joiner had been exposed to furans and dioxins. This was also incorrect, said the Court of Appeals, because testimony in the record supported the proposition that there had been such exposure.

We granted petitioners' petition for a writ of certiorari, 520 U.S. 1114, 117 S.Ct. 1243, 137 L.Ed.2d 325 (1997), and we now reverse....

II

We have held that abuse of discretion is the proper standard of review of a district court's evidentiary rulings. *Old Chief v. United States*, 519 U.S. 172, 174 n. 1, 117 S.Ct. 644, 647 n. 1, 136 L.Ed.2d 574 (1997); *United States v. Abel*, 469 U.S. 45, 54, 105 S.Ct. 465, 470, 83 L.Ed.2d 450 (1984). Indeed, our cases on the subject go back as far as *Spring Co. v. Edgar*, 99 U.S. 645, 658, 25 L.Ed. 487 (1879), where we said that "[c]ases arise where it is very much a matter of discretion with the court whether to receive or exclude the evidence; but the appellate court will not reverse in such a case, unless the ruling is manifestly erroneous." The Court of Appeals suggested that *Daubert* somehow altered this general rule in the context of a district court's decision to exclude scientific evidence. But *Daubert* did not address the standard of appellate review for evidentiary rulings at all. It did hold that the "austere" *Frye* standard of "general acceptance" had not been carried over into the Federal Rules of Evidence. But the opinion also said:

> That the *Frye* test was displaced by the Rules of Evidence does not mean, however, that the Rules themselves place no limits on the admissibility of purportedly scientific evidence. Nor is the trial judge disabled from screening such evidence. To the contrary, under the Rules the trial judge must ensure that any and all scientific testimony or evidence admitted is not only relevant, but reliable. 509 U.S., at 589, 113 S.Ct., at 2794–2795 (footnote omitted).

Thus, while the Federal Rules of Evidence allow district courts to admit a somewhat broader range of scientific testimony than would have been admissible under *Frye*, they leave in place the "gatekeeper" role of the trial judge in screening such evidence. A court of appeals applying "abuse-of-discretion" review to such rulings may not categorically distinguish between rulings allowing expert testimony and rulings disallowing it. Compare *Beech Aircraft Corp. v. Rainey*, 488 U.S. 153, 172, 109 S.Ct. 439, 451, 102 L.Ed.2d 445 (1988) (applying abuse-of-discretion review to a lower court's decision to exclude evidence), with *United States v. Abel, supra*, at 54, 105 S.Ct., at 470 (applying abuse-of-discretion review to a lower court's decision to admit evidence). We likewise reject respondent's argument that because the granting of summary judgment in this case was "outcome determinative," it should have been subjected to a more searching standard of review. On a motion for summary judgment, disputed issues of fact are resolved against the moving party—here, petitioners. But the question of admissibility of expert testimony is not such an issue of fact, and is reviewable under the abuse-of-discretion standard.

We hold that the Court of Appeals erred in its review of the exclusion of Joiner's experts' testimony. In applying an overly "stringent" review to that ruling, it failed to give the trial court the deference that is the hallmark of abuse-of-discretion review.

III

We believe that a proper application of the correct standard of review here indicates that the District Court did not abuse its discretion. Joiner's theory of liability was that his exposure to PCB's and their derivatives "promoted" his development of small-cell lung cancer. In support of that theory he proffered the deposition testimony of expert witnesses. Dr. Arnold Schecter testified that he believed it "more likely than not that Mr. Joiner's lung cancer was causally linked to cigarette smoking and PCB exposure." Dr. Daniel Teitelbaum testified that Joiner's "lung cancer was caused by or contributed to in a significant degree by the materials with which he worked."

Petitioners contended that the statements of Joiner's experts regarding causation were nothing more than speculation. Petitioners criticized the testimony of the experts in that it was "not supported by epidemiological studies ... [and was] based exclusively on isolated studies of laboratory animals." Joiner responded by claiming that his experts had identified "relevant animal studies which support their opinions." He also directed the court's attention to four epidemiological studies on which his experts had relied.

The District Court agreed with petitioners that the animal studies on which respondent's experts relied did not support his contention that exposure to PCB's had contributed to his cancer. The studies involved infant mice that had developed cancer after being exposed to PCB's. The infant mice in the studies had had massive doses of PCB's injected directly into their peritoneums or stomachs. Joiner was an adult human being whose alleged exposure to PCB's was far less than the exposure in the animal studies. The PCB's were injected into the mice in a highly concentrated form. The fluid with which Joiner had come into contact generally had a much smaller PCB concentration of between 0-to-500 parts per million. The cancer that these mice developed was alveologenic adenomas; Joiner had developed small-cell carcinomas. No study demonstrated that adult mice developed cancer after being exposed to PCB's. One of the experts admitted that no study had demonstrated that PCB's lead to cancer in any other species.

Respondent failed to reply to this criticism. Rather than explaining how and why the experts could have extrapolated their opinions from these seemingly far-removed animal studies, respondent chose "to proceed as if the only issue [was] whether animal studies can ever be a proper foundation for an expert's opinion." 864 F.Supp., at 1324. Of course, whether animal studies can ever be a proper foundation for an expert's opinion was not the issue. The issue was whether *these* experts' opinions were sufficiently supported by the animal studies on which they purported to rely.

STEVENS, J (concurring in part and dissenting in part). The question that we granted certiorari to decide is whether the Court of Appeals applied the correct standard of review. That question is fully answered in Parts I and II of the Court's opinion. Part III answers the quite different question whether the District Court properly held that the testimony of plaintiff's expert witnesses was inadmissible. Because I am not sure that the parties have adequately briefed that question, or that the Court has adequately explained why the Court of Appeals' disposition was erroneous, I do not join Part III. Moreover, because a proper answer to that question requires a study of the record that can be performed more efficiently by the Court of Appeals than by the nine Members of this Court, I would remand the case to that court for application of the proper standard of review....

It does seem clear ... that the Court has not adequately explained why its holding is consistent with Federal Rule of Evidence 702, as interpreted in *Daubert v. Merrell Dow Pharmaceuticals, Inc.* In general, scientific testimony that is both relevant and reliable must be admitted and testimony that is irrelevant or unreliable must be excluded. *Id.*, at 597, 113 S.Ct., at 2798–2799. In this case, the District Court relied on both grounds for exclusion. The relevance ruling was straightforward. The District Court correctly reasoned that an expert opinion that exposure to PCB's, "furans" and "dioxins" together may cause lung cancer would be irrelevant unless the plaintiff had been exposed to those substances. Having already found that there was no evidence of exposure to furans and dioxins, it necessarily followed that this expert opinion testimony was inadmissible. Correctly applying *Daubert*, the District Court explained that the experts' testimony "manifestly does not fit the facts of this case, and is therefore inadmissible." 864 F.Supp., at 1322. Of course, if the evidence raised a genuine issue of fact on the question of Joiner's exposure to furans and dioxins—as the Court of Appeals held that it did—then this basis for the ruling on admissibility was erroneous, but not because the District Judge either abused her discretion or misapplied the law.

The reliability ruling was more complex and arguably is not faithful to the statement in *Daubert* that "[t]he focus, of course, must be solely on principles and methodology, not on the conclusions that they generate." 509 U.S., at 595, 113 S.Ct., at 2797–2798. Joiner's experts used a "weight of the evidence" methodology to assess whether Joiner's exposure to transformer fluids promoted his lung cancer. They did not suggest that any one study provided adequate support for their conclusions, but instead relied on all the studies taken together (along with their interviews of Joiner and their review of his medical records). The District Court, however, examined the studies one by one and concluded that none was sufficient to show a link between PCB's and lung cancer. The focus of the opinion was on the separate studies and the conclusions of the experts, not on the experts' methodology.

Unlike the District Court, the Court of Appeals expressly decided that a "weight of the evidence" methodology was scientifically acceptable. To this extent, the Court of Appeals' opinion is persuasive. It is not intrinsically "unscientific" for experienced professionals to arrive at a conclusion by weighing all available scientific evidence—this is not the sort of "junk science" with which *Daubert* was concerned. After all, as Joiner points out, the Environmental Protection Agency (EPA) uses the same methodology to assess risks, albeit using a somewhat different threshold than that required in a trial. Petitioners' own experts used the same scientific approach as well. And using this methodology, it would seem that an expert could reasonably have concluded that the study of workers at an Italian capacitor plant, coupled with data from Monsanto's study and other studies, raises an inference that PCB's promote lung cancer.

The Court of Appeals' discussion of admissibility is faithful to the dictum in *Daubert* that the reliability inquiry must focus on methodology, not conclusions. Thus, even though I fully agree with both the District Court's and this Court's explanation of why each of the studies on which the experts relied was by itself unpersuasive, a critical question remains unanswered: when qualified experts have reached relevant conclusions on the basis of an acceptable methodology, why are their opinions inadmissible?

Note

Judges versus juries revisited. The dissent by Justice Stevens highlights the problem inherent in the abuse-of-discretion standard. The point of the rules in both *Daubert* and *Frye* is to enable the judge to act as "gatekeeper" to avoid unreliable testimony being presented to the jury, who might then reach unwarranted and unpredictable verdicts. Yet if the application of these rules is not uniform throughout the jurisdiction—and the effect of *Joiner* is that it might not be uniform even within one (federal) judicial district—then it is arguable that all that has been achieved is to replace unpredictable jury verdicts with unpredictable decisions by trial judges.

Questions

1. Was the expert testimony whose exclusion in *Joiner* was problematic for Justice Stevens concerned with proving general causation or specific causation?

2. Is it right that the standard of review of a trial judge's rulings on the admissibility or otherwise of expert evidence should be on the basis of abuse of discretion?

3. While abuse of discretion is the standard for appellate review, is there, in fact, any need for the standards of admissibility of evidence that *Daubert* set out?

Kumho Tire Co. v. Carmichael

526 U.S. 137 (1999) (Supreme Court of the United States)

BREYER, J. This case requires us to decide how *Daubert* applies to the testimony of engineers and other experts who are not scientists. We conclude that *Daubert*'s general holding—setting forth the trial judge's general "gatekeeping" obligation—applies not only to testimony based on "scientific" knowledge, but also to testimony based on "technical" and "other specialized" knowledge. See Fed. Rule Evid. 702. We also conclude that a trial court may consider one or more of the more specific factors that Daubert mentioned when doing so will help determine that testimony's reliability. But, as the Court stated in *Daubert*, the test of reliability is "flexible," and *Daubert*'s list of specific factors neither necessarily nor exclusively applies to all experts or in every case. Rather, the law grants a district court the same broad latitude when it decides how to determine reliability as it enjoys in respect to its ultimate reliability determination. See *General Electric Co. v. Joiner*, 522 U.S. 136, 143. Applying these standards, we determine that the District Court's decision in this case—not to admit certain expert testimony—was within its discretion and therefore lawful.

SCALIA, J (joined by O'CONNOR and THOMAS, JJ, concurring). I join the opinion of the Court, which makes clear that the discretion it endorses—trial-court discretion in choosing the manner of testing expert reliability—is not discretion to abandon the gatekeeping function. I think it worth adding that it is not discretion to perform the function inadequately. Rather, it is discretion to choose among *reasonable* means of excluding expertise that is *fausse* and science that is junky. Though, as the Court makes clear today, the *Daubert* factors are not holy writ, in a particular case the failure to apply one or another of them may be unreasonable, and hence an abuse of discretion.

Questions

1. Does Justice Scalia's concurrence address adequately the possibility of trial judges reaching unpredictable conclusions as to the admissibility of evidence?

2. Do the Notes on the 2000 Amendment to Rule 702 of the Federal Rules of Evidence (below) address adequately the possibility of trial judges reaching unpredictable conclusions as to the admissibility of evidence?

Advisory Committee on Rules, Notes on 2000 Amendment

Rule 702 has been amended in response to *Daubert v. Merrell Dow Pharmaceuticals, Inc.*, 509 U.S. 579 (1993), and to the many cases applying *Daubert*, including *Kumho Tire Co. v. Carmichael*, 119 S.Ct. 1167 (1999).... Consistently with *Kumho*, the Rule as amended provides that all types of expert testimony present questions of admissibility for the trial court in deciding whether the evidence is reliable and helpful. Consequently, the admissibility of all expert testimony is governed by the principles of Rule 104(a). Under that Rule, the proponent has the burden of establishing that the pertinent admissibility requirements are met by a preponderance of the evidence. See *Bourjaily v. United States*, 483 U.S. 171 (1987).

Daubert set forth a non-exclusive checklist for trial courts to use in assessing the reliability of scientific expert testimony. The specific factors explicated by the *Daubert* Court are (1) whether the expert's technique or theory can be or has been tested—that is, whether the expert's theory can be challenged in some objective sense, or whether it is instead simply a subjective, conclusory approach that cannot reasonably be assessed for reliability; (2) whether the technique or theory has been subject to peer review and publication; (3) the known or potential rate of error of the technique or theory when applied; (4) the existence and maintenance of standards and controls; and (5) whether the technique or theory has been generally accepted in the scientific community. The Court in *Kumho* held that these factors might also be applicable in assessing the reliability of nonscientific expert testimony, depending upon "the particular circumstances of the particular case at issue." 119 S.Ct. at 1175.

No attempt has been made to "codify" these specific factors. *Daubert* itself emphasized that the factors were neither exclusive nor dispositive. Other cases have recognized that not all of the specific *Daubert* factors can apply to every type of expert testimony....

Courts both before and after *Daubert* have found other factors relevant in determining whether expert testimony is sufficiently reliable to be considered by the trier of fact. These factors include:

(1) Whether experts are "proposing to testify about matters growing naturally and directly out of research they have conducted independent of the litigation, or whether they have developed their opinions expressly for purposes of testifying." *Daubert v. Merrell Dow Pharmaceuticals, Inc.*, 43 F.3d 1311, 1317 (9th Cir. 1995).

(2) Whether the expert has unjustifiably extrapolated from an accepted premise to an unfounded conclusion. See *General Elec. Co. v. Joiner*, 522 U.S. 136, 146 (1997) (noting that in some cases a trial court "may conclude that there is simply too great an analytical gap between the data and the opinion proffered").

(3) Whether the expert has adequately accounted for obvious alternative explanations. See *Claar v. Burlington N.R.R.*, 29 F.3d 499 (9th Cir. 1994) (testimony excluded where the expert failed to consider other obvious causes for the plaintiff's condition). Compare *Ambrosini v. Labarraque*, 101 F.3d 129 (D.C.Cir. 1996) (the possibility of some uneliminated causes presents a question of weight, so long as the most obvious causes have been considered and reasonably ruled out by the expert).

(4) Whether the expert "is being as careful as he would be in his regular professional work outside his paid litigation consulting." *Sheehan v. Daily Racing Form, Inc.*, 104 F.3d 940, 942 (7th Cir. 1997). See *Kumho Tire Co. v. Carmichael*, 119 S.Ct. 1167, 1176 (1999) (*Daubert* requires the trial court to assure itself that the expert "employs in the courtroom the same level of intellectual rigor that characterizes the practice of an expert in the relevant field").

(5) Whether the field of expertise claimed by the expert is known to reach reliable results for the type of opinion the expert would give. See *Kumho Tire Co. v. Carmichael*, 119 S.Ct. 1167, 1175 (1999) (*Daubert's* general acceptance factor does not "help show that an expert's testimony is reliable where the discipline itself lacks reliability, as, for example, do theories grounded in any so-called generally accepted principles of astrology or necromancy."); *Moore v. Ashland Chemical, Inc.*, 151 F.3d 269 (5th Cir. 1998) (*en banc*) (clinical doctor was properly precluded from testifying to the toxicological cause of the plaintiff's respiratory problem, where the opinion was not sufficiently grounded in scientific methodology); *Sterling v. Velsicol Chem. Corp.*, 855 F.2d 1188 (6th Cir. 1988) (rejecting testimony based on "clinical ecology" as unfounded and unreliable).

All of these factors remain relevant to the determination of the reliability of expert testimony under the Rule as amended. Other factors may also be relevant. See *Kumho*, 119 S.Ct. 1167, 1176 ("(W)e conclude that the trial judge must have considerable leeway in deciding in a particular case how to go about determining whether particular expert testimony is reliable."). Yet no single factor is necessarily dispositive of the reliability of a particular expert's testimony. See, e.g., *Heller v. Shaw Industries, Inc.*, 167 F.3d 146, 155 (3d Cir., 1999) ("not only must each stage of the expert's testimony be reliable, but each stage must be evaluated practically and flexibly without bright-line exclusionary (or inclusionary) rules.") ...

A review of the caselaw after *Daubert* shows that the rejection of expert testimony is the exception rather than the rule. *Daubert* did not work a "seachange over federal evidence law," and "the trial court's role as gatekeeper is not intended to serve as a replacement for the adversary system." *United States v. 14.38 Acres of Land Situated in Leflore County, Mississippi*, 80 F.3d 1074, 1078 (5th Cir. 1996). As the Court in *Daubert* stated: "Vigorous cross-examination, presentation of contrary evidence, and careful instruction on the burden of proof are the traditional and appropriate means of attacking shaky but admissible evidence." 509 U.S. at 595. Likewise, this amendment is not intended to provide an excuse for an automatic challenge to the testimony of every expert. See *Kumho Tire Co. v. Carmichael*, 119 S.Ct. 1167, 1176 (1999) (noting that the trial judge has the discretion "both to avoid unnecessary 'reliability' proceedings in ordinary cases where the reliability of an expert's methods is properly taken for granted, and to require appropriate proceedings in the less usual or more complex cases where cause for questioning the expert's reliability arises.").

When a trial court, applying this amendment, rules that an expert's testimony is reliable, this does not necessarily mean that contradictory expert testimony is unreliable.

The amendment is broad enough to permit testimony that is the product of competing principles or methods in the same field of expertise. See, e.g., *Heller v. Shaw Industries, Inc.*, 167 F.3d 146, 160 (3d Cir. 1999) (expert testimony cannot be excluded simply because the expert uses one test rather than another, when both tests are accepted in the field and both reach reliable results). As the court stated in *In re Paoli R.R. Yard PCB Litigation*, 35 F.3d 717, 744 (3d Cir. 1994), proponents "do not have to demonstrate to the judge by a preponderance of the evidence that the assessments of their experts are correct, they only have to demonstrate by a preponderance of evidence that their opinions are reliable.... The evidentiary requirement of reliability is lower than the merits standard of correctness." See also *Daubert v. Merrell Dow Pharmaceuticals, Inc.*, 43 F.3d 1311, 1318 (9th Cir. 1995) (scientific experts might be permitted to testify if they could show that the methods they used were also employed by "a recognized minority of scientists in their field."); *Ruiz-Troche v. Pepsi Cola*, 161 F.3d 77, 85 (1st Cir. 1998) ("*Daubert* neither requires nor empowers trial courts to determine which of several competing scientific theories has the best provenance.").

The Court in *Daubert* declared that the "focus, of course, must be solely on principles and methodology, not on the conclusions they generate." 509 U.S. at 595. Yet as the Court later recognized, "conclusions and methodology are not entirely distinct from one another." *General Elec. Co. v. Joiner*, 522 U.S. 136, 146 (1997). Under the amendment, as under *Daubert*, when an expert purports to apply principles and methods in accordance with professional standards, and yet reaches a conclusion that other experts in the field would not reach, the trial court may fairly suspect that the principles and methods have not been faithfully applied. See *Lust v. Merrell Dow Pharmaceuticals, Inc.*, 89 F.3d 594, 598 (9th Cir. 1996). The amendment specifically provides that the trial court must scrutinize not only the principles and methods used by the expert, but also whether those principles and methods have been properly applied to the facts of the case. As the court noted in *In re Paoli R.R. Yard PCB Litig.*, 35 F.3d 717, 745 (3d Cir. 1994), "any step that renders the analysis unreliable ... renders the expert's testimony inadmissible. This is true whether the step completely changes a reliable methodology or merely misapplies that methodology."

If the expert purports to apply principles and methods to the facts of the case, it is important that this application be conducted reliably. Yet it might also be important in some cases for an expert to educate the factfinder about general principles, without ever attempting to apply these principles to the specific facts of the case. For example, experts might instruct the factfinder on the principles of thermodynamics, or bloodclotting, or on how financial markets respond to corporate reports, without ever knowing about or trying to tie their testimony into the facts of the case. The amendment does not alter the venerable practice of using expert testimony to educate the factfinder on general principles. For this kind of generalized testimony, Rule 702 simply requires that: (1) the expert be qualified; (2) the testimony address a subject matter on which the factfinder can be assisted by an expert; (3) the testimony be reliable; and (4) the testimony "fit" the facts of the case....

Nothing in this amendment is intended to suggest that experience alone—or experience in conjunction with other knowledge, skill, training or education—may not provide a sufficient foundation for expert testimony. To the contrary, the text of Rule 702 expressly contemplates that an expert may be qualified on the basis of experience....

The amendment makes no attempt to set forth procedural requirements for exercising the trial court's gatekeeping function over expert testimony. See Daniel J. Capra, *The Daubert Puzzle*, 38 Ga. L. Rev. 699, 766 (1998) ("Trial courts should be allowed substantial discretion in dealing with *Daubert* questions; any attempt to codify procedures will likely give rise to unnecessary changes in practice and create difficult questions for appellate review."). Courts have shown considerable ingenuity and flexibility in considering challenges to expert testimony under *Daubert*, and it is contemplated that this will continue under the amended Rule. See, e.g., *Cortes-Irizarry v. Corporacion Insular*, 111 F.3d 184 (1st Cir. 1997) (discussing the application of *Daubert* in ruling on a motion for summary judgment); *In re Paoli R.R. Yard PCB Litig.*, 35 F.3d 717, 736, 739 (3d Cir. 1994) (discussing the use of in limine hearings); *Claar v. Burlington N.R.R.*, 29 F.3d 499, 502–05 (9th Cir. 1994) (discussing the trial court's technique of ordering experts to submit serial affidavits explaining the reasoning and methods underlying their conclusions).

McClain v. Metabolife International, Inc.
401 F.3d 1233 (11th Cir. 2005)

ROYAL, J. This is an appeal of a jury verdict in a products liability action against Metabolife International, Inc. At trial Plaintiffs claimed that they suffered serious medical problems after taking Metabolife 356, an herbal weight-loss supplement, manufactured, marketed, and sold by Metabolife. After hearing the evidence, a jury returned a verdict in Plaintiffs' favor. Metabolife now appeals that verdict on the ground that the trial court erred in admitting the testimony of Plaintiffs' experts on the issue of causation....

Before trial Metabolife moved to exclude Plaintiffs' experts' testimony on medical causation asserting that Plaintiffs' experts' opinions lacked a reliable foundation for admission under the standards of *Daubert v. Merrell Dow Pharmaceuticals, Inc.*, 509 U.S. 579, 113 S.Ct. 2786, 125 L.Ed.2d 469 (1993). The trial court held a *Daubert* hearing, and Plaintiffs offered two expert witnesses to prove causation: James O'Donnell, Pharm. D., and Hashim Hakim, M.D., a neurologist. Dr. O'Donnell primarily offered opinions on general causation. Dr. Hakim offered testimony on both general and individual causation.

In its brief written order on the motion, the district court acknowledged its role as a gatekeeper under Fed.R.Evid. 702, but concluded that it lacked sufficient knowledge on the scientific subject matter to exclude the testimony presented and that Defendant had not produced competing testimony for it to determine that, as a matter of law, testimony from Plaintiffs' experts was inadmissible. Metabolife later filed a motion for reconsideration on the issue, and it was denied. The two experts testified at trial on the issues covered by Defendant's motion, and the jury returned a verdict for Plaintiffs. Defendant appealed contending that the district court abused it discretion in admitting Plaintiffs' experts' testimony on medical causation.

This is a toxic tort case. Plaintiffs contend that the toxic combination of ephedrine and caffeine in the Metabolife 356 that they ingested harmed them. To prove their toxic tort claims, Plaintiffs must prove the toxicity of the ephedrine/caffeine combination and that it had a toxic effect on them causing the injuries that they suffered—ischemic strokes in three Plaintiffs and a heart attack in the other.

This type of proof requires expert testimony, and when a party offers expert testimony and the opposing party raises a *Daubert* challenge, the trial court must "make certain that an expert, whether basing testimony upon professional studies or personal experience, employs in the courtroom the same level of intellectual rigor that characterizes the practice of an expert in the relevant field." *Kumho Tire Co., Ltd. v. Carmichael*, 526 U.S. 137, 152, 119 S.Ct. 1167, 143 L.Ed.2d 238 (1999). This requirement for proof of the reliability of the expert's method comes from Fed.R.Evid. 702, which authorizes the admission of expert opinion testimony "if (1) the testimony is based upon sufficient facts or data,

(2) the testimony is the product of reliable principles and methods, and (3) the witness has applied the principles and methods reliably to the facts of the case." Rule 702 lays the foundation for the trial court's *Daubert* analysis.

Daubert requires the trial court to act as a gatekeeper to insure that speculative and unreliable opinions do not reach the jury. As a gatekeeper the court must do "a preliminary assessment of whether the reasoning or methodology underlying the testimony is scientifically valid and of whether that reasoning or methodology properly can be applied to the facts in issue." The proposed testimony must derive from the scientific method; good grounds and appropriate validation must support it. The court must consider the testimony with the understanding that "[t]he burden of establishing qualification, reliability, and helpfulness rests on the proponent of the expert opinion...."

The court of appeals reviews a trial court's *Daubert* rulings under an abuse of discretion standard. *Gen. Elec. Co. v. Joiner*, 522 U.S. 136, 140, 118 S.Ct. 512, 139 L.Ed.2d 508 (1997). A "district court enjoys 'considerable leeway' in making [reliability] determinations" under *Daubert*. *Kumho*, 526 U.S. at 152, 119 S.Ct. 1167. Thus, "[w]hen applying [the] abuse of discretion standard, we must affirm unless we at least determine that the district court has made a 'clear error of judgment,' or has applied an incorrect legal standard."

A trial court, however, abuses its discretion by failing to act as a gatekeeper. In this case the trial court essentially abdicated its gatekeeping role. Although the trial court conducted a *Daubert* hearing, and both witnesses were subject to a thorough and extensive examination, the court ultimately disavowed its ability to handle the *Daubert* issues. In ruling on the *Daubert* motion, the trial court stated:

> Trying to cope in this case without a pharmacological, or a medical, or a chemical, or a scientific background, the court cannot fully and fairly appreciate and evaluate the methodology employed by either of these witnesses as they reached the conclusions they reached, conclusions that a jury could not reach without some expert opinion testimony. Neither can the court fully appreciate or evaluate the criticisms made by defendant of the proposed testimony of these witnesses, especially when the criticisms do not come from competing proposed experts. This court does not pretend to know enough to formulate a logical basis for a preclusionary order that would necessarily find, as a matter of law, that these witnesses cannot express to a jury the opinions they articulated to the court.

This abdication was in itself an abuse of discretion.

Yet, even had the trial court fully accepted its role, it would have abused its discretion by admitting the experts' testimony. The record of their testimony in the pretrial hearing demonstrates that their testimony failed to satisfy the standards of reliability required under *Daubert* and its progeny. The admission of their testimony on medical causation in this toxic tort case substantially prejudiced Metabolife and authorizes reversal of the judgment.

In analyzing the experts' testimony, we note that toxic tort cases usually come in two broad categories: first, those cases in which the medical community generally recognizes the toxicity of the drug or chemical at issue, and second, those cases in which the medical community does not generally recognize the agent as both toxic and causing the injury plaintiff alleges. Examples of the first type include toxins like asbestos, which causes asbestosis and mesothelioma; silica, which causes silicosis; and cigarette smoke, which causes cancer. This case, involving Metabolife's combination of ephedrine and caffeine, falls into the second category. The medical community does not generally recognize the toxicity of this drug combination or ephedrine alone as causing the injuries Plaintiffs allege.

The court need not undertake an extensive *Daubert* analysis on the general toxicity question when the medical community recognizes that the agent causes the type of harm a plaintiff alleges. The battleground in this first category of cases focuses on plaintiff-specific questions: was plaintiff exposed to the toxin, was plaintiff exposed to enough of the toxin to cause the alleged injury, and did the toxin in fact cause the injury? A *Daubert* analysis in the first type of case deals with questions of individual causation to plaintiff.

In the second category of toxic tort cases, the *Daubert* analysis covers not only the expert's methodology for the plaintiff-specific questions about individual causation but also the general question of whether the drug or chemical can cause the harm plaintiff alleges. This is called general causation. "General causation is concerned with whether an agent increases the incidence of disease in a group and not whether the agent caused any given individual's disease." Michael D. Green *et al.*, *Reference Guide on Epidemiology*, in Reference Manual on Scientific Evidence 392 (Federal Judicial Center, 2d ed., 2000). Thus, in this case, Plaintiffs' experts must offer reliable opinions about Metabolife's general toxicity for the harm Plaintiffs allege and that it in fact harmed them. The court will consider, therefore, the reliability of Plaintiffs' experts' opinions on the question of general causation and also the question of individual causation.

Reversed and remanded.

Much Ado about Nothing?

We have already seen that the adoption of the Products Liability Restatement, and particularly its notion of a risk-utility standard to prove a defective product design, has proved to be extremely controversial. Adoption of the *Daubert* standard for expert evidence, especially when coupled with the reiteration in *Joiner* of the abuse of discretion standard for appellate review, has been no less controversial. The ramifications of both cases have been bitterly criticized by the plaintiff bar, while defense counsel are happy to applaud them. Attorneys on both sides of the debate have anecdotes aplenty as to why *Daubert* and its progeny are right or wrong. The odd thing is that there currently is no empirical evidence to support the idea that the *Daubert* trilogy really changed anything.

In fact, such research has struggled to find any clear evidence of change at all. In a huge study comparing the practices of state courts before and after they adopted *Daubert*— and with the practices of states which have not adopted *Daubert*—Eric Helland & Jonathan Klick, *Does Anyone Get Stopped at the Gate? An Empirical Assessment of the Daubert Trilogy in the States*, University of Pennsylvania, Institute for Law & Economics Research Paper 09-12 (2009), concluded (at p. 28):

> The *Daubert* trilogy creates a new standard for determining the admissibility of expert evidence in federal courts. With its focus on methodological rigor, many tort reformers trumpet the *Daubert* standards as a way to get rid of junk science in the courtroom. Conventional wisdom holds that *Daubert* led to stronger scrutiny of expert evidence in the federal courts, seemingly supporting the tort reformers' view. This has led to a related effort to encourage state courts to adopt the *Daubert* standard. Despite all of these efforts, as well as the efforts of those opposing adoption on the grounds that *Daubert* is overly restrictive, there is virtually no systematic evidence supporting the view that adoption of *Daubert* makes any difference at all.

Because the existing evidence either focuses on the federal courts or a very limited range of state courts, we examine this issue using a large dataset that spans almost every state over a wide range of civil case types. In this more comprehensive analysis, we too find very little evidence that adoption of the *Daubert* trilogy has any systematic effect on who is offered as an expert in state court disputes. This is true even when we examine more detailed data in the area of products liability disputes where *Daubert* is thought to be particularly important. While we cannot determine exactly why *Daubert* seems to have no systematic effect, our results are consistent with other empirical studies on this topic. While none of these studies is perfect, their imperfections are largely orthogonal to each other, making it unlikely that design flaws or data limitations are driving this non-effect. While courts may be scrutinizing expert evidence more carefully, as suggested by the RAND research at the federal level, it seems unlikely that this has anything to do with *Daubert* per se.

Questions

1. Might it be that *Daubert* and subsequent cases have produced arbitrary decision-making at trial level, but that studies like the one by Helland and Klick are unable to detect this degree of arbitrariness because they are looking at averages?

2. Does the Helland and Klick study suggest that *Daubert* and subsequent cases have had little effect in practice, or that their effect has been felt outside of the courtroom?

3. Do the differing criteria for the admissibility of expert evidence effectively mirror the controversy as to whether the "consumer expectations" or "risk-utility" test should be employed to determine the existence or otherwise of a design defect?

4. In what cases is expert testimony not required?

Ortiz-Martinez v. Hyundai Motor Co.
602 F.Supp.2d 311 (2009) (US District Court, Puerto Rico)

[The plaintiff was injured when the vehicle he was driving struck the wall of a McDonald's drive-through at low speed. The case turned on whether the air bag deployed before or after the impact with the wall.]

BESOSA, J. On January 2, 2009, Hyundai Motor Company ("Hyundai") moved for summary judgment claiming that plaintiffs could not establish a viable products liability claim without an expert witness. On February 3, 2009, plaintiffs filed their opposition to the summary judgment motion. On February 6, 2009, United States Magistrate Judge Marcos E. Lopez issued a report and recommendation, recommending that the defendants' motion for summary judgment be denied. Hyundai filed its objection to the report and recommendation on February 17, 2009. For the following reasons, the Court now adopts the report and recommendation in full.

A district court may refer pending dispositive motions to a magistrate judge for a report and recommendation. See 28 U.S.C. § 636(b)(1)(B); Fed.R.Civ.P. 72(b); L.Civ.R. 72(a). Any party may file written objections to the report and recommendation within ten days of being served with the magistrate judge's report. See 28 U.S.C. § 636(b)(1). The party that files a timely objection is entitled to a *de novo* determination of "those portions of the report or specified proposed findings or recommendations to which specific objection is made." Failure to comply with this rule waives each party's right to review in the district court. In conducting its review, the Court may "accept, reject, or modify, in whole or in part, the findings or recommendations made by the magistrate judge." 28 U.S.C. §636(b)(1).

After reviewing the report and recommendation issued by the magistrate judge and the objection filed to it by Hyundai, the Court finds that only one issue needs to be addressed. That issue is whether the magistrate judge properly relied on a particular case in recommending that Hyundai's motion for summary judgment be denied.

Hyundai's summary judgment motion presented a single issue for the Court's determination—whether plaintiffs can establish a viable products liability claim under Puerto Rico law without expert testimony....

The magistrate judge then pointed out that in *Perez-Trujillo v. Volvo Car Corp. (Sweden)*, 137 F.3d 50, 55 (1st Cir. 1998)

> the First Circuit [Court of Appeals] stated with regard to Puerto Rico law on products liability, jurisdictions which model their decisional law along Restatement lines uniformly hold that a strict liability claimant may demonstrate an unsafe defect through direct eyewitness observation of a product malfunction, and need not adduce expert testimony to overcome a motion for summary judgment.

Based on his analysis of prior First Circuit Court of Appeals case law regarding the treatment of evidence arising in product liability cases in Puerto Rico, the magistrate judge ultimately determined that the plaintiffs in this case could overcome Hyundai's summary judgment motion without offering an expert witness....

Expert testimony is not required to prove that the vehicle involved in the accident "differs from the manufacturer's intended result or from other ostensibly identical units of the same product." Whether plaintiffs have lay testimony sufficiently credible to support the conclusion that a product defect caused the airbag's deployment is clearly something for the jury to decide; if no lay evidence exists to support that conclusion, then Hyundai will prevail.

Accordingly, defendants' objection is deemed unconvincing, and the Court adopts in full the magistrate judge's report and recommendation to allow plaintiffs' case to proceed to trial without an expert witness. Hyundai's motion for summary judgment is denied.

Questions

1. Is lay testimony likely to be sufficient only in cases of an alleged manufacturing defect?

2. Is a jury more likely to believe the testimony of a lay eye-witness, who claims to have seen what happened, or an expert who claims to be able to reconstruct the likely narrative of events from evidence gained after the fact?

Chapter 15

Mass Torts Litigation Devices

Introduction

Most lay persons have little or no interest—or even knowledge—of most of the law of torts. Few, however, can have failed to notice the widely-publicized mass torts cases involving products such as asbestos, Bendectin (a drug used to treat morning sickness in pregnant women), cigarettes, the Dalkon Shield (an intrauterine contraceptive device), diethylstilbestrol (more commonly known as DES, a drug used to reduce a variety of conditions, including complications with pregnancy), HIV-infected blood, and silicone breast implants. The power of these mass torts cases—often known as "toxic torts" cases—can be gauged from the fact that asbestos, Bendectin, and the Dalkon Shield have all been withdrawn from use in the United States, although Bendectin continues to be prescribed in both Canada and Europe (where it is known as Diclectin, except in the United Kingdom, where it is known as Debendox). While DES is still on the market, it is no longer licensed for use by pregnant women.

This Chapter discusses three mass torts litigation devices: class actions, multi-district litigation (MDLs), and market share liability. All are indigenous creations of American tort law. None featured in the common law imported from England, and English law still does not recognize them. Even within the United States, the courts originally maintained their innate hostility to anything that might open the floodgates (whether to claims or trials), and resisted the idea that a claim in tort should be treated differently simply because there was a large number of would-be plaintiffs. Indeed, some states (like Virginia) still refuse to recognize class actions, while others restrict the type of claim that may be brought using this device. In addition, the majority of states do not recognize the concept of market share liability. MDLs, by contrast, are mandated by federal law.

It is usually the case that mass torts litigation involves either or both a class action and/or an MDL. Class actions may be certified when a large number of claims are made together (usually in one district court); MDLs may also be appropriate in such circumstances, although they are applicable too where multiple claims are made separately in a number of different courts. Many class actions are consolidated for pre-trial purposes through an MDL.

Multidistrict Litigation:
Federalism or Uniformity?

The legal relationship between the federal government and state governments is quite complex. The Constitution of the United States grants a set of powers to the federal government, but the Tenth Amendment points out that:

> The powers not delegated to the United States by the Constitution, nor prohibited by it to the States, are reserved to the States respectively, or to the people.

In other words, unless a power is constitutionally granted to the federal government, it has no jurisdiction, in which case the relevant law-making bodies will be the states. However, when such a power is granted to the federal government, the apposite provision is to be found in the second paragraph of Article VI of the Constitution—generally known as the "Supremacy Clause"—which provides:

> This Constitution, and the Laws of the United States which shall be made in Pursuance thereof; and all Treaties made, or which shall be made, under the Authority of the United States, shall be the supreme Law of the Land; and the Judges in every State shall be bound thereby, any Thing in the Constitution or Laws of any State to the Contrary notwithstanding.

Nothing in the Constitution grants any branch of the federal government the power to make or amend the law of torts (although federal courts have original, but non-exclusive, jurisdiction over admiralty law under section 2 of Article III of the Constitution, and what would otherwise be considered issues of torts are decided in such cases from time to time. Indeed, *United States v. Carroll Towing Co.*, 159 F.2d 169 (2d. Cir. 1947), (in)famous for Judge Learned Hand's formula for ascertaining negligence, was an admiralty case). For this reason, tort law remains essentially a matter for the states.

Erie Railroad Co. v. Tompkins
304 U.S. 64, 58 S.Ct. 817 (1938) (SCOTUS)

BRANDEIS, J. Tompkins, a citizen of Pennsylvania, was injured on a dark night by a passing freight train of the Erie Railroad Company while walking along its right of way at Hughestown in that state. He claimed that the accident occurred through negligence in the operation, or maintenance, of the train; that he was rightfully on the premises as licensee because on a commonly used beaten footpath which ran for a short distance alongside the tracks; and that he was struck by something which looked like a door projecting from one of the moving cars. To enforce that claim he brought an action in the federal court for Southern New York, which had jurisdiction because the company is a corporation of that state. It denied liability; and the case was tried by a jury.

The Erie insisted that its duty to Tompkins was no greater than that owed to a trespasser. It contended, among other things, that its duty to Tompkins, and hence its liability, should be determined in accordance with the Pennsylvania law; that under the law of Pennsylvania, as declared by its highest court, persons who use pathways along the railroad right of way—that is, a longitudinal pathway as distinguished from a crossing—are to be deemed trespassers; and that the railroad is not liable for injuries to undiscovered trespassers resulting from its negligence, unless it be wanton or willful. Tompkins denied that any such rule had been established by the decisions of the Pennsylvania courts; and contended that, since there was no statute of the state on the subject, the railroad's duty and liability is to be determined in federal courts as a matter of general law.

The trial judge refused to rule that the applicable law precluded recovery. The jury brought in a verdict of $30,000; and the judgment entered thereon was affirmed by the Circuit Court of Appeals, which held (2 Cir., 90 F.2d 603, 604), that it was unnecessary to consider whether the law of Pennsylvania was as contended, because the question was one not of local, but of general, law, and that

> upon questions of general law the federal courts are free, in absence of a local statute, to exercise their independent judgment as to what the law is; and it is well settled that the question of the responsibility of a railroad for injuries caused by its servants is one of general law....

The Erie had contended that application of the Pennsylvania rule was required, among other things, by section 34 of the Federal Judiciary Act of September 24, 1789, c. 20, 28 U.S.C. s 725, 28 U.S.C.A. s 725, which provides:

> The laws of the several States, except where the Constitution, treaties, or statutes of the United States otherwise require or provide, shall be regarded as rules of decision in trials at common law, in the courts of the United States, in cases where they apply.

Because of the importance of the question whether the federal court was free to disregard the alleged rule of the Pennsylvania common law, we granted certiorari.

Swift v. Tyson, 16 Pet. 1, 18, 10 L.Ed. 865, held that federal courts exercising jurisdiction on the ground of diversity of citizenship need not, in matters of general jurisprudence, apply the unwritten law of the state as declared by its highest court; that they are free to exercise an independent judgment as to what the common law of the state is—or should be; and that, as there stated by Mr. Justice Story,

> the true interpretation of the 34th section limited its application to state laws, strictly local, that is to say, to the positive statutes of the state, and the construction thereof adopted by the local tribunals, and to rights and titles to things having a permanent locality, such as the rights and titles to real estate, and other matters immovable and intra-territorial in their nature and character. It never has been supposed by us, that the section did apply, or was designed to apply, to questions of a more general nature, not at all dependent upon local statutes or local usages of a fixed and permanent operation, as, for example, to the construction of ordinary contracts or other written instruments, and especially to questions of general commercial law, where the state tribunals are called upon to perform the like functions as ourselves, that is, to ascertain, upon general reasoning and legal analogies, what is the true exposition of the contract or instrument, or what is the just rule furnished by the principles of commercial law to govern the case.

The fallacy underlying the rule declared in *Swift v. Tyson* is made clear by Mr. Justice Holmes. The doctrine rests upon the assumption that there is "a transcendental body of law outside of any particular State but obligatory within it unless and until changed by statute," that federal courts have the power to use their judgment as to what the rules of common law are; and that in the federal courts "the parties are entitled to an independent judgment on matters of general law":

> But law in the sense in which courts speak of it today does not exist without some definite authority behind it. The common law so far as it is enforced in a

State, whether called common law or not, is not the common law generally but the law of that State existing by the authority of that State without regard to what it may have been in England or anywhere else....

The authority and only authority is the State, and if that be so, the voice adopted by the State as its own (whether it be of its Legislature or of its Supreme Court) should utter the last word.

Thus the doctrine of *Swift v. Tyson* is, as Mr. Justice Holmes said, "an unconstitutional assumption of powers by the Courts of the United States which no lapse of time or respectable array of opinion should make us hesitate to correct." In disapproving that doctrine we do not hold unconstitutional section 34 of the Federal Judiciary Act of 1789 or any other act of Congress. We merely declare that in applying the doctrine this Court and the lower courts have invaded rights which in our opinion are reserved by the Constitution to the several states....

The defendant contended that by the common law of Pennsylvania as declared by its highest court in *Falchetti v. Pennsylvania* R. Co., 307 Pa. 203, 160 A. 859, the only duty owed to the plaintiff was to refrain from willful or wanton injury. The plaintiff denied that such is the Pennsylvania law.

In support of their respective contentions the parties discussed and cited many decisions of the Supreme Court of the state. The Circuit Court of Appeals ruled that the question of liability is one of general law; and on that ground declined to decide the issue of state law. As we hold this was error, the judgment is reversed and the case remanded to it for further proceedings in conformity with our opinion.

Notes

1. *Substantive law. Erie* thus lays down that, even when a case is to be tried in federal court, the substantive law to be applied is that of the state most relevant to the case at hand.

2. *Procedural law.* However, *Erie* has nothing to say about questions of procedure. That is, in fact, governed by the so-called "Necessary and Proper Clause" in Section 8 of Article I of the federal Constitution, which says:

The Congress shall have Power ... To make all Laws which shall be necessary and proper for carrying into Execution the foregoing Powers, and all other Powers vested by this Constitution in the Government of the United States, or in any Department or Officer thereof.

United States Code — Title 28: Judiciary and Judicial Procedure

§ 1407. Multidistrict Litigation

(a) When civil actions involving one or more common questions of fact are pending in different districts, such actions may be transferred to any district for coordinated or consolidated pretrial proceedings. Such transfers shall be made by the judicial panel on multidistrict litigation authorized by this section upon its determination that transfers for such proceedings will be for the convenience of parties and witnesses and will promote the just and efficient conduct of such actions. Each action so transferred shall be remanded by the panel at or before the conclusion of such pretrial proceedings to the district from which it was transferred unless it shall have been previously terminated: Provided, however, That the panel may separate any claim, cross-claim, counter-claim, or third-party claim and remand any of such claims before the remainder of the action is remanded.

(b) Such coordinated or consolidated pretrial proceedings shall be conducted by a judge or judges to whom such actions are assigned by the judicial panel on multidistrict litigation. For this purpose, upon request of the panel, a circuit judge or a district judge may be designated and assigned temporarily for service in the transferee district by the Chief Justice of the United States or the chief judge of the circuit, as may be required, in accordance with the provisions of Chapter 13 of this title. With the consent of the transferee district court, such actions may be assigned by the panel to a judge or judges of such district. The judge or judges to whom such actions are assigned, the members of the judicial panel on multidistrict litigation, and other circuit and district judges designated when needed by the panel may exercise the powers of a district judge in any district for the purpose of conducting pretrial depositions in such coordinated or consolidated pretrial proceedings.

(c) Proceedings for the transfer of an action under this section may be initiated by—

(i) the judicial panel on multidistrict litigation upon its own initiative, or

(ii) motion filed with the panel by a party in any action in which transfer for coordinated or consolidated pretrial proceedings under this section may be appropriate. A copy of such motion shall be filed in the district court in which the moving party's action is pending.

The panel shall give notice to the parties in all actions in which transfers for coordinated or consolidated pretrial proceedings are contemplated, and such notice shall specify the time and place of any hearing to determine whether such transfer shall be made. Orders of the panel to set a hearing and other orders of the panel issued prior to the order either directing or denying transfer shall be filed in the office of the clerk of the district court in which a transfer hearing is to be or has been held. The panel's order of transfer shall be based upon a record of such hearing at which material evidence may be offered by any party to an action pending in any district that would be affected by the proceedings under this section, and shall be supported by findings of fact and conclusions of law based upon such record. Orders of transfer and such other orders as the panel may make thereafter shall be filed in the office of the clerk of the district court of the transferee district and shall be effective when thus filed. The clerk of the transferee district court shall forthwith transmit a certified copy of the panel's order to transfer to the clerk of the district court from which the action is being transferred. An order denying transfer shall be filed in each district wherein there is a case pending in which the motion for transfer has been made.

(d) The judicial panel on multidistrict litigation shall consist of seven circuit and district judges designated from time to time by the Chief Justice of the United States, no two of whom shall be from the same circuit. The concurrence of four members shall be necessary to any action by the panel.

(e) No proceedings for review of any order of the panel may be permitted except by extraordinary writ pursuant to the provisions of title 28, section 1651, United States Code. Petitions for an extraordinary writ to review an order of the panel to set a transfer hearing and other orders of the panel issued prior to the order either directing or denying transfer shall be filed only in the court of appeals having jurisdiction over the district in which a hearing is to be or has been held. Petitions for an extraordinary writ to review an order to transfer or orders subsequent to transfer shall be filed only in the court of appeals having jurisdiction over the transferee district. There shall be no appeal or review of an order of the panel denying a motion to transfer for consolidated or coordinated proceedings.

(f) The panel may prescribe rules for the conduct of its business not inconsistent with Acts of Congress and the Federal Rules of Civil Procedure.

(g) Nothing in this section shall apply to any action in which the United States is a complainant arising under the antitrust laws....

Notes

1. *Purpose.* This transfer or "centralization" process is designed to avoid duplication of discovery, to prevent inconsistent pretrial rulings, and to conserve the resources of the parties, their counsel and the judiciary. Transferred actions not terminated in the transferee district are remanded to their originating transferor districts at or before the conclusion of centralized pretrial proceedings.

2. *MDL docket.* By October 2008, the judicial panel on multidistrict litigation had dealt with motions in over 2,000 dockets involving more than 300,000 cases and millions of claims therein. Such motions have related not just to mass torts claims such as those involving asbestos, but also claims involving airplane crashes, train wrecks, hotel fires, patent validity and infringement, antitrust price fixing, securities fraud, and employment practices.

3. *Multi-state law.* Cases may be transferred from all over the nation. This can lead to the transferee court's having to determine (or even predict) the law in many different states.

In Re: Methyl Tertiary Butyl Ether (MTBE) Products Liability Litigation

379 F.Supp.2d 348 (2005) (US District Court, S.D. New York)

SCHEINDLIN, J. In this consolidated multi-district litigation, plaintiffs seek relief from defendants' alleged contamination, or threatened contamination, of groundwater with the gasoline additive methyl tertiary butyl ether ("MTBE"). The parties have already engaged in extensive motion practice, and familiarity with the Court's previous opinions is assumed. Defendants now move, pursuant to Federal Rule of Civil Procedure 12(b)(6), for the complete dismissal of all the complaints filed in fifteen states: Connecticut, Florida, Illinois, Indiana, Iowa, Kansas, Louisiana, Massachusetts, New Hampshire, New Jersey, New York, Pennsylvania, Vermont, Virginia, and West Virginia.

While raising many issues, defendants' motions to dismiss focus in particular on the problem of product identification. Defendants argue that the complaints from all fifteen states must be dismissed because plaintiffs have failed to identify which defendant's MTBE-containing gasoline proximately caused their harm. In each of the relevant jurisdictions, plaintiffs must establish which product was responsible for causing their injuries in order to be granted relief. If plaintiffs cannot do so, their cases cannot survive unless they can proceed on a theory of collective liability. Plaintiffs concede that they cannot identify the offending product due to its fungible nature, as well as the commingling of many suppliers' petroleum products during transportation and distribution. Thus, the primary question addressed in this decision is whether plaintiffs may proceed on their state law claims based on theories of collective liability.

An important point must be highlighted at the outset, which raises the delicate consideration of the dual sovereignty of the federal and state courts. In the absence of a definitive ruling by the highest court of a particular state, this Court is called upon to predict what that court would decide if presented with the issue of collective liability. This is the duty of a federal court when faced with an undecided issue of state law. States have the primary responsibility to construe their own laws. The Tenth Amendment states: "The powers not delegated to the United States by the Constitution, nor prohibited by it to the States, are reserved to the States respectively, or to the people." ...

Therefore, some federal courts—especially in diversity cases—have exercised great restraint in ruling on novel issues of state law. While not adopting the Seventh Circuit's refusal to "speculat[e] about trends" in state law, the Second Circuit has stated that the role of the federal court is to "construe and apply state law as [it] believe[s] the state's highest court would, not to adopt innovative theories that may distort established state law." Courts have noted that such caution is especially appropriate where plaintiffs choose to bring an action in federal court.

Here, plaintiffs did not bring these actions in federal court in the hope of obtaining a broader interpretation of state law than they might reasonably expect to obtain from the state. All of these actions were originally brought in state court but removed to federal court over plaintiffs' vigorous objections. Thus, plaintiffs sought to have a state court interpret state law and should not be prejudiced by a removal they opposed.

When a defendant removes a case from state to federal court, a liberal construction of state law protects the principle of dual sovereignty by protecting a party who sought to obtain a resolution of state law claims from state courts. If this Court were to adopt a more restrictive reading of state law than the highest courts of the relevant states would be likely to adopt, the parties would be treated differently than they would be in a state court—a result directly contrary to the fundamental goals of *Erie*, namely the "discouragement of forum-shopping and avoidance of inequitable administration of laws." Therefore, while a court may not adopt "innovative theories" without support in state law, or "distort" existing state law, when a case is removed to federal court, the plaintiff is entitled to the same treatment it would receive in state court—no more, and no less....

A motion to dismiss pursuant to Rule 12(b)(6) should be granted only if "it appears beyond doubt that the plaintiff can prove no set of facts in support of [its] claim which would entitle [it] to relief." At the motion to dismiss stage, the issue "is not whether a plaintiff is likely to prevail ultimately, but whether the claimant is entitled to offer evidence to support the claims. Indeed it may appear on the face of the pleading that a recovery is very remote and unlikely but that is not the test."

The task of the court in ruling on a Rule 12(b)(6) motion is "merely to assess the legal feasibility of the complaint, not to assay the weight of the evidence which might be offered in support thereof." When deciding a motion to dismiss, courts must accept all factual allegations in the complaint as true, and draw all reasonable inferences in plaintiff's favor. Although the plaintiff's allegations are taken as true, the claim may still fail as a matter of law if it appears beyond doubt that the plaintiff can prove no set of facts in support of its claim which would entitle it to relief, or if the claim is not legally feasible.

It is now well-established that a plaintiff need not "set out in detail the facts upon which [it] bases [its] claim," nor allege a prima facie case. Pursuant to Rule 8, "a complaint must include only 'a short and plain statement of the claim showing that the pleader is entitled to relief.'" The issue is not whether a plaintiff has alleged certain facts, but whether the facts asserted give the defendant fair notice of the claim and the basis for such claim. Fair notice is "that which will enable the adverse party to answer and prepare for trial, allow the application of res judicata, and identify the nature of the case so that it may be assigned the proper form of trial." This notice pleading standard "relies on liberal discovery rules and summary judgment motions to define disputed facts and issues and to dispose of unmeritorious claims." "If a pleading fails to specify the allegations in a manner that provides sufficient notice, a defendant can move for a more definite statement under Rule 12(e) before responding." Accordingly, a claim can only be dismissed if "no relief could be granted under any set of facts that could be proved consistent with the allegations." ...

When a plaintiff alleges fraud, on the other hand, the defendant must be given more than notice of the claim. Rule 9(b) requires that "[i]n all averments of fraud or mistake, the circumstances constituting fraud or mistake shall be stated with particularity. Malice, intent, knowledge, and other condition of mind of a person may be averred generally." The objectives of the Rule are (1) to provide a defendant with fair notice of the plaintiff's claim to enable preparation of a defense; (2) to protect a defendant from harm to its reputation or goodwill; and (3) to reduce the number of strike suits. Rule 9(b) must be read in conjunction with Rule 8's requirement of a "short and plain statement" of the claim.

A fraud claim should specify the who, what, when, where, and how of the alleged fraud. "Where multiple defendants are asked to respond to allegations of fraud, the complaint should inform each defendant of the nature of [its] alleged participation in the fraud." Although scienter may be averred generally, the plaintiff must allege facts that give rise to a strong inference of fraudulent intent.

> The requisite "strong inference" of fraud may be established either (a) by alleging facts to show that defendants had both a motive and opportunity to commit fraud, or (b) by alleging facts that constitute strong circumstantial evidence of conscious misbehavior or recklessness.

An exception to Rule 9(b) is that fraud allegations may be based upon information and belief as to facts peculiarly within the opposing party's knowledge. However, "the allegations must be accompanied by a statement of the facts upon which the belief is based."

"Where the substantive law of the forum state is uncertain or ambiguous, the job of the federal courts is carefully to predict how the highest court of the forum state would resolve uncertainty or ambiguity" In making a prediction of state law, federal courts "look to the state's decisional law, as well as to its constitution and statutes." The "fullest weight" is accorded to the pronouncements of the state's highest court, while "proper regard" is given to the relevant rulings of the state's lower courts. A court may consider cases from other jurisdictions on the same or analogous issues. If the state has not passed on the question but the federal appeals court in the circuit where the state is located "has essayed its own prediction of the course of state law..., the federal courts of other circuits should defer to that holding." However, a court is not bound by the relevant circuit court's decision if it is

> persuaded that the holding ha[s] been superceded by a later pronouncement from state legislative or judicial sources, or that prior state court decisions had been inadvertently overlooked by the pertinent court of appeals ... [,] the pertinent court of appeals [ ] disregarded clear signals emanating from the state's highest court pointing toward a different rule ... [or the sitting court] can point to a clear basis in [state] law for predicting that the [state] courts, when confronted with a case such as [the one before it], would conclude that the [circuit court's] prediction was incorrect....

Defendants contend that because none of the fifteen states recognize the theories of concert of action, alternative, enterprise, or market share liability, plaintiffs will not be able to sustain their burden of proving causation. Plaintiffs respond that Rule 8 does not require them to plead theories of causation, but in any event, each state would adopt collective liability theories in the MTBE context. Plaintiffs add that in addition to the theories named by defendants, certain states might also apply the joint and several liability principle of concurrent negligence. Although Rule 8 does not require plaintiffs to plead a theory of causation, it does not protect a legally insufficient claim. The issue is whether plaintiffs can prove any set of facts that would entitle them to relief.

Plaintiffs argue in the alternative that if the Court rejects all theories of collective liability, their claims should still not be dismissed because they may, following discovery, be able to prove causation through traditional proof of product identification. Defendants object to that argument on the ground that plaintiffs are bound by the admissions in their complaints that product identification is impossible. According to defendants, because these fifteen states do not recognize collective liability theories, plaintiffs have pled themselves out of court. The arguments made by both plaintiffs and defendants are devoid of merit.

First, plaintiffs' claims cannot survive these motions to dismiss based on the mere possibility of plaintiffs identifying the manufacturer of the offending product during discovery. To accept this argument would be akin to granting pre-action discovery to plaintiffs, which would impose onerous burdens on defendants and would encourage strike suits against participants in certain industries. It is not fair to require more than two hundred companies to defend against these MTBE claims if plaintiffs cannot name the actual tortfeasors, and the fifteen states do not relieve plaintiffs of that burden.

Second, plaintiffs' statements of impossibility are not judicial admissions because they pertain to facts peculiarly in the knowledge and control of defendants. While "[a] party's assertion of fact in a pleading is a judicial admission by which it normally is bound throughout the course of the proceeding," judicial admissions generally pertain to matters that a party is uniquely positioned to know and concede, as opposed to facts uniquely known or controlled by an adverse party. Trial judges are given broad discretion to relieve the parties from the consequences of judicial admissions in the appropriate circumstances.

Plaintiffs assert that they cannot identify the wrongdoer based on the fungible nature of the MTBE-containing gasoline. However, if plaintiffs' claims survive based on theories of collective liability, then discovery will proceed. During that discovery, evidence might reveal that the offending product can be traced to a specific tortfeasor through the sales and distribution records of defendants. It would be unfair to treat plaintiffs' assertions as binding when defendants are in a better position to know who manufactured the injury-causing product, but have little incentive to provide that information. Plaintiffs' statements were based on an incomplete understanding of the relevant facts—many of which may surface in the course of discovery. If plaintiffs are able to discover which defendants caused their injuries, they will not be permitted to proceed on a theory of collective liability, but must pursue the actual wrongdoers and dismiss the remaining defendants. Accordingly, plaintiffs are not precluded from proving their case through individualized proof of product identification if they eventually discover whose products caused their harm.

Defendants' motions to dismiss complaints filed in Florida, Kansas, Massachusetts, New York, Pennsylvania, Vermont, Virginia, and West Virginia denied in their entirety. Defendants' motions to dismiss complaints filed in Connecticut, Illinois, Indiana, Iowa, Louisiana, New Hampshire, and New Jersey granted in part and denied in part.

Questions

1. Is it appropriate to seek consistency among different cases in pre-trial determinations?

2. The predictions that a federal court makes at an MDL about state law will often effectively determine the outcome of the whole litigation. Is this appropriate, especially as regards the laws of states that do not fall within the same federal circuit?

3. Do MDLs lead to consistency, or cause duplication of pre-trial motions?

Burton v. Wyeth-Ayerst Laboratories
513 F.Supp.2d 708 (2007) (US District Court, N.D. Texas)

FISH, C.J. This case stems from the ingestion by the plaintiff Cindy Burton ("Burton" or "the plaintiff") of certain diet drugs manufactured by the defendant Wyeth-Ayerst Laboratories ("Wyeth" or "the defendant"). Between 1996 and 1997, Burton was prescribed and used two products manufactured by Wyeth—Pondimin and Redux—to combat obesity. Burton claims that as a result of such use, she now suffers from two ailments: heart valve regurgitation and pulmonary arterial hypertension ("PAH"). Originally filed in state court, the case was removed to this court in February 1999; in October 1999, the Judicial Panel on Multidistrict Litigation ordered the case transferred to the United States District Court for the Eastern District of Pennsylvania for coordinated and consolidated pretrial proceedings. The case remained before the transferee court until August 2, 2006, when it was conditionally remanded to this court. Following a status conference and the entry of a scheduling order, the instant motions, among others, were filed.

Both of the instant motions in limine seek to exclude proposed expert testimony under Fed.R.Evid. 702 and *Daubert v. Merrell Dow Pharmaceuticals, Inc.*, 509 U.S. 579, 113 S.Ct. 2786, 125 L.Ed.2d 469 (1993). Fed.R.Evid. 702 provides that a duly qualified individual may provide opinion testimony as to "scientific, technical, or other specialized knowledge" if such information "will assist the trier of fact to understand the evidence or to determine a fact in issue." According to the rule, such evidence is limited to testimony that is both based upon sufficient facts or data and is the product of reliable principles and methods. Furthermore, the expert witness must have applied the principles and methods reliably to the facts of the case. These prerequisites to the admissibility of expert testimony have been applied as a two-part test: reliability and "fit."

Following the Supreme Court's decision in *Daubert*, it is the duty of the trial court to serve a gatekeeping function, excluding from the jury unreliable or irrelevant expert testimony. Courts are to apply this gatekeeping function to all expert testimony, not just science-based expert testimony. To aid in the exercise of this gatekeeping function, the Supreme Court set forth a non-exhaustive list of factors for trial courts to consider: (1) "whether [the theory or technique] can be (and has been) tested"; (2) "whether the theory or technique has been subjected to peer review and publication"; (3) "the known or potential rate of error"; (4) "the existence and maintenance of standards controlling the [theory or] technique's operation"; and (5) whether the theory or technique has "general acceptance" within the scientific community.

Application of the *Daubert* factors and any other relevant factors used to determine the admissibility of expert testimony is left to the judgment of the trial court and reviewed only under an abuse of discretion standard. In determining the admissibility of expert testimony, the trial court is not to consider the conclusions generated by an expert witness, but only the principles and methodology used to reach those conclusions. When the principles and methodology are sufficient to allow the expert opinion to be presented to the jury, the party challenging the testimony must resort to "[v]igorous cross-examination, presentation of contrary evidence, and careful instruction on the burden of proof" as the means to attack "shaky but admissible evidence." ...

Dr. Jerome L. Avorn ("Avorn") is a medical doctor and pharmaco-epidemiologist. Wyeth seeks the exclusion of Avorn's testimony regarding ... (4) his reading of "various documents" into the record....

Avorn's testimony regarding how he would have treated the adverse drug experience reports and his opinion regarding the intent of Wyeth based on its handling of these reports concerns the corporate intent of Wyeth. The transferee court found Avorn's testimony regarding Wyeth's corporate intent to be inadmissible. This court will not displace the ruling of the transferee court. This court further reiterates the finding of the transferee court — though Burton cannot introduce evidence of Wyeth's intent through this expert, she is not generally precluded from introducing evidence of Wyeth's intent. Because the transferee court previously ruled on the issue of Avorn's testimony regarding the corporate intent of Wyeth, the motion to limit his testimony is denied as moot.

The final issue with regard to Avorn's testimony is whether he will be permitted to read "various documents" into evidence. Wyeth argues that Avorn lacks personal knowledge of the content of these documents and that Burton is merely "funnel[ing]" these documents through Avorn's expert testimony as a means to get the contents of those documents before the jury. When this argument was previously raised before the transferee court, it held, "Whether a particular document can be introduced through a witness as a basis for his expert opinion will, of course, be left to the trial judge in the transferor court." The transferee court continued, stating that if a document in question is admitted into evidence, then the trial judge will likely allow the expert to discuss the document. This court does not disagree with this uncontroversial decision of the transferee court. On the instant motion, Wyeth has done little to further its argument. This court cannot address the issue of whether Avorn can read from unnamed "various documents" until first determining the admissibility of these documents. Thus, while the court notes the defendant's objection to the use of this testimony, the court must deny the motion at this time.

Accordingly, Wyeth's motion to limit the testimony of Dr. Avorn is denied. Under the existing pretrial order, Avorn's testimony regarding his opinions as to the thoughts of other physicians, his reactions to the FDA documents, and his opinion regarding the intent of Wyeth has already been deemed inadmissible. Thus, the motion to exclude these portions of Avorn's testimony is denied as moot....

However, the defendant shall have leave to reassert its objection to Avorn's reading of the "various documents" at trial following a decision by this court on the admissibility of the specific documents at issue....

Dr. Robyn J. Barst ("Barst") is a medical doctor with expertise in the treatment and diagnosis of primary pulmonary hypertension ("PPH"). Dr. Stuart Rich ("Rich") is an internist and cardiologist, with expertise in the diagnosis and treatment of PPH. Wyeth seeks to exclude from evidence Barst's and Rich's testimony regarding (1) FDA regulations; (2) the efficacy of prescribing Pondimin and Redux for the treatment of obesity; and (3) the drug Aminorex (an anorexigen marketed in Europe in the 1960's that was determined to cause PPH).... The transferee court addressed both issues [(1) and (2)] and found the testimony to be inadmissible. Thus, the court denies as moot Wyeth's motion regarding these two challenges.

With regard to Barst's and Rich's testimony about Aminorex, the court will not exclude such testimony. The transferee court refused to exclude similar testimony about Aminorex proffered by Dr. Lewis J. Rubin. Because "the Aminorex experience in the 1960's may support evidence of notice to the pharmaceutical community," the transferee court left the ultimate decision of the Aminorex testimony to the discretion of this court at trial. Under Texas state law, when a plaintiff asserts a claim of negligence, notice can serve to establish the foreseeability of the harmful consequences alleged. Thus, the issue of notice goes to the threshold element of duty. Accordingly, testimony regarding Aminorex is admissible for the purpose of establishing notice to Wyeth.

Therefore, Wyeth's motion to limit the testimony of Barst and Rich is denied. The motion is denied as moot with regard to Wyeth's challenge to their testimony about the FDA regulations and the efficacy of Pondimin and Redux. As to their testimony regarding Aminorex, the motion is denied. To the extent that this last challenge seeks to exclude causation testimony about Aminorex, the motion is denied as moot because the transferee court previously found such testimony to be inadmissible. . . .

Dr. Colin M. Bloor ("Bloor") is a pathologist specializing in the cardiovascular and pulmonary systems. Between 1998 and 1990, a Dr. Boivin conducted a study known as Study 1781 in which rats were exposed to dexfenfluramine (Redux) to study its effects. In March and July of 1999, Bloor used the slides from Study 1781 to conduct a separate study in which he visually observed portions of the exposed rats' hearts. . . .

In PTO 1685, the transferee court stated it

> perceive[d] no *Daubert* problem with testimony by Dr. Bloor that, based on his experience in cardiac pathology, the levels of nd location of fibrosis reported by Dr. Boivin in Study 1781, if assumed to be accurate, warranted further investigation with regard to the potential of fenfluramines to cause cardiac fibrosis.

Thus, the transferee court found that testimony regarding the conclusions Bloor drew from his study were inadmissible, but his testimony regarding Study 1781 itself was admissible. Again, Wyeth presents this court with no reason to deviate from the pretrial order. . . .

Dr. John L. Gueriguian ("Gueriguian") is a medical doctor, pharmacologist, endocrinologist, and chemist. . . .

[H]is testimony shall be limited to the extent described in PTO 1685 and no further; the motion to limit Gueriguian's testimony is denied as moot.

Dr. Arthur Hull Hayes, Jr. ("Hayes") is a medical doctor and former commissioner of the FDA. Wyeth seeks to exclude his testimony in three respects[.] . . . The transferee court . . . excluded the testimony regarding the defendant's corporate intent. Thus, the first challenge is denied as moot.

As to the second point of contention, the court agrees with the transferee court—the challenge to Hayes reading certain documents is co-extensive with the similar challenge made to Avorn's testimony. . . . Accordingly, as was determined on the similar issue with regard to Avorn's testimony, the motion to limit this portion of Hayes' testimony is denied, but the defendant is granted leave to reassert this challenge following determination of the admissibility of the underlying documents.

Dr. Barry Sears ("Sears") has a Ph.D. in biological chemistry with a background in the study of the molecular structure of lipids and the role of lipids in artherosclerosis. . . .

Burton does note that she may call Sears to testify about the effectiveness of Pondimin and Redux in treating obesity—an area for which the transferee court found Sears' testimony to be admissible. In light of these stipulations and PTO 1685, the court finds that no further discussion regarding Sears' testimony is necessary. Accordingly, Wyeth's motion to limit Sears' testimony regarding whether Pondimin and Redux met the FDA efficacy requirements and regarding the marketing obligations of Wyeth is denied as moot.

Under Texas law, one factor for consideration by the jury when assessing punitive damages is the net worth of the defendant. Wyeth previously designated Patrick A. Gaughan ("Gaughan"), Ph.D., to serve as an expert witness to testify at trial regarding the net worth of Wyeth. The plaintiff designated Michael P. Elkin ("Elkin"), a certified public accountant ("CPA"), as a rebuttal witness on the issue of punitive damages. As best the court can ascertain, Wyeth does not challenge Elkin's testimony to the extent that his calculations of net worth may differ from Gaughan's calculations, but rather challenges Elkin's testimony on the ground that he intends to improperly suggest to the jury a range within which to assign punitive damages. To the extent that Elkin's testimony makes such improper assertions, the court agrees with Wyeth.

There are two specific pieces of information that should be excluded from the evidence: (1) Elkin's "Schedule of Relevant Financial Measurements," attached to Expert Witness Report of Michael P. Elkin ("Elkin Report") as Exhibit E, attached to Appendix to Wyeth's Motion to Exclude Expert Testimony of Michael P. Elkin as Exhibit 1; and (2) Elkin's statement that the jury could "award well in excess of $1 billion without jeopardizing the company's financial condition or ongoing operations."

With regard to the Schedule of Relevant Financial Measurements, the problem lies not in the calculations or the method through which the figures were arrived at but in the implicit reference to a range of punitive damage amounts for the jury to consider. The schedule is a simple chart. On the horizontal axis, Elkin lists several financial measurements for the defendant: net worth, total assets, working capital, etc. Wyeth does not object to the values Elkin assigned to each of these measurements. On the vertical axis, Elkin list the dollar amount of potential punitive damage awards, ranging from $100 million on the low end to $2.5 billion at the other extreme. The substance of the chart provides the reader with a simple arithmetical calculation—the proposed punitive damage award listed on the vertical axis is divided by the financial measurement on the horizontal axis. This calculation produces a schedule of percentages so that the user could choose a number along the vertical axis and convert it to a percentage of the various financial measures. For example, the schedule illustrates that a punitive damage award of $500 million would be equal to 3.4 percent of Wyeth's net worth, 1.4 percent of Wyeth's total assets, and 13.7 percent of Wyeth's net income.

To the extent that this schedule provides various financial measurements, the court finds no fault. To the extent that this schedule provides the jury with an illustration of how to ascertain percentages, again the court finds no fault. But to the extent that the schedule suggests to the jury that it should assess a punitive damage award (if any) in the range of $100 million to $2.5 billion the schedule is wholly prejudicial. As best the court can determine, Elkin merely chose these numbers, among others, because they "appeared" to him to be "significant" percentages. With all due respect to Elkin, his unsupported opinion, without more, does not constitute a proper basis for expert testimony.

The second objectionable portion of Elkin's report—that a $1 billion award of punitive damages will have no affect on Wyeth—is a similarly improper form of expert testimony. In *Hayes v. Wal-Mart Stores, Inc.*, 294 F.Supp.2d 1249 (E.D.Okla., 2003), the district court excluded expert testimony regarding the economic impact of certain amounts suggested by the plaintiff's expert economist. The Hayes court held that economic impact testimony was unreliable under the *Daubert* factors because such conclusions "ha[ve] not been tested or subjected to peer review, ha[ve] no known error rate and ha[ve] not been accepted in the community of economists." In the instant case, Elkin's report states, "Based upon my review and analysis Wyeth has more than adequate resources to pay a punitive award well in excess of $1 billion without jeopardizing the company's financial condition or ongoing operations." He does not state how he came to the conclusion that such an award would not jeopardize the company's financial condition and in response to the motion to exclude such testimony, Burton provides no further elaboration. The court cannot allow such random speculation to be presented to the jury under the guise of expert testimony.

In addition to these two specific challenges to Elkin's testimony, Wyeth argues that his entire testimony should be stricken because under *State Farm v. Campbell*, 538 U.S. 408, 123 S.Ct. 1513 (2003), and *BMW of North America, Inc. v. Gore*, 517 U.S. 559, 116 S.Ct. 1589 (1996), the introduction of evidence regarding Wyeth's net worth is unconstitutional. As stated previously, Tex. Civ. Prac. & Rem.Code § 41.011(a)(6) provides that the net worth of the defendant is a relevant factor when determining punitive damages. Wyeth's argument in this respect comes from an overly broad reading of *State Farm* and *Gore*. The main point of Wyeth's confusion on the issue stems from the fact that it attempts to read State Farm and Gore as placing restrictions on the admissibility of evidence. However, neither *State Farm* nor *Gore* addressed the factual question of what amount of punitive damages can be awarded; rather, these cases imposed a gatekeeping function on the trial court to limit as a matter of law the amount of punitive damages awarded....

It is true that both *Gore* and *State Farm* warn that the "presentation of evidence of a defendant's net worth creates the potential that juries will use their verdicts to express biases against big businesses, particularly those without strong local presences." However, neither case requires the exclusion of such evidence. In fact, the *State Farm* majority cited Justice Breyer's concurring opinion from *Gore* in which he wrote, "[Wealth] provides an open-ended basis for inflating awards when the defendant is wealthy. That does not make its use unlawful or inappropriate; it simply means that this factor cannot make up for the failure of other factors, such as 'reprehensibility,' to constrain significantly an award that purports to punish a defendant's conduct."

This court refuses to declare unconstitutional the provision of the Texas statutes permitting the consideration of net worth. While the court takes note of the concern expressed by the Supreme Court in *State Farm* and *Gore* about the use of net worth as a factor in deciding whether or not to award punitive damages, that concern is mitigated by the Supreme Court's own recognition of the usefulness of such a measure and the trial court's role in reviewing the constitutionality of any such punitive damage award. Accordingly, to the extent Wyeth seeks to exclude Elkin's testimony in its entirety, the motion is denied.

For the reasons stated above, the defendant's motion to limit the testimony of plaintiff's generic experts is denied. The defendant's motion to exclude the expert testimony of Michael P. Elkin is granted in part and denied in part.

Note

Constitutionality of punitive damages. The cases of *State Farm v. Campbell* and *BMW of North America, Inc. v. Gore* are discussed at greater length in Chapter 18, together with other cases which set out the Supreme Court's position on the constitutional limits of punitive damages.

Class Actions

The idea of a class action is to avoid having the courts flooded with a huge number of cases which all deal with the same set of issues. One of their ostensible advantages is, therefore, that they can provide a more efficient form of dispute resolution than expecting the courts to handle an "avalanche of litigation." (*Jenkins v. Raymark Industries, Inc.*, 782 F.2d 468, 470 (5th Cir., 1986)). In *Jenkins*, for example, the court noted that "[a]bout 5,000 asbestos-related cases are pending in this circuit" so that the Fifth Circuit found that:

> Judge Parker's plan is clearly superior to the alternative of repeating, hundreds of times over, the litigation of the . . . issues with, as that experienced judge says, "days of the same witnesses, exhibits and issues from trial to trial." (782 F.2d at 470, 473.)

Such efficiency may benefit not just the courts, but also both plaintiffs and defendants, who can then concentrate their resources on dealing with one large claim, rather than having to deal with a multitude of simultaneous or repetitive claims in different courts. In *Jenkins* itself, class certification was affirmed in order to have settled the viability or otherwise of the defendants' "state of the art" defense, "[b]ecause the trial of that issue consistently consumed substantial resources in every asbestos trial." (782 F.2d at 470.)

So far as federal law is concerned, the certification of a class action is governed by Rule 23 of the Federal Rules of Procedure. The states have similar, if not identical, rules.

Federal Rules of Procedure

Rule 23(a). Class Actions — Prerequisites

One or more members of a class may sue or be sued as representative parties on behalf of all members only if:

(1) the class is so numerous that joinder of all members is impracticable,

(2) there are questions of law or fact common to the class,

(3) the claims or defenses of the representative parties are typical of the claims or defenses of the class; and

(4) the representative parties will fairly and adequately protect the interests of the class.

Notes

1. *Classes of plaintiffs — and of defendants.* Although it is far more common to have a class of plaintiffs certified by the courts, it is worth noting that Rule 23(a) also permits the certification of a class of defendants.

2. *Necessary, but not sufficient.* All four factors outlined in Rule 23(a) must be satisfied in order for a class to be certified. However, one additional factor must also be satisfied: it can be any one of the factors set out in Rule 23(b).

Federal Rules of Procedure

Rule 23(b). Class Actions—Types of Class Actions

A class action may be maintained if Rule 23(a) is satisfied and if:

(1) prosecuting separate actions by or against individual class members would create a risk of:

(A) inconsistent or varying adjudications with respect to individual class members that would establish incompatible standards of conduct for the party opposing the class; or

(B) adjudications with respect to individual class members that, as a practical matter, would be dispositive of the interests of the other members not parties to the individual adjudications or would substantially impair or impede their ability to protect their interests;

(2) the party opposing the class has acted or refused to act on grounds that apply generally to the class, so that final injunctive relief or corresponding declaratory relief is appropriate respecting the class as a whole; or

(3) the court finds that the questions of law or fact common to class members predominate over any questions affecting only individual members, and that a class action is superior to other available methods for fairly and efficiently adjudicating the controversy. The matters pertinent to these findings include:

(A) the class members' interests in individually controlling the prosecution or defense of separate actions;

(B) the extent and nature of any litigation concerning the controversy already begun by or against class members;

(C) the desirability or undesirability of concentrating the litigation of the claims in the particular forum; and

(D) the likely difficulties in managing a class action.

Notes

1. *Enhancing consistency.* The first type of class action envisioned in Rule 23(b) is that designed to enhance consistency where an adjudication would have implications for parties in other cases. Questions of general causation are good examples of such an issue, for once it is held that a particular agent can (or cannot) be a cause of the injury which is the subject of litigation, then it will mean either that future defendants will be denied the ability to plead a lack of general causation, or else that future plaintiffs will be denied the ability to bring their case at all. See *Engle v. Liggett Group Inc,.* 945 Sn. 2d 1246 (Fla. 2006), discussed further below. Class certification thus provides those who may not be the first to bring or defend a claim with the opportunity to ensure that their positions are properly represented in the litigation.

2. *Predominance.* Most class actions fall, however, under Rule 23(b)(3). This still means, though, that the cases involved must have issues of fact and/or law in common. In an action concerned with exposure to asbestos fibers, *In re Fibreboard Corp.*, 893 F.2d 706, 712 (1990), the Fifth Circuit denied certification of a class on the grounds that:

> [Too many disparities exist] among the various plaintiffs for their common concerns to predominate. The plaintiffs suffer from different diseases, some of which are more likely to have been caused by asbestos than others. The plaintiffs were

exposed to asbestos in various manners and to varying degrees. The plaintiffs' lifestyles differed in material respects. To create the requisite commonality for trial, the discrete components of the class members' claims and the asbestos manufacturers' defenses must be submerged.

Nevertheless, as the Supreme Court of Appeals of West Virginia noted in *In Re West Virginia Rezulin Litigation*, 585 S.E.2d 52, 72 (2003):

> The predominance requirement does not demand that common issues be dispositive, or even determinative; it is not a comparison of the amount of court time needed to adjudicate common issues versus individual issues; nor is it a scale-balancing test of the number of issues suitable for either common or individual treatment. Rather, "[a] single common issue may be the overriding one in the litigation, despite the fact that the suit also entails numerous remaining individual questions." The presence of individual issues may pose management problems for the circuit court, but courts have a variety of procedural options under Rule 23(c) and (d) to reduce the burden of resolving individual damage issues, including bifurcated trials, use of subclasses or masters, pilot or test cases with selected class members, or even class decertification after liability is determined...."That class members may eventually have to make an individual showing of damages does not preclude class certification." *Smith v. Behr Process Corp.*, 113 Wash.App. 306, 323, 54 P.3d 665, 675 (2002) (citations omitted).

3. *Individualized determinations.* Where the cases involved require individualized, fact-specific determinations, class certification will not normally be appropriate, since each case will be more or less unique, and they will have little in common with one another. Thus, while adjudication of general causation may well be apt for a class action, adjudication upon issues of specific causation may not be so amenable. For example, in *Castano v. American Tobacco Co.*, 160 F.R.D. 544, 556 (La. 1995), (reversed on other grounds by *Castano v. American Tobacco Co.*, 84 F.3d 734 (5th Cir. 1996)), a federal district court—which was considering an application for class certification of claims by smokers against tobacco manufacturers—found that:

> [T]he following issues are so overwhelmingly replete with individual circumstances that they quickly outweigh predominance and superiority. First is whether a person suffered emotional injury, if any, as a result of addiction. Second is whether a person's addiction was caused by any actions of the defendants. Third is whether each plaintiff relied on defendants' representations, whether they be omissions or commissions, in beginning or continuing to smoke cigarettes. Fourth is whether affirmative defenses unique to each class member preclude plaintiffs' recovery in any manner.
>
> Thus, because individual issues, not common issues, predominate and are superior in regard to injury-in-fact, proximate cause, reliance and affirmative defenses, class certification is improper as to these issues.

4. *Superiority and multi-state cases.* Appellate courts, in particular, have been at pains to emphasize that simply demonstrating common issues is not enough to fulfill the requirements of Rule 23(b)(3). It is also necessary that a class action be a superior means of prosecuting the cases concerned in comparison to having them all litigated individually. In *Castano v. American Tobacco Co.*, 84 F.3d 734, 737, 740 (1996), the Fifth Circuit rejected the idea that a class action could be a superior method of adjudicating upon the disputes at hand because the class included "all nicotine-dependent persons in the United States," and yet the law in each state was not identical.

5. *Opt-in or opt-out?* The procedure preferred in most states requires that potential parties be notified of the class action and be given the opportunity to opt out by a given deadline if they so choose. Nevertheless, the procedure sometimes chosen requires that the parties notified opt *in* to the class by the stated deadline if they wish their interests to be settled in the class action. In *Salmonsen v. CGD, Inc.*, 377 S.C. 442 (2008), however, the Supreme Court of South Carolina ruled that a trial court's decision to establish such a procedure was an abuse of discretion, and that the "opt-out" class action and notification procedure is the exclusive method of class action litigation in that state.

6. *Settlement-only class actions. Amchem Products, Inc. v. Windsor*, 521 U.S. 591, 620 (1997), was a case where class certification was clearly more beneficial to the defendants than to potential plaintiffs. Asbestos products manufacturers had obtained district court approval for their proposed global settlement of claims by persons exposed to asbestos (whether already manifesting symptoms or not), and moved to enjoin actions against them by individuals who had failed in timely fashion to opt out of the class. Writing for a majority of the Supreme Court, Justice Ginsburg held that a district court need not inquire whether the case, if tried, would present intractable management problems under Fed. Rule Civ. Proc. 23(b)(3)(D), since a settlement-only class certification proposes that there be no trial. But other specifications of the Rule — specifically, those designed to protect absentees by blocking unwarranted or overbroad class definitions:

> demand undiluted, even heightened, attention in the settlement context. Such attention is of vital importance, for a court asked to certify a settlement class will lack the opportunity, present when a case is litigated, to adjust the class, informed by the proceedings as they unfold. See Rule 23(c), (d).

On this basis, the "sprawling class" certified by the District Court did not satisfy Rule 23.

7. *Desirability of concentrating litigation?* One circumstance in which class actions are often proposed as superior alternatives to individual litigation is where victims of small injuries can join together in a large class to make a series of economically unviable claims into one larger claim that is now both economic and practicable. As the Seventh Circuit has put it:

> The policy at the very core of the class action mechanism is to overcome the problem that small recoveries do not provide the incentive for any individual to bring a solo action prosecuting his or her rights. A class action solves this problem by aggregating the relatively paltry potential recoveries into something worth someone's (usually an attorney's) labor. (*Mace v. Van Ru Credit Corp.*, 109 F.3d 338, 344 (1997)).

This is often justified on the basis that it provides a greater incentive to manufacturers to produce safe products, rather than allowing them effectively to get away with causing a succession of low-level injuries that could be avoided. But, from the defendants' perspective, it could be said that leads to the "skewing [of] trial outcomes." (*Castano v. American Tobacco Co.*, 84 F.3d 734, 746 (1996)). In the same case, the Fifth Circuit also observed that:

> Class certification magnifies and strengthens the number of unmeritorious claims. Aggregation of claims also makes it more likely that a defendant will be found liable and results in significantly higher damage awards ... [and] creates insurmountable pressure on defendants to settle, whereas individual trials would not. The risk of facing an all-or-nothing verdict presents too high a risk, even when the probability of an adverse judgment is low. These settlements have been referred to as judicial blackmail. (84 F.3d at 746.)

8. *Coupon settlements.* Moreover, there is a danger inherent in class actions (especially when small claims are involved) that they can end up benefitting no-one but the attorneys, and may even bring the legal system itself into disrepute. So-called "coupon settlements" have proved particularly problematic. These occur where the members of a victorious class of plaintiffs receive a low-value coupon for goods or services instead of the usual monetary award. A court may ask an independent expert to provide information on the actual value to the class members of the coupons that are redeemed before deciding whether to approve the settlement. (28 U.S.C.A. 1712(d)). Moreover, the portion of any attorney's fee that is attributable to the award of the coupons must be based on the value to class members of the coupons that are redeemed. (28 U.S.C.A. 1712(a)).

9. *Judicial blackmail.* The Fifth Circuit was quoted above as saying in *Castano* that class actions sometimes amount to "judicial blackmail." Yet the Fifth Circuit's use of that phrase is actually somewhat misleading. In *In re General Motors Corp. Pick-Up Truck Fuel Tank Products Liability Litigation*, 55 F.3d 768, 784 (1995), the Third Circuit commented:

> The law favors settlement, particularly in class actions and other complex cases where substantial judicial resources can be conserved by avoiding formal litigation. The parties may also gain significantly from avoiding the costs and risks of a lengthy and complex trial. These economic gains multiply when settlement also avoids the costs of litigating class status — often a complex litigation within itself. Furthermore, a settlement may represent the best method of distributing damage awards to injured plaintiffs, especially where litigation would delay and consume the available resources and where piecemeal settlement could result, in the Rule 23(b)(1)(B) limited fund context, in a sub-optimal distribution of the damage awards.

The last point is especially well made. In cases where there the defendant and its insurers are unlikely to have the resources to meet all the claims in full (as in the Bendectin and asbestos litigation), the device of a class action helps to ensure that all the victims get a proportion of the available funds, instead of those funds going only to those who filed their claims first.

10. *Judicial blackmail (again).* The Third Circuit in *In re General Motors Corp.* did not quite refer to class action settlements as "judicial blackmail." What it actually said was that:

> [C]lass actions create the opportunity for a kind of legalized blackmail: a greedy and unscrupulous plaintiff might use the *threat* (*sic.*) of a large class action, which can be costly to the defendant, to extract a settlement far in excess of the individual claims' actual worth. Because absentees are not parties to the action in any real sense, and probably would not have brought their claims individually, attorneys or plaintiffs can abuse the suit nominally brought in the absentees' names....
>
> The drafters designed the procedural requirements of Rule 23, especially the requisites of subsection (a), so that the court can assure, to the greatest extent possible, that the actions are prosecuted on behalf of the actual class members in a way that makes it fair to bind their interests. The rule thus represents a measured response to the issues of how the due process rights of absentee interests can be protected and how absentees' represented status can be reconciled with a litigation system premised on traditional bipolar litigation. (55 F.3d at 784–85.)

11. *Undesirability of concentrating litigation.* One obvious circumstance where it might be considered undesirable to concentrate products liability litigation into one class action is where a number of individual actions have already been brought but lost by the plaintiffs.

Matter of Rhone-Poulenc Rorer, Inc.
51 F.3d 1293 (7th Cir. 1995)

POSNER, J. The suit to which the petition for mandamus relates arises out of the infection of a substantial fraction of the hemophiliac population of this country by the AIDS virus because the blood supply was contaminated by the virus before the nature of the disease was well understood or adequate methods of screening the blood supply existed. The AIDS virus (HIV-human immunodeficiency virus) is transmitted by the exchange of bodily fluids, primarily semen and blood. Hemophiliacs depend on blood solids that contain the clotting factors whose absence defines their disease. These blood solids are concentrated from blood obtained from many donors. If just one of the donors is infected with the AIDS virus the probability that the blood solids manufactured in part from his blood will be infected is very high unless the blood is treated with heat to kill the virus....

First identified in 1981, AIDS was diagnosed in hemophiliacs beginning in 1982, and by 1984 the medical community agreed that the virus was transmitted by blood as well as by semen. That year it was demonstrated that treatment with heat could kill the virus in the blood supply and in the following year a reliable test for the presence of the virus in blood was developed. By this time, however, a large number of hemophiliacs had become infected. Since 1984 physicians have been advised to place hemophiliacs on heat-treated blood solids, and since 1985 all blood donated for the manufacture of blood solids has been screened and supplies discovered to be HIV-positive have been discarded. Supplies that test negative still are heat-treated, because the test is not infallible and in particular may fail to detect the virus in persons who became infected within six months before taking the test.

The plaintiffs have presented evidence that 2,000 hemophiliacs have died of AIDS and that half or more of the remaining U.S. hemophiliac population of 20,000 may be HIV-positive. Unless there are dramatic breakthroughs in the treatment of HIV or AIDS, all infected persons will die from the disease. The reason so many are infected even though the supply of blood for the manufacture of blood solids (as for transfusions) has been safe since the mid-80s is that the disease has a very long incubation period; the median period for hemophiliacs may be as long as 11 years. Probably most of the hemophiliacs who are now HIV-positive, or have AIDS, Some 300 lawsuits, involving some 400 plaintiffs, have been filed, 60 percent of them in state courts, 40 percent in federal district courts under the diversity jurisdiction, seeking to impose tort liability on the defendants for the transmission of HIV to hemophiliacs in blood solids manufactured by the defendants. Obviously these 400 plaintiffs represent only a small fraction of the hemophiliacs (or their next of kin, in cases in which the hemophiliac has died) who are infected by HIV or have died of AIDS. One of the 300 cases is *Wadleigh*, filed in September 1993, the case that the district judge certified as a class action. Thirteen other cases have been tried already in various courts around the country, and the defendants have won twelve of them. All the cases brought in federal court (like *Wadleigh*) — cases brought under the diversity jurisdiction — have been consolidated for pretrial discovery in the Northern District of Illinois by the panel on multidistrict litigation.

The plaintiffs advance two principal theories of liability. The first is that before any-one had heard of AIDS or HIV, it was known that Hepatitis B, a lethal disease though less so than HIV-AIDS, could be transmitted either through blood transfusions or through injection of blood solids. The plaintiffs argue that due care with respect to the risk of in-fection with Hepatitis B required the defendants to take measures to purge that virus from their blood solids, whether by treating the blood they bought or by screening the donors—perhaps by refusing to deal with paid donors, known to be a class at high risk of being infected with Hepatitis B. The defendants' failure to take effective measures was, the plaintiffs claim, negligent. Had the defendants not been negligent, the plaintiffs fur-ther argue, hemophiliacs would have been protected not only against Hepatitis B but also, albeit fortuitously or as the plaintiffs put it "serendipitously," against HIV.

The plaintiffs' second theory of liability is more conventional. It is that the defendants, again negligently, dragged their heels in screening donors and taking other measures to prevent contamination of blood solids by HIV when they learned about the disease in the early 1980s. The plaintiffs have other theories of liability as well, including strict prod-ucts liability, but it is not necessary for us to get into them....

We do not want to be misunderstood as saying that class actions are bad because they place pressure on defendants to settle. That pressure is a reality, but it must be balanced against the undoubted benefits of the class action that have made it an authorized pro-cedure for employment by federal courts.... But the plan ... devised for the HIV-he-mophilia litigation exceeds the bounds of allowable judicial discretion. Three concerns, none of them necessarily sufficient in itself but cumulatively compelling, persuade us to this conclusion.

The first is a concern with forcing these defendants to stake their companies on the outcome of a single jury trial, or be forced by fear of the risk of bankruptcy to settle even if they have no legal liability, when it is entirely feasible to allow a final, authoritative de-termination of their liability for the colossal misfortune that has befallen the hemophil-iac population to emerge from a decentralized process of multiple trials, involving different juries, and different standards of liability, in different jurisdictions; and when, in addi-tion, the preliminary indications are that the defendants are not liable for the grievous harm that has befallen the members of the class. These qualifications are important. In most class actions—and those the ones in which the rationale for the procedure is most com-pelling—individual suits are infeasible because the claim of each class member is tiny relative to the expense of litigation. That plainly is not the situation here. A notable fea-ture of this case, and one that has not been remarked upon or encountered, so far as we are aware, in previous cases, is the demonstrated great likelihood that the plaintiffs claims, despite their human appeal, lack legal merit. This is the inference from the defendants' having won 92.3 percent (12/13) of the cases to have gone to judgment. Granted, thirteen is a small sample and further trials, if they are held, may alter the pattern that the sam-ple reveals. But whether they do or not, the result will be robust if these further trials are permitted to go forward, because the pattern that results will reflect a consensus, or at least a pooling of judgment, of many different tribunals.

For this consensus or maturing of judgment the district judge proposes to substitute a single trial before a single jury instructed in accordance with no actual law of any ju-risdiction—a jury that will receive a kind of Esperanto instruction, merging the negli-gence standards of the 50 states and the District of Columbia. One jury, consisting of six persons (the standard federal civil jury nowadays consists of six regular jurors and two al-ternates), will hold the fate of an industry in the palm of its hand. This jury, jury num-ber fourteen, may disagree with twelve of the previous thirteen juries—and hurl the industry into bankruptcy. That kind of thing can happen in our system of civil justice (it is not likely to happen, because the industry is likely to settle—whether or not it really is liable) without violating anyone's legal rights. But it need not be tolerated when the alternative exists of submitting an issue to multiple juries constituting in the aggregate at much larger and more diverse sample of decision-makers. That would not be a feasible option if the stakes to each class member were too slight to repay the cost of suit, even though the aggregate stakes were very large and would repay the costs of a consolidated proceeding. But this is not the case with regard to the HIV-hemophilia litigation. Each plaintiff if successful is apt to receive a judgment in the millions. With the aggregate stakes in the tens or hundreds of millions of dollars, or even in the billions, it is not a waste of judicial resources to conduct more than one trial, before more than six jurors, to determine whether a major segment of the international pharmaceutical industry is to follow the asbestos manufacturers into Chapter 11.

We have hinted at the second reason for concern that the district judge exceeded the bounds of permissible judicial discretion. He proposes to have a jury determine the negligence of the defendants under a legal standard that does not actually exist anywhere in the world. One is put in mind of the concept of "general" common law that prevailed in the era of *Swift v. Tyson*. The assumption is that the common law of the 50 states and the District of Columbia, at least so far as bears on a claim of negligence against drug companies, is basically uniform and can be abstracted in a single instruction. It is no doubt true that at some level of generality the law of negligence is one, not only nationwide but worldwide. Negligence is a failure to take due care, and due care a function of the probability and magnitude of an accident and the costs of avoiding it. A jury can be asked whether the defendants took due care. And in many cases such differences as there are among the tort rules of the different states would not affect the outcome. The Second Circuit was willing to assume *dubitante* that this was true of the issues certified for class determination in the Agent Orange litigation. *In re Diamond Shamrock Chemicals Co.*, 725 F.2d 858, 861 (2d Cir.1984).

We doubt that it is true in general, and we greatly doubt that it is true in a case such as this in which one of the theories pressed by the plaintiffs, the "serendipity" theory, is novel. If one instruction on negligence will serve to instruct the jury on the legal standard of every state of the United States applicable to a novel claim, implying that the claim despite its controversiality would be decided identically in all 50 states and the District of Columbia, one wonders what the Supreme Court thought it was doing in the *Erie* case when it held that it was unconstitutional for federal courts in diversity cases to apply general common law rather than the common law of the state whose law would apply if the case were being tried in state rather than federal court. The law of negligence, including subsidiary concepts such as duty of care, foreseeability, and proximate cause, may as the plaintiffs have argued forcefully to us differ among the states only in nuance, though we think not, for a reason discussed later. But nuance can be important, and its significance is suggested by a comparison of differing state pattern instructions on negligence and differing judicial formulations of the meaning of negligence and the subordinate concepts.

Questions

1. How is it possible in practice to know in advance whether a class action will prove superior to traditional, individual litigation in any particular instance?

2. Is the fundamental departure of a class action from the traditional pattern of individual litigation justified in principle?

3. Is a class action best treated as a sort of Hobbesian Leviathan, whereby an undesirable power is invoked to take on an even more undesirable problem?

4. Are class actions really more suitable for suits brought by financial investors or alleged victims of employment discrimination than for claims brought by the alleged victims of defective products?

5. If it is appropriate to determine together in an MDL pre-trial motions of cases filed in jurisdictions throughout the nation, why is it not also appropriate (a) to have the substance of such cases tried in one class action, or (b) to have a class comprised of citizens throughout the nation?

6. If a number of individual suits are brought against a product manufacturer in respect of a specific product, and all are lost, but then some new evidence emerges about the safety of the product that was unavailable to those unsuccessful plaintiffs, would a class action brought by others claiming to have been harmed by the product in question still be precluded?

7. Judge Posner is probably best known as the *doyen* of the economic approach to law, which argues that the objective of the common law of contracts and torts is to pursue the most efficient outcome. Is his judgment in *Rhone-Poulenc* consistent with that approach?

Federal Rules of Procedure

Rule 23(c). Class Actions—Certification Order; Notice to Class Members; Judgment; Issues Classes; Subclasses.

(1) Certification Order.

(A) Time to Issue. At an early practicable time after a person sues or is sued as a class representative, the court must determine by order whether to certify the action as a class action.

(B) Defining the Class; Appointing Class Counsel. An order that certifies a class action must define the class and the class claims, issues, or defenses, and must appoint class counsel under Rule 23(g).

(C) Altering or Amending the Order. An order that grants or denies class certification may be altered or amended before final judgment.

(2) Notice.

(A) For (b)(1) or (b)(2) Classes. For any class certified under Rule 23(b)(1) or (b)(2), the court may direct appropriate notice to the class.

(B) For (b)(3) Classes. For any class certified under Rule 23(b)(3), the court must direct to class members the best notice that is practicable under the circumstances, including individual notice to all members who can be identified through reasonable effort. The notice must clearly and concisely state in plain, easily understood language:

(i) the nature of the action;

(ii) the definition of the class certified;

(iii) the class claims, issues, or defenses;

(iv) that a class member may enter an appearance through an attorney if the member so desires;

(v) that the court will exclude from the class any member who requests exclusion;

(vi) the time and manner for requesting exclusion; and

(vii) the binding effect of a class judgment on members under Rule 23(c)(3).

(3) Judgment.

Whether or not favorable to the class, the judgment in a class action must:

(A) for any class certified under Rule 23(b)(1) or (b)(2), include and describe those whom the court finds to be class members; and

(B) for any class certified under Rule 23(b)(3), include and specify or describe those to whom the Rule 23(c)(2) notice was directed, who have not requested exclusion, and whom the court finds to be class members.

(4) Particular Issues.

When appropriate, an action may be brought or maintained as a class action with respect to particular issues.

(5) Subclasses.

When appropriate, a class may be divided into subclasses that are each treated as a class under this rule.

Notes

1. *Standard for appellate review.* A district court's decision to certify (or not) a particular class is, strictly speaking, open to appellate review only under an abuse of discretion standard: see *In Re West Virginia Rezulin Litigation*, 585 S.E.2d 52 (2003). However, in the same case, the Supreme Court of Appeals of West Virginia pointed out that:

> Of course, the circuit court's discretion must be exercised in the context of the appropriate rules of procedure. In the instant case, the circuit court was called upon to apply and interpret Rule 23 of the West Virginia Rules of Civil Procedure. As we stated in Syllabus Point 4 of *Keesecker v. Bird*, 200 W.Va. 667, 490 S.E.2d 754 (1997), "An interpretation of the West Virginia Rules of Civil Procedure presents a question of law subject to a *de novo* review."

The Eighth Circuit took the same view in *In re Baycol Products Litigation*, 593 F.3d 716, 722 (2010). In other words, interpretation of the rules is a question of law subject to *de novo* review, whereas *application* of those rules, once interpreted, is subject only to abuse of discretion review.

2. *Effect of decertification on appeal.* Appellate courts have become more vigilant in recent years about whether classes have been appropriately certified, so that a number of cases where judgment has apparently been rendered have subsequently been overturned on appeal because of inappropriate class certification. Such a decision means, of course, that the individual plaintiffs are required to start their cases all over again in a new trial. It is thus extremely important to ensure that the requirements for class certification are strictly adhered to.

3. *Class Action Fairness Act of 2005.* The Class Action Fairness Act (CAFA) of 2005, incorporated into Title 28 of the U.S. Code as §§ 1332(d), 1453, 1711–15, enables defendants to remove a certified class action to federal court (irrespective of the defendant's citizenship or place of incorporation) where the amount at stake exceeds the sum or value of $5 million, exclusive of interest and costs.

It is not yet clear whether CAFA has had the effect of reducing the readiness of plaintiffs' attorneys to seek class certification, which is clearly one of the aims of those supporting the legislation (the other being to have federal courts decertify classes). But CAFA may prove counter-productive in encouraging plaintiff attorneys to find larger classes of plaintiffs, including those out of state. If the case will be removed to federal court in any event, some attorneys may feel that there is little to be lost in so doing, although they will then clearly face an enhanced burden in showing that the common issues predominate to an extent not significantly undermined by the differences in state law.

Perhaps, however, the most likely result will prove to be that little has changed. Indeed, if the defendant is a citizen of, or incorporated in, another state, then CAFA is essentially irrelevant, since diversity jurisdiction under 28 U.S.C. § 1332 will mean that the case can be removed to federal court in any event.

Engle v. Liggett Group
945 So.2d 1246 (2006) (Supreme Court of Florida)

PER CURIAM. On October 31, 1994, the trial court certified as a nationwide class action a group of smokers and their survivors under Florida Rule of Civil Procedure 1.220(b)(3). The class representatives on behalf of themselves, and all others similarly situated, filed an amended class action complaint seeking compensatory and punitive damages against major domestic cigarette companies and two industry organizations (hereinafter collectively referred to as "Tobacco") for injuries allegedly caused by smoking.

The trial court defined the class as: "All United States citizens and residents, and their survivors, who have suffered, presently suffer or who have died from diseases and medical conditions caused by their addiction to cigarettes that contain nicotine." Tobacco filed an interlocutory appeal of the trial court's order certifying the *Engle* Class pursuant to Florida Rule of Appellate Procedure 9.130(a)(6). On January 31, 1996, the Third District affirmed the trial court's order certifying the class but reduced the class to include only Florida smokers. Tobacco's petition for review by this Court was denied.

On February 4, 1998, the trial court issued a trial plan, dividing the trial proceedings into three phases. Phase I consisted of a year-long trial to consider the issues of liability and entitlement to punitive damages for the class as a whole. The jury considered common issues relating exclusively to the defendants' conduct and the general health effects of smoking. On July 7, 1999, at the conclusion of Phase I, the jury rendered a verdict for the *Engle* Class and against Tobacco on all counts.

Phase II was divided into two subparts-Phase II-A and Phase II-B. Phase II-A was intended to resolve the issues of entitlement and amount of compensatory damages, if any, that the three individual class representatives—Frank Amodeo, Mary Farnan, and Angie Della Vecchia should receive. Phase II-B was designed to result in a jury determination of a total lump sum punitive damage award, if any, that should be assessed in favor of the class as a whole.

At the conclusion of Phase II-A, the jury determined that the three individual class representatives were entitled to compensatory damages in varying amounts, which were offset by their comparative fault. The total award was $12.7 million. The jury subsequently determined in Phase II-B the lump-sum amount of punitive damages for the entire class to be $145 billion, without allocation of that amount to any class member. Tobacco filed several post-verdict motions, including a motion at the conclusion of phase II-B for a new trial or remittitur, a motion to set aside the verdict, and for entry of judgment, and another motion to decertify the class.

On November 6, 2000, the trial court entered a final judgment and amended omnibus order, in which it granted judgment in Tobacco's favor in two respects. First, the trial court granted Tobacco's motion for directed verdict on a statute of limitations basis with regard to named plaintiff Frank Amodeo on the counts based on strict liability, implied warranty, express warranty, negligence, and intentional infliction of emotional distress. However, the trial court ruled that Amodeo's fraud and conspiracy claims were not time-barred. Second, the court granted Tobacco's motion for directed verdict with regard to count seven of the complaint, in which the *Engle* Class sought equitable relief, upon the basis that the count had previously been dismissed by the court. The court entered judgment in favor of the *Engle* Class on all other counts, ordered immediate payment to the individual plaintiffs, and directed Tobacco to pay the $145 billion in punitive damages into the registry of the Dade County Circuit Court for the benefit of the entire class.

According to the trial plan, in Phase III, new juries are to decide the individual liability and compensatory damages claims for each class member (estimated to number approximately 700,000). Thereafter, the plan contemplated that the trial court would divide the punitive damages previously determined equally among any successful class members. Pursuant to the omnibus order, interest on the punitive award began accruing immediately.

Tobacco filed an appeal and the Third District reversed the final judgment with instructions that the class be decertified.

1. Res Judicata

In 1995, the State of Florida and others (hereinafter "State") filed a complaint against many of the defendants involved in the present action (hereinafter "FSA Defendants"). This earlier action was initiated by the State under the Medicaid Third-Party Liability Act, section 409.910, Florida Statutes (1995). In its complaint, the State alleged counts of negligence, strict liability in tort, injunctive relief, various statutory and criminal violations, and violations of the Florida RICO Act. The State sought reimbursement of Medicaid monies expended in treating the victims of tobacco-related illnesses as well as other damages permitted by law, including punitive damages where available. Subsequent to the filing of the State's complaint, the circuit court granted the FSA Defendants' motion for summary judgment and dismissed all claims by the State for punitive damages with the exception of its claim for punitive damages contained in count four of the complaint alleging only statutory and criminal violations.

In 1997, the State and the FSA Defendants entered into the Florida Settlement Agreement, which resolved "all present and future civil claims against *all parties to [the] litigation* relating to the subject matter of [the] litigation, which [were] or could have been asserted by *any of the parties [thereto]*" (emphasis supplied). Pursuant to the terms of the FSA, in exchange for agreeing to resolve these claims, the State received $550 million for unspecified purposes, $200 million for a pilot program by the State of Florida aimed at the reduction of the use of tobacco products by minors, several billion dollars paid out over a period of time for the benefit of the State of Florida, and injunctive relief. As stated by the FSA, the monies received "constitute[d] not only reimbursement for Medicaid expenses incurred by the State of Florida, but also settlement of all of Florida's other claims, including those for punitive damages, RICO and other statutory theories." Also included in the FSA was a "Non-Admissibility" provision which provided:

> These settlement negotiations have been undertaken by the parties in good faith and for settle ment purposes only, and neither this Settlement Agreement nor any evidence of negotiations hereunder, shall be offered or received in evidence in this Action, or any other action or proceeding, for any purpose other than in an action or proceeding arising under this Settlement Agreement....

The reasoning in *In re Exxon Valdez*, 270 F.3d 1215 (9th Cir.2001), is instructive. In that case, the defendants appealed a punitive damages award for claims arising out of the Exxon Valdez oil spill. The plaintiffs consisted of separate classes of commercial fishermen, Alaskan natives, and landowners affected by the spill. These distinct classes sought compensatory and punitive damages for injuries resulting from the Exxon Valdez spill. The jury returned a verdict in favor of the plaintiffs which assessed $287 million in compensatory damages and $5 billion in punitive damages. Exxon appealed the resulting judgment, asserting that the punitive damages award was barred by the res judicata effect of a consent decree between Exxon and the United States and the State of Alaska that settled claims in a previous action filed under the Clean Water Act. In holding that the award was not barred by the previous settlement, the court concluded that the interests asserted by the plaintiffs were distinct from those asserted by the United States and Alaska in the prior action. The court, relying on *Satsky*, noted that the prior consent decree addressed harms caused to the environment and the general public whereas the claims in the class action were to vindicate wrongs that resulted in individual injuries. Moreover, the court stressed that although the consent decree "released all government claims, [it] provides explicitly that 'nothing in this agreement, however, is intended to affect legally the claims, if any, of any person or entity not a Party to this Agreement.'" The FSA expressly provided that neither the agreement itself "nor any evidence of negotiations [t]hereunder, shall be offered or received in evidence in this Action, or any other action or proceeding, for any purpose other than in an action or proceeding arising under this Settlement Agreement." The facts of *In re Exxon* are similar to the circumstances presented in this case and support our conclusion that the Third District erred in holding that the FSA barred the *Engle* Class's punitive damages claim.

2. Punitive Damages Award

Although we conclude that the Third District erred in applying the doctrine of res judicata to bar the *Engle* Class's punitive damages claim, we must vacate the classwide punitive damages award because we unanimously agree with the Third District that the trial court erred in allowing the jury to determine a lump sum amount before it determined the amount of total compensatory damages for the class. As a matter of law, the punitive damages award violates due process because there is no way to evaluate the reasonableness of the punitive damages award without the amount of compensatory damages having been fixed. The amount awarded is also clearly excessive because it would bankrupt some of the defendants. A majority of the Court further concludes that the trial court erred in allowing the jury to consider entitlement to punitive damages during the Phase I trial....

4. Three-Phase Trial Plan—Decertification

We agree with the Third District that problems with the three-phase trial plan negate the continued viability of this class action. We conclude that continued class action treatment for Phase III of the trial plan is not feasible because individualized issues such as legal causation, comparative fault, and damages predominate....

Although no Florida cases address whether it is appropriate under rule 1.220(d)(4)(A) to certify class treatment for only limited liability issues, several decisions by federal appellate courts applying a similar provision in the Federal Rules of Civil Procedure provide persuasive authority for this approach.

Federal Rule of Civil Procedure 23(c)(4)(A) provides that "[w]hen appropriate ... an action may be brought or maintained as a class action with respect to particular issues." In determining whether the predominance requirement of Federal Rule of Civil Procedure 23(b)(3) has been met, several United States Courts of Appeals have concluded that under federal rule 23(c)(4)(A) a trial court can properly separate liability and damages issues, certifying class treatment of liability while leaving damages to be determined on an individual basis. The Second and Seventh Circuits have also stated that the determination that class treatment of damages issues is inappropriate can be made after a finding on liability....

In this case, the Phase I trial has been completed. The pragmatic solution is to now decertify the class, retaining the jury's Phase I findings other than those on the fraud and intentional infliction of emotion distress claims, which involved highly individualized determinations, and the finding on entitlement to punitive damages questions, which was premature. Class members can choose to initiate individual damages actions and the Phase I common core findings we approved above will have res judicata effect in those trials....

In this case, although the jury decided issues common to all class members, none involved whether, or the degree to which, the defendants' conduct was the sole or contributing cause of the class members' injuries, which is the pertinent question in applying the doctrine of comparative negligence.

We approve the Phase I findings for the class as to Questions 1 (that smoking cigarettes causes aortic aneurysm, bladder cancer, cerebrovascular disease, cervical cancer, chronic obstructive pulmonary disease, coronary heart disease, esophageal cancer, kidney cancer, laryngeal cancer, lung cancer (specifically, adenocarinoma, large cell carcinoma, small cell carcinoma, and squamous cell carcinoma), complications of pregnancy, oral cavity/tongue cancer, pancreatic cancer, peripheral vascular disease, pharyngeal cancer, and stomach cancer), 2 (that nicotine in cigarettes is addictive), 3 (that the defendants placed cigarettes on the market that were defective and unreasonably dangerous), 4(a) (that the defendants concealed or omitted material information not otherwise known or available knowing that the material was false or misleading or failed to disclose a material fact concerning the health effects or addictive nature of smoking cigarettes or both), 5(a) (that the defendants agreed to conceal or omit information regarding the health effects of cigarettes or their addictive nature with the intention that smokers and the public would rely on this information to their detriment), 6 (that all of the defendants sold or supplied cigarettes that were defective), 7 (that all of the defendants sold or supplied cigarettes that, at the time of sale or supply, did not conform to representations of fact made by said defendants), and 8 (that all of the defendants were negligent). Therefore, these findings in favor of the *Engle* Class can stand.

The class consists of all Florida residents fitting the class description as of the trial court's order dated November 21, 1996. However, we conclude for the reasons explained in this opinion that continued class action treatment is not feasible and that upon remand the class must be decertified. Individual plaintiffs within the class will be permitted to proceed individually with the findings set forth above given res judicata effect in any subsequent trial between individual class members and the defendants, provided such action is filed within one year of the mandate in this case. We remand this case to the Third District for further proceedings consistent with this opinion.

Notes

1. *General and specific causation.* *Engle* demonstrates once again the distinction between general and specific causation. The Supreme Court of Florida was prepared to allow jury findings as to general causation to stand from the class action because they must inevitably be issues common to all those seeking to prove that they had suffered injury as a result of smoking. However, significant factual differences between the differ-

ent plaintiffs made it inappropriate for a class action to continue, since it would not enable the issues of specific causation to be properly addressed and determined.

2. *The never-ending story.* The class in *Engle* had originally been certified as those throughout the nation who had contracted a smoking-related disease by the class cut-off date of November 21, 1996. Members of the class were subsequently narrowed on appeal to include only Florida residents and citizens. After the Supreme Court's decision in *Engle*, the plaintiffs—once estimated to number somewhere between 300,000 and 700,000—were required to file suit individually by January 10, 2008 if they wished to continue with their cases. It is difficult to know how many potentially valid claims have been deterred by this long-drawn-out, attritional litigation, although (as will be seen below) there have already been some trials on the merits of such individual claims.

3. *Comparative fault as a sword, not a shield.* As we saw in Chapter 11, plaintiffs' attorneys in many of the tobacco cases in Florida have adopted the strategy of pleading their client's comparative fault. This is done to encourage the jury to apportion fault, and so award the plaintiff something, rather than asking that an all-or-nothing decision be made in favor of one or other party (where the plaintiff might be the one to get nothing). The tobacco companies have fought this strategy, but the Florida Second District Court of Appeal ruled in *Philip Morris v. Arnitz*, 933 So.2d 693, 698 (2006) that it was acceptable, even though the defendant had retracted its plea of comparative fault as an affirmative defense. The court held:

> Philip Morris asserts that it must be allowed the choice in which defenses it raises. However, … [the] plaintiff[] must be allowed to choose the theory under which his case is tried. Arnitz admitted that he was partly responsible for his injuries because he continued to smoke after he became aware of the health risks associated with smoking; but he also contended that Philip Morris brand cigarettes had a design defect that made them even more dangerous and that he and other consumers were unaware of this increased health risk. We conclude that the trial court did not err in allowing Arnitz to present his theory of the case to the jury and, based on the pleadings, in instructing the jury on comparative negligence.

4. *Escrow.* In order to appeal the original $145 billion punitive award, the tobacco companies would normally have had to post a bond equal to the award amount. Yet this was the largest punitive award in United States history, and the tobacco companies were understandably reluctant to post such a large bond. State legislators proposed a bill to create a "bond cap" of $100 million, but Stanley and Susan Rosenblatt, the attorneys for the class, threatened to challenge the bill's constitutionality. The parties compromised: the tobacco companies agreed to put $709 million in an escrow account—money which would be paid to the class regardless of the outcome of the appeal—while the Rosenblatts agreed not to challenge the law. The defendants contributed to this escrow account according to their proportion of the damages award. Philip Morris contributed $500 million, Lorillard $200 million, and Liggett $9 million.

Questions

1. Since the *Engle* class has now been decertified, to whom is the escrow money payable, and when?

2. Can the Rosenblatts claim to be paid out of the escrow funds?

3. Does the existence of the escrow account preclude further awards by juries of punitive damages?

R.J. Reynolds Tobacco Co. v. Martin

53 So. 3d 1060 (2010) (First DCA, Florida)

MARSTILLER, J. This is the first so-called "*Engle* progeny" case to reach a district court of appeal following the Florida Supreme Court's decision in *Engle v. Liggett Group*, Inc., 945 So. 2d 1246 (Fla. 2006). *Engle* began as a smokers' class action lawsuit filed in 1994 against cigarette companies and tobacco industry organizations seeking damages for smoking-related illnesses and deaths. The class included all Florida "'citizens and residents, and their survivors, who have suffered, presently suffer or who have died from diseases and medical conditions caused by their addiction to cigarettes that contain nicotine.'" *Id.* at 1256. The tobacco company defendants included the appellant in this case, R.J. Reynolds Tobacco Company ("RJR"). In *Engle*, the supreme court decertified the class, but allowed certain jury findings from the class action to have res judicata effect in any subsequent lawsuits by individual class members seeking damages from the defendants. RJR appeals from a final judgment in one such action, seeking reversal of the compensatory and punitive damage awards.

RJR primarily contends that the trial court gave the findings approved in *Engle* overly broad preclusive effect and thus relieved the plaintiff below, Matilde Martin, of her burden to prove legal causation on her negligence and strict liability claims. RJR also asserts Mrs. Martin failed to prove the reliance element of her fraudulent concealment claim, and that the punitive damage award is excessive and unconstitutional. For the reasons that follow, we find the trial court correctly applied *Engle* and Mrs. Martin produced sufficient independent evidence to prove RJR's liability for her husband's death....

In support of its argument, RJR points out the Eleventh Circuit's decision in *Brown v. R.J. Reynolds Tobacco Co.*, an interlocutory appeal in an *Engle* progeny lawsuit pending in the United States District Court, Middle District of Florida. The plaintiff in *Brown* appealed a pretrial order ruling that "the *Engle* Phase I findings may not be used to establish any element of an individual *Engle* plaintiff's claim." *Brown v. R.J. Reynolds Tobacco Co.*, 576 F. Supp. 2d 1328, 1347–48 (M.D. Fla. 2008). The Eleventh Circuit vacated the order, reasoning that the Florida Supreme Court's decision in *Engle* must be given the same preclusive effect in federal courts it would have in state courts. *Brown*, 611 F.3d at 1331. The court then explained what it believes are the scope of the preclusive effect of *Engle* and the burden individual plaintiffs in federal court must carry in proving applicability of the *Engle* findings to their claims. It determined the supreme court, in giving the Phase I findings res judicata effect in subsequent lawsuits by *Engle* class members, necessarily meant issue preclusion rather than claim preclusion—both of which are included in the concept of "res judicata"—because "factual issues and not causes of action were decided in Phase I." *Id.* at 1333. Then the court concluded individual *Engle* plaintiffs may only use the Phase I findings to establish elements of their claims in federal court if they can demonstrate with a "reasonable degree of certainty" which facts were "actually adjudicated." *Brown*, 611 F.3d at 1334–35. This they can do by pointing to relevant parts of the class action trial transcript. *Id.* at 1335.

While we generally agree with the Eleventh Circuit's analysis of issue preclusion versus claim preclusion, we find it unnecessary to distinguish between the two or to define what the supreme court meant by "res judicata" to conclude the factual determinations made by the Phase I jury cannot be relitigated by RJR and the other *Engle* defendants. More importantly, we do not agree every *Engle* plaintiff must trot out the class action trial transcript to prove applicability of the Phase I findings. Such a requirement undercuts the supreme court's ruling. The Phase I jury determined "*common issues* relating exclusively to the defendants' conduct …" but not "whether any class members relied on Tobacco's misrepresentations or were injured by Tobacco's conduct." *Engle*, 945 So. 2d at 1256 (emphasis added). The common issues, which the jury decided *in favor of the class*, were the "conduct" elements of the claims asserted by the class, and not simply, as characterized by the Eleventh Circuit, a collection of facts *relevant* to those elements.…

As does the Eleventh Circuit, we interpret the supreme court's ruling in *Engle* to mean individual class plaintiffs, when pursuing RJR and the other class defendants for damages, can rely on the Phase I jury's factual findings. But unlike the Eleventh Circuit, we conclude the Phase I findings establish the conduct elements of the asserted claims, and individual *Engle* plaintiffs need not independently prove up those elements or demonstrate the relevance of the findings to their lawsuits, assuming they assert the same claims raised in the class action. For that reason, we find the trial court in Mrs. Martin's case correctly construed *Engle* and instructed the jury accordingly on the preclusive effect of the Phase I findings.…

As a corollary to its argument on the preclusive effect of *Engle*, RJR asserts the trial court did not require Mrs. Martin to prove legal causation on her negligence and strict liability claims.… RJR stipulated pretrial that nicotine in cigarettes is addictive and smoking cigarettes causes lung cancer. RJR further stipulated that Mr. Martin smoked Lucky Strike cigarettes, every Lucky Strike cigarette he smoked contained nicotine, and Mr. Martin did not smoke any brand of cigarettes other than Lucky Strike and Camel (another RJR brand). At trial Mrs. Martin produced evidence showing that: Mr. Martin started smoking at age 14 and by age 23 was smoking two packs of non-filtered Lucky Strike cigarettes every day; he tried unsuccessfully several times over the years to quit smoking and was distraught over it; Mr. Martin was diagnosed by a physician as being addicted to nicotine; his treating pulmonologist determined his decades of smoking caused him to contract lung cancer which in turn caused his death. The record thus demonstrates Mrs. Martin was required to prove legal causation, and she produced sufficient evidence for a jury to find that Mr. Martin's addiction to RJR's cigarettes was the legal cause of his death.

Judgment affirmed.

Notes

1. *Comparative fault as a sword revisited.* Attorneys for Mrs. Martin pleaded from the outset that her husband shared some of the blame for his own demise. The jury determined that his share of the fault amounted to 34%, and so their award of $5 million in compensatory damages was reduced by that proportion.

2. *Punitive damages.* The Court of Appeal in *Martin* also upheld the jury's decision to award punitive damages of $25 million. The issues involved in such a substantial award are considered in greater detail in Chapter 18.

3. *The never-ending story (continued).* In July 2011, the Supreme Court of Florida declined to take an appeal from *Martin*. Other cases are still being heard in the Florida courts.

Market Share Liability

We saw in Chapters 9 and 10 that a lack of information frequently hampers victims' ability to prove that their injuries were caused by a defective product manufactured or distributed by the defendant(s). Sometimes their problem is that scientific knowledge is insufficient to establish that the allegedly toxic agent is capable of causing this type of harm; this is an issue of general causation. Sometimes the problem is in establishing that the toxic agent caused the particular plaintiff's injuries; that is a matter of specific causation.

But there is also another problem. Even if the plaintiff succeeds in establishing both general and specific causation with regard to the causative agent, this does not mean that s/he can necessarily establish *who* was responsible for the defective product's manufacture or distribution. Chapter 10 showed how the courts are often prepared to overcome this hurdle so far as the signature asbestos diseases of mesothelioma and asbestosis are concerned, by treating them both (despite inconclusive scientific knowledge) as indivisible diseases. This allows the courts to designate multiple defendants as jointly and severally liable in states that still recognize that doctrine. In states that have moved to comparative fault, the courts can instead apportion liability among the defendants according to their degree of fault, regardless of their precise contribution to the harm suffered by the plaintiff.

Those types of asbestos cases are, however, unique. No other causative agent has ever been identified for mesothelioma and asbestosis. Other forms of harm, by contrast, may be caused by a variety of agents. As a result, courts are typically reluctant to adopt a similar strategy so far as proof of causation is concerned in non-asbestos cases.

This does not mean, however, that no alternative approaches have been explored. Far from it. Indeed, perhaps the principal form of "collective liability" to which the court was alluding in *In Re: Methyl Tertiary Butyl Ether (MTBE) Products Liability Litigation*, above, is market share liability.

Sindell v. Abbott Laboratories
607 P.2d 924 (1980) (Supreme Court of California)

MOSK, J. This case involves a complex problem both timely and significant: may a plaintiff, injured as the result of a drug administered to her mother during pregnancy, who knows the type of drug involved but cannot identify the manufacturer of the precise product, hold liable for her injuries a maker of a drug produced from an identical formula?

Plaintiff Judith Sindell brought an action against eleven drug companies and Does 1 through 100, on behalf of herself and other women similarly situated. The complaint alleges as follows:

Between 1941 and 1971, defendants were engaged in the business of manufacturing, promoting, and marketing diethylstilbesterol (DES), a drug which is a synthetic compound of the female hormone estrogen. The drug was administered to plaintiff's mother and the mothers of the class she represents, for the purpose of preventing miscarriage. (The plaintiff class alleged consists of "girls and women who are residents of California and who have been exposed to DES before birth and who may or may not know that fact or the dangers" to which they were exposed. Defendants are also sued as representatives of a class of drug manufacturers which sold DES after 1941.) In 1947, the Food and Drug Administration authorized the marketing of DES as a miscarriage preventative, but only on an experimental basis, with a requirement that the drug contain a warning label to that effect.

DES may cause cancerous vaginal and cervical growths in the daughters exposed to it before birth, because their mothers took the drug during pregnancy. The form of cancer from which these daughters suffer is known as adenocarcinoma, and it manifests itself after a minimum latent period of 10 or 12 years. It is a fast-spreading and deadly disease, and radical surgery is required to prevent it from spreading. DES also causes adenosis, precancerous vaginal and cervical growths which may spread to other areas of the body. The treatment for adenosis is cauterization, surgery, or cryosurgery. Women who suffer from this condition must be monitored by biopsy or colposcopic examination twice a year, a painful and expensive procedure. Thousands of women whose mothers received DES during pregnancy are unaware of the effects of the drug.

In 1971, the Food and Drug Administration ordered defendants to cease marketing and promoting DES for the purpose of preventing miscarriages, and to warn physicians and the public that the drug should not be used by pregnant women because of the danger to their unborn children.

During the period defendants marketed DES, they knew or should have known that it was a carcinogenic substance, that there was a grave danger after varying periods of latency it would cause cancerous and precancerous growths in the daughters of the mothers who took it, and that it was ineffective to prevent miscarriage. Nevertheless, defendants continued to advertise and market the drug as a miscarriage preventative. They failed to test DES for efficacy and safety; the tests performed by others, upon which they relied, indicated that it was not safe or effective. In violation of the authorization of the Food and Drug Administration, defendants marketed DES on an unlimited basis rather than as an experimental drug, and they failed to warn of its potential danger.

Because of defendants' advertised assurances that DES was safe and effective to prevent miscarriage, plaintiff was exposed to the drug prior to her birth. She became aware of the danger from such exposure within one year of the time she filed her complaint. As a result of the DES ingested by her mother, plaintiff developed a malignant bladder tumor which was removed by surgery. She suffers from adenosis and must constantly be monitored by biopsy or colposcopy to insure early warning of further malignancy....

We begin with the proposition that, as a general rule, the imposition of liability depends upon a showing by the plaintiff that his or her injuries were caused by the act of the defendant or by an instrumentality under the defendant's control. The rule applies whether the injury resulted from an accidental event or from the use of a defective product.

There are, however, exceptions to this rule. Plaintiff's complaint suggests several bases upon which defendants may be held liable for her injuries even though she cannot demonstrate the name of the manufacturer which produced the DES actually taken by her mother. The first of these theories, classically illustrated by *Summers v. Tice* (1948) 33 Cal.2d 80, 199 P.2d 1, places the burden of proof of causation upon tortious defendants in certain circumstances. The second basis of liability emerging from the complaint is that defendants acted in concert to cause injury to plaintiff. There is a third and novel approach to the problem, sometimes called the theory of "enterprise liability," but which we prefer to designate by the more accurate term of "industry-wide" liability, which might obviate the necessity for identifying the manufacturer of the injury-causing drug. We shall conclude that these doctrines, as previously interpreted, may not be applied to hold defendants liable under the allegations of this complaint. However, we shall propose and adopt a fourth basis for permitting the action to be tried, grounded upon an extension of the *Summers* doctrine....

In our contemporary complex industrialized society, advances in science and technology create fungible goods which may harm consumers and which cannot be traced to any specific producer. The response of the courts can be either to adhere rigidly to prior doctrine, denying recovery to those injured by such products, or to fashion remedies to meet these changing needs. Just as Justice Traynor in his landmark concurring opinion in *Escola v. Coca Cola Bottling Company* (1944) 24 Cal.2d 453, 467–468, recognized that in an era of mass production and complex marketing methods the traditional standard of negligence was insufficient to govern the obligations of manufacturer to consumer, so should we acknowledge that some adaptation of the rules of causation and liability may be appropriate in these recurring circumstances.

The most persuasive reason for finding plaintiff states a cause of action is that advanced in *Summers*: as between an innocent plaintiff and negligent defendants, the latter should bear the cost of the injury. Here, as in *Summers*, plaintiff is not at fault in failing to provide evidence of causation, and although the absence of such evidence is not attributable to the defendants either, their conduct in marketing a drug the effects of which are delayed for many years played a significant role in creating the unavailability of proof.

From a broader policy standpoint, defendants are better able to bear the cost of injury resulting from the manufacture of a defective product. As was said by Justice Traynor in *Escola*, "(t)he cost of an injury and the loss of time or health may be an overwhelming misfortune to the person injured, and a needless one, for the risk of injury can be insured by the manufacturer and distributed among the public as a cost of doing business." (24 Cal.2d p. 462.) The manufacturer is in the best position to discover and guard against defects in its products and to warn of harmful effects; thus, holding it liable for defects and failure to warn of harmful effects will provide an incentive to product safety. These considerations are particularly significant where medication is involved, for the consumer is virtually helpless to protect himself from serious, sometimes permanent, sometimes fatal, injuries caused by deleterious drugs.

Where, as here, all defendants produced a drug from an identical formula and the manufacturer of the DES which caused plaintiff's injuries cannot be identified through no fault of plaintiff, a modification of the rule of *Summers* is warranted. As we have seen, an undiluted *Summers* rationale is inappropriate to shift the burden of proof of causation to defendants because if we measure the chance that any particular manufacturer supplied the injury-causing product by the number of producers of DES, there is a possibility that none of the five defendants in this case produced the offending substance and that the responsible manufacturer, not named in the action, will escape liability.

But we approach the issue of causation from a different perspective: we hold it to be reasonable in the present context to measure the likelihood that any of the defendants supplied the product which allegedly injured plaintiff by the percentage which the DES sold by each of them for the purpose of preventing miscarriage bears to the entire production of the drug sold by all for that purpose. Plaintiff asserts in her briefs that Eli Lilly and Company and 5 or 6 other companies produced 90 percent of the DES marketed. If at trial this is established to be the fact, then there is a corresponding likelihood that this comparative handful of producers manufactured the DES which caused plaintiff's injuries, and only a 10 percent likelihood that the offending producer would escape liability.

Reversed.

Notes

1. Other states applying market share liability to DES cases. Wisconsin, Washington, New York, and Florida have all applied some form of market share liability in DES cases. See *Collins v. Eli Lilly & Co.*, 342 N.W.2d 37 (1984), *Martin v. Abbott Laboratories*, 689 P.2d

368 (1984), *Hymowitz v. Eli Lilly & Co.*, 539 N.E.2d 1069 (1989), and *Conley v. Boyle Drug Co.*, 570 So.2d 275 (1990) respectively.

2. *Two grounds for resistance to market share liability.* The notion of market share liability has always been controversial—for essentially two reasons. First, it departs from orthodox doctrine in that it relieves a plaintiff of the need to prove specific causation. Instead, it relies on the idea that tortiously exposing persons to a significant risk of harm is enough. As we saw in Chapter 10, such a radical departure from orthodox causation doctrine is highly controversial. Indeed, it has often been held to be more properly a matter for a state's legislature rather than its courts: see, *e.g.*, *Mulcahy v. Eli Lilly & Co.*, 386 N.W.2d 67, 75 (Iowa, 1986).

Secondly, it almost certainly means that, in any case where it is applied, the defendant who really did cause (most of) the victim's injury pays less than it would in a case were causation proved by regular means, while this shortfall is made up by other defendants who played little or no role in causing the particular plaintiff's injury. In *Sutowski v. Eli Lilly & Co.*, 696 N.E.2d 187, 190 (1998), for example, the Supreme Court of Ohio rejected the theory on the grounds that:

> Under market share theory, the plaintiff is discharged from proving the important causal link. The defendant actually responsible for the plaintiff's injuries may not be before the court. Such a result collides with the traditional tort notions of liability by virtue of responsibility, and imposes a judicially created form of industry wide insurance upon those manufacturers subject to market share liability.

3. *Asbestos.* As we saw in *Black v. Abex Corporation*, 603 N.W.2d 182 (N.D., 1999), in Chapter 10, the courts have not been prepared to apply the theory of market share liability to asbestos cases.

4. *Fungibility.* One of the problems has been that, even if the idea of market share liability were acceptable in principle, it requires that the courts can clearly define the market in which each putative defendant has a share. This has proved highly problematic in asbestos-related cases because there are many different types of asbestos, and many different types of products made from these various forms of asbestos. No court has been prepared to apply market share liability to non-fungible products.

5. *Three types of fungibility.* In *Thomas v. Mallet*, 701 N.W.2d 523, 560–61 (2005), the Supreme Court of Wisconsin observed:

> Allen Rostron, *Beyond Market Share Liability: A Theory of Proportional Share Liability for Nonfungible Products*, 52 UCLA L. Rev. 151 (2004) ... writes that a product can be fungible in at least three different senses....
>
> First, a product can be "functionally interchangeable." Under this meaning, whether a product is fungible is a matter of degree and heavily dependent on the context of whatever "function" is at issue. For example, " 'for signaling New Year's Eve, a blast from an auto horn and one from a saxophone may be equivalent as noise, but few would want to dance to the former.' " *Id.* at 163–64 (quoting *Hamilton v. Accu-Tek*, 32 F.Supp.2d 47, 51 (E.D.N.Y.1998))....
>
> Second, a product can be fungible in the sense that it is "physically indistinguishable." *Id.* at 164. Because appearances can be deceiving, the degree of physical similarity required, as with functional interchangeability, depends heavily on context ...
>
> Third, a product can be fungible as it presents a "uniformity of risk." *Id.* at 165. Under this meaning, "[a]s a result of sharing an identical or virtually identical

chemical formula, each manufacturer's product posed the same amount of risk as every other manufacturer's product. The products therefore were 'identically defective,' with none being more or less defective than the rest." *Id.* However, "whether a product poses a uniform risk can depend on the choice of the unit for which risk is measured. While each milligram of DES presented the same amount of risk, each DES pill did not, because the pills came in different dosages." *Id.* at 166. Thus, as products may contain different concentrations of the hazardous substance, there is leeway to conclude that strict chemical uniformity does not render all substances fungible. *Id.* at 166–67. Nevertheless, this was important to market-share liability as it defined "the market" by concretely establishing the risk undertaken by the manufacturers.

Thomas itself concerned exposure to lead paint, the toxic ingredient of which was white lead carbonate. The Court applied market share liability, but declined to identify which form of fungibility was involved on the grounds that white lead carbonate was fungible according to all three tests.

6. *Arguments in favor of market share liability.* Proponents of market share liability argue that, as *Sindell* and *Thomas* demonstrate, reliance on orthodox doctrine would mean that those who truly caused the victim's injury would often be immune from paying anything at all (since there would be insufficient evidence to establish specific causation), while those defendants who might be said to be "overpaying" in a particular case where liability is apportioned according to market share have probably injured another victim anyway. In other words, market share liability is simply a relatively straightforward, common sense way of deciding cases where information is scarce apart from our knowledge that the victim was injured by a particular causative agent.

7. *Joint and several liability.* It should be noted that, in those jurisdictions that recognize market share liability, the concept works quite differently from the "causal fictions" identified by Professor Stapleton in relation to asbestos. In those cases, the fictions mean that multiple defendants are held liable for an indivisible injury. Such defendants are therefore held jointly and severally liable in those states that have retained that doctrine.

With market share liability, by contrast, the point is that it cannot actually be established that all the defendants actually contributed to the victim's injury. Instead, each defendant is held liable according to its contribution to the risk that the market in that product posed overall.

Questions

1. Is market share liability another type of "causal fiction"? Is it any better or worse than the fictions applied in relation to cases of asbestosis and mesothelioma?

2. Which of the three types of fungibility identified by the Supreme Court of Wisconsin is the true legal test so far as market share liability is concerned?

3. What other products, if defective, might lend themselves to the application of market share liability?

4. If a court is considering applying market share liability, how is it to draw the geographical boundaries of the relevant market?

Part VI

Role of Federal Law

Chapter 16

Defendants in Bankruptcy Protection

Stays of Proceedings

It is well known that a debtor may utilize the Bankruptcy Code to gain protection from being pursued for the full sum of debts owed. The purpose of bankruptcy protection is to facilitate the negotiation of a plan of repayment and/or reorganization which will allow the debts to be discharged for only a fraction of what is owed. What is somewhat less widely known is that the Bankruptcy Code can be utilized in precisely the same way by a business seeking protection from products liability claims. Examples of corporations that have sought bankruptcy protection from products liability litigation include A.H. Robins Co., which was responsible for the development and marketing of the now-notorious Dalkon Shield contraceptive intrauterine device (IUD), and Dow Corning Corporation, which was a major manufacturer of what turned out to be defective breast implants. But probably the best-known examples involved manufacturers, such as Johns-Manville Corporation, of products made from asbestos.

In such instances, successful or potentially successful plaintiffs are treated like any other creditor of the bankrupt defendant. This inevitably means that, unless they can access the defendant's liability insurance, such plaintiffs will receive only a fraction—sometimes a very small fraction—of the sum of compensation to which they would have been entitled if the defendant had not entered bankruptcy protection.

Sometimes, as the case of the Johns-Manville Corporation demonstrates, utilization of the Bankruptcy Code is inevitable because of the sheer weight of claims compared to the financial resources of the business facing litigation. In such instances, the Code at least ensures that all victims receive a proportion of the value of their claims, rather than having to face the prospect of the pool of available resources from which any compensation may be paid being exhausted by the first plaintiff to settle or litigate successfully. Moreover, the fact that all claims against a defendant in bankruptcy protection must be removed to the same federal Bankruptcy Court ensures that they will all be dealt with on a consistent basis, rather than case-by-case by a jury, as would normally be the practice in an ordinary civil trial.

On other occasions, by contrast, defendants file for bankruptcy protection so as to be permitted to reorganize themselves. This is often referred to as a "prepackaged bankruptcy." While such reorganization must certainly include the drawing up of a plan, which the Court will need to approve, to repay the outstanding creditors (including successful and potentially successful plaintiffs), this does enable defendants to invoke bankruptcy protection (or the threat of it) as a means of forestalling litigation and/or encouraging settlements. This is because a defendant's entering bankruptcy protection means that any proceedings against it are immediately and automatically stayed.

United States Code—Title 11: Bankruptcy

§ 362. *Automatic Stay*

(a) Except as provided in subsection (b) of this section, a petition filed under section 301, 302, or 303 of this title, or an application filed under section 5(a)(3) of the Securities Investor Protection Act of 1970, operates as a stay, applicable to all entities, of—

(1) the commencement or continuation, including the issuance or employment of process, of a judicial, administrative, or other action or proceeding against the debtor that was or could have been commenced before the commencement of the case under this title, or to recover a claim against the debtor that arose before the commencement of the case under this title;

(2) the enforcement, against the debtor or against property of the estate, of a judgment obtained before the commencement of the case under this title;

(3) any act to obtain possession of property of the estate or of property from the estate or to exercise control over property of the estate;

(4) any act to create, perfect, or enforce any lien against property of the estate;

(5) any act to create, perfect, or enforce against property of the debtor any lien to the extent that such lien secures a claim that arose before the commencement of the case under this title;

(6) any act to collect, assess, or recover a claim against the debtor that arose before the commencement of the case under this title;

(7) the setoff of any debt owing to the debtor that arose before the commencement of the case under this title against any claim against the debtor ...

(c) Except as provided in subsections (d), (e), (f), and (h) of this section—

(1) the stay of an act against property of the estate under subsection (a) of this section continues until such property is no longer property of the estate;

(2) the stay of any other act under subsection (a) of this section continues until the earliest of—

(A) the time the case is closed;

(B) the time the case is dismissed; or

(C) if the case is a case under chapter 7 [liquidation], of this title concerning an individual or a case under chapter 9 [municipal reorganizations], 11 [business reorganizations], 12 [family farms], or 13 [consumer repayment] of this title, the time a discharge is granted or denied ...

Notes

1. *Application.* As § 362(c)(2)(C) implies, this provision is contained in a chapter of the Bankruptcy Code which is "generally applicable," and thus applies to different types of bankruptcies. While there are practical differences from chapter to chapter, the effect on products liability claims against defendants in each category is much the same. The Administrative Office of the U.S. Courts has reported that, in 2011, there were 1,410,653 filings, of which 47,806 were business filings (around 15% fewer than in 2010). In 2006, by contrast, there were 19,695 business filings for bankruptcy.

2. *Actual and potential claims.* It is important to understand the breadth of the automatic stay. Note that it applies not just to cases already filed, but also to actions that "*could*

have been commenced before the commencement of the case under this title" (emphasis added). As a result, if a product defect manifested itself before the manufacturer or distributor entered bankruptcy protection, the victim injured by the defective product will be unable to pursue his or her case irrespective of whether or not a lawsuit has already been filed.

3. *Judgments already entered.* The breadth of the automatic stay even extends to some judgments that have already been entered. Not only is the enforcement stayed of judgments already entered but not yet enforced, but the trustee in bankruptcy also has the power to avoid satisfying any judgment entered up to ninety days before the filing of the bankruptcy petition. This is because, according to §547(f): "For the purposes of this section, the debtor is presumed to have been insolvent on and during the 90 days immediately preceding the date of the filing of the petition."

4. *Co-defendants.* The automatic stay does not apply to any co-defendants who are not in bankruptcy protection, so that litigation against those defendants may continue.

5. *Lifting of the automatic stay.* The Bankruptcy Court, to which any pending case must be removed, has discretion to lift the automatic stay.

Questions

1. Is the breadth of the automatic stay appropriate?

2. Does it undermine the rule of law if a petition for bankruptcy can lead to the unraveling of a judgment entered within the previous ninety days?

3. Should bankruptcy judges have the power effectively to determine the outcome of many products liability suits, even before they have been filed or evidence has been heard?

4. Is it appropriate to have products liability claims, which typically involve matters of state law, removed to a federal court simply because the defendant has entered bankruptcy protection?

Gorran v. Atkins Nutritionals, Inc.

464 F.Supp.2d 315 (2006) (U.S. District Court, S.D. New York)

[On July 31, 2005, Atkins Nutritional, Inc. (ANI) commenced voluntary bankruptcy proceedings in the United States Bankruptcy Court for the Southern District of New York. The plaintiff's action, which had been commenced in Florida, was thereby stayed as to ANI pursuant to 11 U.S.C. §362. On November 1, 2005, defendants removed the action to the Bankruptcy Court for the Southern District of Florida. The action was then transferred to this court, by stipulation of the parties, on November 22, 2005. The stay was lifted on January 10, 2006.]

CHIN, J. Plaintiff Jody Gorran, a 53-year old businessman, went on the popular low-carbohydrate Atkins Diet (the "Diet") in the spring of 2001. Six months earlier, his cholesterol level was only 146 and he had a "very low risk" of heart disease. After just two months on the Diet, however, his cholesterol level shot up to 230. Nonetheless, he remained on the Diet until October 2003, when he experienced severe chest pain. As a consequence, he had an angioplasty—a surgical procedure—to unclog one of his coronary arteries, and a stent was placed into the artery to help keep it open.

Gorran now sues defendants Atkins Nutritionals, Inc. ("ANI"), and Paul D. Wolf, co-executor of the Estate of Robert C. Atkins, M.D. (the "Estate"), for products liability, negligent misrepresentation, and deceptive conduct under Florida law. Gorran contends that the Diet is dangerous because it calls for a high-fat, high-protein, low-carbohydrate diet that increases the risk of coronary heart disease, diabetes, stroke, and certain types of cancer. He alleges that products sold by defendants—books, food products, and nutritional supplements—are "defective and unreasonably dangerous." He seeks money damages as well as an injunction requiring defendants to put warning labels on all Atkins products and the ANI website.

Defendants move pursuant to Rule 12(c) of the Federal Rules of Civil Procedure for judgment on the pleadings dismissing the complaint. The motions are granted, for Gorran's claims are meritless. Defendants' books and food products are not defective or dangerous products within the meaning of products liability law. Pastrami and cheesecake—large amounts of which Gorran admittedly consumed—may present risks, but these are risks of which consumers are aware. The average consumer surely anticipates that these and other high-fat or high-protein foods may increase cholesterol levels and the risk of heart disease. Moreover, the Diet consists of advice and ideas. The concepts may be controversial and the subject of criticism, but they are protected by the First Amendment. For these and other reasons set out below, Gorran's claims are dismissed.

Notes

1. *Books. As* we saw in Chapter 1 in *Way v. Boy Scouts of America*, 856 S.W.2d 230 (1993), words in books are not considered to be products.

2. *Busiest courts.* The Southern District of New York boasts one of the two busiest bankruptcy courts in the nation; the other is in Delaware. Since 2005, over 70% of the 200 or so large corporations that have filed for bankruptcy have done so in of these two courts. They have developed a particular reputation for prepackaged bankruptcies.

Questions

1. The court dismissed Gorran's claims because it held that consumers would be aware of the risks of a high-fat, high-protein diet. In a footnote, Judge Chin commented: "The Court notes that it has had success with its own, much simpler diet, which can be described in four words: 'Run more, eat less.'" Does this robust approach simply give license to authors to make a fast buck by preying on those with low self-esteem by dreaming up some new, "revolutionary," and perhaps even dangerous, diet?

2. If the plaintiff still wishes to pursue the claim, and as an alternative to lifting the automatic stay, the Bankruptcy Court may decide to adjudicate upon liability and compensation (if any) itself in a bench trial. In the circumstances, does this seem an appropriate way to proceed?

Bankruptcy and Liability Insurance

One of the most common reasons for the Bankruptcy Court to exercise its discretion to lift the automatic stay is that the claims involved can be defended, and any awards of compensation paid for, by the bankrupt defendant's liability insurance. (Indeed, some states require that liability insurance policies contain wording to indicate expressly that the bankruptcy of the insured will not relieve the insurer of its coverage obligations.) In such cases, the automatic stay will be lifted only to the extent of the policy limits since, beyond that point, any award of compensation would become an additional debt of the original, bankrupt defendant.

The position becomes significantly more complicated, however, where a defendant in bankruptcy protection is self-insured. As its name suggests, self-insurance means putting some money aside, as though paying insurance premiums, to meet potential liability claims, but retaining that money in a designated account of one's own. For this reason, the terminology of "self-insurance" has been subject to judicial criticism. In *Aerojet-General Corp. v. Transport Indem. Co.*, 17 Cal.4th 38, 72, fn. 20 (1997), the Supreme Court of California declared:

> In a strict sense, "self-insurance" is a "misnomer." (*Nabisco, Inc. v. Transport Indemnity Co.* (1983) 143 Cal.App.3d 831, 836.) "Insurance is a contract whereby one undertakes to indemnify another against loss, damage, or liability arising from a contingent or unknown event." (Ins. Code, § 22.) "[S]elf-insurance ... is equivalent to no insurance...." (*Richardson v. GAB Business Services, Inc.*, (1984) 161 Cal.App.3d 519, 523.) As such, it is "repugnant to the [very] concept of insurance...." (*Ibid.*) If insurance requires an undertaking by one to indemnify another, it cannot be satisfied by a self-contradictory undertaking by one to indemnify oneself.

Nevertheless, the practice of "self-insuring" is widespread. Businesses who take this option obviously do so to save money, but they also typically "top-up" such self-insurance with liability insurance designed to provide coverage for amounts in excess of the coverage that self-insurance provides.

Figure 16.1 Layers of Liability Insurance

	LAYER	EFFECT	WHO IS LIABLE TO PAY
$$$$$	Uninsured layer	Award of compensation exceeds policy limits, and must therefore be sought from defendant rather than insurer	Defendant
$$$$	Second excess layer	Larger businesses may have a second (or more) layers of insurance over and above the self-insurance and first excess layers	Insurer(s)
$$$	Excess layer	Awards of compensation that exceed the level of self-insurance may be claimed from those providing excess insurance coverage	Insurer(s)
$$	Self-insurance layer	Awards within this range (as well as this part of larger awards) are self-insured, and so must be claimed from the defendant, and not the insurer	Defendant
$0			

It may be tempting to see excess liability insurance as much the same as regular liability insurance, albeit with a somewhat larger deductible in the shape of the self-insurance coverage. In fact, however, there is a very significant difference. With regular liability insurance, the insurer is "on risk" as soon as its insured (the defendant) receives notice of a claim being made against it. The significance of the deductible is simply that the insurer can seek reimbursement of that amount of its liability from the defendant (although, if the latter is in bankruptcy protection, this might not be a right worth having). But since the insurer is on risk from the moment the claim is made, the plaintiff will be able to receive whatever compensation s/he is awarded, subject to the policy limits—and s/he will not even be denied the deductible, since that is a purely contractual matter between the insured defendant and its insurer.

Self-insurance works very differently. In effect, the defendant business will have insurance coverage divided into two or more layers, as Figure 16.1 demonstrates. The first layer of coverage is provided by the business's own self-insurance. Since this layer will be on risk for every claim, it is the most expensive layer to insure, and businesses can therefore make considerable cost savings in taking on that level of risk themselves. Coverage for the next layer of risk, known as the "excess layer," is then typically provided by outside insurers, who will charge lower premiums than they would have charged for the first layer because they will be on risk only for claims that exceed the limits of the insured defendant's self-insurance. Excess insurance is often purchased through a policy that refers to a "self-insured retention" (SIR): this is essentially (with potentially one important difference, noted below) just another name for the self-insurance layer.

Depending on the nature of the defendant's business and the potential costs for which it might be held liable to a third party, it might also take out a second (or even more) layers of excess insurance in order to increase its coverage. For example, *In re September 11th Liab. Ins. Coverage Cases*, 458 F. Supp. 2d 104 (N.Y. 2006), involved five layers of excess insurance. Premiums charged by insurers for the higher layers will diminish as their likelihood of coming on risk also diminishes.

The significance of a bankrupt defendant's being self-insured is this. Unlike regular liability insurers—who come on risk as soon as a claim is made, and to whom the automatic stay cannot apply because the insurer is not itself bankrupt—excess insurers come on risk only once the self-insured layer (or SIR) has been exhausted: see *In re Amatex Corp.*, 107 B.R. 856 (Pa. 1989). Yet claims against the bankrupt defendant itself are automatically stayed. As a result, the self-insured layer (or SIR) cannot be called upon at all, let alone become exhausted, and so the excess insurers cannot come on risk. In other words, the automatic stay has the effect of immunizing the excess insurers from claims just as much as the self-insured defendant.

That, at least, is the effect when standard principles of excess insurance are strictly applied. The problem is that this leaves a products liability victim uncompensated while allowing the excess insurers to escape the liability for which they have already received a premium. As a result, courts are sometimes willing to stretch a point in order to achieve what they consider to be a more equitable outcome.

In *In re Keck, Mahin & Cate*, 241 B.R. 583 (Ill. 1999), for example, a court was faced with an excess liability insurance policy that required that an SIR of $1 million for each claim be "paid" by the bankrupt insured before the insurance company would be required to satisfy the remaining insurance obligation. The court decided, however, that this SIR could be satisfied by granting to the claimants an unsecured claim for the SIR portion of any amount owed to them. This then obligated the excess liability insurers, within the policy limits, to satisfy any claims that went over and above the SIR. In effect, this enabled claimants to recover in full for that portion of their losses that fell within the excess layer, while restricting them to the prospect of pennies on the dollar for the self-insurance layer because of the bankruptcy of the defendant itself.

By contrast, actual payment of an amount equivalent to the SIR by a party other than the defendant itself has been held not to amount to exhaustion of the SIR. In *Forecast Homes, Inc. v. Steadfast Ins. Co.*, 181 Cal.App.4th 1466 (2010), a California Court of Appeal accepted that there was nothing wrong, in principle, with permitting a third party to satisfy the SIR. But the Court held in the instant case that the policy wording was clear that the SIR could be satisfied only by payments made by the insured itself, and not by others (even co-insureds). It also held that such provisions were not contrary to public policy, although they clearly had the effect of denying claims for which the excess insurer would have been responsible if the insured defendant had remained solvent.

This brings us to the one significant difference between an SIR and a self-insurance layer. The latter is a form of primary insurance, so that it must always be "exhausted" (however the courts choose to define that occurrence) before other, effectively secondary, insurance becomes implicated. An SIR can, however, itself be satisfied by another insurance policy taken out by the defendant insured, provided that the policy wording does not prohibit it: *Vons Companies, Inc. v. United States Fire Ins. Co.*, 78 Cal.App.4th 52 (Cal. 2000).

Thus in *Montgomery Ward & Company, Inc. v. Imperial Cas. & Indem. Co.*, 181 Cal.App.4th 1466 (Cal. 2010), a different California appellate court found that the wording of the excess insurance policy with which it was presented effectively treated the SIR as tantamount to a deductible. It held that the substance of the policy terms trumped any label applied to it, and so the excess insurer was on risk even without exhaustion of the SIR. Such collapsing of the distinction between insured and self-insured defendants means that excess liability insurers are always on risk when a claim is made, even when the defendant is in bankruptcy protection.

Questions

1. Should the terms of a defendant's liability insurance arrangements determine the viability of a products liability claim, or should there simply be a rule governing the liability of excess insurers irrespective of the policy terms?

2. Does your answer to question (1) depend on whether the defendant is solvent or in bankruptcy protection?

3. Should SIRs be treated differently from self-insurance layers?

Note

Direct liability of insurer. Irrespective of whether the defendant was wholly insured or partially self-insured, the liability of the liability insurers (including any excess liability insurers) that we have been discussing so far is secondary liability. It is always parasitic to the direct liability of the insured defendant, and arises only through a contract between liability insurer and insured defendant.

Occasionally, however, a plaintiff may argue that the liability insurer is itself somehow directly responsible for the victim's injuries caused by the alleged product defect.

This will normally involve claims of fraudulent misrepresentation and/or failures to warn by the insurer. The point of bringing such claims is likely twofold.

First, since a claim against the insurer directly represents an entirely new cause of action that is not parastic on any claim against the insured manufacturer or distributor, any award of compensation made cannot be capped by the insurance policy limits. It is, instead, a regular claim where the amount of compensation is at large.

Secondly, since the defendant will be the insurer itself, who is solvent, the plaintiff will, in principle, be able to circumvent the automatic stay, including any associated issues that arise when the product manufacturer or distributor is partially self-insured. That was precisely the issue at stake in the following case.

The Travelers Indemnity Co. v. Pearlie Bailey
129 S.Ct. 2195 (2009) (SCOTUS)

SOUTER, J. As an element of the 1986 reorganization plan of the Johns-Manville Corporation (Manville), the United States Bankruptcy Court for the Southern District of New York enjoined certain lawsuits against Manville's insurers, including The Travelers Indemnity Company and its affiliates (Travelers). The question is whether the injunction bars state-law actions against Travelers based on allegations either of its own wrongdoing while acting as Manville's insurer or of its misuse of information obtained from Manville as its insurer. We hold that the terms of the injunction bar the actions and that the finality of the Bankruptcy Court's orders following the conclusion of direct review generally stands in the way of challenging the enforceability of the injunction.

From the 1920s to the 1970s, Manville was, by most accounts, the largest supplier of raw asbestos and manufacturer of asbestos-containing products in the United States, and for much of that time Travelers was Manville's primary liability insurer. As studies began to link asbestos exposure to respiratory disease and thousands of lawsuits were filed against Manville, Travelers, as the insurer, worked closely with Manville to learn what its insured knew and to assess the dangers of asbestos exposure; it evaluated Manville's potential liability and defenses, and paid Manville's litigation costs.

It thus became incumbent on the Bankruptcy Court to devise

> a plan of reorganization for [Manville] which would provide for payment to holders of present or known asbestos health related claims ... and [to] those persons who had not yet manifested an injury but who would manifest symptoms of asbestos-related illnesses at some future time.

The ensuing reorganization plan created the Manville Personal Injury Settlement Trust (Trust) to pay all asbestos claims against Manville, which would be channeled to the Trust.

In the period leading up to the reorganization, Manville and its insurers litigated over the scope and limits of liability coverage, and Travelers faced suits by third parties, such as Manville factory workers and vendors of Manville products, seeking compensation under the insurance policies. There was also litigation among the insurers themselves, who brought various indemnity claims, contribution claims, and cross-claims. In a settlement described as the "cornerstone" of the Manville reorganization, the insurers agreed to provide most of the initial corpus of the Trust, with a payment of $770 million to the bankruptcy estate, $80 million of it from Travelers.

There would have been no such payment without the injunction at the heart of the present dispute. The December 18, 1986, order of the Bankruptcy Court approving the insurance settlement agreements (Insurance Settlement Order) provides that, upon the insurers' payment of the settlement funds to the Trust, "all Persons are permanently restrained and enjoined from commencing and/or continuing any suit, arbitration or other proceeding of any type or nature for Policy Claims against any or all members of the Settling Insurer Group." The Insurance Settlement Order goes on to provide that the insurers are "released from any and all Policy Claims," which are to be channeled to the Trust. The order defines "Policy Claims" as "any and all claims, demands, allegations, duties, liabilities and obligations (whether or not presently known) which have been, or could have been, or might be, asserted by any Person against ... any or all members of the Settling Insurer Group based upon, arising out of or relating to any or all of the Policies." The insurers were entitled "to terminate the settlements if the injunctive orders [were] not issued or if they [were] set aside on appeal." ...

Nonetheless, over a decade later plaintiffs started filing asbestos actions against Travelers in various state courts, cases that have been spoken of in this litigation as Direct Actions. They are of two sorts. The Statutory Direct Actions are brought under state consumer-protection statutes, and allege that Travelers conspired with other insurers and with asbestos manufacturers to hide the dangers of asbestos and to raise a fraudulent "state of the art" (or "no duty to warn") defense to personal injury claims. The Common Law Direct Actions claim that Travelers violated common law duties by failing to warn the public about the dangers of asbestos or by acting to keep its knowledge of those dangers from the public. It is undisputed that many of the plaintiffs seek to recover from Travelers, not indirectly for Manville's wrongdoing, but for Travelers' own alleged violations of state law.

In 2002, Travelers invoked the terms of the 1986 Orders in moving the Bankruptcy Court to enjoin 26 Direct Actions pending in state courts. The court issued a temporary restraining order, repeatedly extended, and referred the parties to mediation, which led to settlements between Travelers and three sets of plaintiffs in both Statutory and Common Law Direct Actions. Under the settlement terms Travelers would pay more than $400 million to settlement funds to compensate Direct Action claimants, contingent upon the entry of an order by the Bankruptcy Court clarifying that the Direct Actions were, and remained, prohibited by the 1986 Orders. The settlement requires claimants seeking payment from the settlement funds to grant Travelers a release from further liability, separate and apart from Travelers' protection under the 1986 Orders.

After notice of the settlement was given to potential claimants, the Bankruptcy Court (the same judge who had issued the 1986 Orders) held an evidentiary hearing and made extensive factual findings that are not challenged here. The court determined that

> Travelers['] knowledge of the hazards of asbestos was derived from its nearly three decade insurance relationship with Manville and the performance by Travelers of its obligations under the Policies, including through the underwriting, loss control activities, defense obligations and generally through its lengthy and confidential insurance relationship under the policies.

In sum, the Bankruptcy Court found that "Travelers learned virtually everything it knew about asbestos from its relationship with Manville."

As for the Direct Actions, the court saw "[t]he gravamen of the Statutory Direct Action Lawsuits" as "center[ing] on Travelers['] defense of Manville in asbestos-related claims." The court read the "alleged factual predicate" of the Common Law Direct Actions as being "essentially identical to the statutory actions: Travelers ... influence[d] Manville's purported failure to disclose knowledge about asbestos hazards; Travelers defended Manville; Travelers advanced the state of the art defense; and Travelers coordinated Manville's national defense effort." The court understood "the direct action claims against Travelers [to be] inextricably intertwined with Travelers['] long relationship as Manville's insurer," and found that "[a]fter the Court preliminarily enjoined prosecution of Direct Action Claims against Travelers pending final ruling on the merits, certain plaintiffs' lawyers violated the letter and the spirit of this Court's rulings by simply deleting the term 'Manville' from their complaints—but leaving the substance unchanged."

Hence, the court's conclusion that "[t]he evidence in this proceeding establishes that the gravamen of Direct Action Claims were acts or omissions by Travelers arising from or relating to Travelers['] insurance relationship with Manville." Finding that the "claims against Travelers based on such actions or omissions necessarily 'arise out of' and [are] 'related to'" the insurance policies, which compelled Travelers to defend Manville against asbestos-related claims, the Bankruptcy Court held that the Direct Actions "are—and always have been—permanently barred" by the 1986 Orders.

The settlement was accordingly approved and an order dated August 17, 2004 (Clarifying Order), was entered, providing that the 1986 Orders barred the pending Direct Actions and "[t]he commencement or prosecution of all actions and proceedings against Travelers that directly or indirectly are based upon, arise out of or relate to Travelers['] insurance relationship with Manville or Travelers['] knowledge or alleged knowledge concerning the hazards of asbestos," including claims for contribution or indemnification....

Some individual claimants and Chubb Indemnity Insurance Company (Chubb), respondents before this Court, objected to the settlement and subsequently appealed. So far as it matters here, the District Court affirmed, but the Court of Appeals for the Second Circuit reversed....

If it is black-letter law that the terms of an unambiguous private contract must be enforced irrespective of the parties' subjective intent, it is all the clearer that a court should enforce a court order, a public governmental act, according to its unambiguous terms. This is all the Bankruptcy Court did.

Given the Clarifying Order's correct reading of the 1986 Orders, the only question left is whether the Bankruptcy Court had subject-matter jurisdiction to enter the Clarifying Order. The answer here is easy: as the Second Circuit recognized, and respondents do not dispute, the Bankruptcy Court plainly had jurisdiction to interpret and enforce its own prior orders. What is more, when the Bankruptcy Court issued the 1986 Orders it explicitly retained jurisdiction to enforce its injunctions.

The Court of Appeals, however, went on to a different jurisdictional enquiry. It held that the 1986 Orders could not be enforced according to their terms because, as the panel saw it, the Bankruptcy Court had exceeded its jurisdiction when it issued the orders in 1986. We think, though, that it was error for the Court of Appeals to reevaluate the Bankruptcy Court's exercise of jurisdiction in 1986.

On direct appeal of the 1986 Orders, anyone who objected was free to argue that the Bankruptcy Court had exceeded its jurisdiction, and the District Court or Court of Appeals could have raised such concerns sua sponte. In fact, one objector argued just that. In *MacArthur*, a distributor of Manville asbestos claimed to be a coinsured under certain Manville insurance policies and argued that the 1986 Orders exceeded the Bankruptcy Court's jurisdiction by preventing the distributor from recovering under the policies; the Second Circuit disagreed, concluding that the Bankruptcy Court had not stepped outside its jurisdiction or statutory authority. But once the 1986 Orders became final on direct review (whether or not proper exercises of bankruptcy court jurisdiction and power), they became res judicata to the "parties and those in privity with them, not only as to every matter which was offered and received to sustain or defeat the claim or demand, but as to any other admissible matter which might have been offered for that purpose." ...

Our holding is narrow. We do not resolve whether a bankruptcy court, in 1986 or today, could properly enjoin claims against nondebtor insurers that are not derivative of the debtor's wrongdoing. As the Court of Appeals noted, in 1994 Congress explicitly authorized bankruptcy courts, in some circumstances, to enjoin actions against a nondebtor "alleged to be directly or indirectly liable for the conduct of, claims against, or demands on the debtor to the extent such alleged liability ... arises by reason of ... the third party's provision of insurance to the debtor or a related party," and to channel those claims to a trust for payments to asbestos claimants. 11 U. S. C. §524 (g)(4)(A)(ii). On direct review today, a channeling injunction of the sort issued by the Bankruptcy Court in 1986 would have to be measured against the requirements of §524 (to begin with, at least). But owing to the posture of this litigation, we do not address the scope of an injunction authorized by that section.

Nor do we decide whether any particular respondent is bound by the 1986 Orders. We have assumed that respondents are bound, but the Court of Appeals did not consider this question. Chubb, in fact, relying on *Amchem Products, Inc. v. Windsor*, 521 U.S. 591 (1997), and *Ortiz v. Fibreboard Corp.*, 527 U.S. 815 (1999), has maintained that it was not given constitutionally sufficient notice of the 1986 Orders, so that due process absolves it from following them, whatever their scope. The District Court rejected this argument, but the Court of Appeals did not reach it. On remand, the Court of Appeals can take up this objection and any others that respondents have preserved.

We reverse the judgment of the Court of Appeals and remand for further proceedings consistent with this opinion.

So ordered.

Questions

1. Should it be possible to bring suit against a liability insurer for its own alleged wrongdoing when the underlying cause of the plaintiff's injuries was a defective product?

2. Does the answer to question (1) depend on whether the insured manufacturer or distributor is solvent or in bankruptcy protection?

3. Is such an insurer's direct liability properly the subject of orders by the Bankruptcy Court when the insured manufacturer or distributor seeks to emerge from bankruptcy protection?

Discharge from Bankruptcy Protection

One of the objectives of bankruptcy protection is to enable the debtor to be released from outstanding debts. This typically means that the pre-petition products liability claims will be stayed indefinitely. There are some exceptions, however: claims of fraud or of intentional injury will not be stayed.

Straight discharges are, however, granted only to individual debtors. So far as businesses are concerned, they are discharged from bankruptcy protection only after having a plan of reorganization approved by the court. Such a plan might simply treat products liability plaintiffs like other unsecured creditors, and enable them to claim pennies on the dollar for their injuries. Another possibility—if the Bankruptcy Court agrees—is that the plan might make provision (as in *Travelers*, above, and *Johns-Manville*, below) for the setting aside of specified funds to pay claims for injuries caused by products that were defective at the time of the defendant's entering bankruptcy protection. In the case of defective products known to cause latent injury (such as asbestos, whose signature diseases do not manifest themselves for years), this means that any such fund will need to be structured, so far as is possible, to be able to meet claims that have yet to be brought (and which might not be brought for some time).

United States Code—Title 11: Bankruptcy

§ 524. *Effect of discharge*

(a) A discharge in a case under this title—

(1) voids any judgment at any time obtained, to the extent that such judgment is a determination of the personal liability of the debtor with respect to any debt discharged under section 727, 944, 1141, 1228, or 1328 of this title, whether or not discharge of such debt is waived;

(2) operates as an injunction against the commencement or continuation of an action, the employment of process, or an act, to collect, recover or offset any such debt as a personal liability of the debtor, whether or not discharge of such debt is waived; …

(g)(1)(A) After notice and hearing, a court that enters an order confirming a plan of reorganization under chapter 11 may issue, in connection with such order, an injunction in accordance with this subsection to supplement the injunctive effect of a discharge under this section.

(B) An injunction may be issued under subparagraph (A) to enjoin entities from taking legal action for the purpose of directly or indirectly collecting, recovering, or receiving payment or recovery with respect to any claim or demand that, under a plan of reorganization, is to be paid in whole or in part by a trust…, except such legal actions as are expressly allowed by the injunction, the confirmation order, or the plan of reorganization.

In re Johns-Manville Corporation

36 B.R. 743 (1984) (U.S. Bankruptcy Court, S.D. New York)

LIFLAND, J. Keene Corp. has put before this Court a motion to appoint a legal representative for asbestos-exposed future claimants in the Manville reorganization case. It is abundantly clear that the Manville reorganization will have to be accountable to future asbestos claimants whose compelling interest must be safeguarded in order to leave a residue of assets sufficient to accommodate a meaningful resolution of the Manville asbestos-related health problem. The term "future asbestos claimants" is defined for these purposes to include all persons and entities who, on or before August 26, 1982, came into contact with asbestos or asbestos-containing products mined, fabricated, manufactured, supplied or sold by Manville and who have not yet filed claims against Manville for personal injuries or property damage. These claimants may be unaware of their entitlement to recourse against Manville due to the latency period of many years characterizing manifestation of all asbestos related diseases.

Exposure to asbestos dust may result in one of three diseases: asbestosis, a chronic disease of the lungs causing shortness of breath similar to emphysema; mesothelioma, a fatal cancer of the lining of the chest, abdomen or lung, and lung or other cancers. However, it is contended by Manville that it was not until recently that the full extent of the dangers due to asbestos exposure was clarified. Thus, the enhanced safety programs which eventuated because of the new discoveries regarding the damages of asbestos were too late to have any effect on those who had previously been exposed. Accordingly, Manville expects a proliferation of claims in the next 30 years by those previously exposed who will manifest these diseases in this period....

From the inception of this case, it has been obvious to all concerned that the very purpose of the initiation of these proceedings is to deal in some fashion with claimants exposed to the ravages of asbestos dust who have not as of the filing date manifested symptoms of asbestos disease. Indeed, but for this continually evolving albeit amorphous constituency, it is clear that an otherwise economically robust Manville would not have commenced these reorganization proceedings. It is the spectre of proliferating, overburdening litigation to be commenced in the next 20–30 years, which litigation would be beyond the company's ability to manage, control, and pay for, which has prompted this filing....

Accordingly, a resolution of the interests of future claimants is a central focus of these reorganization proceedings. Any plan emerging from this case which ignores these claimants would serve the interests of neither the debtor nor any of its other creditor constituencies in that the central short and long-term economic drain on the debtor would not have been eliminated. Manville might indeed be forced to file again and again if this eventuated. Each filing would leave attenuated assets available to deal with interests of emerging future claimants. Manville could also be forced into liquidation. The liquidation of this substantial corporation would be economically inefficient in not only leaving many asbestos claimants uncompensated, but also in eliminating needed jobs and the productivity emanating from an ongoing concern. It fosters the key aims of Chapter 11 to avoid liquidation at all reasonable costs....

Section 1109(b) of the Code, 11 U.S.C. § 1109(b), makes clear that any "party in interest" may appear and be heard in a Chapter 11 case. It provides: "Any party in interest, including the debtor, the trustee, a creditors' committee, an equity security holders' committee, an equity holder, or any indenture trustee, may raise and may appear and be heard on any issue in a case under this chapter."

The term "party in interest" has no specific definition in the Code and its applicability must be determined on an "ad hoc" basis....

While the precise contours of Code Section 1109(b) have yet to be fixed, they are certainly broad enough to embrace the interests of future claimants as affected parties. Future claimants are undeniably parties in interest to these reorganization proceedings pursuant to the broad, flexible definition of that term enunciated by the foregoing authorities. The drafting of "party in interest" as an elastic concept was designed for just this kind situation. As detailed above, future claimants are indeed the central focus of the entire reorganization. Any plan not dealing with their interests precludes a meaningful and effective reorganization and thus inures to the detriment of the reorganization body politic. Any meaningful plan will either provide funding for future claimants directly or provide for the continuation of some form of responsive, ongoing entity post-confirmation, from which to glean assets with which to pay them. If they are denied standing as parties in interest, they will be denied all opportunity either to help design the ship that sails away from these reorganization proceedings with their cargo on board or to assert their interests during a pre-launching distribution. In either event, the direct impact on these claimants will be enormous as declared by the Seventh Circuit in *In re UNR*. Thus, because none of the existing committees of unsecured creditors and present asbestos claimants represents this key group, a separate and distinct representative for these parties in interest must be established so that these claimants have a role in the formulation of such a plan. This is especially so given that any plan of reorganization must necessarily balance the rights and needs of prepetition creditors against the anticipated rights and needs of post-petition creditors with Manville's purportedly limited assets and further economic prospects apportioned accordingly.

Motion for the appointment of a legal representative granted.

Notes

1. *Flowchart.* The stages of bankruptcy proceedings and their effect on products liability claims are depicted in the flowchart in Figure 16.2.

2. *Non-mandatory trusts.* As has already been noted, defendants in bankruptcy are not required to set up trusts to fund the compensation of those injured by their defective products. The following piece explores this issue further.

Susan Power Johnston & Katherine Porter, Extension of Section 524(g) of the Bankruptcy Code to Nondebtor Parents, Affiliates, and Transaction Parties
59 Bus. Lawyer 510 (2004)

In 1994, Congress amended the Bankruptcy Code to provide a restructuring model for asbestos-related bankruptcies. Section 524(g) represents a congressional response to the need for an effective mechanism to facilitate reorganization of companies facing massive numbers of asbestos claims. A variety of efforts to achieve such relief outside Chapter 11 had not proven successful. Section 524(g) codifies the approach that Johns-Manville Corporation ("Johns-Manville") used in its bankruptcy in the mid-1980s to deal with the asbestos claims against it. The statute does not apply to non-asbestos liabilities. The keystone of § 524(g) is the creation of a trust as part of the debtor's plan of reorganization. The trust is vested with, among other things, the reorganized debtor's stock, from which present and future asbestos-related claims will be paid. In return for funding this trust, and subject to a myriad of requirements detailed below, the debtor, its predecessors and successors in interest, and its past or present affiliates receive broad protection from any asbestos-related liabilities through the bankruptcy court's issuance of a channeling injunction directing asbestos claims exclusively to the trust....

Section 524(g) also contains a heightened requirement for approval by creditors. To be confirmed, the plan must designate a separate class of present claimants, of which seventy-five percent of those voting must approve the plan....

The trust must satisfy certain standards in order to qualify for the court's issuing a broad channeling injunction to direct claimants to the trust....

If a debtor's situation and the proposed trust satisfy ... the ... requirements, § 524(g) authorizes the bankruptcy court to issue a channeling injunction requiring asbestos claimants to seek payment solely from the trust. The injunction may direct that future claims are also limited to the trust for compensation, but only if a future-claims representative

Figure 16.2 The Effect of Bankruptcy Protection on Products Liability Claims

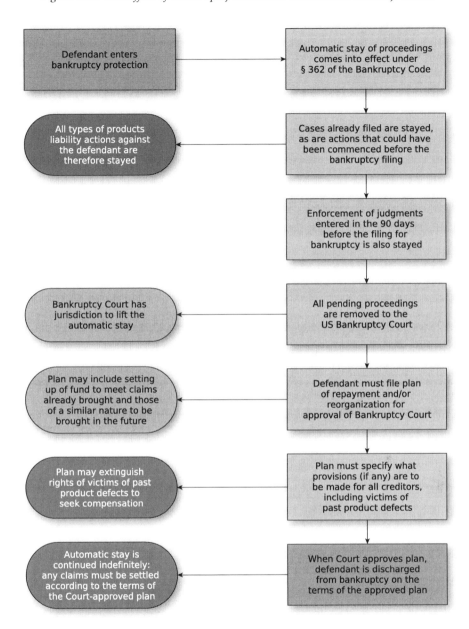

is appointed in the bankruptcy process and only if the court determines that the application of the injunction to future claimants is "fair and equitable … in light of the benefits provided, or to be provided, to such trust on behalf of such debtor or debtors or such third party."

The most remarkable, and desirable, power of § 524(g) is the statute's authorization of a broad channeling injunction that offers protection to a broad group of parties in interest, in addition to protecting the debtor. To help the debtor move forward without risk from its tort liabilities, the Bankruptcy Code allows the channeling injunction to shield from liability any entity that becomes a direct or indirect transferee of or successor to any assets of the reorganized debtor or trust. Debtors are also aided in their efforts to obtain credit after reorganization by a court's power to protect from liability any entity that makes a loan to the debtor or trust. The injunction also shields certain third parties from asbestos liability if such parties are identifiable from the terms of the injunction. Parties may be protected if their alleged liability arises from "the third party's ownership ... in the debtor, a past or present affiliate of the debtor, or a predecessor in interest of the debtor." ...

Section 524(g) offers corporations facing asbestos liability relief from the continuing stream of new multijurisdictional lawsuits that characterize mass tort litigation, by providing that the injunction "may not be revoked or modified by any court except through appeal." This ability to end all tort litigation against the debtors and its affiliates and to segregate such activity into actions against the trust gives § 524(g) the power to put a complete rest to asbestos litigation that has plagued a debtor for years.

The scope of this protection has rendered § 524(g) the only guaranteed method for containing asbestos liability for corporate parents and buyers....

Even when the asbestos trusts turn out to be underfunded, there has been no suggestion that asbestos plaintiffs have recourse against the reorganized debtors or their parents or affiliates. Although few trusts have existed long enough to test this issue, the experience in *Johns-Manville* indicates that insulating a company from liability by confirming a plan with a § 524(g) trust cannot be undone merely because hindsight reveals the trust to be insufficient.

Section 524(g) is by its terms limited to debtors facing current asbestos or asbestos-related liabilities. Because § 524 merely reflects a codification of the approach used in Johns-Manville's plan of reorganization, which was confirmed under the Bankruptcy Code's equitable powers, a *Johns-Manville*/section 524(g) model could arguably be applied in nonasbestos contexts despite the express limitation of § 524(g) to asbestos cases. Notably, in the legislative history to § 524(g), Congress expressed no opinion on a bankruptcy court's authority to issue a channeling injunction in a nonasbestos case under the court's equitable powers. The nature of the solution offered in § 524(g) should appeal to companies faced with class-action litigation other than asbestos claims.

Several debtors have filed bankruptcy to address products liability arising from the sale or manufacture of consumer products. For example, Dow Corning Corporation's ("Dow Corning") bankruptcy was triggered by widespread class-action lawsuits for tort claims based on the company's manufacture of breast implants. A.H. Robins Co. ("A.H. Robins") faced similar suits stemming from its development and marketing of the Dalkon Shield I.U.D. Other bankruptcies driven by tort liability include those of U.S. Brass Corporation, which was facing lawsuits for its manufacture of plastic plumbing pipe, and Piper Aircraft Corporation ("Piper Aircraft"), which was named in several lawsuits alleging the defective manufacture of aircraft or aircraft parts. At the peak of class-action activity against tobacco manufacturers, speculation also occurred as to whether tobacco companies would seek refuge in bankruptcy court.

A Chapter 11 bankruptcy reorganization that uses a trust with a channeling injunction is a powerful tool for resolving any situation in which present and future liabilities are widespread, liability is impossible to determine fully at the time of the bankruptcy, and insurance companies and affiliates of the debtor face lawsuits based on the debtor's alleged liability. A trust and channeling injunction could be useful in other types of products liability cases, such as those brought against pharmaceutical manufacturers or firearm manufacturers.... In theory, any company facing widespread and massive liability could attempt to consolidate and pay off tort claimants by using a trust....

For example, A.H. Robins confirmed a plan of reorganization that created three trusts to resolve the claims of Dalkon Shield users, their families, and third parties. As part of its plan, A.H. Robins was merged into a subsidiary of American Home Products Corporation, which contributed $2.475 billion to pay Dalkon Shield claims as partial consideration for gaining ownership of A.H. Robins. In sharp contrast to the experience of Johns-Manville, the Dalkon Shield trusts were solvent after paying all claims. Dow Corning did not use a trust to pay its mass tort liabilities, but instead created Settlement and Litigation Facilities that claimants could look to for recovery of tort damages. Dow Corning's plan contained a release of all tort liability as against the debtor (Dow Corning), The Dow Company and Corning Inc., the insurance companies, and certain health-care providers. The extension of releases to the nondebtor entities was challenged, but it was upheld by the bankruptcy court only as to creditors that accepted the plan. The court analogized the releases in Dow Corning's plan of reorganization to the channeling injunction power of § 524(g) but noted that the provision was not applicable, because, *inter alia*, the detailed requirements for a supplemental injunction in § 524(g)(2)(B) had not been met.

Asbestos defendants have dominated the landscape of mass tort bankruptcies, however, and have led the way in challenging the limits of § 524(g). Several reasons, aside from the express limitation on asbestos harms in § 524(g), may explain why the trust and channeling injunction concepts have not become widely used or well integrated in nonasbestos contexts. One explanation is that a § 524(g)-type solution is most useful if a debtor or its affiliates are not committed to contesting their ultimate liability. When a company wants to litigate the merits of its liability, bankruptcy is ostensibly still helpful because of the stay of pending litigation and the consolidation of the cases in one district. Nonetheless, a company that believes it can achieve dismissal on a large fraction of the claims against it may not be willing to make the substantial contribution necessary for a § 524(g) trust.

Question

Should the setting up of a fund or trust to handle current and foreseeable products liability claims for pre-petition defects be a mandatory requirement imposed on any business seeking to exit bankruptcy protection?

Effective Date of Claim

As we saw under § 362, the automatic stay applies to any action "that was or could have been commenced before" the defendant entered bankruptcy protection. As we have now seen under § 524, that stay is continued indefinitely against all such claims when the defendant exits bankruptcy protection. Unfortunately, however, the date on which a claim arises is not quite as clear-cut as it might, at first, appear.

Grady v. A.H. Robins Co., Inc.
839 F.2d 198 (4th Cir. 1988)

WIDENER, J. Rebecca Grady and the Legal Representative of the Future Claimants appeal an order of the district court deciding that Mrs. Grady's claim against A.H. Robins

Co., Inc. (Robins) arose prior to the date Robins sought protection under the Bankruptcy Code and therefore was subject to the automatic stay provision of 11 U.S.C. § 362(a)(1). We affirm.

Robins, a pharmaceutical company, was the manufacturer and marketer of the Dalkon Shield, an interuterine contraceptive device, from 1971 to 1974. Production was discontinued in 1974 because of mounting concerns about the device's safety. Because of the overwhelming number of claims filed against it because of the Dalkon Shield, Robins filed a petition for reorganization under Chapter 11 of the Bankruptcy Code, 11 U.S.C. § 1101 et seq, on August 21, 1985.

Mrs. Grady had had inserted a Dalkon Shield some years before but thought that the device had fallen out. On August 21, 1985, she was admitted to Salinas Valley Memorial Hospital, Salinas, California, complaining of abdominal pain, fever and chills. X-rays and sonograms revealed the presence of the Dalkon Shield. On August 28, 1985, the Dalkon Shield was surgically removed. Mrs. Grady was discharged from the hospital but not long after returned to her physician, complaining of persistent pain, fever and chills. She was again admitted to the hospital on November 14, 1985, on which admission she was diagnosed as having pelvic inflammatory disease, and underwent a hysterectomy. She blames the Dalkon Shield for those injuries. The facts surrounding Mrs. Grady's claims have not been ascertained by trial. At this stage we proceed, as did the bankruptcy court, on her complaint and an affidavit filed by her.

On October 15, 1985 (almost two months after Robins filed its petition for reorganization), Mrs. Grady filed a civil action against Robins in the United States District Court for the Northern District of California. The case was subsequently transferred to the Eastern District of Virginia.

Mrs. Grady then filed a motion in the bankruptcy court, seeking a decision that her claim did not arise before the filing of the petition so that it would not be stayed by the automatic stay provision of the Code. If the claim arose when the Dalkon Shield was inserted into her, the district court reasoned, then it would be considered a claim under the Bankruptcy Code and its prosecution would be stayed by the provisions of 11 U.S.C. § 362(a)(1). If, however, the claim was found to arise when the injuries became apparent, then it might not be a claim for bankruptcy purposes and the automatic stay provision would be inapplicable.

The bankruptcy court determined that Mrs. Grady's claim against Robins arose when the acts giving rise to Robins' liability were performed, not when the harm caused by those acts was manifested. The court rejected Mrs. Grady's contention that the court must look to state law to determine when her cause of action accrued and equate that with a right to payment. It concluded that the court must follow federal law in determining when the claim arose. It held that the right to payment under 11 U.S.C. § 101(4)(A) of Mrs. Grady's claim arose when the acts giving rise to the liability were performed and thus the claim was pre-petition under 11 U.S.C. § 362(a)(1)....

We commence with the proposition that "... except where federal law, fully apart from bankruptcy, has created obligations by the exercise of power granted to the federal government, a claim implies the existence of an obligation created by State law." ... So, the bankruptcy Code is superimposed upon the law of the State which has created the obligation. Congress has the undoubted power under the bankruptcy article, U.S. Const. Art. I, § 8 cl. 4, to define and classify claims against the estate of a bankrupt. In the case of a claim as noted above, the legislative history shows that Congress intended that all legal obligations of the debtor, no matter how remote or contingent, will be able to be dealt with in bankruptcy. The Code contemplates the broadest possible relief in the bankruptcy court. Also, that history tells us that the automatic stay is one of the fundamental debtor protections provided by the bankruptcy laws. It provides a breathing spell to the debtor to restructure his affairs, which could hardly be done with hundreds or thousands of creditors persevering in different courts all over the country for a first share of a debtor's assets. Absent a stay of litigation against the debtor, dismemberment rather than reorganization would, in many or even most cases, be the inevitable result....

Mrs. Grady's claim, as well as whatever rights the other Future Tort Claimants have, is undoubtedly "contingent." It depends upon a future uncertain event, that event being the manifestation of injury from use of the Dalkon Shield. We do not believe that there must be a right to the immediate payment of money in the case of a tort or allied breach of warranty or like claim, as present here, when the acts constituting the tort or breach of warranty have occurred prior to the filing of the petition, to constitute a claim under §362(a)(1). It is at once apparent that there can be no right to the immediate payment of money on account of a claim, the existence of which depends upon a future uncertain event. But it is also apparent that Congress has created a contingent right to payment as it has the power to create a contingent tort or like claim within the protection of §362(a)(1). We are of opinion that it has done so.

Order affirmed.

Notes

1. *Claims relating to pre-petition product defects.* It is extremely important to understand that the indefinite stay applies to pre-petition product *defects* rather than pre-petition products. This might sound like a meaningless distinction since, by definition, it is impossible to have a defective product without having a product at all. Indeed, so far as manufacturing defects and failures to warn are concerned, there will be no practical difference in distinguishing between pre-petition defects and pre-petition products. In both cases, any defect is a characteristic of a specific item: the one cannot exist without the other.

2. *Pre-petition design defects.* The significance of the distinction becomes apparent, however, in the case of design defects. The point is that any designs alleged to be defective but drawn up before the defendant entered bankruptcy protection must have been defective at the time they were created. While products may be manufactured according to such designs for some time after the defendant exits bankruptcy protection, the date of their manufacture will be relevant only for claims of a manufacturing defect or a failure to warn. For claims of design defect, the relevant date is, naturally, the date of design. Since that was before the defendant entered bankruptcy, such claims will be stayed indefinitely as part of the plan of reorganization that must accompany the defendant's exit from bankruptcy, unless expressly permitted by the plan in accordance with §524(g)(1)(B).

This has happened repeatedly in the asbestos context, albeit that, in those cases, the plan of reorganization incorporated the setting up of special funds designed to pay the future claims that will inevitably be brought. But many reorganization plans include no such provision.

3. *Chrysler.* One recent example involves the emergence from bankruptcy protection in 2009 of the car manufacturer, Chrysler. As part of its plan of reorganization following its abandonment by DaimlerBenz—a plan that also involved a federal bailout to the final tune of an estimated $1.3 billion—Chrysler proposed to the Bankruptcy Court that claims

for design defects should continue to be stayed. The Court agreed, meaning that anyone injured as a result of the defective design of a Chrysler vehicle—and no matter whether they were the owner, passenger, or a complete stranger—is now barred from bringing a claim against the manufacturer for such a defect if the design was drawn up before Chrysler entered bankruptcy protection. Nor do these victims have the ability to make a claim on a trust fund, since the approved plan of reorganization made no provision for the establishment of such a fund. There are around 10 million Chrysler vehicles currently on American roads.

4. *Lemons.* The one concession made in the Chrysler plan was that claims under warranties, "lemon" laws, and rebates would be honored, along with remedial work following a recall. As the Center for Justice and Democracy put it in a Press Release issued in June 2009: "The new company will replace a defective part, but if the part causes an accident or leads to a catastrophic injury or death, the company is off the hook."

5. *Fiat.* The Treasury's decision to go along with this plan while injecting hundreds of millions of dollars of taxpayers' money into Chrysler seems all the odder since the ultimate goal of the reorganization was to make Chrysler a worthwhile acquisition for the Italian manufacturer, Fiat. Yet Fiat had already agreed to assume liability for product liability claims. It appears that the Treasury simply made an unsolicited offer to Fiat that it would have Chrysler ask the Bankruptcy Court to continue the stay.

6. *General Motors.* Chrysler emerged from bankruptcy before its much larger competitor, General Motors (GM), which boasts around 30 million vehicles currently on the road. GM also benefited from Treasury bailout money. At the time, it was widely expected that the plan of reorganization for GM would also involve continuing to stay all product liability actions for defects that occurred before the manufacturer entered bankruptcy protection. In the event, however, the plan that enabled GM to emerge *does* permit *new* products liability claims to be brought. Even so, those who had already filed claims have again been left with no trust fund to pay them, and are simply to be treated as unsecured creditors who can expect no more than pennies on the dollar (if they receive anything at all).

7. *The Asbestos Bankruptcy Paradox.* S. Todd Brown, *Section 524(g) Without Compromise: Voting Rights and the Asbestos Bankruptcy Paradox*, 2008 Col. Bus. L. Rev. 101, 106–107, 109–11 (2008), has highlighted the paradox at the heart of the use of the Bankruptcy Code by manufacturers of defective products:

> When Johns-Manville petitioned for bankruptcy protection in 1982, stunned lawyers and victims' rights advocates were up in arms. As the largest bankruptcy in history at the time, Manville's Chapter 11 was an easy target. Critics railed against the filing as an abuse of the bankruptcy process and an unconscionable tactic to delay payment to the sick and dying. On the surface, these seemingly healthy company with assets in excess of $2 billion and fixed liabilities of roughly $1 billion possibly be a candidate for bankruptcy?

> Unlike its predecessor, however, the new bankruptcy law did not require imminent or actual insolvency for a debtor to be eligible for relief. This was no mere oversight; the insolvency requirement was omitted to serve the goals of "preserving going concerns and maximizing property available to satisfy creditors" by ensuring timely access to the bankruptcy process. And as the principal asbestos personal injury litigation defendant, Manville faced potentially limitless liability …

> Even if the Bankruptcy Code authorized courts to enjoin future claimants from suing the reorganized companies, due process ordinarily requires giving parties

an opportunity to contest the modification of their rights, and it is not possible to provide this opportunity to those who may not become aware of their injury until months or years after plan confirmation. And as much as bankruptcy may vary from ordinary litigation, the mere happenstance that proceedings occur in a bankruptcy forum does not eliminate the obligation to satisfy the dictates of due process. On the other hand, the inability to address future asbestos liability could force an otherwise viable company into liquidation and thereby undermine future victims' prospects for recovery. The preservation of customary due process would come at the cost of the very property rights due process is intended to protect. Thus, binding future claimants in spite of their absence would be to their benefit, as it presumably would be to other constituencies.

Questions

1. What is the explanation for the different treatment of products liability claims in the discharge from bankruptcy of Chrysler and General Motors? Are the differences justifiable?

2. If someone injured by a defective Chrysler is unable to bring an action against the manufacturer, is that person left entirely without a remedy, or can s/he instead seek a remedy elsewhere?

3. Is it appropriate for federal bankruptcy law to trump state products liability laws?

4. Is the Bankruptcy Code being used improperly as a means for businesses who have made bad products to evade their responsibilities?

Chapter 17

Pre-Emption by Federal Law

Sphere of Federal Government

As we saw in Chapter 15, *Erie Railroad Co. v. Tompkins*, 304 U.S. 64, 58 S.Ct. 817 (1938), established that, even when a case is to be tried in federal court, the substantive tort law to be applied is that of the state most relevant to the case at hand. However, the federal Constitution provides that state law will be overridden (or, as it is more commonly expressed, "pre-empted") when Congress has passed a statute which conflicts with state law but which regulates an area within the competence of the federal government.

Constitution of the United States (1788)

Article I, Section 8 — "Commerce Clause"

The Congress shall have Power … To regulate Commerce with foreign Nations, and among the several States, and with the Indian Tribes.

Article I, Section 8 — "Necessary and Proper Clause"

The Congress shall have Power … To make all Laws which shall be necessary and proper for carrying into Execution the foregoing Powers, and all other Powers vested by this Constitution in the Government of the United States, or in any Department or Officer thereof.

Article VI, Clause 2 — "Supremacy Clause"

This Constitution, and the Laws of the United States which shall be made in Pursuance thereof; and all Treaties made, or which shall be made, under the Authority of the United States, shall be the supreme Law of the Land; and the Judges in every State shall be bound thereby, any Thing in the Constitution or Laws of any State to the Contrary notwithstanding.

Notes

1. *Areas of competence.* These three Clauses essentially dictate that, if Congress passes legislation regulating inter-state commerce, then the provisions of that legislation will override, or "pre-empt," any state law — whether created through case law or legislation — with which they conflict. If a state law is pre-empted, this means that is rendered invalid and thus ineffective.

2. *Pre-emption of different types of defect.* It should be noted that pre-emption can work to pre-empt either *all* types of product defect claims, or only certain types of claims (such as design defect claims, or post-sale failure-to-warn claims). The extent of any pre-emption depends on the wording and context of the federal law in question.

3. *Two-part test*. Any argument alleging pre-emption must pass both limbs of a two-part test. First, it must be established that the federal law in question deals with interstate commerce. Apart from the question of damages, tackled in Chapter 15, this test normally presents few problems so far as the laws on products liability are concerned.

The second test, however, is far more problematic: it requires that there is a conflict between federal law and state law. If there is no conflict, then state law can be applied in the usual manner; if there is, the state law in question is effectively rendered null and void. But ambiguity in the drafting of much federal legislation, coupled with controversy over what such a conflict entails, mean that it is often far from clear whether a conflict exists. This is evident from the rash of recent cases before the Supreme Court.

Bruesewitz v. Wyeth
131 S.Ct. 1068 (2011) (SCOTUS)

SCALIA, J. We consider whether a preemption provision enacted in the National Childhood Vaccine Injury Act of 1986 (NCVIA) bars state-law design-defect claims against vaccine manufacturers.

I A

For the last 66 years, vaccines have been subject to the same federal premarket approval process as prescription drugs, and compensation for vaccine-related injuries has been left largely to the States. Under that regime, the elimination of communicable diseases through vaccination became "one of the greatest achievements" of public health in the 20th century. But in the 1970's and 1980s vaccines became, one might say, victims of their own success.

They had been so effective in preventing infectious diseases that the public became much less alarmed at the threat of those diseases, and much more concerned with the risk of injury from the vaccines themselves.

Much of the concern centered around vaccines against diphtheria, tetanus, and pertussis (DTP), which were blamed for children's disabilities and developmental delays. This led to a massive increase in vaccine-related tort litigation. Whereas between 1978 and 1981 only nine product-liability suits were filed against DTP manufacturers, by the mid-1980's the suits numbered more than 200 each year. This destabilized the DTP vaccine market, causing two of the three domestic manufacturers to withdraw; and the remaining manufacturer, Lederle Laboratories, estimated that its potential tort liability exceeded its annual sales by a factor of 200. Vaccine shortages arose when Lederle had production problems in 1984. Despite the large number of suits, there were many complaints that obtaining compensation for legitimate vaccine-inflicted injuries was too costly and difficult. A significant number of parents were already declining vaccination for their children,10 and concerns about compensation threatened to depress vaccination rates even further. This was a source of concern to public health officials, since vaccines are effective in preventing outbreaks of disease only if a large percentage of the population is vaccinated.

To stabilize the vaccine market and facilitate compensation, Congress enacted the NCVIA in 1986. The Act establishes a no-fault compensation program "designed to work faster and with greater ease than the civil tort system." *Shalala v. Whitecotton*, 514 U. S. 268, 269 (1995). A person injured by a vaccine, or his legal guardian, may file a petition for compensation in the United States Court of Federal Claims, naming the Secretary of Health and Human Services as the respondent. A special master then makes an informal adjudication of the petition within (except for two limited exceptions) 240 days. The Court of Federal Claims must review objections to the special master's decision and enter final judgment under a similarly tight statutory deadline. At that point, a claimant has two options: to accept the court's judgment and forgo a traditional tort suit for damages, or to reject the judgment and seek tort relief from the vaccine manufacturer. Fast, informal adjudication is made possible by the Act's Vaccine Injury Table, which lists the vaccines covered under the Act; describes each vaccine's compensable, adverse side effects; and indicates how soon after vaccination those side effects should first manifest themselves. Claimants who show that a listed injury first manifested itself at the appropriate time are prima facie entitled to compensation. No showing of causation is necessary; the Secretary bears the burden of disproving causation. A claimant may also recover for unlisted side effects, and for listed side effects that occur at times other than those specified in the Table, but for those the claimant must prove causation. Unlike in tort suits, claimants under the Act are not required to show that the administered vaccine was defectively manufactured, labeled, or designed.

Successful claimants receive compensation for medical, rehabilitation, counseling, special education, and vocational training expenses; diminished earning capacity; pain and suffering; and $250,000 for vaccine-related deaths. Attorney's fees are provided, not only for successful cases, but even for unsuccessful claims that are not frivolous. These awards are paid out of a fund created by an excise tax on each vaccine dose.

The *quid pro quo* for this, designed to stabilize the vaccine market, was the provision of significant tort-liability protections for vaccine manufacturers. The Act requires claimants to seek relief through the compensation program before filing suit for more than $1,000. Manufacturers are generally immunized from liability for failure to warn if they have complied with all regulatory requirements (including but not limited to warning requirements) and have given the warning either to the claimant or the claimant's physician. They are immunized from liability for punitive damages absent failure to comply with regulatory requirements, "fraud," "intentional and wrongful withholding of information," or other "criminal or illegal activity." And most relevant to the present case, the Act expressly eliminates liability for a vaccine's unavoidable, adverse side effects:

> No vaccine manufacturer shall be liable in a civil action for damages arising from a vaccine-related injury or death associated with the administration of a vaccine after October 1, 1988, if the injury or death resulted from side effects that were unavoidable even though the vaccine was properly prepared and was accompanied by proper directions and warnings.

B

The vaccine at issue here is a DTP vaccine manufactured by Lederle Laboratories. It first received federal approval in 1948 and received supplemental approvals in 1953 and 1970. Respondent Wyeth purchased Lederle in 1994 and stopped manufacturing the vaccine in 1998. Hannah Bruesewitz was born on October 20, 1991. Her pediatrician administered doses of the DTP vaccine according to the Center for Disease Control's recommended childhood immunization schedule. Within 24 hours of her April 1992 vaccination, Hannah started to experience seizures. She suffered over 100 seizures during the next month, and her doctors eventually diagnosed her with "residual seizure disorder" and "developmental delay." Hannah, now a teenager, is still diagnosed with both conditions.

In April 1995, Hannah's parents, Russell and Robalee Bruesewitz, filed a vaccine injury petition in the United States Court of Federal Claims, alleging that Hannah suffered from on-Table residual seizure disorder and encephalopathy injuries. A Special Master denied their claims on various grounds, though they were awarded $126,800 in attorney's fees and costs. The Bruesewitzes elected to reject the unfavorable judgment, and in October 2005 filed this lawsuit in Pennsylvania state court. Their complaint alleged (as relevant here) that defective design of Lederle's DTP vaccine caused Hannah's disabilities, and that Lederle was subject to strict liability, and liability for negligent design, under Pennsylvania common law.

II A

We set forth again the statutory text at issue:

> No vaccine manufacturer shall be liable in a civil action for damages arising from a vaccine-related injury or death associated with the administration of a vaccine after October 1, 1988, if the injury or death resulted from side effects that were unavoidable even though the vaccine was properly prepared and was accompanied by proper directions and warnings.

The "even though" clause clarifies the word that precedes it. It delineates the preventative measures that a vaccine manufacturer must have taken for a side-effect to be considered "unavoidable" under the statute. Provided that there was proper manufacture and warning, any remaining side effects, including those resulting from design defects, are deemed to have been unavoidable. State-law design-defect claims are therefore preempted.

If a manufacturer could be held liable for failure to use a different design, the word "unavoidable" would do no work. A side effect of a vaccine could always have been avoidable by use of a differently designed vaccine not containing the harmful element. The language of the provision thus suggests that the design of the vaccine is a given, not subject to question in the tort action. What the statute establishes as a complete defense must be unavoidability (given safe manufacture and warning) with respect to the particular design. Which plainly implies that the design itself is not open to question.

A further textual indication leads to the same conclusion. Products-liability law establishes a classic and well known triumvirate of grounds for liability: defective manufacture, inadequate directions or warnings, and defective design. If all three were intended to be preserved, it would be strange to mention specifically only two, and leave the third to implication. It would have been much easier (and much more natural) to provide that manufacturers would be liable for "defective manufacture, defective directions or warning, and defective design." It seems that the statute fails to mention design-defect liability "by deliberate choice, not inadvertence." *Barnhart v. Peabody Coal Co.*, 537 U. S. 149, 168 (2003). *Expressio unius, exclusio alterius.*

Judgment of the Court of Appeals affirmed.

Questions

1. If it had been found that the vaccine given to Hannah had not conformed to its intended design, could the manufacturer have been liable for a manufacturing defect, or would such a claim have been pre-empted too?

2. If no-fault compensation programs are "designed to work faster and with greater ease than the civil tort system," why are there not more of them? Are there other types of product that would be just as amenable to a no-fault scheme as vaccines?

Types of Pre-Emption

Bruesewitz is an example of express pre-emption: although the statute was not exactly crystal clear, it did expressly pre-empt a regular (state law) claim in tort. However, federal law may not only pre-empt state law expressly; it may also do so by implication. In fact, the bigger issue has been that three competing theories currently vie for adoption by the courts as to what constitutes implied pre-emption. These are:

1. Conflict pre-emption, which requires that there must be an actual conflict between what federal law and state law either permit or require, such that it is impossible to comply with both;

2. Frustration pre-emption, where the application of state law conflicts with (and therefore would frustrate) the objectives of a federal statute; and

3. Field pre-emption, where the fact that the federal government has legislated within a given field means that it is now off-limits to state law.

Conflict pre-emption is not particularly controversial, since virtually everyone recognizes that state law must be pre-empted when compliance with it would make it impossible to comply with federal law at the same time. There is, however, significant controversy over the appropriate answers to the following questions:

1. Should the notion of implied pre-emption should go further than just conflict pre-emption?

2. If it should, should it stop at frustration pre-emption, or should it go all the way to field pre-emption?

3. If frustration pre-emption is recognized, how are the purposes of a federal law (whether in the form of a primary statute or regulations) to be identified, and what is meant by the notion of "frustration"?

4. If field pre-emption is recognized, how is the relevant "field" to be identified, and what sort of "trigger" for pre-empting that field is required?

The case below illustrates some of the differences between express pre-emption and the first two approaches (conflict and frustration pre-emption respectively) to implied pre-emption.

Geier v. American Honda Motor Co.
529 U.S. 861 (2000) (SCOTUS)

BREYER, J. This case focuses on the 1984 version of a Federal Motor Vehicle Safety Standard promulgated by the Department of Transportation under the authority of the National Traffic and Motor Vehicle Safety Act of 1966, 80 Stat. 718, 15 U.S.C. § 1381 et seq. (1988 ed.). The standard, FMVSS 208, required auto manufacturers to equip some but not all of their 1987 vehicles with passive restraints. We ask whether the Act pre-empts a state common-law tort action in which the plaintiff claims that the defendant auto manufacturer, who was in compliance with the standard, should nonetheless have equipped a 1987 automobile with airbags. We conclude that the Act, taken together with FMVSS 208, pre-empts the lawsuit.

In 1992, petitioner Alexis Geier, driving a 1987 Honda Accord, collided with a tree and was seriously injured. The car was equipped with manual shoulder and lap belts which Geier had buckled up at the time. The car was not equipped with airbags or other passive restraint devices.

Geier and her parents, also petitioners, sued the car's manufacturer, American Honda Motor Company, Inc., and its affiliates (hereinafter American Honda), under District of Columbia tort law. They claimed, among other things, that American Honda had designed its car negligently and defectively because it lacked a driver's side airbag. The District Court dismissed the lawsuit. The court noted that FMVSS 208 gave car manufacturers a choice as to whether to install airbags. And the court concluded that petitioners' lawsuit, because it sought to establish a different safety standard—i.e., an airbag requirement—was expressly pre-empted by a provision of the Act which pre-empts "any safety standard" that is not identical to a federal safety standard applicable to the same aspect of performance, 15 U.S.C. § 1392(d) (1988 ed.); Civ. No. 95-CV-0064 (D.D.C., Dec. 9, 1997), App. 17. (We, like the courts below and the parties, refer to the pre-1994 version of the statute throughout the opinion; it has been recodified at 49 U.S.C. § 30101 et seq.)

The Court of Appeals agreed with the District Court's conclusion but on somewhat different reasoning. It had doubts, given the existence of the Act's "saving" clause, 15 U.S.C. § 1397(k) (1988 ed.), that petitioners' lawsuit involved the potential creation of the kind of "safety standard" to which the Safety Act's express pre-emption provision refers. But it declined to resolve that question because it found that petitioners' state-law tort claims posed an obstacle to the accomplishment of FMVSS 208's objectives. For that reason, it found that those claims conflicted with FMVSS 208, and that, under ordinary pre-emption principles, the Act consequently pre-empted the lawsuit. The Court of Appeals thus affirmed the District Court's dismissal.

Several state courts have held to the contrary, namely, that neither the Act's express pre-emption nor FMVSS 208 pre-empts a "no airbag" tort suit.... All of the Federal Circuit Courts that have considered the question, however, have found pre-emption. One rested its conclusion on the Act's express pre-emption provision. See, e.g., *Harris v. Ford Motor Co.*, 110 F.3d 1410, 1413–1415 (C.A.9 1997). Others, such as the Court of Appeals below, have instead found pre-emption under ordinary pre-emption principles by virtue of the conflict such suits pose to FMVSS 208's objectives, and thus to the Act itself.... We granted certiorari to resolve these differences. We now hold that this kind of "no airbag" lawsuit conflicts with the objectives of FMVSS 208, a standard authorized by the Act, and is therefore pre-empted by the Act.

In reaching our conclusion, we consider three subsidiary questions. First, does the Act's express pre-emption provision pre-empt this lawsuit? We think not. Second, do ordinary pre-emption principles nonetheless apply? We hold that they do. Third, does this lawsuit actually conflict with FMVSS 208, hence with the Act itself? We hold that it does.

We first ask whether the Safety Act's express pre-emption provision pre-empts this tort action. The provision reads as follows:

> Whenever a Federal motor vehicle safety standard established under this subchapter is in effect, no State or political subdivision of a State shall have any authority either to establish, or to continue in effect, with respect to any motor vehicle or item of motor vehicle equipment[,] any safety standard applicable to the same aspect of performance of such vehicle or item of equipment which is not identical to the Federal standard. 15 U.S.C. § 1392(d) (1988 ed.).

American Honda points out that a majority of this Court has said that a somewhat similar statutory provision in a different federal statute—a provision that uses the word "requirements"—may well expressly pre-empt similar tort actions. See, e.g., *Medtronic, Inc. v. Lohr*, 518 U.S. 470, 502–504, (1996) (plurality opinion). Petitioners reply that this statute speaks of pre-empting a state-law "safety standard," not a "requirement," and that a tort action does not involve a safety standard. Hence, they conclude, the express pre-emption provision does not apply.

We need not determine the precise significance of the use of the word "standard," rather than "requirement," however, for the Act contains another provision, which resolves the disagreement. That provision, a "saving" clause, says that "[c]ompliance with" a federal safety standard "does not exempt any person from any liability under common law." 15 U.S.C. § 1397(k) (1988 ed.). The saving clause assumes that there are some significant number of common-law liability cases to save. And a reading of the express pre-emption provision that excludes common-law tort actions gives actual meaning to the saving clause's literal language, while leaving adequate room for state tort law to operate — for example, where federal law creates only a floor, *i.e.*, a minimum safety standard. See, *e.g.*, Brief for United States as Amicus Curiae 21 (explaining that common-law claim that a vehicle is defectively designed because it lacks antilock brakes would not be pre-empted by 49 C.F.R. § 571.105 (1999), a safety standard establishing minimum requirements for brake performance). Without the saving clause, a broad reading of the express pre-emption provision arguably might pre-empt those actions, for, as we have just mentioned, it is possible to read the pre-emption provision, standing alone, as applying to standards imposed in common-law tort actions, as well as standards contained in state legislation or regulations. And if so, it would pre-empt all nonidentical state standards established in tort actions covering the same aspect of performance as an applicable federal standard, even if the federal standard merely established a minimum standard. On that broad reading of the pre-emption clause little, if any, potential "liability at common law" would remain. And few, if any, state tort actions would remain for the saving clause to save. We have found no convincing indication that Congress wanted to pre-empt, not only state statutes and regulations, but also common-law tort actions, in such circumstances. Hence the broad reading cannot be correct. The language of the pre-emption provision permits a narrow reading that excludes common-law actions. Given the presence of the saving clause, we conclude that the pre-emption clause must be so read.

We have just said that the saving clause at least removes tort actions from the scope of the express pre-emption clause. Does it do more? In particular, does it foreclose or limit the operation of ordinary pre-emption principles insofar as those principles instruct us to read statutes as pre-empting state laws (including common-law rules) that "actually conflict" with the statute or federal standards promulgated thereunder? Petitioners concede, as they must in light of *Freightliner Corp. v. Myrick*, 514 U.S. 280, 115 S.Ct. 1483 (1995), that the pre-emption provision, by itself, does not foreclose (through negative implication) "any possibility of implied [conflict] pre-emption". But they argue that the saving clause has that very effect.

We recognize that, when this Court previously considered the pre-emptive effect of the statute's language, it appeared to leave open the question of how, or the extent to which, the saving clause saves state-law tort actions that conflict with federal regulations promulgated under the Act. We now conclude that the saving clause (like the express pre-emption provision) does not bar the ordinary working of conflict pre-emption principles.

Nothing in the language of the saving clause suggests an intent to save state-law tort actions that conflict with federal regulations. The words "[c]ompliance" and "does not exempt," 15 U.S.C. § 1397(k) (1988 ed.), sound as if they simply bar a special kind of defense, namely, a defense that compliance with a federal standard automatically exempts a defendant from state law, whether the Federal Government meant that standard to be an absolute requirement or only a minimum one. See Restatement (Third) of Torts: Products Liability § 4(b), Comment e (1997) (distinguishing between state-law compliance defense and a federal claim of pre-emption). It is difficult to understand why Congress would have insisted on a compliance-with-federal-regulation precondition to the provision's applicability had it wished the Act to "save" all state-law tort actions, regardless of their potential threat to the objectives of federal safety standards promulgated under that Act. Nor does our interpretation conflict with the purpose of the saving provision, say, by rendering it ineffectual. As we have previously explained, the saving provision still makes clear that the express pre-emption provision does not of its own force pre-empt common-law tort actions. And it thereby preserves those actions that seek to establish greater safety than the minimum safety achieved by a federal regulation intended to provide a floor.

Moreover, this Court has repeatedly "decline[d] to give broad effect to saving clauses where doing so would upset the careful regulatory scheme established by federal law." We find this concern applicable in the present case. And we conclude that the saving clause foresees—it does not foreclose—the possibility that a federal safety standard will pre-empt a state common-law tort action with which it conflicts. We do not understand the dissent to disagree, for it acknowledges that ordinary pre-emption principles apply, at least sometimes. . . .

The basic question, then, is whether a common-law "no airbag" action like the one before us actually conflicts with FMVSS 208. We hold that it does. In petitioners' and the dissent's view, FMVSS 208 sets a minimum airbag standard. As far as FMVSS 208 is concerned, the more airbags, and the sooner, the better. But that was not the Secretary's view. The Department of Transportation's (DOT's) comments, which accompanied the promulgation of FMVSS 208, make clear that the standard deliberately provided the manufacturer with a range of choices among different passive restraint devices. Those choices would bring about a mix of different devices introduced gradually over time; and FMVSS 208 would thereby lower costs, overcome technical safety problems, encourage technological development, and win widespread consumer acceptance—all of which would promote FMVSS 208's safety objectives. . . .

In effect, petitioners' tort action depends upon its claim that manufacturers had a duty to install an airbag when they manufactured the 1987 Honda Accord. Such a state law—*i.e.*, a rule of state tort law imposing such a duty—by its terms would have required manufacturers of all similar cars to install airbags rather than other passive restraint systems, such as automatic belts or passive interiors. It thereby would have presented an obstacle to the variety and mix of devices that the federal regulation sought. It would have required all manufacturers to have installed airbags in respect to the entire District-of-Columbia-related portion of their 1987 new car fleet, even though FMVSS 208 at that time required only that 10% of a manufacturer's nationwide fleet be equipped with any passive restraint device at all. It thereby also would have stood as an obstacle to the gradual passive restraint phase-in that the federal regulation deliberately imposed. In addition, it could have made less likely the adoption of a state mandatory buckle-up law. Because the rule of law for which petitioners contend would have stood "as an obstacle to the accomplishment and execution of" the important means-related federal objectives that we have just discussed, it is pre-empted.

Judgment of the Court of Appeals affirmed.

Notes

1. *Interpreting Geier.* In *Williamson v. Mazda Motor of America, Inc.*, 131 S.Ct. 1131, 1135–36 (2011), the Supreme Court considered an updated version of FMVSS 208 in re-

lation to seatbelts. This gave manufacturers a choice as to whether to install either simple lap belts or lap-and-shoulder belts on rear inner seats. In a judgement given once again by Justice Breyer, the Court noted that, just as in *Geier*, the statute's express pre-emption clause could not pre-empt the common-law tort action; but neither could its saving clause foreclose or limit the operation of ordinary conflict pre-emption principles. The Court consequently turned to the question of, whether, in fact, the state tort action conflicted with the federal regulation.

In an opinion which demonstrates the significance of identifying the purposes underlying a federal law in order to determine whether upholding a state law claim would frustrate them, Justice Breyer opined, 131 S.Ct. at 1136–37:

> At the heart of *Geier* lies our determination that giving auto manufacturers a choice among different kinds of passive restraint devices was a significant objective of the federal regulation. We reached this conclusion on the basis of our examination of the regulation, including its history, the promulgating agency's contemporaneous explanation of its objectives, and the agency's current views of the regulation's pre-emptive effect....
>
> We turn now to the present case. Like the regulation in *Geier*, the regulation here leaves the manufacturer with a choice. And, like the tort suit in *Geier*, the tort suit here would restrict that choice. But unlike *Geier*, we do not believe here that choice is a significant regulatory objective.

Because the Court held that there was no regulatory objective to maintain manufacturer choice, the state tort claim could not be pre-empted. *Geier* and *Williamson* are thus cases where the theory of frustration pre-emption has been applied, but where the identification of different federal objectives has led to different conclusions being drawn by a majority of the Supreme Court.

2. *Justice Sotomayor's concurrence.* Justice Sotomayor spelt out the distinction between *Geier* and *Williamson* a little more starkly. She wrote, 131 S.Ct. at 1140:

> *Geier* does not stand, as the California Court of Appeal, other courts, and some of respondents' *amici* seem to believe, for the proposition that any time an agency gives manufacturers a choice between two or more options, a tort suit that imposes liability on the basis of one of the options is an obstacle to the achievement of a federal regulatory objective and may be pre-empted. Rather, *Geier* turned on the fact that the agency, via Federal Motor Vehicle Safety Standard 208, "deliberately sought variety—a mix of several different passive restraint systems." 529 U.S., at 878. As the United States notes, "a conflict results only when the Safety Act (or regulations implementing the Safety Act) does not just set out options for compliance, but also provides that the regulated parties must remain free to choose among those options." Brief for United States as *Amicus Curiae* 8. In other words, the mere fact that an agency regulation allows manufacturers a choice between options is insufficient to justify implied pre-emption; courts should only find pre-emption where evidence exists that an agency has a regulatory objective—*e.g.*, obtaining a mix of passive restraint mechanisms, as in *Geier*—whose achievement depends on manufacturers having a choice between options. A link between a regulatory objective and the need for manufacturer choice to achieve that objective is the lynchpin of implied pre-emption when there is a saving clause.

3. *Justice Thomas's concurrence.* Justice Thomas thought that, while *Williamson* was correctly decided, *Geier* was wrong. Indeed, he thought both cases were much more straightforward than his fellow justices had made them. He argued, 131 S.Ct. at 1141–42:

The plain text of the Safety Act resolves this case. Congress has instructed that "[c]ompliance with a motor vehicle safety standard prescribed under this chapter does not exempt a person from liability at common law." This saving clause "explicitly preserv[es] state common-law actions." *Wyeth v. Levine*, 129 S.Ct. 1187, 1214, (2009) (THOMAS, J., concurring in judgment). Here, Mazda complied with FMVSS 208 when it chose to install a simple lap belt. According to Mazda, the Williamsons' lawsuit alleging that it should have installed a lap-and-shoulder seatbelt instead is pre-empted. That argument is foreclosed by the saving clause; the Williamsons' state tort action is not pre-empted.

The majority does not rely on the Safety Act's saving clause because this Court effectively read it out of the statute in *Geier v. American Honda Motor Co.*, 529 U.S. 861, 120 S.Ct. 1913 (2000). In *Geier*, the Court interpreted the saving clause as simply cancelling out the statute's express pre-emption clause with respect to common-law tort actions. This left the Court free to consider the effect of conflict pre-emption principles on such tort actions.

But it makes no sense to read the express pre-emption clause in conjunction with the saving clause. The express pre-emption clause bars States from having any safety "standard applicable to the same aspect of performance" as a federal standard unless it is "identical" to the federal one. § 30103(b). That clause pre-empts States from establishing "objective rule[s] prescribed by a legislature or an administrative agency" in competition with the federal standards; it says nothing about the tort lawsuits that are the focus of the saving clause. Read independently of the express pre-emption clause, the saving clause simply means what it says: FMVSS 208 does not pre-empt state common-law actions.

Questions

1. What is the difference between the antilock brake example and the case brought by Alexis Geier?

2. Do you accept the reasoning of the majority in *Williamson* as to the difference between that case and *Geier*, or do you prefer the view of Justice Thomas?

3. If, in *Geier*, (a) FMVSS 208 had, instead, mandated that every car be fitted with airbags, and that these must comply with a specific set of standards, and (b) Honda had complied with this version of FMVSS 208, would it be possible for someone injured in a car accident (despite the deployment of the airbags as designed) to claim that the design was defective because it was not as good as that fitted in other automobiles, or would such a claim also be pre-empted?

4. How ready should the courts be to find implied pre-emption of a state common-law action?

Restatement (Third) of Torts: Products Liability (1998)

§ 4. Noncompliance and Compliance with Product Safety Statutes or Regulations

In connection with liability for defective design or inadequate instructions or warnings:

(a) a product's noncompliance with an applicable product safety statute or administrative regulation renders the product defective with respect to the risks sought to be reduced by the statute or regulation; and

(b) a product's compliance with an applicable product safety statute or regulation is properly considered in determining whether the product is defective with respect to the risks sought to be reduced by the statute or regulation, but such compliance does not preclude as a matter of law a finding of product defect.

Comment e. Compliance with product safety statute or administrative regulation.

An important distinction must be drawn between the subject addressed in Subsection (b) and the matter of federal preemption of state products liability law. Subsection (b) addresses the question of whether and to what extent, as a matter of state tort law, compliance with product safety statutes or administrative regulations affects liability for product defectiveness. When a court concludes that a defendant is not liable by reason of having complied with a safety design or warnings statute or regulation, it is deciding that the product in question is not defective as a matter of the law of that state. The safety statute or regulation may be a federal provision, but the decision to give it determinative effect is a state-law determination. In contrast, in federal preemption, the court decides as a matter of federal law that the relevant federal statute or regulation reflects, expressly or impliedly, the intent of Congress to displace state law, including state tort law, with the federal statute or regulation. The question of preemption is thus a question of federal law, and a determination that there is pre-emption nullifies otherwise operational state law.

Notes

1. ***Compliance with federal standards as a defense.*** One of the points in *Geier* was considered again in *Bic Pen Corp. v. Carter*, 171 S.W.3d 657, 666 (Tex.App.2005). The mother of a girl, who was severely burned after her younger brother set fire to her dress with a child-resistant disposable lighter, brought an action which alleged manufacturing and design defects against the lighter's manufacturer. The jury found for the plaintiff and made a multimillion-dollar award of compensation. The verdict was affirmed on appeal, where it was held that sufficient factual and legal evidence existed to show that the lighter contained a design defect that resulted in the child's injuries, despite the defendant's claim that it was entitled to a presumption that there was no design defect because of its compliance with the federal child-safety regulations issued under the Consumer Product Safety Act (CPSA) of 1972. The court pointed out that the CPSA expressly stated that compliance with federal standards did not relieve a party from liability at common law.

2. ***Consumer Product Safety Commission and pre-emption.*** The CPSA does, however, mean that many allegations regarding post-sale failures to warn (including claims that certain products should have been recalled because of known defects) will be pre-empted. The CPSA created the Consumer Product Safety Commission (CSPC), an independent federal regulatory agency, to act as the Act's "gatekeeper" in order to:

1.   Protect the public against unreasonable risks of injury associated with consumer products;

2.   Assist in evaluating the comparative safety of consumer products;

3.   Develop uniform safety standards for consumer products and to minimize conflicting State and local regulations; and

4.   Promote research and investigation into the causes and prevention of product-related deaths, illnesses, and injuries.

With a remit that covers around 15,000 types of consumer products, the CPSC has the ability to insist on manufacturers' issuing recalls. This sets out when manufacturers, importers, distributers, and retailers must report hazards in consumer products. If the CPSC determines a product is "substantially hazardous," it will enter into negotiations with the relevant company or companies to assess the logistics of any recall campaign. It is clear that any allegation that a product within the CPSC's remit should have been subject to a post-sale duty to warn or a recall will be subject to implied or conflict pre-emption by the CPSA. Nevertheless, in response to growing concerns over the cumbersome nature of this system, the CPSC instituted in 1997 a Fast-Track Recall Process, which permits companies to begin a recall process without the CPSC's making the preliminary determination that a product is substantially hazardous. A company simply proposes a recall plan within twenty days of reporting the danger to the CPSC and, if the Commission accepts it, the company can begin the recall campaign immediately.

3. *Recalls revisited.* Similarly, a United States District Court for the District of Massachusetts held, in *National Women's Health v. A.H. Robins Co.*, 545 F. Supp 1177 (1982), that the plaintiffs' application for a court-ordered recall of the Dalkon Shield I.U.D. was pre-empted by the Federal Food, Drug and Cosmetic Act. The court held that:

> As the legislative history discussed previously indicates, Congress intended the Secretary of the FDA to have discretion as to when to seek recall. Since the federal interest in this area is "dominant" and the regulatory scheme is "pervasive," pre-emption must follow. Under the FDCA it is apparent that medical devices, and IUDs in particular, are to be regulated by the FDA through federal law.

Riegel v. Medtronic, Inc.
128 S.Ct. 999 (2008) (SCOTUS)

SCALIA, J. We consider whether the pre-emption clause enacted in the Medical Device Amendments of 1976, 21 U.S.C. § 360k, bars common-law claims challenging the safety and effectiveness of a medical device given premarket approval by the Food and Drug Administration (FDA).

The Federal Food, Drug, and Cosmetic Act (FDCA), 52 Stat. 1040, as amended, 21 U.S.C. § 301 et seq., has long required FDA approval for the introduction of new drugs into the market. Until the statutory enactment at issue here, however, the introduction of new medical devices was left largely for the States to supervise as they saw fit. See *Medtronic, Inc. v. Lohr*, 518 U.S. 470, 475–476, 116 S.Ct. 2240 (1996).

The regulatory landscape changed in the 1960's and 1970's, as complex devices proliferated and some failed. Most notably, the Dalkon Shield intrauterine device, introduced in 1970, was linked to serious infections and several deaths, not to mention a large number of pregnancies. Thousands of tort claims followed. In the view of many, the Dalkon Shield failure and its aftermath demonstrated the inability of the common-law tort system to manage the risks associated with dangerous devices. Several States adopted regulatory measures, including California, which in 1970 enacted a law requiring premarket approval of medical devices. 1970 Cal. Stats. ch. 1573, §§ 26670–26693; see also Leflar & Adler, The Pre-emption Pentad: Federal Pre-emption of Products Liability Claims After *Medtronic*, 64 Tenn. L. Rev. 691, 703, n. 66 (1997) (identifying 13 state statutes governing medical devices as of 1976).

Congress stepped in with passage of the Medical Device Amendments of 1976 (MDA), 21 U.S.C. § 360c et seq., which swept back some state obligations and imposed a regime of detailed federal oversight. The MDA includes an express pre-emption provision that states:

> Except as provided in subsection (b) of this section, no State or political subdivision of a State may establish or continue in effect with respect to a device intended for human use any requirement—
>
> (1) which is different from, or in addition to, any requirement applicable under this chapter to the device, and
>
> (2) which relates to the safety or effectiveness of the device or to any other matter included in a requirement applicable to the device under this chapter. § 360k(a)....

The new regulatory regime established various levels of oversight for medical devices, depending on the risks they present. Class I, which includes such devices as elastic bandages and examination gloves, is subject to the lowest level of oversight: "general controls," such as labeling requirements. Class II, which includes such devices as powered wheelchairs and surgical drapes, is subject in addition to "special controls" such as performance standards and postmarket surveillance measures, § 360c(a)(1)(B).

The devices receiving the most federal oversight are those in Class III, which include replacement heart valves, implanted cerebella stimulators, and pacemaker pulse generators. In general, a device is assigned to Class III if it cannot be established that a less stringent classification would provide reasonable assurance of safety and effectiveness, and the device is "purported or represented to be for a use in supporting or sustaining human life or for a use which is of substantial importance in preventing impairment of human health," or "presents a potential unreasonable risk of illness or injury." § 360c(a)(1)(C)(ii)....

The agency's review of devices for substantial equivalence is known as the § 510(k) process, named after the section of the MDA describing the review. Most new Class III devices enter the market through § 510(k). In 2005, for example, the FDA authorized the marketing of 3,148 devices under § 510(k) and granted premarket approval to just 32 devices.

Premarket approval is a "rigorous" process. A manufacturer must submit what is typically a multivolume application. It includes, among other things, full reports of all studies and investigations of the device's safety and effectiveness that have been published or should reasonably be known to the applicant; a "full statement" of the device's "components, ingredients, and properties and of the principle or principles of operation"; "a full description of the methods used in, and the facilities and controls used for, the manufacture, processing, and, when relevant, packing and installation of, such device"; samples or device components required by the FDA; and a specimen of the proposed labeling. § 360e(c)(1). Before deciding whether to approve the application, the agency may refer it to a panel of outside experts, and may request additional data from the manufacturer, § 360e(c)(1)(G).

The FDA spends an average of 1,200 hours reviewing each application, and grants premarket approval only if it finds there is a "reasonable assurance" of the device's "safety and effectiveness," § 360e(d). The agency must "weig[h] any probable benefit to health from the use of the device against any probable risk of injury or illness from such use." § 360c(a)(2)(C). It may thus approve devices that present great risks if they nonetheless offer great benefits in light of available alternatives. It approved, for example, under its Humanitarian Device Exemption procedures, a ventricular assist device for children with failing hearts, even though the survival rate of children using the device was less than 50 percent. The premarket approval process includes review of the device's proposed labeling. The FDA evaluates safety and effectiveness under the conditions of use set forth on the label, § 360c(a)(2)(B), and must determine that the proposed labeling is neither false nor misleading, § 360e(d)(1)(A).

After completing its review, the FDA may grant or deny premarket approval. § 360e(d). It may also condition approval on adherence to performance standards, 21 CFR § 861.1(b)(3), restrictions upon sale or distribution, or compliance with other requirements, § 814.82. The agency is also free to impose device-specific restrictions by regulation. § 360j(e)(1). If the FDA is unable to approve a new device in its proposed form, it may send an "approvable letter" indicating that the device could be approved if the applicant submitted specified information or agreed to certain conditions or restrictions. 21 CFR § 814.44(e). Alternatively, the agency may send a "not approvable" letter, listing the grounds that justify denial and, where practical, measures that the applicant could undertake to make the device approvable. § 814.44(f).

Once a device has received premarket approval, the MDA forbids the manufacturer to make, without FDA permission, changes in design specifications, manufacturing processes, labeling, or any other attribute, that would affect safety or effectiveness. § 360e(d)(6)(A)(i). If the applicant wishes to make such a change, it must submit, and the FDA must approve, an application for supplemental premarket approval, to be evaluated under largely the same criteria as an initial application. § 360e(d)(6); 21 CFR § 814.39(c).

After premarket approval, the devices are subject to reporting requirements. § 360i. These include the obligation to inform the FDA of new clinical investigations or scientific studies concerning the device which the applicant knows of or reasonably should know of, 21 CFR § 814.84(b)(2), and to report incidents in which the device may have caused or contributed to death or serious injury, or malfunctioned in a manner that would likely cause or contribute to death or serious injury if it recurred, § 803.50(a). The FDA has the power to withdraw pre-market approval based on newly reported data or existing information and must withdraw approval if it determines that a device is unsafe or ineffective under the conditions in its labeling. § 360e(e)(1); see also § 360h(e) (recall authority).

Except as otherwise indicated, the facts set forth in this section appear in the opinion of the Court of Appeals. The device at issue is an Evergreen Balloon Catheter marketed by defendant-respondent Medtronic, Inc. It is a Class III device that received premarket approval from the FDA in 1994; changes to its label received supplemental approvals in 1995 and 1996. Charles Riegel underwent coronary angioplasty in 1996, shortly after suffering a myocardial infarction. His right coronary artery was diffusely diseased and heavily calcified. Riegel's doctor inserted the Evergreen Balloon Catheter into his patient's coronary artery in an attempt to dilate the artery, although the device's labeling stated that use was contraindicated for patients with diffuse or calcified stenoses. The label also warned that the catheter should not be inflated beyond its rated burst pressure of eight atmospheres. Riegel's doctor inflated the catheter five times, to a pressure of 10 atmospheres; on its fifth inflation, the catheter ruptured. Riegel developed a heart block, was placed on life support, and underwent emergency coronary bypass surgery.

Riegel and his wife Donna brought this lawsuit in April 1999, in the United States District Court for the Northern District of New York. Their complaint alleged that Medtronic's catheter was designed, labeled, and manufactured in a manner that violated New York common law, and that these defects caused Riegel to suffer severe and permanent injuries. The complaint raised a number of common-law claims. The District Court held that the MDA pre-empted Riegel's claims of strict liability; breach of implied warranty; and negligence in the design, testing, inspection, distribution, labeling, marketing, and sale of the catheter. It also held that the MDA pre-empted a negligent manufacturing claim insofar as it was not premised on the theory that Medtronic violated federal law. Finally, the court concluded that the MDA pre-empted Donna Riegel's claim for loss of consortium to the extent it was derivative of the pre-empted claims.

The United States Court of Appeals for the Second Circuit affirmed these dismissals. The court concluded that Medtronic was "clearly subject to the federal, device-specific requirement of adhering to the standards contained in its individual, federally approved" premarket approval application. The Riegels' claims were pre-empted because they "would, if successful, impose state requirements that differed from, or added to" the device-specific federal requirements. We granted certiorari.

Since the MDA expressly pre-empts only state requirements "different from, or in addition to, any requirement applicable … to the device" under federal law, § 360k(a)(1), we must determine whether the Federal Government has established requirements applicable to Medtronic's catheter. If so, we must then determine whether the Riegels' common-law claims are based upon New York requirements with respect to the device that are "different from, or in addition to" the federal ones, and that relate to safety and effectiveness. § 360k(a).

We turn to the first question. In *Lohr*, a majority of this Court interpreted the MDA's pre-emption provision in a manner "substantially informed" by the FDA regulation set forth at 21CFR § 808.1(d). That regulation says that state requirements are pre-empted "only when the Food and Drug Administration has established specific counterpart regulations or there are other specific requirements applicable to a particular device…." 21 CFR § 808.1(d). Informed by the regulation, we concluded that federal manufacturing and labeling requirements applicable across the board to almost all medical devices did not pre-empt the common-law claims of negligence and strict liability at issue in *Lohr*. The federal requirements, we said, were not requirements specific to the device in question—they reflected "entirely generic concerns about device regulation generally." While we disclaimed a conclusion that general federal requirements could never pre-empt, or general state duties never be pre-empted, we held that no pre-emption occurred in the case at hand based on a careful comparison between the state and federal duties at issue.

Even though substantial-equivalence review under § 510(k) is device specific, *Lohr* also rejected the manufacturer's contention that § 510(k) approval imposed device-specific "requirements." We regarded the fact that products entering the market through § 510(k) may be marketed only so long as they remain substantial equivalents of the relevant pre-1976 devices as a qualification for an exemption rather than a requirement.

Premarket approval, in contrast, imposes "requirements" under the MDA as we interpreted it in *Lohr*. Unlike general labeling duties, premarket approval is specific to individual devices. And it is in no sense an exemption from federal safety review—it *is* federal safety review. Thus, the attributes that *Lohr* found lacking in § 510(k) review are present here. While § 510(k) is "focused on equivalence, not safety," pre-market approval is focused on safety, not equivalence. While devices that enter the market through § 510(k) have "never been formally reviewed under the MDA for safety or efficacy," the FDA may grant premarket approval only after it determines that a device offers a reasonable assurance of safety and effectiveness, § 360e(d). And while the FDA does not "require" that a device allowed to enter the market as a substantial equivalent "take any particular form for any particular reason," the FDA requires a device that has received premarket approval to be made with almost no deviations from the specifications in its approval application, for the reason that the FDA has determined that the approved form provides a reasonable assurance of safety and effectiveness.

We turn, then, to the second question: whether the Riegels' common-law claims rely upon "any requirement" of New York law applicable to the catheter that is "different from, or in addition to" federal requirements and that "relates to the safety or effectiveness of

the device or to any other matter included in a requirement applicable to the device."
§ 360k(a). Safety and effectiveness are the very subjects of the Riegels' common-law claims,
so the critical issue is whether New York's tort duties constitute "requirements" under the
MDA....

Congress is entitled to know what meaning this Court will assign to terms regularly used
in its enactments. Absent other indication, reference to a State's "requirements" includes
its common-law duties. As the plurality opinion said in *Cipollone*, common-law liability
is "premised on the existence of a legal duty," and a tort judgment therefore establishes that
the defendant has violated a state-law obligation. And while the common-law remedy is
limited to damages, a liability award "can be, indeed is designed to be, a potent method
of governing conduct and controlling policy."

In the present case, there is nothing to contradict this normal meaning. To the contrary, in the context of this legislation excluding common-law duties from the scope of
pre-emption would make little sense. State tort law that requires a manufacturer's catheters

Figure 17.1 Express and Implied Pre-Emption

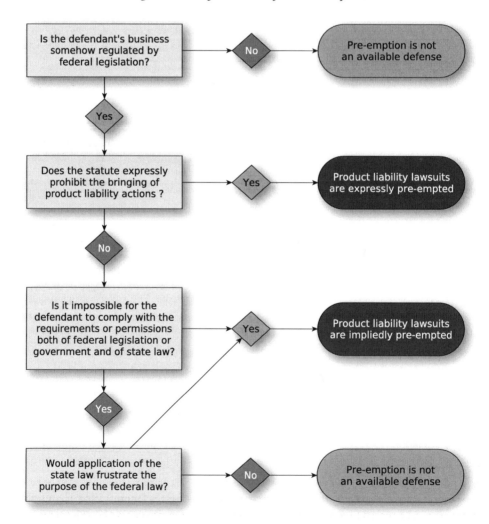

to be safer, but hence less effective, than the model the FDA has approved disrupts the federal scheme no less than state regulatory law to the same effect. Indeed, one would think that tort law, applied by juries under a negligence or strict-liability standard, is less deserving of preservation. A state statute, or a regulation adopted by a state agency, could at least be expected to apply cost-benefit analysis similar to that applied by the experts at the FDA: How many more lives will be saved by a device which, along with its greater effectiveness, brings a greater risk of harm? A jury, on the other hand, sees only the cost of a more dangerous design, and is not concerned with its benefits; the patients who reaped those benefits are not represented in court. As Justice BREYER explained in *Lohr*, it is implausible that the MDA was meant to "grant greater power (to set state standards 'different from, or in addition to' federal standards) to a single state jury than to state officials acting through state administrative or legislative lawmaking processes." That perverse distinction is not required or even suggested by the broad language Congress chose in the MDA, and we will not turn somersaults to create it.

Judgment of the Court of Appeals affirmed.

Note

The application of the theory of express pre-emption, and of the two theories of implied pre-emption that have been addressed so far, is depicted in Figure 17.1.

Questions

1. Does the explanation, in *Comment e* to § 4 of the Products Liability Restatement, of the distinction between different federal and state safety standards on the one hand and federal pre-emption of state law on the other, make sense?

2. Does the recognition of federal pre-emption effectively undermine the whole point of § 4? If so, is that result justifiable?

3. We saw that, in *Bic Pen Corp.*, the CPSA of 1972 expressly stated that compliance with federal standards did not relieve a party from liability at common law. Should the courts adopt the presumption (rebuttable by express statutory wording) that federal law creates (a) a "floor" of standards below which it is always unlawful for a manufacturer or distributor to go, but (b) permits state law products liability claims that effectively demand higher standards, and (c) refuses to treat them as pre-empted, so long as (d) those higher standards are reasonable?

Field Pre-Emption

Although there is nothing explicit in the text of the judgment in that *Riegel* to suggest this, some commentators seem to believe that it implicitly opened the way to the much more far-reaching theory of field pre-emption. The advantage of this approach is that it would ensure that there is a uniform set of standards throughout the nation in any field upon which Congress has decided to legislate. This accords strongly with the idea of having Congress regulate inter-state commerce, since it means that manufacturers and distributors need concern themselves only with meeting the requirements of one legal regime rather than fifty.

In *Rice v. Santa Fe Elevator Corp.*, 331 U.S. 218, 230–31; 67 S.Ct. 1146, 1152 (1947), however, Justice Douglas preferred to presume the contrary:

> [W]e start with the assumption that the historic police powers of the States were not to be superseded by the Federal Act unless that was the clear and manifest purpose of Congress. Such a purpose may be evidenced in several ways. The scheme of federal regulation may be so pervasive as to make reasonable the inference that Congress left no room for the States to supplement it. Or the Act of Congress may touch a field in which the federal interest is so dominant that the federal system will be assumed to preclude enforcement of state laws on the same subject. Likewise, the object sought to be obtained by the federal law and the character of obligations imposed by it may reveal the same purpose. Or the state policy may produce a result inconsistent with the objective of the federal statute. It is often a perplexing question whether Congress has precluded state action or by the choice of selective regulatory measures has left the police power of the States undisturbed except as the state and federal regulations collide.

To this day, the question remains whether field pre-emption is a doctrine recognized by the courts or not. As the following, recent decision of the Supreme Court suggests, the answer to this question seems to be "Yes and No."

Kurns v. Railroad Friction Products Corp.

565 U. S. _____ (2012) (SCOTUS)

THOMAS, J. This case requires us to determine whether petitioners' state-law tort claims for defective design and failure to warn are pre-empted by the Locomotive Inspection Act (LIA), 49 U. S. C. § 20701 et seq. The United States Court of Appeals for the Third Circuit determined that petition ers' claims fall within the field pre-empted by that Act, as that field was defined by this Court's decision in *Napier v. Atlantic Coast Line R. Co.*, 272 U. S. 605 (1926). We agree.

I

George Corson was employed as a welder and machinist by the Chicago, Milwaukee, St. Paul & Pacific Railroad from 1947 until 1974. Corson worked in locomotive repair and maintenance facilities, where his duties included installing brakeshoes on locomotives and stripping insulation from locomotive boilers.

In 2005, Corson was diagnosed with malignant mesothelioma. In 2007, Corson and his wife filed suit in Pennsylvania state court against 59 defendants, including respondents Railroad Friction Products Corporation (RFPC) and Viad Corp (Viad). According to the complaint, RFPC distributed locomotive brakeshoes containing asbestos, and Viad was the successor-in-interest to a company that manufactured and sold locomotives and locomotive engine valves containing asbestos. Corson alleged that he handled this equipment and that he was injured by exposure to asbestos. The complaint asserted state-law claims that the equipment was defectively designed because it contained asbestos, and that respondents failed to warn of the dangers of asbestos or to provide instructions regarding its safe use. After the complaint was filed, Corson passed away, and the executrix of his estate, Gloria Kurns, was substituted as a party. Corson's widow and the executrix are petitioners here.

Respondents removed the case to the United States District Court for the Eastern District of Pennsylvania and moved for summary judgment. Respondents argued that petitioners' state-law claims were pre-empted by the LIA. The District Court agreed and granted summary judgment for respondents. We granted certiorari.

II

Congress enacted the predecessor to the LIA, the Boiler Inspection Act (BIA), in 1911. The BIA made it unlawful to use a steam locomotive "unless the boiler of said locomotive and appurtenances thereof are in proper condition and safe to operate ... without unnecessary peril to life or limb." Act of Feb. 17, 1911, ch. 103, §2, 36 Stat. 913–914. In 1915, Congress amended the BIA to apply to "the entire locomotive and tender and all parts and appurtenances thereof."1 Act of Mar. 4, 1915, ch. 169, §1, 38 Stat. 1192. The BIA as amended became commonly known as the Locomotive Inspection Act. As relevant here, the LIA provides:

> A railroad carrier may use or allow to be used a locomotive or tender on its railroad line only when the locomotive or tender and its parts and appurtenances—
>
> (1) are in proper condition and safe to operate without unnecessary danger of personal injury;
>
> (2) have been inspected as required under this chapter and regulations prescribed by the Secretary of Transportation under this chapter; and
>
> (3) can withstand every test prescribed by the Secretary under this chapter. 49 U. S. C. §20701.2

The issue presented in this case is whether the LIA pre-empts petitioners' state-law claims that respondents defectively designed locomotive parts and failed to warn Corson of dangers associated with those parts....

III B

We do not, however, address the LIA's pre-emptive effect on a clean slate, because this Court addressed that issue 85 years ago in *Napier*....

To determine whether the state requirements were pre empted, this Court asked whether the LIA "manifest[s] the intention to occupy the entire field of regulating loco motive equipment[.]" *Id.*, at 611. The Court answered that question in the affirmative, stating that "[t]he broad scope of the authority conferred upon the [ICC]" by Congress in the LIA led to that conclusion. *Id.*, at 613. The power delegated to the ICC, the Court explained, was a "general one" that "extends to the design, the construction and the material of every part of the locomotive and tender and of all appurtenances." *Id.*, at 611.

The Court rejected the States' contention that the scope of the pre-empted field was to "be determined by the object sought through the legislation, rather than the physical elements affected by it." *Id.*, at 612. The Court found it dispositive that "[t]he federal and the state statutes are directed to the same subject—the equipment of locomotives." *Ibid.* Because the States' requirements operated upon the same physical elements as the LIA, the Court held that the state laws, "however commendable or how ever different their purpose," *id.*, at 613, fell within the LIA's pre-empted field....

IV B

Petitioners do not ask us to overrule Napier and thus do not seek to over come the presumption of stare decisis that attaches to this 85-year-old precedent. See *Global-Tech Appliances, Inc. v. SEB S.A.*, 563 U. S. ___, ___ (2011) (slip op., at 9) (noting the "special force of the doctrine of *stare decisis* with regard to questions of statutory interpretation" (internal quotation marks omitted)). Instead, petitioners advance several arguments aimed at demonstrating that their claims fall outside of the field pre-empted by the LIA, as it was defined in *Napier*. Each is unpersuasive.

Petitioners, along with the Solicitor General as amicus curiae, first argue that petitioners' claims do not fall with in the LIA's pre-empted field because the claims arise out of the repair and maintenance of locomotives, rather than the use of locomotives on a railroad line. Specifically, they contend that the scope of the field pre-empted by the LIA is coextensive with the scope of the Federal Government's regulatory authority under the LIA, which, they argue, does not extend to the regulation of hazards arising from the repair or maintenance of locomotives. Therefore, the argument goes, state-law claims arising from repair or maintenance — as opposed to claims arising from use on the line — do not fall within the pre-empted field.

We reject this attempt to redefine the pre-empted field. In *Napier*, the Court held that Congress, in enacting the LIA, "manifest[ed] the intention to occupy the entire field of regulating locomotive equipment," and the Court did not distinguish between hazards arising from repair and maintenance as opposed to those arising from use on the line. 272 U. S., at 611. The pre-empted field as defined by *Napier* plainly encompasses the claims at issue here. Petitioners' common-law claims for defective design and failure to warn are aimed at the equipment of locomotives....

For the foregoing reasons, we hold that petitioners' state-law design-defect and failure-to-warn claims fall within the field of locomotive equipment regulation pre empted by the LIA, as that field was defined in *Napier*. Accordingly, the judgment of the Court of Appeals is affirmed.

KAGAN, J. (concurring). Like JUSTICE SOTOMAYOR, *post*, at 1 (opinion concurring in part and dissenting in part), I doubt this Court would decide *Napier v. Atlantic Coast Line R. Co.*, 272 U. S. 605 (1926), in the same way today. The *Napier* Court concluded that Congress had "manifest[ed] the intention to occupy the entire field of regulating locomotive equipment," based on nothing more than a statute granting regulatory authority over that subject matter to a federal agency. *Id.*, at 611. Under our more recent cases, Congress must do much more to oust all of state law from a field. Viewed through the lens of modern preemption law, *Napier* is an anachronism.

But *Napier* governs so long as Congress lets it — and that decision provides a straightforward way to determine whether state laws relating to locomotive equipment are preempted. According to *Napier*, the scope of the agency's power under the Locomotive Inspection Act (LIA) determines the boundaries of the preempted field. And under that test, none of the state-law claims at issue here can survive.

Affirmed.

Questions

1. Justice Sotomayor, with whom Justices Ginsburg and Breyer joined, dissented as to the determination of the plaintiff's failure-to-warn claim. She argued that the statutory language referred to "the physical composition of locomotive equipment." It could not, therefore, pre-empt a failure-to-warn claim unless such a warning had been somehow affixed or engraved onto the equipment at issue. She rejected the majority's approach as "treat[ing] defective-design and failure-to-warn claims as congruent, reasoning that each asserts a product defect" but, while that "may be true at a high level of generality," the two claims "rest on different factual allegations and distinct legal concepts." How persuasive do you find this view?

2. In *Altria Group, Inc. v. Good*, 555 U. S. 70 (2008), a bare majority of the Supreme Court found that smokers' claims that tobacco manufacturers' fraudulent advertising had

misled them into purchasing "light" cigarettes were not pre-empted. Writing for the majority, Justice Stevens distinguished *Riegel* on the grounds that it concerned a regular products liability claim, whereas *Altria* was concerned with fraudulent misrepresentation. Indeed, an interesting feature of *Altria* was that the plaintiffs sought compensation only for their financial expenditure in buying the cigarettes, rather than for any physical harm (which raises the question of how any damages should be calculated). Justice Stevens held that, while section 5(b) of the Labeling Act of 1965 provided that "[n]o requirement or prohibition based on smoking and health shall be imposed under State law with respect to the advertising or promotion of any cigarettes the packages of which are labeled in conformity with the provisions of this chapter," this did not "encompass the more general duty not to make fraudulent statements." Does *Altria* lend support to Justice Sotomayor's dissent in *Kurns*?

3. The Justices in *Kurns* were unanimous in dismissing the design defect claim. But does it make sense to apply the precedent from *Napier* to a product liability case at all, when *Napier* was decided long before the law recognized a discrete body of law on products liability? (The landmark case of *Greenman v. Yuba Power Products, Inc.*, 377 P.2d 897, was decided in 1963.)

Notes

1. *An anachronism, or the new normal?* Justice Kagan referred to the *Napier* approach to the question of pre-emption as "an anachronism." However, the policy of federal agencies towards pre-emption changed markedly during the presidency of George W. Bush. Previously, they had not claimed that their very existence, coupled with the regulations that they are empowered to promulgate, pre-empted the whole field of activity from the province of state law, unless there was some express term in the primary legislation to that effect. Attempts to claim implied pre-emption were limited instead to specific types of product liability claims, and according to the wording of specific regulations, as in *Geier* and *Williamson*.

Under President Bush, however, agencies began to adopt the policy of claiming in preambles to their regulations that the whole field of activity was now pre-empted—even though the text of the regulations themselves said nothing about pre-emption. The Food and Drug Administration (FDA) is a good example of this significant change in practice. Since 1930, it had made no claims that its existence pre-empted state tort law claims against pharmaceutical manufacturers until 2002, when it first argued in an *amicus* brief that the federal Food, Drug, and Cosmetic Act (FDCA) of 1938 impliedly preempts failure-to-warn claims based on product labeling that it has approved. It subsequently formalized this position in 2006 in the preamble to a new regulation on product labeling.

A former Commissioner of the FDA, David A. Kessler—who had been appointed by President George H.W. Bush, and reappointed by President William J. Clinton—was extremely critical of the FDA's new position. Together with a Georgetown law professor, David C. Vladeck, he wrote a scathing article, *A Critical Examination of the FDA's Efforts to Preempt Failure-To-Warn Claims*, 96 Geo. L.J. 461, 465–66 (2008), which includes the following comments:

> [T]he FDA's pro-preemption arguments are based on what we see as an unrealistic assessment of the agency's practical ability—once it has approved the marketing of a drug—to detect unforeseen adverse effects of the drug and to take prompt and effective remedial action. After all, there are 11,000 FDA-regulated

drugs on the market (including both prescription and over-the-counter drugs), with nearly one hundred more approved each year. The reality is that the FDA does not have the resources to perform the Herculean task of monitoring comprehensively the performance of every drug on the market. Recent regulatory failures, such as the agency's ineffectual response to Vioxx, have demonstrated the FDA's shortcomings in this regard. Given the FDA's inability to police drug safety effectively on its own, we question the wisdom of the FDA's efforts to restrict or eliminate the complementary discipline placed on the market by failure-to-warn litigation....

Of course, the moment the FDA approves a new drug is the one moment the agency is in the best position to be the exclusive arbiter of a drug's safety and effectiveness. On that day, the FDA has had access to and has devoted considerable resources to reviewing carefully all of the extant health and safety data relating to the drug. On that day, and that day only, we agree that the FDA's determinations about labeling ought not be subject to re-examination by courts or juries in failure-to-warn cases.

But in our view, the FDA is wrong to focus on the moment of approval as determinative of the preemption question. The relevant timeframe is postapproval, and the question, in our opinion, is what did the FDA and the drug company know about a drug's risks at the time the patient-plaintiff sustained the injury. After all, the FDA's knowledge-base of the risks posed by a new drug is far from static. At the time of approval, the FDA's knowledge-base may be close to perfect, but it is also highly limited because, at that point, the drug has been tested on a relatively small population of patients. Once the drug enters the marketplace, risks that are relatively rare, that manifest themselves only after an extended period of time, or that affect vulnerable subpopulations, begin to emerge. These are often not risks foreseen by the drug's manufacturer or the FDA and, for that reason, are not addressed on the label.

2. *Fraudulent misrepresentation on an agency.* One problem is that a federal agency may be the victim of fraudulent misrepresentations made to it by a product manufacturer. Even then, however, it is likely that a claim brought by a victim on a theory of fraud on a federal agency will be considered to be pre-empted. See *Buckman v. Plaintiffs' Legal Committee* 531 U.S. 341, 121 S.Ct. 1012 (2001), discussed in Chapter 4. Any agency that believes that it might have been misled by a manufacturer is, of course, in a position to take appropriate action, but this will not necessarily enable those harmed by the product concerned to obtain compensation.

3. *Seismic shift back?* Kessler and Vladeck refer to a "seismic shift" in FDA policy in favor of claiming that its own work impliedly pre-empts state law in the field in which the FDA operates. A year later, however, President Barack Obama issued a memorandum which arguably marks an equally seismic shift back to the position previously taken by federal agencies.

The White House: Office of the Press Secretary, Memorandum for the Heads of Executive Departments and Agencies—Subject: Preemption

May 20, 2009

From our Nation's founding, the American constitutional order has been a Federal system, ensuring a strong role for both the national Government and the States. The Federal Government's role in promoting the general welfare and guarding individual liberties is critical, but State law and national law often operate concurrently to provide independent safeguards for the public. Throughout our history, State and local governments have frequently protected health, safety, and the environment more aggressively than has the national Government.

An understanding of the important role of State governments in our Federal system is reflected in longstanding practices by executive departments and agencies, which have shown respect for the traditional prerogatives of the States. In recent years, however, notwithstanding Executive Order 13132 of August 4, 1999 (Federalism), executive departments and agencies have sometimes announced that their regulations preempt State law, including State common law, without explicit preemption by the Congress or an otherwise sufficient basis under applicable legal principles.

The purpose of this memorandum is to state the general policy of my Administration that preemption of State law by executive departments and agencies should be undertaken only with full consideration of the legitimate prerogatives of the States and with a sufficient legal basis for preemption. Executive departments and agencies should be mindful that in our Federal system, the citizens of the several States have distinctive circumstances and values, and that in many instances it is appropriate for them to apply to themselves rules and principles that reflect these circumstances and values. As Justice Brandeis explained more than 70 years ago, "[i]t is one of the happy incidents of the federal system that a single courageous state may, if its citizens choose, serve as a laboratory; and try novel social and economic experiments without risk to the rest of the country."

To ensure that executive departments and agencies include statements of preemption in regulations only when such statements have a sufficient legal basis:

1. Heads of departments and agencies should not include in regulatory preambles statements that the department or agency intends to preempt State law through the regulation except where preemption provisions are also included in the codified regulation.

2. Heads of departments and agencies should not include preemption provisions in codified regulations except where such provisions would be justified under legal principles governing preemption, including the principles outlined in Executive Order 13132.

3. Heads of departments and agencies should review regulations issued within the past 10 years that contain statements in regulatory preambles or codified provisions intended by the department or agency to preempt State law, in order to decide whether such statements or provisions are justified under applicable legal principles governing preemption. Where the head of a department or agency determines that a regulatory statement of preemption or codified regulatory provision cannot be so justified, the head of that department or agency should initiate appropriate action, which may include amendment of the relevant regulation.

Executive departments and agencies shall carry out the provisions of this memorandum to the extent permitted by law and consistent with their statutory authorities. Heads of departments and agencies should consult as necessary with the Attorney General and the Office of Management and Budget's Office of Information and Regulatory Affairs to determine how the requirements of this memorandum apply to particular situations.

This memorandum is not intended to, and does not, create any right or benefit, substantive or procedural, enforceable at law or in equity by any party against the United States, its departments, agencies, or entities, its officers, employees, or agents, or any other person.

The Director of the Office of Management and Budget is authorized and directed to publish this memorandum in the Federal Register.

BARACK OBAMA

Note

High-water mark? It now seems possible that *Riegel v. Medtronic* represents the high-water mark for the notion of implied pre-emption. For, barely a year later, the Supreme Court arrived—to the eyes of many commentators, very unexpectedly—at a very different conclusion in *Wyeth v. Levine*, 129 S.Ct 1187 (2009), below. However, one of the reasons that it did so was precisely because the FDA's new view in support of pre-emption, which was made known to the Court, was very different from the "FDA's own longstanding position"—to which, presumably, President Obama's memo has now encouraged it to return.

Wyeth v. Levine
129 S.Ct. 1187 (2009) (SCOTUS)

STEVENS, J. Directly injecting the drug Phenergan into a patient's vein creates a significant risk of catastrophic consequences. A Vermont jury found that petitioner Wyeth, the manufacturer of the drug, had failed to provide an adequate warning of that risk and awarded damages to respondent Diana Levine to compensate her for the amputation of her arm. The warnings on Phenergan's label had been deemed sufficient by the federal Food and Drug Administration (FDA) when it approved Wyeth's new drug application in 1955 and when it later approved changes in the drug's labeling. The question we must decide is whether the FDA's approvals provide Wyeth with a complete defense to Levine's tort claims. We conclude that they do not.

Phenergan is Wyeth's brand name for promethazine hydrochloride, an antihistamine used to treat nausea. The injectable form of Phenergan can be administered intramuscularly or intravenously, and it can be administered intravenously through either the "IV-push" method, whereby the drug is injected directly into a patient's vein, or the "IV-drip" method, whereby the drug is introduced into a saline solution in a hanging intravenous bag and slowly descends through a catheter inserted in a patient's vein. The drug is corrosive and causes irreversible gangrene if it enters a patient's artery.

Levine's injury resulted from an IV-push injection of Phenergan. On April 7, 2000, as on previous visits to her local clinic for treatment of a migraine headache, she received an intramuscular injection of Demerol for her headache and Phenergan for her nausea. Because the combination did not provide relief, she returned later that day and received a second injection of both drugs. This time, the physician assistant administered the drugs by the IV-push method, and Phenergan entered Levine's artery, either because the needle penetrated an artery directly or because the drug escaped from the vein into surrounding tissue (a phenomenon called "perivascular extravasation") where it came in contact with arterial blood. As a result, Levine developed gangrene, and doctors amputated first her right hand and then her entire forearm. In addition to her pain and suffering, Levine incurred substantial medical expenses and the loss of her livelihood as a professional musician.

After settling claims against the health center and clinician, Levine brought an action for damages against Wyeth, relying on common-law negligence and strict-liability theories. Although Phenergan's labeling warned of the danger of gangrene and amputation following inadvertent intra-arterial injection, Levine alleged that the labeling was defective because it failed to instruct clinicians to use the IV-drip method of intravenous administration instead of the higher risk IV-push method. More broadly, she alleged that Phenergan is not reasonably safe for intravenous administration because the foreseeable risks of gangrene and loss of limb are great in relation to the drug's therapeutic benefits.

Wyeth filed a motion for summary judgment, arguing that Levine's failure-to-warn claims were pre-empted by federal law. The court found no merit in either Wyeth's field pre-emption argument, which it has since abandoned, or its conflict pre-emption argument. With respect to the contention that there was an "actual conflict between a specific FDA order," and Levine's failure-to-warn action, the court reviewed the sparse correspondence between Wyeth and the FDA about Phenergan's labeling and found no evidence that Wyeth had "earnestly attempted" to strengthen the intra-arterial injection warning or that the FDA had "specifically disallowed" stronger language. The record, as then developed, "lack[ed] any evidence that the FDA set a ceiling on this matter." The evidence presented during the 5-day jury trial showed that the risk of intra-arterial injection or perivascular extravasation can be almost entirely eliminated through the use of IV-drip, rather than IV-push, administration. An IV drip is started with saline, which will not flow properly if the catheter is not in the vein and fluid is entering an artery or surrounding tissue. By contrast, even a careful and experienced clinician using the IV-push method will occasionally expose an artery to Phenergan. While Phenergan's labeling warned against intraarterial injection and perivascular extravasation and advised that "[w]hen administering any irritant drug intravenously it is usually preferable to inject it through the tubing of an intravenous infusion set that is known to be functioning satisfactorily," the labeling did not contain a specific warning about the risks of IV-push administration.

The trial record also contains correspondence between Wyeth and the FDA discussing Phenergan's label. The FDA first approved injectable Phenergan in 1955. In 1973 and 1976, Wyeth submitted supplemental new drug applications, which the agency approved after proposing labeling changes. Wyeth submitted a third supplemental application in 1981 in response to a new FDA rule governing drug labels. Over the next 17 years, Wyeth and the FDA intermittently corresponded about Phenergan's label. The most notable activity occurred in 1987, when the FDA suggested different warnings about the risk of arterial exposure, and in 1988, when Wyeth submitted revised labeling incorporating the proposed changes. The FDA did not respond. Instead, in 1996, it requested from Wyeth the labeling then in use and, without addressing Wyeth's 1988 submission, instructed it to "[r]etain verbiage in current label" regarding intra-arterial injection. After a few further changes to the labeling not related to intra-arterial injection, the FDA approved Wyeth's 1981 application in 1998, instructing that Phenergan's final printed label "must be identical" to the approved package insert.

Based on this regulatory history, the trial judge instructed the jury that it could consider evidence of Wyeth's compliance with FDA requirements but that such compliance did not establish that the warnings were adequate. He also instructed, without objection from Wyeth, that FDA regulations "permit a drug manufacturer to change a product label to add or strengthen a warning about its product without prior FDA approval so long as it later submits the revised warning for review and approval."

Answering questions on a special verdict form, the jury found that Wyeth was negligent, that Phenergan was a defective product as a result of inadequate warnings and instructions, and that no intervening cause had broken the causal connection between the product defects and the plaintiff's injury. It awarded total damages of $7,400,000, which the court reduced to account for Levine's earlier settlement with the health center and clinician.

On August 3, 2004, the trial court filed a comprehensive opinion denying Wyeth's motion for judgment as a matter of law. After making findings of fact based on the trial record (supplemented by one letter that Wyeth found after the trial), the court rejected Wyeth's pre-emption arguments. It determined that there was no direct conflict between FDA regulations and Levine's state-law claims because those regulations permit strengthened warnings without FDA approval on an interim basis and the record contained evidence of at least 20 reports of amputations similar to Levine's since the 1960's. The court also found that state tort liability in this case would not obstruct the FDA's work because the agency had paid no more than passing attention to the question whether to warn against IV-push administration of Phenergan. In addition, the court noted that state law serves a compensatory function distinct from federal regulation.

The Vermont Supreme Court affirmed. It held that the jury's verdict "did not conflict with FDA's labeling requirements for Phenergan because [Wyeth] could have warned against IV-push administration without prior FDA approval, and because federal labeling requirements create a floor, not a ceiling, for state regulation." In dissent, Chief Justice Reiber argued that the jury's verdict conflicted with federal law because it was inconsistent with the FDA's conclusion that intravenous administration of Phenergan was safe and effective.

The importance of the pre-emption issue, coupled with the fact that the FDA has changed its position on state tort law and now endorses the views expressed in Chief Justice Reiber's dissent, persuaded us to grant Wyeth's petition for certiorari. The question presented by the petition is whether the FDA's drug labeling judgments "preempt state law product liability claims premised on the theory that different labeling judgments were necessary to make drugs reasonably safe for use."

Wyeth makes two separate pre-emption arguments: first, that it would have been impossible for it to comply with the state-law duty to modify Phenergan's labeling without violating federal law, and second, that recognition of Levine's state tort action creates an unacceptable "obstacle to the accomplishment and execution of the full purposes and objectives of Congress," because it substitutes a lay jury's decision about drug labeling for the expert judgment of the FDA....

The trial court proceedings established that Levine's injury would not have occurred if Phenergan's label had included an adequate warning about the risks of the IV-push method of administering the drug. The record contains evidence that the physician assistant administered a greater dose than the label prescribed, that she may have inadvertently injected the drug into an artery rather than a vein, and that she continued to inject the drug after Levine complained of pain. Nevertheless, the jury rejected Wyeth's argument that the clinician's conduct was an intervening cause that absolved it of liability. In finding Wyeth negligent as well as strictly liable, the jury also determined that Levine's injury was foreseeable. That the inadequate label was both a but-for and proximate cause of Levine's injury is supported by the record and no longer challenged by Wyeth.

The trial court proceedings further established that the critical defect in Phenergan's label was the lack of an adequate warning about the risks of IV-push administration.

Levine also offered evidence that the IV-push method should be contraindicated and that Phenergan should never be administered intravenously, even by the IV-drip method. Perhaps for this reason, the dissent incorrectly assumes that the state-law duty at issue is the duty to contraindicate the IV-push method. But, as the Vermont Supreme Court explained, the jury verdict established only that Phenergan's warning was insufficient. It did not mandate a particular replacement warning, nor did it require contraindicating IV-push administration: "There may have been any number of ways for [Wyeth] to strengthen the Phenergan warning without completely eliminating IV-push administration." We therefore need not decide whether a state rule proscribing intravenous administration would be pre-empted. The narrower question presented is whether federal law pre-empts Levine's claim that Phenergan's label did not contain an adequate warning about using the IV-push method of administration. . . .

Wyeth first argues that Levine's state-law claims are pre-empted because it is impossible for it to comply with both the state-law duties underlying those claims and its federal labeling duties. The FDA's premarket approval of a new drug application includes the approval of the exact text in the proposed label. See 21 U.S.C. §355; 21 CFR §314.105(b) (2008). Generally speaking, a manufacturer may only change a drug label after the FDA approves a supplemental application. There is, however, an FDA regulation that permits a manufacturer to make certain changes to its label before receiving the agency's approval. Among other things, this "changes being effected" (CBE) regulation provides that if a manufacturer is changing a label to "add or strengthen a contraindication, warning, precaution, or adverse reaction" or to "add or strengthen an instruction about dosage and administration that is intended to increase the safe use of the drug product," it may make the labeling change upon filing its supplemental application with the FDA; it need not wait for FDA approval. §§314.70(c)(6)(iii)(A), (C).

Wyeth argues that the CBE regulation is not implicated in this case because a 2008 amendment provides that a manufacturer may only change its label "to reflect newly acquired information." 73 Fed.Reg. 49609. Resting on this language (which Wyeth argues simply reaffirmed the interpretation of the regulation in effect when this case was tried), Wyeth contends that it could have changed Phenergan's label only in response to new information that the FDA had not considered. And it maintains that Levine has not pointed to any such information concerning the risks of IV-push administration. Thus, Wyeth insists, it was impossible for it to discharge its state-law obligation to provide a stronger warning about IV-push administration without violating federal law. Wyeth's argument misapprehends both the federal drug regulatory scheme and its burden in establishing a pre-emption defense.

We need not decide whether the 2008 CBE regulation is consistent with the FDCA and the previous version of the regulation, as Wyeth and the United States urge, because Wyeth could have revised Phenergan's label even in accordance with the amended regulation. As the FDA explained in its notice of the final rule, "newly acquired information" is not limited to new data, but also encompasses "new analyses of previously submitted data." The rule accounts for the fact that risk information accumulates over time and that the same data may take on a different meaning in light of subsequent developments . . .

Wyeth argues that if it had unilaterally added such a warning, it would have violated federal law governing unauthorized distribution and misbranding. Its argument that a change in Phenergan's labeling would have subjected it to liability for unauthorized distribution rests on the assumption that this labeling change would have rendered Phenergan a new drug lacking an effective application. But strengthening the warning about IV-push administration would not have made Phenergan a new drug. See 21 U.S.C.

§ 321(p)(1) (defining "new drug"); 21 CFR § 310.3(h). Nor would this warning have rendered Phenergan misbranded. The FDCA does not provide that a drug is misbranded simply because the manufacturer has altered an FDA-approved label; instead, the misbranding provision focuses on the substance of the label and, among other things, proscribes labels that fail to include "adequate warnings." 21 U.S.C. § 352(f). Moreover, because the statute contemplates that federal juries will resolve most misbranding claims, the FDA's belief that a drug is misbranded is not conclusive. See §§ 331, 332, 334(a)–(b). And the very idea that the FDA would bring an enforcement action against a manufacturer for strengthening a warning pursuant to the CBE regulation is difficult to accept—neither Wyeth nor the United States has identified a case in which the FDA has done so.

Wyeth's cramped reading of the CBE regulation and its broad reading of the FDCA's misbranding and unauthorized distribution provisions are premised on a more fundamental misunderstanding. Wyeth suggests that the FDA, rather than the manufacturer, bears primary responsibility for drug labeling. Yet through many amendments to the FDCA and to FDA regulations, it has remained a central premise of federal drug regulation that the manufacturer bears responsibility for the content of its label at all times. It is charged both with crafting an adequate label and with ensuring that its warnings remain adequate as long as the drug is on the market. See, e.g., 21 CFR § 201.80(e) (requiring a manufacturer to revise its label "to include a warning as soon as there is reasonable evidence of an association of a serious hazard with a drug"); § 314.80(b) (placing responsibility for post-marketing surveillance on the manufacturer); 73 Fed.Reg. 49605 ("Manufacturers continue to have a responsibility under Federal law ... to maintain their labeling and update the labeling with new safety information")....

Wyeth also argues that requiring it to comply with a state-law duty to provide a stronger warning about IV-push administration would obstruct the purposes and objectives of federal drug labeling regulation. Levine's tort claims, it maintains, are pre-empted because they interfere with "Congress's purpose to entrust an expert agency to make drug labeling decisions that strike a balance between competing objectives." We find no merit in this argument, which relies on an untenable interpretation of congressional intent and an overbroad view of an agency's power to pre-empt state law.

Wyeth contends that the FDCA establishes both a floor and a ceiling for drug regulation: Once the FDA has approved a drug's label, a state-law verdict may not deem the label inadequate, regardless of whether there is any evidence that the FDA has considered the stronger warning at issue. The most glaring problem with this argument is that all evidence of Congress' purposes is to the contrary. Building on its 1906 Act, Congress enacted the FDCA to bolster consumer protection against harmful products. See *Kordel v. United States*, 335 U.S. 345, 349, 69 S.Ct. 106, 93 L.Ed. 52 (1948); *United States v. Sullivan*, 332 U.S. 689, 696, 68 S.Ct. 331, 92 L.Ed. 297 (1948). Congress did not provide a federal remedy for consumers harmed by unsafe or ineffective drugs in the 1938 statute or in any subsequent amendment. Evidently, it determined that widely available state rights of action provided appropriate relief for injured consumers. It may also have recognized that state-law remedies further consumer protection by motivating manufacturers to produce safe and effective drugs and to give adequate warnings.

If Congress thought state-law suits posed an obstacle to its objectives, it surely would have enacted an express pre-emption provision at some point during the FDCA's 70-year history. But despite its 1976 enactment of an express pre-emption provision for medical devices, Congress has not enacted such a provision for prescription drugs. See *Riegel*, 128 S.Ct., at 1009 ("Congress could have applied the pre-emption clause to the entire FDCA. It did not do so, but instead wrote a pre-emption clause that applies only to medical devices"). Its silence on the issue, coupled with its certain awareness of the prevalence of state tort litigation, is powerful evidence that Congress did not intend FDA oversight to be the exclusive means of ensuring drug safety and effectiveness. As Justice O'Connor explained in her opinion for a unanimous Court: "The case for federal pre-emption is particularly weak where Congress has indicated its awareness of the operation of state law in a field of federal interest, and has nonetheless decided to stand by both concepts and to tolerate whatever tension there [is] between them." *Bonito Boats, Inc. v. Thunder Craft Boats, Inc.*, 489 U.S. 141, 166–167, 109 S.Ct. 971, 103 L.Ed.2d 118 (1989)....

In prior cases, we have given "some weight" to an agency's views about the impact of tort law on federal objectives when "the subject matter is technica[l] and the relevant history and background are complex and extensive." *Geier*, 529 U.S., at 883, 120 S.Ct. 1913. Even in such cases, however, we have not deferred to an agency's conclusion that state law is pre-empted. Rather, we have attended to an agency's explanation of how state law affects the regulatory scheme. While agencies have no special authority to pronounce on pre-emption absent delegation by Congress, they do have a unique understanding of the statutes they administer and an attendant ability to make informed determinations about how state requirements may pose an "obstacle to the accomplishment and execution of the full purposes and objectives of Congress." The weight we accord the agency's explanation of state law's impact on the federal scheme depends on its thoroughness, consistency, and persuasiveness.

Under this standard, the FDA's 2006 preamble does not merit deference. When the FDA issued its notice of proposed rulemaking in December 2000, it explained that the rule would "not contain policies that have federalism implications or that preempt State law." 65 Fed.Reg. 81103; see also 71 id., at 3969 (noting that the "proposed rule did not propose to preempt state law"). In 2006, the agency finalized the rule and, without offering States or other interested parties notice or opportunity for comment, articulated a sweeping position on the FDCA's pre-emptive effect in the regulatory preamble. The agency's views on state law are inherently suspect in light of this procedural failure.

Further, the preamble is at odds with what evidence we have of Congress' purposes, and it reverses the FDA's own longstanding position without providing a reasoned explanation, including any discussion of how state law has interfered with the FDA's regulation of drug labeling during decades of co-existence. The FDA's 2006 position plainly does not reflect the agency's own view at all times relevant to this litigation. Not once prior to Levine's injury did the FDA suggest that state tort law stood as an obstacle to its statutory mission. To the contrary, it cast federal labeling standards as a floor upon which States could build and repeatedly disclaimed any attempt to pre-empt failure-to-warn claims. For instance, in 1998, the FDA stated that it did "not believe that the evolution of state tort law [would] cause the development of standards that would be at odds with the agency's regulations." It further noted that, in establishing "minimal standards" for drug labels, it did not intend "to preclude the states from imposing additional labeling requirements."

In keeping with Congress' decision not to pre-empt common-law tort suits, it appears that the FDA traditionally regarded state law as a complementary form of drug regulation. The FDA has limited resources to monitor the 11,000 drugs on the market, and manufacturers have superior access to information about their drugs, especially in the postmarketing phase as new risks emerge. State tort suits uncover unknown drug hazards and provide incentives for drug manufacturers to disclose safety risks promptly. They also serve a distinct compensatory function that may motivate injured persons to come forward with information. Failure-to-warn actions, in particular, lend force to the FDCA's premise that manufacturers, not the FDA, bear primary responsibility for their drug labeling at all times. Thus, the FDA long maintained that state law offers an additional, and important, layer of consumer protection that complements FDA regulation. The agency's 2006 preamble represents a dramatic change in position.

Largely based on the FDA's new position, Wyeth argues that this case presents a conflict between state and federal law analogous to the one at issue in *Geier*. There, we held that state tort claims premised on Honda's failure to install airbags conflicted with a federal regulation that did not require airbags for all cars. The Department of Transportation (DOT) had promulgated a rule that provided car manufacturers with a range of choices among passive restraint devices. Rejecting an "all airbag" standard, the agency had called for a gradual phase-in of a mix of passive restraints in order to spur technological development and win consumer acceptance. Because the plaintiff's claim was that car manufacturers had a duty to install airbags, it presented an obstacle to achieving "the variety and mix of devices that the federal regulation sought."

Wyeth and the dissent contend that the regulatory scheme in this case is nearly identical, but, as we have described, it is quite different. In *Geier*, the DOT conducted a formal rulemaking and then adopted a plan to phase in a mix of passive restraint devices. Examining the rule itself and the DOT's contemporaneous record, which revealed the factors the agency had weighed and the balance it had struck, we determined that state tort suits presented an obstacle to the federal scheme. After conducting our own pre-emption analysis, we considered the agency's explanation of how state law interfered with its regulation, regarding it as further support for our independent conclusion that the plaintiff's tort claim obstructed the federal regime.

By contrast, we have no occasion in this case to consider the pre-emptive effect of a specific agency regulation bearing the force of law. And the FDA's newfound opinion, expressed in its 2006 preamble, that state law "frustrate[s] the agency's implementation of its statutory mandate," 71 Fed.Reg. 3934, does not merit deference for the reasons we have explained. Indeed, the "complex and extensive" regulatory history and background relevant to this case, undercut the FDA's recent pronouncements of pre-emption, as they reveal the longstanding co-existence of state and federal law and the FDA's traditional recognition of state-law remedies—a recognition in place each time the agency reviewed Wyeth's Phenergan label.

In short, Wyeth has not persuaded us that failure-to-warn claims like Levine's obstruct the federal regulation of drug labeling. Congress has repeatedly declined to pre-empt state law, and the FDA's recently adopted position that state tort suits interfere with its statutory mandate is entitled to no weight. Although we recognize that some state-law claims might well frustrate the achievement of congressional objectives, this is not such a case.

We conclude that it is not impossible for Wyeth to comply with its state and federal law obligations and that Levine's common-law claims do not stand as an obstacle to the accomplishment of Congress' purposes in the FDCA. Accordingly, the judgment of the Vermont Supreme Court is affirmed.

Questions

1. What do you think of the different methods and theories, according to which federal law can pre-empt state law?

2. Is the Supreme Court's holding in *Wyeth* consistent with its decision in *Riegel*?

3. What is the status, so far as pre-emption is concerned, of claims that allege that harm has been sustained because of a defect in a medical device that is designed to dispense a regular dose of a pharmaceutical?

Note

The Supreme Court had not finished with the subject in *Wyeth*. In the following case, it revisited much of the same ground but, by a majority of 5–4, came to the very opposite conclusion.

PLIVA, Inc. v. Mensing

131 S.Ct. 2567 (2011) (SCOTUS)

THOMAS, J. These consolidated lawsuits involve state tort-law claims based on certain drug manufacturers' alleged failure to provide adequate warning labels for generic metoclopramide. The question presented is whether federal drug regulations applicable to generic drug manufacturers directly conflict with, and thus pre-empt, these state-law claims. We hold that they do.

I

Metoclopramide is a drug designed to speed the movement of food through the digestive system. The Food and Drug Administration (FDA) first approved metoclopramide tablets, under the brand name Reglan, in 1980. Five years later, generic manufacturers also began producing metoclopramide. The drug is commonly used to treat digestive tract problems such as diabetic gastroparesis and gastroesophageal reflux disorder.

Evidence has accumulated that long-term metoclopramide use can cause tardive dyskinesia, a severe neurological disorder. Studies have shown that up to 29% of patients who take metoclopramide for several years develop this condition.

Accordingly, warning labels for the drug have been strengthened and clarified several times. In 1985, the label was modified to warn that "tardive dyskinesia … may develop in patients treated with metoclopramide," and the drug's package insert added that "[t]herapy longer than 12 weeks has not been evaluated and cannot be recommended." Physician's Desk Reference 1635–1636 (41st ed. 1987). In 2004, the brand-name Reglan manufacturer requested, and the FDA approved, a label change to add that "[t]herapy should not exceed 12 weeks in duration." And in 2009, the FDA ordered a black box warning—its strongest—which states: "Treatment with metoclopramide can cause tardive dyskinesia, a serious movement disorder that is often irreversible … Treatment with metoclopramide for longer than 12 weeks should be avoided in all but rare cases." See Physician's Desk Reference 2902 (65th ed. 2011).

Gladys Mensing and Julie Demahy, the plaintiffs in these consolidated cases, were prescribed Reglan in 2001 and 2002, respectively. Both received generic metoclopramide from their pharmacists. After taking the drug as prescribed for several years, both women developed tardive dyskinesia.

In separate suits, Mensing and Demahy sued the generic drug manufacturers that produced the metoclopramide they took (Manufacturers). Each alleged, as relevant here, that long-term metoclopramide use caused her tardive dyskinesia and that the Manufacturers were liable under state tort law (specifically, that of Minnesota and Louisiana) for failing to provide adequate warning labels. They claimed that "despite mounting evidence that long term metoclopramide use carries a risk of tardive dyskinesia far greater than that indicated on the label," none of the Manufacturers had changed their labels to adequately warn of that danger.

In both suits, the Manufacturers urged that federal law pre-empted the state tort claims. According to the Manufacturers, federal statutes and FDA regulations required them to use the same safety and efficacy labeling as their brand-name counterparts. This means, they argued, that it was impossible to simultaneously comply with both federal law and any state tort-law duty that required them to use a different label. The Courts of Appeals for the Fifth and Eighth Circuits rejected the Manufacturers' arguments and held that Mensing and Demahy's claims were not pre-empted. We granted certiorari, consolidated the cases, and now reverse each.

II

Pre-emption analysis requires us to compare federal and state law. We therefore begin by identifying the state tort duties and federal labeling requirements applicable to the Manufacturers.

A

It is undisputed that Minnesota and Louisiana tort law require a drug manufacturer that is or should be aware of its product's danger to label that product in a way that renders it reasonably safe. Under Minnesota law, which applies to Mensing's lawsuit, "where the manufacturer ... of a product has actual or constructive knowledge of danger to users, the ... manufacturer has a duty to give warning of such dangers." Similarly, under Louisiana law applicable to Demahy's lawsuit, "a manufacturer's duty to warn includes a duty to provide adequate instructions for safe use of a product." In both States, a duty to warn falls specifically on the manufacturer.

Mensing and Demahy have pleaded that the Manufacturers knew or should have known of the high risk of tardive dyskinesia inherent in the long-term use of their product. They have also pleaded that the Manufacturers knew or should have known that their labels did not adequately warn of that risk. The parties do not dispute that, if these allegations are true, state law required the Manufacturers to use a different, safer label.

B

Federal law imposes far more complex drug labeling requirements. We begin with what is not in dispute. Under the 1962 Drug Amendments to the Federal Food, Drug, and Cosmetic Act, 76 Stat. 780, 21 U.S.C. § 301 *et seq.*, a manufacturer seeking federal approval to market a new drug must prove that it is safe and effective and that the proposed label is accurate and adequate. See, e.g., 21 U.S.C. §§ 355(b)(1), (d); *Wyeth v. Levine*, 555 U.S. 555, 567. Meeting those requirements involves costly and lengthy clinical testing. §§ 355(b)(1)(A), (d).

Originally, the same rules applied to all drugs. In 1984, however, Congress passed the Drug Price Competition and Patent Term Restoration Act, 98 Stat. 1585, commonly called the Hatch-Waxman Amendments. Under this law, "generic drugs" can gain FDA approval simply by showing equivalence to a reference listed drug that has already been approved by the FDA. 21 U.S.C. § 355(j)(2)(A). This allows manufacturers to develop generic drugs inexpensively, without duplicating the clinical trials already performed on the equivalent brand-name drug. A generic drug application must also "show that the [safety and efficacy] labeling proposed ... is the same as the labeling approved for the [brand-name] drug." § 355(j)(2)(A)(v).

As a result, brand-name and generic drug manufacturers have different federal drug labeling duties. A brand-name manufacturer seeking new drug approval is responsible for the accuracy and adequacy of its label. A manufacturer seeking generic drug approval, on the other hand, is responsible for ensuring that its warning label is the same as the brand name's.

The parties do not disagree. What is in dispute is whether, and to what extent, generic manufacturers may change their labels *after* initial FDA approval. Mensing and Demahy contend that federal law provided several avenues through which the Manufacturers could have altered their metoclopramide labels in time to prevent the injuries here.

The FDA, however, tells us that it interprets its regulations to require that the warning labels of a brand-name drug and its generic copy must always be the same—thus, generic drug manufacturers have an ongoing federal duty of "sameness." The FDA's views are "controlling unless plainly erroneous or inconsistent with the regulation[s]" or there is any other reason to doubt that they reflect the FDA's fair and considered judgment. *Auer v. Robbins*, 519 U.S. 452, 461, 462 (1997).

1

First, Mensing and Demahy urge that the FDA's "changes-being-effected" (CBE) process allowed the Manufacturers to change their labels when necessary. The CBE process permits drug manufacturers to "add or strengthen a contraindication, warning, [or] precaution," 21 CFR § 314.70(c)(6)(iii)(A) (2006), or to "add or strengthen an instruction about dosage and administration that is intended to increase the safe use of the drug product," § 314.70(c)(6)(iii)(C). When making labeling changes using the CBE process, drug manufacturers need not wait for preapproval by the FDA, which ordinarily is necessary to change a label. *Wyeth, supra*, at 568, 129 S.Ct. 1187. They need only simultaneously file a supplemental application with the FDA. 21 CFR § 314.70(c)(6).

The FDA denies that the Manufacturers could have used the CBE process to unilaterally strengthen their warning labels. The agency interprets the CBE regulation to allow changes to generic drug labels only when a generic drug manufacturer changes its label to match an updated brand-name label or to follow the FDA's instructions. The FDA argues that CBE changes unilaterally made to strengthen a generic drug's warning label would violate the statutes and regulations requiring a generic drug's label to match its brand-name counterpart's.

We defer to the FDA's interpretation of its CBE and generic labeling regulations. Although Mensing and Demahy offer other ways to interpret the regulations, we do not find the agency's interpretation "plainly erroneous or inconsistent with the regulation." Nor do Mensing and Demahy suggest there is any other reason to doubt the agency's reading. We therefore conclude that the CBE process was not open to the Manufacturers for the sort of change required by state law.

2

Next, Mensing and Demahy contend that the Manufacturers could have used "Dear Doctor" letters to send additional warnings to prescribing physicians and other healthcare professionals. Again, the FDA disagrees, and we defer to the agency's views.

The FDA argues that Dear Doctor letters qualify as "labeling." Thus, any such letters must be "consistent with and not contrary to [the drug's] approved ... labeling." 21 CFR § 201.100(d)(1). A Dear Doctor letter that contained substantial new warning information would not be consistent with the drug's approved labeling. Moreover, if generic drug manufacturers, but not the brand-name manufacturer, sent such letters, that would inaccurately imply a therapeutic difference between the brand and generic drugs and thus could be impermissibly "misleading."

As with the CBE regulation, we defer to the FDA. Mensing and Demahy offer no argument that the FDA's interpretation is plainly erroneous. Accordingly, we conclude that federal law did not permit the Manufacturers to issue additional warnings through Dear Doctor letters.

3

Though the FDA denies that the Manufacturers could have used the CBE process or Dear Doctor letters to strengthen their warning labels, the agency asserts that a different avenue existed for changing generic drug labels. According to the FDA, the Manufacturers could have proposed—indeed, were required to propose—stronger warning labels to the agency if they believed such warnings were needed. U.S. Brief 20; 57 Fed.Reg. 17961. If the FDA had agreed that a label change was necessary, it would have worked with the brand-name manufacturer to create a new label for both the brand-name and generic drug.

The agency traces this duty to 21 U.S.C. § 352(f)(2), which provides that a drug is "misbranded ... [u]nless its labeling bears ... adequate warnings against ... unsafe dosage or methods or duration of administration or application, in such manner and form, as are necessary for the protection of users." By regulation, the FDA has interpreted that statute to require that "labeling shall be revised to include a warning as soon as there is reasonable evidence of an association of a serious hazard with a drug." 21 CFR § 201.57(e).

According to the FDA, these requirements apply to generic drugs. As it explains, a "central premise of federal drug regulation is that the manufacturer bears responsibility for the content of its label at all times." *Wyeth*, 555 U.S., at 570–571). The FDA reconciles this duty to have adequate and accurate labeling with the duty of sameness in the following way: Generic drug manufacturers that become aware of safety problems must ask the agency to work toward strengthening the label that applies to both the generic and brand-name equivalent drug.

The Manufacturers and the FDA disagree over whether this alleged duty to request a strengthened label actually existed. The FDA argues that it explained this duty in the preamble to its 1992 regulations implementing the Hatch-Waxman Amendments. The Manufacturers claim that the FDA's 19-year-old statement did not create a duty, and that there is no evidence of any generic drug manufacturer ever acting pursuant to any such duty. Because we ultimately find pre-emption even assuming such a duty existed, we do not resolve the matter.

C

To summarize, the relevant state and federal requirements are these: State tort law places a duty directly on all drug manufacturers to adequately and safely label their products. Taking Mensing and Demahy's allegations as true, this duty required the Manufacturers to use a different, stronger label than the label they actually used. Federal drug regulations, as interpreted by the FDA, prevented the Manufacturers from independently changing their generic drugs' safety labels. But, we assume, federal law also required the Manufacturers to ask for FDA assistance in convincing the brand-name manufacturer to adopt a stronger label, so that all corresponding generic drug manufacturers could do so as well. We turn now to the question of pre-emption.

III

The Supremacy Clause establishes that federal law "shall be the supreme Law of the Land ... any Thing in the Constitution or Laws of any State to the Contrary federal drug and medical device laws pre-empted a state tort-notwithstanding." U.S. Const., Art. VI, cl. 2. Where state and federal law "directly conflict," state law must give way. We have held that state and federal law conflict where it is "impossible for a private party to comply with both state and federal requirements." *Freightliner Corp. v. Myrick*, 514 U.S. 280, 287 (1995).

A

We find impossibility here. It was not lawful under federal law for the Manufacturers to do what state law required of them. And even if they had fulfilled their federal duty to ask for FDA assistance, they would not have satisfied the requirements of state law.

If the Manufacturers had independently changed their labels to satisfy their state-law duty, they would have violated federal law. Taking Mensing and Demahy's allegations as true, state law imposed on the Manufacturers a duty to attach a safer label to their generic metoclopramide. Federal law, however, demanded that generic drug labels be the same at all times as the corresponding brand-name drug labels. Thus, it was impossible for the Manufacturers to comply with both their state-law duty to change the label and their federal law duty to keep the label the same.

The federal duty to ask the FDA for help in strengthening the corresponding brand-name label, assuming such a duty exists, does not change this analysis. Although requesting FDA assistance would have satisfied the Manufacturers' federal duty, it would not have satisfied their state tort-law duty to provide adequate labeling. State law demanded a safer label; it did not instruct the Manufacturers to communicate with the FDA about the possibility of a safer label. Indeed, Mensing and Demahy deny that their state tort claims are based on the Manufacturers' alleged failure to ask the FDA for assistance in changing the labels....

C

Wyeth is not to the contrary. In that case, as here, the plaintiff contended that a drug manufacturer had breached a state tort-law duty to provide an adequate warning label. The Court held that the lawsuit was not pre-empted because it was possible for Wyeth, a brand-name drug manufacturer, to comply with both state and federal law. Specifically, the CBE regulation, 21 CFR § 314.70(c)(6)(iii), permitted a brand-name drug manufacturer like Wyeth "to unilaterally strengthen its warning" without prior FDA approval. Thus, the federal regulations applicable to Wyeth allowed the company, of its own volition, to strengthen its label in compliance with its state tort law duty.

We recognize that from the perspective of Mensing and Demahy, finding pre-emption here but not in *Wyeth* makes little sense. Had Mensing and Demahy taken Reglan, the brand-name drug prescribed by their doctors, Wyeth would control and their lawsuits would not be pre-empted. But because pharmacists, acting in full accord with state law, substituted generic metoclopramide instead, federal law pre-empts these lawsuits. We acknowledge the unfortunate hand that federal drug regulation has dealt Mensing, Demahy, and others similarly situated.

But "it is not this Court's task to decide whether the statutory scheme established by Congress is unusual or even bizarre." *Cuomo v. Clearing House Assn., L.L.C.*, 129 S.Ct. 2710, 2733 (2009).

Reversed and remanded.

Questions

1. Should the views of federal agencies be accorded deference regarding the pre-emption of state tort claims?

2. Is the Supreme Court's holding in *Mensing* consistent with its decision in *Wyeth*? Does the juxtaposition of the two decisions "make[] little sense"?

3. Since the generic manufacturers *could* have applied to the FDA to have the warning on the label strengthened, to which the FDA *might* have agreed, and required both the generic and brand-name manufacturers to strengthen the warning on the label in the manner advocated by the plaintiffs in *Mensing*, was the majority in *Mensing* really applying a test of impossibility, or one of improbability?

4. What implications do *Wyeth* and *Mensing* together have for the behavior of pre-scribing doctors, pharmacists, and patients — and/or for Medicare and Medicaid?

Part VII

Damages

Chapter 18

Damages

Compensatory Damages

It is obvious that the primary remedy sought by the victim of a defective product is that of damages to compensate for the injury and loss sustained as a result. However, compensatory damages can be awarded under several different headings. While there is relatively little controversy over the availability and size of such awards to compensate for significant personal injuries, property damage, and consequential economic losses (such as loss of income and medical bills), the same cannot be said for the compensation of other types of harm.

Awards for pain and suffering, and for emotional distress, have proved particularly problematic. There are, no doubt, several reasons for such ambivalence. First, unlike "traditional" personal injuries and property damage, there is nothing inherently tangible about pain, suffering, or distress. Unless such injuries manifest themselves in clear physical symptoms (such as a heart attack, miscarriage, or stroke) they are, therefore, difficult to identify objectively. Indeed, the whole point about claims for pain and suffering and emotional distress is that they are intensely personal and hence subjective: no two persons will suffer pain or emotional trauma in the same way (or even at all) as a result of the same incident.

This, critics argue, opens the door to fraudulent claims, for there is no way to distinguish the real from the fake. This argument is closely associated with — though not identical to — the two floodgates concerns that we first encountered in Chapter 1. The counter-argument questions whether it is right that those genuinely suffering pain, or emotional distress, should have their claims rejected merely because of the possibility that others might make a false claim.

A third concern is that it is impossible to set a meaningful value on a claim for either pain and suffering or emotional distress. Allied to this is the observation that no sum of money can rectify the problems caused. These arguments can, however, be made with just as much validity about damages for personal injuries. There can be no objective way to value the loss of a leg, or the suffering of partial paralysis, nor can any amount of money rectify these injuries, and yet that is the very basis of the law of torts. Indeed, it might be countered that, in some cases, compensation for emotional distress might facilitate the victim's paying for expert counseling, which might then lead to the reduction or even elimination of the distress, in much the same way that "regular" compensation is often used to meet medical bills for traditional, physical injuries.

Fourthly, since there is no objective measure for damages for pain and suffering, and emotional distress, and since each victim suffers these things in a wholly personal way which the rest of us cannot really replicate, awards of damages for such injuries risk empathetic juries making huge, economically unsustainable awards. For these reasons, many states have introduced legislative caps on damages for pain and suffering.

Finally, awards for pain and suffering, and for emotional distress, are often criticized as acting as a deterrent to self-reliance. This is an argument about so-called "moral hazard," where someone insulated from a risk behaves differently from how s/he would behave if fully exposed to the risk. The assertion here is that the availability of damages for pain and suffering, and for emotional distress, is likely to cause plaintiffs to wallow in self-pity and indulge generally in a "victim culture," (and thus increase the award of damages payable) instead of trying proactively to overcome the setbacks that they now face.

Damages for Pain and Suffering

W. Kip Viscusi, Reforming Products Liability
(1991)

The one component that has attracted the attention of products liability reformers is that of pain and suffering damages. The court system has no well-established methodology for setting pain and suffering and other noneconomic damages, and not surprisingly there have been claims that juries have often been inconsistent in establishing such damages. Examination of actual patterns of awards indicates that noneconomic damage compensation is quite substantial, and it varies in systematic fashion with the character of the injury.

Overall, depending on the injury category, pain and suffering and noneconomic damages constitute 30 percent to 50 percent of the total award. This level is not too dissimilar from the normal contingency fee share of one-third. Although legal reform debates may focus on the appropriate levels of pain and suffering compensation and treat such compensation at face value, this noneconomic damage component may simply be the mechanism by which juries compensate accident victims for their legal fees. If limits are imposed on pain and suffering. then juries may provide this compensation in other ways by, for example, increasing the amount of economic damages awarded.

One way to avoid this outcome is to include explicit compensation for reasonable attorney's fees as part of the award. Thus, pain and suffering awards would be governed by an advisory schedule, economic damages procedures would be unchanged, and attorney's fees would be addressed through a separate awards component based on a standardized fee schedule.

Although a wide variety of pain and suffering caps have been proposed, by far the more fundamental reform task is to establish a firm conceptual basis for pain and suffering awards. One such basis is the deterrence value of compensation.

A second conceptual approach would be the insurance value. In general. the insurance value is below the deterrence value, particularly for major injuries. Except for minor injuries, pain and suffering damages are not outcomes that individuals would choose to insure, so the optimal insurance amount for pain and suffering will typically be zero.

The competing objectives of deterrence and compensation in tort liability consequently results in pain and suffering damages that will typically range from zero to the deterrence values associated with the injury. If there were greater emphasis on the deterrence function, juries could be provided with schedules of such deterrence values and descriptions of the health outcomes, and they could then assess where along this schedule the injury suffered by the plaintiff would fall. This scheduling process would assist juries in making these judgments and would also decrease some of the uncertainty now associated with tort liability awards. It would provide structure without imposing arbitrary limits that do not allow variations with injury severity.

This guideline approach appears preferable to a damages cap. Caps will affect very few products liability claims and will have little overall financial impact. Some of the most highly publicized awards will, of course, be influenced by a cap, but the lion's share of the pain and suffering damages is generated by smaller claims, not by the few large claims at the extreme.

Moreover, noneconomic damage caps create a new class of inequities across injury groups. It is the minor injuries that tend to be overcompensated the most. The truly major injuries with substantial losses tend to be relatively undercompensated. Damages caps would leave the minor injuries unaffected and place a disproportionate burden on victims of injuries in only a few categories. such as brain damage and paraplegia.

There is no compelling rationale for caps other than the imposition of discipline. Rather than impose binding constraints on pain and suffering compensation, which does not even appear to be a driving force behind the liability crisis, it would be preferable to use suggested damages schedules that can be applied in a nonbinding manner.

Widespread adoption of deterrence values for pain, suffering, and the loss of life could, however, impose enormous costs. Moreover, even if one were indifferent to the price tag and simply wanted to create the correct incentives for safety, then utilization of the deterrence values of injury across the board is excessive except when firms completely ignore safety. Nevertheless, the courts could utilize the economic deterrence values in a very limited group of situations, as when it is important to establish defective deterrence incentives to promote appropriate recognition of product safety.

Deterrence values of life and health consequently can serve as the conceptual basis for setting punitive damages awards, thus providing greater certainty to a damages area where jury discretion is enormous. In addition, these values can be of general use in assessing whether firms undertook safety precautions sufficient to pass a risk-utility test. Finally, these estimates may be of use in other, very selected damages contexts where the courts' main interest is in establishing deterrence incentives rather than simply providing insurance to accident victims. These award levels would not be punitive in the sense of punishing firms, but they would be designed to redress imbalances when firms are ignoring the safety objectives at stake.

Questions

1. Should damages for pain and suffering be awarded in products liability cases?

2. If so, should they be capped in some way? If such caps should be imposed, what would be appropriate level(s)?

3. Should awards of damages be based on some sort of schedule (as happens, for example, in England)?

4. How could "deterrence values" of various types of harm be calculated?

5. Should attorneys' fees be included as part of an award of compensation to a successful plaintiff?

Emotional Distress

Norfolk & Western Railway Company v. Ayers
538 U.S. 135, 123 S.Ct. 1210 (2003) (SCOTUS)

GINSBURG, J. The Federal Employers' Liability Act (FELA or Act), 35 Stat. 65, as amended, 45 U.S.C. §§ 51–60, makes common carrier railroads liable in damages to employees who suffer work-related injuries caused "in whole or in part" by the railroad's negligence. This case, brought against Norfolk & Western Railway Company (Norfolk) by six former employees now suffering from asbestosis (asbestosis claimants), presents two issues involving the FELA's application. The first issue concerns the damages recoverable by a railroad worker who suffers from the disease asbestosis: When the cause of that disease, in whole or in part, was exposure to asbestos while on the job, may the worker's recovery for his asbestosis-related "pain and suffering" include damages for fear of developing cancer?

The second issue concerns the extent of the railroad's liability when third parties not before the court—for example, prior or subsequent employers or asbestos manufacturers or suppliers—may have contributed to the worker's injury. Is the railroad answerable in full to the employee, so that pursuit of contribution or indemnity from other potentially liable enterprises is the railroad's sole damages-award-sharing recourse? Or is the railroad initially entitled to an apportionment among injury-causing tortfeasors, i.e., a division of damages limiting the railroad's liability to the injured employee to a proportionate share? ...

The jury returned total damages awards for each asbestosis claimant, ranging from $770,000 to $1.2 million. After reduction for three claimants' comparative negligence from smoking and for settlements with non-FELA entities, the final judgments amounted to approximately $4.9 million. It is impossible to look behind those judgments to determine the amount the jury awarded for any particular element of damages. Norfolk, although it could have done so, did not endeavor to clarify the jury's damages determinations; it did not seek a special verdict or interrogatory calling upon the jury to report, separately, its assessments, if any, for fear-of-cancer damages.

The trial court denied Norfolk's motion for a new trial, and the Supreme Court of Appeals of West Virginia denied Norfolk's request for discretionary review. We granted certiorari, and now affirm....

We turn first to the question whether the trial judge correctly stated the law when he charged the jury that an asbestosis claimant, upon demonstrating a reasonable fear of cancer stemming from his present disease, could recover for that fear as part of asbestosis-related pain and suffering damages. In answering this question, we follow the path marked by the Court's decisions in *Consolidated Rail Corporation v. Gottshall*, 512 U.S. 532 (1994), and *Metro-North Commuter R. Co. v. Buckley*, 521 U.S. 424 (1997).

The FELA plaintiff in Gottshall alleged that he witnessed the death of a co-worker while on the job, and that the episode caused him severe emotional distress. He sought to recover damages from his employer, Conrail, for "mental or emotional harm ... not directly brought about by a physical injury." Reversing the Court of Appeals' judgment in favor of the plaintiff, this Court stated that uncabined recognition of claims for negligently inflicted emotional distress would "hol[d] out the very real possibility of nearly infinite and unpredictable liability for defendants." Of the "limiting tests ... developed in the common law," the Court selected the zone-of-danger test to delineate "the proper scope of an employer's duty under [the] FELA to avoid subjecting its employees to negligently inflicted emotional injury". That test confines recovery for stand-alone emotional distress claims to plaintiffs who: (1) "sustain a physical impact as a result of a defendant's negligent conduct"; or (2) "are placed in immediate risk of physical harm by that conduct"— that is, those who escaped instant physical harm, but were "within the zone of danger of physical impact." (internal quotation marks omitted). The Court remanded *Gottshall* for reconsideration under the zone-of-danger test.

In *Metro-North*, the Court applied the zone-of-danger test to a claim for damages under the FELA, one element of which was fear of cancer stemming from exposure to asbestos. The plaintiff in *Metro-North* had been intensively exposed to asbestos while working as a pipefitter for Metro-North in New York City's Grand Central Terminal. At the time of his lawsuit, however, he had a clean bill of health. The Court rejected his entire claim for relief. Exposure alone, the Court held, is insufficient to show "physical impact" under the zone-of-danger test. "[A] simple (though extensive) contact with a carcinogenic substance," the Court observed, "does not ... offer much help in separating valid from invalid emotional distress claims." The evaluation problem would be formidable, the Court explained, "because contacts, even extensive contacts, with serious carcinogens are common." "The large number of those exposed and the uncertainties that may surround recovery," the Court added, "suggest what *Gottshall* called the problem of 'unlimited and unpredictable liability.'"

As in *Gottshall*, the Court distinguished stand-alone distress claims from prayers for damages for emotional pain and suffering tied to a physical injury: "Common-law courts," the Court recognized, "do permit a plaintiff who suffers from a disease to recover for related negligently caused emotional distress ..." When a plaintiff suffers from a disease, the Court noted, common-law courts have made "a special effort" to value related emotional distress, "perhaps from a desire to make a physically injured victim whole or because the parties are likely to be in court in any event."

In sum, our decisions in *Gottshall* and *Metro-North* describe two categories: Stand-alone emotional distress claims not provoked by any physical injury, for which recovery is sharply circumscribed by the zone-of-danger test; and emotional distress claims brought on by a physical injury, for which pain and suffering recovery is permitted. Norfolk, whose position the principal dissent embraces.

Relevant to this characterization question, the parties agree that asbestosis is a cognizable injury under the FELA. Norfolk does not dispute that the claimants suffer from asbestosis, or that asbestosis can be "a clinically serious, often disabling, and progressive disease". As *Metro-North* plainly indicates, pain and suffering damages may include compensation for fear of cancer when that fear "accompanies a physical injury." Norfolk, therefore, cannot plausibly maintain that the claimants here, like the plaintiff in *Metro-North*, "are disease and symptom free." The plaintiffs in *Gottshall* and *Metro-North* grounded their suits on claims of negligent infliction of emotional distress. The claimants before us, in contrast, complain of a negligently inflicted physical injury (asbestosis) and attendant pain and suffering.

Unlike stand-alone claims for negligently inflicted emotional distress, claims for pain and suffering associated with, or "parasitic" on, a physical injury are traditionally compensable. The Restatement (Second) of Torts § 456 (1963–1964) (hereinafter Restatement) states the general rule:

> If the actor's negligent conduct has so caused any bodily harm to another as to make him liable for it, the actor is also subject to liability for "(a) fright, shock, *or other emotional disturbance* resulting from the bodily harm or from the conduct which causes it ..." (emphases added).

A plaintiff suffering bodily harm need not allege physical manifestations of her mental anguish. "The plaintiff must of course present evidence that she has suffered, but otherwise her emotional distress claims, in whatever form, are fully recoverable."

By 1908, when the FELA was enacted, the common law had evolved to encompass apprehension of future harm as a component of pain and suffering. The future harm, genuinely feared, need not be more likely than not to materialize. Physically injured plaintiffs, it is now recognized, may recover for "reasonable fears" of a future disease. As a classic example, plaintiffs bitten by dogs succeeded in gaining recovery, not only for the pain of the wound, but also for their fear that the bite would someday result in rabies or tetanus. The wound might heal, but "[t]he ghost of hydrophobia is raised, not to down during the life-time of the victim."

In the course of the 20th century, courts sustained a variety of other "fear-of" claims. Among them have been claims for fear of cancer. Heightened vulnerability to cancer, as one court observed, "must necessarily have a most depressing effect upon the injured person. Like the sword of Damocles," he knows it is there, but not whether or when it will fall. . . .

Arguing against the trend in the lower courts, Norfolk and its supporting *amici* assert that the asbestosis claimants' alleged cancer fears are too remote from asbestosis to warrant inclusion in their pain and suffering awards. In support of this contention, the United States, one of Norfolk's *amici*, refers to the "separate disease rule," under which most courts have held that the statute of limitations runs separately for each asbestos-related disease. Because the asbestosis claimants may bring a second action if cancer develops, Norfolk and the Government argue, cancer-related damages are unwarranted in their asbestosis suit. The question, as the Government frames it, is not *whether* the asbestosis claimants can recover for fear of cancer, but *when*. The principal dissent sounds a similar theme.

But the asbestosis claimants did not seek, and the trial court did not allow, discrete damages for their increased risk of future cancer. Instead, the claimants sought damages for their current injury, which, they allege, encompasses a present fear that the toxic exposure causative of asbestosis may later result in cancer. The Government's "*when*, not *whether*," argument has a large gap; it excludes recovery for the fear experienced by an asbestosis sufferer who never gets cancer. For such a person, the question is *whether*, not *when*, he may recover for his fear.

Even if the question is *whether*, not simply *when*, an asbestosis sufferer may recover for cancer fear, Norfolk has another string in its bow. To be compensable as pain and suffering, Norfolk maintains, a mental or emotional harm must have been "directly brought about by a physical injury." Because asbestosis itself, as distinguished from asbestos exposure, does not generate cancer, Norfolk insists and the principal dissent agrees, "fear of cancer is too unrelated, as a matter of law, to be an element of [an asbestosis sufferer's] pain and suffering." This argument elides over a key connection between Norfolk's conduct and the damages the asbestosis claimants allege as an element of their pain and suffering: Once found liable for "any bodily harm," a negligent actor is answerable in damages for emotional disturbance "resulting from the bodily harm *or from the conduct which causes it*." Restatement § 456(a) (emphasis added).

There is an undisputed relationship between exposure to asbestos sufficient to cause asbestosis, and asbestos-related cancer. Norfolk's own expert acknowledged that asbestosis puts a worker in a heightened risk category for asbestos-related lung cancer.

Furthermore, the asbestosis claimants' expert testified without contradiction to a risk notably "different in kind from the background risks that all individuals face,": Some "ten percent of the people who have the disease, asbestosis, have died of mesothelioma." In light of this evidence, an asbestosis sufferer would have good cause for increased apprehension about his vulnerability to another illness from his exposure, a disease that inflicts "agonizing, unremitting pain," relieved only by death.

Norfolk understandably underscores a point central to the Court's decision in *Metro-North*. The Court's opinion in *Metro-North* stressed that holding employers liable to workers merely exposed to asbestos would risk "unlimited and unpredictable liability." But as earlier observed, *Metro-North* sharply distinguished exposure-only plaintiffs from "plaintiffs who suffer from a disease," and stated, unambiguously, that "[t]he common law permits emotional distress recovery for [the latter] category." Commentary similarly distinguishes asymptomatic asbestos plaintiffs from plaintiffs who "developed asbestosis and thus suffered real physical harm."

The categorical approach endorsed in Metro-North serves to reduce the universe of potential claimants to numbers neither "unlimited" nor "unpredictable." Relevant here, and as Norfolk recognizes, of those exposed to asbestos, only a fraction will develop asbestosis.

Norfolk presented the question "[w]hether a plaintiff who has asbestosis but not cancer can recover damages for fear of cancer under the [FELA] without proof of physical manifestations of the claimed emotional distress." Brief for Petitioner (i). Our answer is yes, with an important reservation. We affirm only the qualification of an asbestosis sufferer to seek compensation for fear of cancer as an element of his asbestosis-related pain and suffering damages. It is incumbent upon such a complainant, however, to prove that his alleged fear is genuine and serious....

The "elephantine mass of asbestos cases" lodged in state and federal courts, we again recognize, "defies customary judicial administration and calls for national legislation." *Ortiz v. Fibreboard Corp.*, 527 U.S. 815, 821 (1999); see Report of the Judicial Conference Ad Hoc Committee on Asbestos Litigation 3, 27–35 (Mar.1991) ... Courts, however, must resist pleas of the kind Norfolk has made, essentially to reconfigure established liability rules because they do not serve to abate today's asbestos litigation crisis.

KENNEDY, J. (concurring in part and dissenting in part) (joined by REHNQUIST C.J., O'CONNOR and BREYER JJ.) The Court allows compensation for fear of cancer to those who manifest symptoms of some other disease, not itself causative of cancer, though stemming from asbestos exposure. The Court's precedents interpreting FELA neither compel nor justify this result. The Court's ruling is not based upon a sound application of the common-law principles that should inform our decisions implementing FELA. On the contrary, those principles call for a different rule, one which does not yield such aberrant results in asbestos exposure cases. These reasons require my respectful dissent.

It is common ground that the purpose of FELA is to provide compensation for employees protected under the Act. The Court's decision is a serious threat to that objective. Although a ruling that allows compensation for fear of a disease might appear on the surface to be solicitous of employees and thus consistent with the goals of FELA, the realities of asbestos litigation should instruct the Court otherwise.

Consider the consequences of allowing compensation for fear of cancer in the cases now before the Court. The respondents are between 60 and 77 years old. All except one have a long history of tobacco use, and three have smoked for more than 50 years. They suffer from shortness of breath, but only one testified that it affects his daily activities. As for emotional injury, one of the respondents complained that his shortness of breath caused him to become depressed; the others stated, in response to questions from their attorneys, that they have some "concern" about their health and about cancer. For this, the jury awarded each respondent between $770,640 and $1,230,806 in damages, reduced by the trial court to between $523,605 and $1,204,093 to account for the comparative negligence of the respondents' cigarette use.

Contrast this recovery with the prospects of an employee who does not yet have asbestosis but who in fact will develop asbestos-related cancer. Cancers caused by asbestos have long periods of latency. Their symptoms do not become manifest for decades after exposure. These cancers inflict excruciating pain and distress-pain more severe than that associated with asbestosis, distress more harrowing than the fear of developing a future illness.

One who has mesothelioma, in particular, faces agonizing, unremitting pain in the lungs, which spreads throughout the thoracic cavity as tumors expand and metastasize. The symptoms do not subside. Their severity increases, with death the only prospect for relief. And death is almost certain within a short time from the onset of mesothelioma. Yet the majority's decision endangers this employee's chances of recovering any damages for the simple reason that, by the time the worker is entitled to sue for the cancer, the funds available for compensation in all likelihood will have disappeared, depleted by verdicts awarding damages for unrealized fear, verdicts the majority is so willing to embrace.

This Court has recognized the danger that no compensation will be available for those with severe injuries caused by asbestos. In fact the Court already has framed the question that should guide its resolution of this case:

> In a world of limited resources, would a rule permitting immediate large-scale recoveries for widespread emotional distress caused by fear of future disease diminish the likelihood of recovery by those who later suffer from the disease?

The Court ignores this question and its warning. It is only a matter of time before inability to pay for real illness comes to pass. The Court's imprudent ruling will have been a contributing cause to this injustice.

Asbestos litigation has driven 57 companies, which employed hundreds of thousands of people, into bankruptcy, including 26 companies that have become insolvent since January 1, 2000. With each bankruptcy the remaining defendants come under greater financial strain, and the funds available for compensation become closer to exhaustion.

In this particular universe of asbestos litigation, with its fast diminishing resources, the Court's wooden determination to allow recovery for fear of future illness is antithetical to FELA's goals of ensuring compensation for injuries.

Affirmed.

Notes

1. *Negligence at work.* There is no system of workers' compensation statute for employees working on the railroads. Instead, any injury sustained while at work is compensable only if it fits within the parameters of the regular common law, particularly the law of negligence.

2. *Time value of money.* The dissent in *Ayers* is concerned that allowing claims for emotional distress now might mean an inability to compensate for physical injuries later. While this is undoubtedly a genuine concern, the dissent seems not to appreciate the time value of money. Since those who subsequently suffer physical harm are likely to be among the group of plaintiffs who are claiming compensation now for the emotional distress suffered at the prospect of having to endure such injury in the future, it could be argued that it is better for them to receive the compensation sooner rather than later. This might

give them a better quality of life for the intervening period which will offset, to some extent, the subsequent pain and suffering. Moreover (or alternatively), any compensation received now can be invested for the future, so that the subsequent physical trauma can receive expeditious medical treatment without questions over who will pay, whether the individual's health plan coverage limits have been exceeded, or how then to go about bringing a lawsuit. It is true that others are also likely to be compensated for their emotional distress who do not subsequently go on to experience the physical symptoms, but if the choice of who has that money is between such individuals and the corporation who put everyone in this position, it is not clear why the corporation should be favored.

Question

Is the crux of the dispute in *Ayers* between Justices Ginsburg and Kennedy (a) a disagreement over policy as to how available resources should be deployed, or (b) a disagreement as to whether fear of a future injury amounts to a species of pain and suffering endured now (which must therefore be compensable), or mere speculation as to the possible enduring of injury at some time in the future (which cannot be compensable)?

Flax v. DaimlerChrysler Corporation

272 S.W.3d 521 (2008) (Supreme Court of Tennessee)

HOLDER, J. The plaintiffs filed this products liability case against DaimlerChrysler seeking damages for the wrongful death of their son and for emotional distress suffered by the mother. The plaintiffs also sought punitive damages. We granted review to determine: 1) whether a negligent infliction of emotional distress claim brought simultaneously with a wrongful death claim is a "stand-alone" claim that requires expert medical or scientific proof of a severe emotional injury; 2) whether the evidence presented at trial was sufficient to support an award of punitive damages; 3) whether the punitive damages awarded by the trial court were excessive; and 4) whether the trial court erred by recognizing the plaintiffs' second failure to warn claim. We hold that the simultaneous filing of a wrongful death suit does not prevent a negligent infliction of emotional distress claim from being a "stand-alone" claim. Therefore, negligent infliction of emotional distress claims brought under these circumstances must be supported by expert medical or scientific proof of a severe emotional injury. In addition, we conclude that the punitive damages awarded by the trial court were adequately supported by the evidence and were not excessive....

On June 30, 2001, Rachel Sparkman and her eight-month-old son, Joshua Flax, were passengers in a 1998 Dodge Grand Caravan ("the Caravan") operated by Ms. Sparkman's father, Jim Sparkman. Ms. Sparkman was seated in a captain's chair directly behind the driver's seat. Joshua Flax was restrained in a child safety seat in the captain's chair directly behind the front passenger's seat, which Joe McNeil occupied.

As Mr. Sparkman turned left from a private drive onto a public road, the Caravan was rear-ended by a pickup truck driven by Louis Stockell. According to the testimony of the accident reconstruction experts, the pickup truck was traveling between fifty and fifty-six miles per hour at the time of impact. The Caravan was traveling in the same direction at a speed between ten and fifteen miles per hour. At the moment of the impact, the Caravan experienced a change in velocity of approximately seventeen to twenty-three miles per hour. Accident reconstruction experts for both parties testified that Mr. Sparkman was not responsible for the accident and that the accident would not have occurred if Mr. Stockell had not been driving at an excessive speed.

Upon impact, the backs of the seats containing Mr. Sparkman, Ms. Sparkman, and Mr. McNeil yielded rearward into a reclining position. Tragically, the front passenger's seat-back collapsed far enough to allow the back of Mr. McNeil's head to collide with Joshua Flax's forehead. The collision fractured Joshua Flax's skull and caused severe brain damage. None of the other passengers in the Caravan suffered serious injuries. Experts for both parties acknowledged that Joshua Flax would not have been seriously injured if the seat in front of him had not yielded rearward.

Immediately after the Caravan came to a rest, Ms. Sparkman checked on her son's condition and saw that his forehead had been, in her words, "smashed in." Michael Loftis, one of the first people to arrive at the scene of the accident, testified that he saw Ms. Sparkman outside the vehicle holding Joshua Flax. Because he believed Ms. Sparkman was "kind of hysterical" and could have accidentally caused further injury to Joshua Flax, Mr. Loftis offered to hold the child. Although initially reluctant, Ms. Sparkman agreed to give her son to Mr. Loftis. At this point, Mr. Loftis first observed that Joshua Flax had "a hole in his forehead approximately the size of a golf ball and probably a half inch deep." A short time later, Joshua Flax was transported to the hospital by ambulance. He died of his injuries the next day.

On May 7, 2002, Ms. Sparkman and Joshua Flax's father, Jeremy Flax, filed a complaint against Mr. Stockell and DaimlerChrysler Corporation ("DCC"), the manufacturer of the Caravan. The complaint alleged that the Caravan's seats are defective and unreasonably dangerous, that DCC failed to warn consumers that the seats pose a danger to children seated behind them, and that DCC is strictly liable under the Tennessee Products Liability Act of 1978. Tenn.Code Ann. §§ 29-28-101 to -108 (2000). The plaintiffs further alleged that the condition of the seats and the failure to warn proximately caused Joshua Flax's death and caused Ms. Sparkman to suffer severe emotional distress. Finally, the plaintiffs alleged that punitive damages are warranted because DCC acted intentionally and recklessly in manufacturing, marketing, and selling the Caravan.

After a lengthy trial, the jury found that the seats were defective and unreasonably dangerous, that DCC failed to warn the plaintiffs about the dangers of the seats at the time of sale, that DCC failed to warn plaintiffs about the dangers of the seats after the sale, and that DCC acted recklessly such that punitive damages should be imposed. The jury apportioned half of the fault to DCC and the other half to Mr. Stockell. Finally, the jury awarded $5,000,000 to the plaintiffs for the wrongful death of Joshua and $2,500,000 to Ms. Sparkman individually for negligent infliction of emotional distress ("NIED").

After the second stage of the trial, the jury awarded $65,500,000 in punitive damages to the plaintiffs for the wrongful death of Joshua Flax and $32,500,000 in punitive damages to Ms. Sparkman individually for NIED. Following the jury's verdict, the trial court conducted a review of the jury's award of punitive damages as required by *Hodges v. S.C. Toof & Co.*, 833 S.W.2d 896, 902 (Tenn.1992). In its findings of fact and conclusions of law the trial court concluded that "the jury properly found that Daimler Chrysler [sic] acted recklessly and that punitive damages were warranted." The trial court also concluded that the jury's award of punitive damages was excessive because there was a very large discrepancy between the punitive damages, totaling $98,000,000, and the compensatory damages for which DCC was liable, totaling $3,750,000. Accordingly, the trial court reduced the punitive damages to $20,000,000, a remittitur of $78,000,000. In its final order, the trial court indicated that the plaintiffs were entitled to $13,367,345 in punitive damages for the wrongful death of Joshua Flax and that Ms. Sparkman was individually entitled to $6,632,655 in punitive damages for NIED.

On appeal, the Court of Appeals concluded that Ms. Sparkman's NIED claim was subject to the heightened proof requirements set forth in *Camper v. Minor*, 915 S.W.2d 437, 446 (Tenn., 1996). The Court of Appeals reversed the jury's award of compensatory and punitive damages related to Ms. Sparkman's NIED claim against DCC because the plaintiffs did not satisfy the heightened proof requirements for a "stand-alone" NIED claim. In addition, the Court of Appeals concluded that there was not clear and convincing evidence that DCC acted recklessly or intentionally. Accordingly, the Court of Appeals reversed the trial court's award of all remaining punitive damages. Finally, the Court of Appeals affirmed the trial court's award of $5,000,000 in compensatory damages for the wrongful death of Joshua Flax. The plaintiffs appealed the ruling of the Court of Appeals. We granted review.

We begin our analysis with Ms. Sparkman's NIED claim. Our modern jurisprudence concerning NIED began with *Camper*. In that case, ... [w]e began our analysis in *Camper* by recognizing that the law governing NIED is fundamentally concerned with striking a balance between two opposing objectives: first, promoting the underlying purpose of negligence law—that of compensating persons who have sustained emotional injuries attributable to the wrongful conduct of others; and second, avoiding the trivial or fraudulent claims that have been thought to be inevitable due to the subjective nature of these injuries. We then catalogued a variety of approaches used in other jurisdictions to meet these two opposing goals. Some jurisdictions held that a plaintiff could not recover for NIED unless he or she suffered a "physical impact" caused by the defendant's negligent conduct. Other jurisdictions allowed a plaintiff to recover for NIED if the plaintiff suffered a "physical manifestation" of the emotional injury. Still other jurisdictions required that the plaintiff be in the "zone of danger" created by the defendant's negligent conduct....

To increase the fairness, clarity, and predictability of the law governing NIED, we abandoned the "physical manifestation" rule and adopted new requirements designed to distinguish between meritorious and frivolous cases. Specifically, we held that a plaintiff who has not suffered a physical injury must demonstrate through expert medical or scientific proof that he or she has suffered a "severe" emotional injury. We held that an emotional injury is "severe" if "'a reasonable person, normally constituted, would be unable to adequately cope with the mental stress engendered by the circumstances of the case.'" Our holding in *Camper* therefore balances the goals of compensating victims and avoiding fraudulent claims by: 1) allowing a person with emotional injuries to bring NIED claims regardless of whether he or she has suffered any physical injury, and 2) requiring a higher degree of proof for emotional injuries under these circumstances.

In *Ramsey v. Beavers*, 931 S.W.2d 527, 530–31 (Tenn., 1996), we reaffirmed the principles set forth in *Camper*, rejected the argument that the "zone of danger" test could be integrated into our *Camper* analysis, and held that a plaintiff who saw his mother hit by a car could bring a suit for NIED regardless of whether he was physically injured or placed in immediate danger of being physically injured. We emphasized that to prove his claim the plaintiff was required to present expert medical or scientific evidence that he had suffered a severe emotional injury. In addition, we held that to recover for emotional injuries sustained as the result of the death or injury of a third party a plaintiff must establish: 1) that he or she was sufficiently near the injury-causing event to allow sensory observation of the event, and 2) that the injury was, or was reasonably perceived to be, serious or fatal.

We further clarified our holding in *Camper* in *Estate of Amos v. Vanderbilt University*, 62 S.W.3d 133 (Tenn., 2001). *Amos* involved a plaintiff who was infected with HIV during a blood transfusion. The plaintiff received no notice of the possibility that she had been exposed to HIV. Years later, the plaintiff gave birth to a daughter who was infected with HIV in utero. After her daughter died of an AIDS-related virus, the plaintiff was tested and learned that she had HIV. The plaintiff and her husband filed suit for wrongful birth, negligence, and NIED. The defendants in *Amos* cited *Camper* and argued that the plaintiff was not entitled to recover for emotional injuries because she had failed to present expert or scientific testimony of serious or severe emotional injury. We rejected this argument and held that "[t]he special proof requirements in *Camper* are a unique safeguard to ensure the reliability of 'stand-alone' negligent infliction of emotional distress claims." Because "the risk of fraudulent claims is less ... in a case in which a claim for emotional injury damages is one of multiple claims for damages[,]" we held that the heightened proof requirements set forth in *Camper* are inapplicable "[w]hen emotional damages are a 'parasitic' consequence of negligent conduct that results in multiple types of damages." In other words, we recognized a distinction between traditional negligence claims that include damages for emotional injuries and claims that are based solely on NIED.

The plaintiff in *Amos* alleged that she had suffered emotional injuries caused by her infection with HIV and by the subsequent infection of her daughter. Because the plaintiff's claim of emotional damages was not separate from her other claims of negligence, but rather was "parasitic" to those claims, her claim was properly characterized as a negligence claim that included damages for emotional injuries. As her claim was not based solely on NIED, we concluded that the proof requirements of *Camper* were inapplicable.

With this history in mind, we now turn to the facts of the instant case. At trial, the plaintiffs failed to present expert medical or scientific proof that Ms. Sparkman suffered severe emotional injuries. DCC filed motions for directed verdict and judgment notwithstanding the verdict, arguing that Ms. Sparkman's NIED claim was invalid because plaintiffs failed to meet the *Camper* requirements. Plaintiffs argued that the heightened proof requirements of *Camper* were inapplicable because Ms. Sparkman's NIED claim was filed with a wrongful death claim and was therefore not a "stand-alone" claim. The trial court agreed with the plaintiffs and upheld the jury's verdict with respect to Ms. Sparkman's NIED claim.

On appeal, the plaintiffs continue to argue that the NIED claim is not a "stand-alone" claim because the plaintiffs also brought a wrongful death suit on behalf of Joshua Flax. We disagree. It is well settled that a wrongful death action is a claim belonging to the decedent, not the decedent's beneficiaries. Accordingly, the wrongful death claim in the instant case belongs to Joshua Flax rather than to the plaintiffs.

This case is therefore distinguishable from *Amos*, a case in which the plaintiff sought to recover for emotional damages parasitic to negligence and wrongful birth claims that were personal to the plaintiff. Nothing in our opinion in *Amos* was intended to allow plaintiffs to avoid the heightened proof requirements of *Camper* by bringing a separate wrongful death suit on behalf of a decedent. Because Ms. Sparkman's NIED claim is the only claim that is personal to one of the plaintiffs, we must conclude that it is a "stand-alone" claim subject to the requirements of *Camper*.

Furthermore, this case is not meaningfully distinguishable from our decision in *Ramsey*, a case in which the plaintiff saw his mother killed when she was hit by a car. We held that to recover for emotional injuries sustained as the result of the death or injury of a third party a plaintiff must present expert medical or scientific proof of a severe emotional injury and establish proximity to the injury-causing event and severity of the injury to the third party. Like the plaintiff in *Ramsey*, Ms. Sparkman seeks to recover for emotional injuries sustained as a result of witnessing the death of an immediate family member. That the plaintiffs in this case brought a wrongful death suit is not sufficient to exempt the NIED claim from the requirements set forth in *Camper* and Ramsey because the filing of a wrongful death suit does nothing to demonstrate the reliability of an NIED claim.

The plaintiffs also argue that the NIED claim is valid because Ms. Sparkman suffered minor physical injuries in the accident but chose not to bring a claim for those injuries. This argument has two flaws. First, the plaintiff in *Camper* also suffered minor injuries for which he did not file a claim. Clearly, the plaintiff's minor injury in *Camper* did not prevent us from concluding that heightened proof requirements are necessary for NIED claims. Second, the emotional injuries alleged by Ms. Sparkman are not parasitic to the minor injuries she sustained in the accident but rather are the result of witnessing the death of her child. Even if Ms. Sparkman had chosen to bring a claim for her minor physical injuries, her NIED claim would remain a "stand-alone" claim because the emotional injuries sustained from witnessing the death of her child are completely unrelated to any physical injuries she may have sustained. Of course, Ms. Sparkman would not have been required to meet the *Camper* requirements to recover for any mental and emotional suffering resulting from her own physical injuries. When a plaintiff suffers a physical injury there is some indication that allegations of emotional and mental injuries resulting from that injury are not fraudulent. On the other hand, having a potential claim for physical injuries does nothing to ensure the reliability of an NIED claim relating to the emotional injuries resulting from witnessing the death or injury of a third party. Accordingly, there is no good reason to relieve Ms. Sparkman of her burden of meeting the *Camper* requirements.

Finally, the plaintiffs argue that the heightened proof requirements of *Camper* are unnecessary in this case because the severity of Ms. Sparkman's emotional injuries is obvious. Although it is axiomatic that witnessing the death of one's child is a horrific experience, it is not at all obvious what impact such an event will have on any particular individual. Indeed, we constructed the *Camper* requirements precisely because emotional injuries are uniquely subjective. Although sympathy for a particular plaintiff may tempt us to hold that certain circumstances "obviously" result in severe emotional injuries, we must also recognize that such a holding would subvert the principles set forth in *Camper* and would likely lead to the kind of ad hoc decisions that originally made NIED case law unpredictable and incoherent. Furthermore, we do not believe the requirement that a severe emotional injury be proven by expert medical or scientific evidence is unduly burdensome to those plaintiffs who have suffered legitimate "stand-alone" emotional injuries. Accordingly, we decline to create an exception to the *Camper* requirements based on the particular circumstances of this case.

Based on the foregoing considerations, we hold that Ms. Sparkman's NIED claim was governed by the heightened proof requirements of *Camper*. It is uncontested that Ms. Sparkman failed to meet those requirements. We therefore affirm, albeit under slightly different reasoning, the Court of Appeals' reversal of the compensatory and punitive damage awards based on Ms. Sparkman's NIED claim.

Questions

1. The courts in *Ayers* and *Flax* essentially drew a distinction between claims of compensation for stand-alone, "pure" emotional distress and those for parasitic or "consequential" emotional distress. What are the reasons for such a distinction?

2. Do those reasons actually apply in *Flax*?

3. Why should a plaintiff be required to prove additional elements in a case of pure emotional distress over and above those required in a case of consequential emotional distress?

Economic Loss

We have already met the so-called economic loss rule on a number of occasions throughout this book. Damages for economic losses consequential on physical harm—such as medical bills and loss of income—are essentially unproblematic, especially because—unlike damages for pain and suffering, or emotional distress—economic losses can be verified objectively by expert accountants and actuaries.

Stand-alone, or "pure," economic losses are much more controversial, however, even though they are just as objectively verifiable as those that are consequential on physical harm. The reason for this controversy is, as we have seen, often said to be a technical matter of legal doctrine, namely whether purely economic losses be recoverable in torts, or only in contracts. Underlying this technicality, however, are several practical issues. One of those issues is that losses recoverable in contracts for breach of warranty can, as we saw in Chapter 3, be limited or even excluded altogether; another is that such claims cannot raise the prospect of a possible award of punitive damages.

East River Steamship Corp. v. Transamerica Delaval, Inc.
476 U.S. 858, 106 S.Ct. 2295 (1986) (SCOTUS)

BLACKMUN, J. In this admiralty case, we must decide whether a cause of action in tort is stated when a defective product purchased in a commercial transaction malfunctions, injuring only the product itself and causing purely economic loss. The case requires us to consider preliminarily whether admiralty law, which already recognizes a general theory of liability for negligence, also incorporates principles of products liability, including strict liability. Then, charting a course between products liability and contract law, we must determine whether injury to a product itself is the kind of harm that should be protected by products liability or left entirely to the law of contracts....

Damage to a product itself is most naturally understood as a warranty claim. Such damage means simply that the product has not met the customer's expectations, or, in other words, that the customer has received "insufficient product value." The maintenance of product value and quality is precisely the purpose of express and implied warranties. Therefore, a claim of a nonworking product can be brought as a breach-of-warranty action. Or, if the customer prefers, it can reject the product or revoke its acceptance and sue for breach of contract.

Contract law, and the law of warranty in particular, is well suited to commercial controversies of the sort involved in this case because the parties may set the terms of their own agreements. The manufacturer can restrict its liability, within limits, by disclaiming warranties or limiting remedies. In exchange, the purchaser pays less for the product. Since a commercial situation generally does not involve large disparities in bargaining power, we see no reason to intrude into the parties' allocation of the risk.

While giving recognition to the manufacturer's bargain, warranty law sufficiently protects the purchaser by allowing it to obtain the benefit of its bargain. The expectation damages available in warranty for purely economic loss give a plaintiff the full benefit of its bargain by compensating for forgone business opportunities. Recovery on a warranty theory would give the charterers their repair costs and lost profits, and would place them in the position they would have been in had the turbines functioned properly. Thus, both the nature of the injury and the resulting damages indicate it is more natural to think of injury to a product itself in terms of warranty.

A warranty action also has a built-in limitation on liability, whereas a tort action could subject the manufacturer to damages of an indefinite amount. The limitation in a contract action comes from the agreement of the parties and the requirement that consequential damages, such as lost profits, be a foreseeable result of the breach. In a warranty action where the loss is purely economic, the limitation derives from the requirements of foreseeability and of privity, which is still generally enforced for such claims in a commercial setting.

In products-liability law, where there is a duty to the public generally, foreseeability is an inadequate brake. Permitting recovery for all foreseeable claims for purely economic loss could make a manufacturer liable for vast sums. It would be difficult for a manufacturer to take into account the expectations of persons downstream who may encounter its product. In this case, for example, if the charterers—already one step removed from the transaction—were permitted to recover their economic losses, then the companies that subchartered the ships might claim their economic losses from the delays, and the charterers' customers also might claim their economic losses, and so on. "The law does not spread its protection so far."

And to the extent that courts try to limit purely economic damages in tort, they do so by relying on a far murkier line, one that negates the charterers' contention that permitting such recovery under a products-liability theory enables admiralty courts to avoid difficult line drawing.

Judgment affirmed.

Lloyd v. General Motors Corp.

397 Md. 108, A.2d 257 (Court of Appeals of Maryland, 2002)

BELL, CJ. The major issue in this case is whether the cost to repair defective seatbacks, which allegedly have a tendency to collapse in rear-impact collisions, causing, in some cases, serious bodily injury or death to drivers and/or passengers in the class vehicles, constitutes a cognizable injury, in the form of economic loss for claims sounding in tort, contract, and consumer protection.

Inconsistent with the conclusion reached by the Circuit Court for Montgomery County and the Court of Special Appeals, we shall hold that the petitioners, Timothy and Bernadette Lloyd, have sufficiently alleged an injury that is cognizable under each of the petitioners' claims. Accordingly, we shall reverse the judgment of the Court of Special Appeals dismissing the petitioners' claims.

The petitioners are Timothy and Bernadette Lloyd and seven other Maryland residents, who own "class vehicles," automobiles manufactured between 1990 and 1999 by the respondents, General Motors Corporation, Ford Motor Company, Daimler Chrysler Corporation and Saturn Corporation. The petitioners brought this class action to recover from the respondents the cost of repairing and/or replacing the front seats in each class vehicle. They allege that the seats are unsafe because they collapse rearward in moderate and severe rear-impact collisions. None of the petitioners or any putative class members allege that he or she has experienced personal injury as a result of the mechanical failure that caused the alleged defect. Indeed, persons with such experiences were expressly excluded from this class.

The Third Amended Complaint ("TAC") contains seven counts. Count one alleges negligence in the design and manufacture of the seats. Count two, sounding in strict liability, alleges that the seats were in a defective condition, rendering them "inherently dangerous and creating an unreasonable risk of serious injury or death to users" when they left the control of the defendants. Count three alleges breach of the implied warranty of merchantability. Count four alleges negligent failure to disclose, failure to warn, concealment and misrepresentation. Count five alleges fraudulent concealment and intentional failure to warn. Count six alleges unfair or deceptive trade practices under the Maryland Consumer Protection Act (CPA). Count seven alleges civil conspiracy....

The petitioners filed this suit in the Circuit Court for Montgomery County. Before the petitioners filed pleadings seeking certification of a class, the respondents moved, pursuant to Maryland Rule 2-322(b), to dismiss the complaint for failure to state a claim upon which relief could be granted. The trial court granted the motion, holding that

> the economic loss doctrine would not support the cause of action being sought by the plaintiffs in this case, and there is insufficient basis to allow a fraud claim to continue against these defendants.

The petitioners noted an appeal to the Court of Special Appeals. In an unreported opinion, that court affirmed the dismissal of the action....

The petitioners filed a petition for Writ of Certiorari, which we granted....

Ordinarily, as noted, *supra*, damages for economic loss are not available in a tort action and are recoverable, if at all, in contract causes of action and, in the case of fraud, in actions for deceit. We have explained the rationale for this general rule:

> The distinction between tort recovery for physical injury and warranty recovery for economic loss derives from policy considerations which allocate the risks related to a defective product between seller and the purchaser. A manufacturer may be held liable for physical injuries, including harm to property, caused by defects in its products because it is charged with the responsibility to ensure that its products meet a standard of safety creating no unreasonable risk of harm. However, where the loss is purely economic, the manufacturer cannot be charged with the responsibility of ensuring that the product meet [sic] the particular expectations of the consumer unless it is aware of those expectations and has agreed that the product will meet them. Thus, generally, the only recovery for a purely economic loss would be under a contract theory....

There is an exception to the general rule, however:

> Even when a recovery, based on a defective product, is considered to be for purely economic loss, a plaintiff may still recover in tort if this defect creates a substantial and unreasonable risk of death or personal injury.

This Court adopted this exception, an increasingly popular view, in *Council of Co-Owners Atlantis Condominium, Inc. v. Whiting-Turner Contracting Co.*, 517 A.2d 336, 345 (1986). There, we recognized that, in limited circumstances, those in which a product defect presents a substantial, clear and unreasonable risk of death or personal injury, it is inappropriate to draw a distinction

> between mere "economic loss" and personal injury.... When one is personally injured from a defect, he recovers mainly for his economic loss. Similarly, if a wife loses a husband because of injury from a defect in construction, the measure of damages is totally economic loss. We fail to see any rational reason for such a distinction....

Thus, in order to assert a cognizable products liability theory of recovery, an action sounding in tort, but one premised on economic loss alone, the plaintiff must allege facts that demonstrate that the product at issue creates a dangerous condition, one that gives rise to a clear danger of death or personal injury....

[I]n order to determine whether a valid tort claim exists under the exception to the economic loss rule, the court must

> examine both the nature of the damage threatened and the probability of damage occurring to determine whether the two, viewed together, exhibit a clear, serious, and unreasonable risk of death or personal injury.

Furthermore, we expounded on the logic of this two-part approach, vis-a-vis the general rule barring recovery in tort for economic losses:

> This two part approach recognizes the negative effects that could occur if the economic loss rule was abandoned.... It balances these considerations, however, against the public policy of encouraging people to correct dangerous conditions before tragedy results. Accordingly, we do not ordinarily allow tort claims for purely economic loss. But when those losses are coupled with serious risk of death or personal injury resulting from a dangerous condition, we allow recovery in tort to encourage correction of the dangerous condition.

We also explained that, when analyzing the two elements, the critical test is not whether the plaintiff has alleged facts that meet an articulable threshold for both elements, but, rather, whether that plaintiff has met the threshold to satisfy either of the elements so long as, under the facts alleged, both elements are, at a minimum, present....

> Thus, if the possible injury is extraordinarily severe, i.e., multiple deaths, we do not require the probability of the injury occurring to be as high as we would require if the injury threatened were less severe, i.e. a broken leg or damage to property. Likewise, if the probability of the injury occurring is extraordinarily high, we do not require the injury to be as severe as we would if the probability of the injury were lower....

Applying the thresholds established in *Whiting-Turner*, ... we disagree with the intermediate appellate court, that the appellants in the case sub judice asserted insufficient facts to meet the pleading threshold with regard to the risk of serious bodily injury. On the contrary, we believe that the appellants have alleged facts adequate to satisfy both elements of the analysis, the nature of the damage and the probability of damage prongs, for determining when an exception will lie to the general economic loss bar to recovery.

With regard to the first prong, the nature of the damage, the appellants aver that individuals have suffered extremely serious injuries, including paraplegia, quadriplegia and/or death as a result of rear impact collisions in the class vehicles containing the allegedly defective seat-backs. Certainly, ... such injuries rise to the level of "serious injury" ... [A] plaintiff need only allege facts that satisfy one of the prongs of the analysis to an acceptable degree[;] the fact that the severity of the potential injury is so grave, in this case, is sufficient to meet the threshold for the petitioners' recovery of economic losses, even if the probability that the injuries would occur is not as high.

This Court, however, also concludes that the petitioners have alleged sufficient facts to satisfy the second prong of the *Morris* economic loss analysis, as well, the probability that a serious injury, or death, would occur as a result of the allegedly defective seatbacks. In its TAC, the petitioners alleged that thousands of individuals have been injured or killed as a result of the collapse of the class vehicle seatbacks in rear-end collisions. Indeed, the petitioners' exhibit D includes specific records of complaints made to the National Highway Traffic Safety Administration (NHTSA), in which the drivers of class cars experienced the collapse of seatbacks in rear-end collisions resulting in no less than 38 reported injuries and 3 fatalities. The number of these incidents, as alleged, is certainly greater than those alleged in *Morris*, where the appellants alleged no actual record of past injury, a fact to which this Court accorded great weight when holding that the appellants, in that case, did not meet the threshold for economic loss under the *Whiting-Turner* exception. Although we acknowledge the important goal of the general bar to recovery for purely economic losses, to "keep products liability and contract law in separate spheres and to maintain a realistic limitation on damages," it is exactly the risk of serious bodily injury involved in this case that the exception to the economic loss rule was intended to remedy, to "encourag[e] people to correct dangerous conditions before tragedy results."

Reversed and remanded.

Questions

1. Do you agree with the application of the economic loss rule to products liability cases? Why (not)?

2. If the economic loss rule is appropriate, does the decision in *Lloyd* make sense?

Punitive Damages

Punitive damages are, as their name suggests, not awarded to compensate the victim but to punish the defendant. They are also expected to deter others from engaging in similar conduct in the future. Accordingly, they are awarded only where the defendant has behaved in such a way as to warrant punishment. Punitive damages are not, for example, awarded for a defendant's breach of contract, since contractual liability is strict and therefore involves no imputation of fault. A successful products liability claim for breach of warranty will not, therefore, entitle the plaintiff to ask for punitive damages. Moreover, punitive damages are awarded in only about five percent of successful torts actions. This is because 'mere' negligence does not warrant punishment: there must be evidence of the defendant's egregious conduct for punitive damages to be awarded.

The awarding of punitive damages is, perhaps, even more controversial than the awarding of damages for pain and suffering, emotional distress, or pure economic loss. Other nations with common law systems are far more restrictive about when punitive damages may be awarded; in England, for example, it is virtually impossible for someone injured by a defective product to receive punitive damages. The reason for such restrictiveness is that punishment is viewed in those countries as a matter falling within the almost exclusive province of the criminal law.

Even within the United States, state attorneys-general may bring actions against corporations for producing defective products, especially under the Racketeer Influenced and Corrupt Organization Act (RICO), discussed further below, but such cases will still be civil matters rather than criminal prosecutions. The truth is that, while American criminal law can be highly punitive once invoked, the mechanisms for doing so are somewhat cumbersome, and the will to do so is often rather feeble in comparison to many other Western countries. For this reason, it is often said that the law of torts enables ordinary citizens, and their attorneys, to act like private attorneys-general in holding the manufacturers and distributors of defective products to account.

An apparent oddity of permitting awards of punitive damages in a civil action is that the successful plaintiff will essentially gain a windfall, over and above any loss s/he has suffered. Moreover, this windfall will often have been gained because of the harm caused to many other victims of the defective product that is the focus of the case. Thus the plaintiff may be said to be benefiting from an injustice caused to others. Some states have reacted to this by enacting legislation that enables the state, as the embodiment of the people, to claim a proportion of any punitive damages award.

A further problem with awarding punitive damages in a civil case is that the jury is provided with no guidance on how large the sanction should be. If it were a criminal prosecution, the judge would usually have some sentencing guidelines to assist him or her in working out the appropriate sanction. Moreover, that is a judge's job: s/he is experienced in sentencing criminals. But juries have no such experience, and have nothing to guide them. An award of punitive damages may be as large as a piece of string is long.

To supporters of punitive damages, however, this very unpredictability is the strength of punitive damages; it is the fear of a huge award, rather than any actual such awards, that acts as a big deterrent to wrongdoing. This argument exposes an ambiguity in the purpose of punitive damages. Are they really intended as retributive punishment after the event, or as a deterrent to avoid such wrongdoing in the first place?

Whatever view is taken of the appropriateness of punitive damages in products liability cases—whether as a matter of principle, or in a specific case—it can hardly be stressed too much that such awards are paid in very few cases indeed. It is not just that only around five percent of successful torts claims result in such awards; it needs also to be emphasized that only around two percent of those cases actually end with the award intact. Thus only around one in a thousand successful plaintiffs actually receive a punitive damages award.

The reason for the tiny likelihood of receipt is that any award will almost automatically be met by the defendant's deciding to appeal. This can lead to years of protracted litigation, whose outcome is difficult to predict. In reality, it is probably better to see an award of punitive damages as opening a new stage of negotiations between the parties, with the plaintiff often prepared to accept a much smaller sum immediately on the basis that a bird in the hand is worth two (or, perhaps, twenty) in the bush, and with the defendant often prepared to pay such a reduced sum in order to get closure on the case (and, where the agreement is confidential, without any indication to other, prospective plaintiffs that a similar suit will necessarily be worthwhile).

Flax v. DaimlerChrysler Corporation

272 S.W.3d 521 (2008) (Supreme Court of Tennessee)

[For the facts of the case, see above.] HOLDER, J. Several issues relating to punitive damages have been hotly contested throughout the trial and appeal of this case. DCC continues to assert three arguments against the validity of the punitive damages awarded for the wrongful death of Joshua Flax. First, DCC argues that punitive damages are not warranted in this case because the evidence was insufficient to support a finding of recklessness....

DCC argues that the evidence submitted by the plaintiffs was insufficient to support the imposition of punitive damages. A verdict imposing punitive damages must be supported by clear and convincing evidence that the defendant acted intentionally, fraudulently, maliciously, or recklessly. *Hodges v. S.C. Toof & Co.*, 833 S.W.2d 896, 901 (Tenn.1992). In *Hodges*, we held that evidence is clear and convincing when it leaves "no serious or substantial doubt about the correctness of the conclusions drawn." We also held that a person acts recklessly when "the person is aware of, but consciously disregards, a substantial and unjustifiable risk of such a nature that its disregard constitutes a gross deviation from the standard of care that an ordinary person would exercise under all the circumstances." The jury in this case found that there was clear and convincing evidence that DCC's conduct was reckless.

When this Court is called upon to review the reasonableness of a jury's verdict, as we are in this case, we "are limited to determining whether there is material evidence to support the verdict." In making this determination, we do not re-weigh the evidence. Rather, we are "required to take the strongest legitimate view of all of the evidence in favor of the verdict, to assume the truth of all that tends to support it, allowing all reasonable inferences to sustain the verdict, and to discard all to the contrary." The jury's verdict must be affirmed if any material evidence supports it. Therefore, our review of this issue is limited to determining whether any material evidence supports the jury's conclusion that there is no serious or substantial doubt that DCC consciously disregarded a known, substantial, and unjustifiable risk to the plaintiffs.

To determine whether there is any material evidence supporting the jury's verdict, we must summarize the evidence presented at trial in some detail. At trial, the plaintiffs sought to prove that DCC had known for over twenty years that its seats were defective and unreasonably dangerous but failed to remedy the problem or warn consumers of the danger. DCC countered by arguing that it designed the seats to yield rearward in rear-end collisions to absorb energy from the collision and protect the occupant of the seat. According to DCC, the Caravan design protects the greatest number of people in the greatest number of potential accidents and using stronger seatbacks would increase the danger to occupants of the seat. To further support its argument that its seat design was reasonably safe, DCC repeatedly noted that its seatbacks were similar to those used by other manufacturers and exceeded the federal regulation governing seatback strength, Federal Motor Vehicle Safety Standard 207 ("FMVSS 207").

As part of their effort to demonstrate that the Caravan's seatbacks posed a substantial and unjustifiable risk, the plaintiffs introduced the testimony of Dr. Saczalski, an expert on seat engineering. Dr. Saczalski testified that the Caravan's seats were defective and unreasonably dangerous because they posed a threat to children seated behind them. His testimony was based in part on crash testing he conducted in an attempt to recreate the accident underlying this case. During the crash test, Dr. Saczalski used vehicles of the same make and model as those involved in the accident and attempted to account for the weight, speed, and trajectory of each vehicle. The Caravan used in the crash test contained dummies approximating the size and weight of Mr. Sparkman, Mr. McNeil, Ms. Sparkman, and Joshua Flax. Dr. Saczalski replaced the driver's seat of the Caravan with a seat from a 1996 Chrysler Sebring, a DCC vehicle that had seats with backs approximately five times stronger than the seats used in the Caravan. Dr. Saczalski placed the Sebring seat in the crash test vehicle to demonstrate how a stronger seatback would perform under forces equivalent to those suffered by the Caravan in the actual accident.

Consistent with the circumstances of the actual accident, videos of the crash test show that the front passenger's seat yielded rearward allowing the McNeil surrogate's head to impact the head of the Joshua Flax surrogate. The Sebring seat also yielded rearward but to a far lesser degree. Significantly, the Sebring seat did not substantially encroach upon the seating area behind it. Dr. Saczalski concluded from the crash test that Joshua Flax would have survived the accident without serious injury had the Caravan been equipped with seats with backs as strong as those of the Sebring seat. Contrary to DCC's assertion that stronger seatbacks impose greater dangers to their occupants in rear-end collisions, the crash test dummy in the stronger Sebring seat experienced less head and neck acceleration than the dummy in the Caravan seat.

Dr. Saczalski also testified regarding several other crash tests he performed in which Sebring seats were placed side-by-side with other DCC minivan seats. These tests also demonstrated that DCC minivan seats have the capacity to cause injury to children seated behind them. The test results support the view that Sebring seats do not pose the same threat because they do not encroach upon the passenger space behind them. Furthermore, Dr. Saczalski testified that the dummy-occupants of the stronger Sebring seats tended to experience less acceleration to the head and neck than the dummy-occupants of weaker seats.

The plaintiffs also made a considerable effort to demonstrate that DCC was aware that the Caravan seats were defective and unreasonably dangerous for at least twenty years. The minutes from a DCC Engineer Safety Committee meeting dated December 10, 1980, appear to contain the first acknowledgment that yielding seatbacks could be a potential problem. In the meeting it was noted that the seatbacks had yielded to some degree in every crash test and that "improvements could be made, but would require development costs and a piece penalty would result." The Engineer Safety Committee did not make any recommendation to improve seatback strength because the seats performed as well as those of DCC's competitors, complied with federal requirements, and had not been demonstrated "to be a significant injury producing problem." Videos of crash testing performed by DCC confirm that in rear-impact collisions the seats yielded into the occupant space behind them. In addition, plaintiffs presented documentation showing that in at least one crash test conducted in 1989 the front seats were braced to prevent the seatbacks from impacting equipment occupying the back seat.

Although the minutes from the 1980 meeting indicate that there was no evidence that the seats were a "significant injury producing problem," DCC soon began to receive new information. According to an employee in DCC's customer relations department, during the mid-1980s, DCC began to receive reports of children injured by yielding seatbacks in rear-end collisions. DCC's records contained documentation of several rear-end collisions in which a yielding seatback caused a child to suffer skull or facial fractures. Other injuries sustained by children seated behind yielding seatbacks were also reported to DCC. In spite of these reports, DCC did not issue any warning to customers and continued to advertise the Caravan as a vehicle specifically designed to protect children.

The most significant testimony regarding DCC's knowledge of the danger presented by the Caravan seats was provided by Paul Sheridan, a former DCC employee. During his employment with DCC, Mr. Sheridan served as the chair of the Minivan Safety Leadership Team ("MSLT"), a committee formed to address safety concerns in DCC's minivans. The committee was comprised of persons from DCC's safety, engineering, marketing, sales, and design departments. One of the many safety issues the MSLT was formed to address was the issue of seatback strength. According to Mr. Sheridan, the MSLT had available to it complaints regarding injuries caused by yielding seatbacks. At a March 16, 1993, committee meeting, members of the MSLT reached a consensus that it was unacceptable for seats to yield rearward into the passenger space behind them and that the seats were inadequate to protect customers. After the meeting, Mr. Sheridan distributed the minutes of the meeting to various DCC executives. Some time thereafter, Ronald Zarowitz, a member of the MSLT representing DCC's safety office, instructed Mr. Sheridan to retrieve the minutes of the meeting and destroy them. Mr. Zarowitz informed Mr. Sheridan that this order came from Francois Castaing, the head of the engineering department. Mr. Sheridan retrieved the minutes as instructed, but he retained two copies in his office.

After the March 1993 meeting, Mr. Sheridan decided to investigate the seatback issue further. To this end, Mr. Sheridan met with an engineer responsible for seat design and requested the seat design specifications that discussed how the seats were designed to yield. According to Mr. Sheridan, the engineer "didn't know what [he] was asking for" but provided the design specifications of the seats. These specifications did not state that the seats were designed to yield. In fact, Mr. Sheridan testified that he never heard any engineer state that seatbacks were designed to yield rearward as a safety precaution. In September 1994, Mr. Sheridan told his supervisor that he was going to go to regulators with his concerns about the minivan seat backs. In November 1994, the MSLT was disbanded at the direction of Ted Cunningham, the executive with authority over minivan operations. Mr. Sheridan was fired on December 27, 1994, and the minutes from the March 1993 MSLT meeting and the seat design specifications were confiscated from his office.

We find little support in the record for Justice Koch's speculation that Mr. Sheridan's testimony "may very well reflect DaimlerChrysler's over-reaction to the Sixty Minutes story and the existence of some internal dissension regarding how best to respond to the concerns about car seat safety raised by the story." In fact, this characterization of Mr. Sheridan's testimony appears to have been rejected by the jury, which heard his testimony and was charged with resolving issues of credibility. Moreover, DCC presented no testimony that the formation of the MSLT was an "over-reaction," and it is clear from Mr. Sheridan's testimony that he believed the MSLT was necessary to address serious safety concerns. DCC's efforts to destroy the recommendations produced by the MSLT are a further indication of DCC's awareness of the seat-back problem and its determination to hide the problem rather than solve it. In our minds, this represents more than "some internal dissension regarding how best to respond to the concerns about car safety."

Justice Koch's efforts to discount Mr. Sheridan's testimony are inconsistent with our standard of review on appeal. The jury apparently accredited much of Mr. Sheridan's testimony, and, as we have stated, we are required to view his testimony in the light most favorable to the jury's verdict and assume the truth of his assertions that support the jury's verdict. We therefore must assume that Mr. Sheridan was truthful when he denied leaking confidential information to Auto World magazine. We must also make the reasonable inference that Mr. Sheridan in fact was fired because he threatened to go to regulators with his safety concerns. In addition, whether Mr. Sheridan has been excluded from testifying in other cases is irrelevant to our review. The trial court denied DCC's motion to exclude Mr. Sheridan's testimony, and DCC has not appealed that aspect of the trial court's ruling. The actions of another court have no impact on our review of the testimony accredited by the jury.

The plaintiffs also sought to demonstrate that compliance with FMVSS 207 was insufficient to make the Caravan seats reasonably safe. A seat engineer employed by DCC testified that FMVSS 207 requires "inadequate seat strength to insure that the seat does not fail when the car is subject to severe rear impact." In addition, Mr. Sheridan testified that members of the MSLT agreed that compliance with FMVSS 207 was insufficient to ensure safety of consumers. Furthermore, both of DCC's experts on seat design agreed that compliance with FMVSS 207 alone is inadequate to protect passengers.

Finally, the plaintiffs argued that stronger seatbacks would not result in greater injuries to occupants of the seats. Specifically, the plaintiffs claimed that the Sebring seat, which was approximately five times stronger than the Caravan seat, was a reasonably safe seat. The results of Dr. Saczalski's crash testing provide some evidence that the Sebring seat offered a reasonable level of protection to its occupants. In addition, one of DCC's experts on seatback engineering agreed that the Sebring seat was a reasonably safe seat.

In summary, the jury's finding that the Caravan seats posed a substantial and unjustifiable risk to consumers was supported by: 1) expert testimony that the seats were defective and unreasonably dangerous; 2) crash tests demonstrating that the yielding seatbacks consistently encroached upon the occupant space behind them; 3) Mr. Sheridan's testimony that safety officials and engineers employed by DCC believed that the Caravan's seats were unacceptably dangerous; and 4) crash test evidence and expert testimony that Joshua Flax would not have been killed had a stronger seat been in place. The jury's finding that DCC consciously disregarded the risks posed by the Caravan seats was supported by: 1) minutes of DCC meetings noting that seats yielded; 2) DCC crash tests demonstrating that seats consistently encroached upon the passenger space behind them; 3) DCC records of injuries caused by yielding seatbacks; and 4) Mr. Sheridan's testimony that executives ignored the MSLT's warning that the seatbacks were unacceptably dangerous. We conclude that this evidence adequately supports the jury's conclusion that there is no serious or substantial doubt that DCC consciously disregarded a known, substantial, and unjustifiable risk to the plaintiffs. The evidence that DCC executives failed to heed the warnings of the MSLT and ordered the destruction of the committee's findings is particularly compelling. Not only did DCC fail to warn customers or redesign its product, DCC hid the evidence and continued to market the Caravan as a vehicle that put safety first. Because the jury's verdict is supported by clear and convincing material evidence, we must affirm the jury's finding of recklessness.

DCC's argument that risks associated with the Caravan seats were justified by the need for the seat to absorb energy from the collision and protect seat occupants is of no avail. This argument was presented to the jury, and the jury was apparently unconvinced by it. The jury could have reasonably accredited Mr. Sheridan's testimony that the seats were not intentionally designed to yield as a safety mechanism. The jury also could have reasonably concluded from testimony regarding the Sebring seat that seats need not yield as dramatically as the Caravan seats to protect seat occupants. DCC's argument that there is an ongoing debate regarding the optimum level of seatback strength is also without merit. The jury could have reasonably concluded that such a debate exists and simultaneously found that the Caravan's seats were weak enough to fall outside the range of reasonable debate.

With regard to DCC's proposed justification, Justice Koch fails to give proper deference to the jury's conclusions. He concludes that a "genuine principled debate" concerning the proper seatback strength led DCC to design "the front seats of the minivan to yield in a controlled manner in the event of a rear impact." Whether the seats were designed to yield "in a controlled manner" was contested at trial. The jury, apparently convinced by the accident reconstruction, the expert testimony, DCC's crash tests, and Mr. Sheridan's testimony, concluded that the manner in which the seats yielded was unreasonably dangerous and that DCC recklessly disregarded the danger to its customers. While Justice Koch may disagree with that conclusion, this Court is not free to reweigh the evidence or second-guess the jury's conclusions when they are supported by material evidence.

We are also unconvinced by DCC's arguments that compliance with federal regulations and custom within an industry should bar the recovery of punitive damages. It is true that compliance with FMVSS 207 entitled DCC to a rebuttable presumption that its product was not unreasonably dangerous. It is equally true, for the reasons stated above, that the evidence in this case thoroughly rebutted that presumption. Tennessee Code Annotated section 29-28-104 was designed "'to give refuge to the manufacturer who is operating in good faith and [in] compliance of what the law requires him to do.'" The statute was not designed to provide immunity from punitive damages to a manufacturer who is aware that compliance with a regulation is insufficient to protect users of the product. While evidence of compliance with government regulations is certainly evidence that a manufacturer was not reckless, it is not dispositive. To hold otherwise would create an overly inflexible rule that would allow some manufacturers knowingly engaged in reprehensible conduct to escape the imposition of punitive damages.

Similarly, if a manufacturer knows that a common practice in an industry presents a substantial and unjustifiable risk to consumers, then compliance with the common practice is not an absolute bar to the recovery of punitive damages. Evidence that a manufacturer consciously disregarded substantial and unjustifiable risks to the public can, in some rare cases, overcome evidence that the manufacturer's practice was common in the industry. This is such a case. Because the jury could have reasonably concluded from the evidence presented that DCC was aware that compliance with the FMVSS 207 and the industry standard for seat design was insufficient, we hold that punitive damages were not barred in this case.

United States Code — Title 18: The Racketeer Influenced and Corrupt Organization Act (RICO) (1970)

§ 1961. Definitions

As used in this chapter—

(1) "racketeering activity" means (A) any act or threat involving murder, kidnapping, gambling, arson, robbery, bribery, extortion, dealing in obscene matter, or dealing in a controlled substance or listed chemical (as defined in section 102 of the Controlled Substances Act), which is chargeable under State law and punishable by imprisonment for more than one year; (B) any act which is indictable under any of the following provisions of title 18, United States Code: ... section 1341 (relating to mail fraud), section 1343 (relating to wire fraud), ... section 1546 (relating to fraud and misuse of visas, permits, and other documents), ... section 1951 (relating to interference with commerce, robbery, or extortion) ...

(4) "enterprise" includes any individual, partnership, corporation, association, or other legal entity, and any union or group of individuals associated in fact although not a legal entity;

(5) "pattern of racketeering activity" requires at least two acts of racketeering activity, one of which occurred after the effective date of this chapter and the last of which occurred within ten years (excluding any period of imprisonment) after the commission of a prior act of racketeering activity ...

§ 1962. Prohibited activities

(b) It shall be unlawful for any person through a pattern of racketeering activity ... to acquire or maintain, directly or indirectly, any interest in or control of any enterprise which is engaged in, or the activities of which affect, interstate or foreign commerce.

(c) It shall be unlawful for any person employed by or associated with any enterprise engaged in, or the activities of which affect, interstate or foreign commerce, to conduct or participate, directly or indirectly, in the conduct of such enterprise's affairs through a pattern of racketeering activity ...

(d) It shall be unlawful for any person to conspire to violate any of the provisions of subsection ... (b), or (c) of this section.

§ 1964. Civil remedies

(a) The district courts of the United States shall have jurisdiction to prevent and restrain violations of section 1962 of this chapter by issuing appropriate orders, including, but not limited to: ordering any person to divest himself of any interest, direct or indirect, in any enterprise; imposing reasonable restrictions on the future activities or investments of any person, including, but not limited to, prohibiting any person from engaging in the same type of endeavor as the enterprise engaged in, the activities of which affect interstate or foreign commerce; or ordering dissolution or reorganization of any enterprise, making due provision for the rights of innocent persons.

(b) The Attorney General may institute proceedings under this section. Pending final determination thereof, the court may at any time enter such restraining orders or prohibitions, or take such other actions, including the acceptance of satisfactory performance bonds, as it shall deem proper.

(c) Any person injured in his business or property by reason of a violation of section 1962 of this chapter may sue therefor in any appropriate United States district court and shall recover threefold the damages he sustains and the cost of the suit, including a reasonable attorney's fee ...

(d) A final judgment or decree rendered in favor of the United States in any criminal proceeding brought by the United States under this chapter shall estop the defendant from denying the essential allegations of the criminal offense in any subsequent civil proceeding brought by the United States.

Notes

1. *Applicability of RICO.* In *Sedima v. Imrex Co., Inc.*, 473 U.S. 479, 493, 495, 497 (1985), a majority of the Supreme Court held that a plaintiff may bring a civil claim under RICO even if the defendant has not been convicted of a criminal offense. Nor, it held, is there any need to demonstrate a "racketeering injury." Instead: "Where the plaintiff alleges each element of the violation, the compensable injury necessarily is the harm caused by predicate acts sufficiently related to constitute a pattern." Writing for the Court, Justice White held (473 U.S. at 499–500):

> Underlying the Court of Appeals' holding was its distress at the "extraordinary, if not outrageous," uses to which civil RICO has been put. Instead of being used against mobsters and organized criminals, it has become a tool for everyday fraud cases brought against "respected and legitimate 'enterprises.'" Yet Congress wanted to reach both "legitimate" and "illegitimate" enterprises. The former enjoy neither an inherent incapacity for criminal activity nor immunity from its consequences. The fact that § 1964(c) is used against respected businesses allegedly engaged in a pattern of specifically identified criminal conduct is hardly a sufficient reason for assuming that the provision is being misconstrued. Nor does it reveal the "ambiguity" discovered by the court below. "[T]he fact that RICO has been applied in situations not expressly anticipated by Congress does not demonstrate ambiguity. It demonstrates breadth." *Haroco, Inc. v. American National Bank & Trust Co. of Chicago.*

It is true that private civil actions under the statute are being brought almost solely against such defendants, rather than against the archetypal, intimidating mobster. Yet this defect—if defect it is—is inherent in the statute as written, and its correction must lie with Congress. It is not for the judiciary to eliminate the private action in situations where Congress has provided it simply because plaintiffs are not taking advantage of it in its more difficult applications.

We nonetheless recognize that, in its private civil version, RICO is evolving into something quite different from the original conception of its enactors. Though sharing the doubts of the Court of Appeals about this increasing divergence, we cannot agree with either its diagnosis or its remedy. The "extraordinary" uses to which civil RICO has been put appear to be primarily the result of the breadth of the predicate offenses, in particular the inclusion of wire, mail, and securities fraud, and the failure of Congress and the courts to develop a meaningful concept of "pattern." We do not believe that the amorphous standing requirement imposed by the Second Circuit effectively responds to these problems, or that it is a form of statutory amendment appropriately undertaken by the courts.

2. *Example.* Suppose a manufacturer produced an automobile with defective automatic transmission that could easily slip from park into reverse. Suppose also that the manufacturer knew of that defect and sold the car anyway. Normally, a lawsuit would be brought against that manufacturer for various forms of product liability, such as breach of warranty, a defective design, and fraudulent misrepresentation. However, if it could be proven that the manufacturer used the telephone or mail at least twice to discuss the defect, a RICO action may be available, even if the use of the mail or telephone was for purely intra-corporate communication. There is no requirement that the telephone or mail be the instrument of wire or mail fraud, so long as they were involved in the furtherance of the fraud. This type of suit is obviously an attractive prospect for a plaintiff because of the availability of triple damages.

3. *Limitation of* RICO. There is one caveat to using RICO in product liability cases. RICO can only be used to recover damage to business or property. Thus, RICO cannot be used to triple pain and suffering damages. However, since it can be used to gain triple recovery for property damage (and possibly for lost wages and medical bills as well), it can be a very potent weapon when coupled with a product liability case.

4. *RICO and Big Tobacco in Florida.* On August 25, 1997, the five leading cigarette manufacturers in the United States agreed to pay to the State of Florida $11.3 billion in settlement of litigation that had been instituted in February 1995. Originally put forward as a Medicaid cost recovery action, the litigation evolved into a wide-ranging claim that the tobacco companies had violated RICO, thus opening the door to penalties such as the disgorgement of all profits generated by the corrupt practice: namely, the sale of cigarettes. The settlement avoided an imminent trial, and included an agreement by the manufacturers to change tobacco marketing practices in ways that were supposed to protect future generations of Floridians from the adverse health effects of tobacco products. See 25 Fla. St. U.L. Rev. 737 (1997–1999) and *Engle v. Liggett Group, Inc.*, 945 So.2d 1246 (Fla., 2006), discussed in Chapter 12.

5. *RICO and Big Tobacco at the federal level.* In *United States v. Philip Morris USA, Inc.*, 566 F.3d 1095, 1105–06 (2009), while affirming a verdict that Big Tobacco had engaged in multiple violations of RICO, the United States Court of Appeals for the District of Columbia Circuit found that:

The government alleged that Defendants violated and continued to violate RICO by joining together in a decades-long conspiracy to deceive the American public about the health effects and addictiveness of smoking cigarettes. Specifically, the government alleged that Defendants fraudulently denied that smoking causes cancer and emphysema, that secondhand smoke causes lung cancer and endangers children's respiratory and auditory systems, that nicotine is an addictive drug and Defendants manipulated it to sustain addiction, that light and low tar cigarettes are not less harmful than full flavor cigarettes, and that Defendants intentionally marketed to youth. *United States v. Philip Morris USA, Inc.*, 449 F. Supp. 2d 1, 27 (D.D.C. 2006). In addition, the government alleged that Defendants concealed evidence and destroyed documents to hide the dangers of smoking and protect themselves in litigation. The government identified 148 racketeering acts of mail and wire fraud Defendants allegedly committed in furtherance of their scheme....

After years of pretrial proceedings and discovery, the case went to trial in September 2004. The bench trial lasted nine months and included live testimony from 84 witnesses, written testimony from 162 witnesses, and almost 14,000 exhibits in evidence. The government presented evidence that the presidents of Philip Morris, Reynolds, Brown & Williamson, Lorillard, and American assembled together in 1953 to develop a strategic response to growing public concern about the health risks of smoking and jointly retained a public relations firm to assist in the endeavor. From the beginning they agreed that no cigarette manufacturer would "seek a competitive advantage by inferring to its public that its product is less risky than others"; they would make no "claims that special filters or toasting, or expert selection of tobacco, or extra length in the butt, or anything else, makes a given brand less likely to cause you-know-what." (quoting public relations firm's Planning Committee Memorandum). Acting on this agreement, the cigarette manufacturers jointly issued "A Frank Statement to Cigarette Smokers," published as a full-page advertisement in newspapers across the country on January 4, 1954. "The Frank Statement set forth the industry's 'open question' position that it would maintain for more than forty years — that cigarette smoking was not a proven cause of lung cancer; that cigarettes were not injurious to health; and that more research on smoking and health issues was needed." All of the Defendant manufacturers eventually joined this collective effort.

The government presented evidence from the 1950s and continuing through the following decades demonstrating that the Defendant manufacturers were aware — increasingly so as they conducted more research — that smoking causes disease, including lung cancer. Evidence at trial revealed that at the same time Defendants were disseminating advertisements, publications, and public statements denying any adverse health effects of smoking and promoting their "open question" strategy of sowing doubt, they internally acknowledged as fact that smoking causes disease and other health hazards.

The Supreme Court and Due Process

As has already been mentioned, punitive damages tend to be awarded only in products liability only where there has been some degree of egregious conduct by the defendant. In principle, tort law is, of course, a matter for the states — to the extent that, even when a torts case is heard in federal court, the court is required to apply the law of the state most closely connected with the case. Nevertheless, it has also already been seen how a layer of federal law is often superimposed over state tort law—for example, in pretrial matters relating to multidistrict litigation, when a defendant is in bankruptcy, or when a torts claim is potentially preempted by a federal statute or agency.

In addition to the clauses in the Constitution discussed in previous Chapters, the Supreme Court of the United States has held that another provision in the Constitution is relevant to awards of damages in products liability cases. It is Section 1 of the Fourteenth Amendment, which says: "No State shall make or enforce any law which shall abridge the privileges or immunities of citizens of the United States." This means, it has held, that there is a constitutional bar on excessively large awards of punitive damages. The Court's view remains highly controversial, even among recent members of the court. Interestingly, the split does not follow the usual liberal versus conservative lines: on this issue the liberal Justices Stevens and Ginsburg and the conservative Justices Scalia and Thomas have all seemed to be, if not quite of one mind, then certainly on a similar wavelength.

In these cases, the application of the Fourteenth Amendment's "Due Process" Clause actually involves two issues: (a) whether the sum awarded is "grossly excessive," and (b) whether the defendant is being punished for harming persons who are not before the court. In either case a majority of the Supreme Court has held that awards which do so are unconstitutional.

BMW of North America, Inc. v. Gore
517 U.S. 559 (1996) (SCOTUS)

STEVENS, J. The Due Process Clause of the Fourteenth Amendment prohibits a State from imposing a "'grossly excessive'" punishment on a tortfeasor. *TXO Production Corp. v. Alliance Resources Corp.*, 509 U.S. 443, 454, 113 S.Ct. 2711, 2718, 125 L.Ed.2d 366 (1993) (and cases cited). The wrongdoing involved in this case was the decision by a national distributor of automobiles not to advise its dealers, and hence their customers, of predelivery damage to new cars when the cost of repair amounted to less than 3 percent of the car's suggested retail price. The question presented is whether a $2 million punitive damages award to the purchaser of one of these cars exceeds the constitutional limit.

In January 1990, Dr. Ira Gore, Jr. (respondent), purchased a black BMW sports sedan for $40,750.88 from an authorized BMW dealer in Birmingham, Alabama. After driving the car for approximately nine months, and without noticing any flaws in its appearance, Dr. Gore took the car to "Slick Finish," an independent detailer, to make it look "'snazzier than it normally would appear.'" Mr. Slick, the proprietor, detected evidence that the car had been repainted. Convinced that he had been cheated, Dr. Gore brought suit against petitioner BMW of North America (BMW), the American distributor of BMW automobiles. Dr. Gore alleged, inter alia, that the failure to disclose that the car had been repainted constituted suppression of a material fact. The complaint prayed for $500,000 in compensatory and punitive damages, and costs.

At trial, BMW acknowledged that it had adopted a nationwide policy in 1983 concerning cars that were damaged in the course of manufacture or transportation. If the cost of repairing the damage exceeded 3 percent of the car's suggested retail price, the car was placed in company service for a period of time and then sold as used. If the repair cost did not exceed 3 percent of the suggested retail price, however, the car was sold as new without advising the dealer that any repairs had been made. Because the $601.37 cost of repainting Dr. Gore's car was only about 1.5 percent of its suggested retail price, BMW did not disclose the damage or repair to the Birmingham dealer.

Dr. Gore asserted that his repainted car was worth less than a car that had not been refinished. To prove his actual damages of $4,000, he relied on the testimony of a former BMW dealer, who estimated that the value of a repainted BMW was approximately 10 percent less than the value of a new car that had not been damaged and repaired. To support his claim for punitive damages, Dr. Gore introduced evidence that since 1983 BMW had sold 983 refinished cars as new, including 14 in Alabama, without disclosing that the cars had been repainted before sale at a cost of more than $300 per vehicle. Using the actual damage estimate of $4,000 per vehicle, Dr. Gore argued that a punitive award of $4 million would provide an appropriate penalty for selling approximately 1,000 cars for more than they were worth....

The jury returned a verdict finding BMW liable for compensatory damages of $4,000. In addition, the jury assessed $4 million in punitive damages, based on a determination that the nondisclosure policy constituted "gross, oppressive or malicious" fraud.

BMW filed a post-trial motion to set aside the punitive damages award. The company introduced evidence to establish that its nondisclosure policy was consistent with the laws of roughly 25 States defining the disclosure obligations of automobile manufacturers, distributors, and dealers. The most stringent of these statutes required disclosure of repairs costing more than 3 percent of the suggested retail price; none mandated disclosure of less costly repairs. Relying on these statutes, BMW contended that its conduct was lawful in these States and therefore could not provide the basis for an award of punitive damages.

BMW also drew the court's attention to the fact that its nondisclosure policy had never been adjudged unlawful before this action was filed. Just months before Dr. Gore's case went to trial, the jury in a similar lawsuit filed by another Alabama BMW purchaser found that BMW's failure to disclose paint repair constituted fraud. Before the judgment in this case, BMW changed its policy by taking steps to avoid the sale of any refinished vehicles in Alabama and two other States. When the $4 million verdict was returned in this case, BMW promptly instituted a nationwide policy of full disclosure of all repairs, no matter how minor....

The trial judge denied BMW's post-trial motion, holding, inter alia, that the award was not excessive. On appeal, the Alabama Supreme Court also rejected BMW's claim that the award exceeded the constitutionally permissible amount.... Based on its analysis, the court concluded that BMW's conduct was "reprehensible"; the nondisclosure was profitable for the company; the judgment "would not have a substantial impact upon [BMW's] financial position"; the litigation had been expensive; no criminal sanctions had been imposed on BMW for the same conduct; the award of no punitive damages in Yates reflected "the inherent uncertainty of the trial process"; and the punitive award bore a "reasonable relationship" to "the harm that was likely to occur from [BMW's] conduct as well as ... the harm that actually occurred."

The Alabama Supreme Court did, however, rule in BMW's favor on one critical point: The court found that the jury improperly computed the amount of punitive damages by multiplying Dr. Gore's compensatory damages by the number of similar sales in other jurisdictions. Having found the verdict tainted, the court held that "a constitutionally reasonable punitive damages award in this case is $2,000,000," and therefore ordered a remittitur in that amount. The court's discussion of the amount of its remitted award expressly disclaimed any reliance on "acts that occurred in other jurisdictions"; instead, the court explained that it had used a "comparative analysis" that considered Alabama cases, "along with cases from other jurisdictions, involving the sale of an automobile where the seller misrepresented the condition of the vehicle and the jury awarded punitive damages to the purchaser."

Punitive damages may properly be imposed to further a State's legitimate interests in punishing unlawful conduct and deterring its repetition. In our federal system, States necessarily have considerable flexibility in determining the level of punitive damages that they will allow in different classes of cases and in any particular case. Most States that authorize exemplary damages afford the jury similar latitude, requiring only that the damages awarded be reasonably necessary to vindicate the State's legitimate interests in punishment and deterrence. Only when an award can fairly be categorized as "grossly excessive" in relation to these interests does it enter the zone of arbitrariness that violates the Due Process Clause of the Fourteenth Amendment. For that reason, the federal excessiveness inquiry appropriately begins with an identification of the state interests that a punitive award is designed to serve. We therefore focus our attention first on the scope of Alabama's legitimate interests in punishing BMW and deterring it from future misconduct.

No one doubts that a State may protect its citizens by prohibiting deceptive trade practices and by requiring automobile distributors to disclose presale repairs that affect the value of a new car. But the States need not, and in fact do not, provide such protection in a uniform manner. Some States rely on the judicial process to formulate and enforce an appropriate disclosure requirement by applying principles of contract and tort law. Other States have enacted various forms of legislation that define the disclosure obligations of automobile manufacturers, distributors, and dealers. The result is a patchwork of rules representing the diverse policy judgments of lawmakers in 50 States.

That diversity demonstrates that reasonable people may disagree about the value of a full disclosure requirement. Some legislatures may conclude that affirmative disclosure requirements are unnecessary because the self-interest of those involved in the automobile trade in developing and maintaining the goodwill of their customers will motivate them to make voluntary disclosures or to refrain from selling cars that do not comply with self-imposed standards. Those legislatures that do adopt affirmative disclosure obligations may take into account the cost of government regulation, choosing to draw a line exempting minor repairs from such a requirement. In formulating a disclosure standard, States may also consider other goals, such as providing a "safe harbor" for automobile manufacturers, distributors, and dealers against lawsuits over minor repairs.

We may assume, arguendo, that it would be wise for every State to adopt Dr. Gore's preferred rule, requiring full disclosure of every presale repair to a car, no matter how trivial and regardless of its actual impact on the value of the car. But while we do not doubt that Congress has ample authority to enact such a policy for the entire Nation, is clear that no single State could do so, or even impose its own policy choice on neighboring States. Similarly, one State's power to impose burdens on the interstate market for automobiles is not only subordinate to the federal power over interstate commerce, but is also constrained by the need to respect the interests of other States.

We think it follows from these principles of state sovereignty and comity that a State may not impose economic sanctions on violators of its laws with the intent of changing the tortfeasors' lawful conduct in other States. Before this Court Dr. Gore argued that the large punitive damages award was necessary to induce BMW to change the nationwide policy that it adopted in 1983. But by attempting to alter BMW's nationwide policy, Alabama would be infringing on the policy choices of other States. To avoid such encroachment, the economic penalties that a State such as Alabama inflicts on those who transgress its laws, whether the penalties take the form of legislatively authorized fines or judicially imposed punitive damages, must be supported by the State's interest in protecting its own consumers and its own economy. Alabama may insist that BMW adhere to a particular disclosure policy in that State. Alabama does not have the power, however, to punish BMW for conduct that was lawful where it occurred and that had no impact on Alabama or its residents. Nor may Alabama impose sanctions on BMW in order to deter conduct that is lawful in other jurisdictions.

In this case, we accept the Alabama Supreme Court's interpretation of the jury verdict as reflecting a computation of the amount of punitive damages "based in large part on conduct that happened in other jurisdictions." 646 So.2d, at 627. As the Alabama Supreme Court noted, neither the jury nor the trial court was presented with evidence that any of BMW's out-of-state conduct was unlawful. "The only testimony touching the issue showed that approximately 60% of the vehicles that were refinished were sold in states where failure to disclose the repair was not an unfair trade practice." The Alabama Supreme Court therefore properly eschewed reliance on BMW's out-of-state conduct, and based its remitted award solely on conduct that occurred within Alabama. The award must be analyzed in the light of the same conduct, with consideration given only to the interests of Alabama consumers, rather than those of the entire Nation. When the scope of the interest in punishment and deterrence that an Alabama court may appropriately consider is properly limited, it is apparent — for reasons that we shall now address — that this award is grossly excessive.

Elementary notions of fairness enshrined in our constitutional jurisprudence dictate that a person receive fair notice not only of the conduct that will subject him to punishment, but also of the severity of the penalty that a State may impose. Three guideposts, each of which indicates that BMW did not receive adequate notice of the magnitude of the sanction that Alabama might impose for adhering to the nondisclosure policy adopted in 1983, lead us to the conclusion that the $2 million award against BMW is grossly excessive: the degree of reprehensibility of the nondisclosure; the disparity between the harm or potential harm suffered by Dr. Gore and his punitive damages award; and the difference between this remedy and the civil penalties authorized or imposed in comparable cases. We discuss these considerations in turn.

Degree of Reprehensibility

Perhaps the most important indicium of the reasonableness of a punitive damages award is the degree of reprehensibility of the defendant's conduct. As the Court stated nearly 150 years ago, exemplary damages imposed on a defendant should reflect "the enormity of his offense." This principle reflects the accepted view that some wrongs are more blameworthy than others. Thus, we have said that "nonviolent crimes are less serious than crimes marked by violence or the threat of violence." Similarly, "trickery and deceit," are more reprehensible than negligence. In *TXO*, both the West Virginia Supreme Court and the Justices of this Court placed special emphasis on the principle that punitive damages may not be "grossly out of proportion to the severity of the offense." ...

In this case, none of the aggravating factors associated with particularly reprehensible conduct is present. The harm BMW inflicted on Dr. Gore was purely economic in nature. The presale refinishing of the car had no effect on its performance or safety features, or even its appearance for at least nine months after his purchase. BMW's conduct evinced no indifference to or reckless disregard for the health and safety of others. To be sure, infliction of economic injury, especially when done intentionally through affirmative acts of misconduct, or when the target is financially vulnerable, can warrant a substantial penalty. But this observation does not convert all acts that cause economic harm into torts that are sufficiently reprehensible to justify a significant sanction in addition to compensatory damages.

Dr. Gore contends that BMW's conduct was particularly reprehensible because nondisclosure of the repairs to his car formed part of a nationwide pattern of tortious conduct....

We do not think it can be disputed that there may exist minor imperfections in the finish of a new car that can be repaired (or indeed, left unrepaired) without materially affecting the car's value. There is no evidence that BMW acted in bad faith when it sought to establish the appropriate line between presumptively minor damage and damage requiring disclosure to purchasers.... [I]t is also significant that there is no evidence that BMW persisted in a course of conduct after it had been adjudged unlawful on even one occasion, let alone repeated occasions.

Finally, the record in this case discloses no deliberate false statements, acts of affirmative misconduct, or concealment of evidence of improper motive ...

That conduct is sufficiently reprehensible to give rise to tort liability, and even a modest award of exemplary damages does not establish the high degree of culpability that warrants a substantial punitive damages award. Because this case exhibits none of the circumstances ordinarily associated with egregiously improper conduct, we are persuaded that BMW's conduct was not sufficiently reprehensible to warrant imposition of a $2 million exemplary damages award.

Ratio

The second and perhaps most commonly cited indicium of an unreasonable or excessive punitive damages award is its ratio to the actual harm inflicted on the plaintiff. The principle that exemplary damages must bear a "reasonable relationship" to compensatory damages has a long pedigree. Scholars have identified a number of early English statutes authorizing the award of multiple damages for particular wrongs. Some 65 different enactments during the period between 1275 and 1753 provided for double, treble, or quadruple damages. Our decisions in both [*Pacific Mut. Life Ins. Co. v.*] *Haslip*, 499 U.S. 1, 111 S.Ct. 1032 (1991) and *TXO* endorsed the proposition that a comparison between the compensatory award and the punitive award is significant.

In *Haslip* we concluded that even though a punitive damages award of "more than 4 times the amount of compensatory damages" might be "close to the line," it did not "cross the line into the area of constitutional impropriety." *TXO*, following dicta in *Haslip*, refined this analysis by confirming that the proper inquiry is "'whether there is a reasonable relationship between the punitive damages award and the harm likely to result from the defendant's conduct as well as the harm that actually has occurred.'" Thus, in upholding the $10 million award in TXO, we relied on the difference between that figure and the harm to the victim that would have ensued if the tortious plan had succeeded. That difference suggested that the relevant ratio was not more than 10 to 1.

The $2 million in punitive damages awarded to Dr. Gore by the Alabama Supreme Court is 500 times the amount of his actual harm as determined by the jury. Moreover, there is no suggestion that Dr. Gore or any other BMW purchaser was threatened with any additional potential harm by BMW's nondisclosure policy. The disparity in this case is thus dramatically greater than those considered in *Haslip* and *TXO*.

Of course, we have consistently rejected the notion that the constitutional line is marked by a simple mathematical formula, even one that compares actual and potential damages to the punitive award. Indeed, low awards of compensatory damages may properly support a higher ratio than high compensatory awards, if, for example, a particularly egregious act has resulted in only a small amount of economic damages. A higher ratio may also be justified in cases in which the injury is hard to detect or the monetary value of noneconomic harm might have been difficult to determine. It is appropriate, therefore, to reiterate our rejection of a categorical approach. Once again, "we return to what we said ... in *Haslip*: 'We need not, and indeed we cannot, draw a mathematical bright line between the constitutionally acceptable and the constitutionally unacceptable that would fit every case. We can say, however, that [a] general concer[n] of reasonableness ... properly enter[s] into the constitutional calculus."' In most cases, the ratio will be within a constitutionally acceptable range, and remittitur will not be justified on this basis. When the ratio is a breathtaking 500 to 1, however, the award must surely "raise a suspicious judicial eyebrow."

Sanctions for Comparable Misconduct

Comparing the punitive damages award and the civil or criminal penalties that could be imposed for comparable misconduct provides a third indicium of excessiveness. As Justice O'Connor has correctly observed, a reviewing court engaged in determining whether an award of punitive damages is excessive should "accord 'substantial deference' to legislative judgments concerning appropriate sanctions for the conduct at issue." In *Haslip*, the Court noted that although the exemplary award was "much in excess of the fine that could be imposed," imprisonment was also authorized in the criminal context. In this case the $2 million economic sanction imposed on BMW is substantially greater than the statutory fines available in Alabama and elsewhere for similar malfeasance.

The maximum civil penalty authorized by the Alabama Legislature for a violation of its Deceptive Trade Practices Act is $2,000; other States authorize more severe sanctions, with the maxima ranging from $5,000 to $10,000. Significantly, some statutes draw a distinction between first offenders and recidivists; thus, in New York the penalty is $50 for a first offense and $250 for subsequent offenses. None of these statutes would provide an out-of-state distributor with fair notice that the first violation—or, indeed the first 14 violations—of its provisions might subject an offender to a multimillion dollar penalty.

SCALIA, J. (dissenting), (joined by THOMAS, J.). Today we see the latest manifestation of this Court's recent and increasingly insistent "concern about punitive damages that 'run wild.'" Since the Constitution does not make that concern any of our business, the Court's activities in this area are an unjustified incursion into the province of state governments.

In earlier cases that were the prelude to this decision, I set forth my view that a state trial procedure that commits the decision whether to impose punitive damages, and the amount, to the discretion of the jury, subject to some judicial review for "reasonableness," furnishes a defendant with all the process that is "due." I do not regard the Fourteenth Amendment's Due Process Clause as a secret repository of substantive guarantees against "unfairness"—neither the unfairness of an excessive civil compensatory award, nor the unfairness of an "unreasonable" punitive award. What the Fourteenth Amendment's procedural guarantee assures is an opportunity to contest the reasonableness of a damages judgment in state court; but there is no federal guarantee a damages award actually *be* reasonable. ...

One might understand the Court's eagerness to enter this field, rather than leave it with the state legislatures, if it had something useful to say. In fact, however, its opinion provides virtually no guidance to legislatures, and to state and federal courts, as to what a "constitutionally proper" level of punitive damages might be. ...

"Alabama does not have the power," the Court says, "to punish BMW for conduct that was lawful where it occurred and that had no impact on Alabama or its residents." That may be true, though only in the narrow sense that a person cannot be held liable to be punished on the basis of a lawful act. But if a person has been held subject to punishment because he committed an unlawful act, the degree of his punishment assuredly can be increased on the basis of any other conduct of his that displays his wickedness, unlawful or not. Criminal sentences can be computed, we have said, on the basis of "information concerning every aspect of a defendant's life," *Williams v. New York*, 337 U.S. 241, 250–252 (1949). The Court at one point seems to acknowledge this, observing that, although a sentencing court "[cannot] properly punish lawful conduct," it may in assessing the penalty "consider ... lawful conduct that bears on the defendant's character." That concession is quite incompatible, however, with the later assertion that, since "neither the jury nor the trial court was presented with evidence that any of BMW's out-of-state conduct was unlawful," the Alabama Supreme Court "therefore properly eschewed reliance on BMW's out-of-state conduct, ... and based its remitted award solely on conduct that occurred within Alabama." Why could the Supreme Court of Alabama not consider lawful (but disreputable) conduct, both inside and outside Alabama, for the purpose of assessing just how bad an actor BMW was?

The Court follows up its statement that "Alabama does not have the power ... to punish BMW for conduct that was lawful where it occurred" with the statement: "Nor may Alabama impose sanctions on BMW in order to deter conduct that is lawful in other jurisdictions." The Court provides us no citation of authority to support this proposition—other than the barely analogous cases cited earlier in the opinion—and I know of none.

These significant issues pronounced upon by the Court are not remotely presented for resolution in the present case. There is no basis for believing that Alabama has sought to control conduct elsewhere. The statutes at issue merely permit civil juries to treat conduct such as petitioner's as fraud, and authorize an award of appropriate punitive damages in the event the fraud is found to be "gross, oppressive, or malicious," Ala.Code § 6-11-20(b)(1) (1993). To be sure, respondent did invite the jury to consider out-of-state conduct in its calculation of damages, but any increase in the jury's initial award based on that consideration is not a component of the remitted judgment before us. As the Court several times recognizes, in computing the amount of the remitted award the Alabama Supreme Court—whether it was constitutionally required to or not—"expressly disclaimed any reliance on acts that occurred in other jurisdictions." Thus, the only question presented by this case is whether that award, limited to petitioner's Alabama conduct and viewed in light of the factors identified as properly informing the inquiry, is excessive. The Court's sweeping (and largely unsupported) statements regarding the relationship of punitive awards to lawful or unlawful out-of-state conduct are the purest dicta.

In Part III of its opinion, the Court identifies "[t]hree guideposts" that lead it to the conclusion that the award in this case is excessive ...

Of course it will not be easy for the States to comply with this new federal law of damages, no matter how willing they are to do so. In truth, the "guideposts" mark a road to nowhere; they provide no real guidance at all. As to "degree of reprehensibility" of the defendant's conduct, we learn that "'nonviolent crimes are less serious than crimes marked by violence or the threat of violence,'" and that "trickery and deceit" are "more reprehensible than negligence." As to the ratio of punitive to compensatory damages, we are told that a "general concer[n] of reasonableness ... enter[s] into the constitutional calculus,"—though even "a breathtaking 500 to 1" will not necessarily do anything more than "'raise a suspicious judicial eyebrow,'" 1603 (quoting *TXO, supra,* at 481, 113 S.Ct., at 2732 (O'-Connor, J., dissenting), an opinion which, when confronted with that "breathtaking" ratio, approved it). And as to legislative sanctions provided for comparable misconduct, they should be accorded "substantial deference." One expects the Court to conclude: "To thine own self be true."

These crisscrossing platitudes yield no real answers in no real cases. And it must be noted that the Court nowhere says that these three "guideposts" are the only guideposts; indeed, it makes very clear that they are not—explaining away the earlier opinions that do not really follow these "guideposts" on the basis of additional factors, thereby "reiterat[ing] our rejection of a categorical approach." In other words, even these utter platitudes, if they should ever happen to produce an answer, may be overridden by other unnamed considerations. The Court has constructed a framework that does not genuinely constrain, that does not inform state legislatures and lower courts—that does nothing at all except confer an artificial air of doctrinal analysis upon its essentially ad hoc determination that this particular award of punitive damages was not "fair."

BMW of North America, Inc. v. Gore
701 So.2d 507 (1997) (Supreme Court of Alabama)

PER CURIAM. The United States Supreme Court announced, for the first time and by a 5–4 vote, that a punitive damages award, even one that is the product of a fair trial, may be so large as to violate the Due Process Clause of the Fourteenth Amendment of the United States Constitution. The Supreme Court determined that, under the Due Process Clause, a defendant has the right to fair notice not only of the conduct that may subject him to punishment, but also of the severity of the penalty that a state may impose for such conduct.

Until the United States Supreme Court released its decision in BMW, it was generally assumed that a statute stating that intentional fraud would subject a tortfeasor to such punitive damages as a jury might assess in a fair trial was sufficient notice of the severity of the punishment that might be inflicted....

Although it is difficult to determine case by case what ratio of punitive damages to compensatory damages is excessive, we reject the easy answer of adopting one ratio that would apply to all and would therefore give a wrongdoer precise notice of the penalty that his misconduct might incur. To do so would frustrate the purpose of punitive damages, which is to punish and deter a defendant's misconduct. A ratio that could be deemed reasonable in many cases might well be insufficient in cases where the defendant has reaped great profit from its conduct, or where its conduct is particularly reprehensible....

After carefully reconsidering this case ... in the light of the United States Supreme Court's opinion in BMW, and incorporating the guideposts articulated therein, we agree that the $2 million award of punitive damages against BMW was grossly excessive....

In [*German Auto, Inc. v.*] *Tamburello*, 565 So.2d 238 (Ala., 1990), the plaintiff bought a BMW automobile that was represented and warranted to be new and undamaged. After the purchase, the plaintiff discovered that the left rear fender of the automobile had been damaged and repainted. The plaintiff ultimately sued the BMW dealer, alleging fraud, among other claims. The jury awarded the plaintiff $2,350 in compensatory damages and $10,815 in punitive damages, and this Court affirmed a judgment based on that verdict. In *Tamburello*, as in the instant case, the damage to the automobile had no effect on its safety features or performance and the repairs necessitated by the damage were merely cosmetic. Moreover, the loss to the plaintiff was purely economic, and there was no evidence that the plaintiff was financially vulnerable. The ratio of punitive damages to compensatory damages was only in the range of 5:1....

We do not imply that the 5:1 ratio in *Tamburello* should be the benchmark of every case ...

The trial court's order denying BMW's motion for a new trial is affirmed on the condition that the plaintiff file with this Court within 21 days a remittitur of damages to the sum of $50,000; otherwise, the judgment will be reversed and this cause remanded for a new trial.

ALMON, J. (concurring). Although I did not vote in *BMW of North America, Inc. v. Gore*, 646 So.2d 619 (Ala., 1994), I now vote to concur with the majority opinion issued today after the remand from the Supreme Court of the United States. I write specially to note that, while I agree under all the circumstances with the remittitur ordered today, it appears to me that the deterrent effect of the original award, which changed BMW's national policy in a way that benefited purchasers of its automobiles, has been unduly minimized as this case has proceeded through successive stages of review.

HOUSTON, J. (concurring). On remand, this Court faces the twin tasks of complying with express United States Supreme Court precedent indicating that there is no precise definition of the "outer limit" of federal due process protection, and, at the same time, providing practical guidance for Alabama's trial judges to review the amounts of punitive damages awards. An examination of the origin of the conflict between state law and federal due process requirements reveals that these objectives can be achieved by returning to Alabama's historic common law reasonableness standard, applied strictly, through a reinvigoration of the protective factors that prompt judicial remittitur orders.

Before its decision in this case, the Supreme Court had never overturned a state court's award of punitive damages as violating federal due process requirements. The apparent reason for this is that state law reasonableness standards for determining the amount of the award had historically been stricter than the federal excessiveness standard.

The state law reasonableness standard derives from the judicial mechanism of remittitur, which plays an integral role in the procedure for respecting and controlling the jury's function to punish tortfeasors. Common law judges traditionally accorded jury awards of punitive damages a rebuttable presumption of correctness. See, e.g., *Leith v. Pope*, 2 Black. W. 1327, 1328, 96 Eng. Rep. 777, 778 (C.P.1779) ("[I]n cases of tort the Court will not interpose on account of the largeness of damages, unless they are so flagrantly excessive as to afford an internal evidence of the prejudice and partiality of the jury"). At some point, however, when the facts indicated that the presumption of correctness waned and was finally overcome, common law judges used remittitur to reduce unreasonable awards that resulted from the passion or prejudice of the jury. Numerous English cases upheld the power of common law courts to order a new trial if the judges deemed the punitive damages unreasonable. See, e.g., *Gilbert v. Burtenshaw*, 1 Cowper 230, 98 Eng. Rep. 1059 (K.B.1774) (Mansfield, J.) (recognizing judicial power to grant new trial when jury awards of damages are excessive).

American courts adopted the same procedure. In *Whipple v. Cumberland Mfg. Co.*, 29 F. Cas. 934, 937–38 (C.C.Me.1843), Justice Story, sitting as a Circuit Justice, acknowledged the judicial duty to set aside a jury verdict for unreasonable damages. He had previously stated the American doctrine as follows:

> As to the question of excessive damages, I agree, that the court may grant a new trial for excessive damages.... It is indeed an exercise of discretion full of delicacy and difficulty. But if it should clearly appear that the jury have committed a gross error, or have acted from improper motives, or have given damages excessive in relation to the person or the injury, it is as much the duty of the court to interfere, to prevent the wrong, as in any other case. *Blunt v. Little*, 3 F. Cas. 760, 761–62 (C.C.Mass.1822) (Story, J., sitting as Circuit Justice).

In *National Surety Co. v. Mabry*, 139 Ala. 217, 225, 35 So. 698, 701 (1903), this Court recognized the judicial duty to reduce unreasonable awards of punitive damages, by citing with approval Lord Mansfield's opinion in *Gilbert, supra*, and Justice Story's opinion in *Whipple, supra*....

To resolve the present conflict between the state law reasonableness standard and the federal law excessiveness standard, I would return to the traditional, restrictive Alabama reasonableness standard. Although the Supreme Court, and thus, this Court, cannot precisely define the "outer limit" of federal due process, we can more precisely define the "inner boundary" of state law reasonableness. To the extent this definition comports with history by producing a common law reasonableness standard that is stricter than the federal law excessiveness standard, it would both avoid conflict with binding Supreme Court precedent and provide a more workable standard for Alabama courts to apply....

Although the Supreme Court rejected any fixed ratio, it recognized that punitive damages "must bear a 'reasonable relationship' to compensatory damages." I agree with the majority that this Court should not adopt a specific ratio as a judicially imposed cap on punitive damages. At the same time ... [b]oth the Alabama Legislature and Congress have established treble damages as the most common punitive standard. I would therefore adopt that three-to-one ratio, not as any kind of rigid restraint, but to serve as a benchmark against which to measure reasonableness. Significant deviations above the three-to-one benchmark should require special justification.

Note

Final resolution. Dr. Gore accepted the award of $50,000 in punitive damages.

Questions

1. As Justice Almon pointed out, after being sued by Dr. Gore and a number of other plaintiffs, BMW had changed its policy to inform any prospective purchasers of any car that is re-painted before sale. Do you think that BMW did so because of the size of the punitive damages award in this case, or because of the bad publicity which the case generated? Would the case have generated similar bad publicity for BMW if the punitive damages award had been much lower (say $50,000)?

2. The Alabama Supreme Court suggested in *Gore* that making the size of punitive damages awards predictable would undermine their deterrence function. If that is so, is it contradictory to lay down any kind of ratio as a benchmark for punitive damages awards?

3. Awards of damages, whether compensatory or punitive, have historically been set by juries. Is this intervention by judges evidence that juries have become unreliable? If so, why are judges likely to be more reliable? Why are juries apparently considered unreliable only in relation to damages? Is it indeed time to consider whether jury trials are appropriate in civil cases? (Juries are rarely used in civil cases in common law jurisdictions outside the US.)

4. Alternatively, is this intervention by the courts simply evidence that some judges are developing a tendency to trust juries only when the latter reach a conclusion which is more or less the same as the judges themselves would have reached? If this is true, are the judges acting in an appropriate "gatekeeping" capacity, or are they unconstitutionally usurping the role of the jury?

Flax v. DaimlerChrysler Corporation

272 S.W.3d 521 (2008) (Supreme Court of Tennessee)

[For the facts of the case, see above.] HOLDER, J. Having concluded that punitive damages were warranted in this case, we now review whether the size of the punitive damage award is excessive in violation of the due process standards announced by the United States Supreme Court in *Gore* and [*State Farm Mutual Automobile Ins. Co. v.*] *Campbell* [538 U.S. 408, 123 S.Ct. 1513]. We begin our analysis of this issue by reviewing the United States Supreme Court's punitive damage jurisprudence.

In *Gore*, the United States Supreme Court was called upon to determine the constitutionality of a punitive damage award. The Court concluded that due process requires that "a person receive fair notice not only of the conduct that will subject him to punishment, but also of the severity of the penalty that a State may impose." *Gore*, 517 U.S. at 574 (1996). Accordingly, the Court adopted three guideposts for determining whether a defendant has adequate notice of the magnitude of the sanction that may be imposed. The first and most important guidepost is the reprehensibility of the defendant's conduct. The Court indicated that the presence of violence, deceit, reckless disregard for the safety of others, or repeated misconduct may be aggravating factors that increase the reprehensibility of the defendant's conduct. The second guidepost is the ratio between the punitive damage award and the actual harm suffered by the plaintiff. Although the Court declined to adopt any strict mathematical formula, it repeated the suggestion from a previous case that "a punitive damages award of 'more than 4 times the amount of compensatory damages' might be 'close to the line'" of constitutional impropriety. *Id.* at 581–82 (quoting *Pac. Mut. Life Ins. Co. v. Haslip*, 499 U.S. 1, 23–24 (1991)). The final guidepost requires courts to compare the punitive damage award to civil or criminal penalties that could be imposed for similar conduct.

> [A] reviewing court engaged in determining whether an award of punitive damages is excessive should "accord 'substantial deference' to legislative judgments concerning appropriate sanctions for the conduct at issue."

These legislative judgments are relevant because they provide defendants with notice of the severity of the penalty that may be imposed upon them.

The United States Supreme Court next considered the due process requirements for punitive damages in *Campbell*. The Court again observed that the reprehensibility of the defendant's conduct is the most important guidepost. *Campbell*, 538 U.S. at 419. In an effort to provide guidance to lower courts, the Court stated that courts should determine reprehensibility by considering whether: the harm caused was physical as opposed to economic; the tortious conduct evinced an indifference to or a reckless disregard of the health or safety of others; the target of the conduct had financial vulnerability; the conduct involved repeated actions or was an isolated incident; and the harm was the result of intentional malice, trickery, or deceit, or mere accident. The Court further stated, "The existence of any one of these factors weighing in favor of a plaintiff may not be sufficient to sustain a punitive damages award; and the absence of all of them renders any award suspect." With regard to the second guidepost, the Court stated, "[I]n practice, few awards exceeding a single-digit ratio between punitive and compensatory damages, to a significant degree, will satisfy due process." In addition, "[w]hen compensatory damages are substantial, then a lesser ratio, perhaps only equal to compensatory damages, can reach the outermost limit of the due process guarantee." The Court then qualified its previous statement by observing that "[t]he precise award in any case, of course, must be based upon the facts and circumstances of the defendant's conduct and the harm to the plaintiff." Finally, when discussing the third guidepost, the Court held that [t]he existence of a criminal penalty does have bearing on the seriousness with which a State views the wrongful action. When used to determine the dollar amount of the award, however, the criminal penalty has less utility. Great care must be taken to avoid use of the civil process to assess criminal penalties that can be imposed only after the heightened protections of a criminal trial have been observed, including, of course, its higher standards of proof. Punitive damages are not a substitute for the criminal process, and the remote possibility of a criminal sanction does not automatically sustain a punitive damages award. Unlike the deferential standard of review employed when reviewing a jury's factual conclusions, we conduct a de novo review of the amount of a punitive damages award to determine whether the award meets due process requirements in light of the three guideposts.

Having reviewed the applicable United States Supreme Court precedents, we now turn to the application of the principles set forth therein. The evidence in this case clearly demonstrates that DCC's conduct was reprehensible. Obviously, the harm suffered in this case was physical rather than economic. The death of a child is undoubtedly a tragic experience that is far more serious than a mere economic loss. Furthermore, as we have summarized above, DCC's conduct evinces a conscious disregard for the safety of others. In addition, DCC deceitfully covered up evidence of the deficiencies of its seat design while simultaneously advertising the Caravan as a vehicle that put children's safety first. Finally, DCC's wrongdoing was not an isolated incident because DCC had knowledge of the danger its seats posed to the public for years and yet continued to sell its vehicles in an unreasonably dangerous condition throughout the State of Tennessee. We therefore conclude that under this first, most important guidepost DCC had fair notice that its conduct could subject it to a severe penalty.

We now turn to the second guidepost, the ratio between the punitive damages and compensatory damages. The trial court in this case remitted the punitive damages for the wrongful death of Joshua Flax to $13,367,345. We must compare this punitive damage award to the $2,500,000 in compensatory damages for which DCC is liable for the wrongful death of Joshua Flax. The ratio between these two awards is 1 to 5.35. This ratio is not clearly impermissible because it does not exceed a single digit ratio. There is, however, some doubt as to the propriety of a ratio of 1 to 5.35 because the United States Supreme Court has suggested [in *Campbell*] that a ratio of more than 1 to 4 approaches the outer limits of constitutionality. The Court has also suggested [in *Campbell*] that a ratio of 1 to 1 may be all that is permissible in cases where compensatory damages are "substantial." None of these ratios, however, present "rigid benchmarks," and the United States Supreme Court has thus far declined to adopt any fixed mathematical formula to determine the appropriateness of punitive damages. Instead, the Court has held that "[t]he precise award in any case, of course, must be based upon the facts and circumstances of the defendant's conduct and the harm to the plaintiff."

In light of the first two guideposts, we believe that a ratio of 1 to 5.35 would be warranted in this case. Although the United State Supreme Court has made no effort to demonstrate when damages are "substantial," we do not believe that an award of $2,500,000 is so large as to require a ratio of 1 to 1. Furthermore, a punitive damage award of $13,367,345 is consistent with the concept that the reprehensibility of a defendant's conduct is the most important of the due process guideposts and is justified by DCC's long-term pattern of conduct that resulted in severe injuries to the plaintiffs and showed a conscious disregard for the safety of Tennessee citizens. Accordingly, in light of the first two guideposts we would hold that a punitive damage award approaching the maximum ratio permitted by the due process clause is appropriate.

The third guidepost set forth in *Gore* seems to compel a dramatically different conclusion. The statute that most closely expresses the Tennessee General Assembly's judgment concerning the wrongfulness of DCC's conduct is the reckless homicide statute codified at Tennessee Code Annotated section 39-13-215 (2006). According to that statute, reckless homicide is "a reckless killing of another." Tenn.Code Ann. § 39-13-215. The meaning of the word "reckless" as it is used in that statute is identical to the meaning of "reckless" in a punitive damage context. Compare *Hodges*, 833 S.W.2d at 901, with Tenn.Code Ann. § 39-11-302(c) (2006). Because DCCs reckless conduct resulted in the death of Joshua Flax, reckless homicide is the criminal act most analogous to DCC's conduct. The maximum statutory punishment for corporations that commit reckless homicide is a fine of $125,000. Tenn.Code Ann. § 40-35-111(c)(4) (2006).

Pursuant to the holding of the United States Supreme Court, we must accord "substantial deference" to the General Assembly's decision that $125,000 is an appropriate sanction against corporations guilty of reckless homicide. Furthermore, we must "avoid use of the civil process to assess criminal penalties that can be imposed only after the heightened protections of a criminal trial have been observed." *Campbell*, 538 U.S. at 428, 123 S.Ct. 1513. Although the United States Supreme Court has never held that the third guidepost is dispositive, it appears that under this guidepost $125,000 would be the maximum punitive damage award that could be imposed in this case. Arguably, this is because DCC never had notice that it could be held liable for an amount greater than $125,000. Clearly, the result recommended by the third guidepost is dramatically at odds with the result suggested by the first two. We are unfortunately left with little guidance as to how to resolve this discrepancy because both *Gore* and *Campbell* are cases in which all of the guideposts suggest the same result. Other courts have experienced similar frustrations when attempting to apply the third guidepost, and some have chosen to ignore the third guidepost altogether. See, e.g., *In Re Exxon Valdez*, 490 F.3d 1066, 1094 (9th Cir.2007) (noting that if the Court of Appeals for the Ninth Circuit mentions the third guidepost at all, it does not review the amounts of legislative penalties but determines "whether or not the misconduct was dealt with seriously under state civil or criminal laws").

Although we are somewhat unsure how to reconcile the third guidepost with the first two, we are inclined to give the first two guideposts considerably more weight. The Unites States Supreme Court has held that the first guidepost is the most important and has never stated that the third guidepost is dispositive. Furthermore, we are unaware of any state or federal case that has invalidated a punitive damage award solely because the award was greater than that contemplated by statutory penalties. In addition, the trial court's award in this case is far less drastic than the awards rejected in *Gore* and *Campbell*, which were 1,000 and 14,500 times greater, respectively, than the maximum civil or criminal penalty. Finally, we do not believe that a punitive damage award of $125,000 would adequately punish DCC or deter future instances of similar conduct. For these reasons, we conclude that a punitive damage award of $13,367,345 is constitutionally permissible in this case.

Questions

1. Does the reasoning of the Supreme Court of Tennessee in *Flax* comply with the guidance on punitive damages provided by the Supreme Court of the United States?

2. Does *Flax* lend support to Justice Scalia's assertion in *Gore* that the US Supreme Court's guidance inevitably leads to an "essentially ad hoc determination that this particular award of punitive damages was not 'fair'"?

What Conduct Is to Be Punished by Punitive Damages?

Philip Morris v. Williams
127 S.Ct. 1057 (2007) (SCOTUS)

BREYER, J. The question we address today concerns a large state-court punitive damages award. We are asked whether the Constitution's Due Process Clause permits a jury